To

_____

From

_____

Date

_____

STREAMS
IN THE DESERT

MORNING AND EVENING

365 Devotions

STREAMS
IN
THE DESERT

MORNING AND EVENING

365 Devotions

L. B. COWMAN

16 17 18 19 20 21 22 /DSC/ 29 28 27 26 25 24 23 22 21 20 19 18 17 16 15 14 13 12 11 10 9 8 7 6 5 4 3 2 1

CONTENTS

For the LORD your God is bringing you into a good land—a land with brooks,
streams, and deep springs gushing out into the valleys and hills; a land with
wheat and barley, vines and fig trees, pomegranates, olive oil and honey; a land
where bread will not be scarce and you will lack nothing; a land where the
rocks are iron and you can dig copper out of the hills. When you have eaten and
are satisfied, praise the LORD your God for the good land he has given you.

DEUTERONOMY 8:7–10

We are entering upon a new year—surely we cannot but believe, a new age. If we have rightly learned the lessons of the past, there lies before us a heritage of unspeakable blessing, which none of these vivid metaphors can too strongly describe; infinite sources of blessing, for the fountains and waterbrooks are but the figures of God's illimitable grace. For *with Him* is the fountain of life.

A Fountain Fed by Eternal Springs!

They tell us of boundless supply: "Bread without scarceness" (Deuteronomy 8:9 KJV), the olive oil that speaks of the Holy Ghost, the honey that tells of the sweetness of His love, and the pomegranates that are the seed fruit, which speak of a life that reproduces itself in the blessing of others.

They tell of the "nether springs," which flow from the depths of sorrow in the hard places, in the desert places, in the lone places, in the common places which seem farthest from all that is sacred and Divine.

How delightful it is to have His gladness in the low places of sorrow, and to be able to *glory even in tribulation also.*

They tell us of pleasures that come out of the very heart of trial, treasures wrung from the grasp of the enemy.

How precious the springs that flow into the places of temptation, for there is nothing in life so trying as the touch of Satan's hand and the breath of the destroyer. Oh, how sweet it is, *even there,* to find that the light is as deep as the shadow, and heaven is nearest when we are hard by the gates of hell, so that we can *count it all joy when we fall into diverse temptations* and can say, "Blessed is the man that endureth temptation:

for when he is tried, he shall receive the crown of life, which the Lord hath promised to them that love him" (James 1:12 KJV).

How blessed to drink from the springs of health and find our strength renewed day by day and the life of God flowing into even our physical organs and functions!

"All my fresh *springs are in thee!"*

Beloved, God has for us these springs, and we need them every day. Let us drink of the living waters. Nay, let us receive them into our very hearts so that we shall carry the fountain with us wherever we go. A. B. SIMPSON

We shall never be "springs" until God comes to us. We shall never be fresh or fruitful or useful to others till God comes to us. If we do not have constant visitations of God, we shall soon cease to be "springs," and shall go back to the old dry and barren days. HELENA GARRATT

Let us claim our inheritance in these coming days, and find the hardest places of life's experience God's greatest opportunities and faith's mightiest challenge.

Springs in the valley are very unusual; but He will give us both the upper and the nether springs!

<hr>

JANUARY 1

Evening

The land you are . . . to take possession of is a land of mountains and valleys that drinks rain from heaven. It is a land the LORD your God cares for; the eyes of the LORD your God are continually on it from the beginning of the year to its end.

DEUTERONOMY 11:11–12

Today we stand at the threshold of the unknown. Before us lies a new year, and we are going forward to take possession of it. Who knows what we will find? What new experiences or changes will come our way? What new needs will arise? In spite of the uncertainty before us, we have a cheerful and comforting message from our heavenly Father: "The LORD your God cares for [it]; the eyes of the LORD . . . are continually on it from the beginning of the year to its end." The Lord is to be our Source of supply. In Him are springs, fountains, and streams that will never be cut off or run dry. To those who are anxious comes the gracious promise of our heavenly Father: if He is the Source of our mercies, mercy will never fail us. No heat or drought can dry the "river whose streams make glad the city of God" (Psalm 46:4). Yet the land we are to possess is a land of valleys and hills. It is not all flat or downhill. If life were always smooth and level, the boring sameness would weigh us down. We need the valleys *and* the hills. The hills collect the rain for hundreds of fruitful valleys. And so it is with us! It is the difficulty encountered on the hills that drives us to the throne of grace and brings the showers of blessing. Yes, it is the hills, the cold and seemingly barren hills of life that we question and complain about, that bring down the showers. How many people have perished in the wilderness valley, buried under its golden sand, who would have thrived in the hills? And how many would have been killed by the cold, destroyed or swept desolate of their fruitfulness by the wind, if not for the hills—stern, hard, rugged, and so steep to climb? God's hills are a gracious protection for His people against their foes! We cannot see what loss, sorrow, and trials are accomplishing. We need only to trust. The Father comes near to take our hand and lead us on our way today. It will be a good and blessed New Year!

> *He leads us on by paths we did not know;*
> *Upward He leads us, though our steps be slow,*
> *Though oft we faint and falter on the way,*
> *Though storms and darkness oft obscure the day;*
> > *Yet when the clouds are gone,*
> > *We know He leads us on.*
>
> *He leads us on through all the unquiet years;*
> *Past all our dreamland hopes, and doubts and fears,*
> *He guides our steps, through all the tangled maze*
> *Of losses, sorrows, and o'er clouded days;*
> > *We know His will is done;*
> > *And still He leads us on.*
>
> NICHOLAUS LUDWIG ZINZENDORF

Morning

Jesus himself came up and walked along with them.

LUKE 24:15

A night in Spring . . . and two men walking the Emmaus road—saddened by their master's death—bowed down beneath their load, when suddenly *Another* overtakes them as they walk. A *Stranger* falls in step with them, and earnestly they talk—of what is in their hearts—moved by a warm soul-stirring glow—and when they reach Emmaus, they are loath to let Him go; and so they bid Him stay awhile and share their simple board. And as He breaks the bread . . . *they know.* They know it is the Lord.

Oh, may He *overtake* us as the Path of Life we tread! Along our way of sorrow may His radiant Light be shed . . . Oh, may He come to warm the heart and ease the heavy load—and walk with us as long ago He walked the Emmaus Road.

Take the road . . . the lonely road—courageous, unafraid; ready for the journey when the twilight shadows fade . . . God whose Love is Omnipresent—will He fail us then?—or forget the covenant that He has made with men? PATIENCE STRONG

Jesus never sends a man ahead alone. He blazes a clear way through every thicket and woods, and then softly calls, "Follow Me. Let's go on together, you and I." He has been everywhere that we are called to go. His feet have trodden down smooth a path through every experience that comes to us. He knows each road and knows it well: the valley road of disappointment with its dark shadows; the steep path of temptation down through the rocky ravines and slippery gullies; the narrow path of pain, with the brambly thornbushes so close on each side, with their slash and sting; the dizzy road along the heights of victory; the old beaten road of commonplace daily routine. *Everyday paths He has trodden and glorified, and will walk anew with each of us. The only safe way to travel is with Him alongside and in control.* S. D. GORDON

> *Come, share the road with Me, My own,*
> *Through good and evil weather;*

Two better speed than one alone,
So let us go together.

Come, share the road with Me, My own,
You know I'll never fail you,
And doubts and fears of the unknown
Shall never more assail you.

Come, share the road with Me, My own,
I'll share your joys and sorrows.
And hand in hand we'll seek the throne
And God's great glad tomorrows.

Come, share the road with Me, My own,
And where the black clouds gather,
I'll share thy load with thee, My son,
And we'll press on together.

And as we go we'll share also
With all who travel on it.
For all who share the road with Me
Must share with all upon it.

So make we—all one company,
Love's golden cord our tether,
And, come what may, we'll climb the way
Together—aye, together!

"ROADMATES" BY JOHN OXENHAM

After a long, trying march over perilous Antarctic mountains and glaciers, a South Pole explorer said to his leader, "I had a curious feeling on the march that there was another Person with us!"

Another Person! He is ever there to march side by side with those who trust Him! Take His Hand and Walk with Him!

Evening

The side rooms all around the temple were wider at each successive level.
The structure surrounding the temple was built in ascending stages,
so that the rooms widened as one went upward. A stairway went up
from the lowest floor to the top floor through the middle floor.

EZEKIEL 41:7

Still upward be your onward course:
    For this I pray today;
    Still upward as the years go by,
    And seasons pass away.

Still upward in this coming year,
    Your path is all untried;
    Still upward may you journey on,
    Close by your Savior's side.

Still upward although sorrow come,
    And trials crush your heart;
    Still upward may they draw your soul,
    With Christ to walk apart.

Still upward till the day shall break,
    And shadows all have flown;
    Still upward till in Heaven you wake,
    And stand before the throne.

We should never be content to rest in the mists of the valley when the summit of Mount Tabor awaits us. How pure is the dew of the hills, how fresh is the mountain air, how rich the food and drink of those who dwell above, whose windows look into the New Jerusalem! Many saints are content to live like people in coal mines, who never see the sun. Tears sadden their faces when they could be anointed with heavenly oil. I am convinced that many believers suffer in a dungeon when they could walk on a palace roof, viewing the lush landscape and Lebanon. Wake up, believers, from your lowly condition! Throw away your laziness, sluggishness, coldness, or whatever is interfering with your pure love for Christ. Make Him the Source, the Center, and the One who encompasses every delight of your soul. Refuse to be satisfied any longer with your meager accomplishments. Aspire to a higher, a nobler, and a fuller life. Upward to heaven! Nearer to God! CHARLES H. SPURGEON

I want to scale the utmost height,
And catch a gleam of glory bright;
But still I'll pray, till heaven I've found,
Lord, lead me on to higher ground!

Not many of us are living at our best. We linger in the lowlands because we are afraid to climb the mountains. The steepness and ruggedness discourage us, so we stay in the mist of the valleys and never learn the mystery of the hills. We do not know what is lost by our self-indulgence, what glory awaits if we only have the courage to climb, or what blessings we will find if we will only ascend the mountains of God! J. R. M.

Too low they build who build beneath the stars.

~~~~~ JANUARY 3 ~~~~~

Morning

Therefore do not worry about tomorrow, for tomorrow will worry
about itself. Each day has enough trouble of its own.
MATTHEW 6:34

There are two golden days in the week, upon which, and about which, I never worry—two carefree days, kept sacredly free from fear and apprehension.

One of these days is Yesterday; Yesterday, with its cares and frets, all its pains and aches, all its faults, mistakes, and blunders, has passed forever beyond my recall. I cannot undo an act that I wrought nor unsay a word that I said. All that it holds of my life, of wrong, regret, and sorrow, is in the hands of the Mighty Love that can bring honey out of the rock and sweetest waters out of the bitterest desert. Save for the beautiful memories—sweet and tender—that linger like the perfume of roses in the heart of that day that is gone, I have nothing to do with Yesterday. It *was* mine! It *is* God's!

And the other day that I do not worry about is Tomorrow; Tomorrow, with all its possible adversities, its burdens, its perils, its large promise and poor performance, its failures and mistakes, is as far beyond my mastery as its dead sister, Yesterday. It is a day of God's. Its sun will rise in roseate splendor or behind a mask of weeping clouds—*but it will rise.*

Until then, the same Love and Patience that held Yesterday holds Tomorrow. Save for the star of hope that gleams forever on the brow of Tomorrow, shining with tender promise into the heart of Today, I have no possession in that unborn day of grace. All else is in the safe keeping of the Infinite Love that is higher than the stars, wider than the skies, deeper than the seas. Tomorrow *is* God's day! It *will be* mine!

There is left for myself, then, but one day in the week—Today. *Any man can fight the battles of Today! Any woman can carry the burdens of just one day! Any man can resist the temptations of Today!* Oh, friends, *it is when we willfully add the burdens of those two awful eternities—Yesterday and Tomorrow—such burdens as only the Mighty God can sustain—that we break down.* It isn't the experience of Today that drives men mad. It is the remorse for something that happened Yesterday; the dread of what Tomorrow may disclose.

These are God's days! Leave them with Him!

Therefore, I think and I do, and I journey *but one day* at a time! That is the easy way. That is Man's Day. Dutifully I run my course and work my appointed task on that Day of ours. God—the All-Mighty and All-Loving—takes care of Yesterday and Tomorrow. BOB BURDETTE

> *—But, Lord, tomorrow!*
> *Did I not die for thee?*
> *Do I not live for thee?*
> *Leave Me tomorrow!*

CHRISTINA ROSSETTI

"Tomorrow is God's secret—but today is yours to live."

All the tomorrows of our lives have to pass Him before they
can get to us. I heard a voice at evening softly say,
"Bear not thy yesterday into tomorrow;
Nor load this week with last week's load of sorrow. Lift
all thy burdens as they come, nor try
To weight the present with the by and by. One step,
and then another, take thy way—
Live by the day."

JULIA HARRIS MAY

~~~ JANUARY 3 ~~~
Evening

I [will] move along slowly at the pace of the flocks and
herds before me and the pace of the children.
GENESIS 33:14

What a beautiful picture of Jacob's thoughtfulness for the cattle and the children! He would not allow them to be driven too hard for even one day. He would not lead them at a pace equal to what a strong man like Esau could keep or expected them to keep, but only one as fast as *they* were able to endure. He knew exactly how far they could go in a day, and he made that his only consideration in planning their travel. He had taken the same wilderness journey years before and knew from personal experience its roughness, heat, and distance. And so he said, "I will move along slowly, since you have never been this way before" (Joshua 3:4).

We "have never been this way before," but the Lord Jesus has. It is all untraveled and unknown ground to us, but He knows it all through personal experience. He knows the steep places that take our breath away, the rocky paths that make our feet ache, the hot and shadeless stretches that bring us to exhaustion, and the rushing rivers that we have to cross—Jesus has gone through it all before us. As John 4:6 shows,

"Jesus, tired as he was from the journey, sat down." He was battered by every possible torrent, but all the floodwaters coming against Him never quenched His love. Jesus was made a perfect leader by the things He suffered. "He knows how we are formed, *he remembers that we are dust*" (Psalm 103:14). Think of that when you are tempted to question the gentleness of His leading. He *remembers* all the time and will never make you take even one step beyond what your feet are able to endure. Never mind if you think you are unable to take another step, for either He will strengthen you to make you able, or He will call a sudden halt, and you will not have to take it at all. FRANCES RIDLEY HAVERGAL

> In *"pastures green"? Not always; sometimes He*
> *Who knowest best, in kindness leadeth me*
> *In weary ways, where heavy shadows be.*
> *So, whether on the hilltops high and fair*
> *I dwell, or in the sunless valleys, where*
> *The shadows lie, what matter? He is there.*
> BARRY

～～～ JANUARY 4 ～～～

Morning

Whoever drinks the water I give them will never thirst.
JOHN 4:14

My heart needs Thee, O Lord, my heart needs Thee! No part of my being needs Thee like my heart. All else within me can be filled by Thy gifts. My hunger can be satisfied by daily bread. My thirst can be allayed by earthly waters. My cold can be removed by household fires. My weariness can be relieved by outward rest. But no outward thing can make my heart pure. The calmest day will not calm my passions. The fairest scene will not beautify my soul. The richest music will not make harmony within. The breezes can cleanse the air, but no breeze can cleanse a spirit. This world has not provided for my heart. It has provided for my eye; it has provided for my ear;

it has provided for my touch; it has provided for my taste; it has provided for my sense of beauty, but it has not provided for my heart.

Lift up your eyes unto the hills! Make haste to Calvary, "Calvary's awful mountain-climb," and on the way there visit the slopes of Mount Olivet, where grow the trees of Gethsemane. Contemplate there the agony of the Lord, where He already tasted the tremendous cup, which He drank to the dregs the next noontide on the Cross. *There* is the answer to your need.

Provide Thou for my heart, O Lord. It is the only unwinged bird in all creation. *Give it wings!* O *Lord, give it wings!* Earth has failed to give it wings; its very power of loving has often drawn it into the mire. Be Thou the strength of my heart. Be Thou its fortress in temptation, its shield in remorse, its covert in the storm, its star in the night, its voice in the solitude. Guide it in its gloom; help it in its heat; direct it in its doubt; calm it in its conflict; fan it in its faintness; prompt it in its perplexity; lead it through its labyrinth; raise it from its ruins.

I cannot rule this heart of mine; keep it under the shadow of Thine own wings.

George Matheson

> *None other Lamb! none other name!*
> *None other hope in heaven, or earth, or sea!*
> *None other hiding-place for sin and shame!*
> *None beside Thee!*
>
> *My faith burns low; my hope burns low;*
> *Only my soul's deep need comes out in me*
> *By the deep thunder of its want and woe,*
> *Calls out to Thee.*
>
> *Lord, Thou art life though I be dead!*
> *Love's Flame art Thou, however cold I be!*
> *Nor heaven have I, nor place to lay my head,*
> *Nor home, but Thee.*
>
> Christina Rossetti

"Come to me . . . and I will give you rest" (Matthew 11:28).

Evening

*"Go," Jesus replied, "your son will live." The man
took Jesus at his word and departed.*
JOHN 4:50

Whatever you ask for in prayer, believe.
MARK 11:24

When you are confronted with a matter that requires immediate prayer, pray until you believe God—until with wholehearted sincerity you can thank Him for the answer. If you do not see the external answer immediately, do not pray for it in such a way that it is evident you are not definitely believing God for it. This type of prayer will be a hindrance instead of a help to you. And when you are finished praying, you will find that your faith has been weakened or has entirely gone. The urgency you felt to offer this kind of prayer is clearly from self and Satan. It may not be wrong to mention the matter to the Lord again, if He is keeping you waiting for His answer, but be sure to do so in a way that shows your faith.

Never pray in a way that diminishes your faith. You may tell Him you are waiting, still believing and therefore praising Him for the answer. There is nothing that so fully solidifies faith as being so sure of the answer that you can thank God for it. Prayers that empty us of faith deny both God's promises from His Word and the "Yes" that He whispered to our hearts. Such prayers are only the expression of the unrest of our hearts, and unrest implies unbelief that our prayers will be answered. "Now we who have believed enter that rest" (Hebrews 4:3).

The type of prayer that empties us of faith frequently arises from focusing our thoughts on the difficulty rather than on God's promise. Abraham, "without weakening in his faith . . . faced the fact that his body was as good as dead. . . . Yet he did not waver through unbelief regarding the promise of God, but was strengthened in his faith and gave glory to God" (Romans 4:19–20). May we "watch and pray so that [we] will not fall into [the] temptation" (Matthew 26:41) of praying faith-diminishing prayers. C. H. P.

Faith is not a sense, nor sight, nor reason, but simply taking God at His word. CHRISTMAS EVANS

The beginning of anxiety is the end of faith, and the beginning of true faith is the end of anxiety. GEORGE MUELLER

You will never learn faith in comfortable surroundings. God gives us His promises in a quiet hour, seals our covenants with great and gracious words, and then steps back, waiting to see how much we believe. He then allows the Tempter to come, and the ensuing test seems to contradict all that He has spoken. This is when faith wins its crown. This is the time to look up through the storm, and among the trembling, frightened sailors declare, "I have faith in God that it will happen just as he told me" (Acts 27:25).

> *Believe and trust; through stars and suns,*
> *Through life and death, through soul and sense,*
> *His wise, paternal purpose runs;*
> *The darkness of His Providence*
> *Is starlit with Divine intents.*

～～～ JANUARY 5 ～～～
Morning

And why do you worry . . . ?
MATTHEW 6:28

When a man is living on God's plan he has no need to worry himself about his trade or about his house or about anything that belongs to him.

Do not look at your own faith; look at God's faithfulness! Do not look around on circumstances; keep on looking at the resources of the Infinite God!

The only thing a man may be anxious about in this life is whether he is working on God's plan, doing God's work; and if that is so, all the care of everything else is back on God.

There are some things which we cannot definitely claim in prayer because we do not know whether they are in God's mind for us. They may or may not be, but it is only by praying that we can tell. I am perfectly sure that in praying, there comes to men who dwell with God a kind of holy confidence; and when they get hold of a promise in God's Word, they look on that promise as granted.

Let us yield ourselves to God, that the living Godhead may flow through our poor, mean, frail human minds.

If the Lord careth for thee, be thyself at rest. ARCHBISHOP LEIGHTON

> *When we see the lilies*
> *Spinning in distress,*
> *Taking thought to*
> *Manufacture loveliness;*
> *When we see the birds all*
> *Building barns for store,*
> *'Twill be time for us to worry—*
> *Not before!*

If the Pilot has come on board, why should the captain also pace the deck with weary foot?

JANUARY 5
Evening

*Then Asa . . . said, "*LORD*, there is no one like you*
to help the powerless against the mighty."
2 CHRONICLES 14:11

Remind God of His exclusive responsibility: "There is no one like you to help." The odds against Asa's men were enormous. "Zerah the Cushite marched out against them with an army of thousands upon thousands and three hundred chariots" (v. 9). It seemed impossible for Asa to hold his own against that vast multitude. There were no allies who would come to his defense. Therefore his only hope was in God.

It may be that your difficulties have come to such an alarming level that you may be compelled to refuse all human help. In lesser trials, you may have had that recourse, but now you must cast yourself on your almighty Friend. *Put God between yourself and the enemy.*

Asa, realizing his lack of strength, saw Jehovah as standing between the might of Zerah and himself. And he was not mistaken. We are told that the Cushites "were crushed before the LORD *and his forces*" (v. 13), as though heavenly warriors threw themselves against the enemy on Israel's behalf. God's forces so overwhelmed the vast army of the enemy that they fled. Then all Israel had to do was follow up and gather the plunder. Our God is "the Lord of hosts" (Isaiah 10:16 KJV), who can summon unexpected reinforcements at any moment to help His people. Believe that He is between you and your difficulty, and what troubles you will flee before Him, as clouds in the wind. F. B. MEYER

> *When nothing on which to lean remains,*
> *When strongholds crumble to dust;*
> *When nothing is sure but that God still reigns,*
> *That is just the time to trust.*

> *It's better to walk by faith than sight,*
> *In this path of yours and mine;*
> *And the darkest night, when there's no outer light*
> *Is the time for faith to shine.*

"Abraham believed God" (Romans 4:3), and said to his eyes, "Stand back!" and to the laws of nature, "Hold your peace!" and to an unbelieving heart, "Silence, you lying tempter!" He simply "*believed* God." JOSEPH PARKER

JANUARY 6
Morning

Have faith in God.
MARK 11:22

In the catacombs, we are told, explorers take a thread with them through all the dark passages and tortuous windings, and by this thread they find their way back again to the light. There is such a thread running through all the dark corridors which we tread; and if we simply, practically trust in God, we shall steer past every peril and land in the world of light. This is the counsel to remember in all the perplexities of our actual lives.

There is an answer to every questioning "Why?" It is this: *Have faith in God.*

Have faith that *He knows all, sympathizes with all, can rectify what is amiss in all!*

Have faith in the outworking of His beneficent purpose: that the ruin will become a magnificent pile that the desert will blossom into a garden. *Have faith in God.* Keep close to Him—His side, His will—and He will teach us the true thing, the right way. Have faith that God knows and that we shall know, by and by, why things are as they are.

> *We ask and are answered not,*
> *And so we say, God has forgot,*
> *Or else, there is no God.*
>
> *The years*
> *Roll back and through a mist of tears,*
> *I see a child turn from her play,*
> *And seek with eager feet, the way*
> *That led her to her father's knee.*
>
> *"If God is wise and kind," said she,*
> *"Why did He let my roses die?"*
> *A moment's pause, a smile, a sigh,*
> *And then, "I do not know, my dear,*
> *Some questions are not answered here."*
>
> *"But is it wrong to ask?" "Not so,*
> *My child; that we should seek to know*
> *Proves right to know, beyond a doubt;*
> *And someday we shall yet find out*
> *Why roses die."*
>
> *And then I wait,*
> *Sure of my answer, soon or late;*

Secure that love doth hold for me
The key to life's great mystery;
And oh, so glad to leave it there,
Tho' my dead roses were so fair.

AUTHOR UNKNOWN

~~~ JANUARY 6 ~~~
Evening

When you pass through the waters . . . they will not sweep over you.

ISAIAH 43:2

God does not open paths for us before we come to them, or provide help before help is needed. He does not remove obstacles out of our way before we reach them. Yet when we are at our point of need, God's hand is outstretched.

Many people forget this truth and continually worry about difficulties they envision in the future. They expect God to open and clear many miles of road before them, but He promises to do it step by step, only as their need arises. You must be in the floodwaters before you can claim God's promise. Many people dread death and are distressed that they do not have "dying grace." Of course, they will never have the grace for death when they are in good health. Why should they have it while in the midst of life's duties, with death still far away? Living grace is what is needed for life's work and calling, and then dying grace when it is time to die. J. R. M.

> *"When you pass through the waters"*
>   *Deep the waves may be and cold,*
> *But Jehovah is our refuge,*
>   *And His promise is our hold;*
> *For the Lord Himself has said it,*
>   *He, the faithful God and true:*
> *"When you come to the waters*
>   *You will not go down,* BUT THROUGH.*"*

Seas of sorrow, seas of trial,
    Bitter anguish, fiercest pain,
Rolling surges of temptation
    Sweeping over heart and brain—
They will never overflow us
    For we know His word is true;
All His waves and all His billows
    He will lead us safely THROUGH.

Threatening breakers of destruction,
    Doubt's insidious undertow,
Will not sink us, will not drag us
    Out to ocean depths of woe;
For His promise will sustain us,
    Praise the Lord, whose Word is true!
We will not go down, or under,
    For He says, "You will pass THROUGH."
ANNIE JOHNSON FLINT

JANUARY 7

Morning

Take up twelve stones. . . . to serve as a sign among you. In the future, when your children ask you, "What do these stones mean?" tell them that . . . the waters of the Jordan were cut off. These stones are to be a memorial to the people of Israel forever.

JOSHUA 4:3, 6–7

You will never get anywhere with God unless you take definite steps. God was very definite in His dealings with Abraham. *He brought him to a definite place, and Abraham marked the spot.*

When the children of Israel crossed over Jordan, they marked the spot on the shore with twelve stones, and also placed twelve stones in the riverbed, which were later covered with water—a hidden place.

God wants us, as Christians, *to take definite steps* and to *mark* these steps. There are places in your heart over which the Jordan's waters roll—hidden places which no one sees or of which no one knows the meaning, but He knows. When you have committed them unto Him that He might have His say, saying, "Search me, O God, and know my heart: try me, and know my thoughts: and see if there be any wicked way in me" (Psalm 139:23–24 KJV), *He knows and answers prayer.*

Is this a crisis hour in *your* life? If it is, settle it *now.*

We must never go back on our transactions with God.

It remains to be seen what God can do with a man irrevocably given to Him. It is because we are but partially His that His work in us and for us is incomplete.

If you have given yourself to God, you have just to *reckon* that He takes what you give. A time comes when you have to *cease praying and believe.* Some Christians say, "O Lord, come and fill me." They keep on praying, and He says, "Believe I have come; reckon that I am come; if you reckon, I will come."

A friend said, "If God tells me to reckon, *He pledges Himself to make the reckoning good.*" As we go on reckoning, we will go on realizing. No man makes a mistake who does what the Lord bids him do. THOMAS COOK

Reckon some special time when you fully surrendered your life to the Lord. Build a pile of stones there to mark the spot, and then build another on the life side—the resurrection side! Do this today! Build a heap of stones to mark the time, and never fight the old battle again. We should not be dying and rising, and dying and rising again; we should build our memorials of stones once for all, and then *ever date from that time!*

~~~~~ JANUARY 7 ~~~~~

Evening

I have learned to be content whatever the circumstances.
PHILIPPIANS 4:11

Paul, while being denied every comfort, wrote the above words from a dark prison cell.

A story is told of a king who went to his garden one morning, only to find everything withered and dying. He asked the oak tree that stood near the gate what the trouble was. The oak said it was tired of life and determined to die because it was not tall and beautiful like the pine tree. The pine was troubled because it could not bear grapes like the grapevine. The grapevine was determined to throw its life away because it could not stand erect and produce fruit as large as peaches. The geranium was fretting because it was not tall and fragrant like the lilac.

And so it went throughout the garden. Yet coming to a violet, the king found its face as bright and happy as ever and said, "Well, violet, I'm glad to find one brave little flower in the midst of this discouragement. You don't seem to be the least disheartened." The violet responded, "No, I'm not. I know I'm small, yet I thought if you wanted an oak or a pine or a peach tree or even a lilac, you would have planted one. Since I knew you wanted a violet, I'm determined to be the best little violet I can be."

> *Others may do a greater work,*
> *But you have your part to do;*
> *And no one in all God's family*
> *Can do it as well as you.*

People who are God's without reservation "have learned to be content whatever the circumstances." His will becomes their will, and they desire to do for Him whatever He desires them to do. They strip themselves of everything, and in their nakedness find everything restored a hundredfold.

JANUARY 8
Morning

He made me into a polished arrow.
ISAIAH 49:2

Our daughters will be like pillars carved to adorn a palace.
PSALM 144:12

Cut . . . to Shine!

When in Amsterdam, Holland, last summer," says a traveler, "I was much interested in a visit we made to a place then famous for polishing diamonds. We saw the men engaged in the work. When a diamond is found, it is rough and dark like a common pebble. It takes a long time to polish it, and it is very hard work. It is held by means of a piece of metal close to the surface of a large wheel, which is kept going round and round. Fine diamond dust is put on this wheel, nothing else being hard enough to polish the diamond. This work is kept up for months, and sometimes for several years, before it is finished. If the diamond is intended for a king, then greater time and trouble are spent on it."

What though the precious jewel may be torn and cut until its carats are reduced tenfold! When the cutting and polishing are completed, it will shine with a thousand flashes of reflected light—every carat will be multiplied a hundredfold in value by the process of reduction and threatened destruction!

Let us *wait His time*—let us *trust His love*—that "the proven genuineness of your faith . . . may result in praise, glory and honor when Jesus Christ is revealed" (1 Peter 1:7).

JANUARY 8
Evening

I will send down showers in season; there will be showers of blessing.
EZEKIEL 34:26

What is your *season* today? Are you experiencing a season of drought? If so, then it is the season for showers. Are you going through a season of great heaviness with dark clouds? Then that too is the season for showers. "Your strength will equal your days" (Deuteronomy 33:25). "I will send . . . *showers* of blessing." Notice that the word *showers* is plural.

God will send all kinds of blessings. And all His blessings go together like links in a golden chain. If He gives you saving grace, He will also give you comforting gr[ace]. God will send "*showers* of blessings." Look up today, you who are dried and wi[thered] plants. Open your leaves and flowers and receive God's heavenly watering.
H. SPURGEON

Let but your heart become a valley low,
And God will rain on it till it will overflow.

You, O Lord, can transform my thorn into a flower. And I *do* want my thorn transformed into a flower. Job received sunshine after the rain, but was the rain all wasted? Job wants to know, and I want to know, if the rain is related to the sunshine. Only You can tell me—Your cross can tell me. You have crowned Your sorrow. Let this be my crown, O Lord. I will only triumph in You once I have learned the radiance of the rain. GEORGE MATHESON

The fruitful life seeks rain as well as sunshine.
The landscape, brown and dry beneath the sun,
Needs but the cloud to lift it into life;
The dews may dampen the tree and flower,
But it requires the cloud-distilled shower
To bring rich greenness to the lifeless life.
Ah, how like this, the landscape of a life:
Dews of trial fall like incense, rich and sweet;
But meaning little in the crystal tray—
Like moths of night, dews lift at break of day
And fleeting impressions leave, like lips that meet.
But clouds of trials, bearing burdens rare,
Leave in the soul, a moisture settled deep:
Life stirs by the powerful law of God;
And where before the thirsty camel trod,
There richest beauties to life's landscape leap.
Then re____ ___u in each cloud that comes to you
____ ___Paul, in letters large and clear:
____ ___uds your soul with blessing feed,
____ ___ant trust as you do read,
____ ___ work for good. Fret not, nor fear!

So Jacob was left alone, and a man wrestled with him till daybreak. Then the man said, "You have struggled with God and with humans and have overcome."
GENESIS 32:24, 28

If you saw one of the intimates of the King on his knees, you would marvel at the sight. Look! He is in the Audience Chamber. He has a seat set for him among the peers. He is set down among the old nobility of the Empire. The King will not put on his signet ring to seal a command, till his friend has been heard. "Command Me," the King says to him. "Ask of Me," He says, "for the things of My sons: command the things to come concerning them!" And, as if that were not enough, that man-of-all-prayer is still on his knees. He is wrestling there. There is no enemy that I can see, yet he wrestles like a mighty man. What is he doing with such a struggle? Doing? Do you not know what he is doing? He is moving Heaven and earth. He is casting this mountain, and that, into the midst of the sea. He is casting down thrones. He is smiting old empires of time to pieces. Yes, he is wrestling indeed. ALEXANDER WHYTE

> *Break through to God,*
> *He fully understands*
> *Thou art in His dear Hands,*
> *To fulfill all His commands,*
> *Break through to God!*
>
> *Break through to God,*
> *Be dauntless, faithful, strong,*
> *E'en though the fight is long,*
> *Raise to Him the victor's song,*
> *Break through to God.*
>
> *Break through to God,*
> *Though thy heart may quail,*

And the foe may rail,
Calvary's victory shall not fail,
Break through to God!

Looking back over the Welsh Revival about 1904, the Revelation Seth Joshua wrote: "The secret of the Lord was with many even before the blessing came. I know a man, who, for five years, was carried out by the Spirit, and made to weep and pray along the banks of a Welsh river. At last the travail ceased, and calm expectation followed the soul pangs of this man about whom I now write. *He lived to see the answer to his heart-cries unto the Lord.* He was present in the services in which the first historical incidents took place." *Break through to God!*

—— ~~~ —— JANUARY 9 —— ~~~ ——

Evening

I consider that our present sufferings are not worth comparing
with the glory that will be revealed in us.
ROMANS 8:18

I once kept a bottle-shaped cocoon of an emperor moth for nearly one year. The cocoon was very strange in its construction. The neck of the "bottle" had a narrow opening through which the mature insect forces its way. Therefore the abandoned cocoon is as perfect as one still inhabited, with no tearing of the interwoven fibers having taken place. The great disparity between the size of the opening and the size of the imprisoned insect makes a person wonder how the moth ever exits at all. Of course, it is never accomplished without great labor and difficulty. It is believed the pressure to which the moth's body is subjected when passing through such a narrow opening is nature's way of forcing fluids into the wings, since they are less developed at the time of emerging from the cocoon than in other insects.

I happened to witness the first efforts of my imprisoned moth to escape from its long confinement. All morning I watched it patiently striving and struggling to be free. It never seemed able to get beyond a certain point, and at last my patience was exhausted. The confining fibers were probably drier and less elastic than if the cocoon had been left all winter in its native habitat, as nature meant it to be. In any case, I thought I was wiser and more compassionate than its Maker, so I resolved to give it a helping hand. With the point of my scissors, I snipped the confining threads to make the exit just a little easier. Immediately and with perfect ease, my moth crawled out, dragging a huge swollen body and little shriveled wings! I watched in vain to see the marvelous process of expansion in which these wings would silently and swiftly develop before my eyes. As I examined the delicately beautiful spots and markings of various colors that were all there in miniature, I longed to see them assume their ultimate size. I looked for my moth, one of the loveliest of its kind, to appear in all its perfect beauty. But I looked in vain. My misplaced tenderness had proved to be its ruin. The moth suffered an aborted life, crawling painfully through its brief existence instead of flying through the air on rainbow wings.

I have thought of my moth often, especially when watching with tearful eyes those who were struggling with sorrow, suffering, and distress. My tendency would be to quickly alleviate the discipline and bring deliverance. O shortsighted person that I am! How do I know that one of these pains or groans should be relieved? The farsighted, perfect love that seeks the perfection of its object does not weakly shrink away from present, momentary suffering. Our Father's love is too steadfast to be weak. Because He loves His children, He "disciplines us . . . that we may share in his holiness" (Hebrews 12:10). With this glorious purpose in sight, He does not relieve our crying. Made perfect through suffering, as our Elder Brother was, we children of God are disciplined to make us obedient, and brought to glory through much tribulation.
FROM A TRACT

~~~~~~~ JANUARY 10 ~~~~~~~

Morning

Peter went up on the roof to pray.
ACTS 10:9

He went up upon the housetop to pray, probably *for further light*. What was to be the next step in the fulfillment of his lifework? Was the cloud to move forward?

Was some new development of the Divine pattern at hand which he must realize for himself? And for others?

While he prayed the heavens were opened, and God gave him a real vision of His will. Then when he was very much perplexed in himself at what the vision meant, the knocking at the gate, the voices of men that rose at noon-silence calling his name, together with the assurance of the Spirit that there was no need for fear or further hesitation—all indicated that the hour of Destiny had struck; that a new epoch was inaugurated; and that he was to lead the Church into the greatest revolution she had known since the Ascension of her Lord.

What a lesson for our perplexed and anxious hearts! We find it difficult to wait our Lord's leisure; like imprisoned birds, we beat our breasts against the wires of the cage. Though we pray, we do not trust. We find it hard to obey the injunction of our Lord—to roll our care, our way, ourselves, onto God.

> *Give to the winds thy fears;*
> *hope and be undismayed;*
> *God hears thy sighs, and counts thy tears;*
> *God shall lift up thy head.*
>
> *Leave to His sovereign sway to choose*
> *and to command;*
> *With wonder filled, thou soon shall own*
> *how wise, how strong His Hand!*
>
> *Through waves and clouds and storms, He gently*
> *clears thy way.*
> *Wait thou His time, so shall thy night*
> *soon end in joyous day.*
>
> *He everywhere hath sway, and all things serve*
> *His might.*
> *His every act pure blessing is*
> *His path unsullied light.*

Evening

Paul and his companions . . . [were] kept by the Holy Spirit
from preaching the word in the province of Asia.
ACTS 16:6

It is interesting to study the way God extended His guidance to these early messengers of the Cross. It consisted mainly in prohibiting their movement when they attempted to take a course other than the right one. When they wanted to turn to the left, toward Asia, He stopped them. When they sought to turn to the right, toward Bithynia in Asia Minor, He stopped them again. In his later years, Paul would do some of his greatest work in that very region, yet now the door was closed before him by the Holy Spirit. The time was not yet ripe for the attack on these apparently impregnable bastions of the kingdom of Satan. Apollos needed to go there first to lay the groundwork. Paul and Barnabas were needed more urgently elsewhere and required further training before undertaking this responsible task.

Beloved, whenever you are in doubt as to which way to turn, submit your judgment absolutely to the Spirit of God, asking Him to shut every door but the right one. Say to Him, "Blessed Spirit, I give to You the entire responsibility of closing every road and stopping every step that is not of God. Let me hear Your voice behind me whenever I 'turn aside to the right or to the left' [Deuteronomy 5:32]."

In the meantime, continue along the path you have already been traveling. Persist in your calling until you are clearly told to do something else. O traveler, the Spirit of Jesus is waiting to be to you what He was to Paul. Just be careful to obey even His smallest nudging or warning. Then after you have prayed the prayer of faith and there are no apparent hindrances, go forward with a confident heart. Do not be surprised if your answer comes in doors closing before you. But when doors are shut to the right and left, an open road is sure to lead to Troas. Luke waits for you there, and visions will point the way to where vast opportunities remain open, and faithful friends are waiting. F. B. MEYER

Is there some problem in your life to solve,
    Some passage seeming full of mystery?
God knows, who brings the hidden things to light.
    He keeps the key.

Is there some door closed by the Father's hand
    Which widely opened you had hoped to see?
Trust God and wait—for when He shuts the door
    He keeps the key.

Is there some earnest prayer unanswered yet,
    Or answered not as you had thought 'twould be?
God will make clear His purpose by and by.
    He keeps the key.

Have patience with your God, your patient God,
    All wise, all knowing, no long lingerer He,
And of the door of all your future life
    He keeps the key.

Unfailing comfort, sweet and blessed rest,
    To know of every door He keeps the key.
That He at last when just he sees is best,
    Will give it thee.

ANONYMOUS

～～～ JANUARY 11 ～～～

Morning

Dying, and yet we live on.
2 CORINTHIANS 6:9

To one who asked him the secret of service, Mr. George Mueller replied: "There was a day when I died, utterly died to George Mueller"—and, as he spoke, he bent lower and lower until he almost touched the floor—"to his opinions, preferences, tastes, and will; died to the world, its approval or censure; died to the approval or blame of even my brethren and friends. Since then I have *studied to show myself approved only unto God.*"

> We may not understand nor know
> Just how the giant oak trees throw
> Their spreading branches wide,
> Nor how upon the mountainside
> The dainty wildflowers grow.
>
> We may not understand nor see
> Into the depth and mystery
> Of suffering and tears;
> Yet, through the stress of patient years
> The flowers of sympathy
>
> Spring up and scatter everywhere
> Their perfume on the fragrant air—
> But lo! the seed must die,
> If it would bloom and multiply
> And ripened fruitage bear.

THOMAS KIMBER

Look at that splendid oak! Where was it born? In a grave. The acorn was put into the ground, and in that grave it sprouted and sent up its shoots. And was it only one day that it stood in the grave? No, every day for a hundred years it has stood there, and in that place of death it has found its life. *"The creation of a thousand forests is in one acorn."*

How shall my leaves fly singing in the wind unless my roots shall wither in the dark?
PERSIAN POET

Evening

Comfort, comfort my people, says your God.
ISAIAH 40:1

Store up comfort. This was the prophet Isaiah's mission. The world is full of hurting and comfortless hearts. But before you will be competent for this lofty ministry, you must be trained. And your training is extremely costly, for to make it complete, you too must endure the same afflictions that are wringing countless hearts of tears and blood. Consequently, your own life becomes the hospital ward where you are taught the divine art of comfort. You will be wounded so that in the binding up of your wounds by the Great Physician, you may learn how to render first aid to the wounded everywhere. Do you wonder why you are having to experience some great sorrow? Over the next ten years you will find many others afflicted in the same way. You will tell them how you suffered and were comforted. As the story unfolds, God will apply the anesthetic He once used on you to them. Then in the eager look followed by the gleam of hope that chases the shadow of despair from the soul, *you will know why* you were afflicted. And you will bless God for the discipline that filled your life with such a treasure of experience and helpfulness. SELECTED

God comforts us not to make us comfortable but to make us *comforters.* JOHN HENRY JOWETT

> *They tell me I must bruise*
> *The rose's leaf,*
> *Ere I can keep and use*
> *Its fragrance brief.*

> *They tell me I must break*
> *The skylark's heart,*
> *Ere her cage song will make*
> *The silence start.*

They tell me love must bleed,
And friendship weep,
Ere in my deepest need
I touch that deep.

Must it be always so
With precious things?
Must they be bruised and go
With beaten wings?

Ah, yes! by crushing days,
By caging nights, by scar
Of thorn and stony ways,
These blessings are!

$\sim\sim\sim$ JANUARY 12 $\sim\sim\sim$

Morning

I have lost all things. . . . that I may gain Christ.
PHILIPPIANS 3:8

Every great life has had in it some great renunciation.

Abraham began by letting go, and going out, and all the way it was just giving up: first his home, his father, and his past; next his inheritance to Lot, his selfish nephew; and finally the very child of promise on the altar of Moriah; but he became the father of the faithful, whose inheritance was as the sands of the sea and the stars of the heavens.

Hear David saying, "Neither will I offer burnt offerings unto the LORD my God of that which doth cost me nothing" (2 Samuel 24:24 KJV). David paid the full price. And we read, "The throne of David shall be established before the LORD for ever" (1 Kings 2:45 KJV).

Hannah gave up her boy, and he became the prophet of the restoration of ancient Israel.

Paul not only suffered the loss of all things but also counted them but refuse that he might win Christ. And Paul stood before the common people and in the palaces of kings.

So it is always: *real sacrifice, unto complete surrender of self, brings to us the revelation of God in His fullness.* As we have already seen, it was only on condition of Jacob's releasing and the brothers' bringing the best they had, Benjamin, that they could even see Joseph's face again. And when Judah went farther than this and offered himself to be Joseph's slave forever, then it was that Joseph could keep back nothing, but found himself compelled to reveal everything to those for whom his heart yearned. It is God's own way with us. God in Jesus Christ does not, and apparently cannot, make Himself fully known in His personality and love, until we have surrendered to Him unconditionally and forever not only all we have, but all we are. *Then God can refrain no longer, but lavishes upon us, in Christ, such a revealing of Himself that it cannot be told in words.*

But the supreme sacrifice!

God had to sacrifice Himself, in Christ, in order thus to reveal Himself to us; but His sacrifice alone will not suffice. Not until we in turn have sacrificed ourselves to Him is the revelation possible and complete. But what a revelation it is! *What glory God gives us in the life that is Christ as our lives!* How it changes everything for us thereafter *from famine to royal abundance!* MESSAGES FOR THE MORNING WATCH

I heard a voice so softly calling:
"Take up thy cross and follow me."
A tempest o'er my heart was falling,
A living cross this was to me.

His cross I took, which, cross no longer,
A hundredfold brings life to me;
My heart is filled with joy o'erflowing,
His love and life are light to me.

SELECTED

Evening

Reckon it nothing but joy . . . whenever you find yourselves hedged in by the various trials. Be assured that the testing of your faith leads to power of endurance.

JAMES 1:2–3 WNT

God hedges in His own in order to protect them. Yet often they only see the wrong side of the hedge and therefore misunderstand His actions. And so it was with Job when he asked, "Why is life given to a man whose way is hidden, whom God has hedged in?" (Job 3:23). Ah, but Satan knew the value of that hedge! He challenged the Lord by saying, "Have you not put a hedge around [Job] and his household and everything he has?" (Job 1:10).

Onto the pages of every trial there are narrow shafts of light that shine. Thorns will not prick you until you lean against them, and not one will touch you without God knowing. The words that hurt you, the letter that caused you pain, the cruelty of your closest friend, your financial need—they are all known to Him. He sympathizes as no one else can and watches to see if, through it all, you will dare to trust Him completely.

> *The hawthorn hedge that keeps us from intruding,*
> *Looks very fierce and bare*
> *When stripped by winter, every branch protruding*
> *Its thorns that would wound and tear.*
>
> *But springtime comes; and like the rod that budded,*
> *Each twig breaks out in green;*
> *And cushions soft of tender leaves are studded,*
> *Where spines alone were seen.*
>
> *The sorrows, that to us seem so perplexing,*
> *Are mercies kindly sent*
> *To guard our wayward souls from sadder vexing,*
> *And greater ills prevent.*

To save us from the pit, no screen of roses
    Would serve for our defense,
The hindrance that completely interposes
    Stings back like thorny fence.

At first when smarting from the shock, complaining
    Of wounds that freely bleed,
God's hedges of severity us paining,
    May seem severe indeed.

But afterwards, God's blessed springtime cometh,
    And bitter murmurs cease;
The sharp severity that pierced us bloometh,
    And yields the fruits of peace.

Then let us sing, our guarded way thus wending
    Life's hidden snares among,
Of mercy and of judgment sweetly blending;
    Earth's sad, but lovely song.

~~~~~~~~ JANUARY 13 ~~~~~~~~

Morning

You will sing.
ISAIAH 30:29

Someone writes of sitting one winter evening by an open wood fire and listening to the singing of the green logs as the fire flamed about them. All manner of sounds came out of the wood as it burned, and the writer, with poetic fancy, suggests that they were imprisoned songs, long sleeping in silence in the wood, brought out now by the fire.

When the tree stood in the forest, the birds came and sat on its boughs and sang their songs. The wind, too, breathed through the branches making a weird, strange music. One day a child sat on the moss by the tree's root and sang its happy gladness in a snatch of sweet melody. A penitent sat under the tree's shade and with trembling tones, amid falling leaves, sang the fifty-first Psalm. And all these notes of varied song sank into the tree as it stood there, and they hid away in its trunk. There they slept until the tree was cut down and part of it became a backlog in the cheerful evening fire. Then the flames brought out the music.

This is but a poet's fancy as far as the tree and the songs of the backlog are concerned. But is there not here a little parable which may be likened to many a human life? Life has its varied notes and tones—some glad, some choked in tears. Years pass, and the life gives out no music of praise, sings no songs to bless others. But, at length, grief comes, and in the flames the long-imprisoned music is set free and sings its praise to God and its notes of love to cheer and bless the world. Gathered in life's long summer and stored away in the heart, it is given out in the hours of suffering and pain.

Many a rejoicing Christian never learned to sing till the flames kindled upon him.
J. R. MILLER
Gather the driftwood that will light the winter fire!

JANUARY 13

Evening

In all these things we are more than conquerors through him who loved us.
ROMANS 8:37

This is more than victory. This is a triumph so complete that we not only have escaped defeat and destruction but also have destroyed our enemies and won plunder so rich and valuable that we can actually thank God for the battle. How can we be "more than conquerors"? We can receive from the conflict a spiritual discipline that will greatly strengthen our faith and establish our spiritual character. Temptation is necessary to establish and ground us in our spiritual life. It is like the fierce winds that cause the mighty cedars on the mountainside to sink their roots more deeply into the soil. Our spiritual conflicts are among our most wonderful blessings, and the Adversary is used to train us for his own ultimate defeat. The ancient Phrygians of Asia Minor had a legend that every time they conquered an enemy, they absorbed the physical strength of their victims and added to their own strength and bravery. And in truth, meeting temptation victoriously doubles our spiritual strength and weaponry. Therefore it is possible not only to defeat our enemy but also to capture him and make him fight in our ranks.

The prophet Isaiah tells of "fly[ing] upon the shoulders of the Philistines" (Isaiah 11:14 KJV). These Philistines were their deadly foes, but this passage suggests that they would be able not only to conquer the Philistines but also to ride on their backs to further triumphs. Just as a skilled sailor can use a head wind to carry him forward, by using its impelling power to follow a zigzag course, it is possible for us in our spiritual life, through the victorious grace of God, to turn completely around the things that seem most unfriendly and unfavorable. Then we will be able to say continually, "What has happened to me has actually served to advance the gospel" (Philippians 1:12).

Early sailors believed the coral-building animals instinctively built up the great reefs of the Atoll Islands in order to protect themselves in the inner waterway. He has shown these organisms can only live and thrive facing the open ocean in the highly oxygenated foam of the combative waves. It is commonly thought that a protected and easy life is the best way to live. Yet the lives of all the noblest and strongest people prove exactly the opposite and that the endurance of hardship is the making of the person. It is the factor that distinguishes between merely existing and living a vigorous life. Hardship builds character. SELECTED

But thanks be to God, who always leads us in triumphal procession in Christ and through us spreads everywhere the fragrance of the knowledge of him (2 Corinthians 2:14).

~~~~~ JANUARY 14 ~~~~~
Morning

*For I resolved to know nothing while I was with you
except Jesus Christ and him crucified.*
1 CORINTHIANS 2:2

*For no one can lay any foundation other than the
one already laid, which is Jesus Christ.*
1 CORINTHIANS 3:11

In the Cross of Christ I glory,
Tow'ring o'er the wrecks of time—

Martin Luther preached the doctrine of Atoning Blood to slumbering Europe, and Europe awoke from the dead.

Amid all his defenses of Divine Sovereignty, *Calvin* never ignored or belittled the Atonement.

Cowper sang of it among the water lilies of the Ouse.

Spurgeon thundered this glorious doctrine of Christ Crucified into the ears of peer and peasant with a voice like the sound of many waters.

John Bunyan made the Cross the starting-point to the Celestial City.

Moody's bells all chimed to the keynote of Calvary.

Napoleon, after conquering almost the whole of Europe, put his finger on the red spot on the map representing the British Isles, and said, "Were it not for that red spot, I'd conquer the world!"

So says Satan about the place called Calvary, where Jesus Christ shed His Blood.

Beneath the Cross of Jesus
I fain would take my stand,
The shadow of a mighty rock
Within a weary land;
A home within the wilderness,
A rest upon the way,
From the burning of the noontide heat,
And the burden of the day.
Upon the Cross of Jesus
Mine eye at times can see
The very dying form of One
Who suffered there for me.
And from my smitten heart with tears,
These wonders I confess,
The wonder of His glorious love,
And my own worthlessness.

I take, O Cross, thy shadow
For my abiding place;
I ask no other sunshine than
The sunshine of His face;
Content to let the world go by,
To know no gain nor loss,
My sinful self my only shame,
My glory all the Cross.

Every true preacher of the Gospel strings all his pearls on the Red Cord of the Atonement.
T. L. CUYLER

Calvary covers it all!

~~~~~ JANUARY 14 ~~~~~
Evening

When he has brought out all his own, he goes on ahead of them.
JOHN 10:4

This is intensely difficult work for Him and us—it is difficult for us to go, but equally difficult for Him to cause us pain. Yet it must be done. It would not be in our best interest to always remain in one happy and comfortable location. Therefore He moves us forward. The shepherd leaves the fold so the sheep will move on to the vitalizing mountain slopes. In the same way, laborers must be driven out into the harvest, or else the golden grain would spoil.

But take heart! It could never be better to stay once He determines otherwise; if the loving hand of our Lord moves us forward, it must be best. Forward, in His name, to green pastures, quiet waters, and mountain heights (Psalm 23:2)! *"He goes on ahead of [us]."* So whatever awaits us is encountered first by Him, and the eye of faith can always discern His majestic presence out in front. When His presence cannot be seen, it is dangerous to move ahead. Comfort your heart with the fact that the Savior has

Himself experienced all the trials He asks you to endure; He would not ask you to pass through them unless he was sure that the paths were not too difficult or strenuous for you.

This is the blessed life—not anxious to see far down the road nor overly concerned about the next step, not eager to choose the path nor weighted down with the heavy responsibilities of the future, but quietly following the Shepherd, *one step at a time.*

> *Dark is the sky! and veiled the unknown morrow!*
> *Dark is life's way, for night is not yet o'er;*
> *The longed-for glimpse I may not meanwhile borrow;*
> *But, this I know and trust, he goes before.*
>
> *Dangers are near! and fears my mind are shaking;*
> *Heart seems to dread what life may hold in store;*
> *But I am His—He knows the way I'm taking,*
> *More blessed even still—he goes before.*
>
> *Doubts cast their weird, unwelcome shadows o'er me,*
> *Doubts that life's best—life's choicest things are o'er;*
> *What but His Word can strengthen, can restore me,*
> *And this blest fact; that still he goes before.*
>
> *He goes before! Be this my consolation!*
> *He goes before! On this my heart would dwell!*
> *He goes before! This guarantees salvation!*
> *He goes before! And therefore all is well.*
>
> J. Danson Smith

The oriental shepherd always walked *ahead* of his sheep. He was always *out in front.* Any attack upon the sheep had to take him into account first. Now God is out in front. He is in our tomorrows, and it is tomorrow that fills people with fear. *Yet God is already there.* All the tomorrows of our life have to pass through Him before they can get to us. F. B. Meyer

God is in every tomorrow,
　Therefore I live for today,
Certain of finding at sunrise,
　Guidance and strength for my way;
Power for each moment of weakness,
　Hope for each moment of pain,
Comfort for every sorrow,
　Sunshine and joy after rain.

～～～ JANUARY 15 ～～～

Morning

He said to me: "It is done."
REVELATION 21:6

How many persons are everlastingly *doing,* but how few ever *get through* with it! How few settle a thing and know that it is accomplished and can say, "It is done!"

The moment we really believe, we are conscious that there is power. We can touch God at such times, and the fire in our souls makes us sure that something is settled forever.

Faith must be a clear-cut taking hold of God, a grasping Him with fingers of iron, with an uncompromising commitment of all to God. In learning to float you must utterly abandon yourself to the water; you must believe that the water is able to hold you up. So you must take this step of commitment and then look up to God with confidence and say, "It is done." Our part is *to commit;* God's part is *to work.* The very moment that we commit, that very moment He undertakes. We must believe that He has undertaken what we have committed. Faith must re-echo God's promise and dare to say, *"It is done."*

　The thing is as good as done, since He has taken it in hand.

Step out upon a bare promise right now and "calleth those things which be not as though they were" (Romans 4:17 KJV), and God will make your reckoning real. It will be done by actual experience. DAYS OF HEAVEN UPON EARTH

My old professor, Lord Kelvin, once said in class a very striking thing. He said that there came a point in all his great discoveries when he had to take a leap into the dark. And nobody who is afraid of such a leap from the solid ground of what is demonstrated will know the exhilaration of believing!

To commit ourselves unreservedly to Christ is just the biggest venture in the world! The wonderful thing is that when, with a certain daring, we take Lord Kelvin's "leap into the dark" we discover it is not dark at all, but life abundant, and liberty and peace.
GEORGE H. MORRISON

Believe that it is settled because God says so!

~~~~ JANUARY 15 ~~~~

Evening

That night the LORD appeared to [Isaac].
GENESIS 26:24

It was the same night Isaac went to Beersheba. Do you think this revelation from God was an accident? Do you think the *time* of it was an accident? Do you believe it could have happened any other night as well as this one? If so, you are grievously mistaken. Why did it come to Isaac the night he reached Beersheba? Because that was the night he reached *rest*. In his old land he had been tormented. There had been a whole series of petty quarrels over the ownership of insignificant wells. There is nothing like *little* worries, particularly when there are many of them. Because of these little worries, even after the strife was over, the place held bad memories for Isaac. Therefore he was determined to leave and seek a change of scenery. He pitched his tent far away from the place of his former strife. That very night the revelation came. God spoke to him when there was no inner storm. He could not speak to Isaac when his mind was troubled. God's voice demands the silence of the soul. Only in the *quiet* of the spirit could Isaac hear the garments of his God brush by him. His *still* night became his *shining* night.

My soul, have you pondered these words: "Be still, and know" (Psalm 46:10)? In the hour of distress, you cannot hear the answer to your prayers. How often has the answer seemed to come much later! The heart heard no reply during the moment of its crying, its thunder, its earthquake, and its fire. But once the crying stopped, once the stillness came, once your hand refrained from knocking on the iron gate, and once concern for *other* lives broke through the tragedy of your own life, the long-awaited reply appeared. You must rest, O soul, to receive your heart's desire. Slow the beating of your heart over concerns for your personal care. Place the storm of your individual troubles on God's altar of everyday trials, and the same night, the Lord will appear to you. His rainbow will extend across the subsiding flood, and in your stillness you will hear the everlasting music. GEORGE MATHESON

> *Tread in solitude your pathway,*
> > *Quiet heart and undismayed.*
> *You will know things strange, mysterious,*
> > *Which to you no voice has said.*
>
> *While the crowd of petty hustlers*
> > *Grasps at vain and meager things,*
> *You will see a great world rising*
> > *Where soft sacred music rings.*
>
> *Leave the dusty road to others,*
> > *Spotless keep your soul and bright,*
> *As the radiant ocean's surface*
> > *When the sun is taking flight.*
>
> FROM THE GERMAN OF V. SCHOFFEL

JANUARY 16
Morning

Set a guard over my mouth, LORD; keep watch over the door of my lips.
PSALM 141:3

Let me no wrong or idle word,
Unthinking say;
Set Thou a seal upon my lips—
Just for today.

Keep still! When trouble is brewing, keep still! When slander is getting on its legs, keep still! When your feelings are hurt, keep still till you recover from your excitement at any rate! Things look different through an unagitated eye.

In a commotion once I wrote a letter and sent it, and wished I had not. In my later years I had another commotion and wrote another long letter; my life had rubbed a little sense into me, and I kept that letter in my pocket until I could look it over without agitation, and without tears, and I was glad I did—less and less it seemed necessary to send it. I was not sure it would do any harm, but in my doubtfulness I learned reticence, and eventually it was destroyed.

Time works wonders! Wait till you can speak calmly and then perhaps you will not need to speak. Silence is the most powerful thing conceivable, sometimes. It is strength in its grandeur; it is like a regiment ordered to stand still in the mad fury of battle. To plunge in were twice as easy. *Nothing is lost by learning to keep still.* HANNAH WHITALL SMITH

Lord, keep me still,
Though stormy winds may blow,
And waves my little bark may overflow,
Or even if in darkness I must go,
Yet keep me still, yet keep me still.

Lord, keep me still,
The waves are in Thy hand,
The roughest winds subside at Thy command.
Steer Thou my bark in safety to the land,
And keep me still, and keep me still.

Lord, keep me still,
And may I ever hear Thy still small voice
To comfort and to cheer;

So shall I know and feel Thee ever near.
And keep me still, and keep me still.

Silence is a great peacemaker. HENRY WADSWORTH LONGFELLOW

~~~~~ JANUARY 16 ~~~~~

Evening

A furious squall came up.
MARK 4:37

Some of life's storms—a great sorrow, a bitter disappointment, a crushing defeat—
suddenly come upon us. Others may come *slowly*, appearing on the uneven edge
of the horizon no larger than a person's hand. But trouble that seems so insignificant
spreads until it covers the sky and overwhelms us.

Yet it is in the storm that God equips us for service. When God wants an oak tree,
He plants it where the storms will shake it and the rains will beat down upon it. It is
in the midnight battle with the elements that the oak develops its rugged fiber and
becomes the king of the forest.

When God wants to make a person, He puts him into some storm. The history of
humankind has always been rough and rugged. No one is complete until he has been
out into the surge of the storm and has found the glorious fulfillment of the prayer "O
God, take me, break me, make me."

A Frenchman painted a picture of universal genius. In his painting stand famous
orators, philosophers, and martyrs, all of whom have achieved preeminence in various
aspects of life. The remarkable fact about the picture is this: every person who is pre-
eminent for his ability was first preeminent for suffering. In the foreground stands the
figure of the man who was denied the Promised Land: Moses. Beside him, feeling his
way, is blind Homer. Milton is there, blind and heartbroken. Then there is the form of
One who towers above them all. What is His characteristic? His face is marred more
than any other. The artist might have titled that great picture *The Storm*.

The beauties of nature come after the storm. The rugged beauty of the mountain is born in a storm, and the heroes of life are the storm-swept and battle-scarred.

You have been in the storms and swept by the raging winds. Have they left you broken, weary, and beaten in the valley, or have they lifted you to the sunlit summits of a richer, deeper, more abiding manhood or womanhood? Have they left you with more sympathy for the storm-swept and the battle-scarred? SELECTED

> *The wind that blows can never kill*
> *The tree God plants;*
> *It blows toward east, and then toward west,*
> *The tender leaves have little rest,*
> *But any wind that blows is best.*
> *The tree that God plants*
>
> *Strikes deeper root, grows higher still,*
> *Spreads greater limbs, for God's good will*
> *Meets all its wants.*
>
> *There is no storm has power to blast*
> *The tree God knows;*
> *No thunderbolt, nor beating rain,*
> *Nor lightning flash, nor hurricane;*
> *When they are spent, it does remain,*
> *The tree God knows,*
> *Through every storm it still stands fast,*
> *And from its first day to its last*
> *Still fairer grows.*
>
> SELECTED

～～ JANUARY 17 ～～
Morning

In the year that King Uzziah died, I saw the LORD.
ISAIAH 6:1

We have to get our eyes off others before we can have the full vision of Jesus. Moses and Elijah had to pass to make possible the vision of Jesus only. *In the year that King Uzziah died*, Isaiah says, *I saw the Lord.* His eyes and hopes had been upon the mighty and victorious earthly leader, and with his death all these hopes had sunk in despair. But *the stars come out when the lights of earth fade.* It was then Isaiah's true vision and life began.

It is not enough to see Jesus along with other things and persons. What we need is to have Him fill *all* our vision, *all* our sky, *all* our heart, *all* our plans, and *all* our future. What He wants from us is *"first love,"* that is, the supreme place; and He cannot really be anything to us satisfactorily until He is everything. He is able to fill every capacity of our being and without displacing any rightful affection or occupation, yet so blend with all, so control all, so become the very essence of all thought and all delight that we can truly say, "For to me to live is Christ" (Philippians 1:21 KJV), for "the love of Christ constraineth" me (2 Corinthians 5:14 KJV), shuts me up and in from everything else as a pent-up torrent in its narrow course, to live not unto myself but unto him "who loved me, and gave himself for me" (Galatians 2:20 KJV).

Holy Spirit, bring us our transfiguration, take us apart to our Mount of vision, let Moses and Elijah pass, and let us see no man save *Jesus only.* ECHOES OF A NEW CREATION

> *Am I not enough, Mine own? Enough,*
> *Mine own, for thee?*
> *Hath the world its palace towers,*
> *Garden glades of magic flowers,*
> *Where thou wouldst be?*
> *Fair things and false are there,*
> *False things but fair,*
> *All things thou findst at last*
> *Only in Me.*
> *Am I not enough, Mine own? I, forever*
> *and alone? I, needing thee?*
>
> SUSO

Evening

Daniel, servant of the living God, has your God, whom
you serve continually, been able to rescue you?
DANIEL 6:20

We find the expression *"the living God"* many times in the Scriptures, and yet it is the very thing we are so prone to forget. We know it is written *"the living God,"* but in our daily life there is almost nothing we lose sight of as often as the fact that God is *the living God.* We forget that He is now exactly what He was three or four thousand years ago, that He has the same sovereign power, and that He extends the same gracious love toward those who love and serve Him. We overlook the fact that He will do for us now what He did thousands of years ago for others, simply because He is the unchanging, *living God.* What a great reason to confide in Him, and in our darkest moments to never lose sight of the fact that He *is* still, and ever will be, *the living God*!

Be assured, if you walk with Him, look to Him, and expect help from Him, He will never fail you. An older believer who has known the Lord for forty-four years wrote the following as an encouragement to you: "God has never failed me. Even in my greatest difficulties, heaviest trials, and deepest poverty and need, He has never failed me. Because I was enabled by God's grace to trust Him, He has always come to my aid. I delight in speaking well of His name." GEORGE MUELLER

Martin Luther, deep in thought and needing to grasp hidden strength during a time of danger and fear in his life, was seen tracing on the table with his finger the words, "He lives! He lives!" This is our hope for ourselves, His truth, and humankind. People come and go. Leaders, teachers, and philosophers speak and work for a season and then fall silent and powerless. He abides. They die but He lives. They are lights that glow yet are ultimately extinguished. But He is the true Light from which they draw their brightness, and He shines forevermore. ALEXANDER MACLAREN

"One day I came to know Dr. John Douglas Adam," wrote Charles Gallaudet Trumbull. "I learned he considered his greatest spiritual asset to be his *unwavering awareness of the actual presence of Jesus.* Nothing sustained him as much, he said, as the realization that Jesus was *always* actually present with him. This realization was totally independent of his own feelings, his worthiness, and his perceptions as to how Jesus would demonstrate His presence.

"Furthermore, he said Christ was the center of his thoughts. Whenever his mind was free from other matters, it would turn to Christ. Whenever he was alone, and no matter where he was, he would talk aloud to Christ as easily and as naturally as to any human friend. That is how very real Jesus' *actual presence* was to him."

JANUARY 18

Morning

*I have come down from heaven not to do my will
but to do the will of him who sent me.*

JOHN 6:38

When he was crossing the Irish Channel one dark starless night, says Dr. F. B. Meyer, he stood on the deck by the captain and asked him, "How do you know Holyhead Harbor on so dark a night as this?" He said, "You see those three lights? Those three must line up behind each other as one, and when we see them so united we know the exact position of the harbor's mouth."

When we want to know God's will there are three things which always concur: the inward impulse, the Word of God, and the trend of circumstances! God in the heart, impelling you forward; God in the Book, corroborating whatever He says in the heart; and God in circumstances, which are always indicative of His will. *Never start until these three things agree.*

> *Stand still at the crossroads ready to walk or run,
> and you will not be kept waiting long.*

When we're not quite certain if we turn to left or right—isn't it a blessing when a *signpost* looms in sight! If there were no *signposts* we should wander miles astray—in the wrong direction if we didn't know the way.

God has set His *signposts* on Life's strange and winding road. When we're blindly stumbling with the burden of our load—He will lead our footsteps though the pathway twist and bend—in some form He guides us, through The Book, a song, a friend. . . . In the dark uncertain hours, we need not be afraid—when we're at the crossroads, and decisions must be made. . . . Though the track is unfamiliar, and the light is gray—rest assured, there's bound to be a *signpost on the way.* PATIENCE STRONG

Let us be silent unto Him and believe that, even now, messengers are hastening along the road with the summons, or direction, or help which we need.

~~~~~ JANUARY 18 ~~~~~
Evening

Thanks be to God, who always leads us as captives in christ's triumphal procession.
2 CORINTHIANS 2:14

God wins His greatest victories through apparent defeats. Very often the enemy seems to triumph for a season, and God allows it. But then He comes in and upsets the work of the enemy, overthrows the apparent victory, and as the Bible says, "frustrates the ways of the wicked" (Psalm 146:9). Consequently, He gives us a much greater victory than we would have known had He not allowed the enemy seemingly to triumph in the first place.

The story of the three Hebrew young men who were thrown into the fiery furnace is a familiar one. There was an apparent victory for the enemy. It *looked* as if the servants of the living God were going to suffer a terrible defeat. We have all been in situations where it seemed as though we were defeated, and the enemy rejoiced. We can only imagine what a complete defeat this appeared to be for Daniel's friends. They were thrown into the terrible flames while their enemies watched to see them burn. Yet the enemy was greatly astonished to see them walking around in the fire, enjoying themselves. Then King Nebuchadnezzar told them to come out of the fire. The enemy "crowded around them. They saw that the fire had not harmed their bodies, nor was a hair of their heads singed; their robes were not scorched, and there was no smell of fire on them . . . for no other god can save in this way" (Daniel 3:27, 29).

This apparent defeat resulted in a miraculous victory.

Suppose these three men had lost their faith and courage and had complained, saying, "*Why* didn't God keep us out of the furnace?" They would have been burned, and God would not have been glorified. If there is a great trial in your life today, do not acknowledge it as a *defeat*. Instead, continue by faith to claim the victory through Him who is able to make you "more than conquerors" (Romans 8:37), and a glorious victory will soon be apparent. May we learn that in all the difficult places God takes us, He is giving us opportunities to exercise our faith in Him that will bring about blessed results and greatly glorify His name. LIFE OF PRAISE

> *Defeat may serve as well as victory*
> *To shake the soul and let the glory out.*
> *When the great oak is straining in the wind,*
> *The limbs drink in new beauty, and the trunk*
> *Sends down a deeper root on the windward side.*
> *Only the soul that knows the mighty grief*
> *Can know the mighty rapture. Sorrows come*
> *To stretch out spaces in the heart for joy.*

JANUARY 19
Morning

Can God?
PSALM 78:19

> *"Can God?" the subtle Tempter breathes within,*
> *When all seems lost, excepting sure defeat,*
> *"Can God roll back the raging seas of sin?"*
> *"Can God?" the fainting heart doth quick repeat.*

> *"God can!" in trumpet tones rings faith's glad cry,*
> *And, David-like, it fears no giant foe,*
> *For faith dwells on the Mount, serene, and high,*
> *While unbelief's dark clouds roll far below.*

"God can!" His Saints of old did ever give
Their fullest confirmation o'er and o'er,
And He who made the long-dead bones to live,
E'en now can bring the dead to life once more.

"God can!" Then let us fear not, but arise!
Our motto be this word that He doth give,
If we have faith, before our wondering eyes
a mighty army shall arise and live!

J. A. R.

"Can God?" Oh, fatal question! It shut Israel out of the Land of Promise. And we are in danger of making the same mistake. Can God find me a situation or provide food for my children? Can God keep me from yielding to that besetting sin? Can God extricate me from this terrible snare in which I am entangled? We look at the difficulties, the surges that are rolling high, and we say, *"If* Thou canst do anything, help us!" They said, "Can God?" It hurt and wounded God deeply. Say no more, "Can God?" Rather say this, "God Can!" That will clear up many a problem. That will bring you through many a difficulty in your life.

There is no strength in unbelief.

Has the life of God's people reached the utmost limit of what God can do for them? *Surely not!* God has new places and new developments and new resources. *He can do new things, unheard-of things, hidden things! Let us enlarge our hearts and not limit Him.*

"When thou didst terrible things which we looked not for, thou camest down, the mountains flowed down at thy presence" (Isaiah 64:3 KJV).

We must desire and believe. We must ask and expect that God will do *unlooked-for things!* We must set our faith on a God of whom men do not know what He hath prepared for them that wait for Him. *The Wonder-doing God . . . must be the God of our confidence.* ANDREW MURRAY

The Wonder-doing God can surpass all our expectation!

Evening

Then Jesus told his disciples . . . that they
should always pray and not give up.
LUKE 18:1

O bserve the ant," the great Oriental conqueror Tamerlane told his friends. In relating a story from his early life, he said, "I once was forced to take shelter from my enemies in a dilapidated building, where I sat alone for many hours. Wishing to divert my mind from my hopeless situation, I fixed my eyes on an ant carrying a kernel of corn larger than itself up a high wall. I counted its attempts to accomplish this feat. The corn fell sixty-nine times to the ground, but the insect *persevered.* The seventieth time it reached the top. The ant's accomplishment gave me courage for the moment, and I never forgot the lesson." THE KING'S BUSINESS

Prayer that uses previously unanswered prayers as an excuse for laziness has already ceased to be a prayer of faith. To someone who prays in faith, unanswered prayers are simply the evidence that the answer is *much closer.* From beginning to end, our Lord's lessons and examples teach us that prayer that is not steadfast and persistent, nor revived and refreshed, and does not gather strength from previous prayers is not the prayer that will triumph. WILLIAM ARTHUR

Arthur Rubinstein, the great pianist, once said, "If I neglect practicing one day, I notice; two days, my friends notice; three days, the public notices." It is the old principle *"Practice makes perfect."* We must continue believing, praying, and doing His will. In any of the arts, when the artist ceases to practice, we know the result. If we would only use the same level of common sense in our faith that we use in our everyday life, we would be moving on toward perfection.

David Livingstone's motto was, "I resolved never to stop until I had come to the goal and achieved my purpose." He was victorious through unwavering persistence and faith in God.

Morning

And he went and lived in a town called Nazareth.
MATTHEW 2:23

Our Lord Jesus lived for thirty years amid the happenings of the little town of Nazareth. Little villages spell out their stories in small events. *And He, the young Prince of Glory, was in the carpenter's shop!* He moved amid humdrum tasks, petty cares, village gossip, trifling trade, *and He was faithful in that which was least.*

If these smaller things in life afford such riches of opportunity for the finest loyalty, all of our lives are wonderfully wealthy in possibility and promise. Even though our house is furnished with commonplaces it can be the home of the Lord all the days of our life. J. H. JOWETT

When I am tempted to repine
That such a lowly lot is mine,
There comes to me a voice which saith,
"Mine were the streets of Nazareth."

So mean, so common and confined,
And He the Monarch of mankind!
Yet patiently He traveleth
Those narrow streets of Nazareth.

It may be I shall never rise
To place or fame beneath the skies—
But walk in straitened ways till death,
Narrow as streets of Nazareth.

But if through honor's arch I tread
And there forget to bend my head,

Ah! let me hear the voice which saith,
"Mine were the streets of Nazareth."
NETTIE ROOKER

There's sometimes a good hearty tree growin' out o' the bare rock, out o' some crack that just holds the roots, right on one o' them hills where you can't seem to see a wheelbarrowful o' good earth, but that tree'll keep a green top in the driest summer. You lay your ear down to the ground, and you'll hear a little stream runnin'. Every such tree has got its own livin' spring; there's folks made to match 'em. SARAH ORNE JEWETT

From the desire of being great, good Lord deliver us! A MORAVIAN PRAYER

~~~~~ JANUARY 20 ~~~~~

Evening

Frustration is better than laughter, because a sad face is good for the heart.
ECCLESIASTES 7:3

Sorrow, under the power of divine grace, performs various ministries in our lives. Sorrow reveals unknown depths of the soul, and unknown capacities for suffering and service. Lighthearted, frivolous people are always shallow and are never aware of their own meagerness or lack of depth. Sorrow is God's tool to plow the depths of the soul, that it may yield richer harvests. If humankind were still in a glorified state, having never fallen, then the strong floods of divine joy would be the force God would use to reveal our souls' capacities. But in a fallen world, sorrow, yet with despair removed, is the power chosen to reveal us to ourselves. Accordingly, it is sorrow that causes us to take the time to think deeply and seriously.

Sorrow makes us move more slowly and considerately and examine our motives and attitudes. It opens within us the capacities of the heavenly life, and it makes us willing to set our capacities afloat on a limitless sea of service for God and for others.

Imagine a village of lazy people living at the foot of a great mountain range, yet who have never ventured out to explore the valleys and canyons back in the mountains.

One day a great thunderstorm goes careening through the mountains, turning the hidden valleys into echoing trumpets and revealing their inner recesses, like the twisted shapes of a giant seashell. The villagers at the foot of the hills are astonished at the labyrinths and the unexplored recesses of a region so nearby and yet so unknown. And so it is with many people who casually live on the outer edge of their own souls until great thunderstorms of sorrow reveal hidden depths within, which were never before known or suspected.

God never uses anyone to a great degree until He breaks the person completely. Joseph experienced more sorrow than the other sons of Jacob, and it led him into a ministry of food for all the nations. For this reason, the Holy Spirit said of him, "Joseph is a fruitful vine . . . near a spring, whose branches climb over a wall" (Genesis 49:22). It takes sorrow to expand and deepen the soul. THE HEAVENLY LIFE

The dark brown soil is turned
By the sharp-pointed plow;
And I've a lesson learned.

My life is but a field,
Stretched out beneath God's sky,
Some harvest rich to yield.

Where grows the golden grain?
Where faith? Where sympathy?
In a furrow cut by pain.

MALTBIE D. BABCOCK

Every person and every nation must endure lessons in God's school of adversity. In the same way we say, "Blessed is the night, for it reveals the stars to us," we can say, "Blessed is sorrow, for it reveals God's comfort." A flood once washed away a poor man's home and mill, taking with it everything he owned in the world. He stood at the scene of his great loss, brokenhearted and discouraged. Yet after the waters had subsided, he saw something shining in the riverbanks that the flood had washed bare. "It looks like gold," he said. And it was gold. The storm that had impoverished him made him rich. So it is oftentimes in life. HENRY CLAY TRUMBULL

> *Do not move an ancient boundary*
> *stone set up by your ancestors.*
> PROVERBS 22:28

Among the property owned jointly by two young brothers who were carpenters was the old tumbledown place of their birth. One of the brothers was soon to be married, and the old house was to be torn down and a new one erected on its site. For years neither of the brothers had visited the cottage, as it had been leased.

As they entered now and started the work of demolishing the place, again and again floods of tender memories swept over them. By the time they reached the kitchen they were well-nigh overcome with their emotions. There was the place where the old kitchen, table had stood—with the family Bible—where they had knelt every evening. They were recalling now with a pang how in later years they had felt a little superior to that time-honored custom carefully observed by their father.

Said one: "We're *better off* than he was, but we're not *better men*."

The other agreed, saying, "I'm going back to the old church and the old ways, and in my new home I'm going to make room for worship as Dad did."

The strength of a nation lies in the homes of its people. ABRAHAM LINCOLN

Says Dr. J. G. Paton: "No hurry for market, no rush for business, no arrival of friends or guests, no trouble or sorrow, no joy or excitement, ever prevented us from kneeling around the family altar while our high priest offered himself and his children to God." And on his father's life in his home was based Dr. Paton's decision to follow the Lord wholly. "He walked with God—why not I?"

"Stand ye in the . . . old paths, where is the good way" (Jeremiah 6:16 KJV).

*I consider my life worth nothing to me; my only aim is to finish the
race and complete the task the LORD Jesus has given me.*

ACTS 20:24

We read in 2 Samuel 5:17, "When the Philistines heard that David had been anointed king over Israel, they went up in full force to search for him." The moment we receive anything from the Lord worth fighting for, the Devil comes seeking to destroy us.

When the Enemy confronts us at the threshold of any great work for God, we should accept it as evidence of our salvation, and claim double the blessing, victory, and power. Power is developed through resistance. The force and the amount of damage created by an exploding artillery shell appear to be greater because of the resistance at the point of impact. A power plant produces additional electricity by using the friction of the rotating turbines. And one day, we too will understand that even Satan has been used as one of God's instruments of blessing. DAYS OF HEAVEN UPON EARTH

> *A hero is not fed on sweets,*
> *Daily his own heart he eats;*
> *Chambers of the great are jails,*
> *And head winds right for royal sails.*
> RALPH WALDO EMERSON

Tribulation is the door to triumph. The valley leads to the open highway, and tribulation's imprint is on every great accomplishment. *Crowns are cast in crucibles*, and the chains of character found at the feet of God are forged in earthly flames. No one wins the greatest victory until he has walked the winepress of woe. With deep furrows of anguish on His brow, the "man of sorrows" (Isaiah 53:3 NASB) said, "In this world you will have trouble" (John 16:33). But immediately comes the psalm of promise, "Take heart! I have overcome the world."

The footprints are visible everywhere. The steps that lead to thrones are stained with spattered blood, and scars are the price for scepters. We will wrestle our crowns from the giants we conquer. It is no secret that grief has always fallen to people of greatness.

> *The mark of rank in nature*
> *Is capacity for pain;*
> *And the anguish of the singer*
> *Makes the sweetest of the strain.*

Tribulation has always marked the trail of the true reformer. It was true in the story of Paul, Luther, Savonarola, Knox, Wesley, and the rest of God's mighty army. They came through great tribulation to their point of power.

Every great book has been written with the author's blood. "These are they who have come out of the great tribulation" (Revelation 7:14). In spite of his blindness, wasn't Homer the unparalleled poet of the Greeks? And who wrote the timeless dream of *Pilgrim's Progress*? Was it a prince in royal robes seated on a couch of comfort and ease? No! The lingering splendor of John Bunyan's vision gilded the dingy walls of an old English jail in Bedford, while he, a princely prisoner and a glorious genius, made a faithful transcript of the scene.

> *Great is the easy conqueror;*
> *Yet the one who is wounded sore,*
> *Breathless, all covered o'er with blood and sweat,*
> *Sinks fainting, but fighting evermore—*
> *Is greater yet.*
> SELECTED

～～～ JANUARY 22 ～～～
Morning

And when they climbed into the boat, the wind died down.
MATTHEW 14:32

Faith can conquer every obstacle!

Some people insist upon holding Christ at a distance, waiting before going to Him until obstacles have been removed. *When economic skies are brighter, when doubts have been cleared, when the edge of sorrow has been dulled, then they will go to Jesus.*

Peter, knowing that the Master was near, in sublime faith asked to be permitted to go to Him across the surging waters. *Fear almost conquered him, but even then Jesus lifted him by the hand.*

There are always storms of difficulty and of assailing doubts. Unanswered questions and the problems of hideous wrongs are always battling against the good purposes of Christ. Do not let the storms keep *you* from the consoling presence of Christ. Build *a bridge out of the storms, and go to Him!* SELECTED

"Get into the boat!" Thou didst whisper.
At first how I feared to obey;
I looked not at Thee, but the storm clouds,
The darkness, the waves, and the spray.

But then came the words, "Will you trust Him?
Will you claim and receive at His hand
All His definite fullness of blessing?
Launch out at thy Master's command!"

Thou art willing, my Lord, could I doubt Thee?
Hast Thou ever proved untrue?
Nay! out at Thy word I have ventured,
I have trusted. Thy part is to do.

LAURA A. BARTER-SNOW

When Jesus rises, the storm stops. The calm comes from the power of His Presence. As a strong quiet man steps in majestically among a crowd of noisy brawlers, his very appearance makes them ashamed and hushes their noise; so Jesus steps in among the elements, and they are still in a moment.

Evening

He withdrew . . . to a solitary place.
MATTHEW 14:13

There is no music during a musical rest, but the rest is part of the making of the music. In the melody of our life, the music is separated here and there by rests. During those rests, we foolishly believe we have come to the end of the song. God sends us times of forced leisure by allowing sickness, disappointed plans, and frustrated efforts. He brings a sudden pause in the choral hymn of our lives, and we lament that our voices must be silent. We grieve that our part is missing in the music that continually rises to the ear of our Creator. Yet how does a musician read the rest? He counts the break with unwavering precision and plays his next note with confidence, as if no pause were ever there.

God does not write the music of our lives without a plan. Our part is to learn the tune and not be discouraged during the rests. They are not to be slurred over or omitted, nor used to destroy the melody or to change the key. If we will only look up, God Himself will count the time for us. With our eyes on Him, our next note will be full and clear. If we sorrowfully say to ourselves, "There is no music in a rest," let us not forget that the rest is part of the making of the music. The process is often slow and painful in this life, yet how patiently God works to teach us! And how long He waits for us to learn the lesson! JOHN RUSKIN

> Called aside—
> *From the glad working of your busy life,*
> *From the world's ceaseless stir of care and strife,*
> *Into the shade and stillness by your Heavenly Guide*
> *For a brief time you have been called aside.*
>   Called aside—
> *Perhaps into a desert garden dim;*
> *And yet not alone, when you have been with Him,*
> *And heard His voice in sweetest accents say:*
> *"Child, will you not with Me this still hour stay?"*

Called aside—
In hidden paths with Christ your Lord to tread,
Deeper to drink at the sweet Fountainhead,
Closer in fellowship with Him to roam,
Nearer, perhaps, to feel your Heavenly Home.
Called aside—
Oh, knowledge deeper grows with Him alone;
In secret oft His deeper love is shown,
And learned in many an hour of dark distress
Some rare, sweet lesson of His tenderness.
Called aside—
We thank You for the stillness and the shade;
We thank You for the hidden paths Your love has made,
And, so that we have wept and watched with Thee,
We thank You for our dark Gethsemane.
Called aside—
O restful thought—He doeth all things well;
O blessed sense, with Christ alone to dwell;
So in the shadow of Your cross to hide,
We thank You, Lord, to have been called aside.

JANUARY 23

Morning

When I called him he was only one man, and I blessed him.

ISAIAH 51:2

A celebrated Scottish nobleman and statesman once replied to a correspondent that he was *"plowing his lonely furrow."* Whenever God has required someone to do a big thing for Him, He has sent him to a *lonely furrow.* He has called him to go alone.

You may have to become the loneliest person on earth, but if you do, you will be able always to see around you the chariots of God, even twenty thousand, and thousands of thousands, *and then you will forget your loneliness.*

The soil is hard,
And the plow goes heavily.
The wind is fierce
And I toil on wearily—
But His hands made the yoke!
Ah wonder—that I should bear His yoke—
It is enough, if I may but plow the furrow,
For the Sower to sow the seed.

If you have taken hold of the plow, *hold on until the field is finished.* "Let us not become weary" (Galatians 6:9).

Says Theodore L. Cuyler, "After long and painful perplexities about accepting a certain attractive call, I opened the Book and read: *'Why gaddest thou about so much to change thy way?'*" (Jeremiah 2:36 KJV).

Your present field may be limited, but you are not limited by your field. Great men have sprung from the furrows. Great men have plowed and harrowed, and leaving these things have written their names deep in history. There are heights undreamed of, ecstasies unthought of, for the one who follows on. So follow on in the valley, *looking for hills.* One day you will look back with surprise, and then turning go forward with fresh courage.

You were made to mount and not to crawl!

"One lonely soul on fire with the love of God may set the whole universe ablaze" (Acts 2:41; Revelation 5:11).

~~~~~~~ JANUARY 23 ~~~~~~~

Evening

Why, LORD, do you stand far off?
PSALM 10:1

"God is . . . an ever-present help in trouble" (Psalm 46:1). But He allows trouble to pursue us, as though He were indifferent to its overwhelming pressure, so we may be brought to the end of ourselves. Through the trial, we are led to discover the treasure of darkness and the immeasurable wealth of tribulation.

We may be sure that He who allows the suffering is with us throughout it. It may be that we will only see Him once the ordeal is nearly passed, but we must dare to believe that He never leaves our trial. Our eyes are blinded so we cannot see the One our soul loves. The darkness and our bandages blind us so that we cannot see the form of our High Priest. Yet He is there and is deeply touched. Let us not rely on our feelings but trust in His unswerving faithfulness. And though we cannot see Him, let us talk to Him. Although His presence is veiled, once we begin to speak to Jesus as if He were literally present, an answering voice comes to show us He is in the shadow, keeping watch over His own. Your Father is as close to you when you journey through the darkest tunnel as He is when you are under the open heaven! DAILY DEVOTIONAL COMMENTARY

Although the path be all unknown?
Although the way be drear?
Its shades I travel not alone
When steps of Yours are near.

~~~~~ JANUARY 24 ~~~~~
Morning

There is nothing there.
1 KINGS 18:43

Elijah was a man who hoped perfectly; hoped against hope until the abundant answer came. He continued, in the very face of darkness and perplexity, *to expect,* because the very God of hope lived *in* him and expected *through* him. And he was not ashamed, for it came to pass the seventh time his servant said, "A cloud as small as a man's hand is rising from the sea" (v. 44), and in a little while the heaven was black with clouds, and there was a great rain!

Can *you* count God faithful when only *the still small voice* speaks? When there is neither wind, earthquake, nor fire? Can you start *when you see the cloud no bigger than a man's hand?* Can you say: "'There is nothing,' *but I wait on Thee. My mind is peculiarly in the dark regarding the way I am to take, but Thou knowest. Unto Thee do I look up!*"

*"There is nothing"—though the raindrops needed sorely
and so long
Have been promised by Jehovah, by the Father true and strong.
And the sky is blue and cloudless, and the earth is parched and dry,
Yet no showers are forthcoming from the reservoir on high.*

*"There is nothing"—but the prophet knows and trusts his Master's word;
He is not a senseless idol, but the mighty, powerful God.
He has seen His wondrous working, he believes Him faithful still;
So he humbly waits in patience for Jehovah's perfect will.*

*"There is nothing"—oh, how often doth the enemy declare,
Nothing for your constant wrestlings; nothing for your cries and tears.
And the faithless heart says
"Nothing," though deceived she ne'er has been,
For the little cloud so longed for, at the seventh time is seen.*

*"There is nothing"—but there shall be: God is still the Great "I AM."
He is now Almighty, faithful, and forevermore the same;
And the tears, and cries, and wrestlings, have been recorded on high;
Not forgotten, nor neglected, to be answered by and by.*

JAMES BOOBBYER

"Get thee up, eat and drink; for there is a sound of abundance of rain" (1 Kings 18:41 KJV).

JANUARY 24
Evening

*But the dove could find no place to set its feet . . . so it returned to
Noah in the ark. . . . He waited seven more days and again sent
out the dove from the ark. When the dove returned to him in the
evening, there in its beak was a freshly plucked olive leaf!*

GENESIS 8:9–11 WNT

God knows exactly when to withhold or to grant us any visible sign of encouragement. How wonderful it is when we will trust Him in either case! Yet it is better when all visible evidence that He is remembering us is withheld. He wants us to realize that His Word—His promise of remembering us—is more real and dependable than any evidence our senses may reveal. It is good when He sends the visible evidence, but we appreciate it even more after we have trusted Him without it. And those who are the most inclined to trust God without any evidence except His Word always receive the greatest amount of visible evidence of His love. CHARLES GALLAUDET TRUMBULL

> *Believing Him; if storm clouds gather darkly 'round,*
> *And even if the heavens seem hushed, without a sound?*
> *He hears each prayer and even notes the sparrow's fall.*
>
> *And praising Him; when sorrow, grief, and pain are near,*
> *And even when we lose the thing that seems most dear?*
> *Our loss is gain. Praise Him; in Him we have our All.*
>
> *Our hand in His; e'en though the path seems long and drear*
> *We scarcely see a step ahead, and almost fear?*
> *He guides us right—this way and that, to keep us near.*
>
> *And satisfied; when every path is blocked and bare,*
> *And worldly things are gone and dead which were so fair?*
> *Believe and rest and trust in Him, He comes to stay.*

Delayed answers to prayers are not refusals. Many prayers are received and recorded, yet underneath are the words, "My time has not yet come." God has a fixed time and an ordained purpose, and He who controls the limits of our lives also determines the time of our deliverance. SELECTED

～～～ JANUARY 25 ～～～

Morning

"Present your case," says the LORD. *"Set forth your arguments," says Jacob's King.*
ISAIAH 41:21

Over in Canada there lived an Irish saint called "Holy Ann." She lived to be one hundred years old. When she was a young girl, she was working in a family for very small wages under a very cruel master and mistress. They made her carry water for a mile up a steep hill. At one time there had been a well dug there; it had gone dry, but it stood there year after year. One night she was very tired, and she fell on her knees and cried to God; and while on her knees she read these words: "I will open . . . fountains in the midst of the valleys: I will make . . . the dry land springs of water" (Isaiah 41:18 KJV). "Produce your cause, saith the LORD; bring forth your strong reasons" (v. 21). These words struck Holy Ann, and she produced her cause before the Lord. She told Him how badly they needed the water and how hard it was for her to carry the water up the steep hill; then she lay down and fell asleep. She had pleaded her cause and brought forth her strong reasons. The next morning early she was seen to take a bucket and start for the well. Someone asked her where she was going, and she replied, "I am going to draw water from the well." "Why, it is dry," was the answer. But that did not stop Holy Ann. She knew whom she had believed, and on she went; and, lo and behold, there in the well was eighty-three feet of pure, cold water, and she told me that the well never did run dry! That is the way the Lord can fulfill His promises. "Produce your cause . . . bring forth your strong reasons," and see Him work in your behalf.

How little we use this method of holy argument in prayer, and yet there are many examples of it in Scripture: Abraham, Jacob, Moses, Elijah, Daniel—all used arguments in prayer, and claimed the Divine interposition on the ground of the pleas which they presented.

JANUARY 25

Evening

Your rod and your staff, they comfort me.
PSALM 23:4

At my father's house in the country, there is a little closet near the chimney, where we keep the canes, or walking sticks, of several generations of our family. During my visits to the old house, as my father and I are going out for a walk, we often go to the cane closet and pick out our sticks to suit the occasion. As we have done this, I have frequently been reminded that the Word of God is a staff.

During the war, when we were experiencing a time of discouragement and impending danger, the verse "He will have no fear of bad news; his heart is steadfast, trusting in the LORD" (Psalm 112:7 WNT) was a staff to walk with on many dark days.

When our child died and we were left nearly brokenhearted, I found another staff in the promise: "Weeping may remain for a night, but rejoicing comes in the morning" (Psalm 30:5 WNT).

When I was forced to be away from home for a year due to poor health, not knowing if God would ever allow me to return to my home and work again, I chose this staff, which has never failed: "For I know the plans I have for you, . . . plans to prosper you and not to harm you, plans to give you hope and a future" (Jeremiah 29:11).

In times of impending danger or doubt, when human judgment seems to be of no value, I have found it easy to go forward with this staff: "In quietness and trust is your strength" (Isaiah 30:15). And in emergencies, when there has been no time for deliberation or for action, this staff has never failed me: "He that believeth shall not make haste" (Isaiah 28:16 KJV). BENJAMIN VAUGHAN ABBOTT

Martin Luther's wife said, "I would never have known the meaning of various psalms, come to appreciate certain difficulties, or known the inner workings of the soul; I would never have understood the practice of the Christian life and work, if God had never brought afflictions to my life." It is quite true that God's rod is like a schoolteacher's pointer to a child, pointing out a letter so the child will notice it. In this same way, God points out many valuable lessons to us that we otherwise would never have learned. SELECTED

God always sends His staff with His rod.

"Thy shoes shall be iron and brass; and as thy days, so shall thy strength be" (Deuteronomy 33:25 KJV).

Each of us may be sure that if God sends us over rocky paths, He will provide us with sturdy shoes. He will never send us on any journey without equipping us well. ALEXANDER MACLAREN

I being in the way, the LORD led me.
GENESIS 24:27 KJV

"The way" means God's way, the pathway prepared for us; not our way; not any kind of way (Proverbs 14:12); not man's way; but the direct way of duty and command. In such a way the Lord will be sure to lead and guide us. The Lord answered the servant's prayer *exactly* as he prayed, step by step.

"God never gives guidance for two steps at a time. I must take one step, and then I receive light for the next."

> As thou dost travel down the corridor of Time
> Thou wilt find many doors of usefulness;
> To gain some there are many weary steps to climb,
> And then they will not yield! but onward press,
> For there before thee, in the distance just beyond
> Lies one which yet will open; enter there,
> And thou shalt find all realized thy visions fair
> Of fields more vast than thou hast yet conceived.
> Press on, faint not; though briars strew thy way,
> The greatest things are yet to be achieved;
> And he who falters not will win the day.
> No man can shut the door which God sets wide,
> He bids thee enter there—thy work awaits inside.
> FAIRELIE THORNTON

Keep to your post and watch His signals! Implicitly
rely on the methods of His guidance.

Evening

I have begun to deliver. . . . Now begin to conquer and possess.
DEUTERONOMY 2:31

The Bible has a great deal to say about waiting for God, and the teaching cannot be too strongly emphasized. We so easily become impatient with God's delays. Yet much of our trouble in life is the result of our restless, and sometimes reckless, haste.

We cannot *wait* for the fruit to ripen, but insist on picking it while it is still green. We cannot *wait* for the answers to our prayers, although it may take many years for the things we pray for to be prepared for us. We are encouraged to walk with God, but often God walks very slowly. Yet there is also another side to this teaching: *God often waits for us.*

Quite often we fail to receive the blessing He has ready for us because we are not moving forward with Him. While it is true we miss many blessings by not waiting for God, we also lose numerous blessings by *overwaiting*. There are times when it takes strength simply to sit still, but there are also times when we are to move forward with a confident step.

Many of God's promises are conditional, requiring some initial action on our part. Once we begin to obey, He will begin to bless us. Great things were promised to Abraham, but not one of them could have been obtained had he waited in Chaldea. He had to leave his home, friends, and country, travel unfamiliar paths, and press on in unwavering obedience in order to receive the promises. The ten lepers Jesus healed were told to show themselves to the priest, and *"as they went, they were cleansed"* (Luke 17:14). If they had waited to *see the cleansing* come to their bodies before leaving, they would never have seen it. God was waiting to heal them, and the moment their faith began to work, the blessing came.

When the Israelites were entrapped by Pharaoh's pursuing army at the Red Sea, they were commanded to "go forward" (Exodus 14:15 KJV). No longer was it their duty to wait, but to rise up from bended knees and "go forward" with heroic faith. Years later the Israelites were commanded to show their faith again by beginning their march over the Jordan while the river was at its highest point. They held the key to unlock the gate into the Land of Promise in their own hands, and the gate would not begin to turn on its hinges until they had approached and unlocked it. The key was faith.

We are destined to fight certain battles, and we think we can never be victorious and conquer our enemies. Yet as we enter the conflict, *One* comes who fights by our side. Through Him we are "more than conquerors" (Romans 8:37). If we had waited in fear and trembling for our Helper to come before we would enter the battle, we would have waited in vain. This would have been the *overwaiting* of unbelief. God is waiting to pour out His richest blessings on you. "Go forward" with bold confidence and take what is yours. "I have begun to deliver. . . . Now begin to conquer and possess." J. R. MILLER

～～～ JANUARY 27 ～～～
Morning

And a light shone in the cell. [The angel] struck Peter on
the side and woke him up. "Quick, get up!"
ACTS 12:7

If we fear the Lord, we may look for timely interpositions when our case is at its worst. Angels are not kept from us by storms, nor hindered by darkness. Seraphs think it no humiliation to visit the poorest of the heavenly family. If angels' visits are few and far between at ordinary times, they shall be frequent in our nights of tempest and tossing. Dear reader, is this an hour of distress with you? Then ask for peculiar help. Jesus is the Angel of the Covenant, and if His presence be now earnestly sought it will not be denied. What that presence brings is heart cheer. CHARLES H. SPURGEON

And a light shined in my cell,
And there was not any wall,
And there was no dark at all,
Only Thou, Emmanuel.

Light of love shined in my cell,
Turned to gold the iron bars,

Opened windows to the stars,
Peace stood there as sentinel.

Dearest Lord, how can it be
That Thou art so kind to me?
Love is shining in my cell,
Jesus, my Emmanuel.

A. W. C.

JANUARY 27

Evening

Make you strong, firm and steadfast.
1 PETER 5:10

Before we can establish a new and deeper relationship with Christ, we must first acquire enough intellectual light to satisfy our mind that we have been given the right to stand in this new relationship. Even the shadow of a doubt here will destroy our confidence. Then, having seen the light, we must advance.

We must make our choice, commit to it, and take our rightful place as confidently as a tree is planted in the ground. As a bride entrusts herself to the groom at the marriage altar, our commitment to Christ must be once and for all, without reservation or reversal.

Then there follows a time of establishing and testing, during which we must stand still until the new relationship becomes so ingrained in us that it becomes a permanent habit. It is comparable to a surgeon setting a broken arm by splinting it to keep it from moving. God too has His spiritual splints He wants to put on His children to keep them quiet and still until they pass the first stage of faith. Sometimes the trial will be difficult, but "the God of all grace, who called you to his eternal glory in Christ, after you have suffered a little while, will himself restore you and make you strong, firm and steadfast" (1 Peter 5:10). A. B. SIMPSON

There is a natural law at work in sin and in sickness, and if we just drift along following the flow of our circumstances, we will sink under the power of the Tempter.

— 71 —

But there is another law of spiritual and physical life in Christ Jesus to which we can rise, and through which we can counterbalance and overcome the natural law that weighs us down.

Doing this, however, requires real spiritual energy, a determined purpose, a sure stance, and the habit of faith. It is the same principle as a factory that uses electricity to run its machinery. The switch must be turned on and left in that position. The power is always available, but the proper connection must be made. And as long as that connection is intact, the power will enable all the machinery to stay in operation.

There is a spiritual law of choosing, believing, abiding, and remaining steadfast in our walk with God. This law is essential to the working of the Holy Spirit in our sanctification and in our healing. DAYS OF HEAVEN UPON EARTH

~~~ JANUARY 28 ~~~
Morning

Go out and stand on the mountain in the presence of the LORD.
1 KINGS 19:11

A rebuke is often a blessing in disguise. Elijah needed this form of address in order to arouse him to an understanding of his causeless fear. Such a one as he has no right to be fitful and repining. If he will *go out and stand on the mountain in the presence of the Lord,* instead of hiding away in a cave, he will find new inspiration in a new vision of His power! When we are living on earth's low levels we fail to catch the inspiring visions of God which are the true support of the prophetic life. We must come out into the sunshine and make the ascent of the mountain if we would discern those evidences of God's power which are always available for the re-creation of faith and courage.

The golden-crested wren is one of the tiniest of birds; it is said to weigh only the fifth part of an ounce; and yet, on frailest pinions, it braves hurricanes and crosses northern seas.

It often seems in nature as though Omnipotence works but through the frailest organisms; certainly the Omnipotence of grace is seen to the greatest advantage in the trembling but resolute saint.

On the American prairies the butterflies start westward in their migrations and make steady progress though the wind is against them and the sea in front. The delicate butterflies rebuke me.

> *Step out on the waves*
> *That would crush you!*
> *Step out in the storm*
> *That would hush you!*
> *And you will find,*
> *As you touch the crest*
> *You feared so much,*
> *And walk on its breast,*
> *There was One walking there,*
> *The whole night through,*
> *Walking, watching,*
> *Waiting—for you!*

JANUARY 28

Evening

I am jealous for you with a godly jealousy.
2 CORINTHIANS 11:2

Oh, how the old harpist loves his harp! He cuddles and caresses it, as if it were a child resting on his lap. His life is consumed with it. But watch how he tunes it. He grasps it firmly, striking a chord with a sharp, quick blow. While it quivers as if in pain, he leans forward, intently listening to catch the first note rising from it. Just as he feared, the note is distorted and shrill. He strains the string, turning the torturing thumbscrew, and though it seems ready to snap with the tension, he strikes it again. Then he leans forward again, carefully listening, until at last a smile appears on his face as the first melodic sound arises.

Perhaps this is how God is dealing with you. Loving you more than any harpist loves his harp, He finds you nothing but harsh, discordant sounds. He plucks your heartstrings with torturing anguish. Tenderly leaning over you, he strikes the strings and listens. Hearing only a harsh murmur, He strikes you again. His heart bleeds for you while He anxiously waits to hear the strain "Not my will, but yours be done" (Luke 22:42)—a melody as sweet to His ears as angels' songs. And He will never cease from striking the strings of your heart until your humbled and disciplined soul blends with all the pure and eternal harmonies of His own being. SELECTED

> Oh, the sweetness that dwells in a harp of many strings,
> While each, all vocal with love in a tuneful harmony rings!
> But, oh, the wail and the discord, when one and another is rent,
> Tensionless, broken and lost, from the cherished instrument.
>
> For rapture of love is linked with the pain or fear of loss,
> And the hand that takes the crown, must ache with many a cross;
> Yet he who has never a conflict, wins never a victor's palm,
> And only the toilers know the sweetness of rest and calm.
>
> Only between the storms can the Alpine traveler know
> Transcendent glory of clearness, marvels of gleam and glow;
> Had he the brightness unbroken of cloudless summer days,
> This had been dimmed by the dust and the veil of a brooding haze.
>
> Who would dare the choice, neither or both to know,
> The finest quiver of joy or the agony thrill of woe!
> Never the exquisite pain, then never the exquisite bliss,
> For the heart that is dull to that can never be strung to this.

JANUARY 29
Morning

I will turn all my mountains into roads.
ISAIAH 49:11

Do not try to tunnel under them, nor to squeeze through them, nor to run away from them, but to *claim them*.

Tighten your loins with the promises of God!

These mountains of difficulty are His stepping-stones; walk on them with holy joy. Keep the strong staff of faith well in hand, and *trust God in the dark*.

We are safer with Him in the dark than without Him in the sunshine. *At the end of the gloomy passage beams the heavenly light!* When we reach heaven, we may discover that the richest and most profitable experiences that we had in this world were those gained on the very roads from which we shrank back in dread.

It was because Job was on God's main line that he found so many tunnels.

The great thing to remember is that *God's darknesses are not His goals*. His tunnels must be traveled *to get somewhere else*. Therefore, be patient, my soul! The darkness is not thy bourne; the tunnel is not thy abiding home!

The traveler who would pass from the wintry slopes of Switzerland into the summer beauty of the plains of Italy *must be prepared to tunnel the Alps*.

*Often darkness fills the pathway of the
pilgrim's onward track,
And we shrink from going forward—trembling,
feel like going back:
But the Lord, who plans so wisely, leads us on
both day and night,
Till at last, in silent wonder, we rejoice in
Wisdom's light.*

*Though the tunnel may be tedious through the
narrow, darkened way,
Yet it amply serves its purpose—soon it brings the light of day:
And the way so greatly dreaded, as we backward take a glance,
Shows the skill of careful planning: never the result of chance!*

*Is your present path a tunnel, does the darkness bring you fear?
To the upright, oh, remember, He doth cause a light to cheer.
Press on bravely, resting calmly, though a way you dimly see,
Till, at length, so safely guided, you emerge triumphantly.*

Trust the Engineer Eternal, surely all His works are right,
Though we cannot always trace them, faith will turn at last to sight:
Then no more the deepening shadows of the dark and dismal way,
There forever in clear sunlight, we'll enjoy "the perfect day."
SELECTED

The tunnel is never on a siding—it is planned to lead somewhere!

~~~~~~~~ JANUARY 29 ~~~~~~~~

Evening

</div>

<div align="center">

God is in the midst of her, she will not be moved;
God will help her when morning dawns.
PSALM 46:5 NASB

</div>

"Will not be moved"—what an inspiring declaration! Is it possible for us who are so easily moved by earthly things to come to a point where nothing can upset us or disturb our peace? The answer is yes, and the apostle Paul knew it. When he was on his way to Jerusalem, the Holy Spirit warned him that "prison and hardships" (Acts 20:23) awaited him. Yet he could triumphantly say, "But none of these things move me" (Acts 20:24 KJV).

Everything in Paul's life and experience that could be disturbed had already been shaken, and he no longer considered his life or any of his possessions as having any earthly value. And if we will only let God have His way with us, we can come to the same point. Then, like Paul, neither the stress and strain of little things nor the great and heavy trials of life will have enough power to move us from "the peace of God, which transcends all understanding" (Philippians 4:7). God declares this peace to be the inheritance of those who have learned to rest only on Him.

"The one who is victorious I will make a pillar in the temple of my God. Never again will they leave it" (Revelation 3:12). Becoming as immovable as a pillar in the house of God is such a worthy objective that we would gladly endure all the necessary trials that take us there! HANNAH WHITALL SMITH

When God is the center of a kingdom or a city, He makes it strong "like Mount

<div align="center">

</div>

Zion, which cannot be shaken" (Psalm 125:1). And when God is the center of a soul, although disasters may crowd in on all sides and roar like the waves of the sea, there is a constant calm within. The world can neither give nor take away this kind of peace. What is it that causes people to shake like leaves today at the first hint of danger? It is simply the lack of God living in their soul, and having the world in their hearts instead.
R. LEIGHTON

"*Those who trust in the LORD are like Mount Zion, which cannot be shaken but endures forever*" (Psalm 125:1). There is an old Scottish version of this psalm that strengthens our blood like iron:

> *Who clings to God in constant trust*
> *As Zion's mount he stands full just,*
> *And who moves not, nor yet does reel,*
> *But stands forever strong as steel!*

JANUARY 30
Morning

Go from your country . . . to the land I will show you.
GENESIS 12:1

It was one of the great moments of history when this primitive caravan set out for Haran. As we dimly picture them setting forth in the pale dawn of history, we seem to see the laden camels, pacing slowly, towering above the slow-footed sheep; we hear the drovers' cries and bleating of the flocks, broken by the wail of parting women.

With those who stay behind, we strain wistful eyes across the broad flood of old Euphrates till, in the wilderness beyond, the caravan is lost in a faint dust-haze—a stain and no more on the southern horizon.

Who does not feel that the grandeur of that moment centers in *the loyalty of one human soul to one word of God?*

> *"There's no sense in going further—it's the edge of cultivation."*
> *So they said and I believed it—broke my land and sowed my crop—*

*Built my barns and strung my fences in the little
border station—
Tucked away below the foothills where the trails run out and stop.*

*Till a voice, as bad as conscience, rang interminable changes
On one everlasting whisper, day and night repeated so:
"Something hidden. Go and find it. Go and look behind the Ranges—
Something lost behind the Ranges, lost and waiting for you. Go!"
Anybody might have found it, but—His whisper came to me!*

KIPLING

There remaineth yet very much land to be possessed!

Like the western prairies, there is no limit; it extends beyond the power of the human mind. "What no eye has seen, what no ear has heard, and what no human mind has conceived"—the things God has prepared for those who love him" (1 Corinthians 2:9).

The Holy Ghost is looking for simple-hearted believers *who will claim for Jesus Christ the great stretches of unoccupied places of darkness.*

Who will strike the Trail?

~~~~~~ JANUARY 30 ~~~~~~

Evening

I will be like the dew to Israel.

HOSEA 14:5

The dew is a source of freshness. It is nature's provision for renewing the face of the earth. It falls at night, and without it vegetation would die. It is this great renewal value of the dew that is so often recognized in the Scriptures and used as a symbol of spiritual refreshment. Just as nature is bathed in dew, the Lord renews His people. In Titus 3:5 the same thought of spiritual refreshment is connected with the ministry of the Holy Spirit and referred to as "renewal by the Holy Spirit."

Many Christian workers do not recognize the importance of the heavenly dew in their lives, and as a result lack freshness and energy. Their spirits are withered and droopy for lack of dew.

Beloved fellow worker, you recognize the folly of a laborer attempting to work all day without eating, but do you recognize the folly of a servant of God attempting to minister without eating of the heavenly manna? Neither is it sufficient to have spiritual nourishment only occasionally. Every day you must receive the "renewal by the Holy Spirit." You know the difference between your whole being pulsating with the energy and freshness of God's divine life or feeling worn-out and weary. Quietness and stillness bring the dew. At night when the leaves and grass are still, the plants' pores are open to receive the refreshing and invigorating bath. And spiritual dew comes from quietly lingering in the Master's presence. Get still before Him, for haste will prevent you from receiving the dew. Wait before God until you feel saturated with His presence. Then move on to your next duty with the awareness of the freshness and energy of Christ. DR. PARDINGTON

Dew will never appear while there is either heat or wind. The temperature must fall, the wind cease, and the air come to a point of coolness and rest—absolute rest—before the invisible particles of moisture will become dew to dampen any plant or flower. And the grace of God does not come forth to bring rest and renewal to our soul until we completely reach the *point of stillness* before Him.

> *Drop Your still dews of quietness,*
> *Till all our strivings cease:*
> *Take from our souls the strain and stress;*
> *And let our ordered lives confess*
> *The beauty of Your peace.*
> *Breathe through the pulses of desire*
> *Your coolness and Your balm;*
> *Let sense be mum, its beats expire:*
> *Speak through the earthquake, wind and fire,*
> *O still small voice of calm!*

Morning

They will be like a tree planted by the water.
JEREMIAH 17:8

Trees that brave storms are not propagated in hothouses!

The staunchest tree is not found in the shelter of the forest, but out in the open where the winds from every quarter beat upon it and bend and twist it until it becomes a giant in stature.

It requires storms to produce the rooting.

Out on the meadow it stands to shelter the herds and flocks. The earth about the tree hardens. The rains do little good, for the water runs off.

But the terrific storm strikes. It twists, turns, wrenches, and at times all but tears it out of its place. If the tree could speak it might bitterly complain. Should nature listen and cease the storm process?

The storm almost bends the tree double. It is wrath now. What can such seeming cruelty mean? Is that love? But *wait!*

About the tree the soil is all loosened. Great cracks are opened up way down into the ground. Deep wounds they might appear to the inexperienced. The rain now comes in with its gentle ministry. The *wounds* fill up. The moisture reaches away down deep even to the utmost root. The sun again shines. New and vigorous life bursts forth. The roots go deeper and deeper. The branches shoot forth. Now and again one hears something snap and crack like a pistol: it is getting too big for its clothes! It is growing into a giant! *It is rooting!*

This is the tree from which the mechanic wants his tools made—the tree which the wagon-maker seeks.

When you see a spiritual giant, think of the road over which he has traveled—not the sunny lane where wildflowers ever bloom, but a steep, rocky, narrow pathway where the blasts of hell will almost blow you off your feet, where the sharp rocks cut the feet, where the projecting thorns scratch the brow, and where the venomous serpents hiss on every side.

The Lord provides deep roots when there are
to be wide-spreading branches.

God of the gallant trees
Give to us fortitude:

Give as Thou givest to these,
Valorous hardihood.
We are the trees of Thy planting, O God,
We are the trees of Thy wood.

Now let the life-sap run
Clean through our every vein,
Perfect what Thou hast begun,
God of the sun and rain.
Thou who dost measure the weight of wind,
Fit us for stress and strain!

A. W. C.
Blessed be storms!

〜〜〜〜〜 JANUARY 31 〜〜〜〜〜

Evening

He giveth quietness.
JOB 34:29 KJV

He gives quietness in the midst of the raging storm. As we sail the lake with Him, reaching deep water and far from land, suddenly, under the midnight sky, a mighty storm sweeps down. Earth and hell seem mobilized against us, and each wave threatens to overwhelm our boat. Then He rises from His sleep and rebukes the wind and the waves. He waves His hand, signaling the end of the raging tempest and the beginning of the restful calm. His voice is heard above the screaming of the wind through the ropes and rigging, and over the thrashing of the waves.

"Quiet! Be still!" (Mark 4:39). Can you not hear it? And instantly there is a great calm. "He giveth quietness"—*quietness even in the midst of losing our inner strength and comforts*. Sometimes He removes these because we make too much of them. We are tempted to look at our joys, pleasures, passions, or our dreams, with too much self-satisfaction. Then through His gracious love He withdraws them, leading us to distinguish between them and Himself. He draws near and whispers the assurance of His presence, bringing an infinite calm to keep our hearts and minds. "He giveth quietness."

"He giveth quietness." O Elder Brother,
　　Whose homeless feet have pressed our path of pain,
Whose hands have borne the burden of our sorrow,
　　That in our losses we might find our gain.

Of all Your gifts and infinite consolings,
　　I ask but this: in every troubled hour
To hear Your voice through all the tumults stealing,
　　And rest serene beneath its tranquil power.

Cares cannot fret me if my soul be dwelling
　　In the still air of faith's untroubled day;
Grief cannot shake me if I walk beside you,
　　My hand in Yours along the darkening way.

Content to know there comes a radiant morning
　　When from all shadows I will find release;
Serene to wait the rapture of its dawning—
　　Who can make trouble when You send me peace?

FEBRUARY 1
Morning

Jesus knew that the Father had put all things under his power, and that he had come from God and was returning to God; so he got up from the meal, took off his outer clothing, and wrapped a towel around his waist. After that, he poured water into a basin and began to wash his disciples' feet, drying them with the towel that was wrapped around him.

JOHN 13:3–5

Not to sit on a lifted throne, nor to rule superbly alone; not to be ranked on the left or right in the kingdom's glory, the kingdom's might; not to be great and first of all, not to hold others in humble thrall; not to lord it over the world, a scepter high and a flag unfurled; not with authority, not with pride, vain dominion, mastery wide—nothing to wish for, nothing to do—not, in short, to be ministered to! Ah, but to minister! Lowly to sup with the servant's bread and the servant's cup; down where the waters of sorrow flow; full-baptized in the stream of woe; out where the people of sorrow are, walking brotherly, walking far; known to bitterness, known to sin, to the poor and wretched comrade and kin; so to be helper, the last and the least serf in the kingdom, slave at the feast; so to obey, and so to defer, and so, my Savior, to minister. Yes, for never am I alone: this is Thy glory and this is Thy throne. Infinite Servant, well may I be bondman and vassal and toiler—with Thee. AMOS R. WELLS

I would be simply used,
Spending myself in humble task or great,
Priest at the altar, keeper of the gate,
So be my Lord requireth just that thing
Which at the needful moment I may bring.
O joy of serviceableness Divine!

Of merging will and work, dear Lord, in Thine,
Of knowing that results, however small,
Fitly into Thy stream of purpose fall.
I would be simply used!

ANONYMOUS

I want to be a humble soul commended in the sky.
JOHN SHOBER KIMBER

Evening

This is my doing.
1 KINGS 12:24

The disappointments of life are simply the hidden appointments of love. C. A. FOX
My child, I have a message for you today. Let me whisper it in your ear so any storm clouds that may arise will shine with glory, and the rough places you may have to walk will be made smooth. It is only four words, but let them sink into your inner being, and use them as a pillow to rest your weary head. *"This is my doing."*

Have you ever realized that whatever concerns you concerns Me too? "For whoever touches you touches the apple of [my] eye" (Zechariah 2:8). "You are precious and honored in my sight" (Isaiah 43:4). Therefore it is My special delight to teach you.

I want you to learn when temptations attack you, and the enemy comes in "like a pent-up flood" (Isaiah 59:19), that *"this is my doing"* and that your weakness needs My strength, and your safety lies in letting Me fight for you.

Are you in difficult circumstances, surrounded by people who do not understand you, never ask your opinion, and always push you aside? *"This is my doing."* I am the God of circumstances. You did not come to this place by accident—you are exactly where I meant for you to be.

Have you not asked Me to make you humble? Then see that I have placed you in the perfect school where this lesson is taught. Your circumstances and the people around you are only being used to accomplish My will.

Are you having problems with money, finding it hard to make ends meet? *"This is my doing,"* for I am the One who keeps your finances, and I want you to learn to depend upon Me. My supply is limitless and I "will meet all your needs" (Philippians 4:19). I want you to prove My promises so no one may say, "You did not trust in the LORD your God" (Deuteronomy 1:32).

Are you experiencing a time of sorrow? *"This is my doing."* I am "a man of suffering, and familiar with pain" (Isaiah 53:3). I have allowed your earthly comforters to fail you, so that by turning to Me you may receive "eternal encouragement and good hope" (2 Thessalonians 2:16). Have you longed to do some great work for Me but instead have been set aside on a bed of sickness and pain? *"This is my doing."* You were so busy I could not get your attention, and I wanted to teach you some of My deepest truths. "They also serve who only stand and wait." In fact, some of My greatest workers are those physically unable to serve, but who have learned to wield the powerful weapon of prayer.

Today I place a cup of holy oil in your hands. Use it freely, My child. Anoint with it every new circumstance, every word that hurts you, every interruption that makes you impatient, and every weakness you have. The pain will leave as you learn to see Me in all things. LAURA A. BARTER SNOW

> "This is from Me," the Savior said,
>   As bending low He kissed my brow,
> "For One who loves you thus has led.
>   Just rest in Me, be patient now,
> Your Father knows you have need of this,
>   Though, why perhaps you cannot see—
> Grieve not for things you've seemed to miss.
>   The thing I send is best for thee."
>
> Then, looking through my tears, I plead,
>   "Dear Lord, forgive, I did not know,
> It will not be hard since You do tread,
>   Each path before me here below."
> And for my good this thing must be,
>   His grace sufficient for each test.
> So still I'll sing, "Whatever be
>   God's way for me is always best."

~~~~~ FEBRUARY 2 ~~~~~

Morning

It will be even more fruitful.
JOHN 15:2

Two years ago I set out a rosebush in the corner of my garden. It was to bear yellow roses. And it was to bear them profusely. Yet, during these two years, it has not produced a blossom!

I asked the florist from whom I bought the bush why it was so barren of flowers. I had cultivated it carefully; had watered it often; had made the soil around it as rich as possible. And it had grown well.

"That's just why," said the florist. "That kind of rose needs the poorest soil in the garden. Sandy soil would be best, and never a bit of fertilizer. Take away the rich soil and put gravelly earth in its place. Cut the bush back severely. Then it will bloom."

I did—and the bush blossomed forth in the most gorgeous yellow known to nature. Then I moralized: that yellow rose is just like many lives. Hardships develop beauty in the soul; the soul thrives on troubles; trials bring out all the best in them; ease and comfort and applause only leave them barren. PASTOR JOYCE

> *The bark by tempest vainly tossed*
> *May founder in the calm;*
> *And he who braved the polar frost*
> *Faint by the isles of balm.*
>
> WHITTIER

The finest of flowers bloom in the sandiest of deserts as well as in the hothouses. God is the same Gardener.

~~~ FEBRUARY 2 ~~~

Evening

> *In the shadow of his hand he hid me; he made me into a*
> *polished arrow and concealed me in his quiver.*
> ISAIAH 49:2

In the shadow"—each of us must go there sometimes. The glare of the sunlight is too bright, and our eyes become injured. Soon they are unable to discern the subtle shades of color or appreciate neutral tints, such as the shadowed sickroom, the shadowed house of grief, or the shadowed life where the sunlight has departed.

But fear not! It is the shadow of God's hand. He is leading you, and there are lessons that can be learned only where He leads.

The photograph of His face can only be developed in the dark room. But do not assume that He has pushed you aside.

You are still "in his quiver." He has not thrown you away as something worthless.

He is only keeping you nearby till the moment comes when He can send you quickly and confidently on some mission that will bring Him glory. O shadowed, isolated one, remember how closely the quiver is tied to the warrior. It is always within easy reach of his hand and jealously protected. F. B. MEYER

In some realms of nature, shadows or darkness are the places of greatest growth. The beautiful Indian corn never grows more rapidly than in the darkness of a warm summer night. The sun withers and curls the leaves in the scorching light of noon, but once a cloud hides the sun, they quickly unfold. The shadows provide a service that the sunlight does not. The starry beauty of the sky cannot be seen at its peak until the shadows of night slip over the sky. Lands with fog, clouds, and shade are lush with greenery. And there are beautiful flowers that bloom in the shade that will never bloom in the sun. Florists now have their evening primrose as well as their morning glory. The evening primrose will not open in the noonday sun but only reveals its beauty as the shadows of the evening grow longer.

> If all of life were sunshine,
>   Our face would long to gain
> And feel once more upon it
>   The cooling splash of rain.
>
> HENRY JACKSON VAN DYKE

～～～ FEBRUARY 3 ～～～
Morning

*The chief priests accused him of many things. So again Pilate asked him,
"Aren't you going to answer? See how many things they are accusing
you of." But Jesus still made no reply, and Pilate was amazed.*

MARK 15:3–5

The apostle writes years afterward of this wonderful silence of the God-man: "When they hurled their insults at him, he did not retaliate; when he suffered, he made no threats" (1 Peter 2:23).

His silence was Divine. No mere human could thus remain dumb and innocent and guiltless, allow Himself to be "led like a lamb to the slaughter," to be as a sheep dumb in the hand of the shearers. This silence before Pilate and then the silence on the Cross in the midst of untold agony—silence, broken only seven times, with brief words of wondrous meaning—this silence of Jesus was the climax to a life of God-like silence in circumstances when men must speak; a life of silent waiting until He was thirty years of age ere He entered on public ministry and made His lamb-like way to the Cross; a life of silence over glory unspeakable with His Father and suffering untold at the hands of men; of tender silence over blessing to others and over Judas' traitor path.

This is the pattern for all who would *follow His steps;* the pattern for the one who would walk as He walked, by His walking again in them. And how can it be? Only by seeing the *calling* and accepting it (1 Peter 1:15). And by taking His Cross as *our* Cross, "we having died" *in* Him and *with* Him can thus live unto God, and then the silence of Jesus can be known in truth, and we shall be:

Silent in our lowly service among others, not seeking to be seen of men.

Silent over the glory of the hours on the Mount, lest others think of us above that which is written.

Silent over the depths of the Calvary pathway that led us unto God.

Silent over the human instruments permitted of God to hand us over to the judgment hall and the forsaking of our nearest and our dearest.

Silent whilst we stoop to serve the very ones who have betrayed us.

Silent over the deep things of God revealed in the secret places of the Most High, *impossible to utter* to those who have not yet been *baptized* with that baptism without which they will be *straightened* in spiritual perception *until it be accomplished.*

Silent over questions only to be answered by God, the Holy Ghost, when *that day* dawns for the questioning heart, and silences all doubt by the glorious revelation of Him who is the answer to all our needs.

Silent when forced by others to some position where apparent rivalry with another much-used servant of God seems imminent, only to be hushed by utter self-effacement, and our silent withdrawal without explanation, *irrespective of our rights.*

Silent—yea, silent in the judgment hall of our co-religionists, when criticized and falsely accused of many things. TRACT

Live Thou this life in me.

~~~~~~~~~~ FEBRUARY 3 ~~~~~~~~~~

Evening

At once the Spirit sent him out into the wilderness.

MARK 1:12

This seemed a strange way for God to prove His favor. "At once"—after what? After heaven was opened and the Spirit descended "like a dove" (v. 10), and the Father voiced His blessing, "You are my Son, whom I love; with you I am well pleased" (v. 11). Yet it is not an abnormal experience.

You, my soul, have also experienced it. Aren't your times of deepest depression the moments that immediately follow your loftiest highs? Just yesterday you were soaring high in the heavens and singing in the radiance of the morning. Today, however, your wings are folded and your song is silent. At noon you were basking in the sunshine of the Father's smile, but by evening you were saying from the wilderness, "My way is hidden from the LORD" (Isaiah 40:27).

No, my soul, the actual suddenness of the change is proof that it is not abnormal. Have you considered the comfort of the words "at once," and why the change comes so soon after the blessing? Simply to show that it is the sequel to the blessing. God shines His light on you to make you fit for life's deserts, Gethsemanes, and Calvaries. He lifts you to new heights to strengthen you so that you may go deeper still. He illuminates you so He may send you into the night, making you a help to the helpless.

You are not always worthy of the wilderness—you are only worthy of the wilderness after the splendor of the Jordan River experience. Nothing but the Son's vision can equip you to carry the Spirit's burden, and only the glory of the baptism can withstand the hunger of the desert. GEORGE MATHESON

After blessings comes the battle.

The time of testing that distinguishes and greatly enriches a person's spiritual career

—— 89 ——

is not an ordinary one but a period when it seems as if all hell were set loose. It is a time when we realize our soul is caught in a net, and we know God is allowing us to be gripped by the Devil's hand. Yet it is a period that always ends in certain triumph for those who have committed the keeping of their souls to God. And the testing "later on . . . produces a harvest of righteousness and peace" (Hebrews 12:11) and paves the way for the thirtyfold to one hundredfold increase that is promised to follow (Matthew 13:23).
APHRA WHITE

—— FEBRUARY 4 ——

Morning

We felt we had received the sentence of death. But this
happened that we might not rely on ourselves.

2 CORINTHIANS 1:9

These are weighty words for all Christ's servants, but we must be His servants *in reality* in order to enter into their deep significance. If we are content to live a life of indolence and ease, a life of self-seeking and self-pleasing, it is impossible for us to understand such words or indeed to enter into any of those intense exercises of soul through which Christ's true-hearted servants and faithful witnesses, in all ages, have been called to pass.

We find, invariably, that all those who have been most used of God in public have gone through deep waters in secret. Paul could say to the Corinthians, *"Death is at work in us, but life is at work in you"* (2 Corinthians 4:12). Death working in the poor earthen vessel; but streams of life, heavenly grace, and spiritual power flowing into those to whom he ministered.

How the professing church has departed from the Divine reality of ministry! Where are the Pauls, the Gideons, and the Joshuas? Where are the deep heart-searchings and profound soul exercises which have characterized Christ's servants in other days? Flippant, worldly, shallow, empty, self-sufficient, and self-indulgent are we! *Need we wonder at the small results?*

How can we expect to see life working in others, when we know so little about death working in us?

May the eternal Spirit stir us all up! May He work in us a more powerful sense of what it is to be *true-hearted, single-eyed, devoted servants of the Lord Jesus Christ!*

> *From prayer that asks that I may be*
> *Sheltered from winds that beat on Thee,*
> *From fearing when I should aspire,*
> *From faltering when I should climb higher,*
> *From silken self, O Captain, free*
> *Thy soldier who would follow Thee.*
>
> *From subtle love of softening things,*
> *From easy choices, weakenings,*
> *(Not thus are spirits fortified,*
> *Not this way went the Crucified)*
> *From all that dims Thy Calvary*
> *O Lamb of God, deliver me.*
>
> *Give me the love that leads the way,*
> *The faith that nothing can dismay,*
> *The hope no disappointments tire,*
> *The passion that will burn like fire;*
> *Let me not sink to be a clod:*
> *Make me Thy fuel, Flame of God.*
>
> AMY WILSON CARMICHAEL

Write the death sentence upon self, that the power of resurrection life in Christ may shine forth!

FEBRUARY 4

Evening

I will cause you to ride in triumph on the heights of the land.
ISAIAH 58:14

One of the first rules of aerodynamics is that flying into the wind quickly increases altitude. The wings of the airplane create more lift by flying against the wind. How was this lesson learned? It was learned by watching birds fly. If a bird is simply flying for pleasure, it flies with the wind. But if it senses danger, it turns into the wind to gain altitude, and flies up toward the sun.

The sufferings of life are God's winds. Sometimes they blow against us and are very strong. They are His hurricanes, taking our lives to higher levels, toward His heavens.

Do you remember a summer day when the heat and humidity were so oppressive, you could hardly breathe? But a dark cloud appeared on the horizon, growing larger and larger, until it suddenly brought a rich blessing to your world. The storm raged, lightning flashed, and thunder rumbled. The storm covered your sky, the atmosphere was cleansed, new life was in the air, and your world was changed.

Human life works exactly on the same principle. When the storms of life appear, the atmosphere is changed, purified, filled with new life, and part of heaven is brought down to earth. SELECTED

Facing obstacles should make us sing. The wind finds its voice not when rushing across an open sea but when it is hindered by the outstretched limbs of a pine tree or broken by the strings of an aeolian wind harp. Only then does the harp have songs of power and beauty. Send your soul, which has been set free, sweeping across the obstacles of life. Send it through the relentless forests of pain and against even the smallest hindrances and worries of life, and it too will find a voice with which to sing. SELECTED

> Be like a bird that, halting in its flight,
> Rests on a limb too slight.
> And feeling it give way beneath him sings,
> Knowing he has wings.

~~~~~~~~~ FEBRUARY 5 ~~~~~~~~~

Morning

[Hezekiah] went up to the temple of the LORD and spread it out before the LORD.
ISAIAH 37:14

Does it not often happen that you are in great difficulty how to act in some particular case? Your course is not plain; your way is not open: each side seems equally balanced, and you cannot tell which to choose. Your wishes, perhaps, point one way; your fears, another. You are afraid lest you should decide wrongly, lest you should take what, in the end, may prove hurtful to you.

It is very trying to be brought into this painful conflict. And it adds to our distress if we are forced to go forward at once and take one course or the other. Shall I tell you how you may be sure to find unspeakable relief?

Go and lay your matter before the Lord, as Hezekiah did with the king of Assyria's letter. Do not, however, deceive yourself, as many do, and seek counsel of God, *having determined to act according to your own will, and not according to His.* But, simply and honestly, ask that He would guide you. Commit your case to your Father in heaven; surrender yourself as a little child to be led as He pleases. This is the way to be guided aright, and to realize the blessing of having a heavenly Counselor. A. OXENDEN

Surrendered—led alone by Thee, and wait Thy guidance still.

FEBRUARY 5

Evening

You will not leave in haste.
ISAIAH 52:12

I do not believe we have even begun to understand the wonderful power there is in being still. We are in such a hurry, always doing, that we are in danger of not allowing God the opportunity to work. You may be sure that God will never say to us, "Stand still," "Sit still," or "Be still," unless *He* is going to do something. This is our problem regarding the Christian life: *we* want to do something to be Christians, instead of allowing *Him* to work in us.

Think of how still you stand when your picture is being taken, as the photographer captures your likeness on film. God has one eternal purpose for us: that we should be "conformed to the image of his Son" (Romans 8:29 KJV). But in order for that to happen, we must stand still. We hear so much today about being active, but maybe we need to learn what it means to be quiet. *Crumbs*

Sit still, my children! Just sit calmly still!
Nor deem these days—these waiting days—as ill!
The One who loves you best, who plans your way,
Has not forgotten your great need today!
And, if He waits, it's sure He waits to prove
To you, His tender child, His heart's deep love.

Sit still, my children! Just sit calmly still!
You greatly long to know your dear Lord's will!
While anxious thoughts would almost steal their way
Corrodingly within, because of His delay—
Persuade yourself in simple faith to rest
That He, who knows and loves, will do the best.

Sit still, my children! Just sit calmly still!
Nor move one step, not even one, until
His way has opened. Then, ah then, how sweet!
How glad your heart, and then how swift your feet,
Your inner being then, ah then, how strong!
And waiting days not counted then too long.

Sit still, my daughter! Just sit calmly still!
What higher service could you for Him fill?
It's hard! ah yes! But choicest things must cost!
For lack of losing all how much is lost!
It's hard, it's true! But then—He gives you grace
To count the hardest spot the sweetest place.

J. DANSON SMITH

Morning

Everything is possible for one who believes.
MARK 9:23

Prayer takes the people to the Bank of Faith, and obtains the golden blessing. Mind how you pray! Pray! Make real business of it! Never let it be a dead formality! People pray a long time but do not get what they are supposed to ask for *because they do not plead the promise in a truthful businesslike way.* If you were to go into a bank and stand an hour talking to the clerk, and then come out again without your cash, what would be the good of it? CHARLES H. SPURGEON

Have you ever given God the chance to answer the Prayer of Faith?

Do not let us lose our last chance of believing by waiting till the dawn has broken into day! LILIAS TROTTER

> *If radio's slim finger can pluck a melody*
> *From night, and toss it over a continent or sea;*
> *If the petaled white notes of a violin*
> *Are blown across a mountain or a city's din;*
> *If songs, like crimson roses, are culled from thin*
> *blue air—*
> *Why should mortals wonder if God hears prayer?*
> ETHEL ROMIG FULLER

When all things can be accomplished by prayer, why not yield to the test? Why not pray on? And through?

> *He turned the sea into dry land, they passed through the*
> *waters on foot—come, let us rejoice in him.*
> PSALM 66:6

It is a profound statement that "through *the waters*," the very place where we might have expected nothing but trembling, terror, anguish, and dismay, the children of Israel stopped to "rejoice in him"!

How many of us can relate to this experience? Who of us, right in the midst of our time of distress and sadness, have been able to triumph and rejoice, as the Israelites did?

How close God is to us through His promises, and how brightly those promises shine! Yet during times of prosperity, we lose sight of their brilliance. In the way the sun at noon hides the stars from sight, His promises become indiscernible. But when night falls—the deep, dark night of sorrow—a host of stars begins to shine, bringing forth God's blessed constellations of hope, and promises of comfort from His Word.

Just as Jacob experienced at Jabbok, it is only once the sun sets that the Angel of the Lord comes, wrestles with us, and we can overcome. It was at night, "at twilight" (Exodus 30:8), that Aaron lit the sanctuary lamps. And it is often during nights of trouble that the brightest lamps of believers are set ablaze.

It was during a dark time of loneliness and exile that John had the glorious vision of his Redeemer. Many of us today have our "Isle of Patmos," which produces the brightest memories of God's enduring presence, uplifting grace, and love in spite of solitude and sadness.

How many travelers today, still passing through their Red Seas and Jordan Rivers of earthly affliction, will be able to look back from eternity, filled with memories of God's great goodness, and say, "We 'passed through the waters on foot.' And yet, even in these dark experiences, with waves surging all around, we stopped and said, 'Let us rejoice in him'!" J. R. MACDUFF

"*There* I will give her back her vineyards, and will make the Valley of Achor a door of hope. There she will [sing]" (Hosea 2:15).

Morning

Before they call I will answer; while they are still speaking I will hear.

Isaiah 65:24

In one of his great Gospel campaigns in Chicago, Moody asked his helpers to join him in prayer for $6,000 and to ask that it *might be sent at once.* They prayed long and earnestly, and before they rose from their knees a telegram was brought in. It was in some such words as these:

Your friends at Northfield had a feeling that you needed money for your work in Chicago. We have taken up a collection, and there is $6,000 in the baskets.

"God had prepared the people" (2 Chronicles 29:36 KJV).

In connection with the work of the West London Mission, the Revelation Hugh Price Hughes and his colleagues once found themselves in pressing need of £1,000, and to get quiet they met at midnight to pray for it. After some time of pleading, one of the number burst into praise, being assured that the prayer had been heard and would be answered. Mr. Hughes did not share this absolute confidence. He believed with trembling.

When the day came for announcing the sum received, it was found that £990 had come in within a very short time and in very extraordinary ways—but there was the deficiency of £10. When Mr. Hughes went home he found a letter which he now remembered had been there in the morning, but through pressure he had left it unopened. It contained a check for £10!

I'll trust Thy grace—'tis infinite;
And knows no bound, nor end.

After Dan Crawford had passed to his eternal rest, it was written of him: "He lived (and his work was supported) by strong faith in the unlimited riches of God, and in the power of prayer. He felt, too, *that those riches and that power were available for all Africa, though he knew that not all had the same faith.*"

He had a strong sense of unity of God's work. A certain missionary in Africa, held up in some work for God, wrote to Dan Crawford asking for £100, and excused himself by saying, "You are rich." When he saw that the same weekly mail that had brought the request had brought also contributions amounting to about the sum mentioned, Dan Crawford sent the whole week's income to his correspondent with this reply: "Rich? Yes, I am rich—rich in faith for you all."

"And God is able to bless you abundantly, so that in all things at all times, having all that you need, you will abound in every good work" (2 Corinthians 9:8).

> *He might have doled His blossoms out quite grudgingly,*
> *God might have used His sunset gold so sparingly,*
> *He might have put but one wee star in all the sky—*
> *But since He gave so lavishly, why should not I?*
> A. C. H.

～～～ FEBRUARY 7 ～～～
Evening

Why, my soul, are you downcast?
PSALM 43:5

Is there ever any reason to be downcast? Actually, there are two reasons, but only two. If we were still unbelievers, we would have a reason to be downcast; or if we have been converted but continue to live in sin, we are downcast as a consequence.

Except for these two conditions, there is never a reason to be downcast, for everything else may be brought to God "by prayer and petition, with thanksgiving" (Philippians 4:6). And through all our times of need, difficulty, and trials, we may exercise faith in the power and love of God.

"*Put your hope in God*" (Psalm 43:5). Please remember there is never a time when we cannot hope in God, whatever our need or however great our difficulty may be. Even when our situation appears to be impossible, our work is to "hope in God."

Our hope will not be in vain, and in the Lord's own timing help will come.

Oh, the hundreds, even the thousands, of times I have found this to be true in the past seventy years and four months of my life! When it seemed impossible for help to come, it did come, for God has His own unlimited resources. In ten thousand different ways, and at ten thousand different times, God's help may come to us.

Our work is to lay our petitions before the Lord, and in childlike simplicity to pour out our hearts before Him, saying, "I do not deserve that You should hear me and answer my requests, but for the sake of my precious Lord Jesus; for His sake, answer my prayer. And give me grace to wait patiently until it pleases You to grant my petition. For I believe You will do it in Your own time and way."

"*For I will yet praise him*" (Psalm 43:5). More prayer, more exercising of our faith, and more patient waiting leads to blessings—abundant blessings. I have found it to be true many hundreds of times, and therefore I continually say to myself, "Put your hope in God." GEORGE MUELLER

—————— FEBRUARY 8 ——————

Morning

Then some Jews came [to Lystra] . . . and won the crowd over. They stoned Paul and dragged him outside the city, thinking he was dead. . . . The next day he . . . left for Derbe. They preached the gospel in that city. . . . Then they returned to Lystra.
ACTS 14:19–21

The cruel stones unerring fell upon him—
Until they deemed his bleeding form was dead;
His worth and work they knew not, and they cared not;
Enough, they madly hated what he said.

God touched him! and he rose, with new life given;
Nor in his bosom burned resentful pain;
And, by and by, when need and call both guided,
He to the stoning-place returned again.

Perchance thou, too, hast tasted cruel stoning—
And might'st be glad if call came ne'er again

—— 99 ——

To turn to scenes where surely there awaits thee
The cruel, cutting stones which make life vain.

Yet, if "back to the stones" the Finger pointeth,
Then thou shalt know there is no better way;
And there, just there, shall matchless grace await thee,
And God Himself shall be thy strength and stay.

J. DANSON SMITH

The most sublime moments lie very close to the most painful situations.
Are we familiar with the road that leads back to the stones?

FEBRUARY 8
Evening

Surely I am with you always.
MATTHEW 28:20

Never look ahead to the changes and challenges of this life in fear. Instead, as they arise look at them with the full assurance that God, whose you are, will deliver you out of them. Hasn't He kept you safe up to now? So hold His loving hand tightly, and He will lead you safely through all things. And when you cannot stand, He will carry you in His arms.

Do not look ahead to what *may* happen tomorrow. The same everlasting Father who cares for you today will take care of you tomorrow and every day. Either He will shield you from suffering or He will give you His unwavering strength that you may bear it. Be at peace, then, and set aside all anxious thoughts and worries. FRANCIS DE SALES

"The LORD is my shepherd" (Psalm 23:1).

Not *was*, not *may be*, nor *will be*. "The LORD *is* my shepherd." He *is* on Sunday, on Monday, and through every day of the week. He *is* in January, in December, and every month of the year. He *is* when I'm at home and in China. He *is* during peace or war, and in times of abundance or poverty. J. HUDSON TAYLOR

He will silently plan for you,
His object of omniscient care;
God Himself undertakes to be
Your Pilot through each subtle snare.

He will silently plan for you,
So certainly, He cannot fail!
Rest on the faithfulness of God,
In Him you surely will prevail.

He will silently plan for you
Some wonderful surprise of love.
No eye has seen, no ear has heard,
But it is kept for you above.

He will silently plan for you,
His purposes will all unfold;
Your tangled life will shine at last,
A masterpiece of skill untold.

He will silently plan for you,
Happy child of a Father's care,
As if no other claimed His love,
But you alone to Him were dear.

E. MARY GRIMES

Whatever our faith says God is, He will be.

~~~~ FEBRUARY 9 ~~~~

Morning

God did not lead them on the road through the
Philistine country, though that was shorter.

EXODUS 13:17

Why not? Because the people needed disciplining and molding as a Nation. They would have been destroyed by way of Philistia, but by the way of the wilderness they were trained slowly for the great task at their journey's end. God, who chose the route, also chose the leader. God, who disciplined the people, also disciplined the man who led them.

History and experience seem to point to the fact that God's line for us is not usually a straight line, but a winding zigzag path.

The roundabout way may be the nearest! JOSEPH PARKER

Over the Apennines there is a wonderful railroad—one passes through forty-three tunnels in less than seventy miles—magnificent outlooks, but every few minutes, a tunnel! The road has been built to carry the traveler to his destination by the shortest way; anyone getting off at the first station, simply because he did not like tunnels, and striking into the mountains to find another path would be almost sure of being lost and starving to death.

Can we not believe the same thing of God's way? His way lies through tunnels—long ones often, but it is the best and safest road. And it is not all tunnels; in the region of the high rocks there are most glorious prospects! Places so full of beauty, and commanding such outlooks of love and mercy, as ought to reconcile us to the intervals of darkness.

Be not afraid of the *winding way* if God turns you into it. *Travel the road He points out to you!* God brings men to His consummations *only by His own road.*

> We climbed the height by the zigzag path
> And wondered why—until
> We understood it was made zigzag
> To break the force of the hill.
>
> A road straight up would prove too steep
> For the traveler's feet to tread;
> The thought was kind in its wise design
> Of a zigzag path instead.

It is often so in our daily life;
We fail to understand
That the twisting way our feet must tread
By love alone was planned.

Then murmur not at the winding way,
It is our Father's will
To lead us Home by the zigzag path,
To break the force of the hill.

ANONYMOUS

Simply following God is the true philosophy of life.

FEBRUARY 9

Evening

Jesus did not answer a word.
MATTHEW 15:23

He will quiet you with his love.
ZEPHANIAH 3:17 ESV

Are you reading these verses as a child of God who is experiencing a crushing sorrow, a bitter disappointment, or a heartbreaking blow from a totally unexpected place? Are you longing to hear your Master's voice calling you, saying, "Take courage! It is I. Don't be afraid" (Matthew 14:27)? Yet only silence, the unknown, and misery confront you—"Jesus did not answer a word."

God's tender heart must often ache listening to our sad, complaining cries. Our weak, impatient hearts cry out because we fail to see through our tear-blinded, shortsighted eyes that it is for our own sakes that He does not answer at all or that He answers in a way we believe is less than the best. In fact, the silences of Jesus are as eloquent as His words and may be a sign not of His disapproval but of His approval and His way of providing a deeper blessing for you.

"Why, my soul, are you downcast . . . I will yet praise him" (Psalm 43:5). Yes, praise Him even for His silence. Let me relate a beautiful old story of how one Christian dreamed she saw three other women in prayer.

When they knelt the Master drew near to them. As He approached the first of the three, He bent over her with tenderness and grace. He smiled with radiant love and spoke to her in tones of pure, sweet music. Upon leaving her, He came to the next but only placed His hand upon her bowed head and gave her one look of loving approval. He passed the third woman almost abruptly, without stopping for a word or a glance.

The woman having the dream said to herself, "How greatly He must love the first woman. The second gained His approval but did not experience the special demonstrations of love He gave the first. But the third woman must have grieved Him deeply, for He gave her no word at all, nor even a passing look."

She wondered what the third woman must have done to have been treated so differently. As she tried to account for the actions of her Lord, He Himself came and stood beside her. He said to her, "O woman! How wrongly you have interpreted Me! The first kneeling woman needs the full measure of My tenderness and care to keep her feet on My narrow way. She needs My love, thoughts, and help every moment of the day, for without them she would stumble into failure.

"The second woman has stronger faith and deeper love than the first, and I can count on her to trust Me no matter how things may go or whatever people may do. Yet the third woman, whom I seemed not to notice, and even to neglect, has faith and love of the purest quality. I am training her through quick and drastic ways for the highest and holiest service.

"She knows Me so intimately, and trusts Me so completely, that she no longer depends on My voice, loving glances, or other outward signs to know of My approval. She is not dismayed or discouraged by any circumstances I arrange for her to encounter. She trusts Me when common sense, reason, and even every subtle instinct of the natural heart would rebel, knowing that I am preparing her for eternity, and realizing that the understanding of what I do will come later.

"My love is silent because I love beyond the power of words to express it and beyond the understanding of the human heart. Also, it is silent for your sakes—that you may learn to love and trust Me with pure, Spirit-taught, spontaneous responses. I desire for your response to My love to be without the prompting of anything external."

He "will do wonders never before done" (Exodus 34:10) if you will learn the mystery of His silence and praise Him every time He withdraws His gifts from you. Through this you will better know and love the Giver. SELECTED

~~~~~~~~~~ FEBRUARY 10 ~~~~~~~~~~

Morning

The angel of the LORD encamps around those who fear him, and he delivers them.
PSALM 34:7

A wonderful story is told by a Moravian missionary in connection with angelic protection.

An American missionary and his wife bravely went to their station, where, twenty years before, two missionaries had been killed and eaten by the natives. They said as they took up their work it seemed as if often they were surrounded not only by the hostile natives, but by the very powers of darkness. These latter were so real, that night after night they were forced to get up and strengthen their hearts by reading the Word of God. Again, they would pray.

One day a man came and said, "I would like to see your watchmen close at hand."

The missionary replied: "I have no watchmen; I have only a cook and a little herd boy. What watchmen do you mean?"

The man asked permission to look through the missionaries' home. Every corner of the house was carefully searched, and the man came out of the house greatly disappointed.

Then the missionary asked the man to tell him about the watchmen to whom he referred. Here is the man's answer.

"When you and your wife came here we determined to kill you as we did the missionaries twenty years ago. Night after night we came to carry out our intentions, but *there always stood around your house a double row of watchmen with glittering weapons, and we dared not come near.* At last we hired a professional assassin, who said he feared neither God nor devil. Last night he came close to your house—we followed at a distance—brandishing his spear. *There stood the shining watchmen,* and the killer fled in terror. So we have given up our purpose to kill you, but tell me, *who are the watchmen?*"

The missionary opened the Word of God and read: "The angel of the LORD encampeth round about them that fear him, and delivereth them" (KJV).

"Let the beloved of the LORD rest secure in him" (Deuteronomy 33:12).

"The LORD had hidden them" (Jeremiah 36:26).

<hr>

FEBRUARY 10

Evening

Do not take revenge, my dear friends.
ROMANS 12:19

There are times when doing nothing demands much greater strength than taking action. Maintaining composure is often the best evidence of power. Even to the vilest and deadliest of charges, Jesus responded with deep, unbroken silence. His silence was so profound, it caused His accusers and spectators to wonder in awe. To the greatest insults, the most violent treatment, and to mockery that would bring righteous indignation to the feeblest of hearts, He responded with voiceless, confident calmness. Those who are unjustly accused, and mistreated without cause, know the tremendous strength that is necessary to keep silent and to leave revenge to God.

> *Men may misjudge your aim,*
> *Think they have cause to blame,*
> *Say, you are wrong;*
> *Keep on your quiet way,*
> *Christ is the Judge, not they,*
> *Fear not, be strong.*

The apostle Paul said, "None of these things *move* me" (Acts 20:24 KJV). He did not say, "None of these things *hurt* me." It is one thing to be hurt, and quite another to be moved. Paul had a very tender heart, for we do not read of any other apostle who cried as he did. It takes a strong man to cry. "Jesus wept" (John 11:35), and He was the strongest man that ever lived.

— 106 —

Therefore it does not say, "None of these things hurt me." The apostle Paul had determined not to move from what he believed was right. He did not value things as we are prone to do. He never looked for the easy way, and placed no value on his mortal life. He only cared about one thing, and that was his loyalty to Christ—to gain Christ's smile. To Paul, more than to any other man, doing Christ's work was his earthly pay, but gaining Christ's smile was heaven. MARGARET BOTTOME

～～～～～ FEBRUARY 11 ～～～～～
Morning

The LORD God is my strength, and he will make my feet like hinds' feet, and he will make me to walk upon mine high places.
HABAKKUK 3:19 KJV

In "Marble Faun," Miriam, the brokenhearted singer, puts into a burst of song the pent-up grief of her soul. This was better, surely, than if she had let forth a wild shriek of pain.

It is nobler to sing a victorious song in time of trial than to lie crushed in grief. Songs bless the world more than wails. It is better for our own heart, too, to put our sorrows and pains into songs. *"We shall conquer by song."*

"Our minister is a skylark Christian," boasted one of his people. Fine bird! It sings morning, noon, and evening; sings as it springs from the flowery sod; sings when the ground is white with snow. What a song, too!—a shower of melody and infinite sweetness—*with no undertone of pain.*

If we could only realize the full truth and blessedness of our faith we should continually go up and down singing, until one fine day we would go up singing—up, up, beyond the sun—and come down no more, lost in the eternal light!

Help me to make of all my sorrows music for the world!

Turn your troubles into treasure,
Turn your sorrows into song;

Then all men will know the measure,
In which you to Christ belong.
When they see your bright behavior
Under provocation great,
They may ask what mighty Savior
Can impart that happy state.

Paul and Silas in the prison,
With their feet fast in the stocks,
Praised their glorious Lord, arisen,
Till the earthquake rent the rocks.
There was none to join their singing,
So the earthquake roared "Amen!"
And glad chains fell down a-ringing,
As their voices rang again!

Oh, then sing with us His praises
When there seems least cause to praise;
Faith the sweetest anthem raises
When the darkness hides God's ways;
He brings forth His "new creation"
Only there where ends "the old."
Let us praise Him for salvation,
When all feels most dead and cold.

My soul, keep up thy singing,
Turn thy sorrows into song.

ARTHUR S. BOOTH-CLIBBORN

Let every sigh be changed into a *Hallelujah!* OTTO STOCKMAYER
"None might enter into the king's gate clothed with sackcloth" (Esther 4:2 KJV).

Evening

As soon as the priests . . . set foot in the Jordan, its waters . . . will be cut off.
JOSHUA 3:13

The Israelites were not to wait in the camp until the Jordan was opened but to "walk by faith" (2 Corinthians 5:7 KJV). They were to break camp, pack up their belongings, form a marching line, and actually step into the river before it would be opened.

If they had come down to the riverbank and then stopped, waiting for the water to divide before stepping into it, they would have waited in vain. They were told to "set foot in the Jordan" before "its waters . . . will be cut off."

We must learn to take God at His word and walk straight ahead in obedience, even when we can see no way to go forward. The reason we are so often sidetracked by difficulties is that we expect to see barriers removed before we even try to pass through them.

If we would only move straight ahead in faith, the path would be opened for us. But we stand still, waiting for the obstacle to be removed, when we ought to go forward as if there were no obstacles at all. EVENING THOUGHTS

What a lesson Christopher Columbus taught the world—a lesson of perseverance in the face of tremendous difficulties!

> *Behind him lay the gray Azores,*
>   *Behind the gates of Hercules;*
> *Before him not the ghost of shores,*
>   *Before him only shoreless seas.*
> *The good Mate said: "Now we must pray,*
>   *For lo! the very stars are gone.*
> *Brave Admiral, speak, what shall I say?"*
>   *"Why, say, 'Sail on! sail on! and on!'"*
>
> *"My men grow mutinous day by day;*
>   *My men grow ghastly pale and weak!"*

The strong Mate thought of home; a spray
    Of salt wave washed his sunburned cheek.
"What shall I say, brave Admiral, say,
    If we sight only seas at dawn?"
"Why, you shall say at break of day,
    'Sail on! sail on! sail on! and on!'"

They sailed. They sailed. Then spoke the Mate:
    "This mad sea shows its teeth tonight.
He curls his lip, he lies in wait,
    With lifted teeth, as if to bite!
Brave Admiral, say but one good word;
    What shall we do when hope is gone?"
The words leapt like a leaping sword:
    "Sail on! sail on! sail on! and on!"

Then, pale and worn, he kept his deck
    And peered through darkness. Ah! that night
Of all dark nights! And then a speck—
    A light! A light! A light! A light!
It grew, a starlit flag unfurled!
    It grew to be Time's burst of dawn.
He gained a world; he gave that world
    Its grandest lesson: "On! sail on!"

                          J. R. MILLER

Faith that goes forward triumphs.

～～～ FEBRUARY 12 ～～～

Morning

You, LORD, are my lamp; the LORD turns my darkness into light.

2 SAMUEL 22:29

There are times when a Christian needs to lie still, when our only safety is doing nothing. The voice of our Savior-God is heard beside many a Red-Sea difficulty— "Stand still, and see the salvation of the LORD" (Exodus 14:13 KJV). It is a hard thing to "stand still" in the presence of opposing forces. Jehovah is the *Living God*. Cloud and storm are beneath His feet, and His throne remains unmoved.

"Am I in the dark?" asks Charles H. Spurgeon. "Then Thou, O Lord, 'will lighten my darkness.' Before long things will change. Affairs may grow worse and more dreary, and cloud upon cloud may be piled upon cloud; but if it grows so dark that I cannot see my own hand, still I shall see the Hand of the Lord."

When I cannot find a light within me, or among my friends, or in the whole world, the Lord who said, "Let there be light" and there was light, can say the same thing again. He will speak me into the sunshine yet. The day is already breaking. This sweet text shines like a morning star: "You, LORD, are my lamp; the LORD turns my darkness into light."

Clouds pass; stars remain!

> *My lamp is shattered, I'm deprived of light; my lamp is shattered, and so*
> *dark the night. My lamp is shattered,*
> *yet to my glad sight—a star shines on.*
> *My lamp is shattered, but a star shines bright, and by its glowing*
> *I can wend aright. My lamp is shattered, but I still can fight—*
> *for a star shines on.*
> *My lamp is shattered, sad indeed my plight. My lamp is shattered,*
> *yet I'll reach the height—for a star shines on!*
> WILHELMINA STITCH

～～～ FEBRUARY 12 ～～～
Evening

Your heavenly Father knows.
MATTHEW 6:32

A visitor at a school for the deaf was writing questions on the board for the children. Soon he wrote this sentence: "Why has God made me able to hear and speak, and made you deaf?" The shocking sentence hit the children like a cruel slap on the face. They sat paralyzed, pondering the dreadful word "Why?" And then a little girl arose.

With her lip trembling and her eyes swimming with tears, she walked straight to the board. Picking up the chalk, she wrote with a steady hand these precious words: *"Yes, Father, for this is what you were pleased to do"* (Matthew 11:26). What a reply! It reaches up and claims an eternal truth upon which the most mature believer, and even the youngest child of God, may securely rest—the truth that God is your Father.

Can you state that truth with full assurance and faith? Once you do, your dove of faith will no longer wander the skies in restless flight but will settle forever in its eternal resting place of peace: your Father!

I still believe that a day of understanding will come for each of us, however far away it may be. We will understand as we see the tragedies that today darken and dampen the presence of heaven for us take their proper place in God's great plan—a plan so overwhelming, magnificent, and joyful, we will laugh with wonder and delight.

ARTHUR CHRISTOPHER BACON

Chance has not brought this ill to me;
It's God's own hand, so let it be,
For He sees what I cannot see.
There is a purpose for each pain,
And He one day will make it plain
That earthly loss is heavenly gain.
Like as a piece of tapestry
Viewed from the back appears to be
Only threads tangled hopelessly;
But in the front a picture fair
Rewards the worker for his care,
Proving his skill and patience rare.
You are the Workman, I the frame.
Lord, for the glory of Your Name,
Perfect Your image on the same.

SELECTED

Morning

*Then the cows went straight up . . . keeping on the road and lowing
all the way; they did not turn to the right or to the left.*

1 SAMUEL 6:12

There was another yoke upon those cows that day than the yoke of wood fashioned by the hands of Philistines: they were constrained of God. It was that that made them patient and willing to walk together; that, too, made them choose the new road. Born and stalled in Ekron, familiar with the field and the manger, they herded off to Beth-shemesh, along the road they had never been before.

Why did they do it? *It was God.*

And as surely it is God when men choose the new way and walk along the road to the heavenly kingdom. They are *apprehended of Christ* and not only *born* of the Spirit but *borne* of the Spirit. *Men moved of God have a new instinct.*

Nature would have sent those cows back to their calves, but something has been known to make a man forsake father and mother, renounce life or a love dearer than life, for the Kingdom of God.

Whoso hath felt the Spirit of the Highest cannot confound Him, or doubt Him, or deny.

It means pain. Christ's martyrs, living or dying, though they rejoice to follow in His steps, are not insensible.

The cows went, *lowing all the way.* That was part of the proof; they had not forgotten their calves although they had forsaken them. Every low of the cow was a witness for God, and God who asks His people to sacrifice for His sake does not chide us because we feel it.

The reward of sacrifice is a call to sacrifice still more complete. The Lord never pays spiritual service in earthly currency. The impulse that carried the cows to the destined country led them to pause beside the stone that became an altar. The happy reapers of Beth-shemesh welcomed the Ark, *but the cows who under God's hand had brought it to them were not feasted and garlanded.*

"The people chopped up the wood of the cart and sacrificed the cows as a burnt offering to the LORD" (1 Samuel 6:14). So the service was followed by sacrifice, and the story is in the Book to make us glad when, our active life a thing of the past, we can still render ourselves unto God in a great renunciation. GOD'S HIGHWAY

Measure all by the cross!

~~~~ FEBRUARY 13 ~~~~

Evening

The forested hill country . . . will be yours.
JOSHUA 17:18

There is always room higher in the hills. When the valleys are full of Canaanites, whose mighty iron chariots are slowing your progress, go up to the hills and occupy the higher land. If you find you can no longer do work for God, pray for those who can. You may not be able to move things on earth with your words, but you may move heaven. If it seems that your continued growth is impossible on the lower slopes due to limited areas of service, the constraints of maintaining the day-to-day necessities, or other hindrances, allow your life to burst forth, reaching toward the unseen, the eternal, and the heavenly.

Your faith can level forests. Even if the tribes of Israel had realized what treasures awaited them in the hills above, they would never have dreamed it would be possible to actually harvest the thick forests. But as God instructed them to clear the forests, He also reminded them of the sufficient power they possessed. The sight of seemingly impossible tasks, like leveling these forest-covered hills, are not sent to discourage us. They come to motivate us to attempt spiritual feats that would be impossible except for the great strength God has placed within us through His indwelling Holy Spirit.

Difficulties are sent in order to reveal what God can do in answer to faith that prays and works. Are you being squeezed from all sides in the valley? Then "ride on the heights of the land" and be "nourished . . . with honey from the rock" (Deuteronomy 32:13). Gain wealth from the terraced slopes that are now hidden by the forests. DAILY DEVOTIONAL COMMENTARY

Got any rivers they say are uncrossable,
    Got any mountains they say "can't tunnel through"?
We specialize in the wholly impossible,
    Doing the things they say you can't do.
            SONG OF THE PANAMA CANAL BUILDERS

———————— FEBRUARY 14 ————————

Morning

He makes me lie down in green pastures.
PSALM 23:2

There are times when a Christian needs to lie still, like the earth under the spring rain, letting the lesson of experience and the memories of the Word of God sink down to the very roots of his life and fill the deep reservoirs of his soul.

Those are not always lost days when his hands are not busy, any more than rainy days in summer are lost because they keep the farmer indoors. The Great Shepherd makes his servant to *lie down* there.

There are times when men say they are too busy to stop when they think they are doing God service by going on. Now and then God makes such a one to lie down. He has been driving through the pastures so fast that he has not known their greenness nor apprehended their sweet savor; and God does not mean that he shall lose all that, and so *He makes him lie down.*

Many a man has had to thank God for some such enforced season of rest, in which he first learned the sweetness of meditation on the Word and of lying still in God's hands and waiting God's pleasure.

The soul cannot be hurried!

God is not in a hurry, dear!
The work He chose for you
Can wait, if He is giving you another

task to do,
Or, if He call you from your work
to quietness and rest,
Be sure that in the silence
you may do His bidding best.

You cannot be a joy to Him,
if thus with frown and fret
You turn at each new call of His,
to find new lessons set.

The old familiar tasks were dear,
and ordered by His hand;
But come and tread another way:
it is as He has planned.

And yesterday He led you there;
and now He wants you here;
And what shall be tomorrow's work,
tomorrow shall make clear.
So patiently and faithfully
let each day's course be run;
God is not in a hurry, dear,
His work will all be done.

EDITH HICKMAN DIVALL

There must be a Selah!

FEBRUARY 14

Evening

Rejoice in the LORD always. I will say it again: Rejoice!
PHILIPPIANS 4:4

It is a good thing to "rejoice in the Lord." Perhaps you have tried it but seemed to fail at first. Don't give it a second thought, and forge ahead. Even when you cannot *feel* any joy, there is no spring in your step, nor any comfort or encouragement in your life, continue to rejoice and "*consider it pure joy*" (James 1:2). "Whenever you face trials of many kinds" (James 1:2), regard it as joy, delight in it, and God will reward your faith. Do you believe that your heavenly Father will let you carry the banner of His victory and joy to the very front of the battle, only to calmly withdraw to see you captured or beaten back by the enemy? NEVER! His Holy Spirit will sustain you in your bold advance and fill your heart with gladness and praise. You will find that your heart is exhilarated and refreshed by the fullness within.

Lord, teach me to rejoice in You—to "be always joyful" (1 Thessalonians 5:16 WNT).

> *The weakest saint may Satan rout,*
> *Who meets him with a praiseful shout.*

"Be filled with the Spirit. . . . Sing and make music from your heart to the Lord" (Ephesians 5:18–19).

In these verses, the apostle Paul urges us to use singing as inspiration in our spiritual life. He warns his readers to seek motivation not through the body but through the spirit, not by stimulating the flesh but by exalting the soul.

> *Sometimes a light surprises*
> *The Christian while he sings.*

Let us sing even when we do not feel like it, for in this way we give wings to heavy feet and turn weariness into strength. JOHN HENRY JOWETT

"About midnight Paul and Silas were praying and singing hymns to God, and the other prisoners were listening to them" (Acts 16:25).

O Paul, what a wonderful example you are to us! You gloried in the fact that you "bear on [your] body the marks of Jesus" (Galatians 6:17). You bore the marks from nearly being stoned to death, from three times being "beaten with rods" (2 Corinthians 11:25), from receiving 195 lashes from the Jews, and from being bloodily beaten in the Philippian jail. Surely the grace that enabled you to sing praises while enduring such suffering is sufficient for us. J. ROACH

Oh, let us rejoice in the Lord, evermore,
When darts of the Tempter are flying,
For Satan still dreads, as he oft did before,
Our singing much more than our crying.

FEBRUARY 15

Morning

But the fruit of the Spirit is . . . gentleness.
GALATIANS 5:22 KJV

One day at an auction a man bought a vase of cheap earthenware for a few pennies. He put into the vase a rich perfume—the attar of roses. For a long time the vase held this perfume, and when it was empty it had been so soaked through with the sweet perfume that the fragrance lingered. One day the vase fell and was broken to pieces, but every fragment still smelled of the attar of roses.

We are all common clay—plain earthenware—but if the love of Christ is kept in our hearts it will sweeten all our life, and we shall become as loving as He. That is the way the beloved disciple learned the lesson and grew into such lovingness. He leaned on Christ's breast, and Christ's gentleness filled all his life.

As John upon his dear Lord's breast,
So would I lean, so would I rest;
An empty shell in depths of sea,
So would I sink, be filled with Thee.

Like singing bird in high blue air,
So would I soar, and sing Thee there.
Nor rain, nor stormy wind can be,
When all the air is full of Thee.

And so, though daily duties crowd,
And dust of earth be like a cloud,

Through noise of words, O Lord, my Rest,
Thy John would lean upon Thy breast.
"ROSE FROM BRIER" BY AMY CARMICHAEL

Save me from growing hard!

～～～ FEBRUARY 15 ～～～
Evening

Do not fret because of those who are evil or be envious of those who do wrong.
PSALM 37:1

Never become extremely upset over your circumstances. If worry were ever justified, it would have been during the circumstances surrounding the writing of this psalm. Evil men were "dressed in purple and fine linen and lived in luxury every day" (Luke 16:19). "Those who do wrong" were ascending to the highest places of power and were tyrannizing their brothers who were less fortunate. Sinful men and women strutted through the land with arrogant pride and basked in the light of great prosperity, while good people became fearful and worried.

"Do not fret." Never get unduly upset! Stay cool! Even for a good reason, worrying will not help you. It only heats up the bearings but does not generate any steam. It does not help the locomotive for its axles to become hot; their heat is only a hindrance. The axles become heated because of unnecessary friction.

Dry surfaces are grinding against each other instead of working in smooth cooperation, aided by a thin cushion of oil.

Isn't it interesting how similar the words "fret" and "friction" are? Friction caused by fretting is an indication of the absence of the anointing oil of the grace of God. When we worry, a little bit of sand gets into the bearings. It may be some slight disappointment, ungratefulness, or discourtesy we have experienced—suddenly our life is no longer running smoothly. Friction leads to heat, and heat can lead to very dangerous conditions.

Do not allow your bearings to become heated. Let the oil of the Lord keep you cool so that an unholy heat will not cause you to be regarded as one of the evil men.
THE SILVER LINING

Dear restless heart, be still; don't fret and worry so;
God has a thousand ways His love and help to show;
Just trust, and trust, and trust, until His will you know.

Dear restless heart, be still, for peace is God's own smile,
His love can every wrong and sorrow reconcile;
Just love, and love, and love, and calmly wait awhile.

Dear restless heart, be brave; don't moan and sorrow so,
He has a meaning kind in chilly winds that blow;
Just hope, and hope, and hope, until you braver grow.

Dear restless heart, recline upon His breast this hour,
His grace is strength and life, His love is bloom and flower;
Just rest, and rest, and rest, within His tender power.

Dear restless heart, be still! Don't struggle to be free;
God's life is in your life, from Him you may not flee;
Just pray, and pray, and pray, till you have faith to see.

EDITH WILLIS LINN

~~~~~~~ **FEBRUARY 16** ~~~~~~~

Morning

And we know that in all things God works for the good of those who
love him, who have been called according to his purpose.

ROMANS 8:28

He was weaving.

"That is a strange-looking carpet you are making!" said the visitor.

"Just stoop down and look underneath," was the reply.

—— 120 ——

The man stooped. *The plan was on the other side,* and in that moment a light broke upon his mind.

The Great Weaver is busy with His plan. Do not be impatient; suffice to know that you are part of the plan and that *He never errs.* Wait for the light of the later years and the peep at the other side. *Hope on!*

> *White and black, and hodden-gray,*
> *Weavers of webs are we;*
> *To every weaver one golden strand*
> *Is given in trust by the Master-Hand;*
> *Weavers of webs are we.*
>
> *And that we weave, we know not,*
> *Weavers of webs are we.*
> *The thread we see, but the pattern is known*
> *To the Master-Weaver alone, alone;*
> *Weavers of webs are we.*
>
> JOHN OXENHAM

Of many of the beautiful carpets made in India, it may be said that the weaving is done to music. The designs are handed down from one generation to another, and the instructions for their making are in script that looks not unlike a sheet of music. Indeed, it is more than an accidental resemblance, for each carpet has a sort of tune of its own. The thousands of threads are stretched on a great wooden frame, and behind it on a long bench sit the workers. The master in charge reads the instructions for each stitch in a strange chanting tone, each color having its own particular note.

The story makes us think of our own life web. We are all weavers and day by day we work in the threads—now dark, now bright—that are to go into the finished pattern. But blessed are they who feel sure that there is a pattern; who hear and trust the directing Voice, and so weave the changing threads to music. W. J. HART

Fallen threads I will not search for—I will weave. GEORGE MACDONALD

Although I have afflicted you . . . I will afflict you no more.
NAHUM 1:12

There is a limit to our affliction. God sends it and then removes it. Do you complain, saying, "When will this end?" May we quietly wait and patiently endure the will of the Lord till He comes. Our Father takes away the rod when His purpose in using it is fully accomplished.

If the affliction is sent to test us so that our words would glorify God, it will only end once He has caused us to testify to His praise and honor. In fact, we would not want the difficulty to depart until God has removed from us all the honor we can yield to Him.

Today things may become "completely calm" (Matthew 8:26). Who knows how soon these raging waves will give way to a sea of glass with seagulls sitting on the gentle swells?

After a long ordeal, the threshing tool is on its hook, and the wheat has been gathered into the barn. Before much time has passed, we may be just as happy as we are sorrowful now.

It is not difficult for the Lord to turn night into day. He who sends the clouds can just as easily clear the skies. Let us be encouraged—things are better down the road. *Let us sing God's praises in anticipation of things to come.* CHARLES H. SPURGEON

"The Lord of the harvest" (Luke 10:2) is not always threshing us. His trials are only for a season, and the showers soon pass. "Weeping may stay for the night, but rejoicing comes in the morning" (Psalm 30:5). "Our light and momentary troubles are achieving for us an eternal glory that far outweighs them all" (2 Corinthians 4:17). Trials do serve their purpose.

Even the fact that we face a trial proves there is something very precious to our Lord in us, or else He would not spend so much time and energy on us. Christ would not test us if He did not see the precious metal of faith mingled with the rocky core of our nature, and it is to refine us into purity and beauty that He forces us through the fiery ordeal.

Be patient, O sufferer! The result of the Refiner's fire will more than compensate for our trials, once we see the "eternal glory that far outweighs them all." Just to hear His commendation, "Well done" (Matthew 25:21); to be honored before the holy angels; to be glorified in Christ, so that I may reflect His glory back to Him—ah! that will be more than enough reward for all my trials. TRIED BY FIRE

Just as the weights of a grandfather clock, or the stabilizers in a ship, are necessary for them to work properly, so are troubles to the soul. The sweetest perfumes are obtained only through tremendous pressure, the fairest flowers grow on the most isolated and snowy peaks, the most beautiful gems are those that have suffered the longest at the jeweler's wheel, and the most magnificent statues have endured the most blows from the chisel. All of these, however, are subject to God's law. Nothing happens that has not been *appointed* with consummate care and foresight. DAILY DEVOTIONAL COMMENTARY

~~~~~~~ FEBRUARY 17 ~~~~~~~

Morning

My Presence will go with you, and I will give you rest.
EXODUS 33:14

What *is* rest? To step out of self-life into Christ-life; to lie still, and let Him lift you out of it; to fold your hands close, and hide your face on the hem of His garment; to let Him lay His cooling, soothing, healing hands upon your soul, and draw all the hurry and fever from its veins; to realize that you are not a mighty messenger, an important worker of His, full of care and responsibility, but only a little child, with a Father's gentle bidding to heed and fulfill; to lay your busy plans and ambitions confidently in His hands, as a child brings its broken toys at its mother's call; to serve Him by waiting; to praise Him by saying, "Holy, Holy, Holy"; to cease to hurry, so you may not lose sight of His face; to learn to follow Him, and not to run ahead of orders! To cease to live in self and for self, and to live in Him and for Him; to love His honor more than your own; to be a clear medium for His life-tide to shine and glow through. This is consecration; this is rest.

Thou sweet, beloved will of God,
My anchor ground, my fortress hill,

My spirit's silent, fair abode,
In Thee I hide me and am still.

Thy beautiful sweet will, my God,
Holds fast in its sublime embrace
My captive will, a gladsome bird,
Prison'd in such a realm of grace.

Upon God's will I lay me down,
As child upon its mother's breast,
No silken couch, nor softest bed,
Could ever give me such deep rest.

TERSTEEGEN

FEBRUARY 17

Evening

The land which I do give to them, even to the children of Israel.

JOSHUA 1:2 KJV

God is speaking about something immediate in this verse. It is not something He is *going* to do but something He *does* do, at this very moment. As faith continues to speak, God continues to give. He meets you today in the present and tests your faith. As long as you are waiting, hoping, or looking, you are not believing. You may have hope or an earnest desire, but that is not faith, for "faith is confidence in what we hope for and assurance about what we do not see" (Hebrews 11:1). The command regarding believing prayer is: "Whatever you ask for in prayer, believe that you have received it, and it will be yours" (Mark 11:24). We are to believe that we have received—this present moment. Have we come to the point where we have met God in His everlasting now? A. B. SIMPSON

True faith relies on God and believes before seeing. Naturally, we want some evidence that our petition is granted before we believe, but when we "live by faith"

(2 Corinthians 5:7), we need no evidence other than God's Word. He has spoken, and in harmony with our faith it will be done. We will see because we have believed, and true faith sustains us in the most trying of times, even when everything around us seems to contradict God's Word.

The psalmist said, "I remain confident of this: *I will see* the goodness of the LORD in the land of the living" (Psalm 27:13). He had not yet seen the Lord's answer to his prayers, but he was confident he would see, and his confidence sustained him.

Faith that believes it will see, will keep us from becoming discouraged. We will laugh at seemingly impossible situations while we watch with delight to see how God is going to open a path through our Red Sea. It is in these places of severe testing, with no human way out of our difficulty, that our faith grows and is strengthened.

Dear troubled one, have you been waiting for God to work during long nights and weary days, fearing you have been forgotten? Lift up your head and begin praising Him right now for the deliverance that is on its way to you. LIFE OF PRAISE

~~~~ FEBRUARY 18 ~~~~

Morning

I will go before you and will level the mountains; I will break down gates of bronze and cut through bars of iron.
ISAIAH 45:2

Do I lack the strength to rescue you?
ISAIAH 50:2

If any of you, beloved, seem to be in a knot of difficulty of which you cannot get the thread, look to Him who is perfect wisdom, and *let the tangle go out of your hands into His; turn the matter over to Him.* What is impossible with you is perfectly possible with Him who is Almighty!

A little child at mother's knee
Plies woolen strands and needles bright.

Small, eager hands strive earnestly
To fasten every stitch aright.

But soon perplexing knots appear
Which vex and hinder progress' flow;
Impatient fingers pull and tear,
While ever worse the tangles grow.

How surely then in wiser hands
The roughest places are made plain!
How easy now the task's demands,
How wonderful the lesson's gain!

Thus, God, we bring our snarls to Thee;
Though human sense and stubborn will
Oft clamor loud for mastery,
We hear alone Thy "Peace, be still."

EDITH SHAW BROWN

How tangled some of our problems do become as the days pass and no way appears by which the matter may be straightened out! Perhaps we have been keeping the problems too much in our own hands. No wonder, then, we cannot find the beginning or the end of the line, or how to loosen the knotted strand in just the right places. A young man writing to his father about a personal problem says: "Once again, just yesterday, I have put this whole matter in the Lord's hands, and asked Him to guide me about it all. I often think of how I'd get my fishing line all tangled up. The more I pulled the worse it got. Finally I'd hand the whole thing over to you, and you'd smooth it all out. So I generally do that with my problems now; and I'm trying to learn not to pull at the line much, before I give it to Him." Have you been pulling at the line in that problem that troubles you today? Just hand it over to your heavenly Father, and see how swiftly and lovingly He will untangle the crisscross and knotty impossibility that has troubled you so! SUNDAY SCHOOL TIMES

With thoughtless and
Impatient hands

We tangle up
The plans
The Lord hath wrought.

And when we cry
In pain, He saith,
"Be quiet, dear,
While I untie the knot."

FEBRUARY 18
Evening

Whatever you ask for in prayer, believe that you have received it, and it will be yours.
MARK 11:24

When my little son was about ten years old, his grandmother promised him a stamp collecting album for Christmas. Christmas came and went with no stamp album and no word from Grandma. The matter, however, was not mentioned, until his friends came to see his Christmas presents. I was astonished, after he had listed all the gifts he had received, to hear him add, "And a stamp album from my grandmother."

After hearing this several times, I called my son to me and said, "But, George, you didn't get a stamp album from Grandma. Why did you say you did?"

With a puzzled look on his face, as if I had asked a very strange question, he replied, "Well, Mom, Grandma *said*, and that is the same *as*." Not a word from me would sway his faith.

A month passed and nothing else was said about the album. Finally one day, to test his faith and because I wondered in my own heart why the album had not been sent, I said, "George, I think Grandma has forgotten her promise."

"Oh no, Mom," he quickly and firmly responded. "She hasn't." I watched his sweet, trusting face, which for a while looked very serious, as if he were debating the possibility I had suggested. Soon his face brightened as he said, "Do you think it would do any good for me to write Grandma, *thanking* her for the album?"

"I don't know," I said, "but you might try it." A rich spiritual truth then began to dawn on me.

In a few minutes a letter was written and mailed, as George went off whistling his confidence in his grandma. Soon a letter from Grandma arrived with this message:

My dear George,

I have not forgotten my promise to you for a stamp album. I could not find the one you wanted here, so I ordered one from New York. It did not arrive until after Christmas, and it was not the right one. I then ordered another, but it still has not arrived. I have decided to send you thirty dollars instead so that you may buy the one you want in Chicago.

Your loving Grandma.

As he read the letter, his face was the face of a victor. From the depths of a heart that never doubted came the words, "Now, Mom, didn't I tell you?" George "against all hope . . . in hope believed" (Romans 4:18) that the stamp album would come. And while he was trusting, Grandma was working, and in due time faith became sight.

It is only human to want to see before we step out on the promises of God. Yet our Savior said to Thomas and to a long list of doubters who have followed, "Blessed are those who have not seen and yet have believed" (John 20:29). MRS. ROUNDS

~~~~ FEBRUARY 19 ~~~~
Morning

He heals the brokenhearted and binds up their wounds. He determines
the number of the stars and calls them each by name.
PSALM 147:3–4

A beautiful picture was painted by one of the greatest of the European artists: *The Consoler*. It is a picture of a bedroom in an English cottage. On the bed sits a beautiful little babe, perhaps a year in age, having in his hand a toy soldier that he is holding very lovingly to his body. He is unconscious of anything about him. Back of him on the wall is the picture of a young man in soldier's dress—the baby's father. On her knees, her head in her hands, is the young widow robed in deepest black, sobbing her heart out. One of the saddest pictures the world shall ever know—a baby to forget and never know his father; a young widow to go down through life with burdened, broken heart. But leaning over her, with the light of heaven on His beautiful face, is One who lays His hand lovingly on her shoulder. We do not wonder the great artist has called the picture *The Consoler*.

> With His healing hand on a broken heart,
> And the other on a star,
> Our wonderful God views the miles apart,
> And they seem not very far.
>
> Oh, it makes us cry—then laugh—then sing,
> Tho' 'tis all beyond our ken;
> He bindeth up wounds on that poor crushed thing,
> And He makes it whole again.
>
> Was there something shone from that healed new heart
> Made the Psalmist think of stars—
> That bright as the sun or the lightning's dart,
> Sped away past earthly bars?
>
> In a low place sobbing by death's lone cart,
> Then a flight on whirlwind's cars;
> One verse is about a poor broken heart,
> And the next among the stars.
>
> There is hope and help for our sighs and tears,
> For the wound that stings and smarts;
> Our God is at home with the rolling spheres,
> And at home with broken hearts.
>
> Mamie Payne Ferguson

"Let God cover thy wounds," said Augustine, "do not thou. For if thou wish to cover them being ashamed, the Physician will not come. Let Him cover; for by the covering of the Physician the wound is healed; by the covering of the wounded man the wound is concealed. And from whom? From Him who knoweth all things."

The Great Lover comes close behind the storm,
And whispers softly to the broken mountaintops,
And fills their wounds with clean fresh odors.

The Great Lover knows the pain of blasted trees
And binds up tenderly their broken arms;
The Great Lover has gone through many storms.
MATTHEW BILLER

~~~~~~~ FEBRUARY 19 ~~~~~~~

Evening

Every branch that does bear fruit he prunes so that it will be even more fruitful.
JOHN 15:2

A child of God was once overwhelmed by the number of afflictions that seemed to target her. As she walked past a vineyard during the rich glow of autumn, she noticed its untrimmed appearance and the abundance of leaves still on the vines. The ground had been overtaken by a tangle of weeds and grass, and the entire place appeared totally unkempt. While she pondered the sight, the heavenly Gardener whispered such a precious message to her that she could not help but share it.

The message was this: "My dear child, are you questioning the number of trials in your life? Remember the vineyard and learn from it. The gardener stops pruning and trimming the vine or weeding the soil only when he expects nothing more from the vine during that season. He leaves it alone, because its fruitfulness is gone and further effort now would yield no profit. In the same way, freedom from suffering leads to uselessness. Do you now want me to stop pruning your life? Shall I leave you alone?"

Then her comforted heart cried, "No!" HOMERA HOMER-DIXON

It is the branch that bears the fruit,
 That feels the knife,
To prune it for a larger growth,
 A fuller life.

Though every budding twig be trimmed,
 And every grace
Of swaying tendril, springing leaf,
 May lose its place.

O you whose life of joy seems left,
 With beauty shorn;
Whose aspirations lie in dust,
 All bruised and torn,

Rejoice, though each desire, each dream,
 Each hope of thine
Will fall and fade; it is the hand
 Of Love Divine

That holds the knife, that cuts and breaks
 With tenderest touch,
That you, whose life has borne some fruit,
 Might now bear much.

      Annie Johnson Flint

～～ FEBRUARY 20 ～～
Morning

These were the potters, and those that dwelt among plants and
hedges: there they dwelt with the king for his work.

1 Chronicles 4:23 KJV

Is your place a small place?
Tend it with care!—
He set you there.

Is your place a large place?
Guard it with care!
He set you there.

Whate'er your place, it is
Not yours alone, but His.
He set you there.

JOHN OXENHAM

With infinite care and forethought God has chosen the best place in which you can do your best work for the world. You may be lonely, but you have no more right to complain than the lamp has, which has been placed in a niche to illumine a dark landing or a flight of dangerous stone steps. The master of the house may have put you in a very small corner and on a very humble stand; but it is enough if it be His blessed will. Someday He will pass by, and you shall light His steps as He goes forth to seek and save that which is lost; or you shall kindle some great light that shall shine like a beacon over the storm-swept ocean. Thus the obscure Andrew was the means of igniting his brother Peter, when he brought him to Jesus. SELECTED

When the Master of all the workmen called me into the field,
I went for Him light and happy, the tools of His service to wield;
Expectant of high position, as suited my lofty taste—
When Lo! He set me weeding and watering down in the waste.

Such puttering down in the hedges! A task so thankless and small!
Yet I stifled my vain discomfort and wrought for the Lord of all,
Till, meeker grown, as nightly I sank to my hard-won rest
I cared but to hear in my dreaming, "This one has done his best."

The years have leveled distinctions, there is no more "great" nor "small";
Only faithful service counts with the Lord of all;

And I know that, tilled with patience, the dreariest waste of clod
Shall yield the perfect ideal planned in the heart of God.
SELECTED

Are *you* willing to be a "caulker of seams" (Ezekiel 27:9)?

～～～～ FEBRUARY 20 ～～～～

Evening

Nothing will be impossible for you.
MATTHEW 17:20

It is possible for believers who are completely willing to trust the power of the Lord for their safekeeping and victory to lead a life of readily taking His promises exactly as they are and finding them to be true.

It is possible to daily "cast all your anxiety on him" (1 Peter 5:7) and experience deep peace in the process.

It is possible to have our thoughts and the desires of our hearts purified in the deepest sense of the word.

It is possible to see God's will in every circumstance and to accept it with singing instead of complaining.

It is possible to become strong through and through by completely taking refuge in the power of God and by realizing that our greatest weakness and the things that upset our determination to be patient, pure, or humble provide an opportunity to make sin powerless over us. This opportunity comes through Him who loves us and who works to bring us into agreement with His will, and thereby supplies a blessed sense of His presence and His power.

All these are divine possibilities. Because they are His work, actually experiencing them will always humble us, causing us to bow at His feet and teaching us to hunger and thirst for more.

We will never be satisfied with anything less—each day, each hour, or each moment in Christ, through the power of the Holy Spirit—than walking with God.
H. C. G. MOULE

We are able to have as much of God as we want. Christ puts the key to His treasure chest in our hands and invites us to take all we desire. If someone is allowed into a bank vault, told to help himself to the money, and leaves without one cent, whose fault is it if he remains poor? And whose fault is it that Christians usually have such meager portions of the free riches of God? ALEXANDER MACLAREN

～～～～～ FEBRUARY 21 ～～～～～

Morning

What has happened to me has actually served to advance the gospel.
PHILIPPIANS 1:12

We cannot expect to learn much of the life of trust without passing through hard places. When they come, let us not say as Jacob did: "Everything is against me!" (Genesis 42:36).

Let us rather climb our Hills of Difficulty and say, *"These are faith's opportunities!"*

> *I would not lose the hard things from my life,*
> *The rocks o'er which I stumbled long ago,*
> *The griefs and fears, the failures and mistakes,*
> *That tried and tested faith and patience so.*
>
> *I need them now: they make the deep-laid wall,*
> *The firm foundation-stones on which I raise—*
> *To mount therein from stair to higher stair—*
> *The lofty towers of my House of Praise.*
>
> *Soft was the roadside turf to weary feet,*
> *And cool the meadows where I fain had trod,*
> *And sweet beneath the trees to lie at rest*
> *And breathe the incense of the flower-starred sod;*
>
> *But not on these might I securely build;*

Nor sand nor sod withstand the earthquake shock;
I need the rough hard boulders of the hills,
To set my house on everlasting rock.

ANNIE JOHNSON FLINT

Crises reveal character: when we are put to the test we reveal exactly the hidden resources of our character.

~~~~~~ FEBRUARY 21 ~~~~~~

Evening
</div>

<div align="center">

Be still before the LORD *and wait patiently for him.*

PSALM 37:7
</div>

Have you prayed and prayed, and waited and waited, and still you see no evidence of an answer? Are you tired of seeing no movement? Are you at the point of giving up? Then perhaps you have not waited in the right way, which removes you from the right place—the place where the Lord can meet you.

"*Wait for it patiently*" (Romans 8:25). Patience eliminates worry. The Lord said He would come, and His promise is equal to His presence. Patience eliminates weeping. Why feel sad and discouraged? He knows your needs better than you do, and His purpose in waiting is to receive more glory through it. Patience eliminates self-works. "The work of God is this: to believe" (John 6:29), and once you believe, you may know all is well. Patience eliminates all *want*. Perhaps your desire to receive what you want is stronger than your desire for the will of God to be fulfilled.

Patience eliminates all *weakness*. Instead of thinking of waiting as being wasted time, realize that God is preparing His resources and strengthening you as well. Patience eliminates all *wobbling*. "He touched me and raised me to my feet" (Daniel 8:18). God's foundations are steady, and when we have His patience within, we are steady while we wait. Patience yields *worship*. Sometimes the best part of praiseful waiting is experiencing "great endurance and patience . . . giving joyful thanks" (Colossians 1:11–12). While you wait, "let [all these aspects of] patience have her perfect work" (James 1:4 KJV), and you will be greatly enriched. C. H. P.

<div align="center">

—— 135 ——
</div>

Hold steady when the fires burn,
When inner lessons come to learn,
And from this path there seems no turn—
"Let patience have her perfect work."

L. S. P.

FEBRUARY 22

Morning

Do not lose heart.
2 CORINTHIANS 4:16

One day a naturalist, out in his garden, observed a most unusually large and beautiful butterfly, fluttering as though in great distress; it seemed to be caught as though it could not release itself. The naturalist, thinking to release the precious thing, took hold of the wings and set it free. It flew but a few feet and fell to the ground dead.

He picked up the poor thing, took it into his laboratory, and put it under a magnifying glass to discover the cause of its death. There he found the lifeblood flowing from the tiny arteries of its wings. Nature had fastened it to its chrysalis and was allowing it to flutter and flutter so that its wings might grow strong. It was the muscle-developing process that nature was giving the dear thing so that it might have an unusual range among the flowers and gardens. *If it had only fluttered long enough, the butterfly would have come forth ready for the wide range; but release ended the beautiful dream.*

So with God's children: *how the Father wishes for them wide ranges in experience and truth. He permits us to be fastened to some form of struggle. We would tear ourselves free.* We cry out in our distress and sometimes think Him cruel that He does not release us. He permits us to flutter and flutter on. Struggle seems to be His program sometimes.

Prayer alone will hold us steady while in the struggles, so we keep sweet and learn, oh, such wonderful lessons.

God laid upon my back a grievous load,
A heavy cross to bear along the road.

I staggered on, and lo! one weary day,
An angry lion sprang across my way.

I prayed to God, and swift at His command
The cross became a weapon in my hand.

It slew my raging enemy, and then
Became a cross upon my back again.

I reached a desert. O'er the burning track
I persevered, the cross upon my back.

No shade was there, and in the cruel sun
I sank at last, and thought my days were done.

But lo! the Lord works many a blest surprise—
The cross became a tree before my eyes!

I slept; I woke, to feel the strength of ten.
I found the cross upon my back again.

And thus through all my days from then to this,
The cross, my burden, has become my bliss.

Nor ever shall I lay the burden down,
For God someday will make the cross a crown!

AMOS R. WELLS

You are bound to a cross. I entreat you not to struggle. The more lovingly the cross is carried by the soul, the lighter it becomes!

FEBRUARY 22

Evening

"If you can? . . . Everything is possible for one who believes."
MARK 9:23

I seldom have heard a better definition of faith than that given in one of our meetings, by a sweet, elderly black woman, as she answered a young man who asked, *"How do I obtain the Lord's help for my needs?"*

In her characteristic way, pointing her finger toward him, she said with great insistence, "You just have to believe that He's done it and it's done." The greatest problem with most of us is, after asking Him to do it, we do not believe it is done. Instead, we keep trying to help Him, get others to help Him, and anxiously wait to see how He is going to work.

Faith adds its "Amen" to God's "Yes" and then takes its hands off, leaving God to finish His work. The language of faith is, "Commit your way to the LORD; trust in him and he will do this" (Psalm 37:5). DAYS OF HEAVEN UPON EARTH

> *I simply take Him at His word,*
> *I praise Him that my prayer is heard,*
> *   And claim my answer from the Lord;*
> *I take, He undertakes.*

Active faith gives thanks for a promise even though it is not yet performed, knowing that God's contracts are as good as cash. MATTHEW HENRY

> *Passive faith accepts the Word as true—*
> *   But never moves.*
> *Active faith begins the work to do,*
> *   And thereby proves.*
> *Passive faith says, "I believe it! every word of God is true.*
> *Well I know He has not spoken what He cannot, will not, do.*
> *He has instructed me, 'Go forward!' but a closed-up way I see,*
> *When the waters are divided, soon in Canaan's land I'll be.*

Lo! I hear His voice commanding, 'Rise and walk: take up your bed';
And, 'Stretch to Me your withered hand!' which for so long has been dead.
When I am a little stronger, then, I know I'll surely stand:
When there comes a thrill of healing, I will use with ease my reclaimed hand.
Yes, I know that 'God is able' and full willing all to do:
I believe that every promise, sometime, will to me come true."
Active faith says, "I believe it! and the promise now I take,
Knowing well, as I receive it, God, each promise,
*   real will make.*
So I step into the waters, finding there an open way;
Onward press, the land possessing; nothing can my progress stay.
Yes, I rise at His commanding, walking straight, and joyfully:
This, my hand so sadly shriveled, as I reach, restored will be.
What beyond His faithful promise, would I wish or do I need?
Looking not for 'signs or wonders,' I'll no contradiction heed.
Well I know that 'God is able,' and full willing all to do:
I believe that every promise, at this moment can come true."
Passive faith but praises in the light,
When sun does shine.
Active faith will praise in darkest night—
Which faith is thine?

SELECTED

―――― ∼∼∼∼∼ FEBRUARY 23 ∼∼∼∼∼ ――――

Morning

Put your hope in God, for I will yet praise him.
PSALM 42:5

During a truce in the Civil War in America, when the hostile armies sat sullenly facing each other with a field between them, a little brown bird rose suddenly from the long grass and darted skyward. There, a mere speck in the blue, it poured forth its liquid music of which the lark alone has the secret. And steely eyes melted to tears, and hard hearts grew pitiful and tender. There was a God who cared. There was hope for men.

Hope is like the lark on the battlefield. It will not sing in a gilded cage. It cannot soar in an atmosphere of religious luxury. But brave souls, exposing themselves fearlessly for God and their fellow-men on the battlefield of life, hear its song and are made strong and glad. E. HERMAN

Persons who held on in hope, with seemingly little for which to hope, were known to say: *Then was our mouth filled with laughter. . . . We were like them that dream.*

The tide may turn, the wind may change. New eras have been heard of before now!

In "hope against hope," I wait, Lord,
Faced by some fast-barred gate, Lord,
Hope never says "Too late," Lord,
Therefore in Thee I hope!

Hope though the night be long, Lord,
Hope of a glowing dawn, Lord,
Morning must break in song, Lord,
For we are "saved by hope."
HYMNS OF CONSECRATION AND FAITH

Hope thou in God!

~~~~~~ FEBRUARY 23 ~~~~~~

Evening

And there came a lion.
1 SAMUEL 17:34 KJV

It is a source of inspiration and strength to us to remember how the youthful David trusted God. Through his faith in the Lord, he defeated a lion and a bear and later overthrew the mighty Goliath. When the lion came to destroy his flock, it came as a wonderful *opportunity* for David. If he had faltered and failed, he would have missed

God's opportunity for him and probably would never have been the Lord's chosen king of Israel.

"And there came a lion." Normally we think of a lion not as a special blessing from the Lord but only as a reason for alarm. Yet the lion was God's opportunity in disguise. Every difficulty and every temptation that comes our way, if we receive it correctly, is God's opportunity.

When a "lion" comes to your life, recognize it as an opportunity from the Lord, no matter how fierce it may outwardly seem. Even the tabernacle of God was covered with badger skins and goat hair. No one would think there would be any glory there, yet the Shekinah glory of God was very evident underneath the covering. May the Lord open our eyes to see Him, even in temptations, trials, dangers, and misfortunes. C. H. P.

~~~~ FEBRUARY 24 ~~~~
Morning

*After Paul had seen the vision, we got ready at once to leave for Macedonia,
concluding that God had called us to preach the gospel to them.*

ACTS 16:10

There is a simplicity about God in working out His plans, yet a resourcefulness equal to any difficulty, an unswerving faithfulness to His trusting child, and an unforgetting steadiness in holding to His purpose. Through a fellow prisoner, then a dream, He lifts Joseph from a prison to a premiership. And the length of stay in the prison prevents dizziness in the premier.

It's safe to trust God's methods, and to go by His clock. S. D. GORDON

> *The path was veiled! The Master's will was hidden,*
> *And further progress for the time was stayed;*
> *But in good time he would again be bidden*
> *And, waiting meantime, he was unafraid.*
>
> *Then came that night when, maybe, softly sleeping,*
> *The vision came—the clarion call to move;*

And once again, with all in God's good keeping,
He could step forth, God's faithfulness to prove.

No human voice conveyed the word of leading;
No human hand was sent, his way to guide;
No human heart full knew his depth of needing,
Or could assist him to his steps decide.

And so, without to other minds appealing,
"Assuredly" he "gathered" now God's will,
Yet—to his inner soul there came revealing—
He started forth, God's purpose to fulfill.

Perhaps, O soul, thou waitest for His leading,
Thy longing heart His further will would'st know;
Rest thou in God: His ear hath heard thy pleading,
The "further steps" He yet to thee will show.

Keep looking Himwards—He alone can lead thee;
Nor count from choicest friends thy way to glean;
He knoweth best where He Himself doth need thee,
And He can lead thee on by means unseen.

"Assuredly" thy longing heart shall "gather"
The guidance thou dost long for; therefore wait;
Fret not thyself! Ah, no! But learn this rather—
God's guidance never comes to us too late.

J. Danson Smith

~~~~~ FEBRUARY 24 ~~~~~

Evening

Though John never performed a sign, all that John said about this man was true.

John 10:41

Perhaps you are very dissatisfied with yourself. You are not a genius, have no distinctive gifts, and are inconspicuous when it comes to having any special abilities. Mediocrity seems to be the measure of your existence. None of your days are noteworthy, except for their sameness and lack of zest. Yet in spite of this you may live a great life.

John the Baptist never performed a miracle, but Jesus said of him, "Among those born of women there is no one greater" (Luke 7:28). His mission was to be "a witness to the light" (John 1:8), and that may be your mission and mine. John was content to be only a voice, if it caused people to think of Christ.

Be willing to be only a voice that is heard but not seen, or a mirror whose glass the eye cannot see because it is reflecting the brilliant glory of the Son. Be willing to be a breeze that arises just before daylight, saying, "The dawn! The dawn!" and then fades away.

Do the most everyday and insignificant tasks knowing that God can see. If you live with difficult people, win them over through love. If you once made a great mistake in life, do not allow it to cloud the rest of your life, but by locking it secretly in your heart, make it yield strength and character.

We are doing more good than we know. The things we do today—sowing seeds or sharing simple truths of Christ—people will someday refer to as the first things that prompted them to think of Him. For my part, I will be satisfied not to have some great tombstone over my grave but just to know that common people will gather there once I am gone and say, "He was a good man. He never performed any miracles, but he told me about Christ, which led me to know Him for myself." George Matheson

Thy Hidden Ones

Thick green leaves from the soft brown earth,
Happy springtime has called them forth;
First faint promise of summer bloom
Breathes from the fragrant, sweet perfume,
*   Under the leaves.*

Lift them! what marvelous beauty lies
Hidden beneath, from our thoughtless eyes!

Mayflowers, rosy or purest white,
Lift their cups to the sudden light,
Under the leaves.

Are there no lives whose holy deeds—
Seen by no eye save His who reads
Motive and action—in silence grow
Into rare beauty, and bud and blow
Under the leaves?

Fair white flowers of faith and trust,
Springing from spirits bruised and crushed;
Blossoms of love, rose-tinted and bright,
Touched and painted with Heaven's own light
Under the leaves.

Full fresh clusters of duty borne,
Fairest of all in that shadow grown;
Wondrous the fragrance that sweet and rare
Comes from the flower-cups hidden there
Under the leaves.

Though unseen by our vision dim,
Bud and blossom are known to Him;
Wait we content for His heavenly ray—
Wait till our Master Himself one day
Lifts up the leaves.

God calls many of His most valued workers from the unknown multitude (Luke 14:23).

Morning

*Jesus took with him Peter, James and John the brother of James, and led
them up a high mountain by themselves. There he was transfigured before
them. . . . Peter said to Jesus, "*LORD*, it is good for us to be here."*
MATTHEW 17:1–2, 4

It is good to be the possessor of some mountaintop experience. *Not to know life on the heights is to suffer an impoverishing incompleteness.*

Those times when the Lord's presence is marvelously manifest to you—the moments of self-revelation—*do not despise them.* But beware of *not acting upon what you see in your moments on the mount with God!*

Horizons broaden when we stand on the heights. There is always, we find, the danger that we will make of life too much of a dead-level existence; a monotonous tread of beaten paths; a matter of absorbing, spiritless, deadening routine.

Do not drop your life into the passing current, to be steadily going you scarcely know *where* or *why.*

Christian life, writes one, *is not all a valley of humiliation. It has its heights of vision.*

Abraham saw in the glorious depths of the starry firmament visions that no telescope could ever have revealed! Jacob's stony pillow led up to the ladder of vision!

Joseph's early dreams kept him in the hours of discouragement and despair that followed!

Moses, who spent one-third of his life in the desert, we find crying out: "I beseech thee, show me Thy glory!"

Job's vision showed him God and lifted him out of himself!

The mariner does not expect to see the sun and stars every day, but when he does, he takes his observations and sails by their light for many days to come.

God gives days of special illumination that we may be able to call to memory in the days of shadow and say: "Therefore I will remember you from the land of the Jordan, the heights of Hermon—from Mount Mizar" (Psalm 42:6).

In the life of Paul, we find a few of these blessed interludes—when the Lord gave to him words of promise to remember in his days of trial that followed.

If these special experiences came too often they would lose their flavor! He walks in glory on the hills and longs for men to join Him there.

———————— FEBRUARY 25 ————————

Evening

I will give you every place where you set your foot, as I promised.
JOSHUA 1:3

Besides the literal ground still unoccupied for Christ, there is before us the unclaimed and unwalked territory of *God's promises*. What did God say to Joshua? "I will give you *every place* where you set your foot, *as I promised*." Then He set the boundaries of the Land of Promise—all theirs on one condition: *they must march across its length and breadth*, measuring it off with their own feet.

Yet they never marched across more than one-third of the land, and as a consequence, they never *possessed* more than that one-third. They possessed only what they measured off and no more.

In 2 Peter 1:4 we read, "He has given us his very great and precious promises." The land of God's promises is open before us, and it is His will for us to possess it. We must measure off the territory with the feet of obedient faith and faithful obedience, thereby claiming and appropriating it as our own.

How many of us have ever taken possession of the promises of God in the name of Christ? The land of His promises is a magnificent territory for faith to claim by marching across its length and breadth, but faith has yet to do it.

Let us enter into and claim our total inheritance. Let us lift our eyes to the north, south, east, and west and hear God say, "All the land that you see I will give to you" (Genesis 13:15). ARTHUR TAPPAN PIERSON

Wherever the tribe of Judah set their feet would be theirs, and wherever the tribe of Benjamin set their feet would be theirs, and so on. Each tribe would receive their inheritance by setting foot upon it. Don't you imagine that as each tribe set foot upon a given territory, they instantly and instinctively felt, "This is ours"? An elderly man who had a wonderful testimony of grace was once asked, "Daniel, how is it that you exhibit such peace and joy in your faith?" "Oh, sir!" he replied. "I just fall flat on God's 'very great and precious promises,' and I have all that is in them. Glory! Glory!" One who falls flat on God's promises knows that all the riches abiding in them are his. *Faith Papers*

The Marquis of Salisbury, an English statesman and diplomat, upon being criticized for his colonial policies, replied, "Gentlemen, get larger maps."

FEBRUARY 26

Morning

A woman came with an alabaster jar of very expensive perfume, made of pure nard. She broke the jar and poured the perfume on his head.
MARK 14:3

And the house was filled with the fragrance of the perfume.
JOHN 12:3

Mary wanted it to be known that this act of hers was done *for Him exclusively.* Just for Him, without thought of self, or anything else. Martha was serving, but it was *not exclusively for Him.* It might be in His honor, but it was done for others also. Simon might entertain, but others were included in the entertainment also. What Mary did was for *Him alone.* "When *Jesus understood it,* he said unto them, Why trouble ye the woman?" (Matthew 26:10 KJV).

Jesus understood!

Jesus said to Peter: "Lovest thou Me?" Peter replied: "Thou knowest that I love Thee." Jesus said to him: "Feed my sheep *for Me*. . . . Feed my lambs" (John 21:15–17 KJV).

"Take this baby and nurse him *for me*, and I will pay you" (Exodus 2:9).

Under an Eastern sky
Amid a rabble cry

A Man went forth to die
For me—for me.

Thorn-crowned His blessed Head,
Bloodstained His every tread,
To Calvary He was led
For me—for me.

Pierced were His Hands, His Feet,
Three hours o'er Him did beat
Fierce rays of noonday heat,
For me—for me.

Since Thou wast made all mine,
Lord, make me wholly Thine.
Grant strength and grace Divine
For me—for me.

Thy will to do, Oh, lead
In thought and word and deed
My heart, e'en though it bleed,
To Thee—to Thee.

SELECTED

For me! "For Him! For Him!" the man cries as he planes his boards, sells his goods, adds his figures, or writes his letters. "For Him! For Him!" sings the woman as she plies her needle, makes her bed, cooks her food, or dusts her house.

All day long the hand is outstretched to touch the invisible Christ, and at night the work done is brought to Him for His benediction.

Evening

My grace is sufficient for you.
2 CORINTHIANS 12:9

The other day I was riding home after a hard day's work. I was very tired and deeply depressed, when quickly, and as suddenly as a lightning bolt, the verse came to me: "My grace is sufficient for you." When I arrived home I looked it up in the Word, and it finally came to me this way: *"My grace is sufficient for you."* My response was to say, "Yes, Lord, I should think it is!" Then I burst out laughing.

Until that time, I had never understood what the holy laughter of Abraham was. This verse seemed to make unbelief totally absurd. I pictured a thirsty little fish who was concerned about drinking the river dry, with Father River saying, "Drink away, little fish; my stream is sufficient for you." I also envisioned a mouse afraid of starving after seven years of plenty, when Joseph says to him, "Cheer up, little mouse; my granaries are sufficient for you." Again, I imagined a man high on a mountain peak, saying to himself, "I breathe so many cubic feet of air every year, I am afraid I will deplete all the oxygen in the atmosphere." But the earth says to him, "Breathe away, filling your lungs forever; my atmosphere is sufficient for you."

O people of God, be great believers! Little faith will bring your souls to heaven, but great faith will bring heaven to your souls. CHARLES H. SPURGEON

> *His grace is great enough to meet the great things—*
> *The crashing waves that overwhelm the soul,*
> *The roaring winds that leave us stunned and breathless,*
> *The sudden storms beyond our life's control.*
>
> *His grace is great enough to meet the small things—*
> *The little pinprick troubles that annoy,*
> *The insect worries, buzzing and persistent,*
> *The squeaking wheels that grate upon our joy.*
> ANNIE JOHNSON FLINT

There is always a large balance credited to our account in the bank of heaven. It is waiting for us to exercise our faith to draw upon it. Draw heavily on God's resources.

FEBRUARY 27

Morning

Those who cleanse themselves . . . will be instruments for special purposes,
made holy, useful to the Master and prepared to do any good work.
2 TIMOTHY 2:21

Here, O my Father, is Thy making stuff!
Set Thy wheel going; let it whir and play.
The chips in me, the stones, the straws, the sand,
Cast them out with fine separating hand,
And make a vessel of Thy yielding clay.

Martin Wells Knapp was once undergoing a severe trial, and in his secret devotions he asked God to remove his trial. As he waited before the Lord, the vision of a rough piece of marble rose before him with a sculptor grinding and chiseling. Watching the dust and chips fill the air, he noticed a beautiful image begin to appear in the marble. The Lord spoke to him and said, "Son, you are that block of marble. I have an image in My mind, and I desire to produce it in your character, and will do so if you will stand the grinding; but I will stop now if you so desire." Mr. Knapp broke down and said, *"Lord, continue the chiseling and grinding."*

When God wants to drill a man,
And thrill a man,
And skill a man,
When God wants to mold a man
To play the noblest part;
When He yearns with all His heart
To create so great and bold a man
That all the world shall be amazed,

Watch His methods, watch His ways!
How He ruthlessly perfects
Whom He royally elects!
How He hammers him and hurts him,
And with mighty blows converts him
Into trial shapes of clay which
Only God understands;
While his tortured heart is crying
And he lifts beseeching hands!
How He bends but never breaks
When his good He undertakes;
How He uses whom He chooses,
And with every purpose fuses him;
But every act induces him
To try His splendor out—
God knows what He's about.

SELECTED

Life is a quarry, out of which we are to mold and chisel and complete a character.
GOETHE

FEBRUARY 27

Evening

So Jacob was left alone, and a man wrestled with him till daybreak.
GENESIS 32:24

L eft alone!" What different emotions these words bring to mind for each of us! To some they mean loneliness and grief, but to others they may mean rest and quiet. To be left alone *without* God would be too horrible for words, while being left alone *with* Him is a taste of heaven! And if His followers spent more time alone with Him, we would have spiritual giants again.

Our Master set an example for us. Remember how often He went to be *alone with*

God? And there was a powerful purpose behind His command, "When you pray, go into your room, close the door and pray" (Matthew 6:6).

The greatest miracles of Elijah and Elisha took place when they were alone with God. Jacob was alone with God when he became a prince (Genesis 32:28). In the same way, we too may become royalty and people who are "wondered at" (Zechariah 3:8 KJV). Joshua was alone when the Lord came to him (Joshua 1:1). Gideon and Jephthah were by themselves when commissioned to save Israel (Judges 6:11; 11:29). Moses was by himself at the burning bush (Exodus 3:1–5). Cornelius was praying by himself when the Angel of God came to him (Acts 10:1–4). No one was with Peter on the housetop when he was instructed to go to the Gentiles (Acts 10:9–28). John the Baptist was alone in the wilderness (Luke 1:80), and John the Beloved was alone on the island of Patmos when he was the closest to God (Revelation 1:9).

Earnestly desire to get alone with God. If we neglect to do so, we not only rob ourselves of a blessing but rob others as well, since we will have no blessing to pass on to them. It may mean that we do less outward, visible work, but the work we do will have more depth and power. Another wonderful result will be that people will see "no one except Jesus" (Matthew 17:8) in our lives.

The impact of being alone with God in prayer cannot be overemphasized.

If chosen men had never been alone,
In deepest silence open-doored to God,
No greatness would ever have been dreamed or done.

FEBRUARY 28

Morning

Has not the LORD gone ahead of you?
JUDGES 4:14

God has guided the heroes and saints of all ages to do things which the common sense of the community has regarded as ridiculous and mad. Have *you* ever taken any risks for Christ? CHARLES E. COWMAN

"Am I not sending you?" (Judges 6:14).

God knows, and you know, what He has sent you to do. God sent Moses to Egypt to bring three million bondmen out of the house of bondage into the Promised Land. Did he fail? It looked at first as if he were going to. But *did* he? God sent Elijah to stand before Ahab, and it was a bold thing for him to say that there should be neither dew nor rain: but did he not lock up the heavens for three years and six months? Did he fail?

And you cannot find any place in Scripture where a man was ever sent by God to do a work in which he ever failed. D. L. MOODY

> Had Moses failed to go, had God
> Granted his prayer, there would have been
> For him no leadership to win;
> No pillared fire; no magic rod;
> No wonders in the land of Zion;
> No smiting of the sea; no tears
> Ecstatic, shed on Sinai's steep;
> No Nebo with a God to keep
> His burial; only forty years
> Of desert, watching with his sheep.
>
> J. R. MILLER

Our might is His Almightiness.

～～～ FEBRUARY 28 ～～～
Evening

Let us continually offer to God a sacrifice of praise.
HEBREWS 13:15

An inner-city missionary, stumbling through the trash of a dark apartment doorway, heard someone say, "Who's there, Honey?" Lighting a match, he caught sight of earthly needs and suffering, amid saintly trust and peace. Calm, appealing eyes, etched in ebony, were set within the wrinkles of a weathered black face. On a bitterly cold night in February, she lay on a tattered bed, with no fire, no heat, and no light. Having had no breakfast, lunch, or dinner, she seemed to have nothing at all, except arthritis and faith in God. No one could have been further removed from comfortable circumstances, yet this favorite song of the dear lady played in the background:

> *Nobody knows the trouble I see,*
> *Nobody knows but Jesus;*
> *Nobody knows the trouble I see—*
> > *Sing Glory Hallelu!*

> *Sometimes I'm up, sometimes I'm down,*
> *Sometimes I'm level on the groun',*
> *Sometimes the glory shines aroun'—*
> > *Sing Glory Hallelu!*

And so it continued: "Nobody knows the work I do, Nobody knows the griefs I have," the constant refrain being, "*Glory Hallelu!*" until the last verse rose:

> *Nobody knows the joys I have,*
> *Nobody knows but Jesus!*

"We are hard pressed on every side, but not crushed; perplexed, but not in despair; persecuted, but not abandoned; struck down, but not destroyed" (2 Corinthians 4:8–9). It takes these great Bible words to explain the joy of this elderly black woman.

Do you remember the words of Martin Luther as he lay on his deathbed? Between groans he preached, "These pains and troubles here are like the type that printers set. When we look at them, we see them backwards, and they seem to make no sense and have no meaning. But up there, when the Lord God prints out our life to come, we will find they make splendid reading." Yet we do not have to wait until then. The apostle Paul, walking the deck of a ship on a raging sea, encouraged the frightened sailors, "Be of good cheer" (Acts 27:22 KJV).

Paul, Martin Luther, and the dear black woman were all human sunflowers, seeking and seeing the Light in a world of darkness. WILLIAM C. GARNETT

Go through the camp . . . ready for battle.
JOSHUA 1:11, 14

Pass through, pass through, nor sit among
The hosts encamped around.
The glorious Victor paved the way,
Put all His armor on you may.
With shield of faith held well in view,
Thy song ere long—"He brought me through!"
E. N. P.

After a step of faith most persons are looking for sunny skies and unruffled seas, and when they meet a storm or tempest they are filled with astonishment and perplexity. *But this is just what we must expect if we have received anything of the Lord.* The best token of His presence is the adversary's defiance, and the more real our blessing, the more certainly it will be challenged. It is a good thing to go out looking for the worst, then if it comes we are not surprised; while if our path be smooth and the way unopposed it is all the more delightful because it comes as a glad surprise.

But let us quite understand what we mean by *temptation.* You, especially, who have stepped out with the assurance that you have died to self and sin, may be greatly amazed to find yourself assailed with a tempest of thoughts and feelings that seem to come wholly from within, and you will be impelled to say, "Why, I thought I was dead, but I seem to be alive!" This, beloved, is the time to remember that in temptation the instigation is not your sin but only the voice of the evil one. A. B. SIMPSON

Why does the battle thicken so—
The darts rain fast upon my breast,
While missiles hurled with cruel force
Ring loud against my burnished crest?
Above the din I seem to hear
My Captain's voice in accents clear,

"Because your shield is down!"
Why does the enemy advance
And hem us 'round on every hand
While we, the army of the Lord,
Can scarce his arrogance withstand?
Above the shouts I seem to hear
My Captain's voice in accents clear,
"Because your shields are down!"

Ah! Now it's brighter—now I see
The enemy is taking flight,
And lo, the banner of the Cross
Streams red against the morning light;
But as they flee I seem to hear
My Captain call in accents clear,
"Let not your shields go down!"

THOMAS KIMBER

Failure in our faith is fatal. Faith is our spiritual shield protecting us from the darts of the devil. Lay this shield aside even for a moment, and disaster follows. Any departure from the living God is the result of unbelief.

MARCH 1
Evening

Consider what God has done: Who can straighten what he has made crooked?
ECCLESIASTES 7:13

God often seems to place His children in places of deep difficulty, leading them into a corner from which there is no escape. He creates situations that human judgment, even if consulted, would never allow. Yet the cloudiness of the circumstance itself is used by Him to guide us to the other side. Perhaps this is where you find yourself even now.

Your situation is filled with uncertainty and is very serious, but it is perfectly right. The reason behind it will more than justify Him who brought you here, for it is a platform from which God will display His almighty grace and power.

He not only will deliver you but in doing so will impart a lesson that you will never forget. And in days to come, you will return to the truth of it through singing. You will be unable to ever thank God enough for doing exactly what He has done. SELECTED

We may wait till He explains,
Because we know that Jesus reigns.

It puzzles me; but, Lord, You understandest,
*   And will one day explain this crooked thing.*
Meanwhile, I know that it has worked out Your best—
*   Its very crookedness taught me to cling.*

You have fenced up my ways, made my paths crooked,
*   To keep my wand'ring eyes fixed on You,*
To make me what I was not, humble, patient;
*   To draw my heart from earthly love to You.*

So I will thank and praise You for this puzzle,
*   And trust where I cannot understand.*
Rejoicing You do hold me worth such testing,
*   I cling the closer to Your guiding hand.*
                              F. E. M. I.

MARCH 2

Morning

He did not say anything to them without using a parable. But when
he was alone with his own disciples, he explained everything.
                              MARK 4:34

God may not explain to you a thousand things which puzzle your reason in His dealings with you, but if you always see yourself to be His love-slave, He will awaken in you a jealous love and bestow upon you many blessings which come only to those who are in the inner circle.

I can still believe that a day comes for all of us, however far off it may be, when we shall understand; when these tragedies that now blacken and darken the very air of heaven for us will sink into their places in a scheme so august, so magnificent, so joyful, that we shall laugh for wonder and delight. ARTHUR CHRISTOPHER BENSON

Will not the end explain
The crossed endeavor, earnest purpose foiled,
The strange bewilderment of good work spoiled,
The clinging weariness, the inward strain?
Will not the end explain?

Meanwhile He comforteth
Them that are losing patience. 'Tis His way:
But none can write the words they heard Him say,
For men to read; only they know He saith
Sweet words and comforteth.

Not that He doth explain
The mystery that baffleth; but a sense
Husheth the quiet heart, that far, far hence
Lieth a field set thick with golden grain
Wetted in seedling days by many a rain.
The end—it will explain.

— GOLD CORD

Evening

Be ready in the morning, and then come up. . . . Present yourself to
me there on top of the mountain. No one is to come with you.

EXODUS 34:2–3

The morning is a critically important time of day. You must never face the day until you have faced God, nor look into the face of others until you have looked into His. You cannot expect to be victorious, if you begin your day in your own strength alone.

Begin the work of every day after having been influenced by a few reflective, quiet moments between your heart and God. Do not meet with others, even the members of your own family, until you have first met with the great Guest and honored Companion of your life—Jesus Christ.

Meet with Him alone and regularly, having His Book of counsel open before you. Then face the ordinary, and the unique, responsibilities of each day with the renewed influence and control of His character over all your actions.

Begin the day with God!
He is your Sun and Day!
His is the radiance of your dawn;
To Him address your day.

Sing a new song at morn!
Join the glad woods and hills;
Join the fresh winds and seas and plains,
Join the bright flowers and rills.

Sing your first song to God!
Not to your fellow men;
Not to the creatures of His hand,
But to the glorious One.

Take your first walk with God!
  Let Him go forth with thee;
By stream, or sea, or mountain path,
  Seek still His company.

Your first transaction be
  With God Himself above;
So will your business prosper well,
  All the day be love.

HORATIUS BONAR

Those who have accomplished the most for God in this world are those who have been found on their knees early in the morning. For example, Matthew Henry would spend from four to eight o'clock each morning in his study. Then, after breakfast and a time of family prayer, he would return to his study until noon. After lunch, he would write till four p.m. and then spend the remainder of the day visiting friends.

Philip Doddridge referred to his *Family Expositor* as an example of the difference of rising at five o'clock, as opposed to seven. He realized that increasing his workday by twenty-five percent was the equivalent of adding ten work years to his life over a period of forty years.

Adam Clarke's Commentary on the Bible was penned primarily in the early morning hours. *Barnes' Notes*, a popular and useful commentary by Albert Barnes, was also the fruit of the early morning. And Charles Simeon's *Sketches* were mostly written between four and eight a.m.

~~~~~~~ MARCH 3 ~~~~~~~

Morning

Where there is no vision, the people perish.
PROVERBS 29:18 KJV

We must see something before we make our ventures! Faith must first have visions: faith sees a light, if you will, an imaginary light, and leaps! Faith is always born of vision and hope! We must have the gleam of the thing hoped for shining across the waste before we can have an energetic and energizing faith.

Are we not safe in saying that the majority of people have no fine hopes, are devoid of *the vision splendid,* and therefore, have no spiritual audacity in spiritual adventure and enterprise? Our hopes are petty and peddling, and they don't give birth to crusades. There are no shining towers and minarets on our horizon, no new Jerusalem, and therefore we do not set out in chivalrous explorations.

We need a transformation in the "things hoped for" (Hebrews 11:1 KJV). We need to be *renewed in mind,* and renewed in mind *daily.* We need to have the far-off towering summits of vast and noble possibilities enthroned in our imaginations. Our gray and uninviting horizons must glow with the unfading colors of immortal hopes. SELECTED

> So few men venture out beyond the blazed trail,
> 'Tis he who has the courage to go past this sign
> That cannot in his mission fail.
> He will have left at least some mark behind
> To guide some other brave exploring mind.

No man is of any use until he has dared everything. ROBERT LOUIS STEVENSON

MARCH 3
Evening

The spirit shrieked, convulsed him violently and came out.
MARK 9:26

Evil never surrenders its grasp without a tremendous fight. We never arrive at any spiritual inheritance through the enjoyment of a picnic but always through the fierce conflicts of the battlefield. And it is the same in the deep recesses of the soul. Every human capacity that wins its spiritual freedom does so at the cost of blood. Satan is not put to flight by our courteous request. He completely blocks our way, and our progress must be recorded in blood and tears. We need to remember this, or else we will be held responsible for the arrogance of misinterpretation. When we are born again, it is not into a soft and protected nursery but into the open countryside, where we actually draw our strength from the distress of the storm. "We must go through many hardships to enter the kingdom of God" (Acts 14:22). JOHN HENRY JOWETT

> Faith of our Fathers! living still,
> In spite of dungeon, fire and sword:
> Oh, how our hearts beat high with joy
> Whene'er we hear that glorious word.
> Faith of our Fathers! Holy Faith!
> We will be true to Thee till death!
> Our fathers, chained in prisons dark,
> Were still in heart of conscience free;
> How sweet would be their children's fate,
> If they, like them, could die for Thee!

~~~~~~~ MARCH 4 ~~~~~~~
Morning

[God] will hear.
PSALM 55:19

I was standing at a bank counter in Liverpool waiting for a clerk to come. I picked up a pen and began to print on a blotter in large letters two words which had gripped me like a vise: *"Pray through."* I kept talking to a friend and printing until I had the desk blotter filled from top to bottom with a column. I transacted my business and went away. The next day my friend came to see me and said he had a striking story to tell.

A businessman came into the bank soon after we had gone. He had grown discouraged with business troubles. He started to transact some business with the same clerk, over that blotter, when his eye caught the long column of *"Pray through."* He asked who wrote those words and when he was told exclaimed, "That is the very message I needed.

I will pray through. I have tried in my own strength to worry through, and have merely mentioned my troubles to God; now I am going to pray the situation through until I get light." CHARLES M. ALEXANDER

> *Don't stop praying, but have more trust;*
> *Don't stop praying! for pray we must;*
> *Faith will banish a mount of care;*
> *Don't stop praying! God answers prayer.*
>
> C. M. A.

All I *have seen* teaches me to trust the Creator for *what I have not seen!*

―――――― ~~~ MARCH 4 ~~~ ――――――
Evening

Imitate those who through faith and patience inherit what has been promised.
HEBREWS 6:12

The biblical heroes of faith call to us from the heights they have won, encouraging us that what man once did, man can do again. They remind us not only of the necessity of faith but also of the patience required for faith's work to be perfected. May we fear attempting to remove ourselves from the hands of our heavenly Guide, or missing even one lesson of His loving discipline due to our discouragement or doubt.

An old village blacksmith once said, "There is only one thing I fear: being thrown onto the scrap heap. You see, in order to strengthen a piece of steel, I must first temper it. I heat it, hammer it, and then quickly plunge it into a bucket of cold water. Very soon I know whether it will accept the tempering process or simply fall to pieces. If, after one or two tests, I see it will not allow itself to be tempered, I throw it onto the scrap heap, only to later sell it to the junkman for a few cents per pound.

"I realize the Lord tests me in the same way: through fire, water, and heavy blows of His hammer. If I am unwilling to withstand the test, or prove to be unfit for His tempering process, I am afraid He may throw me onto the scrap heap." When the fire in your life is the hottest, stand still, for "*later on . . . it produces a harvest*" (Hebrews 12:11) of blessings. Then we will be able to say with Job, "When he has tested me, I will come forth as gold" (Job 23:10). SELECTED

Sainthood finds its source in suffering. Remember, it requires eleven tons of pressure on a piano's strings for it to be tuned. And God will tune you to perfect harmony with heaven's theme if you will withstand the strain.

> *Things that hurt and things that mar*
>   *Shape the man for perfect praise;*
> *Shock and strain and ruin are*
>   *Friendlier than the smiling days.*

<hr>

MARCH 5
Morning

So Manasseh and Ephraim, the descendants of Joseph, received their inheritance.
JOSHUA 16:4

A dying judge said to his pastor, "Do you know enough about law to understand what is meant by *joint tenancy?*"

"No," was the reply; "I know nothing about law; I know a little about grace, and that satisfies me."

"Well," he said, "if you and I were joint tenants on a farm, I could not say to you, 'That is your field of corn, and this is mine; that is your blade of grass, and this is mine,' but we would share alike in everything on the place. I have just been lying here and thinking with unspeakable joy that Christ Jesus has nothing apart from me, that everything He has is mine, *and that we will share alike through all eternity.*"

God wants you to have *all* that He has—His Son, His life, His love, His Spirit, His glory. "All [things] are yours, and you are of Christ, and Christ is of God" (1 Corinthians 3:22–23). "My son . . . you are always with me, and everything I have is yours" (Luke 15:31). What a privilege! What a life for a child of God! *Only unbelief can blind us to the Father's love.* Only with a false humility, the children of the King set limitations about their lives that He never appointed. The full table is set for us, and we eat so sparingly, forgetful of the voice that cries, "Eat, O friends; drink, yea, drink abundantly, O beloved" (Song of Songs 5:1 KJV).

"*The resources of the Christian life,*" says Dr. Robert F. Horton, "*are just Jesus Christ.*" He *is our regal provision for the way.* He *is the way.* Let us draw upon these Divine resources. *Whom* should He bless, even on earth, *if not His own?*

Supply yourself from Him!

God is to be adored, but He is also to be *used.* Merely to worship Him in the awe of His greatness and holiness is not to please Him fully. He wants us to draw upon Him as an asset of our practical life and as a priceless possession. We live in Him, but He also lives in us to bring to our souls the power of His own infinite life. *To possess him is to possess all things and to have power to attain our noblest purposes.*

He is always at our service. Use Him, then, for He is there and waits for you to use Him. *All the unclaimed wealth of the forty thousand checks in the bankbook of the Bible is ours!* And "He satisfieth [satiates] the longing soul" (Psalm 107:9 KJV). *God is our God to be used for things we need Him for.*

My need and Thy great fullness meet, and I have all in Thee.

God has a separate inheritance for each one. Do not fail to enter upon *yours.* "It is your right to redeem it and possess it" (Jeremiah 32:8).

MARCH 5

Evening

We have come to share in Christ if indeed we hold our original conviction firmly till the very end.

HEBREWS 3:14

Often the last step is the winning step. In *Pilgrim's Progress* the greatest number of dangers were lurking in the area closest to the gates of the Celestial City. It was in that region the Doubting Castle stood. And it was there the enchanted ground lured the tired traveler to fatal slumber. It is when heaven's heights are in full view that the gates of hell are the most persistent and full of deadly peril. "Let us not become weary in doing good, for at the proper time we will reap a harvest *if we do not give up*" (Galatians 6:9). "Run in such a way as to get the prize" (1 Corinthians 9:24).

> *In the bitter waves of woe*
> > *Beaten and tossed about*
> *By the sullen winds that blow*
> > *From the desolate shores of doubt,*
> *Where the anchors that faith has cast*
> > *Are dragging in the gale,*
> *I am quietly holding fast*
> > *To the things that cannot fail.*
>
> *And fierce though the fiends may fight,*
> > *And long though the angels hide,*
> *I know that truth and right*
> > *Have the universe on their side;*
> *And that somewhere beyond the stars*
> > *Is a love that is better than fate.*
> *When the night unlocks her bars*
> > *I will see Him—and I will wait.*
>
> WASHINGTON GLADDEN

The greatest challenge in receiving great things from God is holding on for the last half hour. SELECTED

~~~~~ MARCH 6 ~~~~~
Morning

For me and thee.
MATTHEW 17:27 KJV

Peter had been a fisherman. Jesus had said, "Follow me," and Peter had given up his fishing business to follow. We read that *straightway* he forsook his nets and followed. That must have been a tremendous experience for Peter—giving up his means of livelihood, upkeep of his home, not to mention the money for those taxes. Peter, the Fisherman, left *all* to follow Christ. The Lord knew that he had given up his means of livelihood to answer His call, and from the very thing that Peter had given up for His sake—*fish*—the Lord met His servant's need when the time for paying the taxes came around.

No servant of Christ will ever be the loser.

So our dear Lord is always thinking in advance of *our* needs, and He loves to save us from embarrassment and anticipate our anxieties and cares by laying up His loving acts and providing before the emergency comes. "For me and thee," He had said, bracketing those words together in a wondrous, sacred intimacy. He puts Himself first in the embarrassing need, and He bears the heavy end of the burden for His distressed and suffering child. He makes our cares, *His* cares; our sorrows, *His* sorrows; our shame, *His* shame.

The tax was due—the Master's and disciple's,
And to the sea the Master strangely sent:
A fish would yield the needful piece of silver!
Strange bank, indeed, from which to pay that rent.
"One piece of silver!" Not two equal portions!

One piece of silver—one, and shining bright;
"That use for Me and thee," thus spoke the Master,
"That claims on Me and thee we thus unite."

Blest, happy bond! May I thus sweetly know Him!
Am I His servant? Hath He use of me?
Then, O my soul, why shouldst thou own law's limit,
If thy dear Lord doth find delight in thee?

If thou art His—joint-heir in all His riches,
Then, O my soul, a simpler spirit grow;

"How shall He not, with Him, why, give us all things,"
All that we need, to do His work below!

J. Danson Smith

~~~~~ MARCH 6 ~~~~~

Evening

We had hoped.
Luke 24:21

I have always been so sorry that the two disciples walking with Jesus on the road to Emmaus did not say to Him, "We *still* hope" instead of "We *had* hoped." The situation is very sad, because in their minds it is over.

Oh, if only they had said, "Everything has come against our hope, and it looks as if our trust were in vain. Yet we will not give up, because we believe we will see Him again." Instead, they walked by His side, declaring their shattered faith. Jesus had to say to them, "How foolish you are, and how slow to believe!" (Luke 24:25).

Are we not in danger of having these same words said to us? We can afford to lose every possession we have, except our faith in the God of truth and love. May we never express our faith, as these disciples did, in the past tense—*"We had hoped."* Yet may we always say, *"I have hope."* Crumbs

The soft, sweet summer was warm and glowing,
Bright were the blossoms on every bough:
I trusted Him when the roses were blooming;
I trust Him now. . . .

Small was my faith should it weakly falter
Now that the roses have ceased to blow;
Frail was the trust that now should alter,
Doubting His love when storm clouds grow.

The Song of a Bird in a Winter Storm

Morning

So they went and saw where he was staying, and they spent that day with him.
JOHN 1:39

I wonder what it was that lured your feet to follow Him upon His homeward way. Was it mere eagerness to see the street, and house in which He sojourned, and to stay at closer quarters with Him for one day?

. . . Or, did you feel a strange attractive Power, which lured you from your boat beside the bay; when, heeding not the passing of the hour, and caring not what other folk might say, you made your home with Him for that brief day?

. . . Perhaps you felt a holy discontent, after the hours spent in that presence fair? Certain it is you thenceforth were intent on fishing men; for, from His side you went, and straightway brought your brother to Him there!

. . . Oh, Andrew! you could never be the same, after the contact of that wondrous day. You ne'er again could play with passion's flame, or harbor pride or hate, or grasp for fame, or give to avarice a place to stay.

. . . Rather, I think, you might be heard to say, "Something about Him burned my pride away, and cooled my hate and changed it for Love's way. . . . *After the healing contact of that stay, I must bring Simon to have one such day!*"

. . . And, ever after, as men passed your way, they would be conscious of some strange, new spell; some unexplained, mysterious miracle. Then, in an awe-filled whisper they would say, *"Andrew is greatly altered since that day!"*

. . . Oh! Wondrous Sojourner on life's dark way. Savior! Who understands what sinners say, *Grant me to come beneath Thy magic sway, lest, rough-edged, loveless, sin-stained, I should stay, lacking the impress of just such a day!* ELEANOR VELLACOTT WOOD

Stradivari of Cremona is said to have marked every one of the priceless violins which he made with the name of Jesus, and so well-known did this become that his work is still called *"Stradivarius del Gesu."*

If our lives might become equally well known because of that sacred mark by which He said that *all men shall know,* there would be more people who, like the blind beggar, would come to Him that they might receive their sight and who, too, would *worship Him.*

Evening

We were harassed at every turn.
2 CORINTHIANS 7:5

Why is it that God leads us in this way, allowing such strong and constant pressure on us? One of His purposes is to show us His all-sufficient strength and grace more effectively than if we were free from difficulties and trials. "We have this treasure in jars of clay to show that this all-surpassing power is from God and not from us" (2 Corinthians 4:7).

Another purpose is to bring us a greater awareness of our dependence upon Him. God is constantly trying to teach us how dependent we are on Him—that we are held completely by His hand and reliant on His care alone.

This is exactly where Jesus Himself stood and where He desires us to stand. We must stand not with self-made strength but always leaning upon Him. And our stand must exhibit a trust that would never dare to take even one step alone. This will teach us to trust Him more.

There is no way to learn of faith except through trials. They are God's school of faith, and it is much better for us to learn to trust Him than to live a life of enjoyment. And once the lesson of faith has been learned, it is an everlasting possession and an eternal fortune gained. Yet without trust in God, even great riches will leave us in poverty.
DAYS OF HEAVEN UPON EARTH

> *Why must I weep when others sing?*
> *"To test the deeps of suffering."*
> *Why must I work while others rest?*
> *"To spend my strength at God's request."*
> *Why must I lose while others gain?*
> *"To understand defeat's sharp pain."*
> *Why must this lot of life be mine*
> *When that which fairer seems is thine?*
> *"Because God knows what plans for me*
> *Will blossom in eternity."*

Morning

God had planned something better for us.
HEBREWS 11:40

Our heavenly Father never takes any earthly thing from His children, unless He means to give them *something better instead.* GEORGE MUELLER

An easy thing, O Power Divine,
To thank Thee for these gifts of Thine!
For summer's sunshine, winter's snow,
For hearts that kindle, thoughts that glow;
But when shall I attain to this:
To thank Thee for the things I miss?

For all young fancy's early gleams,
The dreamed-of joys that still are dreams,
Hope unfulfilled, and pleasures known
Through others' fortunes, not my own,
And blessings seen that are not given,
And ne'er will be—this side of heaven.

Had I, too, shared the joys I see,
Would there have been a heaven for me?
Could I have felt Thy presence near
Had I possessed what I held dear?
My deepest fortune, highest bliss,
Have grown, perchance, from things I miss.

Sometimes there comes an hour of calm;
Grief turns to blessing, pain to balm;
A Power that works above my will
Still leads me onward, upward still;

And then my heart attains to this:
To thank Thee for the things I miss.

THOMAS WENTWORTH HIGGINSON

Instead *of the dry land, springs of water!* Instead *of heaviness, the garment of praise!*
Instead *of the thorn, the fir tree!* Instead *of the brier, the myrtle tree!* Instead *of ashes,*
beauty! (Isaiah 41:18; 55:13; 61:3)

~~~~~~~ MARCH 8 ~~~~~~~

Evening

Do as you promised . . . that your name will be great forever.
1 CHRONICLES 17:23–24

This is one of the most blessed aspects of genuine prayer. Often we ask for things
that God has not specifically promised. Therefore we are not sure if our petitions
are in line with His purpose, until we have persevered for some time in prayer. Yet on
some occasions, and this was one in the life of David, we are fully persuaded that what
we are asking is in accordance with God's will. We feel led to select and plead a promise
from the pages of Scripture, having been specially impressed that it contains a message
for us. At these times, we may say with confident faith, "Do as you promised."

Hardly any stance could be more completely beautiful, strong, or safe than that of
putting your finger on a promise of God's divine Word and then claiming it. Doing so
requires no anguish, struggle, or wrestling but simply presenting the check and asking
for cash. It is as simple as producing the promise and claiming its fulfillment. Nor will
there be any doubt or cloudiness about the request. If all requests were this definitive,
there would be much more interest in prayer. It is much better to claim a few specific
things than to make twenty vague requests. F. B. MEYER

Every promise of Scripture is a letter from God, which we may plead before Him
with this reasonable request: *"Do as you promised."* Our Creator will never cheat those
of us of His creation who depend upon His truth. And even more, our heavenly Father
will never break His word to His own child.

"Remember your word to your servant, for you have given me hope" (Psalm 119:49). This is a very common plea and is a double argument, for it is "your word." Will You not keep it? Why have You spoken it, if You will not make it good? "You have given me hope." Will You now disappoint the hope that You Yourself have brought forth within me? CHARLES H. SPURGEON

"Being fully persuaded that God had power to do what he had promised" (Romans 4:21).

It is the everlasting faithfulness of God that makes a Bible promise "very great and precious" (2 Peter 1:4). Human promises are often worthless, and many broken promises have left broken hearts. But since the creation of the world, God has never broken a single promise to one of His trusting children.

Oh, how sad it is for a poor Christian to stand at the very door of a promise during a dark night of affliction, being afraid to turn the knob and thereby come boldly into the shelter as a child entering his Father's house! GURNAL

Every promise of God's is built on four pillars. The first two are His justice and holiness, which will never allow Him to deceive us. The third is His grace or goodness, which will not allow Him to forget. And the fourth is His truth, which will not allow Him to change, which enables Him to accomplish what He has promised. SELECTED

~~~~ MARCH 9 ~~~~

Morning

Jacob's well was there, and Jesus, tired as he was from the journey, sat down by the well. It was about noon.
JOHN 4:6

I know your deeds, your hard work and your perseverance. I know that you cannot tolerate wicked people, that you have tested those who claim to be apostles but are not, and have found them false. You have persevered and have endured hardships for my name, and have not grown weary.
REVELATION 2:2–3

Our Lord took His apostles aside when they were fatigued, and said, "Let us rest awhile." He never drove His overtired faculties. When tired, He "sat down by the well." He used to go and rest in the home of Martha and Mary after the fatigue of working in Jerusalem. The Scripture shows it was His custom. He tells us all—you, and me, and all—to let tomorrow take care of itself, and merely to meet the evil of the present day.

As Elijah slept under a juniper tree, an angel touched him and said, "Arise and eat" (1 Kings 19:5 KJV). God had sent His wearied servant to sleep. In his overwrought condition sleep was his greatest need, and it is precisely under such conditions that sleep is often wooed in vain. Are we ever astonished at the miracle of sleep? Remember you have to do with the same God who ministered to Elijah, and *Though thy way be long and dreary, Eagle strength He'll still renew.*

Real foresight consists in reserving our own forces. If we labor with anxiety about the future, we destroy that strength which will enable us to meet the future. If we take more in hand now than we can well do, we break up, and the work is broken up with us.

Bakers of bread for others to eat must be very careful to husband their strength. They are not much seen, but much felt; unknown multitudes would feel their loss, and their failing means others famishing.

We need to take lessons of Sir William Cecil, once Lord Mayor of London. Upon throwing off his gown at night he would say to it, "Lay there, Lord Treasurer!" and forget all the cares of State until he resumed his official garb in the morning. THE GOLDEN MILESTONE

"Be still, and know" (Psalm 46:10)!

The Hebrew word for *still* signifies more than quietness and meditation before God; it means to let the tension go out of our life, just as the great cable holds in place the great steamer until the vessel reaches its channel and can go with its own steam. JOHN TIMOTHY STONE

Descend from the crest.
SONG OF SONGS 4:8

Bearing the burden of crushing weight actually gives Christians wings. This may sound like a contradiction in terms, but it is a blessed truth. While enduring a severe trial, David cried, "Oh, that I had the wings of a dove! I would fly away and be at rest" (Psalm 55:6). Yet before he finished his meditation, he seems to have realized that his wish for wings was attainable, for then he said, "Cast your cares on the LORD and he will sustain you" (Psalm 55:22).

The word "burden" is described in my Bible commentary as being "what Jehovah has given you." The saints' burdens are God-given, leading us to wait upon Him. And once we have done so, the burden is transformed into a pair of wings through the miracle of trust, and the one who was weighted down "will soar on wings like eagles" (Isaiah 40:31). SUNDAY SCHOOL TIMES

One day when walking down the street,
On business bent, while thinking hard
About the "hundred cares" which seemed
Like thunderclouds about to break
In torrents, Self-pity said to me:
"You poor, poor thing, you have too much
To do. Your life is far too hard.
This heavy load will crush you soon."
A swift response of sympathy
Welled up within. The burning sun
Seemed more intense. The dust and noise
Of puffing motors flying past
With rasping blast of blowing horn
Incensed still more the whining nerves,
The fabled last back-breaking straw
To weary, troubled, fretting mind.

"Ah yes, it will break and crush my life;
I cannot bear this constant strain
Of endless, aggravating cares;
They are too great for such as I."
So thus my heart consoled itself,
"Enjoying misery," when lo!
A "still small voice" distinctly said,
"'Twas sent to lift you—not to crush."
I saw at once my great mistake.
My place was not beneath the load
But on the top! God meant it not
That I should carry it. He sent
It here to carry me. Full well
He knew my incapacity
Before the plan was made. He saw
A child of His in need of grace
And power to serve; a puny twig
Requiring sun and rain to grow;
An undeveloped chrysalis;
A weak soul lacking faith in God.
He could not help but see all this
And more. And then, with tender thought
He placed it where it had to grow—
Or die. To lie and cringe beneath
One's load means death, but life and power
Await all those who dare to rise above.
Our burdens are our wings; on them
We soar to higher realms of grace;
Without them we must ever roam
On plains of undeveloped faith,
(For faith grows but by exercise
In circumstance impossible).

O paradox of Heaven. The load
We think will crush was sent to lift us

Up to God! Then, soul of mine,
Climb up! Nothing can e'er be crushed
Save what is underneath the weight.
How may we climb! By what ascent
Will we crest the critical cares
Of life! Within His word is found
The key which opens His secret stairs;
Alone with Christ, secluded there,
We mount our loads, and rest in Him.

MARY BUTTERFIELD

~~~ MARCH 10 ~~~

Morning

Without fault and with great joy.

JUDE v. 24

When a young girl, an intense passion for music was awakened within my soul. Father brought great joy into my life by presenting me with a beautiful organ. It would thrill me to the very fiber of my being, as the days slipped by, to be able to draw forth such wonderful harmony from my beloved instrument.

I used to sit at the organ in the early morning hours, just as the birds began to awaken, and through the open windows listen to their sweet little bird notes as they mingled with the melody of the organ, like a paean of praise to our Creator!

Then one morning, quite suddenly, and at a time when I was preparing with girlish enthusiasm for my first concert appearance, one of the notes became faulty. How the discordant sound grated upon my sensitive ear. Father, sensing my grief, said: "Never mind, daughter, I will have the tuner come." Long hours the tuner worked on that faulty note before it again rang out all sweet and true with the others. And the concert was a success *because the tuner was successful!*

Good Tuner, why
This ruthless, slow examination?

Why, on that one poor note,
Expend such careful concentration?
Just pass it by.
How I will let my soul respond to thee!
And see

But, no! Again, and yet again,
With skilled determination,
Rang out that meaningless reiteration.
While, ever and anon, through the great aisle's dim space,
Echoed the reverent chord; the loud harmonious phrase,

Till day began to wane.
And still, more patiently, the Tuner wrought
With that one faulty note; until, with zest,
All sweet and true, it answered like the rest.
Then, as the haloed glories of the sunset
flamed and gleamed,
Swift through the storied windows long shafts of crimson streamed:
And we poor whispering wayfarers heard, round about and o'er us,
The throbbing, thundering triumphs of the Hallelujah Chorus!
"THE TOWER IN THE CATHEDRAL" BY FAY INCHFAWN

MARCH 10
Evening

My righteous one will live by faith.
HEBREWS 10:38

Often our feelings and emotions are mistakenly substituted for faith. Pleasurable emotions and deep, satisfying experiences are part of the Christian life, but they are not the essence of it. Trials, conflicts, battles, and testings lie along the way and are to be counted not as misfortunes but rather as part of our necessary discipline.

In all of these various experiences, we are to rely on the indwelling of Christ in our hearts, regardless of our feelings, as we walk obediently before Him. And this is where many Christians get into trouble. They try to walk by feelings rather than by faith.

A believer once related that it seemed as if God had totally withdrawn Himself from her. His mercy *seemed* completely gone. Her loneliness lasted for six weeks, until the heavenly Lover seemed to say to her, "You have looked for Me in the outside world of emotions, yet all the while I have been waiting inside for you. Meet Me now in the inner chamber of your spirit, *for I am there.*"

Be sure to distinguish between the fact of God's presence and the *feeling* of the fact. It is actually a wonderful thing when our soul feels lonely and deserted, as long as our faith can say, "I do not see You, Lord, nor do I feel Your presence, but I know for certain You are graciously here—exactly where I am and aware of my circumstances." Remind yourself again and again with these words: "Lord, You are here. And though the bush before me does not seem to burn, it *does* burn. I will take the shoes from my feet, 'for the place where [I am] standing is holy ground'" (Exodus 3:5). LONDON CHRISTIAN

Trust God's Word and His power more than you trust your own feelings and experiences. Remember, your Rock is Christ, and it is the sea that ebbs and flows with the tides, not Him. SAMUEL RUTHERFORD

Keep your eyes firmly fixed on the infinite greatness of Christ's finished work and His righteousness. Look to Jesus and believe—look to Jesus and live! In fact, as you look to Him, unfurl your sails and bravely face the raging storms on the sea of life. Do not exhibit your distrust by staying in the security of the calm harbor or by sleeping comfortably through your life of ease. Do not allow your life and emotions to be tossed back and forth against each other like ships idly moored at port. The Christian life is not one of listless brooding over our emotions or slowly drifting our keel of faith through shallow water. Nor is it one of dragging our anchor of hope through the settling mud of the bay, as if we were afraid of encountering a healthy breeze.

Sail away! Spread your sail toward the storm and trust in Him who rules the raging seas. A brightly colored bird is safest when in flight. If its nest is near the ground or if it flies too low, it exposes itself to the hunter's net or trap. In the same way, if we cower in the lowlands of feelings and emotions, we will find ourselves entangled in a thousand nets of doubt, despair, temptation, and unbelief. "How useless to spread a

net where every bird can see it!" (Proverbs 1:17). "Put your hope in God" (Psalm 42:5).
J. R. MACDUFF

When I cannot *feel* the faith of assurance, I live by the *fact* of God's faithfulness.
MATTHEW HENRY

───〜〜〜〜── MARCH 11 ──〜〜〜〜───

Morning

You will be like a well-watered garden, like a spring whose waters never fail.
ISAIAH 58:11

Holiness appeared to me to be of a sweet, pleasant . . . calm nature. It seemed to me . . . that it made the soul like a field or garden of God, with all manner of pleasant flowers—all pleasant, delightful, and undisturbed—enjoying a sweet calm and the gently vivifying beams of the sun.

The soul of a true Christian appeared like such a little white flower as we see in the spring of the year, low and humble on the ground, opening its bosom to receive the pleasant beams of the sun's glory—rejoicing, as it were, in a calm rapture—diffusing around a sweet fragrancy.

Once I rode out into the woods for my health. Having alighted from my horse in a retired place as my manner commonly had been, to walk for Divine contemplation and prayer, I had a view—that was for me extraordinary—of the glory of the Son of God. As near as I can judge, this continued about an hour; and kept me the greater part of the time in a flood of tears and weeping aloud. I felt an ardency of soul to be—what I know not otherwise how to express—*emptied and annihilated; to love Him with a holy and pure love; to serve and follow Him; to be perfectly sanctified, and made pure with a Divine and heavenly purity.* JONATHAN EDWARDS

> *I never thought it could be thus, month after month to know*
> *The river of Thy peace without one ripple in its flow;*
> *Without one quiver in the trust, one flicker in the glow.*

Evening

After the death of Moses the servant of the LORD, *the* LORD *said to
Joshua son of Nun, Moses' aide: "Moses my servant is dead. Now then,
you and all these people, get ready to cross the Jordan River."*
JOSHUA 1:1–2

Yesterday you experienced a great sorrow, and now your home seems empty. Your
first impulse is to give up and to sit down in despair amid your dashed hopes. Yet
you must defy that temptation, for you are at the front line of the battle, and the crisis
is at hand. Faltering even one moment would put God's interest at risk. Other lives will
be harmed by your hesitation, and His work will suffer if you simply fold your hands.
You must not linger at this point, even to indulge your grief.

A famous general once related this sorrowful story from his own wartime experi-
ence. His son was the lieutenant of an artillery unit, and an assault was in progress. As
the father led his division in a charge, pressing on across the battlefield, suddenly his
eye caught sight of a dead artillery officer lying right before him. Just a glance told him
it was his son. The general's fatherly impulse was to kneel by the body of his beloved
son and express his grief, but the duty of the moment demanded he press on with his
charge. So after quickly kissing his dead son, he hurried away, leading his command in
the assault.

Weeping inconsolably beside a grave will never bring back the treasure of a lost
love, nor can any blessing come from such great sadness. Sorrow causes deep scars, and
indelibly writes its story on the suffering heart. We never completely recover from our
greatest griefs and are never exactly the same after having passed through them. Yet
sorrow that is endured in the right spirit impacts our growth favorably and brings us
a greater sense of compassion for others. Indeed, those who have no scars of sorrow or
suffering upon them are poor. "The joy set before" (Hebrews 12:2) us should shine on
our griefs just as the sun shines through the clouds, making them radiant. God has
ordained our truest and richest comfort to be found by pressing on toward the goal.
Sitting down and brooding over our sorrow deepens the darkness surrounding us,
allowing it to creep into our hearts. And soon our strength has changed to weakness.

But if we will turn from the gloom and remain faithful to the calling of God, the light will shine again and we will grow stronger. J. R. MILLER

> Lord, You know that through our tears
>   Of hasty, selfish weeping
> Comes surer sin, and for our petty fears
>   Of loss You have in keeping
> A greater gain than all of which we dreamed;
>   You knowest that in grasping
> The bright possessions which so precious seemed
>   We lose them; but if, clasping
> Your faithful hand, we tread with steadfast feet
>   The path of Your appointing,
> There waits for us a treasury of sweet
>   Delight, royal anointing
> With oil of gladness and of strength.
>   HELEN HUNT JACKSON

MARCH 12

Morning

If we endure, we will also reign with him.
2 TIMOTHY 2:12

There is only one place where we can receive *no answer but peace* to our question "Why?" All torturing questions find answer beneath those old gray olive trees. An hour at the foot of the Cross steadies the soul as nothing else can. Love that loves like that can be trusted with this question.

> O Christ Beloved, Thy Calvary stills all questions.
> For Calvary interprets human life;
> No path of pain but there we meet our Lord;

And all the strain, the terror and the strife
Die down like waves before His peaceful word,
And nowhere but beside the awful Cross,
And where the olives grow along the hill,
Can we accept the unexplained, the loss,
The crushing agony, and hold us still.

ROSE FROM BRIER

Every Gethsemane has beside it the serene, sweet heights of the Mount of Olives and from its summit, the resurrection into the heaven of heavens.

We have missed human history if we have not seen that out of the shadows of suffering have sprung the great literatures, the great paintings, the great philosophies, the great civilizations. All of them have blossomed into the light out of the shadows of suffering.

"Where a great thought is born," said one who knew by bitter experience, "there is always Gethsemane."

> *The mark of rank in nature is capacity for pain, and the anguish*
> *of the singer makes the sweetness of the strain.*

In Scotland there is a battlefield on which the Scots and their Saxon foes met in deadly conflict. A monument marks the spot; and here and there, tradition tells us, a little blue flower grows. It is called the *Flower of Culloden*. The baptism of blood, tradition avers, brought the flower into fertilization.

The choicest flowers are always "Culloden flowers." They spring only from the soil on which lifeblood of a brave heart has been spilt. CHARLES KINGSLEY

MARCH 12

Evening

The LORD made an east wind blow across the land all that day and all
that night. By morning the wind had brought the locusts. . . . Pharaoh
quickly summoned Moses and Aaron. . . . And the LORD changed the

wind to a very strong west wind, which caught up the locusts and carried
them into the Red Sea. Not a locust was left anywhere in Egypt.

EXODUS 10:13, 16, 19

In these verses we see how in ancient times, when the Lord fought for Israel against the cruel Pharaoh, it was *stormy winds* that won their deliverance. And again later, in the greatest display of His power, God struck the final blow to the proud defiance of Egypt with *stormy winds.* Yet at first it seemed that a strange and almost cruel thing was happening to Israel. They were hemmed in by a multitude of dangers: in front, a raging sea defied them; on either side, mountains cut off any hope of escape; and above them, a hurricane seemed to blow. It was as if the first deliverance had come only to hand them over to a more certain death. "The Israelites looked up, and there were the Egyptians, marching after them. They were terrified and cried out to the LORD" (Exodus 14:10).

Only when it seemed they were trapped for the enemy did the glorious triumph come. The *stormy wind* blew forward, beating back the waves. The vast multitude of Israelites marched ahead along the path of the deep sea floor—a path covered with God's protecting love. On either side were crystal walls of water, glowing in the light of the glory of the Lord, and high above them roared the thunder of the storm. And so it continued on through the night, until at dawn the next day, as the last of the Israelites set foot on shore, the work of the *stormy wind* was done.

Then Israel sang a song to the Lord of how the *stormy wind* fulfilled His word: "The enemy boasted, 'I will pursue, I will overtake them. I will divide the spoils. . . .' But you blew with your breath, and the sea covered them. They sank like lead in the mighty waters" (Exodus 15:9–10).

Someday, through His great mercy, we too will stand on "a sea of glass," holding "harps given [to us] by God." Then we will sing "the song of God's servant Moses and of the Lamb: 'Great and marvelous are your deeds, Lord God Almighty. Just and true are your ways, King of the nations'" (Revelation 15:2–3). Then we will know how the *stormy winds* have won our deliverance.

Today only questions surround your great sorrow, but then you will see how the threatening enemy was actually swept away during your stormy night of fear and grief.

Today you see only your loss, but then you will see how God used it to break the evil chains that had begun to restrain you.

Today you cower at the howling wind and the roaring thunder, but then you will see how they beat back the waves of destruction and opened your way to the peaceful Land of Promise. MARK GUY PEARSE

Though winds are wild,
And the gale unleashed,
My trusting heart still sings:
I know that they mean
No harm to me,
He rides upon their wings.

MARCH 13
Morning

That your love may abound more and more.
PHILIPPIANS 1:9

Tradition says that when they carried Saint John for the last time into the church, he lifted up his feeble hands to the listening congregation, and said *"Little children, love one another."* The words are echoing yet throughout the world.

More precious and important even than faith is heavenly love. Without it faith must ultimately wither. Many of God's most powerful workers after a time lose their power *because they lose the spirit of love.* This is the crowning grace of Christian character. *It has a thousand shades, and it is in the finer touches that its glory consists.* Every new experience of life is but a school to learn some lesson of love. Let us not try to expel our teachers. *Let us welcome them* and so learn the lesson, that they may soon pass on and leave us to make new advances.

If mountains can be removed by faith is there less power in love?
The immense arms from either side of the Forth Bridge had been completed;

slowly and steadily they had been built out; all that was now needed at the center of the mighty arch was the final riveting.

The day fixed was cold and chilly, and cold contracts metals. In spite of fires set under the iron to expand it the inch or two required, the union could not be completed and the day's program was a failure.

But the next day the sun rose bright; under its genial warmth the iron expanded, the holes came opposite each other, and the riveters had nothing to do but drive the binding bolts home.

Love unbinds others by its bonds.

> *Love through me, Love of God,*
> *There is no love in me,*
> *O Fire of love, light thou the love,*
> *That burns perpetually.*
>
> *Flow through me, Peace of God,*
> *Calm river, flow until*
> *No wind can blow, no current stir*
> *A ripple of self-will.*
>
> *Shine through me, Joy of God,*
> *Make me like Thy clear air*
> *Which Thou dost pour Thy colors thro'*
> *As though it were not there.*
>
> *O blessed Love of God,*
> *That all may taste and see*
> *How good Thou art, once more I pray:*
> *Love through me, even me.*
>
> A. W. C.

Love never faileth!

Evening

Just and true are your ways, King of the nations.
REVELATION 15:3

The following story was related by Mrs. Charles H. Spurgeon, who suffered greatly with poor health for more than twenty-five years: "At the end of a dull and dreary day, I lay resting on my couch as the night grew darker. Although my room was bright and cozy, some of the darkness outside seemed to have entered my soul and obscured its spiritual vision. In vain I tried to see the sovereign hand that I knew held mine and that guided my fog-surrounded feet along a steep and slippery path of suffering.

"With a sorrowful heart I asked, 'Why does the Lord deal with a child of His in this way? Why does He so often send such sharp and bitter pain to visit me? Why does He allow this lingering weakness to hinder the sweet service I long to render to His poor servants?'

"These impatient questions were quickly answered through a very strange language. Yet no interpreter was needed except the mindful whisper of my heart. For a while silence reigned in the little room, being broken only by the crackling of an oak log burning in the fireplace. Suddenly I heard a sweet, soft sound: a faint, yet clear, musical note, like the tender trill of a robin beneath my window.

"I asked aloud, 'What can that be? Surely no bird can be singing outside at this time of year or night.' But again came the faint, mournful notes, so sweet and melodious, yet mysterious enough to cause us to wonder. Then my friend exclaimed, 'It's coming from the log on the fire!' The fire was unshackling the imprisoned music from deep within the old oak's heart!

"Perhaps the oak had acquired this song during the days when all was well with him—when birds sang merrily on his branches, and while the soft sunlight streaked his tender leaves with gold. But he had grown old and hard since then. Ring after ring of knotty growth had sealed up his long-forgotten melody, until the fiery tongues of the flames consumed his callousness. The intense heat of the fire wrenched from him both a song and a sacrifice at once. Then I realized: when the fires of affliction draw songs of praise from us, we are indeed purified, and our God is glorified!

"Maybe some of us are like this old oak log: cold, hard, unfeeling, and never singing any melodious sounds. It is the fires burning around us that release notes of trust in God and bring cheerful compliance with His will. As I thought of this, the fire burned, and my soul found sweet comfort in the parable so strangely revealed before me.

"Yes, singing in the fire! God helping us, sometimes using the only way He can to get harmony from our hard and apathetic hearts. Then, let the furnace be 'heated seven times hotter than usual' [Daniel 3:19]."

MARCH 14
Morning

Behold, he cometh!
REVELATION 1:7 KJV

The exclamation is a striking one. The Greek word "behold" means "See; look!" It is used to quickly call attention to some striking spectacle which suddenly breaks upon the gaze—as though one should say of some great sight appearing in the heavens before all eyes, "Behold the meteor!" Suddenly in mid-heaven, without a second's warning, is staged by God the most stupendous sight upon which human eyes have ever gazed—the out-flashing, dazzling, awful splendor of the personal coming of the Lord Jesus Christ in His glory.

> *Thus in Thine arms of love, O God, I lie,*
> *Lost, and forever lost to all but Thee.*
> *My happy soul, since it hath learnt to die,*
> *Hath found new life in Thine Infinity.*

The earth beholds and thrills with the first ecstatic moment of her deliverance from the bondage of corruption into the glorious liberty of the sons of God.

The angels behold and cry, "The kingdom of the world has become the kingdom of our Lord and of his Messiah" (Revelation 11:15).

The kings and princes of the world behold and cry to the rocks and hills to fall upon them and hide them from His presence.

The Antichrist beholds and falls palsied and helpless before the breath of His mouth and the glory of His coming.

The nations of the earth behold and wail because of Him.

Behold!

Let *us* study the picture as the Scripture word-paints it. For not since the skies were stretched by the omnipotent hand of God in the ages that are past has their blue canopy been the setting for such a scene as now floods them with its glory. JAMES H. MCCONKEY

"Midnight is past," sings the sailor on the Southern Ocean; "midnight is past; the Cross begins to bend."

It is high time to awake out of sleep. Our Lord will come.

The Morning Cometh!

A shout!
A trumpet note!
A Glorious Presence in the azure sky!
A gasp,
A thrill of joy,
And we are with Him in the twinkling of an eye!
A glance,
An upward look,
Caught up to be with Christ forevermore!
The dead alive!
The living glorified!
Fulfilled are all His promises that came before!

His face!
His joy supreme
Our souls find rapture only at His feet!
Blameless!
Without a spot!
We enter into heaven's joy complete!

Strike harps,
Oh, sound His praise . . .
We know Him as we never knew before!
God's love!
God's matchless grace!
'Twill take eternity to tell while we adore!
ANNE CATHERINE WHITE

~~~~~ MARCH 14 ~~~~~
Evening

Moses approached the thick darkness where God was.
EXODUS 20:21

God still has His secrets—hidden from "the wise and learned" (Luke 10:21). Do not fear these unknown things, but be content to accept the things you cannot understand and to wait patiently. In due time He will reveal the treasures of the unknown to you—the riches of the glory of the mystery. Recognize that the mystery is simply the veil covering God's face.

Do not be afraid to enter the cloud descending on your life, for God is in it. And the other side is radiant with His glory. "Do not be surprised at the fiery ordeal that has come on you to test you as though something strange were happening to you. But rejoice inasmuch as you participate in the sufferings of Christ" (1 Peter 4:12–13). When you feel the most forsaken and lonely, God is near. He is in the darkest cloud. Forge ahead into the darkness without flinching, knowing that under the shelter of the cloud, God is waiting for you. SELECTED

Have you a cloud?
Something that is dark and full of dread;
A messenger of tempest overhead?
A something that is darkening the sky;
A something growing darker by and by;

A something that you're fearful will burst at last;
A cloud that does a deep, long shadow cast?
God's coming in that cloud.

 Have you a cloud?
It is Jehovah's triumph car: in this
He's riding to you, o'er the wide abyss.
It is the robe in which He wraps His form;
For He does dress Him with the flashing storm.
It is the veil in which He hides the light
Of His fair face, too dazzling for your sight.
God's coming in that cloud.

 Have you a cloud?
A trial that is terrible to thee?
A dark temptation threatening to see?
A loss of some dear one long your own?
A mist, a veiling, bringing the unknown?
A mystery that insubstantial seems:
A cloud between you and the sun's bright beams?
God's coming in that cloud.

 Have you a cloud?
A sickness—weak old age—distress and death?
These clouds will scatter at your last faint breath.
Fear not the clouds that hover o'er your boat,
Making the harbor's entrance woeful to float;
The cloud of death, though misty, chill and cold,
Will yet grow radiant with a fringe of gold.
 God's coming in that cloud.

A man once stood on a high peak of the Rocky Mountains watching a raging storm below. As he watched, an eagle came up through the clouds and soared away toward the sun. The water on its wings glistened in the sunlight like diamonds. If not for the storm, the eagle might have remained in the valley. In the same way, the sorrows of life cause us to rise toward God.

Morning

Married to another, even to him.
ROMANS 7:4 KJV

The most joyous moment in the life of the bride ought to be the moment when she loses her own name and self-dependence at the marriage altar, taking her husband's name instead of her own and merging her life in his. And the most blissful moment of our life ought to be that in which we, by renouncing our right to self-ownership, become the bride of Another, the Lord Jesus Christ.

In marriage the wealth of the husband is, of course, placed at the disposal of the wife. Many will recall the story of the Earl of Burleigh, which Tennyson has immortalized. Under the guise of a landscape painter, the Earl won the heart of a simple village maiden. Imagining they were going to the cottage of which he had spoken, in which they were to spend their happy wedded life, they passed one beautiful dwelling after another, until . . .

> *. . . a gateway she discerns*
> *With armorial bearings stately,*
> *And beneath the gate she turns,*
> *Sees a mansion more majestic*
> *Than all those she saw before:*
> *Many a gallant gay domestic*
> *Bows before him at the door.*
> *And they speak in gentle murmur,*
> *When they answer to his call,*
> *While he treads with footstep firmer,*
> *Leading on from hall to hall.*
> *And while now she wonders blindly,*
> *Nor the meaning can divine,*
> *Proudly turns he round and kindly,*
> *"All of this is mine and thine."*

So by the union of hearts and lives the simple village maiden became the Lady of Burleigh, and *all* her husband's wealth was *hers.*

Who shall tell of the wealth which they inherit who are truly united to Jesus?

"The incomparable riches of his grace" (Ephesians 2:7).

"The boundless riches of Christ" (Ephesians 3:8).

> *Oh, sacred union with the Perfect Mind,*
> *Transcendent bliss, which Thou alone canst give;*
> *How blest are they this Pearl of Price who find,*
> *And, dead to earth, have learnt in Thee to live.*
> *Go then, and learn this lesson of the Cross,*
> *And tread the way the saints and prophets trod:*
> *Who, counting life and self and all things loss,*
> *Have found in inward death the life of God.*
> *Give up your identity!*

~~~~~~ MARCH 15 ~~~~~~

Evening

Do not be afraid, you worm Jacob. . . . I will make you into
a threshing sledge, new and sharp, with many teeth.

ISAIAH 41:14–15

Could any two things be in greater contrast than a worm and a threshing tool with sharp teeth? A worm is delicate and is easily bruised by a stone or crushed beneath a passing wheel. Yet a threshing tool with sharp teeth can cut through rock and not be broken, leaving its mark upon the rock. And almighty God can convert one into the other. He can take an individual or a nation, who has all the weakness of a worm, and through the energizing work of His own Spirit, endow that person or nation with strength enough to make a profound mark upon the history of their time.

Therefore a "worm" may take heart. Almighty God can make us stronger than our circumstances and can turn each situation to our good. In God's strength we can make them all pay tribute to our soul. We can even take the darkest disappointment, break it open, and discover a precious jewel of grace inside. When God gives us an iron will, we can cut through difficulties just as an iron plowshare cuts through the hardest soil. As He said in the above verse, "I will make you . . ." Will He not do it? JOHN HENRY JOWETT

Christ is building His kingdom with the broken things of earth. People desire only the strong, successful, victorious, and unbroken things in life to build their kingdoms, but God is the God of the unsuccessful—the God of those who have failed. Heaven is being filled with earth's broken lives, and there is no "bruised reed" (Isaiah 42:3) that Christ cannot take and restore to a glorious place of blessing and beauty. He can take a life crushed by pain or sorrow and make it a harp whose music will be total praise. He can lift earth's saddest failure up to heaven's glory. J. R. MILLER

> *"Follow Me, and I will make you . . ."*
> *Make you speak My words with power,*
> *Make you vessels of My mercy,*
> *Make you helpful every hour.*
>
> *"Follow Me, and I will make you . . ."*
> *Make you what you cannot be—*
> *Make you loving, trustful, godly,*
> *Make you even just like Me.*
>
> L. S. P.

~~~~~~ MARCH 16 ~~~~~~

Morning

And, lo, it was the latter growth after the king's mowings.
AMOS 7:1 KJV

Our Lord is so intent on the life harvest of the saints that He Himself often mows our fields for us and takes away the things that seem to us *good* in order to give us *the best.*

Our great King Himself is far more concerned for the worker than for the work.

When your heart fails you, God sends His sunshine and the rain, and your hopes that were laid low sprout again, new growths appear—fertilized, perhaps, by your tears, perhaps by your heart's blood. Not only is the latter growth given after the King's mowing, but *because* of it. Like a grass lawn, the saints' lives become better the more they are beaten and rolled and mown. Do not think, then, that some strange thing has befallen you when you are tempted or tried. *It is by these things men live.*

There are, it may be, lives where the first growth is the worthiest, but I have seen few, and these—though beautiful—have not been strong.

The second crop of roses is the best, and *the greatest saints are those who have felt the scythe.* But *if the King is He who mows, then welcome the mowing that brings Him into the life.*

Better a bare field *with Christ* than the best harvest *without Him!*

Where He comes, Heaven's verdure springs; where He treads, earth's virtues grow.
GOD'S HIGHWAY

> *They took them all away—my toys—*
> *Not one was left;*
> *They set me here, shorn, stripped of humblest joys,*
> *Anguished, bereft.*
>
> *I wondered why. The years have flown;*
> *Unto my hand*
> *Cling weaker, sadder ones who walk alone—*
> *I understand.*
>
> ANONYMOUS

MARCH 16
Evening

For our good.
HEBREWS 12:10

In one of Ralph Conner's books he tells the story of Gwen. Gwen was an undisciplined and strong-willed girl, always accustomed to having her own way. One day she had a terrible accident that crippled her for life, leading her to become even more rebellious. Once while in a complaining mood, she was visited by a local "sky pilot," or mountaineer missionary. He told her the following parable about the canyon:

"At first there were no canyons but only the vast, open prairie. One day the Master of the prairie, walking across His great grasslands, asked the prairie, 'Where are your flowers?' The prairie responded, 'Master, I have no flower seeds.'

"The Master then spoke to the birds, and they brought seeds of every kind of flower, scattering them far and wide. Soon the prairie bloomed with crocuses, roses, yellow buttercups, wild sunflowers, and red lilies all summer long. When the Master saw the flowers, He was pleased. But He failed to see His favorites and asked the prairie, 'Where are the clematis, columbine, violets, wildflowers, ferns, and the flowering shrubs?'

"So once again He spoke to the birds, and again they brought all the seeds and spread them far and wide. But when the Master arrived, He still could not find the flowers he loved the most, and asked, 'Where are my sweetest flowers?' The prairie cried sorrowfully, 'O Master, I cannot keep the flowers. The winds sweep fiercely across me, and the sun beats down upon my breast, and they simply wither up and blow away.'

"Then the Master spoke to the lightning, and with one swift bolt, the lightning split the prairie through its heart. The prairie reeled and groaned in agony and for many days bitterly complained about its dark, jagged, and gaping wound. But the river poured its water through the chasm, bringing rich, dark soil with it.

"Once again the birds brought seeds and scattered them in the canyon. After a long time the rough rocks were adorned with soft mosses and trailing vines, and all the secluded cliffs were draped with clematis and columbine. Giant elms raised their huge limbs high into the sunlight, while at their feet small cedars and balsam firs clustered together. Everywhere violets, anemones, and maidenhair ferns grew and bloomed, until the canyon became the Master's favorite place for rest, peace, and joy."

Then the "sky pilot" said to her, "'The fruit [or "flowers"] of the Spirit [are] love, joy, peace, patience, kindness, . . . gentleness' [Galatians 5:22–23 NASB], and some of these grow only in the canyon." Gwen softly asked, "Which are the canyon flowers?" The missionary answered, "Patience, kindness, and gentleness. Yet even though love, joy, and peace may bloom in the open spaces, the blossom is never as beautiful, or the perfume as fragrant, as when they are found blooming in the canyon."

Gwen sat very still for quite some time, and then longingly said with trembling lips, "There are no flowers in my canyon—only jagged rocks." The missionary lovingly responded, "Someday they will bloom, dear Gwen. The Master will find them, and we will see them, too."

Beloved, when *you* come to your canyon, remember!

Morning

Doth the plowman plow all day to sow?
ISAIAH 28:24 KJV

Is not the plowing merely a preparation for the seed-sowing to follow and after that, for the wheat which is to feed many? *When the plowshare goes through human hearts, surely it is for something!* Someday we shall see when the ripe ears of corn appear that the plowshare had to come for a season. We thought it would kill us! And no plowshare goes through the earth but some life *is* destroyed, *but only that something better than that life may come.*

Be still, poor heart! God is effectual in working. "Let him do what is good in his eyes" (1 Samuel 3:18).

> *God will not let my field lie fallow.*
> *The plowshare is sharp, the feet of the oxen are heavy.*
> *They hurt.*
> *But I cannot stay God from His plowing.*
> *He will not let my field lie fallow.*
> KARLE WILSON BAKER

I have seen a farmer drive his plowshare through the velvet greensward, and it looked like a harsh and cruel process; but the farmer's eye foresaw the springing blades of wheat, and knew that within a few months that torn soil would laugh with a golden harvest.

Deep soul-plowing brings rich fruits of the Spirit. There are bitter mercies as well as sweet mercies; *but they are all mercies,* whether given in honey or given in wormwood. T. L. CUYLER

The iron plowshare goes over the field of the heart until the nighttime . . . down the deep furrows the angels come and sow.

~~~~ MARCH 17 ~~~~
Evening

Stay there until I tell you.
MATTHEW 2:13

I'll stay where You've put me; I will, dear Lord,
  Though I wanted so badly to go;
I was eager to march with the "rank and file,"
  Yes, I wanted to lead them, You know.
I planned to keep step to the music loud,
  To cheer when the banner unfurled,
To stand in the midst of the fight straight and proud,
  But I'll stay where You've put me.

I'll stay where You've put me; I'll work, dear Lord,
  Though the field be narrow and small,
And the ground be neglected, and stones lie thick,
  And there seems to be no life at all.
The field is Your own, only give me the seed,
  I'll sow it with never a fear;
I'll till the dry soil while I wait for the rain,
  And rejoice when the green blades appear;
I'll work where You've put me.
I'll stay where You've put me; I will, dear Lord;
  I'll bear the day's burden and heat,
Always trusting You fully; when sunset has come
  I'll lay stalks of grain at Your feet.

—— 198 ——

And then, when my earth work is ended and done,
  In the light of eternity's glow,
Life's record all closed, I surely will find
  It was better to stay than to go; I'll stay where You've put me.

O restless heart—beating against the prison bars of your circumstances and long-ing for a wider realm of usefulness—allow God to direct all your days. Patience and trust, even in the midst of the monotony of your daily routine, will be the best preparation to courageously handle the stress and strain of a greater opportunity, which God may someday send.

───～～～～～ MARCH 18 ～～～～～───

Morning

I chose you.
JOHN 15:16

M yron Niesley, California tenor, is called the highest-paid radio singer because he receives £5 for singing *one note*—the final and top one of a theme song, which others in the chorus cannot hit so perfectly.

God has *just one person to come at the right moment,* a place which no one can fill *but that person* and *at that time!*

Toil-worn I stood and said,
"O Lord, my feet have bled, My hands are sore,
I weep, my efforts vainly poor.
With fainting heart I pray of Thee,
Give some brave other, work designed for me."

But my Lord answer made,
"O child of Mine,
I have looked through space and searched through time,
There is none can do the work called thine."

Soul-sick I knelt and cried, "Let me forever hide
My little soul
From sight of Him who made me whole,
My one small spirit in the vast,
Vast throngs of like mean myriads, present, past!"

But my Lord answer made,
"O child of Mine,
I have looked through space and searched through time,
But I find no soul is like to thine!"

FRANCES BENT DILLINGHAM

Ask God if you are in His place for you.
Our life is but a little holding lent to do a mighty labor. We are one
with heaven and the stars when it is spent to do God's will.
It is possible for us to cross God's plan for our lives.

~~~~~~~~ MARCH 18 ~~~~~~~~
Evening

He answered nothing.
MARK 15:3 KJV

There is no scene in all the Bible more majestic than our Savior remaining silent before the men who were reviling Him. With one quick burst of divine power, or one fiery word of rebuke, He could have caused His accusers to be laid prostrate at His feet. Yet He answered not one word, allowing them to say and do their very worst. He stood in THE POWER OF STILLNESS—God's holy silent Lamb.

There is a place of stillness that allows God the opportunity to work for us and gives us peace. It is a stillness that ceases our scheming, self-vindication, and the search for a temporary means to an end through our own wisdom and judgment. Instead, it lets God provide an answer, through His unfailing and faithful love, to the cruel blow we have suffered.

Oh, how often we thwart God's intervention on our behalf by taking up our own cause or by striking a blow in our own defense! May God grant each of us this silent power and submissive spirit. Then once our earthly battles and strife are over, others will remember us as we now remember the morning dew, the soft light of sunrise, a peaceful evening breeze, the Lamb of Calgary, and the gentle and holy heavenly Dove.
A. B. SIMPSON

> *The day when Jesus stood alone*
> *And felt the hearts of men like stone,*
> *And knew He came but to atone—*
> *   That day "He held His peace."*
>
> *They witnessed falsely to His word,*
> *They bound Him with a cruel cord,*
> *And mockingly proclaimed Him Lord;*
> *   "But Jesus held His peace."*
>
> *They spat upon Him in the face,*
> *They dragged Him on from place to place,*
> *They heaped upon Him all disgrace;*
> *   "But Jesus held His peace."*
>
> *My friend, have you for far much less,*
> *With rage, which you called righteousness,*
> *Resented slights with great distress?*
> *   Your Savior "held His peace."*
>
> L. S. P.

I remember hearing Bishop Whipple of Minnesota, who was well known as "The Apostle of the Indians," voice these beautiful words: "For the last thirty years, I have looked for the face of Christ in the people with whom I have disagreed."

When this spirit drives us, we will be immediately protected from a feeble tolerance of others, narrow-mindedness, harsh vindictiveness, and everything else that would damage our testimony for Him who came not to destroy lives but to save them.
W. H. GRIFFITH-THOMAS

Morning

From now on, let no one cause me trouble, for I bear on my body the marks of Jesus.
GALATIANS 6:17

Do *we* carry any wound marks? Have we sought the protected areas while others met clash on clash the onset of the evil one? Has compromise robbed us of our war trophies? *Shall we not have done with such?* Someday we shall see Him face-to-face, shall see the nail prints in His hands. Shall we stand ashamed in His presence because we wear no scars of battle? DAILY COMMUNION

> *Hast thou no scar?*
> *No hidden scar on foot, or side, or hand?*
> *I hear thee sung as mighty in the land,*
> *I hear them hail thy bright ascendant star,*
> *Hast thou no scar?*
>
> *Hast thou no wound?*
> *Yet I was wounded by the archers, spent,*
> *Leaned me against a tree to die; and rent*
> *By ravening wolves that compassed me, I swooned;*
> *Hast thou no wound?*
>
> *No wound? No scar?*
> *Yet, as the Master shall the servant be,*
> *And pierced are the feet that follow Me;*
> *But thine are whole; can he have followed far*
> *Who hath no wound nor scar?*
>
> A. W. C.

Our path does not lie all the way through Beulah.

Garibaldi, the great Italian reformer of a past generation, in a fiery speech urged some thousands of Italy's young men to fight for the freedom of their homeland. One timid young fellow approached him, asking, "If I fight, Sir, what will be my reward?" Swift as a lightning flash came the uncompromising answer: "Wounds, scars, bruises, and perhaps death. But remember that through your bruises Italy will be free."

Are you not willing to endure scars in order to liberate souls?

The roughest road goes straight to the hilltop!

~~~~~~ MARCH 19 ~~~~~~

Evening

Dear friends, do not be surprised at the fiery ordeal that has come on . . . .
But rejoice inasmuch as you participate in the sufferings of Christ.
1 PETER 4:12–13

Many hours of waiting were necessary to enrich David's harp with song. And hours of waiting in the wilderness will provide us with psalms of "thanksgiving and the sound of singing" (Isaiah 51:3). The hearts of the discouraged here below will be lifted, and joy will be brought to our Father's heavenly home.

What was the preparation for Jesse's son, David, to compose songs unlike any others ever heard before on earth? It was the sinful persecution he endured at the hands of the wicked that brought forth his cries for God's help. Then David's faint hope in God's goodness blossomed into full songs of rejoicing, declaring the Lord's mighty deliverances and multiplied mercies. Every sorrow was yet another note from his harp, and every deliverance another theme of praise.

One stinging sorrow spared would have been one blessing missed and unclaimed. One difficulty or danger escaped—how great would have been our loss! The thrilling psalms where God's people today find expression for their grief or praise might never have been known.

Waiting on God and abiding in His will is to know Him in "the fellowship of his sufferings" (Philippians 3:10 KJV) and "to be conformed to the image of his Son" (Romans 8:29). Therefore if God's desire is to enlarge your capacity for spiritual understanding, do not be frightened by the greater realm of suffering that awaits you. The Lord's capacity for sympathy is greater still, for the breath of the Holy Spirit into His new creation never makes a heart hard and insensitive, but affectionate, tender, and true. ANNA SHIPTON

"I thank Christ Jesus our Lord, who has given me strength, that he considered me faithful, appointing me to his service" (1 Timothy 1:12).

MARCH 20

Morning

Grain must be ground to make bread.
ISAIAH 28:28

Be content; ye are the wheat growing in our Lord's field; and, *if* wheat, ye must go under our Lord's threshing instrument on His barn floor, and through His sieve; and through His will be bruised, as was the Prince of your salvation (Isaiah 53:10); that ye may be found good bread in your Lord's house. SAMUEL RUTHERFORD

When the wheat is carried home
And the threshing time has come,
Close the door.
When the flail is lifted high,
Like the chaff I would not fly;
At His feet, oh, let me lie,
On the floor!

All the cares that o'er me steal,
All the sorrows that I feel
Like a dart,
When my enemies prevail,
When my strength begins to fail—
'Tis the beating of the flail,
On my heart!

It becomes me to be still,
Though I cannot all His will
Understand.
I would be the purest wheat
Lying humbly at His feet,
Kissing oft the rod that beats,
In His hand!

By and by I shall be stored
In the garner of my Lord
Like a prize;
Thanking Him for every blow
That in sorrow laid me low,
But in beating made me grow
For the skies!

VOICE OF TRIUMPH

Look at God's method of producing corn, and see something of His method of producing saints.

MARCH 20
Evening

Sorrowful, yet always rejoicing.
2 CORINTHIANS 6:10

A stoic person despises the shedding of tears, but a Christian is not forbidden to weep. Yet the soul may become silent from excessive grief, just as the quivering sheep may remain quiet beneath the scissors of the shearer. Or, when the heart is at the verge of breaking beneath the waves of a trial, the sufferer may seek relief by crying out with a loud voice. *But there is something even better.*

It is said that springs of sweet, fresh water pool up amid the saltiness of the oceans, that the fairest Alpine flowers bloom in the wildest and most rugged mountain passes, and that the most magnificent psalms arose from the most profound agonies of the soul.

May it continue to be! Therefore, amid a multitude of trials, souls who love God will discover reasons for boundless, leaping joy. Even though "deep calls to deep" (Psalm 42:7), the clear cadence of the Lord's song will be heard. And during the most difficult hour that could ever enter a human life, *it will be possible* to bless the God and Father of our Lord Jesus Christ.

Have you learned this lesson yet? Not simply to endure or to choose God's will but to rejoice in it "with an inexpressible and glorious joy" (1 Peter 1:8). TRIED BY FIRE

I will be still, my bruised heart faintly murmured,
 As o'er me rolled a crushing load of woe;
My words, my cries, e'en my low moan was stifled;
 I pressed my lips; I barred the teardrop's flow.

I will be still, although I cannot see it,
 The love that bares a soul and fans pain's fire;
That takes away the last sweet drop of solace,
 Breaks the lone harp string, hides Your precious lyre.

But God is love, so I will stay me, stay me—
 We'll doubt not, Soul, we will be very still;
We'll wait till after while, when He will lift us—
 Yes, after while, when it will be His will.

And I did listen to my heart's brave promise;
 And I did quiver, struggling to be still;
And I did lift my tearless eyes to Heaven,
 Repeating ever, "Yes, Christ, have Your will."

But soon my heart spoke up from 'neath our burden,
 Rebuked my tight-drawn lips, my face so sad:
"We can do more than this, O Soul," it whispered.
 "We can be more than still, we can be glad!"

And now my heart and I are sweetly singing—
Singing without the sound of tuneful strings;
Drinking abundant waters in the desert;
Crushed, and yet soaring as on eagle's wings.
S. P. W.

MARCH 21
Morning

Completely.
Hebrews 7:25

To the uttermost.
KJV

John B. Gough, the world's greatest temperance lecturer, was given a text by his godly mother, which indeed became like buried treasure, for it lay hidden within his heart for seven long years of dissipation. It was *He is also able to save them to the uttermost that come unto God by him* (KJV).

His sins rose mountain-high before him; they seemed indelible; the past could not be undone! But he met Jesus Christ and found that His Blood availed for even him. "I have suffered," he cried, "and come out of the fire scorched and scathed with the marks upon my person and with the memory of it burnt right into my soul." He likened his life to a snowdrift that had been badly stained; no power on earth could restore its former whiteness and purity. "The scars remain! The scars remain!" he used to say with bitter self-reproaches.

Giant Yesterday pointed to the black, black past derisively; held it a threat over the poor penitent's bowed and contrite head; told in tones that sounded like thunderclaps that there was no escape.

Wounds of the soul, though healed, will ache;
The reddening scars remain

And make confession.
Lost innocence returns no more,
We are not what we were
Before transgression!

Jesus is able to save to the uttermost. Says a writer, "God paints in many colors, but He never paints so gorgeously as when He paints in white." The crimson of the sunset; the azure of the ocean; the green of the valleys; the scarlet of the poppies; the silver of the dewdrops; the gold of the gorse: these are exquisite—so perfectly beautiful, indeed, that we cannot imagine an attractive heaven without them. But in the soul of John B. Gough we feel that the Divine art is at its very best.

Forty-four years have passed away since he had that grim struggle with sin. Gough is again in America, addressing a vast audience of young men in Philadelphia.

"Young men," he cries, perhaps with a bitter memory of those seven indelible years. "Young men, keep your record clean!" He pauses—a longer pause than usual, and the audience wonders. But he regains his voice.

"Young men," he repeats, more feebly this time, "keep your record clean!" Another pause—longer than the previous one. But again he finds the power of speech.

"Young men," he cries the third time, but in a thin, wavering voice. "Young men, keep your record clean!"

He falls heavily on the platform. Devout men carry him to his burial, and make lamentation over him. His race is finished; his voyage completed; his battle won. The promise has been literally and triumphantly fulfilled. The grace that saved him has kept him *to the very last inch, of the very last yard, of the very last mile; to the very last minute, of the very last hour, of the very last day! For* "He is able also to save them *to the uttermost* that come unto God by him"! SELECTED

~~~~~~~~ MARCH 21 ~~~~~~~~

Evening

According to your faith let it be done to you.
MATTHEW 9:29

Praying through something might be defined as follows: "Praying your way into full faith; coming to the point of assurance, while still praying, that your prayer has been accepted and heard; and in advance of the event, with confident anticipation, actually becoming aware of having received what you ask."

Let us remember that no earthly circumstances can hinder the fulfillment of God's Word. We must look steadfastly at His immutable Word and not at the uncertainty of this ever-changing world. God desires for us to believe His Word without other evidence, *and then* He is ready to do for us "according to [our] faith."

> *When once His Word is past,*
> > *When He has said, "I will,"* [Hebrews 13:5]
> *The thing will come at last;*
> > *God keeps His promise still.* [2 Corinthians 1:20]

The prayers of the Pentecostal era were prayed with such simple faith that they were like cashing a check. ROBERT ANDERSON

"And God said. . . . And it was so" (Genesis 1:9).

~~~~~~ MARCH 22 ~~~~~~

Morning

They told him, "Joseph is still alive! In fact, he is ruler of all Egypt." . . . "I'm convinced! My son Joseph is still alive. I will go and see him before I die."

GENESIS 45:26, 28

There are *heartbreaks of joy in God's plan for His children.* We can no more imagine the good things He has waiting ahead for us, both in this life and in the life to come, than Jacob could have imagined his lost boy alive and ruling Egypt. *That is the sort of miracle-surprise awaiting me daily in the tingling, vibrant, throbbing life of Jesus Christ who is my life, when I let Him fulfill His will and lavish Himself and His gifts and surprises upon me;* when I let Him become all that there is of me. *What a here and hereafter He gives me,* when I can say, "To me, to live is Christ and to die is gain" (Philippians 1:21)! MESSAGES FOR THE MORNING WATCH

I have a heritage of joy
That yet I must not see;
The Hand that bled to make it mine
Is keeping it for me.
My heart is resting on His truth
Who hath made all things mine,
Who draws my captive will to Him
And makes it one with Thine!

A. L. WARING

"You came to greet him with rich blessings and placed a crown of pure gold on his head" (Psalm 21:3).

~~~~~~ MARCH 22 ~~~~~~

Evening

</div>

After forty years had passed, an angel appeared to Moses in the flames of a burning bush in the desert near Mount Sinai. . . . Then the LORD said to him, ". . . I have indeed seen the oppression of my people in Egypt. I have heard their groaning and have come down to set them free. Now come, I will send you back to Egypt."

<div align="center">

ACTS 7:30, 33–34

</div>

Forty years was a long time to wait in preparation for a great mission. Yet when God delays, He is not inactive. This is when He prepares His instruments and matures our strength. Then at the appointed time we will rise up and be equal to our task.

Even Jesus of Nazareth had thirty years of privacy, growing in wisdom before He began His work. JOHN HENRY JOWETT

God is never in a hurry. He spends years preparing those He plans to greatly use, and never thinks of the days of preparation as being too long or boring.

The most difficult ingredient of suffering is often *time*. A short, sharp pain is easily endured, but when a sorrow drags on its long and weary way year after monotonous year, returning day after day with the same dull routine of hopeless agony, the heart loses its strength. Without the grace of God, the heart is sure to sink into dismal despair.

Joseph endured a long trial, and God often has to burn the lessons he learned into the depths of our being, using the fires of prolonged pain. "He will sit as a refiner and purifier of silver" (Malachi 3:3), yet He knows the specific amount of time that will be needed. Like a true goldsmith, God stops the fire the moment He sees His image in the glowing metal.

Today we may be unable to see the final outcome of the beautiful plan that God has hidden "in the shadow of his hand" (Isaiah 49:2). It may be concealed for a very long time, but our faith may rest in the assurance that God is still seated on His throne. Because of this assurance, we can calmly await the time when, in heavenly delight, we will say, "All things [have] work[ed] together for good" (Romans 8:28 KJV).

As Joseph did, we should be more careful to focus on learning all the lessons in the school of sorrow than to focus anxious eyes toward the time of our deliverance. There is a reason behind every lesson, and when we are ready, our deliverance will definitely come. Then we will know we could never have served in our place of higher service without having been taught the very things we learned during our ordeal. God is in the process of educating us for future service and greater blessings. And if we have gained the qualities that make us ready for a throne, nothing will keep us from it once His timing is right.

Don't steal tomorrow from God's hands. Give Him time to speak to you and reveal His will. He is never late—learn to wait. SELECTED

> He never shows up late; He knows just what is best;
> Fret not yourself in vain; until He comes just rest.

Never run impulsively ahead of the Lord. Learn to await His timing—the second, minute, and hour hand must all point to the precise moment for action.

$\sim\!\sim\!\sim$ MARCH 23 $\sim\!\sim\!\sim$

Morning

God is our refuge and strength, an ever-present help in trouble.
PSALM 46:1

Constrained at the darkest hour to confess humbly that without God's help I was helpless, I vowed a vow in the forest solitude that I would confess His aid before men. A silence as of death was around me; it was midnight and I was weakened by illness, prostrated with fatigue and worn with anxiety for my white and black companions, whose fate was a mystery. In this physical and mental distress I besought God to give me back my people. Nine hours later we were exulting with rapturous joy. In full view of all was the crimson flag with the crescent and beneath its waving folds was the long-lost rear column. HENRY M. STANLEY

My horse was very lame, and my head did ache exceedingly. Now what occurred I here avow as truth—though let each man account for it as he will.

Suddenly I thought, "Cannot God heal man or beast as He will?"

Immediately my weariness and headache ceased, and my horse was no longer lame! JOHN WESLEY

~~~~~ MARCH 23 ~~~~~
Evening

Some of the plunder taken in battle they dedicated
for the repair of the temple of the LORD.
1 CHRONICLES 26:27

Great physical force is stored in the depths of the earth, in places such as coal mines. Coal was produced by the tremendous heat that burned the ancient forests. In the same way, spiritual force is stored in the depths of our being and is brought about by the very pain we cannot understand.

Someday we will see that "the plunder taken in battle" from our trials was simply preparing us to become like Great-heart in *Pilgrim's Progress*, so we too could lead our fellow pilgrims triumphantly through trials to the city of the King. But may we never forget that the source of learning to help others must be the experience of victorious suffering. Whining and complaining about our pain never does anyone any good.

Paul never carried the gloom of a cemetery around with him, but a chorus of victorious praise. The more difficult his trial, the more he trusted and rejoiced, shouting from the very altar of sacrifice. He said, "Even if I am being poured out like a drink offering on the sacrifice and service coming from your faith, I am glad and rejoice with all of you" (Philippians 2:17). Lord, help me today to draw strength from everything that comes to me! DAYS OF HEAVEN UPON EARTH

> *He placed me in a little cage,*
> *Away from gardens fair;*
> *But I must sing the sweetest songs*
> *Because He placed me there.*
> *Not beat my wings against the cage*
> *If it's my Maker's will,*
> *But raise my voice to heaven's gate*
> *And sing the louder still!*

~~~~~ MARCH 24 ~~~~~

Morning

Peace I leave with you; my peace I give you. . . . Do not let
your hearts be troubled and do not be afraid.
JOHN 14:27

The late Bishop Moule told how once, during the war, at the close of an entertainment given for men going out to the front, a young officer arose at his colonel's request to express the thanks of the men. He did so in genial words of charm and humor. Then suddenly, as if in afterthought, and in a different tone, he added: "We are soon crossing to France and to the trenches, and very possibly of course to death. Will any of our friends here tell us how to die?" There was a long, strained silence. Then the answer came. One of the singers made her way quietly forward to the front of the stage and began to sing the great *Aria from Elijah,* "O Rest in the Lord." There were few dry eyes when the song was concluded.

Here, above all else, is what each one of us needs in the battle of life: *a heart that has come to rest in God; a will fully surrendered.* That is the great secret. *That, alone, will bring us through with honor.* JAMES STEWART

When the soldiers of Napoleon were weak and discouraged on the Alpine ascent, we are told that their leader ordered: "Sound the French *Gloria*"; and the music gave the men new heart, and triumphantly they pressed forward. Beloved, whatever your cross, look up to your loving Master and sound the *Gloria!*

> *And when the fight is fierce, the warfare long,*
> *Steals on the air the distant triumph song,*
> *And hearts are brave again, and hands are strong,*
> *Alleluia!*
> *The music of the Gospel leads us Home!*

MARCH 24
Evening

Then Jacob prayed, "O God of my father Abraham, God of my father Isaac, LORD, you who said to me, 'Go back to your country and your relatives, and I will make you prosper. . . . Save me, I pray."
GENESIS 32:9, 11

There are many healthy aspects to Jacob's prayer. In some respects it could serve as a mold into which we pour our own spirits while we are being melted in the fiery furnace of sorrow.

Jacob began by quoting God's promise twice and by saying, "Who said to me" and "You have said" (v. 12). See how he has God in his grasp! God places Himself within our reach through His promises, and when we can actually say to Him, "You have said," He cannot say no. God must do as He has said.

If Jacob was so careful over his words, what great care will God take over His promises? Therefore while in prayer be sure to stand firmly on a promise of God. By doing so, you will obtain enough power to throw open the gates of heaven and to take it by force. PRACTICAL PORTIONS FOR THE PRAYER-LIFE

Jesus desires that we would be very specific in our requests, asking for something definite. "What do you want me to do for you?" (Matthew 20:32) is the question He asks everyone who comes to Him during trials and affliction. Make your requests earnestly and specifically, if you desire definite answers. It is the aimlessness of prayer that accounts for so many seemingly unanswered prayers. Be specific in your petitions. Fill out your check for something definite, and it will be cashed at the bank of heaven when it is presented in Jesus' name. *Dare to be specific with God.* SELECTED

Frances Ridley Havergal once said, "Every year I live—in fact, nearly every day—I seem to see more clearly how all the peace, happiness, and power of the Christian life hinges on one thing. That one thing is taking God at His word, believing He really means exactly what He says, and accepting the very words that reveal His goodness and grace, without substituting other words or changing the precise moods and tenses He has seen fit to use." Take Christ's Word—His promise—and Christ's sacrifice—His blood—with you to the throne of grace through prayer, and not one of heaven's blessings can be denied you. ADAM CLARKE

MARCH 25
Morning

I fill up in my flesh what is still lacking in regard to Christ's afflictions.
COLOSSIANS 1:24

The suggestion is this: *all ministry for the Master must be possessed of the sacrificial spirit of the Master.* If Paul is to help in the redemption of Rome, he must himself incarnate the death of Calvary. If he is to be a minister of Life, he must "die daily" (1 Corinthians 15:31 KJV). The spirit of Calvary is to be reincarnate in Ephesus, in Athens, in Rome . . . the sacrificial succession is to be maintained through the ages, and *we* are to *"fill up in [our] flesh what is still lacking in regard to Christ's afflictions."*

Here, then, is a principle: *the gospel of a broken heart demands the ministry of bleeding hearts. As soon as we cease to bleed, we cease to bless. When our sympathy loses its pangs, we can no longer be the servants of the Passion.* I do not know how any Christian service is to be fruitful if the servant is not primarily baptized in the spirit of a suffering compassion. *We can never heal the needs we do not feel. Tearless hearts can never be the heralds of the Passion. We must bleed if we would be the ministers of the saving blood.* We must, by our own suffering sympathies, "fill up in [our] flesh what is still lacking in regard to Christ's afflictions."

Are we in the succession? J. H. JOWETT

Ignatius said, when facing the lions in the arena, *"I am a grain of God. Let me be ground between the teeth of lions if I may thus become bread to feed God's people."* Were such martyred lives wasted? Thrown away? Is any life wasted that becomes seed-corn to produce bread for the world?

The way to make *nothing* of our lives is to be very careful of them. The way to make our lives an *eternal success* is to do with them just what Christ did with His.

Watch the opportunities to *"fill up . . . what is still lacking in regard to Christ's afflictions."* How many of us can show Him wounds that worship *Him*? SEED THOUGHTS CALENDAR

MARCH 25

Evening

Without faith it is impossible to please God, because anyone who comes to him must believe that he exists and that he rewards those who earnestly seek him.

HEBREWS 11:6

We all need faith for desperate days, and the Bible is filled with accounts of such days. Its story is told with them, its songs are inspired by them, its prophecy deals with them, and its revelation has come through them. Desperate days are the stepping-stones on the path of light. They seem to have been God's opportunity to provide our school of wisdom.

Psalm 107 is filled with stories of God's lavish love. In every story of deliverance, it was humankind coming to the point of desperation that gave God His opportunity to act. Arriving at "their wits' end" (Psalm 107:27) of desperation was the beginning of God's power.

Remember the promise made to a couple "as good as dead," that their descendants would be "as numerous as the stars in the sky and as countless as the sand on the seashore" (Hebrews 11:12). Read once again the story of the Red Sea deliverance, and the story of how "the priests who carried the ark of the covenant of the LORD stood firm on dry ground in the middle of the Jordan" (Joshua 3:17 NASB). Study once more the prayers of Asa, Jehoshaphat, and Hezekiah when they were severely troubled, not knowing what to do. Go over the history of Nehemiah, Daniel, Hosea, and Habakkuk. Stand with awe in the darkness of Gethsemane, and linger by the tomb in Joseph of Arimathea's garden through those difficult days. Call to account the witnesses of the early church, and ask the apostles to relate the story of their desperate days.

Desperation is better than despair. Remember, our faith did not create our desperate days. Faith's work is to sustain us through those days and to solve them. Yet the only alternative to desperate faith is despair. Faith holds on and prevails.

There is not a more heroic example of desperate faith than the story of the three Hebrew young men Shadrach, Meshach, and Abednego. Their situation was desperate, but they bravely answered, "If we are thrown into the blazing furnace, the God we serve is able to deliver us from it, and he will deliver us from Your Majesty's hand. But even if he does not, we want you to know, Your Majesty, that we will not serve your gods or worship the image of gold you have set up" (Daniel 3:17–18). I especially like the words "But even if he does not"!

Let me briefly mention the Garden of Gethsemane and ask you to ponder its "nevertheless." "If it be possible . . . nevertheless . . ." (Matthew 26:39 KJV). Our Lord's soul was overwhelmed by deep darkness. To trust meant experiencing anguish to the point of blood, and darkness to the very depths of hell—Nevertheless! Nevertheless!

Find a hymnal and sing your favorite hymn of desperate faith. S. CHADWICK

> When obstacles and trials seem
>   Like prison walls to be,
> I do the little I can do
>   And leave the rest to Thee.
>
> And when there seems no chance, no change,
>   From grief can set me free,
> Hope finds its strength in helplessness,
>   And calmly waits for Thee.

Morning

Leave here . . . and hide.
1 KINGS 17:3

This is not a very gratifying endorsement of Elijah. Doubtless the man's heart swelled with eagerness to start a great reformation; his mind expanded with dreams of world-empire. To flee now, when the audacious approach to the king has been made, is to contradict all accepted methods of operation. Nothing now but solitude? But God knows His plans and Elijah, his servant. There is wholesome truth here. To trust where we cannot trace is to give our God the full sovereignty that He longs for. The most formidable barrier in His dealings with His children is their self-will. "Let him do what is good in his eyes" (1 Samuel 3:18) is not resignation but triumphant faith, if we trust.

And so by the Kerith Ravine the lonely man abides. It is lost time in the judgment of the flesh-depending critics; here is a thread in the fabric of society capable of great accomplishment, doing nothing. But they who argue so fail to see what God is to do. If we weigh things in the scales of human reasoning, we shall always deal with economics and expediency; but no time is lost if God can have His way. The real truth is, that He is to come into the life of His servant to better qualify him for a more vital revelation of Himself, for with God "the worker is more than the work."

There may be many dear saints of God who doubt their saintship because their activities have been taken from them. Circumstances have closed in upon them; doors have been shut in their faces; funds for the prosecution of their work have ceased. It may be that, physically exhausted, they lie on their beds wondering why He can consent to so unreasonable a situation. Be assured of one thing: Elijah is not to remain in obscurity and inactivity for all time. Our error lies in mentally fixing our future according to present conditions. Let us arouse ourselves from this deadly coma. There is always the afterward of His gracious promising. KENNETH MACKENZIE

He knows, and loves, and cares!

"My immediate response was not to consult any human being," says Paul (Galatians 1:16), and he went away into a desert place. A desert place . . . and rest!

Evening

"Look around from where you are, north and south, to the east
and west. All the land that you see I will give to you."
GENESIS 13:14–15

No desire will ever be placed in you by the Holy Spirit unless He intends to fulfill it. So let your faith rise up and soar away to claim all the land you can discover. S. A. KEEN

Everything you can comprehend through faith's vision belongs to you. Look as far as you can, for it is all yours. All you long to be as a Christian, and all you long to do for God, are within the possibilities of faith. Then draw closer to Him, and with your Bible before you, and your soul completely open to the power of the Spirit, allow your entire being to receive the baptism of His presence. As He opens your understanding, enabling you to see His fullness, believe He has it all for you. Accept for yourself all the promises of His Word, all the desires He awakens within you, and all the possibilities of what you could become as a follower of Jesus. All the land you see is given to you.

The provision of His grace, which helps us along the way to the fulfillment of His promise, is actually tied to the inner vision God has given us. He who puts the natural instinct in the heart of a bird to fly across a continent in search of a warmer climate is too good to deceive it. Just as we are confident He placed the instinct within the bird, we can be assured He has also provided balmy breezes and springlike sun to meet it when it arrives.

And He who breathes heavenly hope into our hearts will not deceive or fail us when we press forward toward its realization. SELECTED

"They left and found things just as Jesus had told them" (Luke 22:13).

~ MARCH 27 ~

Morning

We take captive every thought.
2 CORINTHIANS 10:5

They swarmed around me like bees," the psalmist says (118:12).

Every second we get a sting from some fiery shaft, some imagination, some memory, some foreboding, some fear, some care, and God lets us get them in order that they may be destroyed and we so armed against them that they can never hurt us anymore. The only way to be armed against them is to refuse them and the source from which they come.

There is a world of truth here that most Christians have entirely overlooked. They give their spirits and hearts to the Lord, and they keep their heads to themselves. Our intellect must be sanctified by being slain and replaced by *the mind of Christ*.

The only remedy for bad thoughts is to stop thinking all our own thoughts, to be spiritually decapitated, and to be delivered from the natural mind as well as the natural heart. God will, therefore, put us to school in the difficult task of stopping thinking. We will not only try to think right, but *we will stop our thoughts* and *wait for Him to give us His mind.*

This may seem to you like annihilation, but you will come to it if you are going to enter into the deepest, sweetest, strongest life, until *you shall be afraid to think at all until God first thinks in you.*

Have you given your thoughts to God? Have you learned the meaning of that cry of David, "I hate thoughts, but thy law do I love"? (Psalm 119:113 KJV.)
A. B. SIMPSON

Each sin has its door of entrance.
Keep—that—door—closed!
Bolt it tight!
Just outside, the wild beast crouches
In the night.
Pin the bolt with a prayer,
God will fix it there.

"BEES IN AMBER" BY JOHN OXENHAM

Carelessness with thoughts is as dangerous as toying with explosives!
Bolt that door!

Evening

*I consider that our present sufferings are not worth comparing
with the glory that will be revealed in us.*
ROMANS 8:18

A remarkable event occurred recently at a wedding in England. The bridegroom, a very wealthy young man of high social standing, had been blinded by an accident at the age of ten. In spite of his blindness, he had graduated from the university with honors and had now won the heart of his beautiful bride, although he had never looked upon her face. Shortly before his marriage he underwent a new round of treatments by specialists, and the result was ready to be revealed on the day of his wedding.

The big day arrived, with all the guests and their presents. In attendance were cabinet ministers, generals, bishops, and learned men and women. The groom, dressed for the wedding but with his eyes still covered by bandages, rode to the church with his father. His famous ophthalmologist met them in the vestry of the church.

The bride entered the church on the arm of her white-haired father. She was so moved, she could hardly speak. Would the man she loved finally see her face—a face others admired but he knew only through the touch of his delicate fingertips?

As she neared the altar, while the soft strains of the wedding march floated through the church, she saw an unusual group. There before her stood the groom, his father, and the doctor. The doctor was in the process of cutting away the last bandage.

Once the bandage was removed, the groom took a step forward, yet with the trembling uncertainty of someone who is not completely awake. A beam of rose-colored light from a pane in the window above the altar fell across his face, but he did not seem to see it.

Could he see anything? Yes! Recovering in an instant his steadiness and demeanor, and with a dignity and joy never before seen on his face, he stepped forward to meet his bride. They looked into each other's eyes, and it seemed as if his gaze would never wander from her face.

"At last!" she said. "At last," he echoed solemnly, bowing his head. It was a scene with great dramatic power, as well as one of great joy. Yet as beautiful as this story is, it is but a mere suggestion of what will actually take place in heaven when Christians, who have been walking through this world of trial and sorrow, "shall see [him] face to face" (1 Corinthians 13:12). Selected

Just longing, dear Lord, for you,
Jesus, beloved and true;
Yearning and wondering when
You'll be coming back again,
Under all I say and do,
Just longing, dear Lord, for you.

Some glad day, all watching past,
You will come for me at last;
Then I'll see you, hear your voice,
Be with you, with you rejoice;
How the sweet hope thrills me through,
Sets me longing, dear Lord, for you.

MARCH 28

Morning

The potter formed it into another pot, shaping it as seemed best to him.
Jeremiah 18:4

God wants to make the very best He can of each of His children. He puts us on His wheel, and subjects us to the discipline which He deems most likely to secure our greatest blessedness and usefulness. But alas! How often He finds a marred vessel left on His hands when He desired and sought perfect beauty and strength! This is through no failure on His part, but because some bubble of vanity or grit of self-will has hindered Him.

When this has been the case, He does not cast us utterly away but puts us afresh on the wheel and "forms us into another pot." If He cannot do what He desired at first, He will still make the best of us; and the weakness of God is stronger than men. *Yield yourselves afresh to God.* Confess that you have marred His work. Humbly ask that He should make you again, as He made Jacob again and Peter and John and Mark.

There is simply no limit to the progress and development of the soul which is able to meet God with a never-faltering "Yes." *Be very prompt to obey all that He may impress upon you as being His holy will. Let the lifelike clay in the potter's hands be plastic to the Maker's touch!* DAILY DEVOTIONAL COMMENTARY

> *The potter worked at his task*
> *With patience, love and skill.*
> *A vessel, marred and broken,*
> *He altered again to his will.*
> *It was blackened, bent and old*
> *But with traces of beauty left,*
> *So he worked, this mender of pottery,*
> *To restore the charm bereft,*
> *Till at last it stood transformed*
> *And he viewed it with tender eyes,*
> *The work of his hands and love,*
> *This potter, patient and wise.*
>
> *I know a Mender of broken hearts,*
> *And of lives that are all undone;*
> *He takes them all, as they come to Him*
> *And He loves them, every one.*
> *With patience, love and skill*
> *That surpasses the knowledge of men,*
> *This Master Potter gathers the lost*
> *And restores to His image again.*
> *O Lover of folk with broken lives,*
> *O wonderful Potter Divine,*
> *I bring my soul for Thy healing touch;*
> *In me, let Thy beauty shine.*

There is no type of failure that He has not taken hold of and remade.

As soon as the priests who carry the ark of the LORD —*the*
LORD *of all the earth—set foot in the Jordan, its waters flowing
downstream will be cut off and stand up in a heap.*

JOSHUA 3:13

Who can help but admire those brave Levites! They carried the ark of the covenant right into the water, for the river was not divided until "their feet touched the water's edge" (v. 15). God had promised nothing else.

God honors faith—stubborn faith—that sees His PROMISE and looks to that alone. We can only imagine how bystanders today, watching these holy men of God march on, would say, "You will never catch me running that risk! The ark will be swept away!" Yet "the priests . . . stood on dry ground" (v. 17). We must not overlook the fact that faith on our part helps God to carry out His plans. Be willing to come to the help of the Lord.

The ark of the covenant was equipped with poles so the priests could raise it to their shoulders. So even the ark of God did not move itself but was carried. When God is the architect, men are the bricklayers and laborers. Faith assists God. It can shut the mouths of lions and quench the most destructive fire. Faith still honors God, and God honors faith. Oh, for the kind of faith that will move ahead, leaving God to fulfill His promise when He sees fit! Fellow Levites, let us shoulder our load, without looking as though we were carrying God's coffin. It is the ark of the living God! Sing as you march toward the flood! THOMAS CHAMPNESS

One of the distinguishing marks of the Holy Spirit in the New Testament church was the spirit of boldness. One of the great essential qualities of the kind of faith that will attempt great things for God and expect great things from God is holy boldness and daring. When dealing with a supernatural Being and taking things from Him that are humanly impossible, it is actually easier for us to take a lot than it is to take a little. And it is easier to stand in a place of bold trust than in a place where we cautiously and timidly cling to the shore.

Likewise sailors living a life of faith, let us launch our ships into the deep. We will find that all things are "possible with God" (Luke 18:27), and "everything is possible for one who believes" (Mark 9:23).

Today let us attempt great things for God, taking His faith to believe great things and taking His strength to accomplish them! DAYS OF HEAVEN UPON EARTH

<p style="text-align:center">~~~~~ MARCH 29 ~~~~~</p>

Morning

He who promised is faithful.
HEBREWS 10:23

Oftentimes it is difficult to see how certain promises of God are to be realized. *We have nothing to do with that whatever!* God keeps our hands off His promises quite as surely as He keeps them off His stars. If He will not let us intermeddle with His planets, He will not ask us to have anything to do with the outworking and realization of His promises. He asks that their fulfillment be left to Him; and afterwards He will challenge our own life as the witness and answer, and confirmation of all that is gracious and all that is sure in the outworking of His words of promise. JOSEPH PARKER

The One who rolls the stars along speaks all the promises.

Trust the untraceable ways of God and remember that "these are but the outer fringe of his works" (Job 26:14).

In Thy strong arms I lay me down,
So shall the work be done;
For who can work so wondrously,
As the Almighty One!

Evening

See how the flowers of the field grow.
MATTHEW 6:28

Many years ago there was a monk who needed olive oil, so he planted an olive tree sapling. After he finished planting it, he prayed, "Lord, my tree needs rain so its tender roots may drink and grow. Send gentle showers." And the Lord sent gentle showers. Then the monk prayed, "Lord, my tree needs sun. Please send it sun." And the sun shone, gilding the once-dripping clouds. "Now send frost, dear Lord, to strengthen its branches," cried the monk. And soon the little tree was covered in sparkling frost, but by evening it had died.

Then the monk sought out a brother monk in his cell and told him of his strange experience. After hearing the story, the other monk said, "I also have planted a little tree. See how it is thriving! But I entrust my tree to its God. He who made it knows better than a man like me what it needs. I gave God no constraints or conditions, except to pray, 'Lord, send what it needs—whether that be a storm or sunshine, wind, rain, or frost. You made it, and you know best what it needs.'"

Yes, leave it with Him,
The lilies all do,
*   And they grow—*
They grow in the rain,
And they grow in the dew—
*   Yes, they grow:*
They grow in the darkness, all hid in the night—
They grow in the sunshine, revealed by the light—
*   Still they grow.*
Yes, leave it with Him,
It's more dear to His heart,
*   You will know,*
Than the lilies that bloom,

Or the flowers that start
 'Neath the snow:
Whatever you need, if you seek it in prayer,
You can leave it with Him—for you are His care.
 You, you know.

SELECTED

～～～ MARCH 30 ～～～

Morning

She went up and laid him on the bed of the man of
God, then shut the door and went out.

2 KINGS 4:21

The Shunammite woman had lost her only son who had been given to her as the special gift of God. She held him dead in her arms. What could she do? She had a consecrated room where she entertained the prophet of God, and this room meant to her the very presence of God. She took up her precious burden *and she went up* there. How blessed it is to be able *to go up to the secret place of the Most High* and *to bring our troubles under the shadow of the Almighty!* This is the place of refuge where the weary, helpless, and heartbroken find relief.

"*And [she] laid him on the bed of the man of God.*" This is a beautiful picture of committal—laying our trouble, our business, our whole way over on God.

"*Commit . . . trust . . . and he will do this*" *(Psalm 37:5).*

This poor bereaved mother was laying her burden on the Lord and leaving it there. That is one of the most difficult things to do: to *leave* our burdens with the Lord after we have placed them there.

"*[She] shut the door and went out.*" The temptation is *not* to shut the door. We still see our trouble; we still handle it; we go over it again and again; we think our presence is needed, while His presence is more than sufficient. It takes faith to "*shut the door*" and go out. It takes real confidence for us to let the matter that is troubling us pass entirely *out of our* hands *into God's* hands. *In no other way can God fully work.*

The corn of wheat *must be hidden from the eyes of man if it is to bring forth fruit!*

This Shunammite woman committed her dead son entirely to God and went out, shutting the door. No wonder that she could then say when questioned regarding her son, *"Everything is all right"* (v. 26). There is no safer place in all the universe in which to leave our loved ones than in the hands of God. *No wonder that she received her dead son back to life!*

We certainly believe that there is many a son and daughter given as a special gift of God and now dead in trespasses and sins *who, if fully committed to God in definite faith, would certainly be restored and saved.*

We certainly believe, also, that in every burden, trial, or care, *which we thus fully leave with God and for which we fully trust Him, He will work above all we ask or think.*
C. H. P.

> *When thou hast shut thy door,*
> *Shut out from thee its anxious care*
> *With all its sharp temptations sore,*
> *For He is there.*
>
> *When thou hast shut thy door,*
> *Shut out from thee its pain and grief,*
> *Bereavements—pressures to the core;*
> *He gives relief.*
>
> *When thou hast shut thy door,*
> *And left all there behind that wall*
> *Of God's own care, forevermore—*
> *He takes it all.*
>
> *When thou hast shut thy door,*
> *Shut out thyself—He only in,*
> *Nothing for thee but to adore—*
> *He works within.*
>
> L. S. P.

But now, all you who light fires and provide yourselves with flaming torches,
go, walk in the light of your fires and of the torches you have set ablaze. This
is what you shall receive from my hand: You will lie down in torment.

ISAIAH 50:11

This is a solemn warning to those who walk in darkness and who try to help themselves find the light. They are described as the kindling for a fire that is surrounding itself with sparks. What does this mean?

It means that when we are in darkness, the temptation is to find our own way without trusting in the Lord and relying upon Him. Instead of allowing Him to help us, we try to help ourselves. We seek the light of the natural way and the advice of our friends. We reason out our own conclusions and thereby may be tempted to accept a path of deliverance that would not be of God at all.

The light we see may be the fires from our own kindling, or deceptive beacons leading us toward the danger of the rocks. And God will allow us to walk in the false light of those sparks, but the end will be sorrow.

Beloved, never try to get out of a dark place except in God's timing and in His way. A time of trouble and darkness is meant to teach you lessons you desperately need. Premature deliverance may circumvent God's work of grace in your life. Commit the entire situation to Him, and be willing to abide in darkness, knowing He is present.

Remember, it is better to walk in the dark with God than to walk alone in the light. *The Still Small Voice*

Stop interfering with God's plans and with His will. Touching anything of His mars the work. Moving the hands of a clock to suit you does not change the time. You may be able to rush the unfolding of some aspects of God's will, but you harm His work in the long run. You can force a rosebud open, but you spoil the flower. Leave everything to Him, without exception. "Not what I will, but what you will" (Mark 14:36). STEPHEN MERRITT

God sent me on when I would stay
('Twas cool within the wood);
I did not know the reason why.
I heard a boulder crashing by
'Cross the path where I had stood.

He had me stay when I would go;
"Your will be done," I said.
They found one day at early dawn,
Across the way I would have gone,
A serpent with a mangled head.

I ask no more the reason why,
Although I may not see
The path ahead, His way I go;
For though I know not, He does know,
And He will choose safe paths for me.

SUNDAY SCHOOL TIMES

~~~~~ MARCH 31 ~~~~~

Morning

The Spirit himself intercedes for us.
ROMANS 8:26

The highest ideal of prayer is to have the Holy Spirit pray through us. He is in us *to inspire our desires and longings, to quicken our minds and hearts,* and *giving us prayers, to pray them through us.* A great deal has been said about "praying through," and when it means to pray until we believe God, it is a most helpful and scriptural suggestion.

However, if we approach this subject of prayer from the Divine standpoint, it may be truly said that all effectual prayer is only that which the Holy Spirit *prays through us.*

In His *praying through us* He quickens and uses our individual powers of will, intellect, and affection. His action is just as natural as if it had all originated with and was carried on by ourselves, but He is the *pray-er* for we have yielded ourselves to Him by an act of the will in definite faith for His working.

Although His praying is as natural as our own would be, yet when He is the *pray-er,* there is often the consciousness of a depth and power unutterable. These are God's infinitely loving desires striving to find expression through finite and human channels. Beside, there will be the leading out in prayer for objects and persons that otherwise would have been neglected, and *such spirit of prayer will come upon us just as there is need, and may sometimes even seem to be at the most unlikely time and place.*

How limitless are the possibilities of prayer when we have such a mighty, loving Helper! *How certain we may be of the answer when He breathes the prayer through us!*

What wonderful fellowship this kind of prayer gives!

We can only realize His ideal for our prayer-life by abiding in Him and trusting Him moment by moment *to pray through us with His own mighty intercessions.* C. H .P.

Can it be that some souls are still in sins "retained" because you and I have shrunk from the travail of intercession?

~~~~~~ MARCH 31 ~~~~~~

Evening

The wind was against it.
MATTHEW 14:24

The winds of March are often cruel and blustery. And yet they typify the stormy seasons of my life. Indeed, I should be glad to have the opportunity to come to know these seasons. It is better for the rains to descend and the floods to come than to always live in the legendary land of Lotus or the lush Valley of Avalon, where the sun always shines and strong winds never blow. The storms of temptation may appear cruel, but don't they lead to a greater intensity and earnestness in my prayer life? Don't they compel me to cling to God's promises with a tighter grasp? And don't they leave me with character that is more refined?

The storms of sorrow through bereavement are intense, but they are one of the Father's ways of driving me to Himself. His purpose is to softly and tenderly speak to my heart in the secret, hidden place of His presence. There is a certain glory of the Master that can only be seen when the wind is contrary and my ship is being tossed by the waves.

Jesus Christ is not my security *against* the storms of life, but He is my perfect security *in* the storms. He has never promised me an easy passage, only a safe landing.

> Oh, set your sail to the heavenly gale,
> And then, no matter what winds prevail,
> No reef can wreck you, no calm delay;
> No mist will hinder, no storm will stay;
> Though far you wander and long you roam
> Through salt sea sprays and o'er white sea foam,
> No wind can blow but that will speed you Home.

ANNIE JOHNSON FLINT

APRIL 1

Morning

Their hearts are steadfast, trusting.
PSALM 112:7

Before my window is a beautiful branch of a tree now in full spring dress. Only a few weeks ago that same branch was loaded with ice—it seemed as if it must break! I remember one hour: it seemed it could not keep up. I expected to see it give way, but it did not break. Today it is beautiful!

There are many in this sad world who are as my bare branch was—loaded with ice. Their sorrows seem like hailstorms, and how to keep up, how to hold on, seems to be the one vital question. If one such should read about my branch, let me say to that one, "Don't break; cling for your life to the one truth, *that God has not forgotten you!* He holds the winds in His fists; and the waves that now seem as though they would swallow you up, in the hollow of His hands." You may look up and say,

Thou hast a charge no waves can wash away;
And let the storm that does Thy work
Deal with me as it may.

And so, by simple faith in God's goodness and love, you hold on, and when in the future—like the branch near my window—it shall be all spring with you, you will remember your sorrows as waters that have passed away. "Hold on! It is not always winter; spring is coming. The birds are yet to sing on the very branch loaded with ice. *Only, don't break!*"

My branch did not have a will of its own, but we have wills, and God can energize them. We must use our wills and say, "Though he slay me, yet will I hope in him" (Job 13:15) and "He never slays but to make alive."

Thus trusting, though you may bend to the blast, *you will not break; you will hold on; you will see your Spring!*

And I know not any trouble, for I have the tempest's King
To change my winter's fury to the gladness of His spring.
Blessed is the man who, when the tempest has spent its fury,
recognizes his Father's Voice in the undertone.

〜〜〜〜〜 A P R I L 1 〜〜〜〜〜

Evening

Though he slay me, yet will I hope in him.
JOB 13:15

Because I know whom I have believed.
2 TIMOTHY 1:12

I will not doubt, though all my ships at sea
Come drifting home with broken masts and sails;

I will believe the Hand that never fails,
From seeming evil works to good for me.
And though I weep because those sails are tattered,
Still will I cry, while my best hopes lie shattered:
"I trust in Thee."

I will not doubt, though all my prayers return
Unanswered from the still, white realm above;
I will believe it is an all-wise love
That has refused these things for which I yearn;
And though at times I cannot keep from grieving,
Yet the pure passion of my fixed believing
Undimmed will burn.

I will not doubt, though sorrows fall like rain,
And troubles swarm like bees about a hive.
I will believe the heights for which I strive
Are only reached by anguish and by pain;
And though I groan and writhe beneath my crosses,
Yet I will see through my severest losses
The greater gain.

I will not doubt. Well anchored is this faith,
Like some staunch ship, my soul braves every gale;
So strong its courage that it will not fail
To face the mighty unknown sea of death.
Oh, may I cry, though body leaves the spirit,
"I do not doubt," so listening worlds may hear it,
With my last breath.

An old seaman once said, "In fierce storms we must do one thing, for there is only one way to survive: we must put the ship in a certain position and keep her there." And this, dear Christian, is what you must do.

Sometimes, like Paul, you cannot see the sun or the stars to help you navigate when the storm is bearing down on you. This is when you can do only one thing, for there is only one way. Reason cannot help you, past experiences will shed no light, and even prayer will bring no consolation. Only one course remains: you must put your soul in one position and keep it there.

You must anchor yourself steadfastly upon the Lord. And then, come what may—whether wind, waves, rough seas, thunder, lightning, jagged rocks, or roaring breakers—you must lash yourself to the helm, firmly holding your confidence in God's faithfulness, His covenant promises, and His everlasting love in Christ Jesus. RICHARD FULLER

~~~~~ APRIL 2 ~~~~~
Morning

Be still, and know that I am God.
PSALM 46:10

There is immense power in stillness. A great saint once said, "All things come to him who knows how to trust and be silent." The words are pregnant with meaning. A knowledge of this fact would immensely change our ways of working. Instead of restless struggles, we would "sit down" inwardly before the Lord, and would let the Divine forces of His Spirit work out in silence the ends to which we aspire. You may not see or feel the operations of this silent force, but be assured it is always working mightily, and will work for you, if you only get your spirit still enough to be carried along by the currents of its power. HANNAH WHITALL SMITH

> *There is a stillness in the Christian's life:*
> *An inner stillness only known to him*
> *Who has so gladly laid at Jesus' feet*
> *His all, and now He reigns alone within,*
> *Master of every motion, wish, and plan.*
> *In stillness crowned, He rules supreme as King,*
> *And in that inner chamber of the heart*
> *Has made a little sanctuary within.*

There is a stillness in the Christian's life:
The corn of wheat must fall into the ground
And die, then if it die, out of that death
Life, fullest life, will blessedly abound.
It is a mystery no words can tell,
But known to those who in this stillness rest;
Something Divinely incomprehensible:
That for my nothingness, I get God's best!

Leave it all quietly with Him: failures, fears, foes, future!

APRIL 2
Evening

They looked . . . and there was the glory of the LORD appearing in the cloud.
EXODUS 16:10

You should get into the habit of looking for the silver lining of storm clouds. And once you have found it, continue to focus on it rather than the dark gray of the center. Do not yield to discouragement no matter how severely stressed or surrounded by problems you may be. A discouraged soul is in a helpless state, being neither able to "stand against the devil's schemes" (Ephesians 6:11) himself nor able to prevail in prayer for others. Flee every symptom of the deadly foe of discouragement as you would run from a snake. Never be slow to turn your back on it, unless you desire to eat the dust of bitter defeat.

Search for specific promises of God, saying aloud of each one, "This promise is *mine*." Then if you still experience feelings of doubt and discouragement, pour your heart out to God, asking Him to rebuke the Adversary who is so mercilessly harassing you.

The very instant you wholeheartedly turn away from every symptom of discouragement and lack of trust, the blessed Holy Spirit will reawaken your faith and breathe God's divine strength into your soul. Initially you may be unaware that this is happening, but as you determine to uncompromisingly *shun* every attack of even the tendency toward doubt and depression, you will quickly see the powers of darkness being turned back.

Oh, if only our eyes could see the mighty armies of strength and power that are always behind our turning away from the hosts of darkness toward God, there would be no attention given to the efforts of our cunning Foe to distress, depress, or discourage us! All the miraculous attributes of the Godhead are marshaled on the side of even the weakest believer who, in the name of Christ and in simple, childlike trust, yields himself to God and turns to Him for help and guidance. Selected

One day in autumn, while on the open prairie, I saw an eagle mortally wounded by a rifle shot. With his eyes still gleaming like small circles of light, he slowly turned his head, giving one last searching and longing look toward the sky. He had often swept those starry spaces with his wonderful wings. The beautiful sky was the home of his heart. It was the eagle's domain. It was there he had displayed his splendid strength a thousand times. In those lofty heights, he had played with the lightning and raced the wind. And now, far below his home, the eagle lay dying. He faced death because—just once—he forgot and flew too low.

My soul is that eagle. This is not its home. It must never lose its skyward look. I must keep faith, I must keep hope, I must keep courage, I must keep Christ. It would be better to crawl immediately from the battlefield than to not be brave. There is no time for my soul to retreat. Keep your skyward look, my soul; keep your skyward look!

> Keep looking up—
> The waves that roar around your feet,
> Jehovah-Jireh will defeat
>   When looking up.
>   Keep looking up—
> Though darkness seems to wrap your soul;
> The Light of Light will fill your soul
>   When looking up.
>   Keep looking up—
> When worn, distracted with the fight;
> Your Captain gives you conquering might
> When you look up.

We can never see the sunrise by looking toward the west. Japanese proverb

Morning

Say among the nations, "The LORD reigns."
PSALM 96:10

Home of our hearts, lest we forget
What our redemption meant to Thee,
Let our most reverent thought be set
Upon Thy Calvary.

A. W. C.

When Christ hung on the Cross of Calvary He was, apparently, the biggest failure the world had ever seen; for no other man had even dared to make such astounding claims as He, yet there He hung; nailed to the cross of shame, exposed to the view of a coarse, mocking crowd; cut off in early manhood; betrayed by one of His own personal friends; deserted by all of the other apostles—one of whom, after loud professions of devotion had denied Him with oaths and curses. It seemed as if that most wonderful and touching of all intercessory prayers (recorded in John 17) had never reached the Father's ear; and as if the words "Father, the hour has come. Glorify your Son" (John 17:1) were impossible of fulfillment.

Not one soul, even of those who loved the Savior best, understood Him and His lifework; therefore not one friend could really sympathize with the God-man, who, on His human side, so hungered for sympathy.

If you and I are truly following in the Master's footsteps, we too must be willing to risk apparent failure in the eyes of the world; and, harder still, must often be content to be misunderstood by our fellow-Christians. It is only when we have learned the faith and obedience which leave all consequences with God that we can know the power and deep joy contained in these words, that once sounded so terrible—"I have been crucified with Christ" (Galatians 2:20). E. A. G.

Jesus, Thou living bread,
Ground in the mills of death,

Let me by Thee be fed;
Thy servant hungereth.

Jesus, Thou choicest vine,
Nailed to the Cross of woe,
Now let Thy life Divine
Into my being flow.

Strength for the coming day
Thy Body doth impart,
Thy Blood doth cleanse away
The sins that stain my heart.

Let not my heart be cold,
Nor doubt when faith doth prove
That in my hand I hold
Thy Sacrament of love.

Jesus, be not a guest
That tarrieth but a day;
Come to my longing breast,
Come, and forever stay.

R. F. PECHEY

He reigneth! He reigneth, but let us never forget that it is from the throne on Golgotha!

APRIL 3
Evening

Glorify ye the LORD *in the fires.*
ISAIAH 24:15 KJV

Notice the little word "in"! We are to honor the Lord *in* the trial—*in* the very thing that afflicts us. And although there are examples where God did not allow His saints to even feel the fire, usually the fire causes pain.

It is precisely there, in the heat of the fire, we are to glorify Him. We do this by exercising perfect faith in His goodness and love that has permitted this trial to come upon us. Even more, we are to believe that out of the fire will arise something more worthy of praise to Him than had we never experienced it.

To go through some fires will take great faith, for little faith will fail. We must win the victory *in* the furnace. MARGARET BOTTOME

A person has only as much faith as he shows in times of trouble. The three men who were thrown into the fiery furnace came out just as they went in—*except for the ropes* that had bound them. How often God removes our shackles in the furnace of affliction!

These three men walked through the fire unhurt—their skin was not even blistered. Not only had the fire "not harmed their bodies, nor was a hair of their heads singed; their robes were not scorched, and there was no smell of fire on them" (Daniel 3:27).

This is the way Christians should come out of the furnace of fiery trials—liberated from their shackles but untouched by the flames.

"Triumphing over them in it" (Colossians 2:15 KJV).

This is the real triumph—triumphing over sickness *in* it, triumphing over death *in* dying, and triumphing over other adverse circumstances *in* them. Believe me, there is a power that can make us victors *in* the conflict.

There are heights we can reach where we can look back over the path we have come and sing our song of triumph on this side of heaven. We can cause others to regard us as rich, while we are poor, and make many rich in our poverty. We are to triumph *in it*.

Christ's triumph was *in* His humiliation. And perhaps our triumph will also be revealed through what others see as humiliation. MARGARET BOTTOME

Isn't there something captivating about the sight of a person burdened with many trials, yet who is as lighthearted as the sound of a bell? Isn't there something contagious and valiant in seeing others who are greatly tempted but are "more than conquerors" (Romans 8:37)? Isn't it heartening to see a fellow traveler whose body is broken, yet who retains the splendor of unbroken patience?

What a witness these give to the power of God's gift of grace! JOHN HENRY JOWETT

When each earthly brace falls under,
And life seems a restless sea,
Are you then a God-held wonder,
Satisfied and calm and free?

APRIL 4
Morning

Repair whatever damage is found.
2 KINGS 12:5

A God-fearing Armenian Christian was sending some merchandise to a distant city. There were no railroads in that part of the country, and as it was a valuable lot of goods, the merchant himself accompanied the caravan.

Such caravans usually camp at night, and this is an opportune time for the high-waymen, who make their living by attacking caravans, to steal unnoticed upon the campers. At the chosen time, under cover of the night, the Kurds drew near. All was strangely silent. There seemed to be no guards. But as they pressed closer, imagine their astonishment to find *high walls where walls had never stood before.* The next night they found the same impassable walls. On the third night they found the same walls, but there were breaches in them through which the robbers entered.

The captain of the marauding band was so terrified by the mystery that he woke up the Armenian, asking what it meant. He told how his band had followed intent on robbing them, how they had found the high walls around the caravan on the first and second nights; but on this night they had been able to enter through breaches. "If you will tell us the secret of all this, we will not molest you," said the captain.

The merchant himself was puzzled. "My friends," he said, "I have done nothing to have walls raised about us. All I do is pray every evening, committing myself and those with me to God. I fully trust in Him to keep me from all evil; but tonight, being very tired and sleepy, I made a rather halfhearted prayer. That must be why you were allowed to break through."

The Kurds were overcome by this testimony. Then and there they accepted the

Lord Jesus Christ as their Savior. *But the Armenian never forgot the breach in the wall of prayer.*

Have you broken your tryst with God?

~~~~~~ APRIL 4 ~~~~~~
Evening

Elisha prayed, "Open his eyes LORD, *so that he may see."*
2 KINGS 6:17

This is the prayer we need to pray for ourselves and one another: "Lord, open our eyes so we may see." We are surrounded, just as the prophet Elisha was, by God's "horses and chariots of fire" (2 Kings 6:17), waiting to transport us to places of glorious victory.

Once our eyes are opened by God, we will see all the events of our lives, whether great or small, joyful or sad, as a "chariot" for our souls. Everything that comes to us becomes a chariot the moment we treat it as such. On the other hand, even the smallest trial may become an object crushing everything in its path into misery and despair if we allow it.

The difference then becomes a choice we make. It all depends not on the events themselves but on how we view them. If we simply lie down, allowing them to roll over and crush us, they become an uncontrollable car of destruction. Yet if we climb into them, as riding in a car of victory, they become the chariots of God to triumphantly take us onward and upward. HANNAH WHITALL SMITH

There is not much the Lord can do with a crushed soul. That is why the Adversary attempts to push God's people toward despair and hopelessness over their condition or the condition of the church. It has often been said that a discouraged army enters a battle with the certainty of defeat. I recently heard a missionary say she had returned home sick and disheartened because her spirit had lost its courage, which led to the consequence of an unhealthy body.

We need to better understand these attacks of the Enemy on our spirit and how to resist them. If he can dislodge us from our proper position, he then seeks to "wear out the saints of the most High" (Daniel 7:25 KJV) through a prolonged siege, until we finally, out of sheer weakness, surrender all hope of victory.

<hr>

APRIL 5

Morning

Carrying his own cross, he went out to . . . Golgotha.
JOHN 19:17

When the two single beams were lifted from the Lord's bleeding shoulders and laid on those of the sturdy Cyrenian, Simon became what none ever had been, or ever would be, in all the history of the Lord's Passion—he became for a brief space *the substitute of Jesus!* Simon came into Jerusalem that morning, from the village home where he had been a guest, unconscious of the tragedy enacted there during the night, and was soon caught in the throng accompanying Jesus to Calvary. Through the dense excited mass of life, this heavily-built countryman forced his insistent body till he came to the edge of the procession. From this vantage point he could peer in and get sight of Jesus—could catch the weariness of His face. Was it the merest accident that Simon was taken into the heart of the tragedy? The guard looked round and saw Simon—his prominence and bulk—perhaps an unconscious sympathy growing on his face—and before Simon knew what had happened he had been dragged out from among the people and the cross was on his shoulders, and *he was walking beside Jesus to Calvary.*

O good fortune of the Cyrenian to have a stout body—to be born a countryman—to carry a kindly heart! It had won him an honor *denied to kings and conquerors.*

And none so favored as this Cyrenian, for *they journeyed together* within an iron wall—no man could interrupt or annoy—neither priest nor people; they were so close together *that the cross seemed to be on them both.* That Jesus spoke to Simon as He did to few in all His ministry, there can be little doubt, since no one could render Jesus the slightest service without being instantly repaid, and this man had succored Him in His dire extremity. What Jesus said to *His substitute,* Simon never told. But one thing is certain: in the heart of the tragedy on the way to Calvary, *Simon met Jesus.* And with what kindness Jesus must have spoken to *His cross-bearer* as they went forward together under one cross—one common disgrace! *Alone with the Redeemer* one gathers precious treasure!

For a short while *this man carried the load of wood*. In return, *Jesus carried his sin and that of his children after him;* for by the time this Gospel was given unto the world, Simon was known as the head of a distinguished Christian house—a man honored in his sons, Alexander and Rufus.

Nothing save . . . a few drops of blood on the ground remained of the great tragedy as Simon journeyed homeward that evening; but, in the meantime, *Jesus had accomplished the deliverance of the world*—and *Simon, the Cyrenian, had carried the Lord's cross!*

What a privilege!

Taken from the throng to carry another's cross—Via Dolorosa with Jesus! JOHN WATSON

~~~~~ APRIL 5 ~~~~~

Evening

Go inside and shut the door behind you and your sons.

2 KINGS 4:4

The widow and her two sons were to be alone with God. They were not dealing with the laws of nature, human government, the church, or the priesthood. Nor were they even dealing with God's great prophet, Elisha. They had to be isolated from everyone, separated from human reasoning, and removed from the natural tendencies to prejudge their circumstance. They were to be as if cast into the vast expanse of starry space, depending on God alone—in touch with the Source of miracles.

This is an ingredient in God's plan of dealing with us. We are to enter a secret chamber of isolation in prayer and faith that is very fruitful. At certain times and places, God will build a mysterious wall around us. He will take away all the supports we customarily lean upon, and will remove our ordinary ways of doing things. God will close us off to something divine, completely new and unexpected, and that cannot be understood by examining our previous circumstances. We will be in a place where we do not know what is happening, where God is cutting the cloth of our lives by a new pattern, and thus where He causes us to look to Him.

Most Christians lead a treadmill life—a life in which they can predict almost everything that will come their way. But the souls that God leads into unpredictable and special situations are isolated by Him. All they know is that God is holding them and that He is dealing in their lives. Then their expectations come from Him alone.

Like this widow, we must be detached from *outward* things and *attached inwardly to the Lord alone* in order to see His wonders. SOUL FOOD

It is through the most difficult trials that God often brings the sweetest discoveries of Himself. *Gems*

> *God sometimes shuts the door and shuts us in,*
> *That He may speak, perhaps through grief or pain,*
> *And softly, heart to heart, above the din,*
> *May tell some precious thought to us again.*

APRIL 6

Morning

In all these things we are more than conquerors.
ROMANS 8:37

This is one of the greatest chapters in the Bible. If doubt overtakes you, read it. If your sorrows have been too consuming, this chapter has a message for you. If you are weak, it will give you strength. If you are discouraged, hope will be restored by its inescapable logic. Read it often; become familiar with its truths, its reasoning process, its conclusion. Believe it. Live it. *Here is not only promised victory, but more than victory!*

How can we be "more than conquerors"? The American Indians believed that every foe tomahawked sent fresh strength into the warrior's arm. Temptation victoriously met increases our spiritual strength and equipment. It is possible not only to defeat the enemy but to capture him and make him fight in our ranks. God wants all His children *to turn the storm clouds into chariots.*

The ministry of thorns has often been a greater ministry to man than the ministry of thrones. Appropriate this truth.

Face the forces of darkness today fearlessly!

I dare not be defeated
Since Christ, my conquering King,
Has called me to the battle
Which He did surely win.
Come, Lord, and give me courage,
Thy conquering Spirit give,
Make me an overcomer,
In power within me live.

I dare not be defeated,
Just at the set of sun,
When Jesus waits to whisper,
"Well done, beloved, well done!"
Come, Lord, bend from the Glory,
On me Thy Spirit cast,
Make me an overcomer,
A victor to the last.

THE VERSES OF A PILGRIM

APRIL 6
Evening

I will stand at my watch and station myself on the ramparts;
I will look to see what he will say to me.

HABAKKUK 2:1

Without watchful expectation on our part, what is the sense in waiting on God for help? There will be no help without it. If we ever fail to receive strength and protection from Him, it is because we have not been looking for it. Heavenly help is often offered yet goes right past us. We miss it because we are not standing in the tower, carefully watching the horizon for evidence of its approach, and then are unready to throw the gates of our heart open so it may enter. The person who has no expectations and therefore fails to be on the alert will receive little help. Watch for God in the events of your life.

There is an old saying: "They who watch for the providence of God will never lack the providence of God to watch for." And we could turn the saying around as well and say, "They who never watch for the providence of God will never have the providence of God to watch for." Unless you put the water jars out when it rains, you will never collect the water.

We need to be more businesslike and use common sense with God in claiming His promises. If a man were to go to the bank several times a day, lay his check at the teller's window, and then pick it up and leave without cashing it, it would not be long before the bank would have him ordered from the premises.

People who go to the bank have a purpose in mind. They present their check, receive their cash, and then leave, having transacted real business. They do not lay their check on the counter, discuss the beauty of the signature, and point out the lovely design on it. No, they want to receive money for their check and will not be satisfied without it. These are the people who are always welcome at the bank, unlike those who simply waste the teller's time.

Unfortunately, a great many people also play at praying. They do not expect God to give them an answer, so they simply squander their prayer time. Our heavenly Father desires us to transact real business with Him in our praying. CHARLES H. SPURGEON

"Your hope will not be cut off" (Proverbs 23:18).

APRIL 7
Morning

The LORD is my shepherd.
PSALM 23:1

Who is it that is your Shepherd? The Lord! Oh, my friends, what a wonderful announcement! The Lord God of heaven and earth, and Almighty Creator of all things; He who holds the universe in His Hand as though it were a very little thing. He is your Shepherd, and has charged Himself with the care and keeping of you, as a shepherd is charged with the care and keeping of his sheep. If your hearts could really take in this thought you would never have a fear or a care again; for with such a Shepherd how could it be possible for you ever to want any good thing? HANNAH WHITALL SMITH

Come, my sheep, shadows deep fall over land and sea,
Fast the day fades away;
Come and rest with me. Come, and in my fold abide—
Dangers lurk on every side—till at last night is past;
In my fold abide.

Come, my sheep, I will keep watch the long night through.
Safe from harm and alarm,
I will shelter you. Through the night my lambs shall rest
Safe upon the Shepherd's breast, folded there free from care
Through the night shall rest.

Come, my sheep, calmly sleep sheltered in the fold,
Weary one homeward come—
Winds are blowing cold. Rest until the dawn shall break,
Then with joy my flocks shall wake; pastures new wait for you
When the dawn shall break.

DOROTHY B. POLSUE

The Shepherd is responsible for the sheep, not the sheep for the Shepherd. The worst of it is that we sometimes think we are both the Shepherd and the sheep, and that we have both to guide and follow. Happy are we when we realize that He is responsible, that He goes before, and goodness and mercy follow.

~~~~~ APRIL 7 ~~~~~

Evening

Their strength is to sit still.
ISAIAH 30:7 KJV

Inner stillness is an absolute necessity to truly knowing God. I remember learning this during a time of great crisis in my life. My entire being seemed to throb with anxiety, and the sense of need for immediate and powerful action was overwhelming. Yet the circumstances were such that I could do nothing, and the person who could have helped would not move.

For a time it seemed as if I would fall to pieces due to my inner turmoil. Then suddenly "a still small voice" (1 Kings 19:12 KJV) whispered in the depths of my soul, "Be still, and know that I am God" (Psalm 46:10). The words were spoken with power and I obeyed. I composed myself, bringing my body to complete stillness, and forced my troubled spirit into quietness. Only then, while looking up and waiting, did I know that it was God who had spoken. He was in the midst of my crisis and my helplessness, and I rested in Him.

This was an experience I would not have missed for anything. I would also say it was from the stillness that the power seemed to arise to deal with the crisis, and that very quickly brought it to a successful resolution. It was during this crisis I effectively learned that my "strength is to sit still." Hannah Whitall Smith

There is a perfect passivity that is not laziness. It is a living stillness born of trust. Quiet tension is not trust but simply *compressed anxiety*.

> *Not in the turmoil of the raging storm,*
> > *Not in the earthquake or devouring flame;*
> *But in the hush that could all fear transform,*
> > *The still, small whisper to the prophet came.*
> *O Soul, keep silence on the mount of God,*
> > *Though cares and needs throb around you like a sea;*
> *From prayers, petitions, and desires unshod,*
> > *Be still, and hear what God will say to thee.*
>
> *All fellowship has interludes of rest,*
> > *New strength maturing in each level of power;*
> *The sweetest Alleluias of the blest*
> > *Are silent, for the space of half an hour.*
>
> *O rest, in utter quietude of soul,*
> > *Abandon words, leave prayer and praise awhile;*

Let your whole being, hushed in His control,
Learn the full meaning of His voice and smile.

Not as an athlete wrestling for a crown,
Not taking Heaven by violence of will;
But with your Father as a child sit down,
And know the bliss that follows His "Be Still!"

MARY ROWLES JARVIS

〜〜〜〜〜〜　 APRIL 8 　〜〜〜〜〜〜

Morning

He was oppressed and afflicted.
ISAIAH 53:7

Christ was *chosen out of the people,* that He might know our wants and sympathize with us. I believe some of the rich have no notion whatever of what the distress of the poor is. They have no idea of what it is to labor for their daily bread. They have a very faint conception of what a rise in the price of bread means; they do not *know* anything about it. And when we put men in power who never were of the people, they do not understand the art of governing us. But our great and glorious Jesus Christ is one *chosen out of the people,* and therefore He knows our wants.

Jesus suffered *temptation and pain* before us; our *sicknesses* He bore; *weariness*—He has endured it, for weary He sat by the well; *poverty*—He knows it, for sometimes He had no bread to eat save that bread of which the world knows nothing; *to be house-less*—He knew that, too, for the foxes had holes and the birds of the air had nests, but He had nowhere to lay His head.

My fellow-Christian, there is no place where thou canst go, where Christ has not been before thee—sinful places alone excepted. *He hath been before thee;* He hath smoothed the way; He hath entered the grave, that He might make the tomb the royal bedchamber of the ransomed race, the closet where they lay aside the garments of labor to put on the vestments of eternal rest.

In all places whithersoever we go, the Angel of the covenant has been our forerun-
ner. Each burden we have to carry has once been laid on the shoulders of Immanuel.

His way was much rougher and darker than mine;
Did Christ my Lord suffer and shall I repine?

Dear fellow-traveler, take courage! Christ has consecrated the road. CHARLES H.
SPURGEON

And is Thy spotless life on earth to end
Ere Thy young manhood has but scarce begun?
Will not Thy Father heaven's guardians send?
Thou art His Son.

Is there no other way to save mankind
Without Thine agony and utter loss?
Is there no road which Heavenly Love may find
Beside the Cross?

There is no path His weary feet may know
But that which leads Him to the shameful tree;
That Great Forgiving Love will even go
To Calvary.

"NO OTHER ROAD" BY E. LILLIAN LOWTHER

APRIL 8
Evening

That is why, for Christ's sake, I delight in weaknesses, in insults, in hardships,
in persecutions, in difficulties. For when I am weak, then I am strong.

2 CORINTHIANS 12:10

The literal translation of this verse adds a startling emphasis to it, allowing it
to speak for itself with power we have probably never realized. It is as follows:
"Therefore I take pleasure in being without strength, being insulted, experiencing

emergencies, and being chased and forced into a corner for Christ's sake; for when I am without strength, I am *dynamite*."

The secret of knowing God's complete sufficiency is in coming to the end of everything in ourselves and our circumstances. Once we reach this point, we will stop seeking sympathy for our difficult situation or ill treatment, because we will recognize these things as the necessary conditions for blessings. We will then turn from our circumstances to God, realizing they are the evidence of Him working in our lives. A. B. Simpson

George Matheson, the well-known blind preacher of Scotland, once said, "My dear God, I have never thanked You for my thorns. I have thanked You a thousand times for my roses but not once for my thorns. I have always looked forward to the place where I will be rewarded for my cross, but I have never thought of my cross as a present glory itself.

"Teach me, O Lord, to glory in my cross. Teach me the value of my thorns. Show me how I have climbed to You through the path of pain. Show me it is through my tears I have seen my rainbows."

> *Alas for him who never sees*
> *The stars shine through the cypress trees.*

~~~~~~~~~~ APRIL 9 ~~~~~~~~~~

Morning

> *By reason of breakings they purify themselves.*
> JOB 41:25 KJV

Do you know the lovely fact about the opal: that, in the first place, it is made of desert dust, sand and silica, and owes its beauty and preciousness to a defect? It is a stone with a broken heart. It is full of minute fissures, which admit air, and the air refracts the light. Hence, its lovely hues and that sweet "lamp of fire" that ever burns at its heart, for the breath of the Lord is in it. You are only conscious of the cracks and desert sand, but so He makes His precious opals.

We must be broken in ourselves before we can give back the lovely hues of His light, and the lamp of the Temple can burn in us and never go out. ELLICE HOPKINS

> *Then hush! oh, hush! for the Father knows what thou knowest not,*
> *The need and the thorn and the shadow linked with the fairest lot;*
> *Knows the wisest exemption from many an unseen snare,*
> *Knows what will keep thee nearest, knows what thou could'st not bear.*
>
> *Hush! oh, hush! for the Father portioneth as He will,*
> *To all His beloved children, and shall they not be still?*
> *Is not His will the wisest, is not His choice the best?*
> *And in perfect acquiescence is there not perfect rest?*
>
> *Hush! oh, hush! for the Father, whose ways are true and just,*
> *Knoweth and careth and loveth, and waits for thy perfect trust;*
> *The cup He is slowly filling shall soon be full to the brim,*
> *And infinite compensations forever be found in Him.*
>
> FRANCES RIDLEY HAVERGAL

APRIL 9
Evening

> *Everything is against me!*
> GENESIS 42:36

> *All things God works for the good of those who love him.*
> ROMANS 8:28

Many people are lacking when its comes to power. But how is power produced? The other day, my friend and I were passing by the power plant that produces electricity for the streetcars. We heard the hum and roar of the countless wheels of the turbines, and I asked my friend, "How is the power produced?" He replied, "It simply is generated by the turning of those wheels and the friction they create. The rubbing produces the electric current."

In a similar way, when God desires to create more power in your life, He creates more friction. He uses this pressure to generate spiritual power. Some people cannot handle it, and run from the pressure instead of receiving the power and using it to rise above the painful experience that produced it.

Opposition is essential to maintaining true balance between forces. It is the centripetal and centrifugal forces acting in opposition to each other that keep our planet in the proper orbit. The propelling action coupled with the repelling counteraction keep the earth in orbit around the sun instead of flinging it into space and a path of certain destruction.

God guides our lives in the same way. It is not enough to have only a propelling force. We need an equal repelling force, so He holds us back through the testing ordeals of life. The pressures of temptations and trials and all the things that seem to be against us further our progress and strengthen our foundation.

Let us thank Him for both the weights and the wings He produces. And realizing we are divinely propelled, let us press on with faith and patience in our high and heavenly calling. A. B. SIMPSON

In a factory building there are wheels and gearings,
There are cranks, pulleys, belts either tight or slack—
Some are whirling swiftly, some are turning slowly,
Some are thrusting forward, some are pulling back;
Some are smooth and silent, some are rough and noisy,
Pounding, rattling, clanking, moving with a jerk;

In a wild confusion in a seeming chaos,
Lifting, pushing, driving—but they do their work.
From the mightiest lever to the smallest cog or gear,
All things move together for the purpose planned;
And behind the working is a mind controlling,
And a force directing, and a guiding hand.

So all things are working for the Lord's beloved;
Some things might be hurtful if alone they stood;
Some might seem to hinder; some might draw us backward;
But they work together, and they work for good,
All the thwarted longings, all the stern denials,
All the contradictions, hard to understand.
And the force that holds them, speeds them and retards them,
Stops and starts and guides them—is our Father's hand.

ANNIE JOHNSON FLINT

APRIL 10
Morning

Be filled with the Spirit.
EPHESIANS 5:18

General Gordon regretted that no one had told him when he was a young man that there was a Holy Spirit which he could possess and which could possess him. The knowledge would have saved him weakness, and sorrow, and loss. But when the later loneliness came, Gordon knew the inner strengthening of the Spirit. A power not his own came to his help. He was "strengthened with all power" (Colossians 1:11).

This is the apostle's sense of the magnitude of the Spirit. There is nothing we can need at any time of pressure, whether of duty or of danger, of temptation or of anxiety, but the Divine Ally will make Himself the resource of the soul to meet and endure the strain.

The apostle urges *that the utmost room should be made for the Spirit; that a man possess the Divine gift in its utmost measure.* He seems to suggest that there are degrees of possession; there are measurements we make, limitations we impose, and in his eager way he urges *that we make the utmost room for the Spirit's fullness.* Do not go in for small measures; do not restrict your allowance. The gift of the Spirit is not on a rationing basis. Do not confine yourself to mean and petty degrees of the Spirit. "Be filled with the Spirit." There is no surfeit here, nor need there be any restriction. "THE LIFE OF A CHRISTIAN" BY JOHN MACBEATH

> *There are deep things of God. Push out from shore,*
> *Hast thou found much? Give thanks and look for more.*
> *Dost fear the generous Giver to offend?*
> *Then know His store of bounty hath no end.*
> *He doth not need to be implored or teased;*
> *The more we take the better He is pleased.*

Beside the common inheritance of the land, there are some special possessions. A. B. SIMPSON

"Have ye received the Holy Ghost since ye believed?" (Acts 19:2 KJV)

<hr>

APRIL 10
Evening

Tell me what charges you have against me.
JOB 10:2

O tested soul, perhaps the Lord is sending you through this trial to develop your gifts. You have some gifts that would never have been discovered if not for trials. Do you not know that your faith never appears as great in the warm summer weather as it does during a cold winter? Your love is all too often like a firefly, showing very little light except when surrounded by darkness. And hope is like the stars—unseen in the sunshine of prosperity and only discovered during a night of adversity. Afflictions are often the dark settings God uses to mount the jewels of His children's gifts, causing them to shine even brighter.

Wasn't it just a short time ago that on your knees you prayed, "Lord, I seem to have no faith. Please show me that I do"? Wasn't your prayer, even though you may not have realized it at the time, actually asking for trials? For how can you know if you have faith, until your faith is exercised? You can depend upon the fact that God often sends trials so our gifts may be discovered and so we may be certain of their existence. And there is more than just discovering our gifts—we experience *real growth in grace* as another result of our trials being sanctified by Him.

God trains His soldiers not in tents of ease and luxury but by causing them to endure lengthy marches and difficult service. He makes them wade across streams, swim through rivers, climb mountains, and walk many tiring miles with heavy backpacks.

Dear Christian, could this not account for the troubles you are now experiencing? Could this not be the reason He is dealing with you? CHARLES H. SPURGEON

Being left alone by Satan is not evidence of being blessed.

<hr>

APRIL 11

Morning

Instead of the thornbush will grow the juniper, and instead of briers the myrtle will grow. This will be for the LORD's renown, for an everlasting sign, that will endure forever.

ISAIAH 55:13

At the Jerusalem Conference on Good Friday we were out on the Mount of Olives, and our hearts were deeply and strangely moved as we thought about *His* going out of the city yonder, up the hillside, to die. I said to myself, "I would like to follow in His train, and catch the same passion and the same vision." As the meeting was closing I thought, "I will take something by which to remember this hour." I leaned over to pluck a flower, one of the flowers that bloom in lovely profusion across the hillsides of Palestine. As I was about to pick my wildflower, an inner voice said, "No, not the wild-flower; here is the thornbush yonder; take a piece of that." It was the thornbush from which the crown of thorns was taken, and crushed upon the brow of Jesus. I protested, "The thornbush is not beautiful, it is ugly; I would rather have the flower," and I again leaned over to pick my flower. The voice was more imperious this time and said, "No, not the flower, but the thornbush; there is something in the thornbush you do not see now; take it!"

Rather reluctantly I turned away from the wildflower and plucked a piece from the thornbush and put it in the folds of my Bible. No, deeper; I put it within the folds of my heart and wore it there.

Weeks went by—months. One day I chanced to look at my thornbush I had worn within my heart, and to my amazement I found it was all abloom! The Rose of Sharon was there in lovely profusion. There was something else in the thornbush I had not seen.

From thy brier, dear heart, shall blow a rose for others.

To some people there comes this cross, the *absence* of the Cross. There is always the shadow of the Cross. Suppose God took it away, what then?

> *And shall there be no cross for me*
> *In all this life of mine?*
> *Shall mine be all a flowery path*
> *And all the thorns be Thine?*

APRIL 11
Evening

> *What I tell you in the dark, speak in the daylight; what is*
> *whispered in your ear, proclaim from the roofs.*
> MATTHEW 10:27

Our Lord is constantly taking us into the dark in order to tell us something. It may be the darkness of a home where bereavement has drawn the blinds; the darkness of a lonely and desolate life, in which some illness has cut us off from the light and the activity of life; or the darkness of some crushing sorrow and disappointment.

It is there He tells us His secrets—great and wonderful, eternal and infinite. He causes our eyes, blinded by the glare of things on earth, to behold the heavenly constellations. And our ears suddenly detect even the whisper of His voice, which has been so often drowned out by the turmoil of earth's loud cries.

Yet these revelations always come with a corresponding responsibility: "What I tell you . . . *speak* in the daylight . . . *proclaim* from the roofs." We are not to linger in the darkness or stay in the closet. Soon we will be summoned to take our position in the turmoil and the storms of life. And when that moment comes, we are to *speak* and *proclaim* what we have learned.

This gives new meaning to suffering, the saddest part of which is often the apparent feeling of uselessness it causes. We tend to think, "How useless I am! What am I doing that is making a difference for others? Why is the 'expensive perfume' (John 12:3) of my soul being wasted?" These are the desperate cries of the sufferer, but God has a purpose in all of it. He takes His children to higher levels of fellowship so they may hear Him speaking "face to face, as one speaks to a friend" (Exodus 33:11), and then deliver the message to those at the foot of the mountain. Were the forty days Moses spent on the mountain wasted? What about the time Elijah spent at Mount Horeb or the years Paul spent in Arabia?

There is no shortcut to a life of faith, which is an absolute necessity for a holy and victorious life. We must have periods of lonely meditation and fellowship with God. Our souls must have times of fellowship with Him on the mountain and experience valleys of quiet rest in the shadow of a great rock. We must spend some nights beneath the stars, when darkness has covered the things of earth, silenced the noise of human life, and expanded our view, revealing the infinite and the eternal. All these are as absolutely essential as food is for our bodies.

In this way alone can the sense of God's presence become the unwavering possession of our souls, enabling us to continually say, as the psalmist once wrote, "You are near, LORD" (Psalm 119:151). F. B. MEYER

Some hearts, like evening primroses, open more beautifully in the shadows of life.

〰〰〰   APRIL 12   〰〰〰

Morning

If you had been here.
JOHN 11:21

If only my circumstances and my environment were altered . . .
  "*If* only So-and-So were not trying to live with . . .
  "*If* only I had the opportunities, the advantages, that other people have . . .

"*If* only that insurmountable difficulty, that sorrow, that trouble, could be moved out of my life; then how different things would be! And how different I should be."

Ah, dear friend, you are not the only one who has had such thoughts. No less a person than Paul the Apostle besought the Lord three times that the thorn in the flesh might depart from him; *and yet, it was allowed to remain.*

A certain gentleman had a garden which might have been very beautiful had it not been disfigured by an immense boulder which reached far under the soil. He tried to blast it out with dynamite, but in the attempt only shattered the windows of the house. Being very self-willed he used without success one harsh method after another to get rid of the disfigurement until finally he died of worry and blighted hopes.

The heir, a man who *not only had common sense but used it,* soon perceived the hopelessness of striving to budge the boulder and therefore set to work to convert it into a rockery, which he covered with frescoes, flowers, ferns, and vines. It soon came about that the visitors to the garden commented on its unsurpassed beauty, and the owner could never quite decide which gave him the greater happiness—the harmonious aspect of his garden, or the success in adapting himself to the thing that was too deep to move.

So the unsightly boulder, which could not be removed, proved to be the most valuable asset in that garden *when dealt with by one who knew how to turn its very defects to account.* SELECTED

God often plants His flowers among rough rocks!

<hr>

APRIL 12

Evening

Jesus, full of the Holy Spirit, left the Jordan and was led by the Spirit into the wilderness, where for forty days he was tempted by the devil.
LUKE 4:1–2

Jesus was filled with the Holy Spirit and yet was tempted. The strongest force of temptation often comes upon a person when he is closest to God. Someone once said, "The Devil aims high." In fact, he caused one disciple to say he did not even know Christ.

Why is it that very few people have had as great a conflict with the Devil as Martin Luther had? It is because Martin Luther was shaking the very kingdom of hell itself. And remember the tremendous struggles John Bunyan had!

When a person has the fullness of the Spirit of God, he will experience great conflicts with the Tempter. God allows temptation because it does for us what storms do for oak trees, rooting us deeper, and it does for us what heat does for paint on porcelain, giving us long-lasting endurance.

You will never fully realize the level of strength of your grasp on Christ, or His grasp on you, until the Devil uses all his force to attract you to himself. It is then you will feel the tug of Christ's right hand. SELECTED

Extraordinary afflictions are not always the punishment of extraordinary sins but are sometimes the trials resulting from God's extraordinary gifts. God uses many sharp-cutting instruments, and polishes His jewels with files that are rough. And those saints He especially loves, and desires to make shine the most brilliantly, will often feel His tools upon them. R. LEIGHTON

I willingly bear witness to the fact that I owe more to my Lord's fire, hammer, and file than to anything else in His workshop. Sometimes I wonder if I have ever learned anything except at the end of God's rod. When my classroom is darkest, I see best. CHARLES H. SPURGEON

~~~~~~~ APRIL 13 ~~~~~~~

Morning

He has risen!
MARK 16:6

Arise! for He is risen today;
And shine, for He is glorified!
Put on thy beautiful array,
And keep perpetual Eastertide.

A little lad was gazing intently at the picture in the art store window: the store was displaying a notable picture of the crucifixion. A gentleman approached, stopped, and looked. The boy, seeing his interest, said: "That's Jesus." The man made no reply, and the lad continued: "Them's Roman soldiers." And, after a moment: "They killed Him."

"Where did you learn that?" asked the man.

"In the Mission Sunday school," was the reply.

The man turned and walked thoughtfully away. He had not gone far when he heard a youthful voice calling: "Say, Mister," and quickly the little street lad caught up with him. "Say, Mister," he repeated, "I wanted to tell you that He rose again."

That message, which was nearly forgotten by the boy, is the message which has been coming down through the ages. It is the Easter message—the story of the eternal triumph of life over death, the promise and pledge of man's immortality.

The grave to Him was not a terminus!

This is the day of glad tidings! Go quickly, and tell the message! He has risen! Hallelujah! Christ has risen! Hades could not hold Him! Corruption could not devour Him! "I am the Living One; I was dead, and now look, I am alive for ever and ever! And I hold the keys of death and Hades" (Revelation 1:18). Blessed be God! Jesus lives to die no more! Go quickly, and tell everywhere the glad news!

> *And I think the Shining Ones marvel much*
> *As they gaze from the world above,*
> *To see how slowly we spread the news*
> *Of that Sacrifice of love.*

There is, to my mind, a natural sequence in one of the accounts of that first Easter morning, as beautiful as it is suggestive. It is the story of the women who hastened to the sepulcher, and it says: *"They came unto the sepulcher at the rising of the sun"* (Mark 16:2 KJV).

The glory of Easter morn is the sacrificial red on the morning sky!

Evening

*The hand of the LORD was on me there, and he said to me, "Get
up and go out to the plain, and there I will speak to you."*

EZEKIEL 3:22

Have you ever heard of anyone being greatly used by Christ who did not experience a special time of waiting, or a complete upset of his plans at first? From the apostle Paul's being sent into the Arabian wilderness for three years—during which time he must have been overflowing with the Good News—down to the present day, it seems those who will be used will have a time of waiting. Have you been looking forward to *telling* about trusting Jesus, but instead He is asking you to *show* what trust is, by waiting?

My own experience is far less severe than Paul's but reveals the same principle. Once when I thought the door was being thrown open for me to enter the literary field with a great opportunity, it was just as quickly shut. My doctor stepped in and simply said, "Never! You must choose between writing and living, for you cannot do both." The year was 1860, and I did not come out of my shell of isolation with my book *Ministry of Song* until 1869. By then I saw the distinct wisdom of having been kept waiting for nine years in the shade.

God's love is unchangeable, and He is just as loving even when we do not see or feel it. And His love and His sovereignty are equal and universal. Therefore He often withholds our enjoyment and awareness of our progress, because He knows best what will actually ripen and further His work in us. FRANCES RIDLEY HAVERGAL

> *I laid it down in silence,*
>   *This work of mine,*
> *And took what had been sent me—*
>   *A resting time.*
> *The Master's voice had called me*
>   *To rest apart;*
> *"Apart with Jesus only,"*
>   *Echoed my heart.*

I took the rest and stillness
    From His own hand,
And felt this present illness
    Was what He planned.
How often we choose labor,
    When He says "Rest"—
Our ways are blind and crooked;
    His way is best.

Work He Himself has given,
    He will complete.
There may be other errands
    For tired feet;
There may be other duties
    For tired hands,
The present, is obedience
    To His commands.
There is a blessed resting
    In lying still,
In letting His hand mold us,
    Just as He will.
His work must be completed.
    His lesson set;
He is the Master Workman:
    Do not forget!

It is not only "working."
    We must be trained;
And Jesus "learned" obedience,
    Through suffering gained.
For us, His yoke is easy,
    His burden light.
His discipline most needful,
    And all is right.

We are to be His servants;
We never choose
If this tool or if that one
Our hands will use.
In working or in waiting
May we fulfill
Not ours at all, but only
The Master's will!

SELECTED

God provides resting places as well as working places. So rest and be thankful when He brings you, tired and weary, to streams along the way.

APRIL 14

Morning

Be strong in the grace that is in Christ Jesus. . . . Join with
me in suffering, like a good soldier of Christ Jesus.

2 TIMOTHY 2:1, 3

The post of honor in war is so called because it is attended by difficulties and dangers to which but few are equal; yet generals usually allot these hard services to their favorites and friends, who on their part eagerly take them as tokens of favor and marks of confidence.

Should we not, therefore, account it an honor and a privilege when the Captain of our salvation assigns us a difficult post, since He can and does inspire His soldiers, which no earthly commander can, with wisdom, courage, and strength suitable to their situation?

Listen to Ignatius shouting as the lion's teeth tear his flesh, "Now I begin to be a Christian!"

The Christian's badge of honor here has ever been the Cross.

No church or movement can survive unless it is ready to be crucified. BISHOP OF WINCHESTER

If I did not see that the Lord kept watch over the ship, I should long since have abandoned the helm. But I see Him! through the storm, strengthening the tackling, handling the yards, spreading the sails—aye more, commanding the very winds! Should *I* not be a coward if I abandoned *my* post? Let Him govern, let Him carry us forward, let Him hasten or delay, *we will fear nothing!* MARTIN LUTHER

> *For us, swords drawn, up to the gate of heaven:*
> *Oh, may no coward spirit seek to leaven*
> *The warrior code, the calling that is ours!*
> *Forbid that we should sheathe our sword in flowers!*
>
> *Captain beloved, battle wounds were Thine,*
> *Let me not wonder if some hurt be mine.*
> *Rather, O Lord, let my deep wonder be*
> *That I may share a battle wound with Thee.*
>
> GOLD CORD

APRIL 14

Evening

> *The LORD himself will come down from heaven, with a loud command,*
> *with the voice of the archangel and with the trumpet call of God, and*
> *the dead in Christ will rise first. After that, we who are still alive and*
> *are left will be caught up together with them in the clouds to meet*
> *the LORD in the air. And so we will be with the LORD forever.*
> 1 THESSALONIANS 4:16–17

It was "very early in the morning" (Luke 24:1), "while it was still dark" (John 20:1), that Jesus rose from the dead. Only the morning star, not the sun, shone down upon His tomb as it opened. Jerusalem's shadows had not yet retreated, and its citizens were still asleep. Yes, it was still night, during the hours of darkness and sleep, when He arose, but His rising did not break the slumbering of the city.

And it will be during the darkness of the early morning, while only the morning star is shining, that Christ's body—His church—will arise. Like Him, His saints will awake while the children of the night and darkness are still sleeping their slumber of death. Upon rising, the saints will disturb no one, and the world will not hear the voice that summons them. As quietly as Jesus has laid them to rest—each in their own silent grave, like children held in the arms of their mothers—He will just as quietly and gently awake them when the hour arrives. To each will come the life-giving words, "let those who dwell in the dust, wake up and shout for joy" (Isaiah 26:19). Into their graves the earliest ray of glory will find its way. The saints will soak up the first light of morning, while the clouds of the eastern sky will give only the faintest hints of the uprising. The gentle fragrance of the morning, along with its soothing stillness, invigorating freshness, sweet loneliness, and quiet purity—all so solemn and yet so full of hope—will be theirs.

Oh, how great the contrast between these blessings and the dark night through which they have just passed! Oh, how great the contrast between these blessings and the graves from which they have been freed! They will shake off the dirt of earth that once held them, flinging mortality aside, and will rise with glorified bodies "to meet the Lord in the air." The light of "the bright Morning Star" (Revelation 22:16) will guide them upward along a brand-new path. The beams of that Star of the Morning will, like the star of Bethlehem, direct them to the presence of the King. "Weeping may stay for the night, but rejoicing comes in the morning" (Psalm 30:5).

Horatius Bonar

> While the hosts cry Hosanna, from heaven descending,
>   With glorified saints and the angels attending,
> With grace on His brow, like a halo of glory,
>   Will Jesus receive His own.

"'I am coming soon.' Amen. Come, Lord Jesus" (Revelation 22:20).

A soldier once said, "When I die, do not play taps over my grave. Instead, play reveille, the morning call, the summons to arise."

Morning

Though the fig tree does not bud and there are no grapes on the
vines, though the olive crop fails and the fields produce no food,
though there are no sheep in the pen and no cattle in the stalls, yet I
will rejoice in the LORD, I will be joyful in God my Savior.
HABAKKUK 3:17–18

How irrational it seems! We, with whom God hath dealt bountifully, can understand praising Him, but we should have the greatest respect for a man, who under these circumstances would not repine. To bring it closer home than the time of Habakkuk, translate all this into current experience. Instead of flocks and herds, use profits; instead of figs and olives, read credit balances; for husbandry and its terms, use business and its terms; for flocks and stalls, substitute bank balances and securities; for Chaldean invasion, the economic blizzard which is sweeping through the world—and then see where you stand!

Although there shall be no balances and securities, and all dividends shall be passed, and though I be reduced to utter penury, yet will I rejoice in the Lord!

You say that is impossible! Of course, apart from some supernatural aid he could not have done it, nor can we. Habakkuk learned that life cannot be a solo affair: it is a duet. If life were a solo, it would mean a tragic breakdown when the high notes must be reached, or the low ones melodiously sounded. A duet means harmony—*human life linked on to Divine purpose and power.* Habakkuk's experience shows that *you have lost nothing if you have not lost God.* J. STUART HOLDEN

Pilgrim, look up!

The road is dusty; the journey is long. Look up! *Look up in the early morning* when the sun comes peeping over the horizon, out of the shadows of the night. Look up *in the noontide* when the resting-spot is still afar in the distance. Look up *when you see the evening star. Look up! There shines the City!*

Evening

I trust in your word.
PSALM 119:42

The strength of our faith is in direct proportion to our level of belief that God will do exactly what He has promised. Faith has nothing to do with feelings, impressions, outward appearances, nor the probability or improbability of an event. If we try to couple these things with faith, we are no longer resting on the Word of God, because faith is not dependent on them. *Faith rests on the pure Word of God alone.* And when we take Him at His Word, our hearts are at peace.

God delights in causing us to exercise our faith. He does so to bless us individually, to bless the church at large, and as a witness to unbelievers. Yet we tend to retreat from the exercising of our faith instead of welcoming it. When trials come, our response should be, "My heavenly Father has placed this cup of trials into my hands so I may later have something pleasant."

Trials are the food of faith. Oh, may we leave ourselves in the hands of our heavenly Father! It is the joy of His heart to do good to all His children. Yet trials and difficulties are not the only way faith is exercised and thereby increased. *Reading the Scriptures also acquaints us with God as He has revealed Himself in them.*

Are you able to genuinely say, from your knowledge of God and your relationship with Him, that He is indeed a beautiful Being? If not, let me graciously encourage you to ask God to take you to that point, so you will fully appreciate His gentleness and kindness, so you will be able to say just how good He is, and so you will know what a delight it is to God's heart to do good for His children.

The closer we come to this point in our inner being, the more willing we are to leave ourselves in His hands and the more satisfied we are with all of His dealings with us. Then when trials come, we will say, "I will patiently wait to see the good God will do in my life, with the calm assurance He will do it." In this way, we will bear a worthy testimony to the world and thereby strengthen the lives of others. GEORGE MUELLER

Morning

Tell the Israelites to move on.
EXODUS 14:15

Let us move on and step out boldly, though it be into the night where one can scarcely see the way. The path will open as we press on, like the trail through the forest, or the Alpine pass which discloses but a few rods of its length. There are things God gives us to do without any light or illumination at all except His own command, but *those who know the way to God can find it in the dark.* ALEXANDER MACLAREN

The God of Israel, the Savior, is sometimes a God that hideth Himself, but never a God that absenteth Himself; sometimes in the dark, but never at a distance. MATTHEW HENRY

> *There was a rift tonight;*
> *I saw a gray cloud break and let the light*
> *Shine through—a ray of hope to all the earth;*
> *Long had I waited here; I found it hard to say,*
> *"The clouds will drift apart, the darkness melt away*
> *Before the radiance of the night's new birth."*
>
> *That promised glow to guide a wayward one;*
> *At last, after long hours of doubt and fear,*
> *Came light again and life, and sweet security,*
> *As though a hidden ray from God's eternity*
> *Peeped out, that I might look and see it there.*
> *So, if I can but wait,*
> *I know that God will send it, soon or late—*
> *This break within my life's gray cloud; His gift*
> *To me, one star of perfect love to shine and show*
> *That they who walk by faith are told the way to go,*
> *And after storm will come the blessed rift.*
>
> RUTH M. GIBBS

Evening

By faith Abraham, when called to go to a place he would later receive as his inheritance, obeyed and went, even though he did not know where he was going.
HEBREWS 11:8

Abraham "did not know where he was going"—it simply was enough for him to know he went with God. He did not lean as much on the promises as he did on the Promiser. And he did not look at the difficulties of his circumstances but looked to His King—the eternal, limitless, invisible, wise, and only God—who had reached down from His throne to direct his path and who would certainly prove Himself.

O glorious faith! Your works and possibilities are these: contentment to set sail with the orders still sealed, due to unwavering confidence in the wisdom of the Lord High Admiral; and a willingness to get up, leave everything, and follow Christ, because of the joyful assurance that earth's best does not compare with heaven's least. F. B. MEYER

In no way is it enough to set out cheerfully with God on any venture of faith. You must also be willing to take your ideas of what the journey will be like and tear them into tiny pieces, for nothing on the itinerary will happen as you expect.

Your Guide will not keep to any beaten path. He will lead you through ways you would never have dreamed your eyes would see. He knows no fear, and He expects you to fear nothing while He is with you.

> *The day had gone; alone and weak*
> *I groped my way within a bleak*
> *   And sunless land.*
> *The path that led into the light*
> *I could not find! In that dark night*
> *   God took my hand.*
>
> *He led me that I might not stray,*
> *And brought me by a safe, new way*
> *   I had not known.*

By waters still, through pastures green
I followed Him—the path was clean
    Of briar and stone.

The heavy darkness lost its strength,
My waiting eyes beheld at length
    The streaking dawn.
On, safely on, through sunrise glow
I walked, my hand in His, and lo,
    The night had gone.

ANNIE PORTER JOHNSON

~~~~~~ APRIL 17 ~~~~~~

Morning

It will be good for that servant whose master finds him doing so when he returns.
MATTHEW 24:46

A story is related, which has to do with the Second Coming of our blessed Lord and the general dissemination of this precious truth. At last it reached the workers in the South as they worked in the cotton fields. Said one of the old brethren, What's the use of us picking cotton if the Lord is coming back? And scores of others agreed. The cotton pickers stopped their work, and the cotton wasted in the fields. Everybody else was busy attending conferences and camp meetings, singing the praises of God, and looking for His return.

The following winter was one of great need and privation because their crops had been so woefully neglected.

Then one of their number, an evangelist, began preaching on this text:

"It will be good for that servant whose master finds him doing so when he returns."

Before long the people were once again tilling their ground and picking cotton in the rows. It remained for Bertrand Shadwell to give us the following poem which suggests their change in attitude:

There's a King and Captain high,
Who'll be coming by and by;
And He'll find me hoeing cotton when He comes.
You can hear His legions charging in the thunder of the sky;
And He'll find me hoeing cotton when He comes.
When He comes!
When He comes!
All the dead shall rise, in answer to His drums.
Oh, the fires of His encampment star the firmament on high;
And the heavens shall roll asunder, when He comes.
There's a Man they thrust aside,
Who was tortured till He died;
And He'll find me hoeing cotton when He comes.
He was spat upon and mocked at;
He was scourged and crucified;
And He'll find me hoeing cotton when He comes. When He comes!
When He comes!
He'll be loved by saints and angels when He comes; They'll be
  calling out "Hosanna!" to the Man that men denied;
And I'll kneel among the cotton—When He comes!

"Occupy till I come" (Luke 19:13 KJV).

<hr>

APRIL 17

Evening

The hand of the LORD has done this.
JOB 12:9

A number of years ago the most magnificent diamond in the history of the world was found in an African mine. It was then presented to the king of England to embellish his crown of state. The king sent it to Amsterdam to be cut by an expert stonecutter. Can you imagine what he did with it?

He took this gem of priceless value and cut a notch in it. Then he struck it one hard time with his hammer, and the majestic jewel fell into his hand, broken in two. What recklessness! What wastefulness! What criminal carelessness!

Actually, that is not the case at all. For you see, that one blow with the hammer had been studied and planned for days, and even weeks. Drawings and models had been made of the gem. Its quality, defects, and possible lines along which it would split had all been studied to the smallest detail. And the man to whom it was entrusted was one of the most skilled stonecutters in the world.

Now do you believe that blow was a mistake? No, it was the capstone and the culmination of the stonecutter's skill. When he struck that blow, he did the one thing that would bring that gem to its most perfect shape, radiance, and jeweled splendor. The blow that seemed to be the ruin of the majestic precious stone was actually its perfect redemption, for from the halves were fashioned two magnificent gems. Only the skilled eye of the expert stonecutter could have seen the beauty of two diamonds hidden in the rough, uncut stone as it came from the mine.

Sometimes, in the same way, God lets a stinging blow fall on your life. You bleed, feeling the pain, and your soul cries out in agony. At first you think the blow is an appalling mistake. But it is not, for you are the most precious jewel in the world to God. And He is the most skilled stonecutter in the universe.

Someday you are to be a jewel adorning the crown of the King. As you lie in His hand now, He knows just how to deal with you. Not one blow will be permitted to fall on your apprehensive soul except what the love of God allows. And you may be assured that from the depths of the experience, you will see untold blessings, and spiritual enrichment you have never before imagined. J. H. M.

In one of George MacDonald's books, one of the characters makes this bitter statement: "I wonder why God made me. I certainly don't see any purpose in it!" Another of the characters responds, "Perhaps you don't see any purpose yet, but then, He isn't finished making you. And besides, you are arguing with the process."

If people would only believe they are still in the process of creation, submit to the Maker, allowing Him to handle them as the potter handles clay, and yield themselves in one shining, deliberate action to the turning of His wheel, they would soon find themselves able to welcome every pressure from His hand on them, even if it results in pain. And sometimes they should not only believe but also have God's purpose in sight: "bringing many sons and daughters to glory" (Hebrews 2:10).

Not a single blow can hit,
Till the God of love sees fit.

APRIL 18
Morning

He took him outside and said, "Look up at the sky and count the stars—if
indeed you can count them." Then he said to him, "So shall your offspring be."
GENESIS 15:5

We are profoundly impressed with the unlimited resources of the God of the Bible. He never does anything small. When He makes an ocean, He makes it so deep that no man can fathom it. When He makes a mountain, He makes it so large that no one can measure or weigh it. When He makes flowers, He scatters multiplied millions of them where there is no one to admire them but Himself. When He makes grace, He makes it without sides or bottom and leaves the top off. Instead of giving salvation with a medicine dropper, He pours it forth like a river.

When God sets out to do a thing for us, *He does it with a prodigality of love-prompted abundance that fairly staggers one who reckons things by the coldly calculating standards of earth.*

Whatever blessing is in our cup, it is sure to *run over.* With Him the calf is always the *fatted calf;* the robe is always the *best robe;* the joy is *unspeakable;* the peace *passeth understanding;* the grace is *so abundant that the recipient has all-sufficiency for all things and abounds to every good work.*

There is no grudging in God's benevolence; He does not measure out His goodness as the apothecary counts his drops and measures his drams, slowly and exactly, drop by drop. God's way is always characterized by multitudinous and overflowing bounty, like that in nature which is so profuse in beauty and life that every drop of the ocean, every square inch of the forest glade, every molecule of water, teems with marvels and defies the research and investigation of man. Well may we cry with the apostle, *"I have . . . more than enough"* (Philippians 4:18).

Evening

He will do this.
PSALM 37:5

I once believed that after I prayed, it was my responsibility to do everything in my power to bring about the answer. Yet God taught me a better way and showed me that self-effort always hinders His work. He also revealed that when I prayed and had confident trust in Him for something, He simply wanted me to wait in an attitude of praise and do only what He told me. Sitting still, doing nothing except trusting in the Lord, causes a feeling of uncertainty, and there is often a tremendous temptation to take the battle into our own hands.

We all know how difficult it is to rescue a drowning person who tries to help his rescuer, and it is equally difficult for the Lord to fight our battles for us when we insist upon trying to fight them ourselves. It is not that God will not but that He cannot, for our interference hinders His work. C. H. P.

Spiritual forces cannot work while we are trusting earthly forces.

Often we fail to give God an opportunity to work, not realizing that it takes time for Him to answer prayer. It takes time for God to color a rose or to grow a great oak tree. And it takes time for Him to make bread from wheat fields. He takes the soil, then grinds and softens it. He enriches it and wets it with rain showers and with dew. Then He brings the warmth of life to the small blade of grass, later grows the stalk and the amber grain, and finally provides bread for the hungry.

All this takes time. Therefore we sow the seed, till the ground, and then wait and trust until God's purpose has been fulfilled. We understand this principle when it comes to planting a field, and we need to learn the same lesson regarding our prayer life. It takes time for God to answer prayer. J. H. M.

Morning

When you pray, go into your room.
MATTHEW 6:6

The apostolic men, the saintly men, the heroic servants of God, the strong soldiers of Jesus Christ, have everywhere and always *prayed without ceasing.*

If Francis of Assisi knew how to do battle among men, it was because he loved to "fly away as a bird to its nest in the mountains." John Welsh spent eight hours out of the twenty-four in communion with God; therefore, he was equipped and armed and dared to suffer! David Brainerd rode through the endless American woods praying, and so fulfilled his ministry in a short time. John Wesley came out from his seclusion to change the face of England. Andrew Bonar did not once miss his mercy seat, and his fellowship with heaven made him the winsome Christian that he was. John Fletcher sometimes prayed all night. Adoniram Judson won Burma for Christ through unwearied prayer. Such was *the habit of those who wrought nobly for God.*

If we would attempt great things for God, and achieve something before we die, we must pray at every moment and in every place. *God commits Himself into the hands of those who truly pray.*

> *Alone, dear Lord, in solitude serene,*
> *Thy servant Moses was constrained to go,*
> *Into the silent desert with the sheep;*
> *The silvery stars his lovely vigil know.*
>
> *And Paul, the fiery warrior, zealous, bold,*
> *In desert places, 'neath Arabian skies,*
> *Learned God's own lessons, harkened to His voice,*
> *Grew calm, resourceful, humble, meek and wise.*
>
> *Alone, dear Lord, I fear to be alone;*
> *My heart demands the blest companionship*

Of those that love Thee; friendship's nectar sweet,
With those beloved, I evermore would sip.

But in the desert, Moses, David, Paul,
Were not alone, afar from love or care:
They companied with heav'nly visitors,
They knew no loneliness, for Thou wert there.

ALICE E. SHERWOOD

The first-century Christians were said to be *power conscious*. We are *problem* conscious. What did *they* believe about prayer? What do *we*?

~~~~~~~   APRIL 19   ~~~~~~~

Evening

Stand firm and you will see the deliverance the LORD *will bring you today.*

EXODUS 14:13

This verse contains God's command to me as a believer for those times when I am confronted with dire circumstances and extraordinary difficulties. What am I to do when I cannot retreat or go forward and my way is blocked to the right and to the left?

The Master's word to me is, "Stand firm." And the best thing I can do at these times is to listen only to my Master's word, for others will come to me with their suggestions and evil advice. *Despair* will come, whispering, "Give up—lie down and die." But even in the worst of times, God would have me be cheerful and courageous, rejoicing in His love and faithfulness.

Cowardice will come and say, "You must retreat to the world's ways of acting. It is too difficult for you to continue living the part of a Christian. Abandon your principles." Yet no matter how much Satan may pressure me to follow his course, I cannot, for I am a child of God. The Lord's divine decree has commanded me to go from "strength to strength" (Psalm 84:7). Therefore I will, and neither death nor hell will turn me from my course. And if for a season He calls me to "stand firm," I will acknowledge it as time to renew my strength for greater strides in the future.

Impatience will come, crying, "Get up and do something! To 'stand firm' and wait is sheer idleness." Why is it I think I *must* be doing something right now instead of looking to the Lord? He will not only do *something*—He will do *everything*.

Arrogance will come, boasting, "If the sea is blocking your way, march right into it and expect a miracle." Yet true faith never listens to arrogance, impatience, cowardice, or despair but only hears God saying, "Stand firm." And then it stands as immovable as a rock.

"Stand firm." I must maintain the posture of one who stands, ready for action, expecting further orders, and cheerfully and patiently awaiting the Director's voice. It will not be long until God will say to me, as distinctly as He told Moses to tell the children of Israel, "Move on" (Exodus 14:15). CHARLES H. SPURGEON

> *Be quiet! Why this anxious heed*
>   *About your tangled ways?*
> *God knows them all. He gives you speed*
>   *And He allows delays.*
> *It's good for you to walk by faith*
>   *And not by sight.*
> *Take it on trust a little while.*
> *Soon will you read the mystery aright*
> *In the full sunshine of His smile.*

In times of uncertainty—*wait*. If you have any doubt—*wait*, never forcing yourself into action. If you sense any restraint in your spirit, do not go against it—*wait* until the way is clear.

~~~~~~~ APRIL 20 ~~~~~~~

Morning

He himself went a day's journey into the wilderness. He came to a broom bush, sat down under it and prayed that he might die. "I have had enough,

LORD," he said. . . . "The LORD is about to pass by." Then a great and powerful wind . . . but the LORD was not in the wind. . . . but the LORD was not in the earthquake. . . . but the LORD was not in the fire. And after the fire came a gentle whisper. . . . The LORD said to him, "Go back the way you came, and . . . anoint Hazael king over Aram.

1 KINGS 19:4, 11–12, 15

When a man loses heart, he loses everything. To keep one's heart in the midst of life's stream and to maintain an undiscourageable front in the face of its difficulties is not an achievement that springs from anything that a laboratory can demonstrate or that logic can affirm. *It is an achievement of faith.*

If you lose your sky, you will soon lose your earth.

From under the juniper tree Elijah is called into an audience with the King of Kings. While listening to his own defeated wail, the accents of the still small Voice fall upon his weary ear. God refused him his unworthy request; rested him from his service; reminded him that he was still needed; and returned him to his work. He thought his work was done and that life had left him in the shadows. God says: "No, I am commissioning you to go forth and anoint kings and prophets, and climax the service of other days."

Not till His hour strikes is our day done; as long as we live, we serve the King!

The tempter is always ready to take advantage of a time of weariness and reaction. *He loves to fish in troubled waters.*

Juniper trees make poor sanctuaries.

It is good to have things settled by faith, before they are unsettled by feeling.

APRIL 20

Evening

"Not by might nor by power, but by my Spirit," says the LORD Almighty.

ZECHARIAH 4:6

Once as I walked along the road on a steep hill, I caught sight of a boy on a bicycle near the bottom. He was pedaling uphill against the wind and was obviously working tremendously hard. Just as he was exerting the greatest effort and painfully doing the best he could do, a streetcar, also going up the hill, approached him. It was not traveling too fast for the boy to grab hold of a rail at the rear, and I am sure you can guess the result. He went up the hill as effortlessly as a bird gliding through the sky.

This thought then flashed through my mind: "I am like that boy on the bicycle in my weariness and weakness. I am pedaling uphill against all kinds of opposition and am almost worn out with the task. But nearby there is great power available—the strength of the Lord Jesus. All I must do is get in touch with Him and maintain communication with Him. And even if I grab hold with only one little finger of faith, it will be enough to make His power mine to accomplish the act of service that now overwhelms me."

Seeing this boy on his bicycle helped me to set aside my weariness and to recognize this great truth. THE LIFE OF FULLER PURPOSE

ABANDONED

Utterly abandoned to the Holy Ghost!
Seeking all His fullness, whatever the cost;
Cutting all the moorings, launching in the deep
Of His mighty power—strong to save and keep.

Utterly abandoned to the Holy Ghost!
Oh! The sinking, sinking, until self is lost!
Until the emptied vessel lies broken at His feet;
Waiting till His filling shall make the work complete.

Utterly abandoned to the will of God;
Seeking for no other path than my Master trod;
Leaving ease and pleasure, making Him my choice,
Waiting for His guidance, listening for His voice.

Utterly abandoned! No will of my own;
For time and for eternity, His, and His alone;

All my plans and purposes lost in His sweet will,
Having nothing, yet in Him all things possessing still.

Utterly abandoned! It's so sweet to be
Captive in His bonds of love, yet wondrously free;
Free from sin's entanglements, free from doubt and fear,
Free from every worry, burden, grief, or care.

Utterly abandoned! Oh, the rest is sweet,
As I tarry, waiting, at His blessed feet;
Waiting for the coming of the Guest divine,
Who my inmost being will perfectly refine.

Lo! He comes and fills me, Holy Spirit sweet!
I, in Him, am satisfied! I, in Him, complete!
And the light within my soul will nevermore grow dim
While I keep my covenant—abandoned unto Him!

AUTHOR UNKNOWN

~~~~~~ APRIL 21 ~~~~~~

Morning

God chose the weak things of the world to shame the strong.
1 CORINTHIANS 1:27

We must not be fainthearted because we are consciously poor instruments. The main question is *the mastery of Him who uses the instruments.*

Once Paganini, standing before a vast audience, broke string after string of his violin. Men had come to hear his greatest sonata, "Napoleon." They hissed as he seemed to destroy all hope for continuing his performance. Then the artist held up his violin: "One string—and Paganini," and on that one string he made the first complete manifestation of his greatness!

It would be a poor violin, indeed, out of which Paganini could not bring music, a poor pencil with which Raphael could not create a masterpiece; and *the power of the Spirit behind the least gifted one can work to glorious issues.*

It is said that Gainsborough, the artist, longed also to be a musician. He bought musical instruments of many kinds and tried to play them. He once heard a great violinist bringing ravishing music from his instrument. Gainsborough was charmed and thrown into transports of admiration. He bought the violin on which the master played so marvelously. He thought that if he had the wonderful instrument that he could play, too. But he soon learned that the music was not in the violin, but was in the master who played it.

Are you discouraged because there is so little strength, no ability you can call your own? Are you dejected because you have no resources? Think, then, what this may mean: *one hour, one talent—and God!* Let me put myself wholly at God's service, whatever I may be; *greatness is not required,* but *meetness for the Master's use.*

Only let Him have a free hand!
They called him a genius,
The Fiddler;
But he said, "I am only
The strings
Of God's instrument, He
Playing on it.
It is not I, but the fiddle
That sings."

~~~~~~~~~ APRIL 21 ~~~~~~~~~

Evening

He did not waver . . . regarding the promise . . . being fully
persuaded that God had power to do what he had promised.
ROMANS 4:20–21

Scripture tells us that Abraham, "without weakening in his faith, . . . faced the fact that his body was as good as dead" (v. 19). He was not discouraged, because he was not looking at himself but at almighty God. "He did not *waver* . . . regarding the promise" but stood straight, not bending beneath the staggering load of God's blessing. Instead of growing weak, his faith grew stronger, exhibiting more power, even as more difficulties became apparent. Abraham glorified God for His complete sufficiency and was "fully persuaded that God had power to do what he had promised."

The literal translation of this passage from the Greek expresses the thought in this way: God is not merely able but abundantly able, bountifully and generously able, with an infinite surplus of resources, and eternally able "to do what he had promised."

He is the God of limitless resources—the only limit comes from us. Our requests, our thoughts, and our prayers are too small, and our expectations are too low. God is trying to raise our vision to a higher level, call us to have greater expectations, and thereby bring us to greater appropriation. Shall we continue living in a way that mocks His will and denies His Word?

There is no limit to what we may ask and expect of our glorious El Shaddai—our almighty God. And there is no way for us to measure His blessing, for He is "able to do immeasurably more than all we ask or imagine, according to his power that is at work within us" (Ephesians 3:20). A. B. SIMPSON

The way to find God's treasure-house of blessing is to climb the ladder of His divine promises. Those promises are the key that opens the door to the riches of God's grace and favor.

~~~~~~ APRIL 22 ~~~~~~

Morning

By faith Moses . . . chose to be mistreated.
HEBREWS 11:24–25

By faith Moses. . . . chose." Faith rests on promise; to faith, the promise is *equivalent to fulfillment;* and if only we have the one, we may dare to count on the other as already ours. It matters comparatively little that the thing promised is not given; it is sure and certain because God has pledged His word for it, and in anticipation we may enter on its enjoyment. Had Moses simply acted on what he saw, he would never have left Pharaoh's palace. But his faith told him of things hidden from his contemporaries, and these led him to act in a way which to them was perfectly incomprehensible.

One blow struck when the time is fulfilled is worth a thousand struck in premature eagerness. It is not for thee, O my soul, to know the times and seasons which the Father hath put in His own power; wait thou only upon God; let thy expectation be from Him.

It was a rude surprise when he assayed to adjust a difference between two Hebrews to find himself repulsed from them by the challenge, "Who made you ruler and judge over us?" (Exodus 2:14). *"Moses thought that his own people would realize that God was using him to rescue them"* (Acts 7:25). Evidently, then, God's time had not arrived; nor could it come until the heat of his spirit had slowly evaporated in the desert air, and he had learned the hardest of all lessons, that *"it is not by strength that one prevails"* (1 Samuel 2:9).

Faith is only possible when we are on God's plan and stand on God's promise. It is useless to pray for increased faith until we have fulfilled the conditions of faith. It is useless to waste time in regrets and tears over the failures which are due to our unbelief. *"What are you doing down on your face?"* (Joshua 7:10). Faith is as natural to the right conditions of a soul as a flower is to a plant.

Ascertain your place in God's plan, and get on to it. Feed on God's promises. When each of these conditions is realized, faith comes of itself; and there is absolutely nothing which is impossible. The believing soul will then be as the metal track along which God travels to men in love, grace, and truth.

Oh, for grace to wait and watch with God! F. B. MEYER

Faith is not a magic drug, a spiritual anesthetic: it is the victory that overcometh the world by doing battle with it. E. HERMAN

APRIL 22

Evening

He knows the way that I take.

JOB 23:10

O believer, what a glorious assurance this verse is! What confidence I have because "the way that I take"—this way of trials and tears, however winding, hidden, or tangled—"He knows"! When the "furnace [is] heated seven times hotter than usual" (Daniel 3:19), I can know He still lights my way. There is an almighty Guide who knows and directs my steps, whether they lead to the bitter water at the well of Marah or to the joy and refreshment of the oasis at Elim (Exodus 15:23, 27).

The way is dark to the Egyptians yet has its own pillar of cloud and fire for God's Israel. The furnace may be hot, but not only can I trust the hand that lights the fire, I can also have the assurance the fire will not consume but only refine. And when the refining process is complete, not a moment too soon or too late, "I will come forth as gold" (Job 23:10).

When I feel God is the farthest away, He is often the nearest to me. "*When* my spirit grows faint within me, it is you who watch over my way" (Psalm 142:3). Do we know of another who shines brighter than the most radiant sunlight, who meets us in our room with the first waking light, who has an infinitely tender and compassionate watchfulness over us throughout our day, and who "knows the way that [we] take"?

The world, during a time of adversity, speaks of "providence" with a total lack of understanding. They dethrone God, who is the living, guiding Sovereign of the universe, to some inanimate, dead abstraction. What they call "providence" they see as occurrences of fate, reducing God from His position as our acting, powerful, and personal Jehovah.

The pain would be removed from many an agonizing trial if only I could see what Job saw during his time of severe affliction, when all earthly hope lay dashed at his feet. He saw nothing but the hand of God—God's hand behind the swords of the Sabeans who attacked his servants and cattle, and behind the devastating lightning; God's hand giving wings to the mighty desert winds, which swept away his children; and God's hand in the dreadful silence of his shattered home.

Thus, seeing God in everything, Job could say, "*The* Lord gave and *the* Lord has taken away; may the name of *the* Lord be praised" (Job 1:21). Yet his faith reached its zenith when this once-powerful prince of the desert "sat among the ashes" (Job 2:8) and still could say, "Though he slay me, yet will I hope in him" (Job 13:15). J. R. Macduff

Morning

Faith expressing itself through love.
GALATIANS 5:6

Faith without deeds is dead.
JAMES 2:26

God never gave us faith to play with. It is a sword, but it was not made for presentation on a gala day, nor to be worn on state occasions only, nor to be exhibited upon a parade ground. It is a sword that was meant to cut and wound and slay; and he who has it girt about him may expect that between here and heaven, he shall know what battle means. *Faith is a sound seagoing vessel, and not meant to lie in dock and perish of dry rot.* To whom God has given faith, it is as though one gave a lantern to his friend because he expected it to be dark on his way home. *The very gift of faith is a hint to you that you will want it; that at certain points and places you will especially require it; and that, at all points and in every place you will really need it.*

Faith must begin to use its resources!

Use the faith God has already given you. You have faith, or you could not be a Christian. Use your little faith and it will increase by use. Plant a few grains of it, and you will find it will grow and multiply. George Mueller said that when he began his ministry it was as hard to believe for a pound as it was forty years later to believe for one thousand pounds. He was like the Thessalonians to whom Paul wrote, "Your faith is growing more and more" (2 Thessalonians 1:3).

Do not be satisfied with prayer and desire, but do!

Evening

Though I walk in the midst of trouble, you preserve my life.
PSALM 138:7

The Hebrew of this verse literally means to "go on in the center of trouble." What descriptive words! And once we have called on God during our time of trouble, pleaded His promise of deliverance but not received it, and continued to be oppressed by the Enemy until we are in the very thick of the battle—or the "center of trouble"— others may tell us, "Don't bother the teacher anymore" (Luke 8:49).

When Martha said, "Lord, . . . if you had been here, my brother would not have died" (John 11:21), Jesus countered her lack of hope with His greater promise, "Your brother will rise again" (John 11:23). And when we walk "in the center of trouble" and are tempted to think, like Martha, that we are past the point of ever being delivered, our Lord also answers us with a promise from His Word: "Though I walk in the midst of trouble, you preserve my life."

Although His answer seems so long in coming and we continue to "walk in the midst of trouble," "the center of trouble" is the place where He preserves us, not the place where He fails us. The times we continue to walk in seemingly utter hopelessness are the very times He will "stretch out [His] hand against the anger of [our] foes" (Psalm 138:7). He will bring our trouble to completion, causing the Enemy's attack to cease and to fail.

In light of this, what reason would there ever be for despair? APHRA WHITE

THE EYE OF THE STORM

Fear not that the whirlwind will carry you hence,
Nor wait for its onslaught in breathless suspense,
Nor shrink from the blight of the terrible hail,
But pass through the edge to the heart of the tale,
For there is a shelter, sunlighted and warm,
And Faith sees her God through the eye of the storm.

The passionate tempest with rush and wild roar
And threatenings of evil may beat on the shore,
The waves may be mountains, the fields battle plains,
And the earth be immersed in a deluge of rains,
Yet, the soul, stayed on God, may sing bravely its psalm,
For the heart of the storm is the center of calm.

Let hope be not quenched in the blackness of night,
Though the cyclone awhile may have blotted the light,
For behind the great darkness the stars ever shine,
And the light of God's heavens, His love will make thine,
Let no gloom dim your eyes, but uplift them on high
To the face of your God and the blue of His sky.

The storm is your shelter from danger and sin,
And God Himself takes you for safety within;
The tempest with Him passes into deep calm,
And the roar of the winds is the sound of a psalm.
Be glad and serene when the tempest clouds form;
God smiles on His child in the eye of the storm.

APRIL 24
Morning

LORD, teach us to pray.
LUKE 11:1

Pray ye.
MATTHEW 9:38 KJV

Dr. John Timothy Stone tells of a visit which he paid to the old church of Robert Murray McCheyne. The aged sexton showed him around. Taking Dr. Stone into the study, he pointed to a chair and said, "Sit there; that is where the master used to sit." Then he said, "Now put your elbows on the table." This was done. "Now bow your head upon your hands." Dr. Stone did so. "Now let the tears flow; that is the way the master used to do."

The visitor was then taken up into the pulpit, and the old sexton said, "Stand there behind the pulpit." Dr. Stone obeyed. "Now," said the sexton, "lean your elbows on the pulpit and put your face in your hands." This having been done, he said, "Now let the tears flow; that is the way the master used to do."

Then the old man added a testimony which gripped the heart of his hearer. With tearful eyes and trembling voice he said, *"He called down the power of God upon Scotland, and it is with us still."* Sunday School Times

Oh, that *we* had a passion to save others! It was a compact between that holy Indian missionary known as "Praying Hyde" and God—that each day He should have at least four souls.

And Brainerd tells us that one Sunday night he offered himself to be used by God and for Him. "It was raining and the roads were muddy; but this desire grew so strong, that I kneeled down by the side of the road, and told God all about it. While I was praying, I told Him that my hands should work for Him, my tongue speak for Him, if He would only use me as His instrument—when suddenly the darkness of the night lit up, and I knew that God had heard and answered my prayer; and I felt that I was accepted into the inner circle of God's loved ones."

~~~~~~~~~ APRIL 24 ~~~~~~~~~

Evening

Faith is confidence . . . assurance about what we do not see.
Hebrews 11:1

Genuine faith puts its letter in the mailbox and lets go. Distrust, however, holds on to a corner of the envelope and then wonders why the answer never arrives. There are some letters on my desk that I wrote weeks ago, but I have yet to mail them because of my uncertainty over the address or the contents. Those letters have not done any good for me or anyone else at this point. And they never will accomplish anything until I let go of them, trusting them to the postal service.

It is the same with genuine faith. It hands its circumstance over to God, allowing Him to work. Psalm 37:5 is a great confirmation of this: "Commit your way to the LORD; trust in him and he will do this." He will never work until we *commit*. Faith is receiving—or even more, actually appropriating—the gifts God offers us. We may believe in Him, come to Him, commit to Him, and rest in Him, but we will never fully realize all our blessings until we begin to receive from Him and come to Him having the spirit of abiding and appropriating. DAYS OF HEAVEN UPON EARTH

Dr. Payson, while still a young man, once wrote to an elderly mother who was extremely worried and burdened over the condition of her son. He wrote,

> You are worrying too much about him. Once you have prayed for him, as you have done, and committed him to God, you should not continue to be anxious. God's command, "Do not be anxious about anything" (Philippians 4:6), is unlimited, and so is the verse, "Cast *all* your anxiety on him" (1 Peter 5:7). If we truly have cast our burdens upon another, can they continue to pressure us? If we carry them with us from the throne of grace, it is obvious we have not left them there. In my own life I test my prayers in this way: after committing something to God, if I can come away, like Hannah did, with no more sadness, pain, or anxiety in my heart, I see it as proof that I have prayed the prayer of faith. But if I pray and then still carry my burden, I conclude my faith was not exercised.

<hr>

APRIL 25
Morning

Go to him at midnight.
LUKE 11:5

Summoned to the couch of a dying little girl, the mighty Master had time to tarry by the way until a poor helpless woman was healed by a touch of His garment. Meanwhile that little life had ebbed away, and human unbelief hastened to turn back the visit which was now too late. "Trouble not the Master; she is dead." It was then that His strong and mighty love rose to its glorious height of power and victory. *"Be not afraid,"* is His calm reply; *"Only believe and she shall be made whole."*

"Too late," says Martha. "Four days buried." But He only answers, *"Did I not tell you that if you believe, you will see the glory of God?"* (John 11:40).

"Go to Him at midnight!" Let us go when all other doors are barred and even the heavens seem brass, for the gates of prayer are open evermore; and it is only when the sun is gone down and our pillow is but a stone of the wilderness that we behold the ladder that reaches unto heaven with our Infinite God above it, and the angels of His providence ascending and descending for our help and deliverance. He is a friend in extremity. He is able for the hardest occasions. He is seated on His throne for the very purpose of giving help in time of need.

No matter if the case is wholly hopeless, and your situation one where you have nothing, and the hour is dark as midnight, *"Go to Him."* Go to Him at midnight. *He loves the hour of extremity.* It is His chosen time of Almighty interposition.

"There's a budding morrow in midnight," so fold your griefs away, and wait for the bud to open, a fragrant and fair new day. Wait for the bud to open, cease to worry and grope, "there's a budding morrow in midnight," its name is *The Dawn of Hope.*
A New Trail

~~~~~~ APRIL 25 ~~~~~~
Evening

Mary Magdalene and the other Mary were sitting there opposite the tomb.
MATTHEW 27:61

Oh, how slow grief is to come to understanding! Grief is ignorant and does not even care to learn. When the grieving women "were sitting there opposite the tomb," did they see the triumph of the next two thousand years? Did they see anything except that Christ was gone?

The Christ you and I know today came from their loss. Countless mourning hearts have since seen resurrection in the midst of their grief, and yet these sorrowing women watched at the beginning of this result and saw nothing. What they regarded as the end of life was actually the preparation for coronation, for Christ remained silent that He might live again with tenfold power.

They did not see it. They mourned, wept, went away, and then came again to the sepulcher, driven by their broken hearts. And still it was only a tomb—unprophetic, voiceless, and drab.

It is the same with us. Each of us sits "opposite the tomb" in our own garden and initially says, "This tragedy is irreparable. I see no benefit in it and will take no comfort in it." And yet right in the midst of our deepest and worst adversities, our Christ is often just lying there, waiting to be resurrected.

Our Savior is where our death seems to be at the end of our hope, we find the brightest beginning of fulfillment. Where darkness seems the deepest, the most radiant light is set to emerge. And once the experience is complete, we find our garden is not disfigured by the tomb.

Our joys are made better when sorrow is in the midst of them. And our sorrows become bright through the joys God has planted around them. At first the flowers of the garden may not appear to be our favorites, but we will learn that they are the flowers of the heart. The flowers planted at the grave deep within the Christian heart are love, hope, faith, joy, and peace.

> 'Twas by a path of sorrows drear
>   Christ entered into rest;
> And shall I look for roses here,
>   Or think that earth is blessed?
> Heaven's whitest lilies blow
> From earth's sharp crown of woe:
> Who here his cross can meekly bear,
> Shall wear the kingly purple there.

APRIL 26

Morning

Therefore, I urge you, brothers and sisters, in view of God's mercy, to offer your bodies as a living sacrifice, holy and pleasing to God—this is your true and proper worship.

ROMANS 12:1

Someone has said very pertinently, "There was no rudder to Noah's ark." It was hardly necessary. He had obeyed God and now was shut in, with God only to steer his ark, for he was on God's errand. The man who could endure what he endured for more than a century, while preaching the Word amidst a hostile people, did not have any fears as to where he was going. The fulfillment of the prophecy regarding the deluge must have confirmed a faith already strong.

It is a delightful experience when we really believe that God is steering our little bark over life's tempestuous sea. *Only supreme and absolute abandonment to the will of God will give perfect rest of soul.* It is this that enlarges the soul. Fenelon says: "If there be anything that is capable of setting the soul in a large place it is *absolute abandonment to God.* It diffuses in the soul a peace that flows like a river and the righteousness which is as the waves of the sea" (Isaiah 48:18). If there be anything that can render the soul calm, dissipate its scruples and dispel its fears, sweeten its sufferings by the anointing of love, impart strength to all its actions, and spread abroad the joy of the Holy Ghost in its countenance and words, it is this simple and childlike repose in the arms of God.

God could give to Abraham because he had made such a wide opening into his life. God can give only into an open hand. This hand was opened wide. This door swung clear back. God had a free swing, and He used it. He *could,* and He did. He always does. Let this be our rule: "Give all He asks; then take all He gives." And the cup will be spilling joyously over the brim. S. D. GORDON

Beware of every hesitation to abandon to God!

~~~~~ APRIL 26 ~~~~~

Evening

I consider everything a loss because of the surpassing worth of knowing Christ Jesus my Lord.
PHILIPPIANS 3:8

Light is always costly and comes at the expense of that which produces it. An unlit candle does not shine, for burning must come before the light. And we can be of little use to others without a cost to ourselves. Burning suggests suffering, and we try to avoid pain.

We tend to feel we are doing the greatest good in the world when we are strong and fit for active duty and when our hearts and hands are busy with kind acts of service. Therefore when we are set aside to suffer, when we are sick, when we are consumed with pain, and when all our activities have been stopped, we feel we are no longer of any use and are accomplishing nothing.

Yet if we will be patient and submissive, it is almost certain we will be a greater blessing to the world around us during our time of suffering and pain than we were when we thought we were doing our greatest work. Then we are burning, and shining brightly as a result of the fire. EVENING THOUGHTS

The glory of tomorrow is rooted in the drudgery of today.

Many people want the glory without the cross, and the shining light without the burning fire, but crucifixion comes before coronation.

> *Have you heard the tale of the aloe plant,*
>   *Away in the sunny clime?*
> *By humble growth of a hundred years*
>   *It reaches its blooming time;*
> *And then a wondrous bud at its crown*
>   *Breaks into a thousand flowers;*
> *This floral queen, in its blooming seen,*
>   *Is the pride of the tropical bowers,*
> *But the flower to the plant is sacrifice,*
>   *For it blooms but once, and it dies.*
>
> *Have you further heard of the aloe plant,*
>   *That grows in the sunny clime;*
> *How every one of its thousand flowers,*
>   *As they drop in the blooming time,*
> *Is an infant plant that fastens its roots*
>   *In the place where it falls on the ground,*
> *And as fast as they drop from the dying stem,*
>   *Grow lively and lovely all 'round?*
> *By dying, it liveth a thousandfold*
>   *In the young that spring from the death of the old.*

Have you heard the tale of the pelican,
    The Arabs' Gimel el Bahr,
That lives in the African solitudes,
    Where the birds that live lonely are?
Have you heard how it loves its tender young,
    And cares and toils for their good,
It brings them water from mountains far,
    And fishes the seas for their food.
In famine it feeds them—what love can devise!
    The blood of its bosom—and, feeding them, dies.

Have you heard this tale—the best of them all—
    The tale of the Holy and True,
He dies, but His life, in untold souls
    Lives on in the world anew;
His seed prevails, and is filling the earth,
    As the stars fill the sky above.
He taught us to yield up the love of life,
    For the sake of the life of love.
His death is our life, His loss is our gain;
    The joy for the tear, the peace for the pain.
                  SELECTED

APRIL 27

Morning

Is anything too hard for the LORD?
GENESIS 18:14

God wants us to ask Him for the impossible! God can do things that man cannot do. He would not be God if this were not so. That is why He has graciously made prayer a law of life. *"If ye shall ask . . . I will do"* (John 14:14 KJV). This inviting promise from the Lord means that He will do for us what we cannot do for ourselves; He will do for others what we cannot do for them—*if we but ask Him.* How little do we avail ourselves of this immense privilege!

Someone spoke this searching word at Edinburgh in 1910: "*We have lost the eternal youthfulness of Christianity and have aged into calculating manhood. We seldom pray in earnest for the extraordinary, the limitless, the glorious. We seldom pray with any confidence, for any good to the realization of which we cannot imagine a way. And yet, we suppose ourselves to believe in an Infinite Father.*"

The natural man calculates results. Calculations have no place in our relation with God.

That matter which has been so burdening us just now, and with which we can see no way of dealing, *how are we praying about it? In anxiety, or with thanksgiving?*

Worrying prayer defeats its own answer; rejoicing prayer gets through. "Do not be anxious about anything, but in every situation, by prayer and petition, with thanksgiving, present your requests to God" (Philippians 4:6). Then will come the answer "*immeasurably more than all we ask or imagine*" (Ephesians 3:20).

The more we are cut off from human help, the greater claim we can make on Divine help. The more impossible a thing is to human or mortal power, the more at peace can we be when we look to Him for deliverance.

Only those who see the invisible can do the impossible!

> *God will answer when to thee,*
> *Not a possibility*
> *Of deliverance seems near;*
> *It is then He will appear.*
>
> *God will answer when you pray;*
> *Yea, though mountains block thy way,*
> *At His word, a way will be*
> *E'en through mountains, made for thee.*
>
> *God who still divides the sea,*
> *Willingly will work for thee;*
> *God, before whom mountains fall,*
> *Promises to hear thy call.*

M. E. B.

Evening

I am the Living One; I was dead, and now look, I am alive for ever and ever!
REVELATION 1:18

Flowers! Easter lilies! Speak to me this morning the same sweet lesson of immortality you have been speaking to so many sorrowing souls for years. Wise old Book! Let me read again in your pages the steady assurance that "to die is gain" (Philippians 1:21). Poets! Recite for me your verses that resound the gospel of eternal life in every line. Singers! Break forth once more into hymns of joy—let me hear again my favorite resurrection songs.

Trees, blossoms, and birds; and seas, skies, and winds—whisper it, sound it anew, sing it, echo it, let it beat and resonate through every atom and particle on earth, and let the air be filled with it. Let it be told and retold again and again, until hope rises to become conviction, and conviction becomes the certainty of knowing. Let it be told until, like Paul, even when we face our death, we will go triumphantly, with our faith secure and a peaceful and radiant expression on our face.

> *O sad-faced mourners, who each day are wending*
> *Through churchyard paths of cypress and of yew,*
> *Leave for today the low graves you are tending,*
> *And lift your eyes to God's eternal blue!*
>
> *It is no time for bitterness or sadness;*
> *Choose Easter lilies, not pale asphodels;*
> *Let your souls thrill to the caress of gladness,*
> *And answer the sweet chime of Easter bells.*
>
> *If Christ were still within the grave's low prison,*
> *A captive of the Enemy we dread;*
> *If from that rotting cell He had not risen,*
> *Who then could dry the gloomy tears you shed?*

If Christ were dead there would be need to sorrow,
But He has risen and vanquished death today;
Hush, then your sighs, if only till tomorrow,
At Easter give your grief a holiday.

MAY RILEY SMITH

A well-known preacher was once in his study writing an Easter sermon when this thought gripped him: "My Lord is *living!*" With excitement he jumped up, paced the floor, and began repeating to himself, "Christ is alive. His body is warm. He is not the great 'I was' but the great 'I am.'"

Christ is not only a fact but a *living* fact. He is the glorious truth of Easter Day!

Because of that truth, an Easter lily blooms and an angel sits at every believer's grave. We believe in a risen Lord, so do not look to the past to worship only at His tomb. Look above and within to worship the Christ who lives. Because He lives, we live. ABBOTT BENJAMIN VAUGHAN

~~~~~~~ APRIL 28 ~~~~~~~

Morning

For here we do not have an enduring city, but we
are looking for the city that is to come.

HEBREWS 13:14

Mr. Rothschild was the wealthiest man in the world, but he lived and died in an unfinished mansion. He had power to frighten a nation by calling for gold. Yet one of the cornices of his house was purposely unfinished, to bear testimony that he was a pilgrim in the land. He was an orthodox Jew, and the house of every Jew, according to the Talmud, must be left unfinished. The unfinished cornice says: "Beautiful as this is, it is not my home; I am looking for a city."

Beloved, does the unfinished cornice appear in your life? Do you know that you are a stranger as were our fathers?

One place have I in heaven above—
The glory of His throne;
On this dark earth, whence He is gone,
I have one place alone;
And if His rest in heaven I know,
I joy to find His path below.
One lowly path across the waste,
The lowly path of shame;
I would adore Thy wondrous grace
That I should tread the same.
The Stranger and the Alien, Thou—
And I the stranger, alien, now.

G. T. S.

We bless Thee, that life is a pilgrimage, that the earth is not our rest, that every day brings us nearer our home in the city of God, and that Thou art willing to be our Companion in every step of the desert march!

Am I a pilgrim or a tramp?
Build thee more stately mansions, O my soul!

<hr />

APRIL 28

Evening

When they cried out to the LORD, he raised up for them a deliverer, Othniel . . .
Caleb's younger brother, who saved them. The Spirit of the LORD came on him.

JUDGES 3:9–10

God is continually preparing His heroes, and when the opportunity is right, He puts them into position in an instant. He works so fast, the world wonders where they came fRomans

Dear friend, let the Holy Spirit prepare you, through the discipline of life. And when the finishing touch has been made on the sculpture, it will be easy for God to put you on display in the perfect place.

The day is coming when, like Othniel, we will also judge the nations and will rule and reign with Christ on earth during His millennial kingdom. But before that glorious day, we must allow God to prepare us, as He did Othniel at Kiriath Sepher (Judges 1:11–13). We must allow God to work amid our present trials and in the little victories, the future significance of which we can only imagine. Yet we can be sure that if the Holy Spirit has His way with us, the Lord of heaven and earth has also prepared for us a throne. A. B. SIMPSON

Human strength and human greatness
Spring not from life's sunny side,
Heroes must be more than driftwood
Floating on a waveless tide.

Every highway of life descends into the valley now and then. And everyone must go through the tunnel of tribulation before they can travel on the high road of triumph.

~~~~~~~~~ APRIL 29 ~~~~~~~~~

Morning

God is ever true to His promises.
1 CORINTHIANS 1:9 WNT

God puts Himself within our reach in His promises; and when we can say to Him, "Thou saidst," He cannot say nay—He must do as He has said. In prayer, be sure to *get your feet on a promise*; it will give you purchase enough to force open the gates of heaven and to take it by force! When once you can lay hold of a promise, you have a leverage with God which enables you to count upon the fulfillment of your petition. God cannot go back from His plighted word. F. B. MEYER

"God could no more disappoint faith than He could deny Himself."

A friend gives me a check which reads: "Pay to the order of C. H. Spurgeon the sum of ten pounds." His name is good and his bank is good, but I get nothing from his kindness until I put my own name on the back of the check. It is a very simple act but the signature cannot be dispensed with. There are many nobler names than mine, but none of these can be used instead of my own. If I wrote the Queen's name it would not avail me . . . I must affix my own name.

Even so, each one must personally accept, adopt, and endorse the promise of God by his own individual faith, or he will derive no benefit from it. If you were to write Miltonic lines in honor of the bank, or exceed Tennyson in verses in praise of the generous benefactor, it would avail nothing. The simple, self-written name is demanded, and nothing will be accepted instead of it. We must *believe the promise,* each one for himself, and declare that we know it to be true, or it will bring us no blessing. CHARLES H. SPURGEON

"God is always greater than His promises; He does not only fulfill His promises, He over-fulfills them" (Ephesians 3:20).

Upon Thy Word I rest
Each pilgrim day;
This golden staff is best
For all the way.
What Jesus Christ hath spoken
Cannot be broken!

Upon Thy Word I rest
So strong, so sure!
So full of comfort blest,
So sweet, so pure!
The charter of salvation,
Faith's broad foundation.

Upon Thy Word I stand,
That cannot die;
Christ seals it in my hand,

He cannot lie!
Thy Word that faileth never,
Abideth ever.

FRANCES RIDLEY HAVERGAL

~~~~~ APRIL 29 ~~~~~

Evening

Elijah was a person just like us. He prayed earnestly.

<p align="right">JAMES 5:17 CEB</p>

Thank God Elijah was "just like us"! He sat under a tree, complained to God, and expressed his unbelief—just as we have often done. Yet this was not the case at all when he was truly in touch with God. "Elijah was a man just like us," *yet* "he prayed earnestly." The literal meaning of this in the Greek is magnificent: instead of saying, "earnestly," it says, "He prayed in prayer." In other words, "He kept on praying." The lesson here is that you must *keep praying.*

Climb to the top of Mount Carmel and see that great story of faith and sight. After Elijah had called down fire from heaven to defeat the prophets of Baal, rain was needed for God's prophecy to be fulfilled. And the man who could command fire from heaven could bring rain using the same methods. We are told, "Elijah . . . bent down to the ground and put his face between his knees" (1 Kings 18:42), shutting out all sights and sounds. He put himself in a position, beneath his robe, to neither see nor hear what was happening.

Elijah then said to his servant, "Go and look toward the sea" (1 Kings 18:43). Upon returning, the servant replied, "There is nothing there." How brief his response must have seemed! *"Nothing!"* Can you imagine what we would do under the same circumstances? We would say, "Just as I expected!" and then would stop praying. But did Elijah give up? No. In fact, six times he told his servant, "Go back." Each time the servant returned saying, "Nothing!"

Yet "the seventh time the servant reported, 'A cloud as small as a man's hand is rising from the sea'" (1 Kings 18:44). What a fitting description, for a man's hand had been raised in prayer to God before the rains came. And the rains came so fast and furiously that Elijah warned Ahab to "go down before the rain stops you."

This is a story of faith and sight—faith cutting itself off from everything except God, with sight that looks and yet sees nothing. Yes, in spite of utterly hopeless reports received from sight, this is a story of faith that continues "praying in prayer."

Do you know how to pray in that way—how to prevail in prayer? Let your sight bring you reports as discouraging as possible, but pay no attention to them. Our heavenly Father lives, and even the delays of answers to our prayers are part of His goodness.
ARTHUR TAPPAN PIERSON

Each of three young boys once gave a definition of faith that illustrates the important aspect of tenacity. The first boy defined faith as "taking hold of Christ," the second as "keeping our hold on Him," and the third as "not letting go of Him."

~~~~~~ APRIL 30 ~~~~~~

Morning

John . . . was on the island of Patmos because of the word of God.
REVELATION 1:9

Can we not imagine how eagerly John would lay himself out for a life in incessant service for His Divine Master and Lord? No task would seem too great, no toil too arduous, if only His Lord might be glorified; and we can well imagine how all his plans, ambitions, desires would center round the extension of the kingdom of Jesus Christ. Then, suddenly—Patmos! What now became of all his hopes and longings, his plans and projects? Surely he buried them all as he set foot on Patmos. They died when he first heard his sentence; they were interred with no prospect of a resurrection. Patmos was, for the beloved disciple *The Island of Buried Hopes!*

But John soon discovered that Patmos had its compensations. True, he could no longer entertain the hope of carrying out all his plans, yet he learned in Patmos that truer and nobler service would yet be his than any he had ever contemplated. To him came the assurance that not only has the Lord *loved us, and washed us from our sins in*

His own blood, but He hath set us apart as both kings and priests, and nothing can ever terminate that royal priesthood. John had caught sight of a far greater honor and holier service awaiting him in the land that lies beyond.

It might have been thought that John in his dreary exile was terribly isolated. Someone has said *not isolated, but insulated,* and there is a world of difference between the two. True, the island was small and his confines narrow, but that was only the outer circumstance of his life, his daily environment.

Nothing to see! Alone! Ah, but John found it not so! The overwhelming glory of the sight of his risen Lord robbed him of his strength until he felt the gracious gentle pressure of the pierced Hand resting upon him. Again and again he tells us that he heard a Voice speaking to him. Whilst these things were so he could never feel that there was nothing to see! He could never feel alone! And the Spirit so insulated John *that God's messages might pass through him to the entire world!*

Most of us are well acquainted with this experience. We may not have had to suffer at the hands of any earthly potentate, but there must be comparatively few who have not, at some time, had to bury their fondest hopes, their most eager desires. Oh, weary troubled heart, if God has led *you to the Island of Buried Hopes,* it is that He may show you yet more wonderful things. He has not failed you, nor forgotten you, but has led you into the darkened room because, in His own time and way, *He would reveal to you the unsuspected glory of His grace and power.*

Is our life lonely? Monotonous? We need opened eyes. Standing near us all the time is the same wonderful Lord who stood by John on Patmos. *Oh, the joy, even of Patmos, when it is filled with the presence of Jesus! Patmos has its compensations!*

But if we would share in them, and Patmos is to be a blessing to us, we must fulfill certain conditions. Here is the secret that transforms all disappointments, suffering, monotony, loneliness—*love to Christ,* that impels us to learn of Him day by day, to lean upon Him in constant communion, to look upon Him as the all-sufficient Savior.

To those who fulfill these conditions there is no Patmos that is not irradiated by a glory that is not of earth. SELECTED

Our Father makes no mistakes!

Evening

The cows that were ugly and gaunt ate up the seven sleek, fat cows. . . .
The thin heads of grain swallowed up the seven healthy, full heads.

GENESIS 41:4, 7

These dreams should be a warning to each of us. Yes, it *is* possible for the best years of our life, the best experiences we have enjoyed, the best victories we have won, and the best service we have rendered, to be swallowed up by times of failure, defeat, dishonor, and uselessness in God's kingdom. Some people whose lives offered exceptional promise and achievement have come to such an end. It is certainly terrible to imagine, but it is true. *Yet it is never necessary.*

Samuel Dickey Gordon once said that the only safe assurance against such a tragedy is to have a "fresh touch with God daily—or even hourly." My blessed, fruitful, and victorious experiences of yesterday have no lingering value to me today. In fact, they can be "swallowed up" or reversed by today's failures, unless I see them as incentives to spur me on to even better and richer experiences today.

Maintaining this "fresh touch with God," by abiding in Christ, will be the only thing to keep the "ugly and gaunt . . . cows" and the "thin heads of grain" from consuming my life. MESSAGES FOR THE MORNING WATCH

Morning

He was going there on foot.
ACTS 20:13

Why did Paul prefer to go *on foot?* And how may we account for his desire to go *alone?*

There are times in every man's life when he wants no comrade on the road with him. A precious part of our Creed is "I believe in the communion of saints," but, after all, it is not in such communion that we have the closest fellowship with God in Christ. It is *in secret* that we learn the secret of the Lord.

It was in the eerie solitude of Bethel, and in the gray dawn by the ford Jabbok that Jacob was granted visions of God.

It was when he was alone in the silent desert that Moses was shown the burning bush and received the Divine commission.

It was when Joshua walked unattended under the stars by the wall of Jericho that the Captain of the Lord's hosts stood before him.

It was when Isaiah was alone in the Temple that a live coal touched his lips.

It was when Mary was alone that the angel brought to her the message of the Lord.

It was when Elisha was plowing his lonely furrow that the prophet's mantle fell upon his shoulders.

Noah built and voyaged alone. His neighbors laughed at his strangeness and perished.

Abraham wandered and worshiped alone; Sodomites smiled at the simple shepherd, followed the fashion, and fed the flames.

Daniel dined and prayed alone.

Jesus lived and died alone.

Ah, it is good to go "on foot" sometimes, when even our nearest and dearest go by another road. *For when we are alone we have a better chance of One joining us, and making our hearts burn while He talks with us by the way.*

I love the lonely creative hours with God. MADAME GUYON

> *When storms of life are round me beating,*
> *When rough the path that I have trod,*
> *Within my closet doors retreating,*
> *I love to be alone with God.*
>
> *What tho' the clouds have gathered o'er me*
> *What tho' I've passed beneath the rod?*
> *God's perfect will there lies before me,*
> *When I am thus alone with God.*
>
> *Alone with God the world forbidden,*
> *Alone with Him, O blest retreat!*

Alone with God and in Him hidden,
To hold with Him communion sweet.

MAY 1
Evening

God, who does not lie, promised.
TITUS 1:2

Faith is not conjuring up, through an act of your will, a sense of certainty that something is going to happen. No, it is recognizing God's promise as an actual fact, believing it is true, rejoicing in the knowledge of that truth, and then simply resting because God said it.

Faith turns a promise into a prophecy. A promise is contingent upon our cooperation, but when we exercise genuine faith in it, it becomes a prophecy. Then we can move ahead with certainty that it will come to pass, because "God . . . does not lie."
DAYS OF HEAVEN UPON EARTH

I often hear people praying for more faith, but when I listen carefully to them and get to the essence of their prayer, I realize it is not more faith they are wanting at all. What they are wanting is their faith to be changed to sight.

Faith does not say, "I see this is good for me; therefore God must have sent it." Instead, faith declares, "God sent it; therefore it must be good for me."

Faith, when walking through the dark with God, only asks Him to hold his hand more tightly. PHILLIPS BROOKS

> *The Shepherd does not ask of thee*
> *Faith in your faith, but only faith in Him;*
> *And this He meant in saying, "Come to me."*
> *In light or darkness seek to do His will,*
> *And leave the work of faith to Jesus still.*
> HYMNAL

Morning

Those who look to him are radiant.

PSALM 34:5

How lovely are the faces of
The men who talk with God—
Lit with an inner sureness of
The path their feet have trod;
How gentle is the manner of
A man who walks with Him!
No strength can overcome him, and
No cloud his courage dim.
Keen are the hands and feet—ah yes—
Of those who wait His will,
And clear as crystal mirrors, are
The hearts His love can fill.

Some lives are drear from doubt and fear
While others merely plod;
But lovely faces mark the men
Who walk and talk with God.

"MARKED FOR HIS OWN" BY PAULINE PROSSER-THOMPSON

I presume everybody has known saints whose lives were just radiant. Joy beamed out of their eyes; joy bubbled over their lips; joy seemed to fairly run from their fingertips. You could not come in contact with them without having a new light come into your own life. They were like electric batteries charged with joy.

If you look into the eyes of such radiantly happy persons—not those people who are sometimes on the mountaintop and sometimes in the valley, but people who are always radiantly happy—you will find that every one is a man or a woman who spends a great deal of time in prayer with God alone. *God is the source of all joy, and if we come into contact with Him, His infinite joy comes into our lives.*

Would *you* like to be a radiant Christian? You may be. Spend time in prayer. You cannot be a radiant Christian in any other way. Why is it that prayer in the Name of Christ makes one radiantly happy? It is because prayer makes God real. *The gladdest thing upon earth is to have a real God!* I would rather give up anything I have in the world, or anything I ever may have, than give up my faith in God. You cannot have vital faith in God if you give all your time to the world and to secular affairs, to reading the newspapers and to reading literature, no matter how good it is. *Unless you take time for fellowship with God, you cannot have a real God. If you do take time for prayer you will have a real, living God, and if you have a living God you will have a radiant life.* R. A. TORREY

Of all the lights you carry in your face, Joy will reach the farthest out to sea. H. W. BEECHER

It was said by Chesterfield, the heartless dandy, upon his return from visiting Fenelon, the Archbishop of Cambrai: "If I had stayed another day in his presence, *I am afraid I would have had to become a Christian; his spirit was so pure, so attractive and beautiful.*"

<center>~~~~ MAY 2 ~~~~</center>

Evening

The LORD has established his throne in heaven, and his kingdom rules over all.
PSALM 103:19

Some time ago as I went out my door in the early spring, a blast of easterly wind rounded the corner. It seemed defiant and merciless and was fierce and dry, raising a cloud of dust ahead of it. As I removed the key from the door, I quite impatiently began to say, "*I wish the wind would . . .*" What I was about to say was *change*, but my thought was stopped and the sentence was never finished.

As I continued on my way, this incident became a parable for me. I imagined an angel handing me a key and saying, "My Master sends you His love and asked me to

—— 310 ——

give you this." Wondering, I asked, "What is it?" "It is *the key to the winds*," the angel said and then disappeared.

My first thought was, "This indeed will bring me happiness." So I hurried high into the hills to the source of the winds and stood amid the caves. I proclaimed, "I will do away with the terrible east wind—it will never plague us again!" I summoned that unfriendly wind to me, closed the door behind it, and heard it echoing through the hollow caves. As I turned the key, triumphantly locking it in, I said, "There, I am finished with that." Then looking around me, I asked myself, "What should I put in its place?" I thought of the warm southerly wind and how pleasant it must be to newborn lambs and new flowers and plants of all kinds. But as I put the key in the door, it began to burn my hand. I cried aloud, "What am I doing? Who knows what damage I may cause? How do I know what the fields want and need? Ten thousand problems may result from this foolish wish of mine!"

Bewildered and ashamed, I looked up and asked the Lord to send His angel to take away the key. Then I promised I would never ask for it again. To my amazement, the Lord Himself came and stood by me. He stretched out His hand to take the key, and as I placed it there, I saw it touch that sacred scar.

I was filled with remorse as I wondered how I could ever have complained about anything done by Him who bore such sacred signs of His love. Then He took the key and hung it on His belt. I asked, "Do you keep the key to the winds?" "I do, my child," He graciously answered. And as He spoke, I noticed that all the keys to my life were hanging there as well. He saw my look of amazement and asked, *"Did you not know, dear child, that my 'kingdom rules over all'?"*

"If you rule over all," I questioned, "is it safe to complain about anything?" Then He tenderly laid His hand upon me to say, "My dear child, your only safety comes from loving, trusting, and praising Me through everything." MARK GUY PEARSE

~~~~~~ MAY 3 ~~~~~~

Morning

*No one who puts a hand to the plow and looks back
is fit for service in the kingdom of God.*
LUKE 9:62

Keep me from turning back!
Deep indeed is the world's debt to people who would not quit!

Suppose Columbus had not sailed! Suppose Anne Sullivan, discouraged, had lost hope for Helen Keller! Suppose Louis Pasteur, searching for a cure for rabies, had not said to his weary helpers: "Keep on! The important thing is not to leave the subject!"

Many a race is lost at the last lap! Many a ship is washed on the reefs outside the final port! Many a battle is lost on the last charge!

What hope have *we* of completing the course upon which we have embarked? What hope? Ah! *He is able to keep.* "He is able to save them *to the uttermost* that come unto God by him" (Hebrews 7:25 KJV).

God cannot help us until we stop running away. We must be willing to stand somewhere and trust Him. He has reinforcements to send, but there must be somebody there to meet them when they come, and *fear takes flight as well as fright.* "Fear not" is the first step.

> *Keep me from turning back*
> *My hand is on the plow, my faltering hand:*
> *But all in front of me is untilled land,*
> *The wilderness and solitary place,*
> *The lonely desert with its interspace.*
> *What harvest have I but this paltry grain,*
> *These dwindling husks, a handful of dry corn,*
> *These poor lean stalks? My courage is outworn.*
> *Keep me from turning back.*
> *The handles of my plow with tears are wet,*
> *The shares with rust are spoiled, and yet, and yet,*
> *My God! My God! Keep me from turning back.*
>
> AUTHOR UNKNOWN

MAY 3
Evening

Everyone who calls on the name of the LORD *will be saved.*
JOEL 2:32

So why don't I call on His name? Why do I run to this person or that person, when God is so near and will hear my faintest call? Why do I sit down to plot my own course and make my own plans? Why don't I immediately place myself and my burden on the Lord?

Straight ahead is the best way to run, so why don't I run directly to the living God? Instead, I look in vain for deliverance everywhere else, but with God I will find it. With Him I have His royal promise: "[I] *will* be saved." And with Him I never need to ask if I may call on Him or not, for the word "everyone" is all encompassing. It includes me and means anybody and everybody who calls upon His name. Therefore I will trust in this verse and will immediately call on the glorious Lord who has made such a great promise.

My situation is urgent, and I cannot see how I will ever be delivered. Yet this is not my concern, for He who made the promise will find a way to keep it. My part is simply to obey His commands, not to direct His ways. I am His servant, not His advisor. I call upon Him and He will deliver me. CHARLES H. SPURGEON

MAY 4
Morning

*And the God of all grace, who called you to his eternal glory
in Christ, after you have suffered a little while, will himself
restore you and make you strong, firm and steadfast.*
1 PETER 5:10

What a singular wish! The singular thing about it is the blot in the middle—*after you have suffered a little while.* What would you think of receiving this wish from a friend?

Yet this is what Peter desired for those to whom he wrote: all the gifts and the graces of the Christ-life in perfection, but not until after they had "suffered a little while." Peter wrote out of the bitter experience of his own past: *he* had come into his kingdom too soon; he had obtained his crown before he could support its cares. His faith had been drenched in the brine; his love had been cooled in the judgment hall as he sat by the fire and cried, "I don't know the man!" (Matthew 26:74).

In essence he is saying, "I do not want you to find the keys too soon." He does not want them to be innocent only, pure because there is no temptation, loyal because there is no danger.

There is a peace, which is not the peace of the Son of God. Be not that our peace, O God!

We cannot know Thy stillness until it is broken. There is no music in the silence until we have heard the roar of battle! We cannot see Thy beauty until it is shaded. LEAVES FOR QUIET HOURS

After the shadows, the sunlight will come.

~~~~~~~~ MAY 4 ~~~~~~~~

Evening

He wounds, but he also binds up; he injures, but his hands also heal.
JOB 5:18

The ministry of great sorrow!

As we walk beside the hills that have been so violently shaken by a severe earthquake, we realize that times of complete calm follow those of destruction. In fact, pools of clear, still water lie in the valley beneath the fallen rocks of those hills as water lilies reflect their beauty to the sky. The reeds along the streams whisper in the wind, and the village rises once again, forgetting the graves of the past. And the church steeple, still bright after weathering the storm, proclaims a renewed prayer for protection from Him who holds the corners of the earth in His hands and gives strength to the hills. JOHN RUSKIN

God plowed one day with an earthquake,
    And drove His furrows deep!
The huddled plains upstarted,
    The hills were all aleap!

But that is the mountains' secret,
    Long hidden in their breast;
"God's peace is everlasting,"
    Are the dream words of their rest.

He made them the haunts of beauty,
    The home chosen for His grace;
He spreads forth His mornings upon them,
    His sunsets light their face.

His winds bring messages to them—
    Strong storm-news from the main;
They sing it down the valleys
    In the love song of the rain.

They are nurseries for young rivers,
    Nests for His flying cloud,
Homesteads for newborn races,
    Masterful, free, and proud.

The people of tired cities
    Come up to their shrines and pray;
God freshens them within again,
    As He passes by all day.

And lo, I have caught their secret!
    The beauty deeper than all!
This faith—that life's hard moments,
    When the jarring sorrows befall,

Are but God plowing His mountains;
And those mountains yet will be
The source of His grace and freshness,
And His peace everlasting to me.

WILLIAM C. GARNETT

MAY 5
Morning

When he saw the wagons . . . the spirit of Jacob . . . revived.
GENESIS 45:27 KJV

A very simple sight: just some farm wagons laden with corn—food for the starving household. It was these wagons turning into the courtyard that raised the fast-falling hopes of Jacob to expectancy. They remind me of other wagons laden and sent by another One greater than Joseph, even our Lord Jesus Christ. These wagons of His are a great stimulus to our faith. They come unseen to us in our hours of darkness—when our hopes are dashed to the ground. Yes, *when we are in the awful grips of spiritual starvation, how blessed are these wagons as they are seen approaching!*

Lift up your eyes! Look out for them! When they come, they will not be empty! You will be fed and nourished with the choicest of His stores.

"Blessed be the Lord, who daily loadeth us with benefits" (Psalm 68:19 KJV).

"All these things are against me!" Yet those things,
Those very things, were God's machinery
For working out your heart's imaginings,
For turning hope to blessed certainty.
Oh, man who walked by sight,
You should have known the darkest hour of night
Is just before the earliest streak of gray.
Your wagons, all the time, were on their way!

Faith? Yes, but with a flaw.
Here was a man who trusted when he saw!

And yet,
The Holy One has set
His name beside two men of saintly will,
And calls Himself the "God of Jacob" still!
That you and I,
Lacking in faith, maybe, or gentleness
May yet stretch out weak hands of hopelessness,
And find the God of Jacob very nigh.

Oh, sorrowful soul! Trust just a little longer.
Who knows, but o'er your bare, brown hill
The wagons may be coming nearer still?
Give faith a chance. For soon, how soon it may
Give place to sight; and then
Never again
Will you have opportunity to show
That you can trust, albeit you cannot know.

FAY INCHFAWN

MAY 5

Evening

As they began to sing and praise, the LORD set ambushes against the
men . . . who were invading Judah, and they were defeated.

2 CHRONICLES 20:22

Oh, if only we would worry less about our problems and sing and praise more! There are thousands of things that shackle us that could be turned into instruments of music, if we just knew how to do it. Think of those people who ponder, meditate, and weigh the affairs of life, and who continually study the mysterious inner workings of God's providence, wondering why they suffer burdens and are opposed and battled on every front. How different their lives would be, and how much more joyful, if they would stop indulging in self-centered and inward thinking and instead would daily lift their experiences to God, praising Him for them.

It is easier to sing your worries away than to reason them away. Why not sing in the morning? Think of the birds—they are the first to sing each day, and they have fewer worries than anything else in creation. And don't forget to sing in the evening, which is what the robins do when they have finished their daily work. Once they have flown their last flight of the day and gathered the last bit of food, they find a treetop from which to sing a song of praise.

Oh, that we might sing morning and evening, offering up song after song of continual praise throughout our day! Selected

> Don't let the song go out of your life
>   Although it sometimes will flow
> In a minor strain; it will blend again
>   With the major tone you know.
>
> Although shadows rise to obscure life's skies,
>   And hide for a time the sun,
> The sooner they'll lift and reveal the rift,
>   If you let the melody run.
>
> Don't let the song go out of your life;
>   Though the voice may have lost its trill,
> Though the quivering note may die in your throat,
>   Let it sing in your spirit still.
>
> Don't let the song go out of your life;
>   Let it ring in your soul while here;
> And when you go hence, it will follow you thence,
>   And live on in another sphere.

Morning

Jesus made no reply, not even to a single charge.
MATTHEW 27:14

Not railing for railing; not a word. How much is lost by a word! Be still! Keep quiet! If they smite you on one cheek turn the other also. Never retort! Hush—not a word! *Never mind your reputation or your character; they are in His hands; you mar them by trying to retain them.*

Do not strive. Open not your mouth. Silence! A word will grieve, disturb the gentle dove. Hush—not a word!

Are you misunderstood? Never mind! Will it hurt your influence and weaken your power for good? *Leave it to Him*—His to take care and take charge.

Are you wronged and your good name tarnished? All right! Be it yours to be meek and lowly; simple and gentle—not a word! *Let Him keep you in perfect peace; stay your mind on Him; trust in Him.*

Not a word of argument, debate, or controversy. Mind your own business. Be still!

Never judge, condemn, arraign, censure. Not a word! Never a disparaging remark of another. *As you would others should do to you, so do you.*

Pause! Be still! Selah! Not a word, emphatically; not even a look that will mar the sweet serenity of the soul. Get still! Know God! *Keep silence before Him!* Stillness is better than noise.

Not a word of murmuring or complaining in supplication; not a word of nagging or persuading. Let language be simple, gentle, quiet; you utter not a word, but give Him opportunity to speak. *Hearken to hear His voice.*

This is the way to honor and to know Him. Not a word—not the least word! Listen to obey. Words make trouble. *Be still! This is the voice of the Spirit.*

Restlessness, fret, worry, makes the place of His abiding unpleasant. *He is to keep in perfect peace;* take it not out of His hands.

I rode with a dear brother in the cars, and poured my weighty burdens in his ears. I took his earnest advice to my heart. His counsel was not the mind of the Spirit, and when I returned to my seat in the car the Spirit gently said to me: "So you went to him!

Could you not trust Me?" I confessed, was forgiven, restored. And I determined *never again to take my case out of His hands.*

"You are my witnesses" (Isaiah 43:10). *Witness in love.* Not a word! And, like the dew of the morning, or the sweet breeze of eventide, you will be quietly blessed, and you will be so glad that you uttered—*never a word!* STEPHEN MERRITT

> *Let me no wrong or idle word*
> *Unthinking say;*
> *Set Thou a seal upon my lips,*
> *Just for today.*

~~~~~~~   MAY 6   ~~~~~~~
Evening

The secret of the LORD *is with them that fear him.*
PSALM 25:14 KJV

There are certain secrets of God's providence He allows His children to learn. Often, however, at least on the surface, His dealings with them appear to be harsh and hidden. Yet faith looks deeper and says, "This is God's secret. You are looking only on the outside, but I look deeper and see the hidden meaning."

Remember, diamonds are found in the rough, and their true value cannot be seen. And when the tabernacle was built in the wilderness, there was nothing ornate about its outward appearance. In fact, the outer covering of the thick hides of sea cows gave no hint of the valuable things inside.

Dear friend, God may send you some valuable gifts wrapped in unattractive paper. But do not worry about the wrappings, for you can be sure that inside He has hidden treasures of love, kindness, and wisdom. If we will simply take what He sends *and trust Him* for the blessings inside, we will learn the meaning of the secrets of His providence, even in times of darkness. A. B. SIMPSON

> *Not until each loom is silent,*
> *And the crossthreads cease to fly,*

Will God unroll the pattern
And explain the reason why

The dark threads are as needful
In the Weaver's skillful hand,
As the threads of gold and silver
For the pattern He has planned.

A person who has Christ as his Master is the master of every circumstance. Are your circumstances pressing in on you? Do not push away, for they are the Potter's handstand. You will learn to master them not by stopping their progress but by enduring their discipline. Your circumstances are not only shaping you into a vessel of beauty and honor but also providing you with resources of great value.

~~~~~~~ MAY 7 ~~~~~~~

Morning

Then he went down to Nazareth with them and was obedient to them.
LUKE 2:51

Think of it! Thirty years at home with His brothers and sisters who did not believe in Him! We fix on the three years which were extraordinary, and forget altogether the thirty years of absolute submissiveness. "An extraordinary exhibition of submissiveness! And the disciple is not above his master" (Matthew 10:24 KJV).

If God is putting you through a spell of submission, and you seem to be losing your individuality and everything else, *it is because Jesus is making you one with Him.*

Let Dr. A. J. Gossip, the great gifted Scottish preacher, tell us how once on a day in France, the bonniest of experiences befell him.

He had been for weeks amid the appalling desolation and sickening sights of the war front. Then they had gone back to rest where there were budding hedgerows, a shimmer of green on living trees, grass, and flowers—glorious flowers in the first splendor of spring. It seemed Heaven! Then came the order to return to Passchendaele and the battlefront.

"It reached us," says Dr. Gossip, "on a perfect afternoon of sunshine; and with a heart grown hot and hard I turned down a little land with a brown burn wimpling beside it and a lush meadow—all brave sheets of purple and golden flowers—on either side. The earth was very beautiful, and life seemed very sweet, and it was hard to go back into the old purgatory and face death again. And, with that, through the gap in the hedge there came a shepherd laddie tending his flock of some two dozen sheep. He was not driving them in our rough way, with two barking dogs. He went first, and they were following him; if one loitered he called it by name and it came running to him. So they moved on down the lane, up a little hill, up to the brow and over it, and so out of my life. I stood staring after them, hearing as if the words were spoken aloud, to me first, and to me only: *And when he putteth forth his own sheep, he goeth before them*" (John 10:4 kjv).

Peter, outworn,
And menaced by the sword,
Shook off the dust of Rome;
And, as he fled,
Met one, with eager face,
Hastening cityward,
And, to his vast amaze,
It was the Lord.

"Lord, whither goest Thou?" He cried, importunate; And Christ replied,
"Peter, I suffer loss, I go to take thy place, To bear thy cross."
Then Peter bowed his head,
Discomforted;

Then, at the Master's feet,
Found grace complete,
And courage, and new faith,
And turned, with Him
To death.

JOHN OXENHAM

Evening

*Jesus told his disciples a parable to show them that
they should always pray and not give up.*
LUKE 18:1

The failure to *persevere* is the most common problem in prayer and intercession. We begin to pray for something, raising our petitions for a day, a week, or even a month, but then if we have not received a definite answer, we quickly give up and stop praying for it altogether.

This is a mistake with deadly consequences and is simply a trap where we begin many things but never see them completed. It leads to ruin in every area of life. People who get into the habit of starting without ever finishing form the habit of failure. And those who begin praying about something without ever praying it through to a successful conclusion form the same habit in prayer. Giving up is admitting failure and defeat. Defeat then leads to discouragement and doubt in the power of prayer, and that is fatal to the success of a person's prayer life.

People often ask, "How long should I pray? Shouldn't I come to the place where I stop praying and leave the matter in God's hands?" The only answer is this: *Pray until what you pray for has been accomplished or until you have complete assurance in your heart that it will be.* Only when one of these two conditions has been met is it safe to stop persisting in prayer, for prayer not only is calling upon God but is also a battle with Satan. And because God uses our intercession as a mighty weapon of victory in the conflict, He alone must decide when it is safe to cease from petitioning. Therefore we dare not stop praying until either the answer itself has come or we receive assurance it will come.

In the first instance, we stop because we actually see the answer. In the second, we stop because we believe, and faith in our hearts is as trustworthy as the sight of our eyes, for it is "faith *from* God" (Ephesians 6:23) and the "faith *of* God" (Romans 3:3 KJV) that we have within us.

As we live a life of prayer, we will more and more come to experience and recognize this God-given assurance. We will know when to quietly rest in it or when to continue praying until we receive His answer. THE PRACTICE OF PRAYER

Wait at God's promise until He meets you there, for He always returns by the path of His promises. SELECTED

Morning

Against all hope, Abraham in hope believed.
ROMANS 4:18

When God is going to do something *wonderful*, He begins with a difficulty. If it is going to be something *very wonderful*, He begins with an impossibility.
CHARLES INWOOD

> *O God of the impossible!*
> *Since all things are to Thee*
> *But soil in which Omnipotence*
> *Can work almightily,*
>
> *Each trial may to us become*
> *The means that will display*
> *How o'er what seems impossible*
> *Our God hath perfect sway!*
>
> *The very storms that beat upon*
> *Our little bark so frail,*
> *But manifest Thy power to quell*
> *All forces that assail.*
>
> *The things that are to us too hard,*
> *The foes that are too strong,*
> *Are just the very ones that may*
> *Awake a triumph song.*

O God of the impossible,
When we no hope can see,
Grant us the faith that still believes
all possible to Thee!

J. H. S.

~~~~~~ MAY 8 ~~~~~~

Evening

</div>

<div align="center">

Walking around in the fire.
DANIEL 3:25

</div>

When Shadrach, Meshach, and Abednego were thrown into the furnace, the fire did not stop them from moving, for they were seen "walking around." Actually, the fire was one of the streets they traveled to their destination. The comfort we have from Christ's revealed truth is not that it teaches us freedom *from* sorrow but that it teaches us freedom *through* sorrow.

O dear God, when darkness overshadows me, teach me that I am merely traveling through a tunnel. It will then be enough for me to know that someday it will be all right.

I have been told that someday I will stand at the top of the Mount of Olives and experience the height of resurrection glory. But heavenly Father, I want more—I want Calvary to lead up to it. I want to know that the shadows of darkness are the shade on a road—the road leading to Your heavenly house. Teach me that the reason I must climb the hill is because Your house is there! Knowing this, I will not be hurt by sorrow, if I will only *walk* in the fire. GEORGE MATHESON

> *"The road is too rough," I said;*
> *"It is uphill all the way;*
> *No flowers, but thorns instead;*
> *And the skies overhead are gray."*
> *But One took my hand at the entrance dim,*
> *And sweet is the road that I walk with Him.*

<div align="center">

—— 325 ——

</div>

"The cross is too great," I cried—
    "More than the back can bear,
So rough and heavy and wide,
    And nobody near to care."
And One stooped softly and touched my hand:
"I know. I care. And I understand."

Then why do we fret and cry;
    Cross-bearers all we go:
But the road ends by and by
    In the dearest place we know,
And every step in the journey we
May take in the Lord's own company.

~~~~~~~~~   MAY 9   ~~~~~~~~~
                Morning

Come to me, all you who are weary and burdened, and I will give you rest.
                MATTHEW 11:28

I wonder why the easiest thing in the Christian life is the most difficult? I wonder why I work by a guttering candle when there is an electric light switch within easy reach of my hand? The answer, of course, is that I don't. I am not so foolish—except in one direction, and that is Godward. In our spiritual life many of us seem to be content struggling along with all the poor primitive resources of a weak, human nature, while all the infinite power of the Godhead is at our disposal. There is no condition of human nature, no circumstance of human life, that is not completely provided for in the all-embracing love of our Father God; yet the vast majority of His children struggle along life's road, bearing burdens that He is eager to carry, and has urged them to entrust to Him. I wonder why?

It should be an easy thing, an alluring thing, a thrilling thing to talk to God, to hold converse with Christ. Yet, strange to relate, prayer is the most neglected of all the Christian ministries. The most perfunctory, abbreviated and ofttimes omitted exercise of many a Christian's life is the prayer-time. I wonder why?

Perhaps the difficulty lies in its very ease, its utter simplicity. Just to kneel at your bedside, and with the old abandon of childhood and the same unquestioning faith, leave all burdens and cares and needs with the Father! How childlike, but how difficult! How hard to relax; to spare an hour or even half that time out of our busy, rushing, worried lives, and go quietly to our room, shut the door and be still in His presence! How hard to divest ourselves of our sophistication, of our self-consciousness and self-centeredness, and ever-present feeling that I have to face and meet and shoulder all these cares and responsibilities! How hard just to be a child again, and with a great, happy sigh, settle down carefree at His feet, perfectly assured that He careth; that the government is upon His shoulder. A. STUART M'NAIRN

MAY 9

Evening

Abraham remained standing before the LORD.
GENESIS 18:22

In this chapter, Abraham pleaded with God for the lives of others. A friend of God's can do exactly that. But perhaps you see Abraham's level of faith and his friendship with God as something far beyond your own possibilities. Do not be discouraged, however, for Abraham grew in his faith not by giant leaps but step by step. And we can do the same.

The person whose faith has been severely tested yet who has come through the battle victoriously is the person to whom even greater tests will come. The finest jewels are those that are the most carefully cut and polished, and the most precious metals are put through the hottest fires. You can be sure Abraham would never have been called the Father of Faith had he not been tested to the utmost.

Read Genesis 22. In verse 2 God said to Abraham, "Take your son, your only son—whom you love—Isaac and . . . sacrifice him." We then see him climbing Mount Moriah with his heart heavy and yearning yet humbly obedient. He climbed with Isaac, the object of his great love, who was about to be sacrificed at the command of God—the One whom Abraham faithfully loved and served!

What a lesson this should be to us when we question God's dealings in our lives!

Rebuke all explanations that try to cast doubt on this staggering scene, for this was an object lesson for all ages! Angels also looked on in awe. Will Abraham's faith not stand forever as a strength and a help to all God's people? Will his trial not be a witness to the fact that unwavering faith will always prove the faithfulness of God?

The answer is a resounding—yes! And once Abraham's faith had victoriously endured its greatest test, the Angel of the Lord—the Lord Jesus, Jehovah, and He in whom the "many promises God has made . . . are 'Yes' . . . [and] 'Amen'" (2 Corinthians 1:20)—spoke to him and said, "Now I know that you fear God" (Genesis 22:12). The Lord said to him, in effect, "Because you have trusted me through this great trial, I will trust you, and you will forever be 'my friend' [Isaiah 41:8]." The Lord promised Abraham, "I will surely bless you . . . and through your offspring all nations on earth will be blessed, because you have obeyed me" (Genesis 22:17–18).

It is true, and always will be, that *"those who rely on faith are blessed along with Abraham, the man of faith"* (Galatians 3:9). SELECTED

Having a friendship with God is no small thing.

~~~~~~~   MAY 10   ~~~~~~~

Morning

Offer every part of yourself to [God] as an instrument of righteousness.
ROMANS 6:13

God can do nothing with us if we do not yield. We recall a day of sightseeing in the palace of Genoa. We entered a room seemingly empty; bare walls, floors, and tables greeted us. Presently the guide led us across the room to the wall at the farther side. There we espied a niche in the wall. It was covered with a glass case. Behind the case was a magnificent violin, in perfect preservation—Paganini's favorite violin; the rich old Cremona upon which he loved most of all to display his marvelous skill. We gazed intently upon the superb instrument, with its warm rich tints, sinuous curves, and perfect model. And then we tried to imagine the wondrous strains the touch of the great master would bring forth if he were there in that quiet palace chamber . . . Nay, but this could not be! He could not possibly do so! For it was locked up against him! It gave the master no chance.

It is not how much do you have, but how much of yours does God have.

Present your members as instruments to God. To present means "to place near the hand of one." Yielded, reachable, usable—this gives God a chance.

Make it a real transaction!

God-yielded wills find the God-planned life. JAMES H. McCONKEY

> I owned a little boat a while ago
> And sailed a Morning Sea without a fear,
> And whither any breeze might fairly blow
> I'd steer the little craft afar or near.
>
> Mine was the boat, and mine the air,
> And mine the sea; not mine, a care.
>
> My boat became my place of nightly toil.
> I sailed at sunset to the fishing ground.
> At morn the boat was freighted with the spoil
> That my all-conquering work and skill had found.
>
> Mine was the boat, and mine the net,
> And mine the skill, and power to get.
>
> One day there passed along the silent shore,
> While I my net was casting in the sea,
> A man, who spoke as never man before;
> I followed Him—new life begun in me.
>
> Mine was the boat, but His the voice,
> And His the call; yet mine, the choice.
>
> Ah, 'twas a fearful night out on the lake,
> And all my skill availed not at the helm,

Till Him asleep I waken, crying "Take,
Take Thou command, lest waters overwhelm!"

His was the boat, and His the Sea,
And His the Peace o'er all and me.

Once from His boat He taught the curious throng,
Then bade me let down nets out in the Sea;
I murmured, but obeyed, nor was it long
Before the catch amazed and humbled me.

His was the boat, and His the skill, And His the catch—and His, my will.
JOSEPH ADDISON RICHARDS

Give God a chance!

MAY 10

Evening

I would have despaired unless I had believed that I would see the goodness of the
LORD. . . . *Wait for the* LORD; *be strong and let your heart take courage.*
PSALM 27:13–14 NASB

Do not despair!

Oh, how great the temptation is to despair at times! Our soul becomes depressed and disheartened, and our faith staggers under the severe trials and testing that come into our lives, especially during times of bereavement and suffering. We may come to the place where we say, "I cannot bear this any longer. I am close to despair under these circumstances God has allowed. He tells me not to despair, but what am I supposed to do when I am at this point?"

What have you done in the past when you felt weak physically? You could not *do* anything. You *ceased* from doing. In your weakness, you leaned on the shoulder of a strong loved one. You leaned completely on someone else and rested, becoming still, and trusting in another's strength.

It is the same when you are tempted to despair under spiritual afflictions. Once you have come close to the point of despair, God's message is not, "Be strong and courageous" (Joshua 1:6), for He knows that your strength and courage have run away. Instead, He says sweetly, "Be still, and know that I am God" (Psalm 46:10).

Hudson Taylor was so weak and feeble in the last few months of his life that he told a friend, "I am so weak I cannot write. I cannot read my Bible. I cannot even pray. All I can do is lie still in the arms of God as a little child, trusting Him." This wonderful man of God, who had great spiritual power, came to the point of physical suffering and weakness where all he could do was lie still and trust.

That is all God asks of you as His dear child. When you become weak through the fierce fires of affliction, do not try to "*be strong.*" Just "*be still, and know that [He is] God.*" And know that He will sustain you and bring you through the fire.

God reserves His best medicine for our times of deepest despair.

"Be strong and take heart" (Psalm 27:14).

> Be strong, He has not failed you
>   In all the past,
> And will He go and leave you
>   To sink at last?
> No, He said He will hide you
>   Beneath His wing;
> And sweetly there in safety
>   You then may sing.

SELECTED

MAY 11
Morning

God's field.
1 CORINTHIANS 3:9

The plowing and harrowing are painful processes. And surely the Divine Plowman is at work in the world as never before. He plows *by His Spirit, by His Word, and by His providences.* Though painful be the processes of cultivation, they are essential.

Could the earth speak, it would say, "I felt the hard plow today; I knew what was coming; when the plow-point first struck me, I was full of pain and distress and I could have cried out for very agony, for the point was sharp and driven through me with great energy; but now, I think, *this means the blade, the ear, the full corn in the ear, the golden harvest and harvest-home.*"

When the plow of God's providence first cuts up a man's life, what wonder if the man should exclaim a little; yea, if he should give way to one hour's grief! But the man may come to himself, ere eventide, and say, "Plow on, Lord! I want my life to be *plowed all over,* that it may be sown all over, and *that in every corner there may be the golden grain or the beautiful flowers.* Pity me that I exclaimed when I first felt the plowshare. Thou knowest my frame; Thou rememberest that I am dust. But now I recollect; I put things together; I see Thy meaning; *so drive on, Thou Plowman of Eternity!*"

He does not use the plow and harrow without intention. Where God plows, He intends to sow. *His plowing is a proof He is for and not against you.*

"For, behold, I am for you, and I will turn unto you, and ye shall be tilled and sown" (Ezekiel 36:9 KJV).

Let us never forget that the Husbandman is never so near the land as when He is plowing it, the very time when we are tempted to think He hath forsaken us.

His plowing is a proof that He thinks you *of value* and *worth chastening,* for *He does not waste His plowing on the barren sand.* He will not plow continually, but only for a time and for a definite purpose. Soon He will close that process. "When a farmer plows for planting, does he plow continually? Does he keep on breaking up and working the soil?" (Isaiah 28:24). Verily, No! Soon, aye soon, we shall, through these painful processes and by His gentle showers of grace become *His fruitful land.*

"The desolate land will be cultivated. . . . They will say, 'This land that was laid waste has become like the garden of Eden', and thus we shall be a praise unto Him" (Ezekiel 36:34–35).

> Come ill, come well, the cross, the crown, The rainbow or the thunder—
> I fling my soul and body down For God to plow them under.
> "A PRINCE OF THE CAPTIVITY" BY JOHN BUCHAN

Evening

We went through fire and water, but you brought us to a place of abundance.
PSALM 66:12

It may seem paradoxical, but the only person who is at rest has achieved it through conflict. This peace, born of conflict, is not like the ominous lull before the storm but like the serenity and the quietness following the storm, with its fresh, purified air.

The person who may appear to be blessed, having been untouched by sorrow, is typically not one who is strong and at peace. His qualities have never been tested, and he does not know how he would handle even a mild setback. The safest sailor is certainly not one who has never weathered a storm. He may be right for fair-weather sailing, but when a storm arises, wouldn't you want an experienced sailor at the critical post? Wouldn't you want one at the helm who has fought through a gale and who knows the strength of the ship's hull and rigging, and how the anchor may be used to grasp the rocks of the ocean floor?

Oh, how everything gives way when affliction first comes upon us! The clinging stems of our hopes are quickly snapped, and our heart lies overwhelmed and prostrate, like a vine the windstorm has torn from its trellis. But once the initial shock is over and we are able to look up and say, "It is the Lord" (John 21:7), faith begins to lift our shattered hopes once more and securely binds them to the feet of God. And the final result is confidence, safety, and peace. SELECTED

> *The adverse winds blew against my life;*
> *My little ship with grief was tossed;*
> *My plans were gone—heart full of strife,*
> *And all my hope seemed to be lost—*
> *"Then He arose"—one word of peace.*
> *"There was a calm"—a sweet release.*
>
> *A tempest great of doubt and fear*
> *Possessed my mind; no light was there*

To guide, or make my vision clear.
  Dark night! 'twas more than I could bear—
"Then He arose," I saw His face—
"There was a calm" filled with His grace.

My heart was sinking 'neath the wave
  Of deepening test and raging grief;
All seemed as lost, and none could save,
  And nothing could bring me relief—
"Then He arose"—and spoke one word,
"There was a calm!" "IT IS THE LORD."

L. S. P.

MAY 12

Morning

An eagle . . . stirs up its nest.
DEUTERONOMY 32:11

God, like the eagle, stirs our nest. Yesterday it was the place for us; today there is a new plan. He wrecks the nest, although He knows it is dear to us; perhaps because it *is* dear to us. He loves us too well not to spoil our meager contentment. Let not our minds, therefore, dwell on second causes. It is His doing! Do not let us blame the thorn that pierces us.

Though the destruction of the nest may seem wanton and almost certainly comes at an hour when I do not expect it and though the things happen that I least anticipate—let me guard my heart and be not forgetful of God's care, lest I miss the meaning of the wreckage of my hopes. He has *something better for me.*

God will not spoil our nest and leave us without a nest, *if a nest is best for us.* His seeming cruelty is love; therefore, *let us always sit light with the things of time.*

The eaglet says, *"Teach me to fly!"* The saints often sit idly *wishing that they were like to their Lord.* Neither is likely to recognize that the prayer is heard *when the nest is toppled over!*

The breaking up of a nest an act of God's benevolence? What a startling thought!

Yet, here is an old writer who makes it a subject of praise, blesses God for it, declares it to be the first step of my education! I can understand praising Him for His gifts to body and soul, but I lose my breath in surprise when I am asked to make the first stanza of my hymn the adoration of His mercy in loosing the ties of home!

Nay, my soul, it is to *strengthen these ties* that my Father breaks up the nest, not to get rid of home but to teach thee to fly! Travel with thy Teacher and thou shalt learn that *the Home is wider than any nest!*

He would have thee learn of the many mansions of which thy nest is only one. He would tell thee of a brotherhood in Christ, which includes, yet transcends, thy household fires. He would tell thee of the family altar, which makes thee brother to the outcast, sister to the friendless—in kinship to all.

Thy Father hath given thee wings in the breaking of thy ties!

The storm that shook thy nest taught thee to fly! LEAVES FOR QUIET HOURS

> *God spreads broad wings;*
> *And by His lifting, holy grace,*
> *We find a wider, fairer place,*
> *The freedom of untrammeled space;*
> *Where clearer vision shows us things*
> *The nest-view never brings.*
> *The wing-life is characterized by comprehensiveness.*
> *High soaring gives wide seeing!*
>
> J. H. JOWETT

MAY 12

Evening

Everything is possible for one who believes.

MARK 9:23

The "everything" mentioned here does not always come simply by asking, because God is always seeking to teach you the way of faith. Your training for a life of faith requires many areas of learning, including the trial of faith, the discipline of faith, the patience of faith, and the courage of faith. Often you will pass through many stages before you finally realize the result of faith—namely, the victory of faith.

Genuine moral fiber is developed by enduring the discipline of faith. When you have made your request to God, and the answer still has not come, what are you to do? Keep on believing His Word! Never be swayed from it by what you may see or feel. Then as you stand firm, your power and experience is being developed, strengthened, and deepened. When you remain unswayed from your stance of faith, even in view of supposed contradictions to God's Word, you grow stronger on every front.

God will often purposely delay in giving you His answer, and in fact the delay is just as much an answer to your prayer as is the fulfillment when it comes. He worked this way in the lives of all the great Bible characters. Abraham, Moses, and Elijah were not great in the beginning but made great through the discipline of their faith. Only through that discipline were they then equipped for the work to which God had called them.

Think, for example, of Joseph, whom the Lord was training for the throne of Egypt. Psalm 105:19 (KJV) says, "*The word of the LORD tried him.*" It was not the prison life with its hard beds or poor food that "tried him" but "the word of the LORD." The words God spoke into his heart in his early years, concerning his elevated place of honor above his brothers, were the words that were always before him. He remained alone in prison, in spite of his innocence, and watched others being released who were justly incarcerated. Yet he remembered God's words even when every step of his career made fulfillment seem more and more impossible.

These were the times that tried his soul, but they were also the times of his spiritual growth and development. Then when word of his release from prison finally came, he was found ready and equipped for the delicate task of dealing with his wayward brothers. And he was able to do so with a love and a patience only surpassed by God Himself.

No amount of persecution will try you as much as experiences like these—ones in which you are required to wait on God. Once He has spoken His promise to work, it is truly hard to wait as you see the days go by with no fulfillment. Yet it is this discipline of faith that will bring you into a knowledge of God that would otherwise be impossible.

Morning

A short distance beyond the summit, there was Ziba.

2 SAMUEL 16:1

A little past the top of the hill, behold, Ziba.

KJV

It was a hard climb up that hill for a man with a burdened heart; he was tired and done. Then came God's provision for him through Ziba.

Are you a little past the top of the hill? Feeling tired and almost done? Take heart! God has something ready at the precise moment! God's help will meet you!

Just a little farther on—and all who honor Me with joy shall prove My promise true; they too shall honored be. Full well I know thy heart's desire, the heights to which thou dost aspire; thy love which burns with holy fire—and all to honor Me.

Just a little farther on—the "Victor's song will then be sung by all who honor Me." Thou hast done well, yet still press on—and greater works I'll trust to thee and grander glories thou shalt see; thus thou shalt fully honored be—a little farther on! (John 12:26; Psalm 91:15.)

> *Just over the hill, by the climbing way,*
> *Is a place where all good travelers stay—*
> *Just over the hill and up along.*
>
> *At the side of the road is a garden-gate,*
> *Which is always open, early and late—*
> *Just over the hill and up along.*
>
> *And inside the gate is a House of Rest,*
> *Where the Host will give you His very best—*
> *Just over the hill and up along.*

JOHN OXENHAM

God never permits any of His children to come up a steep hill along life's pathway without having provided at the foot of the hill a cooling spring from which the traveler may drink in refreshment and strength ere he begins to climb.

He climbs beside you; lean upon Him!

God has no road without its springs!

MAY 13

Evening

We do not know what we ought to pray for.
ROMANS 8:26

Often it is simply the answers to our prayers that cause many of the difficulties in the Christian life. We pray for patience, and our Father sends demanding people our way who test us to the limit, "because . . . *suffering produces perseverance*" (Romans 5:3). We pray for a submissive spirit, and God sends suffering again, for we learn to be obedient in the same way Christ "*learned obedience from what he suffered*" (Hebrews 5:8).

We pray to be unselfish, and God gives us opportunities to sacrifice by placing other people's needs first and by laying down our lives for other believers. We pray for strength and humility, and "a messenger of Satan" (2 Corinthians 12:7) comes to torment us until we lie on the ground pleading for it to be withdrawn.

We pray to the Lord, as His apostles did, saying, "Increase our faith!" (Luke 17:5). Then our money seems to take wings and fly away; our children become critically ill; an employee becomes careless, slow, and wasteful; or some other new trial comes upon us, requiring more faith than we have ever before experienced.

We pray for a Christlike life that exhibits the humility of a lamb. Then we are asked to perform some lowly task, or we are unjustly accused and given no opportunity to explain, for "he was led like a lamb to the slaughter, and . . . did not open his mouth" (Isaiah 53:7).

We pray for gentleness and quickly face a storm of temptation to be harsh and irritable. We pray for quietness, and suddenly every nerve is stressed to its limit with tremendous tension so that we may learn that when He sends His peace, no one can disturb it.

We pray for love for others, and God sends unique suffering by sending people our way who are difficult to love and who say things that get on our nerves and tear at our hearts. He does this because "love is patient, love is kind. . . . It does not dishonor others . . . it is not easily angered. . . . *It always protects*, always trusts, always hopes, always perseveres. Love never fails" (1 Corinthians 13:4–5, 7–8).

Yes, we pray to be like Jesus, and God's answer is: "I have tested you in the furnace of affliction" (Isaiah 48:10); "Will your courage endure or your hands be strong?" (Ezekiel 22:14); "Can you drink the cup?" (Matthew 20:22).

The way to peace and victory is to accept every circumstance and every trial as being straight from the hand of our loving Father; to live "with him in the heavenly realms" (Ephesians 2:6), above the clouds, in the very presence of His throne; and to look down from glory on our circumstances as being lovingly and divinely appointed. Selected

I prayed for strength, and then I lost awhile
  All sense of nearness, human and divine;
The love I leaned on failed and pierced my heart,
  The hands I clung to loosed themselves from mine;
But while I swayed, weak, trembling, and alone,
The everlasting arms upheld my own.

I prayed for light; the sun went down in clouds,
  The moon was darkened by a misty doubt,
The stars of heaven were dimmed by earthly fears,
  And all my little candle flames burned out;
But while I sat in shadow, wrapped in night,
The face of Christ made all the darkness bright.

I prayed for peace, and dreamed of restful ease,
  A slumber free from pain, a hushed repose;
Above my head the skies were black with storm,
  And fiercer grew the onslaught of my foes;
But while the battle raged, and wild winds blew,
I heard His voice and perfect peace I knew.

I thank You, Lord, You were too wise to heed
My feeble prayers, and answer as I sought,
Since these rich gifts Your bounty has bestowed
Have brought me more than all I asked or thought;
Giver of good, so answer each request
With Your own giving, better than my best.

ANNIE JOHNSON FLINT

~~~~~ MAY 14 ~~~~~

Morning

Make it your ambition to lead a quiet life.
1 THESSALONIANS 4:11

Beloved! this is our spirit's deepest need. It is thus that we can learn to know God. It is thus that we receive spiritual refreshment and nutriment. It is thus that we are nourished and fed. It is thus that we receive the Living Bread. It is thus that our very bodies are healed, and our spirits drink in the life of our risen Lord, and we go forth to life's conflicts and duties like the flower that has drunk in, through the shades of the night, the cool and crystal drops of dew. But the dew never falls on a stormy night, so the dews of His Grace never come to the restless soul.

We cannot go through life strong and fresh on constant express trains with ten minutes for lunch: we must have quiet hours, secret places of the Most High, times of waiting upon the Lord, when we renew our strength and learn to mount up on wings as eagles, and then come back to run and not be weary, and to walk and not faint.

The best thing about this stillness is that it gives God a chance to work. "Anyone who enters God's rest also rests from their works, just as God did from his" (Hebrews 4:10); and when we cease from our thoughts, God's thoughts come into us; when we get still from our restless activity, "God . . . works in [us] to will and to act in order to fulfill his good purpose" (Philippians 2:13), and we have but to work it out.

Beloved! let us take His stillness! A. B. SIMPSON

Jesus, Deliverer, come Thou to me;
Soothe Thou my voyaging,
Over life's sea!

MAY 14
Evening

On that very day Abraham [did] . . . as God told him.
GENESIS 17:23

Instant obedience is the only kind of obedience there is, for *delayed* obedience is disobedience. Each time God calls upon us to do something, He is offering to make a covenant with us. Our part is to obey, and then He will do His part to send a special blessing.

The only way to be obedient is to obey instantly—*"On that very day,"* as Abraham did. I know we often postpone doing what we know to do, and then later do it as well as we can. Certainly this is better than not doing it at all. By then, however, it is at best only a crippled, disfigured, and partial attempt toward obedience. *Postponed obedience can never bring us the full blessing God intended or what it would have brought had we obeyed at the earliest possible moment.*

What a pity it is how we rob ourselves, as well as God and others, by our procrastination! Remember, "On that very day" is the Genesis way of saying, "Do it now!"
Messages for the Morning Watch

Martin Luther once said, "A true believer will crucify, or put to death, the question, 'Why?' He will simply obey without questioning." And I refuse to be one of those people who "unless . . . [I] see signs and wonders . . . will never believe" (John 4:48). I will obey without questioning.

> *Ours not to make reply,*
> *Ours not to reason why,*
> *Ours but to do and die.*

Obedience is the fruit of faith; patience is the early blossom on the tree of faith.
CHRISTINA ROSSETTI

MAY 15
Morning

He asked this only to test him, for he already had in mind what he was going to do.
JOHN 6:6

At this very hour you may have to come face to face with a most tremendous need, and Christ stands beside you looking at it and questioning you about it. He says, in effect, "How are you going to meet it?"

He is scrutinizing you . . . watching you with a gentle, tender sympathy. How many of us have failed in the test! We have taken out our pencil and our paper and commenced to figure out the two hundred pennyworth of bread; or we have run off hither and thither to strong and wealthy friends to extricate us; or we have sat down in utter despondency; or we have murmured against Him for bringing us into such a position. Should we not have turned a sunny face to Christ saying: *Thou hast a plan! Thine is the responsibility, and Thou must tell me what to do. I have come so far in the path of obedience to Thy Guiding Spirit: and now, what art Thou going to do?*

They understood not how that God by His hand would deliver them (Acts 7:25). *It is so today.*

> *Leave the how with Jesus,*
> *Secret things He knows;*
> *Infinite in wisdom,*
> *Time will all disclose.*

> *Leave the how with Jesus,*
> *He will comfort bring;*
> *Thro' the storm He'll hide thee*
> *Underneath His wing.*
> *"God does not explain to us His technique."*

"My times are in your hands" (Psalm 31:15). If you quote this verse to the native of Congo, he will translate it in the gorgeous words: *"All my life's whys and whens and wheres and wherefores are in God's Hand!"* DAN CRAWFORD

We want to know more than the silent God deems it good to tell; to understand the "why" which He bids us wait to ask; to *see* the path which He has spread on purpose in the dark. The Infinite Father does not stand by us to be catechized and to explain Himself to our vain minds; He is here for our trust.

<hr>

MAY 15
Evening

Men see not the bright light which is in the clouds.
JOB 37:21 KJV

Much of the world's beauty is due to clouds. The unchanging blue of a beautiful, sunlit sky still does not compare to the glory of changing clouds. And earth would become a wilderness if not for their ministry to us.

Human life has its clouds as well. They provide us with shade, refresh us, yet sometimes cover us with the darkness of night. But there is never a cloud without its "bright light." God has told us, "I have set my rainbow in the clouds" (Genesis 9:13). If only we could see clouds from above—in all their billowing glory, bathed in reflective light, and as majestic as the Alps—we would be amazed at their shining magnificence.

We see them only from below, so who will describe for us the "bright light" that bathes their summits, searches their valleys, and reflects from every peak of their expanse? Doesn't every drop of rain in them soak up health-giving qualities, which will later fall to earth?

O dear child of God! If only you could see your sorrows and troubles from above instead of seeing them from earth. If you would look down on them from where you are seated "with Christ . . . in the heavenly realms" (Ephesians 2:6), you would know the beauty of the rainbow of colors they reflect to the hosts of heaven. You would also see the "bright light" of Christ's face and would finally be content to see those clouds cast their deep shadows over the mountain slopes of your life.

Remember, clouds are always moving ahead of God's cleansing wind. SELECTED

Should rage so fiercely round me in its wrath;
But this I know—God watches all my path,
    And I can trust.
I cannot know why suddenly the storm
I may not draw aside the unseen veil
I have no power to look across the tide,
That hides the unknown future from my sight,
Nor know if for me waits the dark or light;
    But I can trust.
To see while here the land beyond the river;
But this I know—I will be God's forever;
    So I can trust.

MAY 16

Morning

In the evening my wife died. The next morning I did as I had been commanded.
EZEKIEL 24:18

"In the evening my wife died." The light of the home went out. Darkness brooded over the face of every familiar thing. The trusted companion who had shared all the changes of the ever-changing way was taken from my side. The light of our fellowship was suddenly extinguished as by some mysterious hand stretched forth from the unseen. I lost "the desire of mine eyes." I was alone. "In the evening my wife died. The next morning . . ." Aye, what about the next morning, when the light broke almost obtrusively upon a world which had changed into a cemetery containing only one grave? *"The next morning I did as I had been commanded."*

The command had been laid upon him in the days before his bereavement. Life in his home had been a source of inspiring fellowship. In the evening-time, after the discharge of the burdensome tasks of the day, he had turned to his home as weary, dust-choked pilgrims turn to a bath; and immersed in the sweet sanctities of wedded life, he had found such restoration of soul as fitted him for the renewed labor of the morrow. But "in the evening my wife died." The home was no longer a refreshing bath, but part of the dusty road; no longer an oasis, but a repetition of the wilderness.

How now shall it be concerning the prophet's command? "In the evening my wife died. The next morning" the commandment? How does the old duty appear in the gloom of the prophet's bereavement? Duty still, clamant and clamorous now in the shadows as it was loud and importunate in the light. What shall the prophet do? Take up the old burden, and faithfully trudge the old road. Go out in his loneliness, and go on with the old tasks. But why? You will find the secret of it all in the last clause of the chapter:

"You will be a sign to them, and they will know that I am the Lord*"* (v. 27).

A brokenhearted prophet patiently and persistently pursuing an old duty and by his manner of doing it, compelling people to believe in the Lord! That is the secret motive of the heavy discipline.

The great God wants our conspicuous crises to be occasions of conspicuous testimony; our seasons of darkness to be opportunities for the unveiling of the Divine. *He wants duty to shine more resplendently because of the environing shadows.* He wants tribulation only to furbish and burnish our signs. He wants us to manifest the sweet grace of continuance amid all the sudden and saddening upheavals of our intensely varied life. This was the prophet's triumph. He made his calamity a witness to the eternal. He made his very loneliness minister to his God. He made his very bereavement intensify his calling. He took up the old task, and in taking it up he glorified it. "In the evening my wife died. The next morning I did as I had been commanded."

The evening sorrow will come to all of us: what shall we be found doing in the morning? We shall have to dig graves; have burials: how shall it be with us when the funeral is over? J. H. Jowett

Make a pulpit of every circumstance.

<hr />

MAY 16

Evening

Do not be afraid, Daniel. Since the first day that you set your mind to gain understanding and to humble yourself before your God, your words were heard, and I have come in response to them. But the prince of the Persian kingdom resisted me twenty-one days.

Daniel 10:12–13

This passage is a wonderful teaching on prayer and shows us the direct hindrance Satan can be in our lives. Daniel had fasted and prayed for twenty-one difficult days. As far as we can tell from the biblical account, the difficulty came not because Daniel was not a good person nor because his prayer was not right but because of a special attack from Satan.

The Lord had sent His angelic messenger to tell Daniel that his prayer was answered the moment he began to pray, but the good angel was hindered by an evil angel who met him along the way and wrestled with him. This conflict occurred in the heavens, yet Daniel experienced the same kind of conflict here on earth as he agonized in prayer.

"Our struggle is not against flesh and blood, but against the rulers, against the authorities, . . . and against the spiritual forces of evil in the heavenly realms" (Ephesians 6:12). Satan's attack and the ensuing struggle delayed the answer three full weeks. Daniel was nearly defeated, and Satan would have been glad to kill him, but God would not allow anything to come upon Daniel beyond what he could bear. (1 Corinthians 10:13.)

Many prayers of believers are hindered by Satan. Yet you do not need to fear when your unanswered prayers are piling up, for soon they will break through like a flood. When that happens, not only will your answers flow through, but they will also be accompanied by new blessings.

Hell works the hardest on God's saints. The most worthy souls will be tested with the most pressure and the highest heat, but heaven will not desert them. William L. Watkinson

MAY 17

Morning

"We have come to live here for a while, because the famine is severe in Canaan and your servants' flocks have no pasture . . . and the land of Egypt is before you; settle your father and your brothers in the best part of the land."

Genesis 47:4, 6

Did you ever come to a time of the most awful famine—spiritual famine—in your life, when there was no pasture upon which to feed? At such a time Christ

Himself takes the matter for us to the throne of God. He tells God we are His own brothers. And what is the answer? "The kingdom of heaven is before you; settle your brothers in the best part of the kingdom." Do you realize what it means to have Jesus Christ intercede for you—the Christ whom you repudiated by your own sin? Pharaoh knew not these men; but he knew Joseph, and nothing was too good for Joseph and every relative of JosEphesians

We are "co-heirs with Christ" (Romans 8:17). Because of Christ, God flings wide open the whole kingdom, and simply asks that we take its best. Out of famine—into the best that the kingdom affords! Not only that, but rulers of the King's own property! Oh, Lord Jesus, forgive my unfaith! Open my sin-bound, self-centered eyes to the wonders of Thy love. Teach me how to receive more. The best of the kingdom: that means Thee. I take Thee, Lord, as my feast of Eternal Life. Messages for the Morning Watch

I am not the brood of the dust and sod,
Nor a shuttled thread in the loom of fate;
But the child Divine of the living God,
With eternity for my life's estate.
I am not a sport of a cosmic night,
Nor a thing of chance that has grown to man;
But a deathless soul on my upward flight,
And my Father's heir in His wondrous plan.

ALVA ROMANES

We are His only heirs.

~~~~~~~~ MAY 17 ~~~~~~~~
Evening

After forty years had passed, an angel appeared to Moses . . . in the desert. . . .
Then the LORD said to him, ". . . Now come, I will send you back to Egypt."
ACTS 7:30, 33–34

Often the Lord calls us aside from our work for a season and asks us to be still and learn before we go out again to minister. And the hours spent waiting are not lost time.

An ancient knight once realized, as he was fleeing from his enemies, that his horse needed a shoe replaced. The prudent course of action seemed to be to hurry on without delay. Yet higher wisdom told him to stop for a few minutes at the blacksmith's along the road. Although he heard the galloping hooves of the enemies' horses close behind, he waited until his steed was reshod before continuing his escape. Just as the enemy appeared, only a hundred yards away, he jumped into the saddle and dashed away with the swiftness of the wind. Then he knew his stopping had actually hastened his escape.

Quite often God will ask us to wait before we go, so we may fully recover from our last mission before entering the next stage of our journey and work. DAYS OF HEAVEN UPON EARTH

Waiting! Yes, patiently waiting!
    Till next steps made plain will be;
To hear, with the inner hearing,
    The Voice that will call for me.

Waiting! Yes, hopefully waiting!
    With hope that need not grow dim;
The Master is pledged to guide me,
    And my eyes are unto Him.

Waiting! Expectantly waiting!
    Perhaps it may be today
The Master will quickly open
    The gate to my future way.

Waiting! Yes, waiting! still waiting!
    I know, though I've waited long,
That, while He withholds His purpose,
    His waiting cannot be wrong.

Waiting! Yes, waiting! still waiting!
The Master will not be late:
Since He knows that I am waiting
For Him to unlatch the gate.

J. Danson Smith

MAY 18
Morning

They do not need to go away.
Matthew 14:16

What a task lay before the Lord on that day! There were five thousand men, besides women and children. To feed such a crowd at a moment's notice might well-nigh seem impossible. Well might the disciples say, "Send the crowds away, so they can go to the villages and buy themselves some food" (v. 15). Well might they look startled when the reply came back. "They do not need to go away. You give them something to eat." Their hearts must have sunk within them as their eyes again and again scanned that surging crowd.

The prospect of feeding that multitude did not alarm the Lord. He asked Philip, indeed, "Where shall we buy bread for these people to eat?" (John 6:5) but we learn immediately that He said this "to test him" (v. 6). The Lord Jesus is perfectly confident that He can meet our needs and He would have us confident, too; for He is the One who for thousands of years has met the needs of those who put their trust in Him. As the God of providence He keeps the barrel of meal from wasting, and the cruse of oil from failing. He draws from one the testimony: "I was young and now I am old, yet I have never seen the righteous forsaken or their children begging bread" (Psalm 37:25). And from another, "Not one word has failed of all the good promises he gave" (1 Kings 8:56). Selected

Say not, my soul, "From whence
Can God relieve my care?"

Remember that Omnipotence
Hath servants everywhere.

His help is always sure,
His methods seldom guessed;
Delay will make our pleasure pure:
Surprise will give it zest.

His wisdom is sublime,
His heart profoundly kind;
God never is before His time,
And never is behind.

Hast thou assumed a load
Which none will bear with thee?
And art thou bearing it for God,
And shall He fail to see?

Be comforted at heart,
Thou art not left alone;
Now thou the Lord's companion art—
Soon thou shalt share His throne.

J. J. LYNCH

Jesus fed the multitude in a desert place.

MAY 18
Evening

We were under great pressure, . . . so that we despaired of life itself. . . . But this
happened that we might not rely on ourselves but on God, who raises the dead.

2 CORINTHIANS 1:8–9

Pressed beyond measure; yes, pressed to great length;
Pressed so intensely, beyond my own strength;
Pressed in my body and pressed in my soul,
Pressed in my mind till the dark surges roll.
Pressure from foes, and pressure from dear friends.
Pressure on pressure, till life nearly ends.

Pressed into knowing no helper but God;
Pressed into loving His staff and His rod.
Pressed into liberty where nothing clings;
Pressed into faith for impossible things.
Pressed into living my life for the Lord,
Pressed into living a Christ-life outpoured.

The pressure of difficult times makes us value life. Every time our life is spared and given back to us after a trial, it is like a new beginning. We better understand its value and thereby apply ourselves more effectively for God and for humankind. And the pressure we endure helps us to understand the trials of others, equipping us to help them and to sympathize with them.

Some people have a shallowness about them. With their superficial nature, they lightly take hold of a theory or a promise and then carelessly tell of their distrust of those who retreat from every trial. Yet a man or woman who has experienced great suffering will never do this. They are very tender and gentle, and understand what suffering really means. This is what Paul meant when he said, "Death is at work in us" (2 Corinthians 4:12).

Trials and difficult times are needed to press us forward. They work in the way the fire in the hold of a mighty steamship provides the energy that moves the pistons, turns the engine, and propels the great vessel across the sea, even when facing the wind and the waves. A. B. SIMPSON

Morning

God, our God, blesses us.
Psalm 67:6

When you pray, say: "Father."
Luke 11:2

It is strange how little use we have of the spiritual blessings which God gives us, but it is stranger still *how little use we make of God Himself.* Though He is "our God," we apply ourselves but little to Him. How seldom do we ask counsel at the hands of the Lord! How often do we go about our business without seeking His guidance! In our troubles how constantly do we strive to bear our burdens ourselves, instead of casting them upon the Lord that He may sustain us! This is not because we *may* not, for the Lord seems to say, "I am thine, soul; come and make use of Me as thou wilt; thou mayst come freely to My store, and the oftener the more welcome." It is our own fault if we do not make free with the riches of our own God.

Then, since thou hast such a Friend, and He invites thee, draw from Him daily. *Never want whilst thou hast a God to go to; never fear or faint whilst thou hast God to help thee; go to thy treasure and take whatever thou needest—there is all that thou canst want.*

Learn the Divine skill of making God all things to thee. He can supply thee with all; or, better still, He can be to thee instead of all. Let me urge thee, then, to make use of thy God. Make use of Him in prayer; go to Him often, because *He is thy God.* Oh, wilt thou fail to use so great a privilege? Fly to Him; tell Him all thy wants. Use Him constantly by faith at all times. If some dark providence has beclouded thee, use thy God as a "sun"; if some strong enemy has beset thee, find in Jehovah a "shield"; *for He is a sun and a shield to His people.* If thou hast lost thy way in the mazes of life, use Him as a "guide"; *for He will direct thee.* Whatever thou art, and wherever thou art, remember God is just *what thou wantest,* and just *where thou wantest* and that He *can do all thou wantest!* Charles H. Spurgeon

The life of faith is the life that uses the Lord. H. C. G. Moule

O little heart of mine! Shall pain
Or sorrow make thee moan,
When all this God is all for thee—

A Father all thine own?

MAY 19
Evening

Before he had finished praying, Rebekah came out with her jar on her shoulder. . . .
Then the man bowed down and worshiped the LORD, *saying, "Praise be to*
the LORD, *. . . who has not abandoned his kindness and faithfulness."*
GENESIS 24:15, 26–27

Every godly prayer is answered before the prayer itself is finished—*"Before* he had finished praying . . ." This is because Christ has pledged in His Word, "My Father will give you whatever you ask in my name" (John 16:23). When you ask in faith and in Christ's name—that is, in oneness with Him and His will—"it will be done for you" (John 15:7).

Since God's Word cannot fail, whenever we meet these simple conditions, the answer to our prayer has already been granted and is complete in heaven *as we pray*, even though it may not be revealed on earth until much later. Therefore it is wise to close every prayer with praise to God for the answer He has already given.

"Praise be to the LORD, . . . who has not abandoned his kindness and faithfulness." (Genesis 24:27) MESSAGES FOR THE MORNING WATCH

When we believe God for a blessing, we must have an attitude of faith and begin to act and pray as if the blessing were already ours. We should respond to God as if He has granted our request. This attitude of trust means leaning upon Him for what we have claimed and simply taking it for granted that He has given us our request and will continue to give it.

When people get married, they immediately have a new perspective and begin to act accordingly. This is how it should be when we take Christ as our Savior, our Sanctifier, our Healer, or our Deliverer. He expects us to have a new perspective, in which we recognize Him in the capacity and the role we have trusted Him for, and in which we allow Him to be everything to us we have claimed by faith. SELECTED

The thing I ask when God leads me to pray,
Begins in that same act to come my way.

MAY 20

Morning

"Father, if you are willing, take this cup from me; yet not my will,
but yours be done." An angel from heaven appeared to him and
strengthened him. And being in anguish, he prayed. . . .
LUKE 22:42–44

There is a story of a woman who had had many sorrows: parents, husband, children, wealth, all were gone. In her great grief she prayed for death, but death did not come. She would not take up any of her wonted work for Christ. One night she had a dream: she thought she had gone to heaven. She saw her husband and ran to him with eager joy, expecting a glad welcome. But, strange to say, no answering joy shone on his face—only surprise and displeasure. "How did you come here?" he asked. "They did not say that you were to be sent for today; I did not expect you for a long time yet." With a bitter cry she turned from him to seek her parents. But instead of the tender love for which her heart was longing, she met from them only the same amazement and the same surprised questions. "I'll go to my Savior," she cried. "He will welcome me if no one else does." When she saw Christ, there was infinite love in His look, but His words throbbed with sorrow as He said: "Child, child, who is doing your work down there?" At last she understood; she had no right yet to be in heaven; her work was not finished; she had fled away from her duty.

This is one of the dangers of sorrow: *that in our grief for those who are gone we lose our interest in those who are living, and slacken our zeal in the work which is allotted to us.* However great our bereavements, we may not drop our tasks until the Master calls us away. J. R. MILLER

Finish thy work, the time is short;
The sun is in the west,
The night is coming down; till then
Think not of rest.

Rest? Finish thy work, then rest;
Till then, rest never.
The rest prepared for thee by God
Is rest forever.

Finish thy work, then sit thee down
On some celestial hill,
And of heaven's everlasting bliss
Take thou thy fill.

Finish thy work, then go in peace,
Life's battle fought and won;
Hear from the throne the Master's voice,
"Well done! Well done!"

Finish Thy work, then take the harp,
Give praise to God above;
Sing a new song of mighty joy
And endless love!

Take not your rest too soon, else you will never enter into *your real rest.* It is not here on this plank amid the billows, but yonder on that shore. GEORGE BOWEN

Nothing ever happens but once in this world. What I do now I do once and forever. It is over, it is gone with a still eternity of solemn meaning.

MAY 20
Evening

Shall I not drink the cup the Father has given me?
JOHN 18:11

God is a thousand times more meticulous with us than even an artist is with his canvas. Using many brush strokes of sorrow, and circumstances of various colors, He paints us into the highest and best image He visualizes, if we will only receive His bitter gifts of myrrh in the right spirit.

Yet when our cup of sorrows is taken away and the lessons in it are suppressed or go unheeded, we do more damage to our soul than could ever be repaired. No human heart can imagine the incomparable love God expresses in His gift of myrrh. However, this great gift that our soul should receive is allowed to pass by us because of our sleepy indifference, and ultimately nothing comes of it.

Then, in our barrenness we come and complain, saying, "O Lord, I feel so dry, and there is so much darkness within me!" My advice to you, dear child, is to open your heart to the pain and suffering, and it will accomplish more good than being full of emotion and sincerity. TAULER

> *The cry of man's anguish went up to God,*
> *   "Lord, take away pain:*
> *The shadow that darkens the world You have made,*
> *   The close, choking chain*
> *That strangles the heart, the burden that weighs*
> *   On the wings that would soar,*
> *Lord, take away pain from the world You have made,*
> *   That it love You the more."*
> *Then answered the Lord to the cry of His world:*
> *   "Shall I take away pain,*
> *And with it the power of the soul to endure,*
> *   Made strong by the strain?*
> *Shall I take away pity, that knits heart to heart*
> *   And sacrifice high?*

Will you lose all your heroes that lift from the fire
   Wisdom toward the sky?
Shall I take away love that redeems with a price
   And smiles at the loss?
Can you spare from your lives that would climb unto Me
   The Christ on His cross?"

MAY 21

Morning

I will fill this valley with pools of water.
2 Kings 3:16

Make this valley full of ditches.
KJV

Do we say, "Lord, I want my life to be a channel through which Thy power may flow"? Then let the spade of His Word go down into the depths of your heart, that the hidden things may be revealed. Blessing must be prepared for. You can hinder it, and shirk it; you can shut your ears to His voice; or you can get alone with the Lord Jesus and let Him have His way. *God has a glorious work to do in every yielded life;* He has a glorious fullness to bestow. But there is also a work for *us* to do; there must be a digging down into the depths of our heart; we must resolve to get rid of all the rubbish, and to prepare for the living water. H. Earnshaw Smith

Lord, spare nothing in me that would hinder the flowing of the rivers of water of life. Carry Thy cross to every root and corner of my most secret being.

Do you recall the bit of teaching brought out in connection with the river of the Sanctuary? *Waters to the ankles—waters to the knees—waters to the loins.* Afterward the prophet measured it again, and it was a *river! Waters to swim in!*

Beware of paddling in the ocean of God's truth, when you should be out swimming!

Go deeper into me, Lord Jesus;
Yes, deeper every day,
Till Thou hast conquered me, Lord Jesus;
Go deeper all the way.

Go deeper into me, Lord Jesus;
Search all the secret springs
Of thought and action, words and feelings,
Of great and little things.

Go deeper into me, Lord Jesus,
Cleanse all the hidden part,
Where pride, or touchiness, or temper,
May lurk within my heart.

Go deeper into me, Lord Jesus,
Till Thou canst really rise,
Out of the depths of this my being,
Through Thy great Sacrifice.

As Thou dost rise in me, Lord Jesus,
The life shall be Thine own,
Till o'er my humbled broken spirit
Thou reignest on Thy throne.

E. E. B. ROGERS

We get no deeper into Christ than we allow Him to get into us.

MAY 21
Evening

I remembered my songs in the night.
PSALM 77:6

I read somewhere of a little bird that will never sing the song its owner desires to hear while its cage is full of light. It may learn a note of this or a measure of that but will never learn an entire song until its cage is covered and the sunlight is shut out.

Many people are the same, never learning to sing until the shadows of darkness fall. We need to remember: the fabled nightingale sings with its breast against a thorn; it was on that Bethlehem night the song of angels was heard; and it was "at midnight the cry rang out: 'Here's the bridegroom! Come out to meet him!'" (Matthew 25:6).

It is indeed extremely doubtful that a person's soul can really know the love of God in its richness and in its comforting, satisfying completeness until the skies are dark and threatening. Light emerges from darkness, and morning is born from the womb of night.

James Creelman once journeyed through the Balkans in search of Natalie, the exiled queen of Serbia. In one of his letters, he described his trip this way:

> During that memorable journey, I learned that the world's supply of rose oil comes from the Balkan Mountains. The thing that interested me most was that the roses had to be gathered during the darkest hours, with the pickers starting at one o'clock and finishing by two. Initially this practice seemed to me to be a relic of superstition or tradition, but as I investigated further, I learned that actual scientific tests had proved that a full forty percent of the fragrance of the roses disappeared in the light of day.

And it is also a real and unquestionable fact of human life and culture that a person's character is strengthened most during the darkest days. MALCOLM J. MCLEOD

~~~~~~~ MAY 22 ~~~~~~~
Morning

He giveth quietness.
JOB 34:29 KJV

The calm sea says more to the thoughtful soul than the same sea in a storm and tumult. But we need the understanding of eternal things, and the sentiment of the Infinite to be able to feel this.

Napoleon, with his arms crossed over his breast, is more expressive than the furious Hercules beating the air with his athletic fists.

People of passionate temperament never understand this. AMIEL'S JOURNEY

> *The lovely things are quiet things*
> *Soft falling snow,*
> *And feathers dropped from flying wings*
> *Make no sound as they go.*
>
> *A petal loosened from a rose,*
> *Quietly seeks the ground,*
> *And love, if lovely, when it goes,*
> *Goes without sound.*

The silent seasons of life are imperative. The winter is the mother of spring; the night is the fountain of the physical forces of the day; the silent soil is the womb where vegetable life is born. The greatest things in our spiritual life come out of our waiting hours, when all activity is suspended and the soul learns to be "silent unto God" while He shapes and molds us for future activities and fruitful years.

The greatest forces in nature are quiet ones. The law of gravitation is silent, yet invincible. So, back of all our activities and actions, the law of faith is the mightiest force of the spiritual world, and mightiest when quietest and least demonstrative. When the soul is anchored to the will of God and His exceeding great and precious promises, with the calm unwavering confidence that His power and love are behind us and can never fail us until all His will for us is accomplished, *our life must be victorious.*

> *In the center of the whirlpool, while the waters rush around,*
> *There's a space of perfect stillness, though with turmoil it is bound:*
> *All is calm, and all is quiet, scarcely e'en a sense of sound.*
> *So with us—despite the conflict—when in Christ His Peace is found.*

There is no other real peace; how comparatively few know the secret.

God's noiseless workers own His calm control. NORA C. USHER

We need not be noisy if we are sure. MARY E. SHANNON

Evening

Commit your way to the LORD; trust in him and he will do this.
PSALM 37:5

The literal meaning of this verse is: "*Roll* your way onto *Jehovah* and trust upon Him, and *He works.*" This brings to our attention the immediacy of God's action once we commit, or "roll," burdens of any kind from our hands into His. Whether our burden is a sorrow, difficulty, physical need, or concern over the salvation of a loved one, "*He works.*"

When does He work? "He works" *now.* We act as if God does not immediately accept our trust in Him and thereby delays accomplishing what we ask Him to do. We fail to understand that "He works" *as we commit.* "He works" now! Praise Him for the fact that this is true.

Our expectation that He will work is the very thing enabling the Holy Spirit to accomplish what we have "rolled" onto Him. At that point it is out of our grasp, and we are not to try to do it ourselves. "He works!" Take comfort from this and do not try to pick it up again. What a relief there is in knowing He really is at work on our difficulty!

And when someone says, "But I don't see any results," pay him no attention.

"He works" if you have "rolled" your burdens onto Him and are "looking unto Jesus" (Hebrews 12:2 KJV) to do it. Your faith may be tested, but "He works." His Word is true! V. H. F.

"I cry out to God Most High, to God, who vindicates me" (Psalm 57:2).

One beautiful old translation of this verse says, "He will perform the cause I hold in my hand." That makes it very real to me today. The very thing "I hold in my hand"—my work today, this concern that is beyond my control, this task in which I have greatly overestimated my own abilities—*this* is what I may "cry out" for Him to do "for me," with the calm assurance He will perform it. "The wise and what they do are in God's hands" (Ecclesiastes 9:1). FRANCES RIDLEY HAVERGAL

The Lord will follow through on His covenant promises. Whatever He takes and holds in His hand, He will accomplish. Therefore, His past mercies are guarantees for the future, and worthy reasons for continuing to cry out to Him. CHARLES H. SPURGEON

Though it linger, wait for it; it will certainly come and will not delay.
HABAKKUK 2:3

Some things have their cycle in an hour and some in a century; but His plans shall complete their cycle whether long or short. The tender annual which blossoms for a season and dies, and the Columbian aloe which develops in a century, each is true to its normal principle. Many of us desire to pluck our fruit in June rather than wait until October, and so, of course, it is sour and immature; but God's purposes ripen slowly and fully, and faith waits while He tarries, knowing He will surely come and will not tarry too long.

It is perfect rest to fully learn and wholly trust this glorious promise. We may know without a question that His purposes shall be accomplished when we have fully committed our ways to Him and are walking in watchful obedience to His every prompting. This faith will give a calm and tranquil poise to the spirit and save us from the restless fret of trying to do too much ourselves.

> *Wait, and every wrong will righten;*
> *Wait, and every cloud will brighten,*
> *If you will only wait.*

A. B. SIMPSON

How much depends upon knowing when the time is exactly ripe! Not to interfere before the crisis arrives, not to let the opportunity pass when the crisis has arrived. This power of discernment, of patience, of promptitude, is a gift of superlative value.

Who knows the psychological moment like the Keeper of Israel? He does not interfere too soon; He allows the enemy rope enough to hang himself; He waits until His people know their weakness and peril and are shut up to Him. He does not interpose too late; at the critical juncture He smites the pride of His people.

We see in nature how precisely God works by the clock; certainly He is not less exact in the times and seasons of human life. We often speak of "the hour and the man"; let us remember "the hour and the God."

They were at their wits' end. Then they cried out to the Lord *in
their trouble, and he brought them out of their distress.*
Psalm 107:27–28

Are you standing at "Wits' End Corner,"
    Christian, with troubled brow?
Are you thinking of what is before you,
    And all you are bearing now?
Does all the world seem against you,
    And you in the battle alone?
Remember—at "Wits' End Corner"
    Is just where God's power is shown.

Are you standing at "Wits' End Corner,"
    Blinded with wearying pain,
Feeling you cannot endure it,
    You cannot bear the strain,
Bruised through the constant suffering,
    Dizzy, and dazed, and numb?
Remember—at "Wits' End Corner"
    Is where Jesus loves to come.

Are you standing at "Wits' End Corner"?
    Your work before you spread,
All lying begun, unfinished,
    And pressing on heart and head,
Longing for strength to do it,
    Stretching out trembling hands?
Remember—at "Wits' End Corner"
    The Burden-Bearer stands.

Are you standing at "Wits' End Corner"?
    Then you're just in the very spot
To learn the wondrous resources
    Of Him who fails you not:
No doubt to a brighter pathway
    Your footsteps will soon be moved,
But only at "Wits' End Corner"
    Is the "God who is able" proved.

ANTOINETTE WILSON

Do not get discouraged—it may be the last key on the ring that opens the door.
STANSIFER

———— ～～～ ～～～ ————

MAY 24

Morning

They went away by themselves in a boat to a solitary place.

MARK 6:32

And they departed into a desert place by ship privately.

KJV

If you have a desert place in your heart to which you must sometimes go, you should depart to it in a ship *privately. No man should make a thoroughfare of his desert.* Keep your grief for the private ship. Never go into company with an abstracted mind; that is to display your desert.

You have sometimes refrained from God's table of communion because your thoughts were away. You did well. Man's table of communion has the same need. If you are bidden to a feast when you are troubled in your mind, try first whether you can carry your burden privately away. If you can, then leave the desert behind you; *"put oil on your head and wash your face, so that it will not be obvious to others that you are fasting"* (Matthew 6:17–18). But if you cannot, if there is no ship that can take away your burden in secret, then *come not yet* to the feast. Journey not while the cloud is resting over the tabernacle. Tarry under the cloud. Watch one hour in the garden. Bury thy sorrow in the silence. Let thy heart be reconciled to the Father, and then come to the world and offer thy gift.

Hide your thorn in the rose. Bury your sigh in the song. Keep your cross, if you will, but keep it hidden away under a wreath of flowers. Keep a singing heart!

O Thou that hast hid Thy thorn beneath a rose, steer the ship in which I conceal my burden! Thou hast gone down to the feast of Cana from the fast in the wilderness; where hast Thou hid the print of the nails? In love. Steer me to that burying ground! Let the ship on its way to my desert touch for an hour at the desert of my brother! Let me feel the fellowship of grief, the community of sorrow, the kindredness of pain! Let me hear the voices from other wildernesses, the sighs from other souls, the groans from other graves! And, when I come to my own landing-place and put down my hand to lift up my burden, I shall meet a wondrous surprise. *It will be there, but it will be there half-sized.* Its heaviness will be gone, its impossibility will have vanished. I shall lift it easily; I shall carry it lightly; I shall bury it swiftly. I shall be ready for Cana in an hour, ready for Calvary in a few minutes. I shall go back to enter into the struggle of the multitude; and the multitude will say, *"There is no desert with him!"*

Give others the sunshine, Tell Jesus the rest. Leaves for Quiet Hours

> *Lie down and sleep,*
> *Leave it with God to keep*
> *This sorrow which is part*
> *Now of thy heart.*
>
> *When thou dost wake*
> *If still 'tis thine to take,*
> *Utter no wild complaint,*
> *Work waits thy hand.*
> *If thou shouldst faint*
> *God understands.*

Evening

Sarah became pregnant and bore a son to Abraham in his
old age, at the very time God had promised him.

GENESIS 21:2

"The plans of the LORD stand firm forever, the purposes of his heart through all generations" (Psalm 33:11). But we must be prepared to wait on God's timing. His timing is precise, for He does things "at the very time" He has set. It is not for us to know His timing, and in fact we cannot know it—we must wait for it.

If God had told Abraham while he was in Haran that he would have to wait thirty years before holding his promised child in his arms, his heart might have failed him. So God, as an act of His gracious love, hid from Abraham the number of weary years he would be required to wait. Only as the time was approaching, with but a few months left to wait, did God reveal His promise: "At the appointed time next year . . . Sarah will have a son" (Genesis 18:14). The "appointed time" came at last, and soon the joyous laughter that filled the patriarch's home caused the now elderly couple to forget their long and tiring wait.

So take heart, dear child, when God requires you to wait. The One you wait for will not disappoint you. He will never be even five minutes behind "the appointed time." And soon "your grief will turn to joy" (John 16:20).

Oh, how joyful the soul that God brings to laughter! Then sorrow and crying flee forever, as darkness flees the dawn. SELECTED

As passengers, it is not for us to interfere with the charts and the compass. We should leave the masterful Captain alone to do His own work. ROBERT HALL

Some things cannot be accomplished in a day. Even God does not make a glorious sunset in a moment. For several days He gathers the mist with which to build His beautiful palaces in the western sky.

Some glorious morn—but when? Ah, who will say?
The steepest mountain will become a plain,
And the parched land be satisfied with rain.
The gates of brass all broken; iron bars,

Transfigured, form a ladder to the stars.
Rough places plain, and crooked ways all straight,
For him who with a patient heart can wait.
These things will be on God's appointed day:
It may not be tomorrow—yet it may.

Morning

Take root below and bear fruit above.
ISAIAH 37:31

Why is it that the mountain hemlocks can attain such stateliness in spite of fierce winter gales and crushing snows? If you look at one of them closely, you will see that it has foliage almost as delicate as a fir, its dark needles being as dainty as fairy feathers. Yet if you try to break a twig or a bough you will learn that therein lies the strength and the tenacious power of the hemlock. It will bend and yield, but it will not break. Winds may whip and toss it this way and that, but they cannot break it—nor can elements, however fierce, pull its roots out of the ground. For months it may have its graceful form held down by a mighty weight of snow, but when the warm breath of summer winds and the melting influence of summer's sun relieve it of its burden, it straightens up as proud and as noble as it was before.

Beautiful, wonderful hemlock of the mountains—what a lesson you bring to us! Though we may be storm-tossed and bent by the winds of sorrow, we need not be crushed and broken *if our souls are anchored to the Rock of Ages.*

> *Lord, make me strong! Let my soul rooted be*
> *Afar from vales of rest,*
> *Flung close to heaven upon a great Rock's breast,*
> *Unsheltered and alone, but strong in Thee.*

> *What though the lashing tempests leave their scars?*
> *Has not the Rock been bruised?*

Mine, with the strength of ages deep infused,
To face the storms, and triumph with the stars!

Lord, plant my spirit high upon the crest
Of Thine eternal strength!
Then, though life's breaking struggles come at length,
Their storms shall only bend me to Thy breast.

DOROTHY CLARK WILSON

MAY 25
Evening

I endure everything for the sake of the elect, that they too may obtain
the salvation that is in Christ Jesus, with eternal glory.

2 TIMOTHY 2:10

Oh, if only Job had known, as he sat in the ashes, troubling his heart over the thought of God's providence, that millions down through history would look back on his trials. He might have taken courage in the fact that his experience would be a help to others throughout the world.

No one lives to himself, and Job's story is like yours and mine, only his was written for all to see. The afflictions Job faced and the trials he wrestled with are the very things for which he is remembered, and without them we would probably never have read of him in God's Word.

We never know the trials that await us in the days ahead. We may not be able to see the light through our struggles, but we can believe that those days, as in the life of Job, will be the most significant we are called upon to live. ROBERT COLLYER

Who has not learned that our most sorrowful days are frequently our best? The days when our face is full of smiles and we skip easily through the soft meadow God has adorned with spring flowers, the capacity of our heart is often wasted.

The soul that is always lighthearted and cheerful misses the deepest things of life. Certainly that life has its reward and is fully satisfied, but the depth of its satisfaction is very shallow. Its heart is dwarfed, and its nature, which has the potential of experiencing the highest heights and the deepest depths, remains undeveloped. And the wick of its life burns quickly to the bottom, without ever knowing the richness of profound joy.

Remember, Jesus said, "Blessed are those who mourn" (Matthew 5:4). Stars shine the brightest during the long dark night of winter. And the gentian wildflowers display their fairest blooms among the nearly inaccessible heights of mountain snow and ice.

God seems to use the pressure of pain to trample out the fulfillment of His promises and thereby release the sweetest juice of His winepress. Only those who have known sorrow can fully appreciate the great tenderness of the "man of suffering" (Isaiah 53:3). SELECTED

You may be experiencing little sunshine, but the long periods of gloomy darkness have been wisely designed for you, for perhaps a lengthy stretch of summer weather would have made you like parched land or a barren wilderness. Your Lord knows best, and the clouds and the sun wait for His command. SELECTED

When told, "It's a gray day," an old Scottish cobbler once replied, "Yes, but didn't ya see the patch of blue?"

MAY 26
Morning

I am the resurrection and the life.
JOHN 11:25

Bishop Foster was one of the leading bishops of the Methodist Church in his day, and was a very godly man. After an earnest search for thirty years he found what is here related in the hope that it may be a help to some other hearts who sought light as he did.

"I have perused all of the books written on the immortality of the soul, bought them at great prices, studied them with great earnestness. I have spent thirty years at it, hoping someday I might be able to present the argument with more force and make its impression stronger upon the mind and heart of the world.

"But when death came to my home and struck down my darlings, when I went and looked into their graves, I saw nothing but utter darkness. With an anguish I cannot express I went out into the deep woods, and looked up into the great vault above, and beat upon my breast and cried to my Father until my heart was crushed and broken. In speechless silence I lay with my face upon the earth to see if I could not hear Him; but I found that it was dark and silent; not a ray, not a voice.

"I went and sat down by the philosophers, but now I found they gave me nothing but husks. I read their arguments which once had cheered me, but now they broke my heart. There was nothing in them, not even enough for me to found a conjecture upon. I was desolate with an utter desolation. I wrung my hands in an agony I cannot describe.

"Nor did I find relief until I heard a Voice coming through the gloom. Out of the darkness and silence, with heavenly music and sweetness in it, it said: *I am Jesus, the resurrection and the life; and thy dead shall live again.*

"And with that single idea that I could rest my hope and my faith upon, He has revealed that great doctrine; He has established the truth which ever eluded mankind till He came down out of heaven telling the story of the Fatherhood of God and the immortality of His own spiritual children."

> *I know not how that Bethlehem's Babe*
> *Could in the Godhead be:*
> *I only know the Manger Child*
> *Has brought God's life to me.*
>
> *I know not how that Calvary's Cross*
> *A world from sin could free:*
> *I only know its matchless love*
> *Has brought God's love to me.*
>
> *I know not how that Joseph's tomb*
> *Could solve death's mystery:*
> *I only know a living Christ,*
> *Our immortality.*
>
> Major Harry W. Farrington

Evening

Spring up, O well! Sing about it.
NUMBERS 21:17

This was a strange song and a strange well. The children of Israel had been traveling over the desert's barren sands, and they were desperate for water, but there was none in sight. Then God spoke to Moses and said, "Gather the people together and I will give them water" (v. 16).

The people then gathered around with their rods. As they began to dig deeply into the burning sand, they sang, *"Spring up, O well! Sing about it."* Soon a gurgling sound was heard, and suddenly a rush of water appeared, filling the well and running along the ground. As they had dug the well in the desert, they had tapped the stream that ran below and that had been unseen for a very long time.

What a beautiful picture this is! And it describes for us the river of blessings that flows through our lives. If only we will respond with faith and *praise*, we will find our needs supplied even in the most barren desert.

Again, how did the children of Israel reach the water of this well? It was through *praise*. While standing on the burning sand and digging the well with their staff of promise, they sang a *praise* song of faith.

Our *praise* will bring forth "water . . . in the wilderness and streams in the desert" (Isaiah 35:6), while complaining will only bring judgment. Even prayer by itself may fail to reach the fountain of blessings.

Nothing pleases the Lord as much as *praise*. There is no greater evidence of faith than the virtue of genuine thanksgiving. *Are you praising God enough?* Are you thanking Him for the countless blessings He has bestowed on you? Are you boldly praising Him even for the trials in your life, which are actually blessings in disguise? And have you learned to praise Him in advance for answers yet to come? SELECTED

You're waiting for deliverance!
O soul, you're waiting long!
Believe that your deliverance
Does wait for you in song!

Complain not till deliverance
Your fettered feet does free:
Through songs of glad deliverance
God now surroundeth thee.

Morning

I rejoice in your promise like one who finds great spoil.
PSALM 119:162

It has pleased the Lord to teach me a truth, the benefit of which I have not lost for more than fourteen years. The point is this: I saw more clearly than ever that the first great and primary business to which I ought to attend every day was *to have my soul happy in the Lord.*

The first thing to be concerned about was not how much I might serve the Lord; but how I might get my soul in a happy state, and how my inner man might be nourished. For I might seek to set the truth before the unconverted, I might seek to benefit believers, I might seek to relieve the distressed, I might in other ways seek to behave myself as it becomes a child of God in this world; and yet, not being happy in the Lord and not being strengthened in my inner man day by day, all this might not be attended to in the right spirit. Before this time my practice had been, at least for ten years previously, as an habitual thing to give myself to prayer after having dressed myself in the morning. Now I saw that the most important thing I had to do was *to give myself to the reading of the Word of God, and to meditate on it,* that thus my heart might be comforted, encouraged, warmed, reproved, instructed; and that thus, by means of the Word of God, whilst meditating on it, my heart might be brought into experimental communion with the Lord.

I began therefore to meditate on the New Testament from the beginning, early in the morning. The first thing I did, after having asked in a few words the Lord's blessing upon His precious Word, was to begin to meditate on the Word of God, searching as it were every verse to get a blessing out of it, not for the sake of the public ministry of the Word, not for the sake of preaching upon what I had meditated upon, but *for obtaining food for my own soul.*

The result I have found to be almost invariably this, that after a few minutes my soul has been led to confession, or to thanksgiving, or to intercession, or to supplication; so that, though I did not as it were give myself to prayer, but to meditation, yet it turned almost immediately more or less into prayer. When thus I have been for a while making confession or intercession or supplication, or have given thanks, I go on to the next words or verse, turning all as I go on into prayer for myself or others as the Word may lead to it, but still continually keeping before me that *food for my own soul is the object of my meditation.*

Formerly, I often spent a quarter of an hour, or half an hour, or even an hour on my knees, before being conscious of having derived comfort, encouragement, humbling of soul, et cetera and often, after having suffered much from wandering of mind for the first ten minutes, or a quarter of an hour, or even half an hour, I only then began to really pray. I scarcely ever suffer now in this way; for my heart being nourished by the truth, being brought into experimental fellowship with God, I speak to my Father and to my Friend (vile though I am and unworthy) about the things that He has brought before me in His precious Word. It often now astonishes me that I did not sooner see this point.

Take the golden key, He calleth thee. Enter into the holy place. GEORGE MUELLER'S SECRET

Do you *know this secret?*

~~~~~   MAY 27   ~~~~~
Evening

Bring them here to me.
MATTHEW 14:18

Do you find yourself at this very moment surrounded with needs, and nearly overwhelmed with difficulties, trials, and emergencies? Each of these is God's way of providing vessels for the Holy Spirit to fill. If you correctly understand their meaning, you will see them as opportunities for receiving new blessings and deliverance you can receive in no other way.

The Lord is saying to you, "Bring them here to me." Firmly hold the vessels before

Him, in faith and in prayer. Remain still before Him, and stop your own restless working until He begins to work. Do nothing that He Himself has not commanded you to do. Allow God time to work and He surely will. Then the very trials that threatened to overcome you with discouragement and disaster will become God's opportunity to reveal His grace and glory in your life, in ways you have never known before.

"Bring [your needs] here to me." A. B. SIMPSON

"My God will meet all your needs according to the riches of his glory in Christ Jesus" (Philippians 4:19).

What a source—"God!" What a supply—"his glorious riches!" What a channel—"Christ Jesus!" It is your heavenly privilege to trust "all your needs" to his glorious riches, and to forget your needs in the presence of his . . . riches. In His great love, He has thrown open to you His exhaustive treasury. Go in and draw upon Him in simple child-like faith, and you will never again have the need to rely on anything else. C. H. M.

My Cup Overflows

There is always something "over,"
When we trust our gracious Lord;
Every cup is overflowing,
His great rivers all are broad.
Nothing narrow, nothing sparing,
Ever springing from His store;
To His own He gives full measure,
Overflowing, evermore.

There is always something "over,"
When we, from the Father's hand,
Take our portion with thanksgiving,
Praising for the path He planned.
Satisfaction, full and deepening,
Fills the soul, and lights the eye,
When the heart has trusted Jesus
All its needs to satisfy.

There is always something "over,"
When we tell of all His love;
Unreached depths still lie beneath us,
Unscaled heights rise far above:
Human lips can never utter
All His wondrous tenderness,
We can only praise and wonder,
And His name forever bless.

MARGARET E. BARBER

"He who did not spare his own Son, but gave him up for us all—how will he not also, along with him, graciously give us all things?" (Romans 8:32).

MAY 28

Morning

In the midst of a very severe trial, their overflowing joy and
their extreme poverty welled up in rich generosity.

2 CORINTHIANS 8:2

Joy is not gush; Joy is not jolliness. Joy is simply perfect acquiescence in God's will, because the soul delights itself in God Himself. "I delight to do thy will," said Jesus, though the cup was the Cross, in such agony as no man knew. *It cost Him blood.* Oh, take the Fatherhood of God in the blessed Son the Savior, and by the Holy Ghost; rejoice in the will of God, and nothing else. Bow down your heads and your hearts before God, and let the will, the blessed will of God, be done. PREBENDARY WEBB-PEPLOE

"Joy and deep poverty!" Truly strange blending.
Fullness and emptiness! Contrasting themes.
Spiritual richness and temporal leanness!
None but the Spirit could wed such extremes.

"Joy and deep poverty!" Servant of Jesus,
Doth it perplex that thy portion is this?
Doth it offend that reward for thy faithfulness
Seemeth to lie much in things thou must miss?

"Joy and deep poverty!" Pause thee, and ponder!
Joy for thy spirit—the world cannot give;
If therewith leanness—extreme limitation—
Mayhap 'tis by e'en such need thou shalt live!
                                    J. DANSON SMITH

One of the happiest men who ever lived—Saint Francis of Assisi—was one of the poorest.

MAY 28
Evening

"I will not let you go unless you bless me." . . . Then he blessed him there.
GENESIS 32:26, 29

Jacob won the victory and the blessing here not by wrestling *but by clinging.* His hip was out of joint and he could struggle no longer, but he would not let go. Unable to wrestle further, he locked his arms around the neck of his mysterious opponent, helplessly resting all his weight upon him, until he won at last.

We too will not win the victory in prayer until we cease our struggling. We must give up our own will and throw our arms around our Father's neck in clinging faith.

What can our feeble human strength take by force from the hand of omnipotence? Are we able to wrestle blessings from God by force? Strong-willed violence on our part will never prevail with Him. What wins blessings and victories is the strength of clinging faith.

It is not applying pressure or insisting upon our own will that brings victory. It is won when humility and trust unite in saying, "Not my will, but yours be done" (Luke 22:42).

We are strong with God only to the degree that self is conquered and is dead. Blessings come not by wrestling but by clinging to Him in faith. J. R. MILLER

An incident from the prayer life of Charles H. Usher illustrates how *"wrestling prayer"* is actually a hindrance to prevailing prayer. He shared this story: "My little boy, Frank, was very ill, and the doctors held out little hope of his recovery. I used all the prayer knowledge I possessed on his behalf, but he continued to worsen. This went on for several weeks.

"One day as I stood watching him while he lay on his bed, I realized he could not live much longer without a quick turn for the better. I said to the Lord, 'Oh, God, I have spent much time in prayer for my son, and yet he is no better. I will now leave him to You and give myself to prayer for others. If it is Your will to take him, I choose Your will—I surrender him entirely to You.'

"I called in my dear wife and told her what I had done. She shed some tears but also handed him over to God. Two days later a godly man came to visit us. He had been very interested in our son Frank and had prayed often for him. He told us, 'God has given me faith to believe that your son will recover. Do you have that faith?'

"I responded, 'I have surrendered him to God, but I will now go again to Him regarding my son.' I did just that and while in prayer discovered I had faith for his recovery. From that time forward he began to get better. I then realized that it was the *'wrestling'* of my prayers that had hindered God's answer, and that if I had continued to wrestle, being unwilling to surrender him to God, he would probably not be here today."

O dear child of God, if you want God to answer your prayers, you must be prepared to walk "in the footsteps of the faith that our father Abraham had" (Romans 4:12), even to the mountain of sacrifice.

~~~~~~~   MAY 29   ~~~~~~~
Morning

There was no one with Joseph when he made himself known.
GENESIS 45:1

In the hiding places on the mountainside, show me your
face, let me hear your voice; for your voice is sweet.
SONG OF SONGS 2:14

There are feelings and experiences too tender and too sacred for the public gaze. Joseph could not reveal himself to his brethren in the face of the Egyptian Court. The stranger could not be allowed to intermeddle with the demonstration of his love.

It is so with Christ's revelation of Himself to the human soul. Not in the busy marketplace, not in the social circle, not even in the crowded sanctuary do we come into the closest touch with the heart of our Elder Brother and our Friend. In the hour of silent communion, when the door is shut; when the world is excluded; in the hush of breathless and holy silence there comes to us the fullest apocalypse of the Divine affection. It is then that we see with clearest vision the glory of the face of Christ and hear most distinctly the melody of the Divine voice as it tells to us the story of His love.

No public feast with Him can compensate for the loss of the private interview.

Make time to be alone with God. He has visions to reveal to us that are not for the eye of the worldling. *Alone with God*—to know the depth and sweetness of our relationship to Him!

> *Precious, gentle, holy Jesus!*
> *Blessed Bridegroom of my heart,*
> *In Thy secret inner chamber*
> *Thou wilt whisper what Thou art.*

A calm hour with God is worth a whole lifetime with man. ROBERT MURRAY MCCHEYNE

~~~~~~ MAY 29 ~~~~~~

Evening

I have called you friends.
JOHN 15:15

Years ago there was an old German professor whose beautiful life was a wonder to his students. Some of them were determined to learn the secret of it, so one night they sent someone to hide in the study where the professor spent his evenings.

It was quite late when the teacher finally came. He was very tired but sat down and spent one hour with his Bible. Then he bowed his head in silent prayer, and finally closing the Book of books, he said, "Well, Lord Jesus, we still have the same old relationship."

"To know Christ" (Philippians 3:10) is life's greatest achievement. At all costs, every Christian should strive to "have the same old relationship" with Him.

The reality of knowing Jesus comes as a result of hidden prayer, and personal Bible study that is devotional and consistent in nature. Christ becomes more real to those who persist in cultivating His presence.

> *Speak unto Him for He hears you,*
> *And Spirit with spirit will meet!*
> *Nearer is He than breathing,*
> *Nearer than hands and feet.*
> MALTBIE D. BABCOCK

MAY 30
Morning

I have finished the race.
2 TIMOTHY 4:7

I have finished my course.
KJV

There is a course prepared for each believer from the moment of his new birth, providing for the fullest maturity of the new life within him, and the highest which God can make of his life in the use of every faculty for His service. To discover that *course* and fulfill it is the one duty of every soul. Others cannot judge what that course is; God alone knows it. And God can just as certainly make known and guide the believer into that course today, as He did with Jeremiah and other prophets, Paul and Timothy and other apostles. J. P. L.

Why do I drift on a storm-tossed sea,
With neither compass, nor star, nor chart,
When, as I drift, God's own plan for me
Waits at the door of my slow-trusting heart?

Down from the heavens it drops like a scroll,
Each day a bit will the Master unroll,
Each day a mite of the veil will He lift.
Why do I falter? Why wander, and drift?

Drifting, while God's at the helm to steer;
Groping, when God lays the course so clear;
Swerving, though straight into port I might sail;
Wrecking, when heaven lies just within hail.

Help me, O God, in the plan to believe;
Help me my fragment each day to receive.
Oh, that my will may with Thine have no strife!
God-yielded wills find the God-planned life.

JAMES H. McCONKEY

Allow God to carry out His plans for you without anxiety or interference.

~~~~~~ MAY 30 ~~~~~~

Evening

No one could learn the song except the 144,000 who
had been redeemed from the earth.

REVELATION 14:3

Certain songs can only be learned in the valley. No music school can teach them, for no theory can cause them to be perfectly sung. Their music is found in the heart. They are songs remembered through personal experience, revealing their burdens through the shadows of the past, and soaring on the wings of yesterday.

In this verse, John tells us that even in heaven there will be a song that will only be sung by those "who had been redeemed from the earth." It is undoubtedly a song of triumph—a hymn of victory to the Christ who set us free. Yet the sense of triumph and freedom will be born from the memory of our past bondage.

No angel, nor even an archangel, will be able to sing the song as beautifully as we will. To do so would require them to pass through our trials, which is something they cannot do. Only the children of the Cross will be equipped to learn the song.

Therefore, dear soul, in this life you are receiving a music lesson from your Father. You are being trained to sing in a choir you cannot yet see, and there will be parts in the chorus that only you can sing. There will be notes too low for the angels to reach, and certain notes so far above the scale that only an angel could reach them. But remember, the deepest notes belong to *you* and will only be reached by you.

Your Father is training you for a part the angels cannot sing, and His conservatory is the school of sorrows. Others have said that He sends sorrow to *test* you, yet this is not the case. He sends sorrow to *educate* you, thereby providing you with the proper training for His heavenly choir.

In the darkest night He is composing your song. In the valley He is tuning your voice. In the storm clouds He is deepening your range. In the rain showers He is sweetening your melody. In the cold He is giving your notes expression. And as you pass at times from hope to fear, He is perfecting the message of your lyrics.

O dear soul, do not despise your school of sorrow. It is bestowing on you a unique part in the heavenly song. GEORGE MATHESON

> *Is the midnight closing 'round you?*
> > *Are the shadows dark and long?*
> *Ask Him to come close beside you,*
> > *And He'll give you a new, sweet song.*
>
> *He'll give it and sing it with you;*
> > *And when weakness slows you down,*
> *He'll take up the broken cadence,*
> > *And blend it with His own.*
>
> *And many a heavenly singer*
> > *Among those sons of light,*

Will say of His sweetest music,
"I learned it in the night."

And many a lovely anthem,
That fills the Father's home,
Sobbed out its first rehearsal,
In the shade of a darkened room.

~~~~~ MAY 31 ~~~~~

Morning

*A woman came with an alabaster jar of very expensive perfume, made of
pure nard. She broke the jar and poured the perfume on his head.*

MARK 14:3

The very nature of God is extravagance. How many sunrises and sunsets does God make?

Gloriously wasteful, O my Lord, art Thou! Sunset faints after sunset into the night . . .

How many flowers and birds, how many ineffable beauties all over the world, lavish desert blossoms that only His eyes see?

Mary's act was one of spontaneous extravagance. Mary of Bethany revealed, in her act of extravagant devotion, that the unconscious sympathy of her life was with Jesus Christ. "She did what she could" (v. 8)—to the absolute limit of what a human can do. It was impossible to do more. The only thing that Jesus Christ ever commended was this act of Mary's, and He said: "Wherever the gospel is preached throughout the world, what she has done will also be told, in memory of her" (v. 9), because in the anointing our Lord saw an exact illustration of what He, Himself, was about to do. He put Mary's act alongside His own Cross. God shattered the life of His own Son to save the world. *Are we prepared to pour out our lives for Him?* Our Lord is carried beyond Himself with joy when He sees any of us doing what Mary of Bethany did. *Have I ever produced in the heart of the Lord Jesus what Mary of Bethany produced?* "She did what she could"—to the absolute limit. *I have not done what I could until I have done the same.*

OSWALD CHAMBERS

Is the precious ointment poured on the feet of the Master ever wasted? Eternity will answer the question. GOLD CORD

The only way to keep a thing is to throw it away!
Seeds which mildew in the garner Scattered, fill with gold the plain.
To keep your treasure is to die—to lose it is to live—
The angels keep the records in God's countinghouse—so give!
PATIENCE STRONG

MAY 31
Evening

You will come to the grave in full vigor, like sheaves gathered in season.
JOB 5:26

A man who once wrote about the salvaging of old ships stated that it was not the age of the wood from the vessel alone that improved its quality. The straining and the twisting of the ship by the sea, the chemical reaction produced by the bilgewater, and the differing cargoes also had an effect.

Several years ago some boards and veneers cut from an oak beam from an eighty-year-old ship were exhibited at a fashionable furniture store on Broadway in New York City. They attracted attention, because of their elegant coloring and beautiful grain. Equally striking were some mahogany beams taken from a ship that sailed the seas sixty years ago. The years of travel had constricted the pores of the wood and deepened its colors, so that they were as magnificent and bright as those of an antique Chinese vase. The wood has since been used to make a cabinet that sits in a place of honor in the living room of a wealthy New York family.

There is also a great difference between the quality of elderly people who have lived listless, self-indulgent, and useless lives and the quality of those who have sailed through rough seas, carrying cargo and burdens as servants of God, and as helpers of others. In the latter group, not only has the stress and strain of life seeped into their lives but the aroma of the sweetness of their cargo has also been absorbed into the very pores of each fiber of their character. LOUIS ALBERT BANKS

When the sun finally drops below the horizon in the early evening, evidence of its work remains for some time. The skies continue to glow for a full hour after its departure.

In the same way, when a good or a great person's life comes to its final sunset, the skies of this world are illuminated until long after he is out of view. Such a person does not die from this world, for when he departs he leaves much of himself behind—and being dead, he still speaks. HENRY WARD BEECHER

When Victor Hugo was more than eighty years old, he expressed his faith in this beautiful way: "Within my soul I feel the evidence of my future life. I am like a forest that has been cut down more than once, yet the new growth has more life than ever. I am always rising toward the sky, with the sun shining down on my head. The earth provides abundant sap for me, but heaven lights my way to worlds unknown.

"People say the soul is nothing but the effect of our bodily powers at work. If that were true, then why is my soul becoming brighter as my body begins to fail? Winter may be filling my head, but an eternal spring rises from my heart. At this late hour of my life, I smell the fragrance of lilacs, violets, and roses, just as I did when I was twenty. And the closer I come to the end of my journey, the more clearly I hear the immortal symphonies of eternal worlds inviting me to come. It is awe-inspiring yet profoundly simple."

JUNE 1
Morning

Pray continually.
1 THESSALONIANS 5:17

Is it hypocritical to pray when we don't feel like it? Perhaps there is no more subtle hindrance to prayer than that of our *moods*. Nearly everybody has to meet that difficulty at times. Even God's prophets were not wholly free from it. Habakkuk felt as if he were facing a blank wall for a long time. What shall we do when moods like this come to *us*? Wait until we *do feel like* praying? It is easy to persuade ourselves that it is hypocrisy to pray when we do not feel like it, but we don't argue that way about other things in life. If you were in a room that had been tightly closed for some time you would, sooner or later, begin to feel very miserable—so miserable, perhaps, that you would not want to make the effort to open the windows, especially if they were difficult to open. But your weakness and listlessness would be proof that you were beginning to need fresh air very desperately—that you would soon be ill without it.

If the soul *perseveres* in a life of prayer, there will come a time when *these seasons of dryness will pass away and the soul will be led out,* as Daniel says, *"into a spacious place"* (Psalm 18:19). Let nothing discourage you. If the soil is dry, *keep cultivating it.* It is said, that in a dry time this harrowing of the corn is equal to a shower of rain.

When we are listless about prayer, *it is the very time when we need most to pray.* The only way we can overcome listlessness in anything is to put more of ourselves, not less, into the task. To pray when you do not feel like praying *is not hypocrisy*—it is faithfulness to the greatest duty of life. Just *tell the Father* that you don't feel like it—ask Him to show you what is making you listless. *He will help us to overcome our moods* and give us courage to persevere in spite of them.

When you cannot pray as you would, pray as you can.

If I feel myself disinclined to pray, then is the time when I need to pray more than ever. Possibly when the soul leaps and exults in communion with God it might more safely refrain from prayer than at those seasons when it drags heavily in devotion.
CHARLES H. SPURGEON

~~~~~~~~~ JUNE 1 ~~~~~~~~~

Evening

He said, "This is the resting place, let the weary rest"; and, "This is the place of repose"—but they would not listen.
ISAIAH 28:12

Why do you worry? What possible use does your worrying serve? You are aboard such a large ship that you would be unable to steer even if your Captain placed you at the helm. You would not even be able to adjust the sails, yet you worry as if you were the captain or the helmsman of the vessel. Be quiet, dear soul—God is the Master!

Do you think all the commotion and the uproar of this life is evidence that God has left His throne? He has not! His mighty steeds rush furiously ahead, and His chariots are the storms themselves. But the horses have bridles, and it is God who holds the reins, guiding the chariots as He wills!

Our God Jehovah is still the Master! Believe this and you will have peace. "Don't be afraid" (Matthew 14:27). CHARLES H. SPURGEON

Tonight, my soul, be still and sleep;
The storms are raging on God's deep—
God's deep, not yours; be still and sleep.

Tonight, my soul, be still and sleep;
God's hands will still the Tempter's sweep—
God's hands, not yours; be still and sleep.

Tonight, my soul, be still and sleep;
God's love is strong while night hours creep—
God's love, not yours; be still and sleep.

Tonight, my soul, be still and sleep;
God's heaven will comfort those who weep—
God's heaven, not yours; be still and sleep.

I implore you to not give in to despair. It is a dangerous temptation, because our Adversary has refined it to the point that it is quite subtle. Hopelessness constricts and withers the heart, rendering it unable to sense God's blessings and grace. It also causes you to exaggerate the adversities of life and makes your burdens seem too heavy for you to bear. Yet God's plans for you, and His ways of bringing about His plans, are infinitely wise. MADAME GUYON

〜〜〜 JUNE 2 〜〜〜

Morning

Cast all your anxiety on him.
1 PETER 5:7

Who among us has not occasionally experienced anxiety? And yet the Bible clearly prohibits it, and as clearly provides an unfailing remedy: "Blessed is the man who trusteth in Jehovah, and whose confidence Jehovah is; for he shall be like a tree . . . which stretcheth forth its roots by the water course, so that it shall not fear when heat cometh, but its leaf shall be verdant; which is not uneasy in the year of drought." SPURRELL

Not uneasy! Not uneasy in the year of drought—in a time of spiritual darkness. Not uneasy about spiritual supplies; not uneasy concerning temporal supplies—food or raiment; not uneasy concerning our lip witness—how, or what to say. Then what is there left about which we may be anxious? Nothing. For the Lord went on to say, "Why do you worry about the rest?" (Luke 12:26). And Paul further says, "Do not be anxious about anything" (Philippians 4:6) or "In nothing be anxious." And again, Peter says, "Do not begin to be anxious."

Anxiety is therefore prohibited in the Bible. But how is it to be prevented? By hurling all your care or worry upon Him, because with Him there is care about you.

Blessed is the man who is not uneasy! APHRA WHITE

~~~~~~~ JUNE 2 ~~~~~~~

Evening

Against all hope, Abraham in hope believed. . . . Without weakening in his faith.
ROMANS 4:18–19

I will never forget the statement which that great man of faith George Mueller once made to a gentleman who had asked him the best way to have strong faith: "The *only* way to know strong faith is to endure great trials. I have learned my faith by standing firm through severe testings."

How true this is! *You must trust when all else fails.*

Dear soul, you may scarcely realize the value of your present situation. If you are enduring great afflictions right now, you are at the source of the strongest faith. God will teach you during these dark hours to have the most powerful bond to His throne you could ever know, if you will only submit. "Don't be afraid; just believe" (Mark 5:36). But if you ever are afraid, simply look up and say, "When I am afraid, I put my trust in you" (Psalm 56:3). Then you will be able to thank God for His school of sorrow that became for you the school of faith. A. B. SIMPSON

Great faith must first endure great trials.

God's greatest gifts come through great pain. Can we find anything of value in the spiritual or the natural realm that has come about without tremendous toil and tears? Has there ever been any great reform, any discovery benefiting humankind, or any soul-awakening revival, without the diligence and the shedding of blood of those whose sufferings were actually the pangs of its birth? For the temple of God to be built, David had to bear intense afflictions. And for the gospel of grace to be extricated from Jewish tradition, Paul's life had to be one long agony.

> Take heart, O weary, burdened one, bowed down
>   Beneath your cross;
> Remember that your greatest gain may come
>   Through greatest loss.
> Your life is nobler for a sacrifice,
>   And more divine.
> Acres of blooms are crushed to make a drop
>   Of perfume fine.
> Because of storms that lash the ocean waves,
>   The waters there
> Keep purer than if the heavens o'erhead
>   Were always fair.
> The brightest banner of the skies floats not
>   At noonday warm;
> The rainbow follows after thunderclouds,
>   And after storm.

JUNE 3
Morning

Its roots may grow old in the ground and its stump die in the soil, yet at the scent of water it will bud and put forth shoots like a plant.

JOB 14:8–9

My roots will reach to the water, and the dew will lie all night on my
branches. My glory will not fade; the bow will be ever new in my hand.
JOB 29:19–20

Once there was an oak tree that clung to a crag on a mountainside. The wind swept its crest, and the snows and rains tore at its soil. Its roots ran along a pathway and were trampled by the feet of men. But the rain and the snows ran down the mountain, and the oak tree was dying of drought. Patiently and persistently its underground tendrils had gone forth in every direction for relief. All its power was put into the quest by which it would save its life. And, by and by, the roots reached the mountain spring. The faithful stream that touched the lips of man and beast ran up the trunk and laved the branches and gave new life to the utmost twig. The tree stood in the same place; it met the same storms; it was trodden by the same hurrying feet. *But it was planted by the rivers of water, and its leaf could not wither.* Out into the same old life *you* must go today as ever, but *down underneath you can be nourished by the everlasting streams of God.*

Travelers returning from Palestine report that beneath the streets of Shechem there are rivers flowing. During the daytime it is impossible to hear the murmuring of the waters because of the noise. But when night comes and the clamor dies away, then can be heard the music of the hidden rivers.

Are there not "hidden rivers" flowing under the crowded streets of our lives today? If we can be assured that there is still the music of deep-flowing waters beneath all the noise and tumult of the working hours, we can walk the way of the conqueror.

Keep your roots deep in the living waters.

~~~~~~~~~ JUNE 3 ~~~~~~~~~
Evening

Let us go over to the other side.
MARK 4:35

Even though we follow Christ's command, we should not expect to escape the storm. In this passage of Scripture, the disciples were obeying His command, yet they encountered the fiercest of storms and were in great danger of being drowned. In their distress, they cried out for Christ's assistance.

Christ may delay coming to us during our times of distress, but it is simply so our faith may be tested and strengthened. His purpose is also that our prayers will be more powerful, our desire for deliverance will be greater, and when deliverance finally comes we will appreciate it more fully.

Gently rebuking His disciples, Christ asked, "Why are you so afraid? Do you still have no faith?" (v. 40). In effect, He was saying, "Why didn't you face the storm victoriously and shout to the raging winds and rolling waves, 'You cannot harm us, for Christ, the mighty Savior, is on board'?"

Of course, it is much easier to trust God when the sun is shining than to trust Him when the storm is raging around us.

Yet we will never know our level of genuine faith until it is tested in a fierce storm, and that is why our Savior is on board.

If you are ever to "be strong in the Lord and in his mighty power" (Ephesians 6:10), your strength will be born during a storm. SELECTED

> With Christ in my vessel,
> I smile at the storm.

Christ said, "Let us go over to the other side"—not "to the middle of the lake to be drowned." DANIEL CRAWFORD

JUNE 4
Morning

The hand of the LORD was on him.
EZEKIEL 1:3

Bones cannot be quickened into life by manipulation. Only the touch of God can give them life.

Some of us must be taught this by bitter experiences of failure. So writes Dr. A. C. Dixon.

"While I was pastor of the Baptist Church in Chapel Hill, the university town of North Carolina, I was made to realize that, as a preacher, I was a dismal failure. Parents all over the state wrote me and requested that I look after the spiritual welfare of their sons in the university. I prepared sermons with the students in mind and was glad to see that they showed their appreciation by attending our Sunday services in large numbers. We appointed a week of prayer and preaching with the single purpose of winning them to Christ, and they attended the evening meetings.

"About the middle of the week their interest seemed to turn into opposition; the spirit of mischief possessed them—one night they tried to put out the lights. As I walked through the grove around the university buildings, I sometimes heard my voice coming from behind a tree: a bright student had caught a part of my sermon the night before, and he was giving it in thought and tone for the benefit of his fellow students, who showed their appreciation by applause and laughter. As I walked before an open window I heard my voice in prayer floating out. I felt I was defeated and was seriously considering resigning the pastorate. Not one had been saved.

"After a restless night I took my Bible and went into the grove and remained there until three o'clock in the afternoon. As I read I asked God to show me what was the matter, and the Word of God searched me through and through giving me a deep sense of sin and helplessness, such as I had never had before.

"That evening the students listened reverently, and at the close two pews were filled with those who had responded to the invitation. The revival continued day after day until more than seventy of the students had confessed Christ.

"Now the practical question is *what did it?* Certainly not I; I fear it was the *I* that kept God from doing it for a long time. There came to me out of the day's experience a clear-cut distinction between influence and power. Influence is made up of many things: intellect, education, money, social position, personality, organization—all of which ought to be used for Christ. Power is God Himself at work *unhindered by our unbelief and other sins.*

"The word *influence* occurs but once in the Bible, and that in Job where Jehovah speaks to the old patriarch of *the sweet influences of the Pleiades*—a good text for a young minister to preach on in the springtime, but not sufficient in dealing with a group of mocking university students.

"The New Testament word *power* holds the secret, and *the power from on high* was no other than God the Holy Spirit *touching the soul through the living word and giving it a birth from above.*

"I had been trusting and testing many other good things, only to fail; *the touch of God* did in a minute what my best efforts could not do."

<hr style="width:30%" />

JUNE 4
Evening

All that night the LORD *drove the sea back.*
EXODUS 14:21

In this verse, there is a comforting message showing how God works during darkness. The real work of God for the children of Israel did not happen when they awoke that morning to find they could cross the Red Sea, but it occurred *"all that night."*

There may be a great work occurring in your life when things seems their darkest. You may see no evidence yet, but God is at work. God was just as much at work "all that night" as He was the next day, when the Israelites finally saw the evidence. The next day simply revealed what God had done during the night.

Are you reading this from a place in your life where everything seems dark? Do you have faith to see but are still not seeing? Are you lacking continual victory in your spiritual growth? Is your daily, quiet communion gone, and there is nothing but darkness all around?

"All that night the LORD drove the sea back." Don't forget—it was *"all that night."* God works through the night until the morning light dawns. You may not see it yet, but through the *night* of your life, as you trust Him, He works. C. H. P.

> *"All that night" the Lord was working,*
> *Working in the tempest blast,*
> *Working with the swelling current,*
> *Flooding, flowing, free and fast.*

> *"All that night" God's children waited—*
> *Hearts, perhaps in agony—*

With the enemy behind them,
And, in front, the cruel sea.

"All that night" seemed blacker darkness
Than they ever saw before,
Though the light of God's own presence
Near them was, and sheltered o'er.

"All that night" that weary vigil
Passed; the day at last did break,
And they saw that God was working
"All that night" a path to make.

"All that night," O child of sorrow,
Can you not your heartbreak stay?
Know your God in darkest midnight
Works, as well as in the day.

L. S. P.

JUNE 5
Morning

God heard their groaning and he remembered his covenant
with Abraham, with Isaac and with Jacob.

EXODUS 2:24

God always hears, and He never forgets. His silence does not mean that He is not listening and is not planning. Probably it means that the best time of deliverance has not come yet, and that He is patiently waiting for the moment to arrive when He may prove His love and His power.

Cromwell said to his soldiers just before a great battle: "Know ye soldiers all, that God always comes to man's help in the nick of time."

Yes, God is always on time; never behind and never ahead. Happy the man who learns to wait as he prays, and never loses patience with God. Men Who Prayed

There is a set time for putting into the furnace, and a set time for taking out of the furnace.

There is a time for pruning the branches of the vine, and there is a time when the husbandman lays aside the pruning hook.

Let us wait His time; "He that believeth shall not make haste" (Isaiah 28:16 kjv). God's time is the best time. But shall we come out the same as we went in? Ah, no! We "will come forth as gold" (Job 23:10). We shall become purer vessels to hold the sweet-smelling incense of praise and prayer. We shall become holy golden vessels for the Master's use in time and in Eternity.

"When a great issue is in the balance and the path is obscure, wait; but with that waiting shirk not the work that lieth before thee, for in that task may be the solution of thy problem."

God will justify you before the universe in His own time. Otto Stockmayer

JUNE 5

Evening

Ask the Lord *your God for a sign, whether in the deepest depths or in the highest heights.*
Isaiah 7:11

Make your petition deep, O heart of mine,
 Your God can do much more Than you can ask;
Launch out on the Divine,
 Draw from His love-filled store.
Trust Him with everything;
 Begin today,
And find the joy that comes
 When Jesus has His way!

Selected

We must continue to *pray* and "*wait* for the LORD" (Isaiah 8:17), until we hear the sound of His mighty rain. There is no reason why we should not ask for great things. Without a doubt, we will receive them if we ask in faith, having the courage to wait with patient perseverance for Him and meanwhile doing those things that are within our power to do.

It is not within our power to create the wind or to change its direction, but we can raise our sails to catch it when it comes. We do not create electricity, yet we can tap into it with a wire that will conduct it, allowing it to work. We do not control God's Spirit, but we can place ourselves before the Lord out of obedience to what He has called us to do, and we will come under the influence and power of His mighty breath. SELECTED

Can't the same great wonders be done today that were done many years ago? Where is the God of Elijah? He is *waiting* for today's Elijah to call on Him.

The greatest Old or New Testament saints who ever lived were on a level that is quite within our reach. The same spiritual force that was available to them, and the energy that enabled them to become our spiritual heroes, are also available to us. If we exhibit the same faith, hope, and love they exhibited, we will achieve miracles as great as theirs. A simple prayer from our mouths will be powerful enough to call down from heaven God's gracious dew or the melting fire of His Spirit, just as the words from Elijah's mouth called down literal rain and fire. All that is required is to speak the words with the same complete assurance of faith with which he spoke. DR. GOULBURN, FORMER DEAN OF NORWICH

JUNE 6

Morning

He gives . . . great victories; he shows unfailing love.
PSALM 18:50

Someone who knew what it was to trust God once said: "During the last two years, though I have said little about them, I have had many a crevasse open up before me. The ice has seemed to split asunder, and I have looked down into the blue depths.

"It is a glorious thing to have a big trouble, a great Atlantic billow, that takes you off your feet and sweeps you right out to sea, and lets you sink down into the depths, into old ocean's lowest caverns, till you get to the foundation of the mountains, and there see God, and then come up again to tell what a great God He is, and how graciously He delivers His people." SELECTED

"He stilled the storm to a whisper" (Psalm 107:29).

Life is to be just hard enough to bring out the heroic! I shall go across battlefields and into twisting storms that I may have an experience of the Father's care, protection, and glorious deliverance. *I am to share in the tremendous experiences of the great!*

Only when Christ opened thine ear to the *storm,* did He open thine ear to the *stillness.* GEORGE MATHESON

Prize your storms!

JUNE 6
Evening

Watch and pray so that you will not fall into temptation.
MATTHEW 26:41

Dear friend, never go out into the danger of the world without praying first. There is always a temptation to shorten your time in prayer. After a difficult day of work, when you kneel at night to pray with tired eyes, do not use your drowsiness as an excuse to resign yourself to early rest. Then when the morning breaks and you realize you have overslept, resist the temptation to skip your early devotion or to hurry through it.

Once again, you have not taken the time to "watch and pray." Your alertness has been sacrificed, and I firmly believe there will be irreparable damage. You have failed to pray, and you will suffer as a result.

Temptations are waiting to confront you, and you are not prepared to withstand them. Within your soul you have a sense of guilt, and you seem to be lingering some distance from God. It certainly is no coincidence that you tend to fall short of your responsibilities on those days when you have allowed your weariness to interfere with your prayer life.

When we give in to laziness, moments of prayer that are missed can never be redeemed. We may learn from the experience, but we will miss the rich freshness and strength that would have been imparted during those moments. FREDERICK WILLIAM ROBERTSON

Jesus, the omnipotent Son of God, felt it necessary to rise each morning before dawn to pour out His heart to His Father in prayer. Should we not feel even more compelled to pray to Him who is the giver of "every good and perfect gift" (James 1:17) and who has promised to provide whatever we need?

We do not know all that Jesus gained from His time in prayer, but we do know this—a life without prayer is a powerless life. It may be a life filled with a great deal of activity and noise, but it will be far removed from Him who day and night prayed to God. SELECTED

JUNE 7
Morning

God was reconciling the world to himself in Christ.
2 CORINTHIANS 5:19

There is on record a story of how a tribe of North American Indians who roamed in the neighborhood of Niagara offered, year by year, a young virgin as a sacrifice to the Spirit of the Mighty River.

She was called *the Bride of the Falls.*

The lot fell one year on a beautiful girl who was the only daughter of an old chieftain. The news was carried to him while he was sitting in his tent, but on hearing it the old man went on smoking his pipe and said nothing of what he felt.

On the day fixed for the sacrifice, a white canoe, full of ripe fruits and decked with beautiful flowers, was ready, waiting to receive "the Bride."

At the appointed hour she took her place in the frail bark, which was pushed out into midstream where it would be carried swiftly toward the mighty cataract.

Then, to the amazement of the crowd which had assembled to watch the sacrifice, a second canoe was seen to dart out from the river's bank a little lower down the stream. In it was seated the old chieftain. With swift strokes he paddled toward the canoe in which sat his beloved child. Upon reaching it he gripped it firmly and held it fast. The eyes of both met in one last long look of love; and then, close together, father and daughter were carried by the racing current until they plunged over the thundering cataract and perished side by side.

In their death they were not divided. The father was *in it* with his child!

"God was reconciling the world to himself in Christ." He did not have to do this. Nobody forced Him. *The only force behind that sacrifice was the force of His seeking love for His lost world.* SELECTED

JUNE 7
Evening

Where is God my Maker, who gives songs in the night?
JOB 35:10

D o you ever experience sleepless nights, tossing and turning and simply waiting for the first glimmer of dawn? When that happens, why not ask the Holy Spirit to fix your thoughts on God, your Maker, and believe He can fill those lonely, dreary nights with song?

Is your night one of bereavement? Focusing on God often causes Him to draw near to your grieving heart, bringing you the assurance that He needs the one who has died. The Lord will assure you He has called the eager, enthusiastic spirit of your departed loved one to stand with the invisible yet liberated, living, and radiant multitude. And as this thought enters your mind, along with the knowledge that your loved one is engaged in a great heavenly mission, a song begins in your heart.

Is your night one of discouragement or failure, whether real or imagined? Do you feel as if no one understands you, and your friends have pushed you aside? Take heart: your Maker "will come near to you" (James 4:8) and give you a song—a song of hope, which will be harmonious with the strong, resonant music of His providence. Be ready to sing the song your Maker imparts to you. SELECTED

> *What then? Shall we sit idly down and say*
> *The night has come; it is no longer day?*

Yet as the evening twilight fades away,
The sky is filled with stars, invisible to day.

The strength of a ship is only fully demonstrated when it faces a hurricane, and the power of the gospel can only be fully exhibited when a Christian is subjected to some fiery trial. We must understand that for God to give "songs in the night," He must first make it night. NATHANIEL WILLIAM TAYLOR

<hr>

JUNE 8

Morning

We also glory in our sufferings, because we know that suffering produces perseverance;
perseverance, character; and character, hope. And hope does not put us to shame.
ROMANS 5:3–5

A story is told of the great artist Turner, that one day he invited Charles Kingsley to his studio to see a picture of a storm at sea. Kingsley was rapt in admiration. "How did you do it, Turner?" he exclaimed. Turner answered: "I wished to paint a storm at sea; so I went to the coast of Holland, and engaged a fisherman to take me out in his boat in the next storm. The storm was brewing, and I went down to the boat and bade him bind me to its mast. Then he drove the boat out into the teeth of the storm. The storm was so furious that I longed to be down in the bottom of the boat and allow it to blow over me. But I could not: I was bound to the mast. *Not only did I see that storm, and feel it, but it blew itself into me until I became part of the storm. And then I came back and painted the picture.*"

His experience is a parable of life: sometimes cloud and sometimes sunshine; sometimes pleasure, sometimes pain. *Life is a great mixture of happiness and tragic storm. He who comes out of it rich in living, is he who dares to accept it all, face it all, and let it blow its power, mystery and tragedy into the inmost recesses of the soul. A victory so won in this life will then be an eternal possession.* CHARLES LEWIS SLATTERY

Evening

*Everyone born of God overcomes the world. This is the
victory that has overcome the world, even our faith.*

1 JOHN 5:4

If a person allows it, he can find something at every turn of the road that will rob him of his victory and his peace of mind. Satan is far from retiring from his work of attempting to deceive and destroy God's children. At each milestone in your life, it is wise to check the temperature of your experience in order to be keenly aware of the surrounding conditions.

If you will do this and firmly exhibit your faith at the precise moment, you can sometimes actually snatch victory from the very jaws of defeat.

Faith can change any situation, no matter how dark or difficult. Lifting your heart to God in a moment of genuine faith in Him can quickly alter your circumstances.

God is still on His throne, and He can turn defeat into victory in a split second, if we will only trust Him.

> *God is mighty! He is able to deliver;*
>   *Faith can victor be in every trying hour;*
> *Fear and care and sin and sorrow be defeated*
>   *By our faith in God's almighty, conquering power.*
>
> *Have faith in God, the sun will shine,*
>   *Though dark the clouds may be today;*
> *His heart has planned your path and mine,*
>   *Have faith in God, have faith alway.*

When you have faith, you need never retreat. You can stop the Enemy wherever you encounter him. MARSHAL FERDINAND FOCH

Morning

They will soar on wings like eagles.

ISAIAH 40:31

Those who wait upon the Lord shall obtain a marvelous addition to their resources: *they shall obtain wings!* They become endowed with power to rise above things. Men who do not soar always have small views of things. Wings are required for breadth of view. The wing-life is characterized by a sense of proportion. To see things aright, we must get away from them. An affliction looked at from the lowlands may be stupendous; looked at from the heights, it may appear little or nothing. These "light and momentary troubles are achieving for us an eternal glory that far outweighs them all" (2 Corinthians 4:17). What a breadth of view!

And here is another great quotation: "Our present sufferings are not worth comparing with the glory that will be revealed in us" (Romans 8:18). This is a bird's-eye view. It sees life as a whole. How mighty the bird from which the picture is taken! "Like eagles!" What strength of wing! Such is to be ours if we wait upon the Lord. We shall be able to soar above disappointment—no matter how great—and to wing our way into the very presence of God. *Let us live the wing-life!*

> *The little bird sat on a slender limb,*
> *Upward swinging,*
> *And though wind and rain were rough with him,*
> *Still kept singing.*
> *"O little bird, quick, seek out your nest!"*
> *I could not keep from calling;*
> *"The bleak winds tear your tender breast,*
> *Your tiny feet are falling."*
> *"More need for song*
> *When things go wrong,*
> *I was not meant for crying;*

No fear for me,"
He piped with glee,
"My wings are made for flying!"
My heart had been dark as the stormy sky.
In my sorrow,
With the weight of troubles long passed by,
And the morrow.
"O little bird, sing!" I cried once more, "The sun will soon be shining.
See, there's a rainbow arching o'er
The storm cloud's silver lining."
I, too, will sing
Through everything;
It will teach blessing double;
Nor yet forget.
When rude winds fret,
To fly above my trouble.

SELECTED

Wing-power gives us the gift of soaring, and we see how things are related one to another.

Wide soaring gives wide seeing!

<div align="center">~~~~~~ JUNE 9 ~~~~~~</div>

Evening

Trust in the LORD and do good; dwell in the land and enjoy safe pasture.
PSALM 37:3

I once met a poor woman who earned a meager living through hard domestic labor but was a joyful, triumphant Christian. Another Christian lady, who was quite sullen, said to her one day, "Nancy, I understand your happiness today, but I would think your future prospects would sober you. Suppose, for instance, you experience a time of illness and are unable to work. Or suppose your present employers move away, and you cannot find work elsewhere. Or suppose—"

"Stop!" cried Nancy. "I never 'suppose.' 'The LORD is my shepherd, I shall not want' [Psalm 23:1 KJV]. And besides," she added to her gloomy friend, "it's all that 'supposing' that's making you so miserable. You'd better give that up and simply trust the Lord."

The following scripture is one that will remove all the "supposing" from a believer's life if received and acted on in childlike faith: "Be content with what you have, because God has said, 'Never will I leave you; never will I forsake you.' So we say with confidence, 'The Lord is my helper; I will not be afraid. What can mere mortals do to me?'" (Hebrews 13:5–6). HANNAH WHITALL SMITH

> There's a stream of trouble across my path;
>   It is dark and deep and wide.
> Bitter the hour the future hath
>   When I cross its swelling tide.
> But I smile and sing and say:
>   "I will hope and trust alway;
> I'll bear the sorrow that comes tomorrow,
>   But I'll borrow none today."
>
> Tomorrow's bridge is a dangerous thing;
>   I dare not cross it now.
> I can see its timbers sway and swing,
>   And its arches reel and bow.
> O heart, you must hope alway;
>   You must sing and trust and say:
> "I'll bear the sorrow that comes tomorrow,
>   But I'll borrow none today."

The eagle that soars at great altitudes does not worry about how it will cross a river. SELECTED

Morning

The LORD *your God will bless you in everything you do.*
DEUTERONOMY 15:18

Art thou suddenly called to occupy a difficult position full of responsibilities? Go forward, counting on *Me!* I am giving thee the position full of difficulties for the reason that Jehovah thy God will bless thee in all thy works and in all the business of thy hands.

This day I place in thy hands a pot of holy oil. Draw from it freely, My child, that all the circumstances arising along thy pathway, each word that gives thee pain, each manifestation of thy feebleness, each interruption trying to thy patience, may be anointed with this oil.

Interruptions are Divine instructions.

The sting will go in the measure in which thou seest *Me* in all things.

"*Take to heart all the words I have solemnly declared to you this day. . . . They are your life*" (Deuteronomy 32:46–47).

"*I will now turn aside, and see this great sight*" (Exodus 3:3 KJV).

Our Father is always trying to get us to the place of spiritual discoveries. God is not interested in getting mere information into our souls; He wants us to have a revelation of Himself. God has challenging futures for us and will go to miracle lengths to get us to pay attention. If God calls me from ease and idleness, it will be that His undergirdings are sufficient for a great service. "*I will turn aside,*" for it is God who calls me.

As "my expectation is from him" (Psalm 62:5 KJV), I will listen today.

Evening

*We know that in all things God works for the good of those who
love him, who have been called according to his purpose.*
ROMANS 8:28

What a tremendous claim Paul makes in this verse! He does not say, "We know that in *some* things," "*most* things," or even "*joyful* things" but "ALL things." This promise spans from the very smallest detail of life to the most important, and from the most humbling of daily tasks to God's greatest works of grace performed during a crisis.

Paul states this in the present tense: "God *works*." He does not say, "*worked*" or "*will work*." It is a continuing operation.

We also know from Scripture that God's "justice [is] like the great deep" (Psalm 36:6); at this very moment the angels in heaven, as they watch with folded wings the development of God's great plan, are undoubtedly proclaiming, "The LORD is righteous in *all* his ways and faithful in *all* he does" (Psalm 145:17).

Then when God orchestrates "*all things . . . for the good,*" it is a beautiful blending. He requires many different colors, which individually may be quite drab, to weave into the harmonious pattern.

Separate tones, notes, and even discords are required to compose melodious musical anthems; a piece of machinery requires many separate wheels, parts, and connections. One part from a machine may be useless, or one note from an anthem may never be considered beautiful, but *taken together, combined, and completed*, they lead to perfect balance and harmony.

We can learn a lesson of faith from this: "You do not realize now what I am doing, but later you will understand" (John 13:7). J. R. MACDUFF

In a thousand trials, it is not just five hundred of them that work "for the good" of the believer, but nine hundred and ninety-nine, *plus one*. GEORGE MUELLER

GOD MEANT IT UNTO GOOD

"God meant it unto good"—O blest assurance,
 Falling like sunshine all across life's way,
Touching with Heaven's gold, earth's darkest storm clouds,
 Bringing fresh peace and comfort day by day.

'Twas not by chance the hands of faithless brothers
 Sold Joseph captive to a foreign land;
Nor was it chance that, after years of suffering,
 Brought him before the pharaoh's throne to stand.

One Eye all-seeing saw the need of thousands,
　　And planned to meet it through that one lone soul;
And through the weary days of prison bondage
　　Was working toward the great and glorious goal.

As yet the end was hidden from the captive,
　　The iron entered even to his soul;
His eye could scan the present path of sorrow,
　　Not yet his gaze might rest upon the whole.

Faith failed not through those long, dark days of waiting,
　　His trust in God was reimbursed at last,
The moment came when God led forth his servant
　　To comfort many, all his sufferings past.

"It was not you but God, that led me to here,"
　　Witnessed triumphant faith in later days;
"God meant it unto good," no other reason
　　Mingled their discord with his song of praise.

"God means it unto good" for you, beloved,
　　The God of Joseph is the same today;
His love permits afflictions strange and bitter,
　　His hand is guiding through the unknown way.

Your Lord, who sees the end from the beginning,
　　Has purposes for you of love untold.
Then place your hand in His and follow fearless,
　　Till you the riches of His grace behold.

There, when you stand firm in the Home of Glory,
　　And all life's path lies open to your gaze,
Your eyes will see the hand that you're now trusting,
　　And magnify His love through endless days.

FREDA HANBURY ALLEN

JUNE 11
Morning

I will awaken the dawn.
PSALM 57:8

Take time. Give God time to reveal Himself to you. Give yourself time to be silent and quiet before Him, waiting to receive through the Spirit the assurance of His presence with you, His power working in you. Take time to read His Word as in His presence; that from it you may know what He asks of you and what He promises you. Let the Word create around you, create within you, a holy heavenly light in which your soul will be refreshed and strengthened for the work of daily life.
ANDREW MURRAY

We repeatedly come upon entries in the diary of Dr. Chalmers, which express what he called the "morning grace of appropriation":

"Began my first waking moments with confident hold upon Christ as my Savior."

"A day of quietness."

"My faith took hold of the precious promises this morning."

"The morning makes the entire day. To think of morning is to think of a bloom and fragrance which if missed, cannot be overtaken later on in the day. The Lord stands upon the shore in the morning and reveals Himself to the weary, disillusioned men who had toiled all night and taken nothing. *He* ever stands upon life's most dreary and time-worn shores, and as we *gaze* upon Him the shadows flee and *it is morning.*"

> *I met God in the morning*
> *When the day was at its best,*
> *And His presence came like glory*
> *Of the sunrise in my breast.*
>
> *All day long the Presence lingered,*
> *All day long He stayed with me,*
> *And we sailed in perfect calmness*
> *O'er a very troubled sea.*

Other ships were blown and battered,
Other ships were sore distressed.
But the winds that seemed to drive them,
Brought to us a peace and rest.

Then I thought of other mornings,
With a keen remorse of mind.
When I too, had loosed the moorings
With the Presence left behind.

And I think I know the secret,
Learned from many a troubled way;
You must seek God in the morning
If you want Him through the day.

RALPH CUSHMAN

The early morning hour has always been a time of visions. What discoveries the saints have made while others slept!

JUNE 11
Evening

The servant of the LORD must . . . be gentle.
2 TIMOTHY 2:24 KJV

When God finally conquers us and changes our unyielding nature, we receive deep insights into the Spirit of Jesus. Then, as never before, we see His extraordinary *gentleness of spirit* at work in this dark and unheavenly world. Yet the *gifts* of "the fruit of the Spirit" (Galatians 5:22) do not automatically become evident in our lives. If we are not discerning enough to recognize their availability to us, to desire them, and then to nourish them in our thoughts, they will never become embedded in our nature or behavior. Every further step of spiritual growth in God's grace must be preceded by acknowledging our lack of a godly attribute and then by exhibiting a prayerful determination to obtain it.

However, very few Christians are willing to endure the suffering through which complete gentleness is obtained. We must die to ourselves before we are turned into gentleness, and our crucifixion involves suffering. It will mean experiencing genuine brokenness and a crushing of self, which will be used to afflict the heart and conquer the mind.

Today many people are attempting to use their mental capacity and logical thinking to obtain sanctification, yet this is nothing but a religious fabrication. They believe that if they just mentally put themselves on the altar and believe the altar provides the gift of sanctification, they can then logically conclude they are fully sanctified. Then they go happily on their way, expressing their flippant, theological babble about the "deep" things of God.

Yet the heartstrings of their old nature have not been broken, and their unyielding character, which they inherited from Adam, has not been ground to powder. Their soul has not throbbed with the lonely, gushing groans of Gethsemane. Having no scars from their death on Calvary, they will exhibit nothing of the soft, sweet, gentle, restful, victorious, overflowing, and triumphant life that flows like a spring morning from an empty tomb. G. D. W.

"And abundant grace was upon them all" (Acts 4:33).

JUNE 12
Morning

Has your God . . . been able to rescue you from the lions?
DANIEL 6:20

Thou servant of the living God,
Whilst lions round thee roar,
Look up and trust and praise His Name,
And all His ways adore;
For even now, in peril dire,
He works to set thee free,

And in a way known but to Him,
Shall thy deliverance be.

Dost wait while lions round thee stand?
Dost wait in gloom, alone,
And looking up above thy head
See but a sealed stone?
Praise in the dark! Yea, praise His Name,
Who trusted thee to see
His mighty power displayed again
For thee, His saints, for thee.

Thou servant of the living God,
Thine but to wait and praise;
The living God, Himself, will work,
To Him thine anthem raise;
Though undelivered thou dost wait,
The God who works for thee,
When His hour strikes, will with a word
Set thee forever free.

M. E. B.

"Believe ye that I am able to do this?" . . . "Yea, Lord" (Matthew 9:28 KJV).

Strengthen yourself in the Omnipotence of God. Do not say, "Is God able?" Say, rather, "God is able." ANDREW MURRAY

The supernatural always slumbers when faith lies sleeping, or dead.

JUNE 12
Evening

In him you have been enriched in every way.
1 CORINTHIANS 1:5

Have you ever seen people who through some disaster were driven to great times of prayer? And have you noticed that once the disaster was long forgotten, a spiritual sweetness remained that warmed their souls?

It reminds me of a severe storm I once saw in late spring—one in which darkness covered the sky, except where the lightning violently split the clouds with its thundering power. The wind blew and the rain fell, as though heaven had opened its windows.

What devastation there was! The storm uprooted even the strongest of oaks, and not one spiderweb escaped the wind, despite being hidden from view. But soon, after the lightning was gone, the thunder ceased and was silent, and the rain was over; a western wind arose with a sweet and gentle breath, chasing the dark clouds away. I saw the retreating storm throw a scarf of rainbows over her fair shoulders and her glowing neck. She looked back at me, smiled, and then passed from my sight.

For many weeks after the storm, the fields raised their hands, full of heavenly, fragrant flowers, toward the sky. And all summer long the grass was greener, the streams were filled, and the trees, because of their lush foliage, cast a more restful shade.

All this—*because the storm had come*. All this—even though the rest of the earth had long forgotten the storm, its rainbows, and its rain. THEODORE PARKER

God may not give us an easy journey to the Promised Land, but He will give us a safe one. HORATIUS BONAR

It was a storm that led to the discovery of the gold mines in India. Have we not seen storms drive people to the discovery of the priceless mines of the love of God in Christ?

Is it raining, little flower?
   Be glad of rain;
Too much sun would wither one;
   It will shine again.
The clouds are very dark, it's true;
But just behind them shines the blue.
   Are you weary, tender heart?
Be glad of pain:
In sorrow, sweetest virtues grow,
   As flowers in rain.
God watches, and you will have sun,
When clouds their perfect work have done.

          LUCY LARCOM

Morning

For the joy set before him he endured the cross, scorning its shame.
HEBREWS 12:2

The joy of the spirit is no cheap joy. It has scars on it—radiant scars! It is joy won out of the heart of pain. Those who know it have found one of life's deepest and most transforming secrets; the transmuting of pain into a paean. Sorrow becomes not something to escape; we can make it sing. We can set our tears to music, and no music is so exquisite, so compelling. The Christians learned immediately and at once the truth which the philosopher Royce puts in these words: "Such ills we remove only as we assimilate them, take them up into the plan of our lives, give them meaning, set them in their place in the whole." When their heartstrings were stretched upon some cross of pain and the winds of persecution blew through them, then from this human aeolian harp men heard the very music of God. They did not *bear pain,* they *used* it. SELECTED

Where the rain does not fall we have deserts. When the soil is not torn up by the plow and the harrow we get no crops.

Joy is a rare plant; it needs much rain for its growth and blossoming.

> *I heard an old farmer talk one day,*
> *Telling his listeners how*
> *In the wide, new country far away*
> *The rainfall follows the plow.*
> *"As fast as they break it up, you see,*
> *And turn the heart to the sun,*
> *As they open the furrow deep and free*
> *And the tillage is begun,*
> *The earth grows mellow, and more and more*
> *It holds and sends to the sky*
> *A moisture it never had before,*
> *When its face was hard and dry.*
> *And so wherever the plowshares run*
> *The clouds run overhead,*

And the soil that works and lets in the sun
With water is always fed."
I wonder if that old farmer knew
The half of his simple word,
Or guessed the message that, heavenly true,
Within it was hidden and heard.
It fell on my ear by chance that day,
But the gladness lingers now,
To think it is always God's dear way
That the rainfall follows the plow.
Endure with faith and courage through the frost,
and you will see a glorious spring.

JUNE 13
Evening

My peace I give you.
JOHN 14:27

Two painters were once asked to paint a picture illustrating his own idea of rest. The first chose for his scene a quiet, lonely lake, nestled among mountains far away. The second, using swift, broad strokes on his canvas, painted a thundering waterfall. Beneath the falls grew a fragile birch tree, bending over the foam. On its branches, nearly wet with the spray from the falls, sat a robin on its nest.

The first painting was simply a picture of *stagnation and inactivity.* The second, however, depicted *rest.*

Outwardly, Christ endured one of the most troubled lives ever lived. Storms and turmoil, turmoil and storms—wave after wave broke over Him until His worn body was laid in the tomb. Yet His inner life was as smooth as a sea of glass, and a great calm was always there.

Anyone could have gone to Him at any time and found rest. Even as the human bloodhounds were dogging Him in the streets of Jerusalem, He turned to His disciples, offering them a final legacy: "My peace."

Rest is not some holy feeling that comes upon us in church. It is a state of calm rising from a heart deeply and firmly established in God. HENRY DRUMMOND

> My peace I give in times of deepest grief,
> Imparting calm and trust and My relief.
>
> My peace I give when prayer seems lost, unheard;
> Know that My promises are ever in My Word.
>
> My peace I give when you are left alone—
> The nightingale at night has sweetest tone.
>
> My peace I give in times of utter loss,
> The way of glory leads right to the cross.
>
> My peace I give when enemies will blame,
> Your fellowship is sweet through cruel shame.
>
> My peace I give in agony and sweat,
> For My own brow with bloody drops was wet.
>
> My peace I give when nearest friend betrays—
> Peace that is merged in love, and for them prays.
>
> My peace I give when there's but death for thee—
> The gateway is the cross to get to Me.
>
> L. S. P.

~~~~~~ JUNE 14 ~~~~~~
Morning

I have directed the ravens. . . . I have directed a widow there.
1 KINGS 17:4, 9

We must be where God desires. Elijah spoke of himself as always standing before the Lord God of Israel. He could as distinctly stand before God when hiding at the Kerith Ravine or sheltering in the widow's house at Zarephath, as when he stood erect on Carmel or listened to the voice of God at Horeb.

If we are where God wants us to be, He will see the supply of our need. It is as easy for Him to feed us by the ravens as by the widow woman. As long as God says *stay here,* or *there,* be sure that He is pledged to provide for you. Though you resemble a lonely sentinel in some distant post of missionary service, God will see to you. The ravens are not less amenable to His command than of old: and out of the stores of widow women He is able to supply your need as He did Elijah's at Zarephath.

When God said to Elijah, "Hide in the Kerith Ravine" (v. 3), a carbon copy of the order was given to the ravens. They brought food morning and evening to *the place of Divine appointment.*

When Jesus said, "Go into all the world and preach the gospel" (Mark 16:15), He placed all the resources of heaven at the disposal of the going group.

When I was ordered toward the front in France, I got permission to remain behind ten days for letters. None came. When I reached my objective, where men were dying without a Chaplain's comfort, I found the last thirty days' post. The commanding officer said:

"In the army, the letters go where the orders read."

In the kingdom of God the blessings and equipment are found only where the orders read. Let us all go and tell the story. JOSIAH HOPKINS

It is in the path of His appointment that we shall find His Presence.

JUNE 14

Evening

I have prayed for you . . . that your faith may not fail.
LUKE 22:32

Dear Christian, remember to take good care of your faith, for *faith is the only way to obtain God's blessings.* Prayer alone cannot bring answers down from His throne, because it is the earnest prayer of one who believes that leads to answers.

Faith is the communication link between heaven and earth. It is on this link of faith that God's messages of love travel so quickly that even before we ask, He answers. And while we are still speaking, "he hears us" (1 John 5:14). So when the connection of faith is broken, how will we obtain His promises?

Am I in trouble? I can receive help by expressing faith. Am I being battered by the Enemy? My soul will find refuge by leaning in faith upon God. But without faith, I call to Him in vain, for faith is the only road between my soul and heaven. If the road is blocked, how can I communicate with the great King?

Faith links me to Holy God and clothes me with the power of Jehovah. Faith ensures me that each of His attributes will be used in my defense, helping me to defy the hosts of hell. It causes me to march triumphantly over the necks of my enemies. So without faith, how can I receive anything from the Lord?

Therefore, O Christian, carefully watch your faith. "Everything is possible for one who believes" (Mark 9:23). CHARLES H. SPURGEON

We as a people take such pride in being so practical that we want something more sure than faith. Yet Paul said, "The promise comes by FAITH, so that it may . . . be GUARANTEED" (Romans 4:16). DANIEL CRAWFORD

Faith honors God, and God honors faith.

JUNE 15
Morning

I sought the LORD, *and he answered me.*
PSALM 34:4

Andrew Murray says: It is one of the terrible marks of the diseased state of the Christian life in these days *that there are so many that rest content without the distinct experience of answered prayer. They pray daily* but know little of direct, definite *answer to prayer as the rule of their daily life.*

And it is this the Father wills. He seeks daily intercourse with His children in *listening to and granting* their petitions. He wills that I should come to Him day by day with distinct requests. He wills day by day to do for me what I ask.

There may be cases in which the answer is a refusal, but our Father lets His child know when He cannot give him what he requests, and like the Son in Gethsemane, he will withdraw his petition.

Whether the request be according to His will or not, God will by His Word and His Spirit *teach those who are teachable* and who will give Him time. Let us withdraw our requests if they are not according to God's mind, or persevere until the answer comes.

Prayer is appointed to obtain the answer!

It is in prayer and its answer that *the interchange of love between the Father and His child takes place.*

Are your prayers answered?

JUNE 15

Evening

God has made me fruitful in the land of my suffering.
GENESIS 41:52

A poet stands by the window watching a summer shower. It is a fierce downpour, beating and pounding the earth. But the poet, in his mind's eye, sees more than a rain shower falling. He sees a myriad of lovely flowers raining down, soon breaking forth from the freshly watered earth, and filling it with their matchless beauty and fragrance. And so he sings:

> *It isn't raining rain to me—it's raining daffodils;*
> *In every dripping drop I see wildflowers upon the hills.*
> *A cloud of gray engulfs the day, and overwhelms the town;*
> *It isn't raining rain to me—it's raining roses down.*

Perhaps you are undergoing some trial as God's child, and you are saying to Him, "O God, it is raining very hard on me tonight, and this test seems beyond my power to endure. Disappointments are pouring in, washing away and utterly defeating my chosen plans. My trembling heart is grieved and is cowering at the intensity of my suffering. Surely the rains of affliction are beating down upon my soul."

Dear friend, you are completely mistaken. God is not raining rain on you—*He is raining blessings.* If you will only believe your Father's Word, you will realize that springing up beneath the pounding rain are spiritual flowers. And they are more beautiful and fragrant than those that ever grew before in your stormless and suffering-free life.

You can see the rain, but can you also see the flowers? You are suffering through these tests, but know that God sees sweet flowers of faith springing up in your life beneath these very trials. You try to escape the pain, yet God sees tender compassion for other sufferers finding birth in your soul. Your heart winces at the pain of heavy grief, but God sees the sorrow deepening and enriching your life.

No, my friend, it is not raining afflictions on you. It is raining tenderness, love, compassion, patience, and a thousand other flowers and fruits of the blessed Holy Spirit. And they are bringing to your life spiritual enrichment that all the prosperity and ease of this world could never produce in your innermost being. J. M. M.

Songs across the Storm

A harp stood in the calm, still air,
Where showers of sunshine washed a thousand fragrant blooms;
A traveler bowed with loads of care
Struggled from morning till the dusk of evening glooms
To strum sweet sounds from the songless strings;
The pilgrim strives in vain with each unanswering chord,
Until the tempest's thunder sings,
And, moving on the storm, the fingers of the Lord
A wondrous melody awakes;
And though the battling winds their soldier deeds perform,
Their trumpet-sound brave music makes
While God's assuring voice sings love across the storm.

Morning

*If only you had paid attention to my commands,
your peace would have been like a river.*

ISAIAH 48:18

Do we not see how God's purposes are thwarted and deferred by human perversity? At the very time when God had determined upon the election and consecration of Aaron to the priesthood, Aaron was spending his time in molding and chiseling the golden calf.

We might have been crowned fifty years ago, but just as the coronation was about to take place we were discovered in the manufacture of an idol. *The Lord was just ready to make kings of us when we made fools of ourselves.* JOSEPH PARKER

> *One small life in God's great plan—*
> *How futile it seems as the ages roll,*
> *Do what it may or strive how it can*
> *To alter the sweep of the infinite whole!*
> *A single stitch in the endless web,*
> *A drop in the ocean's flow or ebb;*
> *But the pattern is rent where the stitch is lost,*
> *Or marred where the tangled threads have crossed:*
> *And each life that fails of true intent*
> *Mars the perfect plan that its Master meant.*

Remember the awful truth *that I can limit Christ's power in the present,* although I can never alter God Almighty's order for a moment. SEED THOUGHTS CALENDAR

> *There is a niche in God's own Temple, it is thine;*
> *And the hand that shapes thee for it, is Divine.*

My hope comes from him.
PSALM 62:5

So often we simply neglect to look for the answers to what we have asked, which shows the lack of earnestness in our petitions. A farmer is never content until he reaps a harvest; a marksman observes whether or not his bullet has hit the target; and a physician examines the effect of the medicine he prescribes. Should a Christian be any less careful regarding the effect of his labor in prayer?

Every prayer of the Christian, whether for temporal or spiritual blessings, will be fully answered if it meets certain biblical requirements. It must be prayed in faith and in accordance with God's will. It must rely on God's promise, be offered up in the name of Jesus Christ, and be prayed under the influence of the Holy Spirit.

God always answers the general intent of His people's prayers. He does so not only to reveal His own glory but also to provide for the Christian's spiritual and eternal welfare. Since we see in Scripture that Jesus Christ never rejected even a single petitioner who came to Him, we can believe that no prayer made in His name will be in vain.

The answer to our prayer may be coming, although we may not discern its approach. A seed that is underground during winter, although hidden and seemingly dead and lost, is nevertheless taking root for a later spring and harvest. BICKERSTETH

Delayed answers to prayer are not only trials of faith; they also give us opportunities to honor God through our steadfast confidence in Him even when facing the apparent denial of our request. CHARLES H. SPURGEON

~~~~~~~~~ JUNE 17 ~~~~~~~~~

Morning

The rough ground shall become level, the rugged places a plain. And the glory of the LORD will be revealed, and all people will see it together.
ISAIAH 40:4–5

And what is God's glory? It is the ministration of love. We are not to wait for a union of *opinions;* we are to begin with a union of hearts. *We are to be united, while yet we do not "see together."* You and I may look at the same stars and call them by different names. You are an astronomer, and I am a peasant; to you they are masses of worlds; to me they are candles in the sky set up to light me home.

What matter? Shall we not enjoy the glory though we do not agree about it? *Let us join hands over the message ere we settle the dispute about the messenger.*

Ye who stand upon the shore and wrangle about the number of the waves, there is meantime a work for you to do, *and to do together.* There are shipwrecked voyagers out yonder, crying and calling. They have folded their hands in prayer, and have heard no answer save the echo of their cry. Shall they call in vain? Shall they wait till you have counted the billows that consume them? Shall they stand shivering in the storm while you are disputing the name of the lifeboat? *What matter how we name the lifeboat if only we each believe in it?*

Come out to the wreck, my brothers. Come to the souls who have lost their compass, to lives that have broken their helm, to hearts that have rent their sails. They will not ask *the name of your lifeboat;* even Jacob's angel had no name. You may not see together, *but you shall reveal together*—reveal the glory of the Lord. You shall be the church of united sympathizers. *You shall see together the face of the Master,* but *you shall touch together the print of the nails. Tomorrow, you shall see Him as He is.* GEORGE MATHESON

> *When crew and captain understand each other to the core,*
> *It takes a gale and more than a gale to put their ship ashore;*
> *For the one will do what the other commands,*
> *although they are chilled to the bone;*
> *And both together can live through weather*
> *that neither could face alone.*
>
> KIPLING

A battleship cannot go into action with a mutiny raging on board.

JUNE 17
Evening

*Then there came a voice from above the vault over their
heads as they stood with lowered wings.*

EZEKIEL 1:25

What is the significance of these words: "They stood with lowered wings"? People often ask, "How can I hear the voice of the Lord?" This is the secret: these "living creatures" (v. 5) heard the voice when "they stood with lowered wings."

We have all seen a bird flutter its wings while standing in place. But in this verse, we are told that "there came a voice . . . as they stood with lowered wings."

Do you ever sit, or even kneel, before the Lord and yet are conscious of a fluttering in your spirit? If so, you are not exhibiting a sense of genuine stillness while in His presence.

A dear person told me of this very thing a few days ago. "I prayed about a certain thing," she said, "but I did not wait for the answer to come." She did not get still enough to hear God speak but instead went away and followed her own thinking in the matter. The result proved disastrous, and she was forced to retrace her steps.

Oh, how much energy we waste! How much time we lose by refusing to lower the wings of our spirit and become totally quiet before Him! Imagine the calm, the rest, and the peace that will come as we wait in His presence until we hear from Him!

Then, and only then, we too may speed "back and forth like flashes of lightning" (v. 14), going directly to "wherever the spirit would go" (v. 20).

> *Be still! Just now be still!*
> *Something your soul has never heard,*
> *Something unknown to any song of bird,*
> *Something unknown to any wind, or wave, or star,*
> *A message from the Father's land afar,*
> *That with sweet joy the homesick soul will thrill,*
> *And comes to you only when you're still.*

Be still! Just now be still!
There comes a presence very mild and sweet;
White are the sandals of His noiseless feet.
It is the Comforter whom Jesus sent
To teach you what the words He uttered meant.
The willing, waiting spirit, He does fill.
If you would hear His message,
Dear soul, be still!

JUNE 18
Morning

He makes the clouds his chariot.
PSALM 104:3

We cannot ride in our own chariots and God's at the same time. God must burn up with the fire of His love *every earthly chariot* that stands in the way of our mounting into His.

Would you mount into God's chariots? Then take each thing that is wrong in your life as one of God's chariots for you. Ask Him daily to *open your eyes,* and you will see His unseen chariots of deliverance.

Whenever we mount into God's chariots we have a translation—not into the heavens above us as Elijah did, but into the heaven *within us;* away from the low, groveling plane of life, up into the heavenly places in Christ Jesus, where we shall ride in triumph over all below. But the chariot that carries the soul over this road is generally some chastening, *that for the present doth not seem joyous but grievous.*

Nevertheless afterward!

No matter what the source of these chastenings, look upon them as God's chariots sent to carry your soul into the high planes of spiritual achievement and uplifting. You will find, to your glad surprise, that it is God's love that sends the chariots—His chariots in which you may *ride prosperously* over all darkness.

Let us be thankful for every trial that will help to destroy our earthly chariots, and will compel us to take refuge in the chariots of God, which always stand ready and waiting beside us in every trial.

"Yes, my soul, find rest in God; my hope comes from him. Truly he [only] is my rock and my salvation; he is my fortress, I will not be shaken" (Psalm 62:5–6).

We have to be brought to the place where all other refuges fail, before we can say *He only.* We say, He *and* my experience; He *and* my church relationships; He *and* my Christian work. All that comes after the *and* must be taken away from us, or must be proved useless, before we can come to the *He only.* Only then we mount into God's chariots.

If we want to ride with God *upon the heavens,* all earth riding must be brought to an end.

He who rides with God rides above all earthborn clouds!

Oh, may no earthborn cloud arise to hide Thee from Thy servant's eyes.

No obstacle can hinder the triumphant course of God's chariots! HANNAH WHITALL SMITH

JUNE 18
Evening

Lift up the hands which hang down, and the feeble knees;
And make straight paths for your feet, lest that which is lame
be turned out of the way; but let it rather be healed.
HEBREWS 12:12–13 KJV

This verse is God's word of encouragement to us to lift the hands of faith and to fortify the knees of prayer. All too often our faith becomes tired, weak, and listless, and our prayers lose their power and effectiveness.

The Lord's illustration here is quite compelling. He is pointing out to us that when we become so discouraged and fearful that even one little obstacle depresses and frightens us, we are tempted to walk around it. We would rather take the easy way than face it. Perhaps there is some physical ailment that God is ready to heal, but it requires exertion on our part. The temptation is to find help from someone else or to walk around the obstacle in some other way.

We tend to find many ways of walking around emergencies instead of walking straight through them. So often we are faced with something that frightens or overwhelms us and seek to evade the problem with the excuse: "I'm not quite ready for that now." It may require some sacrifice, or demand our obedience in some area. Perhaps there is some Jericho we are facing, or we are lacking the courage to help someone else and to pray through his concern that him. Perhaps we have a prayer that awaits completion, or a physical problem that is partially healed and we continue to walk around it.

God says, "Lift up the hands which hang down." March straight through the flood, and behold! The waters will divide, the Red Sea will open, the Jordan will part, and the Lord will lead you through to victory.

Do not allow your feet to "be turned out of the way," but let your body "be healed," and your faith strengthened. Go straight ahead, leaving no Jericho unconquered behind you, and no place where Satan can boast of having overwhelmed you. This is a valuable lesson and is extremely practical. How often we find ourselves in this very situation!

Perhaps this is where you find yourself today. A. B. SIMPSON

Pay as little attention to discouragement as possible. Plow ahead like a steamship, which moves forward whether facing rough or smooth seas, and in rain or shine. Remember, the goal is simply to carry the cargo and to make it to port. MALTBIE D. BABCOCK

<hr />

JUNE 19

Morning

I will be like the dew.
HOSEA 14:5

Hosea leads us to the source of *the dew-drenched life*. It is from *Him* that this priceless gift comes. Those who spend much time with the Master come forth with the dew of blessing upon their lives.

The dew falls in the still night when all nature is hushed to rest. What is true in nature holds true in spiritual things: in this we have the key reason why so many of God's people are living dewless lives. They are restless, anxious, impatient, fussy, busy, with no time at all to be still before the Lord.

The finer things are being sacrificed for the coarser; the things of value for the worthless.

In Job 38:28 the question is asked, "Who fathers the drops of dew?" It is one of God's secrets. It comes quietly, and yet works so mightily. We cannot produce it, but we may receive it and live, moment by moment, in that atmosphere where the Holy Spirit may continually drench us with His presence. W. MALLIS

> *But the sensitive dew and the stillness are friends,*
> *In the storm, it is true that it never descends.*
> *Let me fuss not, nor pine, but on God cast my care,*
> *And the dew shall be mine in the quiet of prayer.*
>
> *Let Him hush the sad riot of temper and will,*
> *Till rested and quiet the cleansed heart is still.*
> *When the atmosphere's so, 'tis attractive to dew,*
> *And the first thing you know 'twill be falling on you.*
> MAMIE PAYNE FERGUSON

> *Thy dew is as the dew of herbs.*

God feeds the wildflowers on the lonely mountainside without the help of any man, and they are as fresh and lovely as those that are daily watched over in our gardens. So God can feed His own planted ones without the help of man, by the sweet falling dew on his spirit. ROBERT MURRAY MCCHEYNE

Wait before the Master until your whole heart is drenched by Him, and then go forth in the power of a fresh, strong, and fragrant life.

Lord, let Thy Spirit bedew my dry fleece!

JUNE 19
Evening

Grain must be ground to make bread.
ISAIAH 28:28

Many of us cannot be used as food for the world's hunger, because we have yet to be broken in Christ's hands. "Grain must be ground to make bread," and being a blessing of His often requires sorrow on our part. Yet even sorrow is not too high a price to pay for the privilege of touching other lives with Christ's blessings. The things that are most precious to us today have come to us through tears and pain. J. R. MILLER

God has made me as bread for His chosen ones, and if it is necessary for me to "be ground" in the teeth of lions in order to feed His children, then blessed be the name of the Lord. IGNATIUS

To burn brightly our lives must first experience the flame.

In other words, we cease to bless others when we cease to bleed.

Poverty, hardship, and misfortune have propelled many a life to moral heroism and spiritual greatness. Difficulties challenge our energy and our perseverance but bring the strongest qualities of the soul to life. It is the weights on the old grandfather clock that keep it running. And many a sailor has faced a strong head wind yet used it to make it to port. God has chosen opposition as a catalyst to our faith and holy service.

The most prominent characters of the Bible were broken, threshed, and ground into bread for the hungry. Because he stood at the head of the class, enduring affliction while remaining obedient, Abraham's diploma is now inscribed with these words: "The Father of Faith."

Jacob, like wheat, suffered severe threshing and grinding. Joseph was beaten and bruised, and was forced to endure Potiphar's kitchen and Egypt's prison before coming to his throne.

David, hunted like an animal of prey through the mountains, was bruised, weary, and footsore, and thereby ground into bread for a kingdom. Paul could never have been bread for Caesar's household if he had not endured the bruising of being whipped and stoned. He was ground into fine flour for the Roman royal family.

Combat comes before victory. If God has chosen special trials for you to endure, be assured He has kept a very special place in His heart just for you. A badly bruised soul is one who is chosen.

Morning

And the singers sang, and the trumpeters sounded: and all
this continued until the burnt offering was finished.
2 CHRONICLES 29:28 KJV

There is a joy that is *attained* and another joy that is *given*. The first joy needs things to make it joy—congenial circumstances, attentive friends; the second joy joys because it is filled with a bubbling spring of internal and eternal gladness—a gladness because it is *always in God, and God is always in it*. It glows and grows under all circumstances—it sings *because it is a song.*

It sings after prayer. "Ask and you will receive, and your joy will be complete" (John 16:24). This implies that there must have been a need, a place to fill. As we believe and receive, *the song sings!*

It sings after faith. "Even though you do not see him now, you believe in him and are filled with an inexpressible and glorious joy" (1 Peter 1:8). Nothing seen and nothing sensed, at least not by natural sense—yet *the song sang* and with a fullness of glory not before known.

It sings after yielding. "Once more the humble will rejoice in the LORD" (Isaiah 29:19). Making room for the Lord is a secret of receiving more of Himself.

It sings after sorrow. "Weeping may stay for the night, but rejoicing [singing] comes in the morning" (Psalm 30:5). He who is *Light,* who gives the morning signal to every feathered songster to tune his song, will also give you a *song that sings.*

It sings after sacrifice. "Neither count I my life dear unto myself, so that I might finish my course with joy" (Acts 20:24 KJV).

Did you ever find *the song that sang of itself* in the quiet of your closet, when you heard His "Yes" to your prayer for His glory to come on earth? When nothing was seen of His working for you and your loved ones, did you hear the sweet strains of *the song that sang?*

The world awaits you—the singer with the new song!

Evening

Whether you turn to the right or to the left, your ears will hear a
voice behind you, saying, "This is the way; walk in it."
Isaiah 30:21

When we have doubts or are facing difficulties, when others suggest courses of action that are conflicting, when caution dictates one approach but faith another, we should be still. We should quiet each intruding person, calm ourselves in the sacred stillness of God's presence, study His Word for guidance, and with true devotion focus our attention on Him. We should lift our nature into the pure light radiating from His face, having an eagerness to know only what God our Lord will determine for us. Soon He will reveal by His secret counsel a distinct and unmistakable sense of His direction.

It is unwise for a new believer to depend on this approach alone. He should wait for circumstances to also confirm what God is revealing. Yet Christians who have had many experiences in their walk with Him know the great value of secret fellowship with the Lord as a means of discerning His will.

Are you uncertain about which direction you should go? Take your question to God and receive guidance from either the light of His smile or the cloud of His refusal. You must get alone with Him, where the lights and the darknesses of this world cannot interfere and where the opinions of others cannot reach you. You must also have the courage to wait in silent expectation, even when everyone around you is insisting on an immediate decision or action. If you will do these things, the will of God will become clear to you. And you will have a deeper concept of who He is, having more insight into His nature and His heart of love.

All this will be your unsurpassed gift. It will be a heavenly experience, a precious eternal privilege, and the rich reward for the long hours of waiting. David

> *"Stand still," my soul, for so your Lord commands:*
> *E'en when your way seems blocked, leave it in His wise hands;*
> *His arm is mighty to divide the wave.*
> *"Stand still," my soul, "stand still" and you will see*

How God can work the "impossible" for thee,
For with a great deliverance He does save.

Be not impatient, but in stillness stand,
Even when surrounded on every hand,
In ways your spirit does not comprehend.
God cannot clear your way till you are still,
That He may work in you His blessed will,
And all your heart and will to Him do bend.

"Be still," my soul, for just when you are still,
Can God reveal Himself to you; until
Through you His love and light and life can freely flow;
In stillness God can work through you and reach
The souls around you. He then through you can teach
His lessons, and His power in weakness show.

"Be still"—a deeper step in faith and rest.
"Be still and know" your Father does know best
The way to lead His child to that fair land,
A "summer" land, where quiet waters flow;
Where longing souls are satisfied, and "know
Their God," and praise for all that He has planned.

SELECTED

<div align="center">~~~~~   JUNE 21   ~~~~~</div>

Morning

This God is our God.

PSALM 48:14

G od is *great* in great things, but *very great* in little things," says Henry Dyer.
A party stood on the Matterhorn admiring the sublimity of the scene, when

—— 430 ——

a gentleman produced a pocket microscope and having caught a fly, placed it under the glass. He reminded us that the legs of the household fly in England are naked, then called attention to the legs of this little fly which were thickly covered with hair; thus showing that the same God who made the lofty Swiss mountain attended to the comfort of His tiniest creatures, even providing socks and mittens for the little fly whose home these mountains were. *This God is our God!*

A doubting soul beheld a robin's nest in a gigantic elm and heard a still small voice saying, "If God spent a hundred years in creating a tree like that for a bird, He will surely take care of you." God is so interested that He takes us one by one and arranges for every detail of our life. To Him, *there are no little things.*

The God of the *infinite* is the God of the *infinitesimal.*

> *I saw a human life ablaze with God,*
> *I felt a power Divine*
> *As through an empty vessel of frail clay*
> *I saw God's glory shine.*
> *Then woke I from a dream, and cried aloud:*
> *"My Father, give to me*
> *The blessing of a life consumed by God*
> *That I may live for Thee."*

JUNE 21
Evening

The people heard that he had come home.

MARK 2:1

The adult coral invertebrates, known as polyps, work underwater constructing coral reefs. They do so never even imagining they are building the foundation of a new island, which will someday support plants and animals and will be a home where the children of God will be born and equipped for eternal glory as "co-heirs with Christ" (Romans 8:17).

Beloved, if your place in God's army is hidden and secluded, do not grumble and complain. Do not seek to run from His will and the circumstances in which He has placed you. Remember, without the polyps, the coral reefs would never be built, and God calls some people to be spiritual polyps. He is looking for those who are willing to serve in places hidden from the sight of others, yet in full view of heaven, and who are sustained by the Holy Spirit.

A day is coming when Jesus will bestow His rewards. On that day some people may wonder how you came to merit a certain reward, since they have never heard of you. But remember, He makes no mistakes. SELECTED

> Just where you stand in the conflict,
>   There is your place.
> Just where you think you are useless,
>   Hide not your face.
> God placed you there for a purpose,
>   Whate'er it be;
> Think He has chosen you for it;
>   Work loyally.
> Put on your armor! Be faithful
>   At toil or rest!
> Whate'er it be, never doubting
>   God's way is best.
> Out in the fight or on lookout,
>   Stand firm and true;
> This is the work that your Master
>   Gives you to do.

SELECTED

With freedom from danger, we can leave a crowded meeting of believers, an inspiring mountaintop experience, or a helpful fellowship with "righteous [men] made perfect" (Hebrews 12:23), in order to return to our modest and simple Emmaus, to the dreaded home of the Colossians, or even to the mission field of distant Macedonia. We can do so with the calm assurance that wherever God has placed us, and in every detail of our daily lives, He has ordained the land we are to possess to its very borders and has ordained the victory to be won. NORTHCOTE DECK

—— 432 ——

Morning

Not I, but Christ.
GALATIANS 2:20 KJV

Full of the Holy Spirit.
ACTS 11:24

"We would in Thee abide, In Thee be glorified, And shine as candles "lighted by the Lord.""

For long the wick of my lamp had served my purpose, silently ministering as I read beside it. I felt ashamed that I had not before noticed its unobtrusive ministry. I said to the wick:

"For the service of many months I thank thee."

"What have I done for thee?"

"Hast thou not given light upon my page?"

"Indeed, no; I have no light to give, in proof whereof take me from my bath of oil, and see how quickly I expire. Thou wilt soon turn from me as a piece of smoking tow. It is not I that burns, but *the oil with which my texture is saturated*. It is this that lights thee. I simply mediate between the oil in the cistern and the fire on my edge. This blackened edge slowly decays, but the light continually burns."

"Dost thou not fear becoming exhausted? See how many inches of coil remain! Wilt thou be able to give light till every inch of this is slowly charred and cut away?"

"I have no fear so long as the supply of oil does not fail, if only some kindly hand will remove from time to time the charred margin . . . exposing a fresh edge to the flame. This is my twofold need: *oil and trimming*. Give me these and I shall burn to the end!"

God has called His children to shine as "lights in the world." Let us, then, beware of hiding our light—whether household candle, street lamp, or lighthouse gleam—lest men stumble to their death.

It is at variance with the teaching of the wick to try to accumulate a stock of grace in a sacrament, a convention, or a night of prayer. The wick has no such stores, but is always supplied!

You may seem altogether helpless and inadequate, but a living fountain of oil is prepared to furnish you with inexhaustible supplies: *Not by your might or power, but by His Spirit.* Hour after hour the oil climbs up the wick to the flame! *You cannot exhaust God!*

Let us not *flinch* when the snuffers are used; they only cut away the black charred debris. He thinks so much of His work that He *uses golden* snuffers! And the Hand that holds the snuffers bears *the nailprint of Calvary!* F. B. MEYER

JUNE 22
Evening

Love covers over all wrongs.
PROVERBS 10:12

Follow the way of love.
1 CORINTHIANS 14:1

When you are troubled, share your problems with God alone. Recently I read the personal experience of a precious child of God. It made such an impression on me that I would like to relate it to you here.

"At midnight I found myself completely unable to sleep," she wrote. "Waves of cruel injustice were sweeping over me, and the covering of love seemed to have been unknowingly removed from my heart. In great agony I cried to God for the power to obey His admonition, 'Love covers over all wrongs.'

"Immediately His Spirit began to work the power into me that ultimately brought about forgetfulness. I mentally dug a grave, deliberately throwing the dirt out until the hole was very deep. With sorrow, I lowered the offense that had wounded me into the grave and quickly shoveled the soil over it. Then I carefully covered the hole with green sod, planted beautiful white roses and forget-me-nots on top, and briskly walked away.

"Suddenly restful sleep came to me. And the wound that had seemed so deadly was healed without a scar. God's love has covered so completely that today I cannot remember what caused my grief."

There was a scar on yonder mountainside,
  Gashed out where once the cruel storm had trod;
A barren, desolate chasm, reaching wide
  Across the soft green sod.

But years crept by beneath the purple pines,
  And veiled the scar with grass and moss once more,
And left it fairer now with flowers and vines
  Than it had been before.

There was a wound once in a gentle heart,
  From which life's sweetness seemed to ebb and die;
And love's confiding changed to bitter smart,
  While slow, sad years went by.

Yet as they passed, unseen an angel stole
  And laid a balm of healing on the pain,
Till love grew purer in the heart made whole,
  And peace came back again.

JUNE 23
Morning

Men ought always to pray, and not to faint.
LUKE 18:1 KJV

That little "ought" is emphatic. It implies obligation as high as heaven. *Jesus* said, "Men ought *always* to pray," and added, "and *not to faint.*"

I confess I do not always *feel* like praying—when, judging by my feelings, there is no one listening to my prayer. And then these words have stirred me to pray: I ought *to pray*—I *ought* always *to pray*—I should not grow faint *in praying.*

Praying is a form of work. The farmer plows his field often when he does not *feel* like it, but he confidently expects a crop for his labors. Now, if prayer is a form of work, and *our labor is not in vain in the Lord,* should we not pray regardless of feelings? Once when I knelt for morning prayers I felt a sort of deadness in my soul, and just then the "accuser of the brethren" became busy reminding me of things that had long since been under the Blood. I cried to God for help, and the blessed Comforter reminded me that my Great High Priest was pleading my case; that I must come boldly to the throne of grace. I did, and the enemy was routed! What a blessed time of communion I had with my Lord! Had I fainted instead of *fighting* I could not have received wages because I had not labored fervently in prayer; I could not have *reaped* because I had not *sown.*

COMMISSIONER BRENGLE

~~~~~~~ JUNE 23 ~~~~~~~

Evening

Peter got down out of the boat, walked on the water and came toward Jesus. But when he saw the wind, he was afraid and, beginning to sink, cried out, "LORD, save me!"

MATTHEW 14:29–30

John Bunyan said that Peter did have a little faith, even in the midst of his doubts. In spite of crying out in fear, it was by getting out of the boat and walking that he got to Jesus.

In this passage of Scripture, we see that Peter's sight was actually a hindrance. Once he had stepped out of the boat, the waves were none of his business. His only concern should have been the path of light shining across the darkness from Christ Himself. Even the glow of a kingdom ten times brighter than that of ancient Egypt should not have diverted Peter's eyes.

When the Lord calls you to come across the water, step out with confidence and joy. And never glance away from Him for even a moment. You will not prevail by measuring the waves or grow strong by gauging the wind. Attempting to survey the danger may actually cause you to fall before it. Pausing at the difficulties will result in the waves breaking over your head.

"Lift up [your] eyes to the mountains" (Psalm 121:1) and go forward. There is no other way.

Do you fear to launch away?
Faith lets go to swim!
Never will He let you go;
It's by trusting you will know
Fellowship with Him.

JUNE 24
Morning

In all these things we are more than conquerors through him who loved us.
ROMANS 8:37

The best steel is subjected to the alternatives of extreme heat and extreme cold. In a cutlery you will notice that knife blades are heated and beaten and then heated again and plunged into the coldest water in order to give them the right shape and temper. You will also observe a large heap of rejected blades, rejected because they would not bear the tempering process; when put upon the grindstone, little flaws appeared in some that up to that point had seemed perfect; others would not bear the tempering process.

Souls are heated in the furnace of affliction, plunged into the cold waters of tribulation, and ground between the upper and nether stones of adversity and disaster.

Some come out ready for the highest services; others are unfit for any but the lowest uses. Would you be of account among the forces which are working out the salvation of the world? *Be still in the Hands of God until He tempers you.*

"Stop now!" says the Knife-blade to the Cutler. "I have been in the fire often enough! Would you burn the life out of me?"

But again it goes into the glowing furnace and is heated to white heat.

"Stop hammering! I have been pounded enough already."

But down comes the sledge.

"Keep me out of this cold water! One moment in the fiery furnace, and the next in ice water. It is enough to kill one!"

But in it goes.

"Keep me off the grindstone! You'll chafe the life out of me!"

But it is made to kiss the stone until the Cutler is satisfied.

Now see! You may bend it double; yet it springs back straight as an arrow. It is as bright as polished silver, hard as a diamond, and will cut like a Damascus blade. *It has been shaped, tempered, and polished; it is worth something.*

Be still, and *let God temper and polish you, and you will be worth something, too. Allow yourself to be prepared for usefulness. He will give you a post of holy renown if you will let Him fit you for it. Be still* in the furnace fire *while the Holy Ghost molds and polishes your soul.* R. V. Lawrence

<hr>

JUNE 24
Evening

Concerning the work of my hands command ye me.
Isaiah 45:11 kjv

The Lord Jesus took this very approach with God when He said, "Father, I want those you have given me to be with me" (John 17:24). Joshua used it during the moment of his greatest victory, when he lifted his spear toward the setting sun and cried aloud, "Sun, stand still" (Joshua 10:12). Elijah employed it when he stopped the rain from heaven and started it again after three and a half years. Martin Luther followed it when, kneeling by his dying colleague, Philipp Melanchthon, he forbid death to take its vicTimothy

This is a wonderful relationship that God invites us to enter. We are certainly familiar with passages of Scripture like the one that follows the above verse: "My own hands stretched out the heavens; I marshaled their starry hosts" (Isaiah 45:12). But knowing that God invites us to command Him to act reveals a surprising change in our normal relationship!

What a distinction there is between this attitude and the hesitancy and uncertainty of our prayers of unbelief, to which we have become so accustomed! The constant repetition of our prayers has also caused them to lose their sharp cutting edge.

Think how often Jesus, during His earthly ministry, put others in a position to command Him. "As Jesus and his disciples were leaving Jericho," Jesus stopped and responded to two blind men who had called out to Him. "What do you want me to do for you?" (Matthew 20:29, 32). It was as though He said, "I am yours to command."

Could we ever forget how Jesus yielded the key to His resources to the Greek woman from Syrian Phoenicia because of her reply to Him? In effect, He told her to help herself to all that she needed. (Mark 7:24–30.)

What human mind can fully realize the total significance of the lofty position to which God lovingly raises His little children? He seems to be saying, "All my resources are at your command." *"And I will do whatever you ask in my name"* (John 14:13). F. B. Meyer

Say to this mountain, "Go,
*   Be cast into the sea";*
And doubt not in your heart
*   That it will be to thee.*
It will be done, doubt not His Word,
Challenge your mountain in the Lord!

Claim your redemption right,
*   Purchased by precious blood;*
The Trinity unite
*   To make it true and good.*
It will be done, obey the Word,
Challenge your mountain in the Lord!

Self, sickness, sorrow, sin,
*   The Lord did meet that day*
On His beloved One,
*   And you are freed away.*
It has been done, rest on His Word,
Challenge your mountain in the Lord!

Surround the rival's wall
*   With silent prayer, then raise—*
Before its ramparts fall—
*   The victor's shout of praise.*
It will be done, faith rests assured,
Challenge your mountain in the Lord!

The massive gates of brass,
  The bars of iron yield,
To let the faithful pass,
  Conquerors in every field.
It will be done, the foe ignored,
Challenge your mountain in the Lord!

Take then the faith of God,
  Free from the taint of doubt;
The miracle-working rod
  That casts all reasoning out.
It will be done, stand on the Word,
Challenge your mountain in the Lord!

Selected

JUNE 25
Morning

I also told them about the gracious hand of my God on me.
NEHEMIAH 2:18

Is the work God's work? Has He called you to do it, and equipped you for it? *Be sure on these points.* Take time to consider and pray and find what the will of the Lord is. Then, when the difficulties have been considered and the needs fairly measured, and the clear conviction remains that God calls you to rise and build, then, *put your hand to the plow and never look back.*

Power to endure to the end—patience to outlast all discouragements—zeal that will not die out, and that will enkindle the zeal of others—*all these are given and secured to him who knows that the work and call are from God.*

For every worker and every work in the kingdom of God the principles are the same. The only way to avoid being repelled and discouraged in the work, so as to give it up in irritation, disgust or despair, is to get the work put upon the *right lines* from the very start. These must *begin* in the secret place of the Most High—the Holy of Holies—*alone with God*. They must *proceed* to the Holy Place, for the light and strength contained therein—the guidance and equipment needed. Then, and not till then can they safely *come out,* their success secure and their permanence established, because they are thus truly *"wrought in God"* (John 3:21 KJV). HUBERT BROOKE

While the yoke of the Lord Jesus is easy and His burden light, nevertheless the furrow that He calls us to undertake is not always by any means easy plowing. There is no yoke that fits so smoothly and handily as His, but there is no work that requires more steady trudging and persistent faithfulness than His. Three stages of that work are strikingly set forth by Hudson Taylor when he says: "Commonly there are three stages in work for God: *Impossible, Difficult, Done!"*

Said General William Booth, *"God loves with a special love the man who has a passion for the impossible."* Are you confronting today the *impossible* in work for God? Praise Him for that because you are in a way to discover the blessing of finding that *work difficult* and then to experience the deep joy of finding it *done,* by the same Lord who started you on the furrow.

> *Am I Thy friend?*
> *And canst Thou count on me,*
> *Lord, to be true to Thee?*
> *Canst Thou depend*
> *On sympathy and help of mine,*
> *In purpose, aim,*
> *Or work of Thine,*
> *And trust me with the honor of Thy name?*

JUNE 25

Evening

The LORD said to Moses, ". . . Tell the Israelites to move on.
Raise your staff and stretch out your hand over the sea."
EXODUS 14:15–16

Dear child of God, just imagine that triumphal march! Picture the excited children being constantly hushed and restrained by their parents from their outbursts of wonder. Think how the women must have experienced an uncontrollable excitement as they found themselves suddenly saved from a fate worse than death. Imagine how the men who accompanied them must have felt ashamed and admonished for mistrusting God and for complaining against Moses. And as you envision the Red Sea's mighty walls of water, separated by the outstretched hand of the Eternal in response to the faith of a single man, learn what God will do for His own.

Never dread any consequence resulting from absolute obedience to His command. Never fear the rough waters ahead, which through their proud contempt impede your progress. God is greater than the roar of raging water and the mighty waves of the sea. "The LORD sits enthroned over the flood; the LORD is enthroned as King forever" (Psalm 29:10). A storm is simply the hem of His robe, the sign of His coming, and the evidence of His presence.

Dare to trust Him! Dare to follow Him! Then discover that the forces that blocked your progress and threatened your life become at His command the very materials He uses to build your street of freedom. F. B. MEYER

Have you come to the Red Sea place in your life,
    Where, in spite of all you can do,
There is no way out, there is no way back,
    There is no other way but through?
Then wait on the Lord with a trust serene
    Till the night of your fear is gone;
He will send the wind, He will heap the floods,
    When He says to your soul, "Move on."

And His hand will lead you through—clear through—
    Ere the watery walls roll down,
No foe can reach you, no wave can touch,
    No mightiest sea can drown;
The tossing billows may rear their crests,
    Their foam at your feet may break,
But o'er the seabed you will walk dry ground
    In the path that your Lord will make.

In the morning watch, 'neath the lifted cloud,
 You will see but the Lord alone,
When He leads you on from the place of the sea
 To a land that you have not known;
And your fears will pass as your foes have passed,
 You will be no more afraid;
You will sing His praise in a better place,
 A place that His hand has made.

ANNIE JOHNSON FLINT

JUNE 26
Morning

I am with you always, to the very end of the age.
MATTHEW 28:20

Many with lacerated feet have come back to tell the story and to testify that when the very foundations of earth seemed giving way, He remained whom no accident could take away, no chance ever change. This is the power of the Great Companionship.

Stretched on a rack, where they were torturing him piteously, one of the martyrs saw with cleansed and opened eyes, a Young Man by his side—*not yet fifty years old*—who kept wiping the beads of sweat from his brow.

When the fire is hottest, He is there. *"And the form of the fourth is like the Son of God"* (Daniel 3:25 KJV). *"He that is near Me is near the fire."* That is why the heart of the Divine furnace is the place of the soul's deepest peace. There is always *one* beside us when we go through the fire.

When John G. Paton stood beside that lonely grave in the South Sea Islands, when he with his own hands made his wife's coffin and with his own hands dug her grave, the savages were looking on. They had never seen it in this fashion. That man must fill in the sepulcher and soon leave it. He says, "If it had not been for Jesus and the Presence that He vouchsafed me there, I would have gone mad and died beside that lonely grave." But John G. Paton found his Master with him through the dire darkness.

Sir Ernest Shackleton and two of his companions spent thirty-six hours among the snow mountains of New Georgia, seeking for a station that meant life or death to them and their waiting crew on Elephant Island. Writing of that journey, he says, *"It seemed to me, often, that we were four, not three."* He refers to the "guiding Presence" that went with them. Then in closing he writes, "A record of our journey would be incomplete without a reference to a subject so near to our hearts."

Paul was not peculiarly privileged when he saw the Living One while en route to Damascus.

Kahlil Gibran, the Syrian, explaining his remarkable modern painting of Jesus, said: "Last night I saw His face again, clearer than I have ever seen it."

Handel, composer of the "Hallelujah Chorus," declared: "I did see God on His throne."

During the terrible stress of war many affirmed positively that they saw "The White Comrade."

Phillips Brooks testified, "He is here. I know Him. He knows me. It is not a figure of speech. It is the realest thing in the world."

No distant Lord have I,
Loving afar to be;
Made flesh for me, He cannot rest
Until He rests in me.

Brother in joy or pain,
Bone of my bone was He;
Now—intimacy closer still—
He dwells Himself in me.

I need not journey far,
This dearest Friend to see;
Companionship is always mine,
He makes His home with me.

MALTBIE D. BABCOCK

Evening

What if some were unfaithful? Will their unfaithfulness nullify God's faithfulness?
ROMANS 3:3

I suspect that the source of every bit of sorrow in my life can be traced to simple unbelief. If I truly believe the past is totally forgiven, the present is supplied with power, and the future is bright with hope, how could I be anything but completely happy?

Yes, the future is bright because of God's faithfulness. His abiding truth does not change with my mood, and He never wavers when I stumble and fall over a promise of His through my unbelief. His faithfulness stands firm and as prominent as mountain peaks of pearl splitting the clouds of eternity. And each base of His hills is rooted at an unfathomable depth on the rock of God.

Mont Blanc does not disappear, becoming a passing vision or a whimsical mist, simply because a climber grows dizzy on its slopes. JAMES SMETHAM

Is it any wonder that we do not receive God's blessing after stumbling over His promise through unbelief? I am not saying that faith merits an answer or that we can work to earn it. But God Himself has made *believing* a condition of receiving, and the Giver has a sovereign right to choose His own terms for His gifts. SAMUEL HART

Unbelief continually asks, "How can this be possible?" It is always full of "hows," yet faith needs only one great answer to even ten thousand "hows." That answer is— GOD! C. H. M.

No one accomplishes *so much* in *so little* time as when he or she is praying. And the following thought certainly aligns well with all that the Lord Jesus Christ taught on prayer: If only ONE BELIEVER WITH TOTAL FAITH rises up, *the history of the world will be changed.*

Will *you* be that one to rise up, submitting yourself to the sovereignty and guidance of God our Father? A. E. MCADAM

Prayer without faith quickly degenerates into an aimless routine or heartless hypocrisy. However, prayer with faith brings the omnipotence of God to the support of our petitions. It is better not to pray until your entire being responds to, and understands, the power of prayer. When genuine prayer is even whispered, earth and heaven, and the past and future, say, "Amen!"

This is the kind of prayer Christ prayed. P. C. M.

Nothing lies beyond the reach of prayer except those things outside the will of God.

JUNE 27

Morning

Stormy winds that do his bidding.
PSALM 148:8

Did you ever go into the woods late in the afternoon on a day of howling wind and driving rain, and did you ever see a drearier spectacle or hear drearier sounds? The sough of the winds through the almost bare branches, the drip, drip of the rain upon the masses of withered leaves, the air filled with flying leaves fluttering down in the gloom of the forest as into a grave, the delicate colors of trunk and moss all changed and stained and blended by the soaking of the rain: how hard to believe that such dreariness is related in any way to the beauty of the summer forest!

And yet we know that it is that very wind which is rocking the trees and howling so dismally—just that streaming rain and those rotting leaves which will help to clothe the forest trees next year with verdure and to make the woods sing with joy and pulsate with life. All winds and weathers are favorable to the development of the sturdy, well-rooted tree; even the hurricane which strips it of its leaves and branches quickens all its vital powers, challenging it to put forth greater strength.

If the tree is cut down in part, the result is a sturdier trunk and a more compact and symmetrical growth. Even if it is toppled over by a storm, its acorns are scattered and become the seeds of the forest. In its ruin it goes back to the soil from which spring other trees.

So you are better and purer and stronger today because of the tears and the sighing and the desolation. You know, and the world knows, that your life is richer, better poised, more trustful, less selfish, more detached from the things of sense—that the whole atmosphere is somehow purer and more vitalizing.

"Stormy winds that do his bidding" and the soul that hears in their tumult the rustling of Almighty Wings praises God for the storm—the storm that swings free from enervating ease, the flood that casts upon the Eternal Rock. *Storms make a strong tree—Sufferings make a strong saint!*

Evening

> *Summon your power, God; show us your strength.*
> PSALM 68:28

The Lord imparts to me the underlying strength of character that gives me the necessary energy and decision-making ability to live my life. He strengthens me "with power through his Spirit in [my] inner being" (Ephesians 3:16). And the strength He gives is continuous, for He is a source of power I cannot exhaust.

"Your strength will equal your days" (Deuteronomy 33:25)—my strength of will, affection, judgment, ideals, and achievement will last a lifetime.

"The LORD is my strength" (Exodus 15:2) *to go on.* He gives me the power to walk the long, straight, and level path, even when the monotonous way has no turns or curves offering pleasant surprises and when my spirit is depressed with the terrible drudgery.

"The LORD is my strength" *to go up.* He is my power to climb the straight and narrow path up the Hill of Difficulty, as Christian did in *Pilgrim's Progress*, and not be afraid.

"The LORD is my strength" *to go down.* It is often once I leave the invigorating heights, where the wind and sunlight have surrounded me, and begin to descend to the more confining, humid, and stifling heat of the valley below that my heart grows faint. In fact, I recently heard someone say, referring to his own increasing physical frailty, "It is coming down that tires me most!"

"The LORD is my strength" *to sit still.* And what a difficult accomplishment this is! I often say to others during those times when I am compelled to be still, "If only I could do something!" I feel like the mother who stands by her sick child but is powerless to heal. What a severe test! Yet to do nothing except to sit still and wait requires tremendous strength.

"The LORD is my strength!" "Our competence comes from God" (2 Corinthians 3:5). THE SILVER LINING

Morning

With God nothing shall be impossible.
LUKE 1:37 KJV

Those who have had the joy of climbing the Swiss mountains in springtime will have learned to love the Soldanella, with its delicate little mauve bells. Many years ago there appeared a booklet by Lilias Trotter, "The Glory of the Impossible," with a sketch of this little plant just above the snow. We have never forgotten her exquisite application of the lesson, as she traced the power of this fragile plant to melt its way through the icy covering into the sunshine overhead.

We love to see the impossible done and so does God!

> *"Canst thou prevail*
> *To pierce the snow?*
> *Thou art so frail,*
> *And icy winds do blow!"*
> *"I will lift up my head*
> *And trusting, onward go."*

> *"Now hard as rock*
> *Frozen and dry,*
> *Thy strength to mock,*
> *What profits it to try?*
> *The snow will bar thy way."*
> *"On God I will rely."*

> *"Thou art so weak,*
> *Tender and fair,*
> *Why not go, seek*
> *A balmier softer air?"*
> *"God chose my lot for me,*
> *And will sustain me there."*

"Wilt thou keep on? Alas! the fight
Is stern from dawn
Till eve." "'Tis not by might
The victory is won;
God puts my foes to flight."

And now above
In blaze of day,
Wonder of love,
We see the flower and say, "Naught is impossible To him who trusts alway."
"JUST TRUSTING" BY J. B. L.

The incense buds of the kiku (chrysanthemum) will open even in the frost.
JAPANESE PROVERB

<hr>

JUNE 28
Evening

There before me was a door standing open in heaven.
REVELATION 4:1

We should remember that John wrote these words while on the island of Patmos. He was there "because of the word of God and the testimony of Jesus" (Revelation 1:9). He had been banished to this island, which was an isolated, rocky, and inhospitable prison. Yet it was here, under difficult circumstances—separated from all his loved ones in Ephesus, excluded from worshiping with the church, and condemned to only the companionship of unpleasant fellow captives—that he was granted this vision as a special privilege. It was as a prisoner that he saw "a door standing open in heaven."

We should also remember Jacob, who laid down in the desert to sleep after leaving his father's house. "He had a dream in which he saw a stairway resting on the earth, with its top reaching to heaven, and . . . above it stood the LORD" (Genesis 28:12–13).

The doors of heaven have been opened not only for these two men but also for many others. And in the world's estimation, it seems as if their circumstances were utterly unlikely to receive such revelations. Yet how often we have seen "a door standing open in heaven" for those who are prisoners and captives, for those who suffer from a chronic illness and are bound with iron chains of pain to a bed of sickness, for those who wander the earth in lonely isolation, and for those who are kept from the Lord's house by the demands of home and family.

But there are conditions to seeing the open door. We must know what it is to be "in the Spirit" (Revelation 1:10). We must be "pure in heart" (Matthew 5:8) and obedient in faith. We must be willing to "consider everything a loss because of the surpassing worth of knowing Christ Jesus" (Philippians 3:8). Then once God is everything to us, so that "in him we live and move and have our being" (Acts 17:28), the door to heaven will stand open before us as well. DAILY DEVOTIONAL COMMENTARY

> God has His mountains bleak and bare,
>   Where He does bid us rest awhile;
> Cliffs where we breathe a purer air,
>   Lone peaks that catch the day's first smile.
>
> God has His deserts broad and brown—
>   A solitude—a sea of sand,
> Where He does let heaven's curtain down,
>   Unveiled by His Almighty hand.

~~~~~ JUNE 29 ~~~~~

Morning

Thy people shall be willing in the day of thy power, in the beauties of holiness from the womb of the morning: thou hast the dew of thy youth.
PSALM 110:3 KJV

This is what the term *consecration* properly means. It is the voluntary surrender or self-offering of the heart, by the constraint of love *to be the Lord's*. Its glad expression is "I am my beloved's" (Song of Songs 6:3).

It must spring, of course, from faith. There must be the full confidence that we are safe in this abandonment; that we are not falling over a precipice or surrendering ourselves to the hands of a judge, but that we are sinking into the Father's arms and stepping into an infinite inheritance. Oh, *it is an infinite inheritance!* Oh, it is an infinite privilege to be permitted thus to give ourselves up to One who pledges Himself to make us all that we would love to be; nay, all that His infinite wisdom, power, and love will delight to accomplish in us!

It is the clay yielding itself to the potter's hands, that it may be shaped into a vessel of honor, meet for the Master's use.

It is the poor street waif consenting to become the child of a prince, that he may be educated and provided for; that he may be prepared to inherit all the wealth of his guardian. DAYS OF HEAVEN UPON EARTH

> *He ventured all: the loss of place,*
> *and power, and love of kin—*
> *O bitter loss! O loneliness and pain!*
> *He gained the Christ! Who would not dare*
> *the loss*
> *Such priceless bliss to win?*
> *Christ for today, and each tomorrow—*
> *Christ!*
>
> "PAUL" BY J. MANNINGTON DEXTER

Make a supreme consecration!

JUNE 29

Evening

There we saw the giants.
NUMBERS 13:33 KJV

Yes, the Israeli spies saw giants, but Joshua and Caleb saw God! Those who doubt still say today, "*We can't attack . . . ; they are stronger than we are*" (v. 31). Yet those who believe say, "*We should go up and take possession . . . for we can certainly do it*" (v. 30).

Giants represent great difficulties, and they stalk us everywhere. They are in our families, our churches, our social life, and even our own hearts. We must overcome them or they will devour us, just as the ancient Israelites, fearing those in Canaan, said, "The land we explored devours those living in it. All the people we saw there are of great size" (v. 32). We should exhibit faith as did Joshua and Caleb, who said, "Do not be afraid . . . , because we will devour them" (Numbers 14:9). In effect, they told the others, "We will be stronger by overcoming them than if there had been no giants to defeat."

In fact, unless we have overcoming faith, we will be swallowed up—consumed by the giants who block our path. With "that same spirit of faith" (2 Corinthians 4:13) that Joshua and Caleb had, let us look to God, and He will take care of the difficulties.
Selected

We encounter giants only when we are *serving* God and *following* Him. It was when Israel was going *forward* that the giants appeared, for when they turned back into the wilderness, they found none.

Many people believe that the power of God in a person's life should keep him from all trials and conflicts. However, the power of God actually brings conflict and struggles. You would think that Paul, during his great missionary journey to Rome, would have been kept by God's sovereignty from the power of violent storms and of his enemies. Yet just the opposite was true. He endured one long, difficult struggle with the Jews who were persecuting him. He faced fierce winds, poisonous snakes, and all the powers of earth and of hell. And finally, he narrowly escaped drowning, by swimming to shore at Malta after a shipwreck nearly sent him to a watery grave.

Does this sound like a God of infinite power? Yes, it is just like Him. And that is why Paul told us that once he took the Lord Jesus Christ as his life in his body, a severe conflict immediately arose. In fact, the conflict never ended. The pressure on Paul was persistent, but from the conflict he always emerged victorious through the strength of Jesus Christ.

Paul described this in quite vivid language: "We are hard pressed on every side, but not crushed; perplexed, but not in despair; persecuted, but not abandoned; struck down, but not destroyed. We always carry around in our body the death of Jesus, so that the life of Jesus may also be revealed in our body" (2 Corinthians 4:8–10).

What a ceaseless and strenuous struggle he related! It is nearly impossible to express in English the impact of the original language. Paul gives us five different images in succession. In the first, he has us picture enemies completely surrounding and pressuring but not crushing him, because the heavenly "police" have protected him and cleared a path just wide enough for him to escape. The literal meaning is, "We are crowded from all sides, but not defeated."

The second image is that of someone whose way is completely blocked or thwarted by the enemy. Yet he has persevered, for there is just enough light for him to see the next step. Paul said, "Perplexed, but not in despair," or as one literal translation put it, "Without a road, but not without a 'side road' of escape."

The third picture, "Persecuted, but not abandoned," is one of the enemy in hot pursuit of him while the divine Defender stands nearby. He is pursued, but not left alone.

The fourth is even more vivid and dramatic. The enemy has overtaken him, struck him, and knocked him down. But it is not a fatal blow—he is able to rise again. He has been "struck down, but not destroyed," or literally, "overthrown, but not overcome." In the fifth and final image, Paul advances the thought still further, giving us a picture that *appears* to be one of death itself: "We always carry around in our body the death of Jesus." Yet he does not die, for "the life of Jesus" comes to his aid, and he lives through Christ's life until his lifework is complete.

The reason so many people fail to experience this divine principle is that they expect to receive it all without a struggle. When conflict comes and the battle rages on, they become discouraged and surrender. God has nothing worth having that is easily gained, for there are no cheap goods on the heavenly market. The cost of our redemption was everything God had to give, and anything worth having is expensive. Difficult times and places are our schools of faith and character. If we are ever to rise above mere human strength, and experience the power of the life of Christ in our mortal bodies, it will be through the process of conflict that could very well be called the "labor pains" of the new life. It is like the story of Moses, who "saw that though the bush was on fire it did not burn up" (Exodus 3:2); although Satan's demons tried to extinguish the flame in Moses' life by continually pouring water on his plans, they could not, because God's angels were ever vigilant, pouring oil on the flame to keep it burning brightly.

Dear child of God, you may be suffering, but you cannot fail if you will only dare to believe, stand firm, and refuse to be overcome. FROM A TRACT

Then there came a voice from above the vault . . . as they stood with lowered wings.

EZEKIEL 1:25

If in God's starry universe there throbbed
No heart but His and mine, I would not plod
With eyes earthbound, hungry of soul, and robbed
Of a sweet sense of nearness to my God.
For mystic notes that issue from His soul
Would wing their shining way in singing showers
Into my waiting heart, when spared the toll
Of intercourse with men that wastes my powers.

Alone with God! My soul, invite the art,
As One who climbed the heights alone to pray,
And in the gentle stillness, heart to heart,
Let Heaven's dew transform this house of clay.
Oh, God is everywhere. Yes, God is here!
Only my faith is dim . . . the world too near.

EDITH ALICE BANG

In the silences I make in the midst of the turmoil of life I have appointments with God. From these silences I come forth with spirit refreshed and with a renewed sense of power. I hear a Voice in the silences and become increasingly aware that it is the Voice of God.

Oh, how comfortable is a little glimpse of God! DAVID BRAINERD

Evening

I heard a hushed voice.
JOB 4:16

S ome twenty years ago a friend gave me a book entitled *True Peace*. It had an old medieval message and this one primary thought—that God was waiting in the depths of my being to speak to me if I would only be still enough to hear His voice.

I assumed this would not be a difficult thing to do, so I tried to be still. No sooner had I begun to do so than complete pandemonium seemed to break loose. Suddenly I heard a thousand voices and sounds from without and within, until I could hear nothing except these incredible noises. Some were my own words, my own questions, and even my own prayers, while others were temptations of the Enemy, and the voices of the world's turmoil.

In every direction I turned, I was pushed, pulled, and confronted with indescribable unrest and overwhelming noises. I seemed compelled to listen to some of them and to respond in some way. But God said, "Be still, and know that I am God" (Psalm 46:10). Then my mind was filled with worries over my responsibilities and plans for tomorrow, and God said again, "Be still."

As I listened and slowly learned to obey, I shut my ears to every other sound. Soon I discovered that once the other voices ceased, or once I ceased to hear them, "a gentle whisper" (1 Kings 19:12) began to speak in the depths of my being. And it spoke to me with an inexpressible tenderness, power, and comfort.

This "gentle whisper" became for me the voice of prayer, wisdom, and service. No longer did I need to work so hard to think, pray, or trust, because the Holy Spirit's "gentle whisper" in my heart was God's prayer in the secret places of my soul. It was His answer to all my questions, and His life and strength for my soul and body. His voice became the essence of all knowledge, prayer, and blessings, for it was the living God Himself as my life and my all.

This is precisely how our spirit drinks in the life of our risen Lord. And then we are enabled to face life's conflicts and responsibilities, like a flower that has absorbed the cool and refreshing drops of dew through the darkness of the night. Yet just as *dew never falls on a stormy night*, the dew of His grace never covers a restless soul. A. B. SIMPSON

Morning

*Having disarmed the powers and authorities, he made a
public spectacle of them, triumphing over them.*

COLOSSIANS 2:15

Here Satan is represented as a conquered foe, and even as a degraded antagonist. He has been "disarmed." One is reminded of the figure of a scarecrow on a farmer's field where the dead birds are hung up as warnings against other depredators. He cannot harm us, although he may alarm us. He is beaten before the battle begins. We enter the fray with the prestige of victors. Let us hold this high place as we meet our adversary. Let us treat him as a defeated enemy. Let us not honor him by our doubts and fears. It is not our valor or our victory. It is *our confidence in Christ, the Victor, that wins.*

"This is the victory that has overcome the world, even our faith" (1 John 5:4). Our triumph has already been won by our Leader, *but we must identify ourselves with His victory. Let us never dare to doubt!*

"And the hostile princes and rulers He shook off from Himself, and *boldly displayed them as His conquests* when by the Cross He triumphed over them" (Colossians 2:15 WNT).

Says Dr. Weymouth: "Stand your ground in the day of battle, and having fought to the end, remain victors on the field!" "Victors on the field"—I am thrilled by the inspiring word. After every temptation—the temptation which comes to me in sunshine or the temptation that comes to me in the gloom—after every fight, victors on the field, the Lord's banner flying, and the evil one and all his hosts in utter rout, and in full and dire retreat!
J. H. JOWETT

Describing the force of the waves which beat on the Eddystone Lighthouse, a writer says: "But without a quiver the lighthouse supports those terrible attacks. Yet it bends toward them as if to render homage to the power of its adversaries."

Let us meet the storms of life with the fixedness and plasticity with which the lighthouse overcomes the wild tempest.

Fastened to the Rock of Ages, I shall not be moved.

Evening

My words . . . will come true at their appointed time.

LUKE 1:20

"Blessed is she who has believed that the Lord would fulfill his promise to her!"

LUKE 1:45

The Lord is sure to accomplish those things
　　A loving heart has waited long to see;
Those words will be fulfilled to which she clings,
　　Because her God has promised faithfully;
And, knowing Him, she ne'er can doubt His Word;
He speaks and it is done. The mighty Lord!

The Lord is sure to accomplish those things,
　　O burdened heart, rest ever in His care;
In quietness beneath His shadowing wings
　　Await the answer to your longing prayer.
When you have "cast your cares," the heart then sings,
The Lord is sure to accomplish those things.

The Lord is sure to accomplish those things,
　　O tired heart, believe and wait and pray;
Peacefully, the evening chime still rings,
　　Though cloud and rain and storm have filled the day.
Faith pierces through the mist of doubt that bars
The coming night sometimes, and finds the stars.

The Lord is sure to accomplish those things,
　　O trusting heart, the Lord to you has told;
Let Faith and Hope arise, and lift their wings,
　　To soar toward the sunrise clouds of gold;

The doorways of the rosy dawn swing wide,
Revealing joys the darkness of night did hide.

BESSIE PORTER

Matthew Henry said, "We can depend on God to fulfill His promise, even when all the roads leading to it are closed. 'For no matter how many promises God has made, they are "Yes" in Christ. And so through him the "Amen" [so be it] is spoken by us to the glory of God' [2 Corinthians 1:20]."

~~~~~~~~ JULY 2 ~~~~~~~~

Morning

Answer me when I call to you, my righteous God. Give me relief
from my distress; have mercy on me and hear my prayer.

PSALM 4:1

It is a little thing to trust God as far as we can see Him, as far as the way lies open before us; but to trust Him when we are hedged in on every side and can see no way to escape, this is good and acceptable with God. This is the faith of Abraham, our father. *"Under . . . hopeless circumstances he hopefully believed"* (Romans 4:18 WNT).

Abraham Lincoln, during the Civil War, once said: "I have been driven many times to my knees by the overwhelming conviction that I had nowhere else to go. My own wisdom and that of all about me seemed insufficient for the day."

The greatest men, without God, are nothing but dismal failures.
The devil may wall you 'round
But he cannot roof you in;
He may fetter your feet and tie your hands
And strive to hamper your soul with bands
As his way has ever been;
But he cannot hide the face of God
And the Lord shall be your light,

And your eyes and your thoughts can rise to the sky,
Where His clouds and His winds and His birds go by,
And His stars shine out at night.

The devil may wall you 'round;
He may rob you of all things dear,
He may bring his hardest and roughest stone
And thinks to cage you and keep you alone,
But he may not press too near;
For the Lord has planted a hedge inside,
And has made it strong and tall,
A hedge of living and growing green;
And ever it mounts and keeps between
The trusting soul and the devil's wall.

The devil may wall you 'round,
But the Lord's hand covers you,
And His hedge is a thick and thorny hedge,
And the devil can find no entering wedge
Nor get his finger through;
He may circle about you all day long,
But he cannot work as he would,
For the will of the Lord restrains his hand,
And he cannot pass the Lord's command
And his evil turns to good.

The devil may wall you 'round,
With his gray stones, row on row,
But the green of the hedge is fresh and fair,
And within its circle is space to spare,
And room for your soul to grow;
The wall that shuts you in
May be hard and high and stout,
But the Lord is sun and the Lord is dew,

And His hedge is coolness and shade for you,
And no wall can shut Him out.

ANNIE JOHNSON FLINT

~~~~~~~ JULY 2 ~~~~~~~
Evening

When you walk, your steps will not be hampered;
when you run, you will not stumble.

PROVERBS 4:12

The Lord only builds a bridge of faith directly under the feet of a faithful traveler. He never builds the bridge a few steps ahead, for then it would not be one of faith. "We live by faith, not by sight" (2 Corinthians 5:7).

Years ago automatic gates were sometimes used on country roads. They would securely block the road as a vehicle approached, and if the traveler stopped before coming to the gate, it would not open. But if the traveler drove straight toward it, the weight of the vehicle would compress the springs below the roadway, and the gate would swing back to let him pass. The vehicle had to keep moving forward, or the gate would remain closed.

This illustrates the way to pass through every barrier that blocks the road of service for God. Whether the barrier is a river, a mountain, or a gate, all a child of Jesus must do is head directly toward it. If it is a river, it will dry up as he comes near it, as long as he still forges ahead. If it is a mountain, it will be removed and "cast into the sea" (Mark 11:23 KJV), providing he approaches it with unflinching confidence.

Is some great barrier blocking your path of service right now? Then head straight for it, in the name of the Lord, and it will no longer be there. HENRY CLAY TRUMBULL

We sit and weep in vain, while the voice of the Almighty tells us to never stop moving upward and onward. Let us advance boldly, whether it is dark and we can barely see the forest in front of us, or our road leads us through the mountain pass, where from any vantage point we can only see a few steps ahead.

Press on! And if necessary, like the ancient Israelites we will find a pillar of clouds and fire to lead the way on our journey through the wilderness. God will provide guides and inns along the road, and we will discover food, clothing, and friends at every stage of our journey. And as Samuel Rutherford, the great Scottish minister, once stated so simply, "Whatever happens, the worst will only be a weary traveler receiving a joyful and heavenly welcome home."

> I'm going by the upper road, for that
>   still holds the sun,
> I'm climbing through night's pastures where
>   the starry rivers run:
> If you should think to seek me in my
>   old dark abode,
> You'll find this writing on the door,
>   "He's on the Upper Road."
>
> SELECTED

~~~~~~~ ## JULY 3 ~~~~~~~
Morning

Your true and proper worship.
ROMANS 12:1

Your reasonable service.
KJV

Why are we saved? We are saved in order *to be sacrificed.* There is a striking lesson in God's saving certain of the clean beasts and clean fowl at the time of the flood. At God's direction, Noah brought these, as well as other beasts and fowl that were not clean, into the ark of salvation. These clean creatures were favored above those that were lost in the flood. It must have been a wonderful experience to step out from the ark onto dry land again. But what happened then?

"Then Noah built an altar to the LORD and, taking some of all the clean animals and clean birds, he sacrificed burnt offerings on it" (Genesis 8:20).

Thus it appears *that certain of these creatures were saved in order to be sacrificed after their salvation was complete.* If this surprises us, have we realized that we who believe in Christ are saved for exactly that purpose?

"I urge you, brothers and sisters, in view of God's mercy, to offer your bodies as a living sacrifice" (Romans 12:1).

This is *acceptable unto God,* and it is *our reasonable service.*

Noah's sacrifice of the clean animals brought great blessing to the earth, as the record goes on to show us; and the "living sacrifice" of God's children brings great blessing to mankind.

Let us thank God, indeed, that we are saved to be sacrificed. SUNDAY SCHOOL TIMES

> *Laid on Thine altar, O my Lord, Divine,*
> *Accept this day my gift for Jesus' sake.*
> *I have no jewels to adorn Thy shrine,*
> *Nor any world-famed sacrifice to make;*
> *But here I bring within my trembling hand*
> *This will of mine: a thing that seemeth small;*
> *And only Thou dear Lord, canst understand*
> *That when I yield Thee this, I yield Thee all.*
> *It hath been wet with tears and dimmed with sighs,*
> *Clenched in my clasp, till beauty it hath none.*
>
> *Now from Thy footstool, where it vanquished lies,*
> *The prayer ascendeth: "Let Thy will be done."*
> *Take it, O Father, ere my courage fail,*
> *And blend it so with Thine own will, that e'en*
> *If in some desperate hour my cry prevail,*
> *And Thou giv'st back my gift, it may have been*
> *So changed, so purified, so fair have grown,*
> *So one with Thee, so filled with peace Divine,*
> *I may not know nor feel it as my own,*
> *But gaining back my will may find it Thine.*

All I have I am bringing to Thee!

Evening

When a farmer plows for planting, does he plow continually?
ISAIAH 28:24

One day in early summer I walked past a lovely meadow. The grass was as soft, thick, and beautiful as an immense green Oriental rug. At one end of the meadow stood a fine old tree that served as a sanctuary for countless wild birds, whose happy songs seemed to fill the crisp, sweet air. I saw two cows who lay in the shade as the very picture of contentment. And down by the road, eye-catching dandelions mingled their gold with the royal purple of the wild violets. I leaned against the fence for a long time, feasting my hungry eyes and thinking in my soul that God never made a more beautiful place than this lovely meadow.

The next day I passed that way again, and to my great dismay, the hand of the destroyer had been there. A farmer with a large tractor, which was now sitting idle in the meadow, had in one day inflicted terrible devastation. Instead of seeing the soft, green grass, I now saw the ugly, bare, and brown earth. Gone were the dandelions and the pretty violets. And instead of the multitude of singing birds, there were now only a few, who were industriously scratching the ground for worms. In my grief I said, "How could anyone spoil something so beautiful?"

Then suddenly my eyes were opened, as if by some unseen hand, and I saw a vision. The vision was that of a field of ripe corn ready for harvest. I could see the giant, heavily laden stalks in the autumn sun, and I could almost hear the music of the wind as it swept across the golden tassels. And before I realized it, the bare earth took on a splendor it did not have the day before.

Oh, if only we would always catch the vision of the abundant harvest when the great Master Farmer comes, as He often does, to plow through our very souls—uprooting and turning under that which we thought most beautiful and leaving only the bare and the unlovely before our agonizing eyes. SELECTED

Why should I be frightened and surprised by the plow of the Lord, which makes deep furrows in my soul? I know He is not some arbitrary or irrational farmer—His purpose is to yield a harvest. SAMUEL RUTHERFORD

Morning

They are the ones who will dwell on the heights, whose refuge will be the mountain fortress. . . . Your eyes will . . . view a land that stretches afar.
Isaiah 33:16–17

Up yonder on the rocky cliff in a rough nest of sticks lies an egg. The eagle's breast-feathers warm it; the sky bends down and invites it; the abysses of the air beckon it, saying: *All our heights and depths are for you; come and occupy them.*

And all the peaks and the roomy places up under the rafters of the sky, where the twinkling stars sit sheltered like twittering sparrows, call down to the pent-up little life, "Come up hither!" and the live germ inside hears through the thin walls of its prison, and is coaxed out of its shell, and out of the nest, and off the cliff, and then up and away into the wide ranges of sunlit air, and down into the deep gulfs that gash mountains apart. A Pilgrim of the Infinite

> *I stand upon the mount of God*
> *With sunlight in my soul;*
> *I hear the storms in vales beneath,*
> *I hear the thunders roll.*
>
> *But I am calm with Thee, my God,*
> *Beneath these glorious skies;*
> *And to the height on which I stand,*
> *No storms, nor clouds, can rise.*
>
> *Oh, this is life! Oh, this is joy!*
> *My God, to find Thee so;*
> *Thy face to see, Thy voice to hear,*
> *And all Thy love to know.*
>
> Horatius Bonar

Evening

The revelation awaits an appointed time. . . . Though it linger,
wait for it; it will certainly come and will not delay.

HABAKKUK 2:3

In the captivating booklet *Expectation Corner*, one of the characters, Adam Slowman, was led into the Lord's treasurehouse. Among the many wonders revealed to him there was the "Delayed Blessing Office," where God stored the answers to certain prayers until it was wise to send them.

For some who pray expecting an answer, it takes a long time to learn that *delays of answers are not denials.* In fact, in the "Delayed Blessing Office," there are deep secrets of love and wisdom that we have never imagined! We tend to want to pick our blessings from the tree while they are still green, yet God wants us to wait until they are fully ripe.

"The LORD longs to be gracious to you. . . . *Blessed are all who wait for him!*" (Isaiah 30:18). The Lord watches over us in all the difficult places, and He will not allow even one trial that is too much for us. He will use His refining fire to burn away our impurities and will then gloriously come to our rescue.

Do not grieve Him by doubting His love. Instead, lift up your eyes and begin praising Him *right now* for the deliverance that is on its way to you. Then you will be abundantly rewarded for the delay that has tried your faith.

> *O you of little faith,*
> *God has not failed you yet!*
> *When all looks dark and gloomy,*
> *You do so soon forget—*
>
> *Forget that He has led you,*
> *And gently cleared your way;*
> *On clouds has poured His sunshine,*
> *And turned your night to day.*

And if He's helped you to this point,
 He will not fail you now;
How it must wound His loving heart
 To see your anxious brow!

Oh! doubt not any longer,
 To Him commit your way,
Whom in the past you trusted,
 And is just the same today.

SELECTED

JULY 5
Morning

I will not fear though tens of thousands assail me on every side.
PSALM 3:6

Evening. Felt much turmoil of spirit, in prospect of having all my plans for the welfare of this great region and this teeming population, knocked on the head by savages tomorrow. But I read that Jesus said: "All power is given unto me in heaven and in earth. Go ye therefore, and teach all nations. . . . and, lo, I am with you always, even unto the end of the world" (Matthew 28:18–20 KJV)! *It is the word of a Gentleman, of the strictest and most sacred honor.* So there's an end of it! I will not cross furtively tonight as I intended. Should such a man as I flee? Nay, verily, I shall take observations for latitude and longitude tonight, though they may be the last. I feel quite calm now, thank God! DIARY OF DAVID LIVINGSTONE

During the terrible days of the Boxer uprising in China, as one report followed another of mission stations destroyed and missionaries massacred, Hudson Taylor sat quietly at his desk singing softly the hymn he loved so dearly: *Jesus, I am resting, resting, In the joy of what Thou art.*

When our confidence is in God, we may be superior to circumstances. "If God is for us, who can be against us?" (Romans 8:31). However impossible it may seem to the reasoning of the earthly-minded, it is nevertheless a blessed reality to the trustful child of God that *"Faith can sing through days of sorrow: 'All, all is well!'"*

"Though I was afraid of many things," said John Buchan, *"the thing I feared most mortally was being afraid."*

> *Fierce was the wild billow,*
> *Dark was the night;*
> *Oars labored heavily;*
> *Foam glimmered white.*
> *Trembled the mariners,*
> *Peril was nigh;*
> *Then said the God of Gods,*
> *"Peace! It is I."*
> *Ridge of the mountain wave,*
> *Lower thy crest.*
> *Wail of the stormy wind,*
> *Be thou at rest.*
> *Peril there none can be;*
> *Sorrow must fly,*
> *Where saith the Light of Life, "Peace! It is I."*
>
> SELECTED

Come into port greatly, or sail with God the seas! RALPH WALDO EMERSON

JULY 5

Evening

I am now going to allure her; I will lead her into the wilderness. . . . There I will give her back her vineyards.

HOSEA 2:14–15

The wilderness is certainly a strange place to find vineyards! Can it be true that the riches of life that we need can be found in the wilderness—a place that symbolizes loneliness, and through which we can seldom find our way? Not only is this true but verse 15 goes on to say, "I . . . will make the Valley of Achor a door of hope. *There she will respond as in the days of her youth.*" "Achor" means "troubled," yet the Valley of Achor is called "a door of hope."

Yes, God knows our need for a wilderness experience. He knows exactly where and how to produce enduring qualities in us. The person who has been idolatrous, has been rebellious, has forgotten God, and has said with total self-will, "I will go after my lovers" (Hosea 2:5), will find her path blocked by God. "She will chase after her lovers but not catch them; she will look for them but not find them" (Hosea 2:7). And once she feels totally hopeless and abandoned, God will say, "I am now going to allure her; I will lead her into the wilderness and speak tenderly to her."

What a loving God we have!

We never know where God has hidden His streams. We see a large stone and have no idea that it covers the source of a spring. We see a rocky area and never imagine that it is hiding a fountain. God leads me into hard and difficult places, and it is there I realize I am where eternal streams abide. SELECTED

<hr>

JULY 6
Morning

*I consider that our present sufferings are not worth comparing
with the glory that will be revealed in us.*
ROMANS 8:18

For developing character an imperfect man needs the stimulus and discipline of a *developing* environment, not yet perfected—a world of struggle and resistance: obstacles to be overcome, battles to be won, baffling problems to be solved. He needs not a soft world of ease to lull him to sleep, but a changing environment of action and reaction: cold and heat, summer and winter, sunshine and shadow, light and darkness, pleasure and pain, prosperity and adversity.

As Dr. Hillis said: "He who would ask release from suffering *would take the winter out of the seasons, the glory of the night out of the round of day, the cloud and rainstorms out of the summer; would expel the furrows from the face of Lincoln; would rob Socrates of his dignity and majesty; would make Saint Paul a mere esthetic feeling; would steal the sweetness from maternity; would rob the Divine Sufferer of His sanctity."*

When the little girl told her music teacher that it hurt her fingers to practice the piano, the teacher answered: *"I know it hurts, but it strengthens them, too."* Then the child packed the philosophy of the ages in her reply: "Teacher, *it seems that everything that strengthens, hurts."*

God never wastes His children's pain!

God loves much those whom He trusts with sorrow, and designs some precious soul enrichment which comes only through the channel of suffering.

There are things which even God cannot do for us unless He allows us to suffer. *He cannot have the result of the process without the process.*

If you are among "them that love God" (v. 28 KJV), *all things are yours!* The stars in their courses fight for you. Every wind that blows can only fill your sails.

God does not test worthless souls!

<hr>

JULY 6
Evening

We do not know what to do, but our eyes are on you.

2 CHRONICLES 20:12

An Israelite named Uzzah lost his life because he "reached out and took hold of the ark of God" (2 Samuel 6:6). He placed his hands on it with the best of intentions—to steady it, "because the oxen stumbled" (2 Samuel 6:6)—but nevertheless, he had overstepped his bounds by touching the Lord's work, and "therefore God struck him down" (2 Samuel 6:7). *Living a life of faith often requires us to leave things alone.*

If we have completely entrusted something to God, we must keep our hands off it. He can guard it better than we can, and He does not need our help. "Be still before the LORD and wait patiently for him; do not fret when people succeed in their ways, when they carry out their wicked schemes" (Psalm 37:7).

Things in our lives may seem to be going all wrong, but God knows our circumstances better than we do. And He will work at the perfect moment, if we will completely trust Him to work in His own way and in His own time. Often there is nothing as godly as inactivity on our part, or nothing as harmful as restless working, for God has promised to work His sovereign will. A. B. SIMPSON

> *Being perplexed, I say,*
> * "Lord, make it right!*
> *Night is as day to You,*
> *Darkness as light.*
> *I am afraid to touch*
> *Things that involve so much;*
> *My trembling hand may shake,*
> *My skilless hand may break;*
> *Yours can make no mistake."*
>
> *Being in doubt I say,*
> * "Lord, make it plain;*
> *Which is the true, safe way?*
> * Which would be gain?*
> *I am not wise to know,*
> *Nor sure of foot to go;*
> *What is so clear to Thee,*
> *Lord, make it clear to me!"*

It is such a comfort to drop the entanglements and perplexities of life into God's hands and leave them there.

JULY 7

Morning

He performeth the thing that is appointed for me.

JOB 23:14 KJV

Let us have confidence in the *purposes of God*. The thought occurs in the writings of Goulburn, Adolph Monod, and others, that the Lord owed that wonderful calmness which marked His life—a calmness which never forsook Him, whether teaching, or traveling, however engaged, however tried—very much to the fact that His Father had a plan for Him; not a plan for a lifetime merely, but a plan for each day; and that He had but to discover what the plan was, and then carry it out; and so, however puzzling and perplexing the maze of duties through which He had to thread His way, nothing ever perplexed or puzzled Him, because, putting His hand in His Father's, *He just walked in the paths prepared for Him.*

Well, now, what if God should have a plan for everyone? What if God should have a plan for *you*? In such a case—surely it is the true case—everything we have to do, everything we have to bear, comes to us as part of a prearranged plan. Things that disturb our work, things that upset our purposes, things that thwart our wishes, interruptions, annoyances—these may all be a part of the plan—God's plan—and should be met accordingly. Living Waters

I doubt not through the ages One Eternal purpose runs.

There's a throne above the world. There's a Man on the throne. He has a plan for things down here during this time of turmoil and strife. His Spirit is down here to get that plan done. He needs each one of us. He puts His Hand on each Christian life and says, "Separate yourself from all else for the bit I need you to do." His Hand is on *you*. Are you doing it? *Anything else classes as failure.* "The Bent-Knee Time" by S. D. Gordon

JULY 7

Evening

He made me into a polished arrow.
Isaiah 49:2

Pebble Beach, on the California coast, has become quite famous for the beautiful pebbles found there. The raging white surf continually roars, thundering and pounding against the rocks on the shore. These stones are trapped in the arms of the merciless waves. They are tossed, rolled, rubbed together, and ground against the sharp edges of the cliffs. Both day and night, this process of grinding continues relentlessly. And what is the result?

Tourists from around the world flock there to collect the beautiful round stones. They display them in cabinets and use them to decorate their homes. Yet a little farther up the coast, just around the point of the cliff, is a quiet cove. Protected from the face of the ocean, sheltered from the storms, and always in the sun, the sands are covered with an abundance of pebbles never sought by the travelers.

So why have these stones been left untouched through all the years? Simply because they have escaped all the turmoil and the grinding of the waves. The quietness and peace have left them as they have always been—rough, unpolished, and devoid of beauty—*for polish is the result of difficulties.*

Since God knows what niche we are to fill, let us trust Him to shape us to it. And since He knows what work we are to do, let us trust Him to grind us so we will be properly prepared.

> *O blows that strike! O hurts that pierce*
> *This fainting heart of mine!*
> *What are you but the Master's tools*
> *Forming a work Divine?*
> *Nearly all of God's jewels are crystallized tears.*

<hr>

JULY 8
Morning

We were under great pressure.
2 CORINTHIANS 1:8

You smell delightfully fragrant," said the Gravel Walk to the bed of Camomile flowers under the window.

"We have been trodden on," replied the Camomiles.

"Does that cause it?" asked the Gravel Walk. "Treading on me produces no sweetness."

"Our natures are different," answered the Camomiles. "Gravel walks become only the harder by being trodden upon; but the effect on our own selves is that, if pressed and bruised when the dew is upon us, we give forth the sweet smell you now delight in."

"Very delightful," replied the Gravel Walk.

Trials come alike to the Christian and to the man of the world. The one grows bitter and hardened under the experience, while the other becomes mellow and Christlike. It is because their natures are different.

> *Oh, beautiful rose, please tell me,*
> *For I would like to know,*
> *Why I must crush your petals*
> *That sweet perfume may flow.*
>
> *Oh, life that is clothed in beauty,*
> *Perhaps like that beautiful rose,*
> *You will need to be crushed by suffering*
> *Ere you give out your best; who knows?*
>
> *A life that is crushed by sorrow*
> *Can feel for another's grief,*
> *And send out that sweet perfume of love*
> *That will bring some heart relief.*
>
> *Oh, do not repine at your testing,*
> *When called to pass under the rod,*
> *It is that life might the sweeter be,*
> *And comes from the Hand of God.*
>
> *He knows how much we are needing,*
> *Of sorrow, or suffering, or test,*
> *And only gives to His children*
> *The things that He knoweth are best.*
>
> *Then let us rejoice when He sendeth*
> *Some sorrow or hardship that tries,*
> *And be glad to be crushed as the rose leaf,*
> *That a sweeter perfume may arise.*

FLORA L. OSGOOD

They will soar on wings like eagles.
ISAIAH 40:31

There is a fable about the way birds first got their wings. The story goes that initially they were made without them. Then God made the wings, set them down before the wingless birds, and said to them, "Take up these burdens and carry them."

The birds had sweet voices for singing, and lovely feathers that glistened in the sunshine, but they could not soar in the air. When asked to pick up the burdens that lay at their feet, they hesitated at first. Yet soon they obeyed, picked up the wings with their beaks, and set them on their shoulders to carry them.

For a short time the load seemed heavy and difficult to bear, but soon, as they continued to carry the burden and to fold the wings over their hearts, the wings grew attached to their little bodies. They quickly discovered how to use them and were lifted by the wings high into the air. *The weights had become wings.*

This is a parable for us. We are the wingless birds, and our duties and tasks are the wings God uses to lift us up and carry us heavenward. We look at our burdens and heavy loads, and try to run from them, but if we will carry them and tie them to our hearts, they will become wings. And on them we can then rise and soar toward God.

There is no burden so heavy that when lifted cheerfully with love in our hearts will not become a blessing to us. God intends for our tasks to be our helpers; to refuse to bend our shoulders to carry a load is to miss a new opportunity for growth. J. R. MILLER

No matter how overwhelming, any burden God has lovingly placed with His own hands on our shoulders is a blessing. FREDERICK WILLIAM FABER

~~~~~~~ JULY 9 ~~~~~~~

Morning

I thirst for you, my whole being longs for you, in a dry and parched land.
PSALM 63:1

An interesting story is told concerning the northern reindeer. It seems that on those far-off plains, a hundred miles from the sea, at a certain season, in the midst of the Laplander's village a young reindeer will raise his broad muzzle to the north wind and stare at the limitless distance for the space of a minute or more. He grows restless from that moment, but he is yet alone. The next day a dozen of the herd look up from cropping the moss, snuffing the breeze. Then the Laps nod to one another, and the camp grows daily more unquiet.

At times the whole herd of young deer stand and gaze, as it were, breathing hard through wide nostrils, then jostling each other and stamping the soft ground. They grow unruly and it is hard to harness them into the light sleds. As the days pass the Laps watch them more and more closely, well knowing what will happen sooner or later.

And then, at last, in the northern twilight, the great herd begins to move! The impulse is simultaneous, irresistible; their heads are all turned in one direction. They move slowly at first, still biting here and there at the bunches of rich moss. Presently the slow step becomes a trot; they crowd more closely together, while the Laps hasten to gather up their last unpacked possessions, their cooking utensils, and their wooden gods.

The great herd together breaks from a trot to a gallop, from a gallop to a breakneck pace; the distant thunder of their united tread reaches the camp for a few minutes, and then they are gone out of sight and hearing, to drink of the Polar Sea.

The Laps follow after them, dragging painfully their laden sledges in the broad track left by the thousands of galloping beasts; a day's journey, and they are yet far from the sea, and the track is yet broad.

On the second day the path grows narrower, and there are stains of blood to be seen; far on the distant plain before them, their sharp eyes distinguish in the direct line a dark, motionless object, another, and yet another. The race has grown more desperate and more wild as the stampede nears the sea. The weaker reindeer have been trampled by their stronger fellows. A thousand sharp hoofs have crushed and cut through hide and flesh and bone. Ever swifter and more terrible in their motion, the ruthless herd has raced onward, careless of the slain, careless of the food, careless of any drink but the sharp, salt water ahead of them. And when the Laplanders reach the shore, their deer are once more quietly grazing, once more tame and docile, once more ready to drag the sled.

Once in its life the reindeer must taste of the sea in one long satisfying draft, and if he is hindered, he perishes! Neither man nor beast dare stand between him and the ocean, in the hundred miles of his arrowlike path!

—— 475 ——

I hear the voice of Jesus say,
"Behold, I freely give
The living water; thirsty one,
Stoop down, and drink, and live!"
I came to Jesus, and I drank
Of that life-giving stream;
My thirst was quenched,
my soul revived,
And now I live in Him.

Come, O come ye to the Waters!

JULY 9

Evening

I have chosen thee in the furnace of affliction.
ISAIAH 48:10 KJV

Doesn't God's Word come to us like a soft rain shower, dispelling the fury of the flames? Isn't it like fireproof armor, against which the heat is powerless? Then let afflictions come, for God has *chosen* me. Poverty, you may walk through my door, but God is already in my house, and He has *chosen* me. Sickness, you may intrude into my life, but I have a cure standing ready—God has *chosen* me. Whatever occurs in the valley of tears, I know He has *chosen* me.

Dear Christian, do not be afraid, for Jesus is with you. Through all your fiery trials, His presence is both your comfort and safety. He will never forsake those He has chosen for His own. "Do not be afraid, for I am with you" (Genesis 26:24) is His unfailing word of promise to His chosen ones who are experiencing "the furnace of affliction." CHARLES H. SPURGEON

Pain's furnace heat within me quivers,
God's breath upon the flame does blow;

And all my heart in anguish shivers
        And trembles at the fiery glow; And yet I whisper,
"As God will!" And in the hottest fire hold still.
He comes and lays my heart, all heated,

On the hard anvil, minded so
        Into His own fair shape to beat it
With His great hammer, blow on blow;
        And yet I whisper, "As God will!"
And at His heaviest blows hold still.
He takes my softened heart and beats it;

The sparks fly off at every blow;
        He turns it o'er and o'er and heats it,
And lets it cool, and makes it glow;
        And yet I whisper, "As God will!"
And in His mighty hand hold still.
Why should I complain? for the sorrow

Then only longer-lived would be;
        The end may come, and will tomorrow,
When God has done His work in me;
        So I say trusting, "As God will!"
And, trusting to the end, hold still.

JULIUS STURM

The burden of suffering seems to be a tombstone hung around our necks. Yet in reality it is simply the weight necessary to hold the diver down while he is searching for pearls. JULIUS RICHTER

JULY 10
Morning

The LORD took me from tending the flock.
AMOS 7:15

Whom have You left behind to carry out the work?" asked the angels. "A little band of men and women who love Me," replied the Lord Jesus.

"But what if they should fail when the trial comes? Will all You have done be defeated?"

"Yes, if they should fail, all I have done will be defeated; but *they will not fail!*"

And the angels wondered as they saw the sublime confidence of love which this betokened!

> *"Wilt thou follow Me?"*
> *The Savior asked.*
> *The road looked bright and fair,*
> *And filled with youthful hope and zeal*
> *I answered, "Anywhere."*
>
> *"Wilt thou follow Me?" Again He asked.*
> *The road looked dim ahead;*
> *But I gave one glance at His glowing face*
> *"To the end, dear Lord," I said.*
>
> *"Wilt thou follow Me?" I almost blanched,*
> *For the road was rough and new,*
> *But I felt the grip of His steady Hand,*
> *And it thrilled me through and through.*
>
> *"Still followest thou?" 'Twas a tender tone,*
> *And it thrilled my inmost heart.*
> *I answered not, but He drew me close,*
> *And I knew we would never part.*
>
> SELECTED

The way lies through Gethsemane, through the city gate, outside the camp. The way lies alone, and the way lies until there is no trace of a foot step, only the Voice, "Follow Me!" But in the end it leads to "the joy set before him" (Hebrews 12:2) and to the Mount of God. SELECTED

The hour is desperately dark; your flame is needed.

Evening

I called him but he did not answer.
SONG OF SONGS 5:6

Once the Lord has given us great faith, He has been known to test it with long delays. He has allowed His servants' voices to echo in their ears, as if their prayers were rebounding from a contemptuous sky. Believers have knocked at the heavenly gate, but it has remained immovable, as though its hinges had rusted. And like Jeremiah, they have cried, *"You have covered yourself with a cloud so that no prayer can get through"* (Lamentations 3:44).

True saints of God have endured lengthy times of patient waiting with no reply, not because their prayers were prayed without intensity, nor because God did not accept their pleas. They were required to wait because it pleased Him who is sovereign and who gives according to "his good purpose" (Philippians 2:13). And if it pleases Him to cause our patience to be exercised, should He not do as He desires with His own?

No prayer is ever lost, or any prayer ever breathed in vain. There is no such thing as prayer unanswered or unnoticed by God, and some things we see as refusals or denials are simply delays. HORATIUS BONAR

Christ sometimes delays His help so He may test our faith and energize our prayers. Our boat may be tossed by the waves while He continues to sleep, but He will awake before it sinks. He sleeps but He never oversleeps, for He is never too late. ALEXANDER MACLAREN

> *Be still, sad soul! lift up no passionate cry,*
> *But spread the desert of your being bare*
> *To the full searching of the All-seeing eye;*
> *Wait! and through dark misgiving, deep despair,*
> *God will come down in pity, and fill the dry*
> *Dead place with light, and life, and springlike air.*
> JOHN CAMPBELL SHAIRP

Morning

He leads me beside quiet waters.
PSALM 23:2

Is it worthwhile, this ceaseless chase by which so many are affected? Does it pay? And, after all, why this exciting pace which has all too truly become a part of our national program?

Must the sons of men be forever driven like so many beasts of prey? Is there no escape from the feverish haste which persists in manifesting itself in all the walks of life?

It is possible for a Christian to make his active life restful. He may carry the atmosphere of the closet into the street. The Shepherd promises to lead him beside still waters; and those are the deepest waters.

This feverish hurried life which too many of us lead is not in God's economy, depend upon it. If we live in this way it is because we push on before the Shepherd instead of letting Him lead us beside still waters.

If we were more docile, we should be more restful.

Only when the soul is brimful of the life of faith does it work in rest. Not until we shall have let our life drop back behind God, to follow at the rate which He prescribes, shall we learn what the words mean, "Thou wilt keep him in perfect peace, whose mind is stayed on thee" (Isaiah 26:3 KJV).

Our little restless earth and our little breathless lives will take on dignity and deeper worth if we catch step with the rhythmic movement of the quiet stars.

Most strong men know times of silence. Abraham, alone with God, was made the father of a nation; Moses, in the quietness and stillness of the desert, received God's message at the burning bush. Most of their training was in the school of silence.

It takes time to be spiritual; it doesn't just happen!

In the deep jungles of Africa, a traveler was making a long trek. Men had been engaged from a tribe to carry the loads. The first day they marched rapidly and went far. The traveler had high hopes of a speedy journey. But the second morning, these jungle tribesmen refused to move. For some strange reason, they just sat and rested. On inquiry as to the reason for this strange behavior, the traveler was informed that they had gone too fast the first day, and that they were now waiting for their souls to catch up with their bodies.

This whirling rushing life which so many of us live does for us what that first march did for those poor jungle tribesmen. The difference: they knew what they needed to restore life's balance; too often we do not.

Jesus calls us o'er the tumult of our life's wild restless sea.

~~~~ JULY 11 ~~~~

Evening

Some time later the brook dried up because there had been no rain in the land.

1 KINGS 17:7

Week after week, with an unwavering and steadfast spirit, Elijah watched the brook dwindle and finally dry up. Often tempted to stumble in unbelief, he nevertheless refused to allow his circumstances to come between himself and God. Unbelief looks at God through the circumstances, just as we often see the sun dimmed by clouds or smoke. But faith puts God between itself and its circumstances, and looks at them through Him.

Elijah's brook dwindled to only a silver thread, which formed pools at the base of the largest rocks. Then the pools evaporated, the birds flew away, and the wild animals of the fields and forests no longer came to drink, for the brook became completely dry. And only then, to Elijah's patient and faithful spirit, did the word of the Lord come and say, "Go at once to Zarephath" (v. 9).

Most of us would have become anxious and tired, and would have made other plans long before God spoke. Our singing would have stopped as soon as the stream flowed less musically over its rocky bed. We would have hung our harps on the willows nearby and begun pacing back and forth on the withering grass, worrying about our predicament. And probably, long before the brook actually dried up, we would have devised some plan, asked God to bless it, and headed elsewhere.

God will often extricate us from the mess we have made, because "his love endures forever" (1 Chronicles 16:34). Yet if we had only been patient and waited to see the unfolding of His plan, we would never have found ourselves in such an impossible maze, seeing no way out. We would also never have had to turn back and retrace our way, with wasted steps and so many tears of shame.

"*Wait* for the LORD" (Psalm 27:14). *Patiently wait!* F. B. MEYER

<hr/>

JULY 12
Morning

I press on. . . . Forgetting what is behind.
PHILIPPIANS 3:12–13

In the very depths of yourself, dig a grave. Let it be like some forgotten spot to which no path leads; and there, in the eternal silence, bury the wrongs that you have suffered. Your heart will feel as if a weight had fallen from it, and a Divine peace come to abide with you. CHARLES WAGNER

To be misunderstood even by those whom one loves is the cross and bitterness of life. It is the secret of that sad melancholy smile on the lips of great men which so few understand. It is what must have oftenest wrung the heart of the Son of Man. AMIEL

> *Blasted rock and broken stone,*
> *Ordinary earth,*
> *Rolled and rammed and trampled on,*
> *Forgotten, nothing worth,*
> *And blamed, but used day after day;*
> *An open road—the king's highway.*
>
> *Often left outside the door,*
> *Sometimes in the rain,*
> *Always lying on the floor,*
> *And made for mud and stain:*
> *Men wipe their feet, and tread it flat,*
> *And beat it clean—the master's mat.*

Thou wast broken, left alone,
Thou wast blamed, and worse,
Thou wast scourged and spat upon,
Thou didst become my curse—
Lord Jesus, as I think of that
I pray, make me Thy road, Thy mat.

GOLD CORD

The power to help others depends upon the acceptance of a trampled life.

JULY 12

Evening

He knows the way that I take; when he has tested me, I will come forth as gold.
JOB 23:10

Faith grows during storms. These are just four little words, but what significance they have to someone who has endured life-threatening storms!

Faith is that God-given ability that, when exercised, brings the unseen into plain view. It deals with the supernatural and makes impossible things possible. And yes, *it grows during storms*—that is, it grows through disturbances in the spiritual atmosphere. Storms are caused by conflicts between the physical elements, and the storms of the spiritual world are conflicts with supernatural, hostile elements. And it is in this atmosphere of conflict that faith finds its most fertile soil and grows most rapidly to maturity.

The strongest trees are found not in the thick shelter of the forest but out in the open, where winds from every direction bear down upon them. The fierce winds bend and twist them until they become giant in stature. These are the trees that toolmakers seek for handles for their tools, because of the wood's great strength.

It is the same in the spiritual world. Remember, when you see a person of great spiritual stature, the road you must travel to walk with him is not one where the sun always shines and wildflowers always bloom. Instead, the way is a steep, rocky, and narrow path, where the winds of hell will try to knock you off your feet, and where sharp rocks will cut you, prickly thorns will scratch your face, and poisonous snakes will slither and hiss all around you.

The path of faith is one of sorrow and joy, suffering and healing comfort, tears and smiles, trials and victories, conflicts and triumphs, and also hardships, dangers, beatings, persecutions, misunderstanding, trouble, and distress. Yet "in all these things we are more than conquerors through him who loved us" (Romans 8:37).

Yes, "in all these"—even *during storms*, when the winds are the most intense—"we are more than conquerors." You may be tempted to run from the ordeal of a fierce storm of testing, but head straight for it! God is there to meet you in the center of each trial. And He will whisper to you His secrets, which will bring you out with a radiant face and such an invincible faith that all the demons of hell will never be able to shake it. E. A. KILBOURNE

<hr>

JULY 13

Morning

The place where you are standing is holy ground.
EXODUS 3:5

We cannot depend upon great events, striking circumstances, exalted moments and great occasions to measure our zeal, courage, faith, and love. These are measured by the commonplace, workaday tasks, the homely hidden paths of common life.

Thank God for the new vision, the beautiful idea, the glowing experience of the mountain; but unless we bring it down to the level of life, and teach it to walk with feet, work with hands, and stand the strain of daily life, we have worse than lost it—we have been hurt by it. *The uncommon life is the product of the day lived in the uncommon way.*

Conspicuous efficiency in a lowly sphere is the best preparation for a higher one.

The incidents of which Jesus' work was made up are, humanly speaking, very humble and unpretentious. Human details fill the compass of His vast experience and work. He might have stilled a tempest every night. He could have walked upon the sea or flown over it, had the need existed. He could have transfigured Himself before

Pilate and the astonished multitude in the Temple. He could have made visible ascensions at noon every day, had He been minded so to do.

The most faithful cannot compare with Jesus in lowliness of manner: He taught only one woman at Jacob's well; He noticed a finger-touch on the hem of His garment; He stooped to take little children up in his arms and bless them; even so small a thing as a cup of cold water, He said, would yield its recompense of a heavenly reward. SELECTED

It may be on a kitchen floor,
Or in a busy shopping store,
Or teaching, nursing, day by day,
Till limb and brain almost give way;
Yet if, just there, by Jesus thou art found,
The place thou standest on is Holy Ground.
M. COLLEY

"*I will make the place of my feet glorious*" (Isaiah 60:13 KJV) said the Lord. Be it never so rough, be it never so steep, be it never so miry—*the place of His feet is glorious!*

Take God on thy route and thou shalt banish wrinkles from thy brow. Gethsemane itself shall not age thee if thou tread by the side of Jesus; for it is not the place of thy travel that makes thee weary—it is the heaviness of thy step. GEORGE MATHESON

JULY 13

Evening

God . . . calls into being things that were not.
ROMANS 4:17

What does this verse mean? It is the very reason why "Abraham in hope believed" (v. 18). That Abraham would become the father of a child at his advanced age seemed absurd and an utter impossibility, yet God called him "the father of many nations" (Genesis 17:4) long before there was any indication of fulfillment. And

Abraham thought of himself as a father, because God had said so. That is genuine faith—believing and declaring what God has said, stepping out on what appears to be thin air and finding solid rock beneath your feet.

Therefore boldly declare what God says you have, and He will accomplish what you believe. You must, however, exhibit genuine faith and trust Him with your entire being. CRUMBS

We must be willing to live by faith, not hoping or desiring to live any other way. We must be willing to have every light around us extinguished, to have every star in the heavens blotted out, and to live with nothing encircling us but darkness and danger. Yes, we must be willing to do all this, if God will only leave within our soul an inner radiance from the pure, bright light that faith has kindled. THOMAS C. UPHAM

The moment has come when you must jump from your perch of distrust, leaving the nest of supposed safety behind and trusting the wings of faith. You must be like a young bird beginning to test the air with its untried wings. At first you may feel as though you will fall to the earth. The fledgling may feel the same way, but it does not fall, for its wings provide support. Yet even if its wings do fail, one of its parents will sweep under it, rescuing it on strong wings.

God will rescue you in the same way. Simply trust Him, for His "right hand sustains" (Psalm 18:35). Do you find yourself asking, "But am I to step out onto nothing?" That is exactly what the bird is seemingly asked to do, yet we know that the *air is there* and that the air is not nearly as insubstantial as it seems. And *you* know that the *promises of God are there*, and they certainly are not insubstantial at all. Do you still respond, "But it seems so unlikely that my poor, helpless soul would be sustained by such strength." Has God said it will? "Do you mean that my tempted, yielding nature will be victorious in the fight?" Has God said it will? "Do you mean that my timid, trembling heart will find peace?" Has God said it will?

If God has said so, surely you do not want to suggest He has lied! If He has spoken, will He not fulfill it? If He has given you His word—His sure word of promise—do not question it but trust it absolutely. You have His promise, and in fact you have even more—you have Him who confidently speaks the words.

"Yes, I tell you" (Luke 12:5). Trust Him! J. B. FIGGIS

Morning

The chariots of God are tens of thousands.
PSALM 68:17

Chariots to victory.
HABAKKUK 3:8

But Lord, they do not *look* like chariots. They look instead like enemies, sufferings, trials, defeats, misunderstandings, disappointments, unkindnesses; juggernaut cars of misery and wretchedness that are only waiting to roll over us and crush us into the earth.

But they *are* chariots; chariots of triumph in which we may rise to those very heights of victory for which our souls have been longing and praying.

Earthly chariots are subject to the laws of matter and may be hindered or overturned; *God's* chariots are controlled by spiritual forces, *and triumph over all hindering things!*

"Tens of thousands" says the text; and although our spiritual eyes may not as yet have been opened to see them, all around us on every side *they must be waiting for us.*

"And Elisha prayed, 'Open his eyes, LORD, so that he may see.' Then the LORD opened the servant's eyes, and he looked and saw the hills full of horses and chariots of fire all around Elisha" (2 Kings 6:17).

Chariots the King of Syria was unable to see, nor could the servant of the prophet see them. But the prophet himself sat calmly in his house without fear—his eyes had been opened to see the invisible. Now, what he asked for his servant was, *"Open his eyes, Lord, so that he may see."*

Open our eyes that we may see!

I have not a shadow of a doubt that if all our eyes were opened today we would see our homes, our places of business, the streets we traverse, filled with the "chariots of God." There is no need for any one of us to walk for lack of a chariot in which to ride: that cross inmate of your household, who has hitherto made life a burden to you and who had been the juggernaut car to crush your soul into the very dust, may henceforth be a glorious chariot to carry you to the heights of heavenly patience and long-suffering; that misunderstanding, that mortification, that unkindness, that disappointment, that loss, that defeat—these are the chariots waiting to carry you to those places of victory you have so often longed to reach.

Somewhere in the trial His will must be hidden, and you must accept His will whether known or unknown, and so hide yourself in His invisible arms of love. Say, "Thy will be done! Thy will be done!" again and again. Shut out every other thought but the one thought of submission to His will and of trust in His love. Thus will you find yourself *riding with God* in a way you never dreamed could be.

No words can express the glorious places to which that soul shall arrive who travels in the chariots of God! *Would you ride on the high places of the earth?*

Then get into the chariots that will take you there! HANNAH WHITALL SMITH

JULY 14
Evening

Bind the festival sacrifice with cords to the horns of the altar.
PSALM 118:27 NASB

Is the altar of sacrifice calling you? Why not ask God to *bind* you to it, so you will never be tempted to turn away from a life of consecration, or dedication, to Him? There are times when life is full of promise and light, and we choose the cross; yet at other times, when the sky is gray, we run from it. Therefore it is wise to be *bound* to the altar.

Dear blessed Holy Spirit, will You bind us to the cross and fill us with such love for it that we will never abandon it? Please bind us with Your scarlet cord of redemption, Your gold cord of love, and the silver cord of hope in Christ's second coming. We ask this so we will not turn from the cross of sacrifice, or desire becoming anything but humble partners with our Lord in His pain and sorrow!

"The horns of the altar" are inviting you. Will you come? Are you willing to continually live a life of total surrender, giving yourself completely to the Lord? SELECTED

I once heard a story of a man who attended a tent revival meeting and tried to give himself to God. Every night at the altar, he would dedicate himself to the Lord. Yet as he left each evening, the Devil would come to him and convince him that since he did not *feel* changed, he was not truly redeemed.

Again and again he was defeated by the Adversary. Finally one evening he came to the meeting carrying an ax and a large wooden stake. After dedicating himself once more, he drove the stake into the ground where he had knelt to pray. As he was leaving the tent, the Devil came to him as usual, trying to make him believe that his commitment to God was not genuine. He quickly returned to the stake, pointed to it, and said, "Devil, do you see this stake? This is my witness that God has forever accepted me."

Immediately the Devil left him, and he never experienced doubts again. THE STILL SMALL VOICE

Beloved, if you are tempted to doubt the finality of your salvation experience, drive a stake into the ground and then let it be your witness before God, and even the Devil, that you have settled the question forever.

> *Are you groping for a blessing,*
>   *Never getting there?*
> *Listen to a word of wisdom,*
>   *Get somewhere.*
>
> *Are you struggling for salvation*
>   *By your anxious prayer?*
> *Stop your struggling, simply trust, and—*
>   *Get somewhere.*
>
> *Does the answer seem to linger*
>   *To your earnest prayer?*
> *Turn your praying into praise, and—*
>   *Get somewhere.*
>
> *You will never know His fullness*
>   *Till you boldly dare*
> *To commit your all to Him, and—*
>   *Get somewhere.*
>
>   SONGS OF THE SPIRIT

Morning

That person will receive the crown of life . . . promised.
JAMES 1:12

The greatest helpers of humanity have been its cross-bearers. The leaders of men have suffered in loneliness; the prophets have learned their lessons in the school of pain. The corals in the sheltered lagoon grow rank and useless; those that are broken and crushed by the surf form the living rock and the foundations of continents. Ease has not produced greatness.

Men who have had to struggle with an unfavorable environment, to fight cold, to buffet the storm, to blast the rock or wring a livelihood from a niggardly soil, have won character by their pains.

The bird rises against a strong head wind, not only in spite of the wind but *because of it*. The *opposing force* becomes a *lifting force* if faced at the right angle.

The storm may buffet ships and rend the rigging, but it makes strong hands and brave hearts. Oh, fellow-voyager amid the storms and calms of life's wide sea, "Spread thy sails to catch the favoring breezes of adversity."

If the greatest character of all time, even He who was the very touchstone of destiny, could be made perfect only through suffering, is it not probable that you and I must be also?

The best things all lie beyond some battle plain: you must fight your way across the field to get them!

> *High natures must be thunder-scarred*
> *With many a scarring wrong!*
> *Naught unmarred with struggle hard*
> *Can make the soul's sinews strong.*
>
> LOWELL

Take the hardest thing in your life—the place of difficulty, outward or inward, and expect God to triumph gloriously in that very spot. Just there He can bring your soul into blossom. LILIAS TROTTER

Evening

This is the victory that has overcome the world, even our faith.
1 JOHN 5:4

It is easy to love Him when the blue is in the sky,
When the summer winds are blowing, and we smell the roses nigh;
There is little effort needed to obey His precious will
When it leads through flower-decked valley, or over sun-kissed hill.

It is when the rain is falling, or the mist hangs in the air,
When the road is dark and rugged, and the wind no longer fair,
When the rosy dawn has settled in a shadowland of gray,
That we find it hard to trust Him, and are slower to obey.

It is easy to trust Him when the singing birds have come,
And their songs of praise are echoed in our heart and in our home;
But it's when we miss the music, and the days are dull and drear,
That we need a faith triumphant over every doubt and fear.

And our blessed Lord will give it; what we lack He will supply;
Let us ask in faith believing—on His promises rely;
He will ever be our Leader, whether smooth or rough the way,
And will prove Himself sufficient for the needs of every day.

Trusting even when it appears you have been forsaken; praying when it seems your words are simply entering a vast expanse where no one hears and no voice answers; believing that God's love is complete and that He is aware of your circumstances, even when your world seems to grind on as if setting its own direction and not caring for life or moving one inch in response to your petitions; desiring only what God's hands have planned for you; waiting patiently while seemingly starving to death, with your only fear being that your faith might fail—"this is the victory that has overcome the world"; this is genuine faith indeed. GEORGE MACDONALD

Morning

In the LORD *I take refuge.*
PSALM 11:1

That is a jubilant bird note, but the bird is singing, not on some fair dewy spring morning, but in a cloudy heaven, and in the very midst of a destructive tempest. A little while ago I listened to a concert of mingled thunder and birdsong. Between the crashing peals of thunder, I heard the clear thrilling note of the lark. The melody seemed to come out of the very heart of the tempest. The environment of this Psalm is stormy. The sun is down. The stars are hid. The waters are out. The roads are broken up. And in the very midst of the darkness and desolation one hears the triumphant cry of the psalmist, "In the LORD I take refuge." The singer is a soul in difficulty. He is the victim of relentless antagonists. He is pursued by implacable foes. The fight would appear to be going against him. The enemies are overwhelming, and, just at this point of seeming defeat and imminent disaster, there emerges this note of joyful confidence in God. "In the LORD I take refuge." It is a song in the night. J. H. JOWETT

There is a bird of the thrush family found in the South of Ireland, called the "Storm Thrush," from its peculiar love of storms. In the wildest storms of rain and wind, it betakes itself to the very topmost twig of the highest tree and there pours out its beautiful song—its frail perch swaying in the wind.

A beautiful story is told of some little birds whose nest had been ruined. As the poet walked among the trees in his garden after the storm, he found a torn nest lying on the ground. He began to brood sadly over it, pitying the birds whose home had thus been wrecked. But as he stood there and mused, he heard a twittering and chattering over his head; looking up he saw the birds *busy building again their ruined nest!*

> *I heard a bird at break of day*
> *Sing from the autumn trees*
> *A song so musical and calm,*
> *So full of certainties,*
> *No man, I think, could listen long*
> *Except upon his knees.*

Yet this was but a simple bird
Alone among dead trees.

Robert Louis Stevenson closes one of his prayers with these words: "Help us with the grace of courage that we be none of us cast down while we sit lamenting over the ruins of our happiness. *Touch us with the fire of Thine altar, that we may be up and doing, to rebuild our city.*"

Begin to build anew!

~~~~~~~~~ **JULY 16** ~~~~~~~~~
Evening

> *Because you have done this and have not withheld your son,*
> *your only son, I will . . . make your descendants as numerous*
> *as the stars in the sky . . . because you have obeyed me.*
> Genesis 22:16–18

From the time of Abraham, people have been learning that when they obey God's voice and surrender to Him whatever they hold most precious, He multiplies it thousands of times. Abraham gave up his one and only son at the Lord's command, and in doing so, all his desires and dreams for Isaac's life, as well as his own hope for a notable heritage, disappeared. Yet God restored Isaac to his father, and Abraham's family became "as numerous as the stars in the sky and as the sand on the seashore" (v. 17). And through his descendants, "when the set time had fully come, God sent his Son" (Galatians 4:4).

This is exactly how God deals with every child of His when we truly sacrifice. We surrender everything we own and accept poverty—then He sends wealth. We leave a growing area of ministry at His command—then He provides one better than we had ever dreamed. We surrender all our cherished hopes and die to self—then He sends overflowing joy and His "life . . . that [we] might have it more abundantly" (John 10:10 KJV).

The greatest gift of all was Jesus Christ Himself, and we can never fully comprehend the enormity of His sacrifice. Abraham, as the earthly father of the family of

Christ, had to begin by surrendering himself and his only son, just as our heavenly Father sacrificed His only Son, Jesus. We could never have come to enjoy the privileges and joys as members of God's family *through any other way.* CHARLES GALLAUDET TRUMBULL

We sometimes seem to forget that *what God takes from us, He takes with fire,* and that the only road to a life of resurrection and ascension power leads us first to Gethsemane, the cross, and the tomb.

Dear soul, do you believe that Abraham's experience was unique and isolated? It is only an example and a pattern of how God deals with those who are prepared to obey Him whatever the cost. "After waiting patiently, Abraham received what was promised" (Hebrews 6:15), and so will you. The moment of your greatest sacrifice will also be the precise moment of your greatest and most miraculous blessing. God's river, which never runs dry, will overflow its banks, bringing you a flood of wealth and grace.

Indeed, there is nothing God will not do for those who will dare to step out in faith onto what appears to be only a mist. As they take their first step, they will find a rock beneath their feet. F. B. MEYER

JULY 17

Morning

God remembered Noah . . . and he sent a wind over the earth, and the waters receded. Now the springs of the deep and the floodgates of the heavens had been closed, and the rain had stopped falling from the sky. The water receded steadily from the earth.

GENESIS 8:1–3

All this because God remembered Noah! The forces of heaven and earth were enlisted, reversed, ordered about, solely because God remembered Noah and had plans for him.

God has not forgotten *you.* He will as readily order about the forces of the universe on your account as He did on Noah's. His plans for Noah were also plans for the whole world through Noah. So they are for you. He will use you for the good of the whole world if you will let Him. SELECTED

We may forget; God does not!

God's time is never wrong,
Never too fast nor too slow;
The planets move to its steady pace
As the centuries come and go.

Stars rise and set by that time,
The punctual comets come back
With never a second's variance,
From the round of their viewless track.

Men space their years by the sun,
And reckon their months by the moon,
Which never arrive too late
And never depart too soon.

Let us set our clocks by God's,
And order our lives by His ways,
And nothing can come and nothing can go
Too soon or too late in our day.

ANNIE JOHNSON FLINT

There are no dates in His fine leisure.

~~~~~~ JULY 17 ~~~~~~
Evening

I will remain quiet and will look on from my dwelling place.
ISAIAH 18:4

In this passage, Assyria is marching against Ethiopia, whose people are described as "tall and smooth-skinned" (v. 2). As the army advances, God makes no effort to stop them, and it appears as though they will be allowed to do as they wish. The Lord is watching from His "dwelling place" while the sun continues to shine on them, yet "before the harvest" (v. 5) the entire proud army is defeated as easily as new growth is pruned from a vine.

Isn't this a beautiful picture of God—remaining quiet and watching? Yet His silence is not to be confused with passive agreement or consent. He is simply biding His time and will arise at the most opportune moment, just when the plans of the wicked are on the verge of success, in order to overwhelm the enemy with disaster. And as we see the evil of this world, as we watch the apparent success of wrongdoers, and as we suffer the oppression of those who hate us, let us remember those miraculous words of God—"I will remain quiet and will look on."

Yes, God does have another point of view, and there is wisdom behind His words. Why did Jesus watch His disciples straining at the oars through the stormy night? Why did He, though unseen by others, watch the sequence of anguishing events unfold in Bethany as Lazarus slowly passed through the stages of his terminal illness, succumbed to death, and was finally buried in a rocky tomb? Jesus was simply waiting for the perfect moment when He could intercede most effectively.

Is the Lord being *quiet* with you? Nevertheless, He is attentive and still sees everything. He has His finger on your pulse and is extremely sensitive to even the slightest change. And He will come to save you when the perfect moment has arrived. DAILY DEVOTIONAL COMMENTARY

Whatever the Lord may ask of us or however slow He may seem to work, we can be absolutely sure He is never a confused or fearful Savior.

> *O troubled soul, beneath the rod,*
> *Your Father speaks, be still, be still;*
> *Learn to be silent unto God,*
> *And let Him mold you to His will.*
>
> *O praying soul, be still, be still,*
> *He cannot break His promised Word;*
> *Sink down into His blessed will,*
> *And wait in patience on the Lord.*
>
> *O waiting soul, be still, be strong,*

And though He tarry, trust and wait;
Doubt not, He will not wait too long,
Fear not, He will not come too late.

JULY 18
Morning

"Sovereign LORD, *how can I know that I will gain possession of it?"*
So the LORD *said to him, "Bring me a heifer." . . . Then birds of*
prey came down on the carcasses, but Abram drove them away.
GENESIS 15:8–9,11

When God promises us a great blessing, and we ask how we may know that we shall have it, the answer is always the same: *By your own sacrifice to Me.* God cannot fulfill His richest promises to any of us until we have offered up to Him, *in utter completeness of surrender, ourselves. Then He can do glorious things for and with our lives.*

And then, also, "the birds of prey" attack a life as never before. The devil does not like to see any life sacrificed to God, *for he knows how mightily God will use that life to defeat the works of darkness.* So the birds of prey come down. We must expect to be attacked and tempted more fiercely and continuously after our life has been *wholly surrendered to God* than we ever were before. MESSAGES FOR THE MORNING WATCH

There is a Chinese legend of a potter who sought for many years to put a certain tint on the vases he made, but all his efforts failed. At last discouraged and in despair, he threw himself into his furnace, and his body was consumed in the fire; then, when the vases were taken out, they bore the exquisite color which he had striven so long to produce.

The legend illustrates that truth that we can do our noblest and best work only at cost of self. The alabaster box must be broken before its odors can flow out.

Christ lifted up and saved the world not by an easy, pleasant, successful life in it; but by suffering and dying for it. And *we* can never bless the world merely by having a good time in it; but only by giving our lives for it.

It takes heart's blood to heal hearts. *Saving of life proves, in the end, the losing of it.*

My wild will was captured, yet under the yoke
There was pain and not peace at the press of the load;
Till the glorious burden the last fiber broke,
And I melted like wax in the furnace of God.

And now I have flung myself recklessly out,
Like a chip on the stream of His infinite will;
I pass the rough rocks with a smile and a shout,
And just let my God His dear purpose fulfill.

JULY 18

Evening

The eyes of the LORD *range throughout the earth to strengthen*
those whose hearts are fully committed to him.

2 CHRONICLES 16:9

God is looking for men and women whose hearts are firmly fixed on Him and who will continually trust Him for all He desires to do with their lives. God is ready and eager to work more powerfully than ever through His people, and the clock of the centuries is striking the eleventh hour.

The world is watching and waiting to see what God can do through a life committed to Him. And not only is the world waiting but God Himself awaits to see who will be the most completely devoted person who has ever lived: willing to be nothing so Christ may be everything; fully accepting God's purposes as his own; receiving Christ's humility, faith, love, and power yet never hindering God's plan but always allowing Him to continue His miraculous work. C. H. P.

There is no limit to what God can do through you, provided you do not seek your own glory.

George Mueller, at more than ninety years of age, in an address to ministers and other Christian workers, said, "*I was converted* in November 1825, but I didn't come to the point *of total surrender of my heart* until four years later, in July 1829. It was then I realized my love for money, prominence, position, power, and worldly pleasure was gone. God, and He alone, became my all in all. In Him I found everything I needed, and I desired nothing else. By God's grace, my understanding of His sufficiency has remained to this day, making me an exceedingly happy man. It has led me to care only about the things of God.

"And so, dear believers, I kindly ask if you have totally surrendered your heart to God, or is there something in your life you refuse to release, in spite of God's call?

"Before the point at which I surrendered my life, I read a little of the Scriptures but preferred other books. Yet since that time, the truth He has revealed to me of Himself has become an inexpressible blessing. Now I can honestly say from the depth of my heart that God is an infinitely wonderful Being.

"Please, never be satisfied until you too can express from your innermost soul, 'God is an infinitely wonderful Being!'" SELECTED

My prayer today is that God would make me an extraordinary Christian. GEORGE WHITEFIELD

~~~~~~~~   JULY 19   ~~~~~~~~

Morning

For no matter how many promises God has made, they are "Yes" in Christ.
2 CORINTHIANS 1:20

Sometimes Christians go for a good while in trouble, not realizing that riches are laid up for them in a familiar promise.

When Christian and Hopeful strayed out of the path upon forbidden ground and found themselves locked up in Doubting Castle by Giant Despair for their carelessness, there they lay for days, until one night they began to pray. "Now a little before it was day, Good Christian, as one half-amazed, broke out in passionate speech: 'What a fool!' quoth he, 'am I, thus to lie in this horrible dungeon, when I may as well walk at liberty. I have a key in my bosom called PROMISE, that will, I am persuaded, open any lock in Doubting Castle.' Then said Hopeful, 'That's good news good brother; pluck it out of thy bosom and try.' Then Christian pulled it out of his bosom, and began to try the dungeon door, whose bolts gave back, and the door flew open with ease, and Christian and Hopeful came out." "PILGRIM'S PROGRESS" BY JOHN BUNYAN

Often you cannot get at a difficulty so as to deal with it aright and find your way to a happy result. You pray, but have not the liberty in prayer which you desire. A definite promise is what you want. You try one and another of the inspired words, but they do not fit. You try again, and in due season a promise presents itself which seems to have been made for the occasion; it fits exactly as a well-made key fits the lock for which it was prepared. Having found the identical word of the living God you hasten to plead it at the throne of grace, saying, "O Lord, Thou hast promised this good thing unto Thy servant; be pleased to grant it!" The matter is ended: sorrow is turned to joy; prayer is heard. CHARLES H. SPURGEON

> *Faith, mighty faith, the promise sees*
> *And looks to God alone,*
> *Laughs at impossibilities,*
> *And cries, "It shall be done."*

Try all your keys! Never despair! God leaves no treasure-house locked against us!

JULY 19

Evening

"Shall I not drink the cup the Father has given me?"
JOHN 18:11

To "drink the cup" was a greater thing than calming the seas or raising the dead. The prophets and apostles could do amazing miracles, but they did not always do the will of God and thereby suffered as a result. Doing God's will and thus experiencing suffering is still the highest form of faith, and the most glorious Christian achievement.

Having your brightest aspirations as a young person forever crushed; bearing burdens daily that are always difficult, and never seeing relief; finding yourself worn down by poverty while simply desiring to do good for others and provide a comfortable living for those you love; being shackled by an incurable physical disability; being completely alone, separated from all those you love, to face the trauma of life alone; yet in all these, still being able to say through such a difficult school of discipline, "Shall I not drink the cup the Father has given me?"—this is faith at its highest, and spiritual success at its crowning point.

Great faith is exhibited not so much in doing as in suffering. CHARLES PARKHURST

In order to have a sympathetic God, we must have a suffering Savior, for true sympathy comes from understanding another person's hurt by suffering the same affliction. Therefore we cannot help others who suffer without paying a price ourselves, because afflictions are the cost we pay for our ability to sympathize. Those who wish to help others must first suffer. If we wish to rescue others, we must be willing to face the cross; experiencing the greatest happiness in life through ministering to others is impossible without drinking the cup Jesus drank and without submitting to the baptism He endured.

The most comforting of David's psalms were squeezed from his life by suffering, and if Paul had not been given "a thorn in the flesh" (2 Corinthians 12:7 KJV), we would have missed much of the heartbeat of tenderness that resonates through so many of his letters.

If you have surrendered yourself to Christ, your present circumstances that seem to be pressing so hard against you are the perfect tool in the Father's hand to chisel you into shape for eternity. So trust Him and never push away the instrument He is using, or you will miss the result of His work in your life.

> Strange and difficult indeed
> We may find it,
> But the blessing that we need
> Is behind it.

The school of suffering graduates exceptional scholars.

JULY 20
Morning

Until now you have not asked for anything in my name. Ask
and you will receive, and your joy will be complete.
JOHN 16:24

Alexander the Great had a famous, but indigent, philosopher in his court. This man adept in science was once particularly straightened in his circumstances. To whom should he apply but to his patron, the conqueror of the world? His request was no sooner made than granted. Alexander gave him a commission to receive of his treasury whatever he wanted. He immediately demanded in his sovereign's name ten thousand pounds. The treasurer, surprised at so large a demand, refused to comply, but waited upon the king and represented to him the affair, adding withal how unreasonable he thought the petition and how exorbitant the sum. Alexander listened with patience, but as soon as he heard the remonstrance replied, "Let the money be instantly paid. I am delighted with this philosopher's way of thinking; he has done me a singular honor: by the largeness of his request he shows the high idea he has conceived both of my superior wealth and my royal munificence."

Saints have never yet reached the limit to the possibilities of prayer. Whatever has been attained or achieved *has touched but the fringe of the garment of a prayer-hearing God*. We honor the riches both of His power and love *only* by large demands. A. T. PIERSON

You cannot think of a prayer so large that God, in answering it, will not wish that you had made it larger. *Pray not for crutches, but for wings!* PHILLIPS BROOKS

Make thy petition deep.
It is thy God who speaks with love o'erflowing,
Thy God who claims the rapture of bestowing,
Thy God who whispers, all thy weakness knowing,
"Wouldst thou in full reap?
Make thy petition deep."

Make thy petition deep.
Now to the fountainhead thy vessel bringing,
Claim all the fullness of its glad upspringing;
At Calvary was proclaimed its boundless measure;
Who spared not then, withholds from thee no treasure;
This word—His token, keep:
Make thy petition deep.

If Alexander gave like a King, shall not Jehovah give like a God?

Since we have a great high priest . . . , Jesus the Son of God, let us hold firmly to the
faith we profess. . . . Let us then approach God's throne of grace with confidence,
so that we may receive mercy and find grace to help us in our time of need.

HEBREWS 4:14, 16

Our great Helper in prayer is the Lord Jesus Christ. He is our Advocate, ever pleading our case before the Father. He is our "great high priest," whose primary ministry has for centuries been intercession and prayer on our behalf. It is He who receives our imperfect petitions from our hands, cleanses them of their defects, corrects their error, and then claims their answer from His Father. And He does so strictly on the basis of His worth and righteousness through the sufficiency of His atonement.

Believer, are you lacking power in prayer? Look to Christ, for your blessed Advocate has already claimed your answer. And if you give up the fight just as the moment of victory approaches, you will grieve and disappoint Him. He has already entered "the Most Holy Place" (Exodus 26:33) on your behalf, holding up your name on the palms of His hands. The messenger is now on his way to bring you your blessing, and the Holy Spirit simply awaits your act of trust, so He may whisper in your heart the echo of the answer from the throne of God, "*It is done*" (Revelation 21:6). A. B. SIMPSON

The Holy Spirit is the one who works to make our prayers acceptable, yet we often forget this truth. He enlightens our mind so we may clearly see our desires, then softens our heart so we may feel them, and finally He awakens and focuses those desires toward godly things. He gives us a clear view of God's power and wisdom, provides grace "in our time of need," and strengthens our confidence in His truth so we will never waver.

Prayer is a wonderful thing, and each person of the Trinity is involved in every acceptable prayer. J. ANGELL JAMES

Morning

Whatever you ask for in prayer . . . it will be yours.
MARK 11:24

O h, the victories of prayer! They are the mountaintops of the Bible.
They take us back to the plains of Mamre, to the fords of Peniel, to the
prison of Joseph, to the triumphs of Moses, to the victories of Joshua, to the deliver-
ances of David, to the miracles of Elijah and Elisha, to the holy story of the Master's
life, to the secret of Pentecost, to the keynote of Paul's unparalleled ministry, to the
lives of saints and the deaths of martyrs, to all that is most sacred and sweet in the his-
tory of the church and the experience of the children of God.

And when for us the last conflict shall have passed, and the *footstool of prayer shall
have given place to the harp of praise,* the scenes of time that shall be gilded with eternal
radiance shall be those linked with deepest sorrow and darkest night, over which we
have written *Jehovah Shammah (the Lord was there).*

> *Beyond thy utmost wants,*
> *His power can love and bless;*
> *To trusting souls He loves to grant*
> *More than they can express.*

Evening

Let me make just one more request. Allow me one more test with the fleece.
JUDGES 6:39

T here are three levels of faith in the Christian experience. The first is being able to
believe only when we see some sign or have some strong emotion. Like Gideon,

we feel the fleece and are willing to trust God if it is wet. This may be genuine faith but it is imperfect. It is continually looking to feelings or some other sign instead of the Word of God. We have taken a great step toward maturity when we trust God without relying on our feelings. It is more of a blessing when we believe without experiencing any emotion.

While the first level of faith believes when our emotions are favorable, the second believes when all feelings are absent. And the third level transcends the other two, for it is faith that believes God and His Word when circumstances, emotions, appearances, people, and human reason all seem to urge something to the contrary. Paul exercised this level of faith when he said, "When neither sun nor stars appeared for many days and the storm continued raging, we finally gave up all hope of being saved" (Acts 27:20), then nevertheless went on to say, "Keep up your courage, men, *for I have faith in God* that it will happen just as he told me" (Acts 27:25).

May God grant us faith to completely trust His Word, even when every other sign points the other way. C. H. P.

> *When is the time to trust?*
> *Is it when all is calm,*
> *When waves the victor's palm,*
> *And life is one glad psalm*
> *Of joy and praise?*
>
> *No! For the time to trust*
> *Is when the waves beat high,*
> *When storm clouds fill the sky,*
> *And prayer is one long cry,*
> *"Oh, help and save!"*
>
> *When is the time to trust?*
> *Is it when friends are true?*
> *Is it when comforts woo,*
> *And in all we say and do*
> *We meet but praise?*

No! For the time to trust
    Is when we stand alone,
    And summer birds have flown,
    And every prop is gone,
    All else but God.

When is the time to trust?
    Is it some future day,
    When you have tried your way,
    And learned to trust and pray
    By bitter woe?

No! For the time to trust
    Is in this moment's need,
    Poor, broken, bruised reed!
    Poor, troubled soul, make speed
    To trust your God.

When is the time to trust?
    Is it when hopes beat high,
    When sunshine gilds the sky,
    And joy and ecstasy
    Fill all the heart?

No! For the time to trust
    Is when our joy has fled,
    When sorrow bows the head,
    And all is cold and dead,
    All else but God.

SELECTED

Morning

*For you who revere my name, the sun of righteousness
will rise with healing in its rays.*

Malachi 4:2

*Unto you that fear my name shall the Sun of
righteousness arise with healing in his wings.*

kjv

A South American traveler tells of a curious conflict which he once witnessed between a little quadruped and a poisonous reptile of great size. The little creature seemed no match for its antagonist that threatened to destroy it by a blow, as well as its helpless young, but it fearlessly faced its mighty enemy and rushing at him, struck him with a succession of fierce and telling blows, but received at the onset a deep and apparently fatal wound from the poisonous fangs, which flashed for a moment with an angry fire, and then fastened themselves deep into the flesh of the daring little assailant.

For a moment it seemed as if all were over, but the wise little creature immediately retired into the forest, and hastening to the plantain tree eagerly devoured some of its leaves, and then hurried back, seemingly fresh and restored, to renew the fray with vigor and determination. Again and again this strange spectacle was repeated: the serpent, although greatly exhausted, ferociously attacked, and again and again wounded its antagonist to death, as it seemed; but the little creature each time repaired to its simple prescription, and returned to renewed victory. In the course of an hour or two the battle was over—the mammoth reptile lay still and dead and the little victor was unharmed, in the midst of the nest and the helpless little ones.

How often we are wounded by the dragon's sting—wounded, it would seem to death! and if we had to go through some long ceremony to reach the source of life, we must faint and die. But blessed be His Name as near at hand as that which the forest holds in its shade, *there is ever for us a Plant of healing to which we may continually repair* and come back refreshed, invigorated, transfigured—like Him who shone with the brightness of celestial light as He prayed in the mount; who, as He prayed in the garden arose triumphant over the fear of death, strengthened from on high to accomplish the mighty battle of our redemption. A. B. SIMPSON

It is His wings that heal our pains,
And soothe the serpent's poisoned stings;
Close to His bosom we must press
To feel His healing wings.

~~~~~~~~   JULY 22   ~~~~~~~~
Evening

Therefore will the LORD *wait, that he may be gracious unto*
you . . . blessed are all they that wait for him.
ISAIAH 30:18 KJV

We should not only understand the importance of our waiting on God but also realize something even more wonderful—the Lord waits on us. And the very thought of His waiting on us will give us renewed motivation and inspiration to "wait for him." It will also provide inexpressible confidence that our waiting will never be in vain. Therefore, in the spirit of waiting on God, let us seek to discover exactly what it means right now.

The Lord has an inconceivably glorious purpose for each of His children. "If this is true," you ask, "why is it that He continues to wait longer and longer to offer His grace and to provide the help I seek, even after I have come and waited on Him?" He does so because He is a wise gardener who "waits for the land to yield its valuable crop" and is [patient] . . . for the autumn and spring rains" (James 5:7). God knows He cannot gather the fruit until it is ripe, and He knows precisely when we are spiritually ready to receive blessings for our gain and His glory. And waiting in the sunshine of His love is what will ripen our soul for His blessings. Also, waiting under the clouds of trials is as important, for they will ultimately produce showers of blessings.

Rest assured that if God waits longer than we desire, it is simply to make the blessings doubly precious. Remember, He waited four thousand years, "but when the set time had fully come, God sent his Son" (Galatians 4:4). Our time is in His hands, and

He will quickly avenge those He has chosen, swiftly coming to our support without ever delaying even one hour too long. ANDREW MURRAY

JULY 23
Morning

Whatever . . . that the Father may be glorified in the Son.
JOHN 14:13

Do we pray for His glory?

This is the privilege and possibility for every man who can speak to God *"in His Name."*

In the Lone Star Mission at Ongole, India, a faithful few had held on believingly and courageously year after year. Now the mission was about to be abandoned. The work had apparently failed; money had failed. The only hope now was God.

Dr. Jowett and his wife took with them that famous old Hindu woman, Julia, nearly one hundred years of age, and ascended the hills above Ongole to ask God to save the Lone Star Mission and the lost souls of India. The old Hindu saint mingled her tears with her description of the most important and most thrilling moment of her life—that memorable sunrise meeting on "Prayer Meeting Hill," as she rehearsed the story one night in Nellore, India, to Dr. Cortland Myers.

"They all prayed, and they all believed! They talked and then they prayed again! They wrestled before heaven's throne in the face of a heathen world, like Elijah on Carmel. At last the day dawned. Just as the sun rose above the horizon, Dr. Jowett arose out of darkness and seemed to see a great light. He lifted his hand heavenward and turned his tear-stained face toward the great Heart of Love. He declared that his vision saw the cactus field below transformed into a church and mission buildings!

"His faith grasped and gripped the great fact! He claimed the promise and challenged God to answer *a prayer that was entirely for His own glory and the salvation of men!*

The money came *immediately,* and *clearly from God's hand!*

The man—God's choice, came *immediately!* Clearly it was of God that Dr. Clough was called to put new life and hope into the almost abandoned mission.

Today on that very cactus field stands the Christian church with the largest membership of any church on earth—20,000 members! If it had not been divided by necessity there would now be 50,000 members—the greatest miracle of the modern missionary world.

On that well-nigh abandoned field, Dr. Clough baptized 10,000 persons in one year; 2,222 in one day!

Prayer Meeting Hill *moved the throne of God,* and made the world to tremble! The battlements of heaven must have been crowded to watch these many workings of a prayer for *His* glory!

JULY 23
Evening

Sing . . . to the LORD, always giving thanks to God the Father for everything.
EPHESIANS 5:19–20

No matter the source of the evil confronting you, if you are in God and thereby completely surrounded by Him, you must realize that it has first passed through Him before coming to you. Because of this, you can thank Him for everything that comes your way. This does not mean thanking Him for the sin that accompanies evil, but offering thanks for what He will bring out of it and through it. May God make our life one of continual thanksgiving and praise, so He will then make everything a blessing.

I once saw a man draw some black dots on a piece of paper. Several of us looked at it yet saw nothing but an irregular arrangement of dots. Then he also drew a few lines, put in a few rests, and added a treble clef at the beginning. Suddenly we realized that the dots were musical notes, and as we began to sound them out, we were singing,

> *Praise God from whom all blessings flow,*
> *Praise Him all creatures here below.*

Each of us has many black dots or spots in our life, and we cannot understand *why* they are there or *why* God permitted them. But when we allow Him into our life to adjust the dots in the proper way, to draw the lines He desires, and to put rests at the proper places to separate us from certain things, then from the black dots and spots He will compose a glorious harmony.

So let us not hinder Him in His glorious work! C. H. P.

> Would we know that the major chords were sweet,
>   If there were no minor key?
> Would the painter's work be fair to our eyes,
>   Without shade on land or sea?
> Would we know the meaning of happiness,
>   Would we feel that the day was bright,
> If we'd never known what it was to grieve,
>   Nor gazed on the dark of night?

Many people owe the grandeur of their lives to their tremendous difficulties. CHARLES H. SPURGEON

When an organist presses the black keys of a great organ, the notes are just as beautiful as when he presses the white ones. Yet to fully demonstrate the capabilities of the instrument, he must press them all. SELECTED

JULY 24
Morning

Blessed are those who have not seen and yet have believed.
JOHN 20:29

There are those to whom no visions come, no moments upon the mount suffused with a glory that never was on land or sea. Do not envy the men of vision. It may be that the vision is given to strengthen a faith that else were weak. It is to the people who can live along the line of what others call the commonplace, and yet trust, that the Master says, "Blessed."

Beware of a life of fitful impulse. Live and act on sustained principle. It is a poor thing—the flash of summer lightning, compared with the steady luster of moon and star.

"The darkest night has stars in it!"

When the low mood comes, open your New Testament. Read it imaginatively: stand on the shore at Capernaum, visit the home at Bethany, sit by Jacob's well and in the Upper Room, look into the eyes of Jesus, listen to His voice, take a walk around by Calvary, remember the crown of thorns, then tell yourself (for it is true), "All this was for me! The Son of God loved me, and gave Himself for me." And see if a passion of praise does not send the low mood flying.

"Praise and service are great healers." When life grows sore and wounding, and it is difficult to be brave, praise God! Sing something, and you will rally your own heart with the song!

You must learn to swim and hold your head above the water even when the sense of His Presence is not with you to hold up your chin. GARDEN OF SPICES

Do not depend on frames or feelings. You cannot always live in the tropics.

~~~~~~ JULY 24 ~~~~~~

Evening

Then they believed his promises and sang his praise. But they soon forgot what he had done and did not wait for his plan to unfold. In the desert they gave in to their craving; in the wilderness they put God to the test. So he gave them what they asked for, but sent a wasting disease among them.

PSALM 106:12–15

In Hebrews 11:27, we read that Moses "persevered because he saw him who is invisible." Yet in the above passage, exactly the opposite was true of the children of Israel. They persevered only when their circumstances were favorable, because they were primarily influenced by whatever appealed to their senses, instead of trusting in the invisible and eternal God.

Even today we have people who live an inconsistent Christian life because they have become preoccupied with things that are external. Therefore they focus on their circumstances rather than focusing on God. And God desires that we grow in our ability to see Him in everything and to realize the importance of seemingly insignificant circumstances if they are used to deliver a message from Him.

We read of the children of Israel, "*Then* they believed his promises." They did not believe until *after* they saw—once they saw Him work, "*then* they believed." They unabashedly doubted God when they came to the Red Sea, but when He opened the way and led them across and they *saw* Pharaoh and his army drowned—"*then* they believed." The Israelites continued to live this kind of up-and-down existence, because their faith was dependent on their circumstances. And this is certainly not the kind of faith God wants us to have.

The world says that "seeing is believing," but God wants us to believe in order to see. The psalmist said, "I would have despaired unless I had *believed that I would see* the goodness of the LORD in the land of the living" (Psalm 27:13 NASB).

Do you believe God only when your circumstances are favorable, or do you believe no matter what your circumstances may be? C. H. P.

Faith is believing what we do not see, and the reward for this kind of faith is to see what we believe. SAINT AUGUSTINE

<hr>

JULY 25
Morning

You must go to everyone I send you to.
JEREMIAH 1:7

Have you ever read George Eliot's poem called "Stradivarius"? Stradivari was the famous old violin maker whose violins, nearly two centuries old, are almost worth their weight in gold today. Says Stradivari in the poem:

> *If my hand slacked,*
> *I should rob God—since He is fullest good,*
> *Leaving a blank instead of violins.*
> *He could not make Antonio Stradivari's violins*
> *Without Antonio.*

You are God's opportunity in your day. He has waited for ages for a person just like you. If you refuse Him, then God loses His opportunity which He sought through you; and He will never have another, for there will never be another person on the earth just like you.

> *Bring to God your gift, my brother,*
> *He'll not need to call another,*
> *You will do;*
> *He will add His blessing to it,*
> *And the two of you will do it,*
> *God and you.*
>
> R. E. NEIGHBOUR

Get taken clear out into the purpose of God and let Him lade you with merchandise for others.

We find scores of people in middle life who are in the unhappy position of doing everyday work which they hate and which does not express the personality, when each one might have done brilliantly in another sphere if he had given a day's prayerful thought to a decision which affected half a century.

JULY 25
Evening

> *You do not realize now what I am doing, but later you will understand.*
> JOHN 13:7

In this life, we have an incomplete view of God's dealings, seeing His plan only half finished and underdeveloped. Yet once we stand in the magnificent temple of eternity, we will have the proper perspective and will see everything fitting gracefully together!

Imagine going to the mountains of Lebanon during the reign of Israel's great king Solomon. Can you see the majestic cedar? It is the pride of all the other trees and has wrestled many years with the cold north winds! The summer sun has loved to smile upon it, while the night has caused its soft leaves to glisten with drops of dew. Birds have built their nests in its branches, and weary travelers and wandering shepherds have rested in its shade from the midday heat or taken shelter from the raging storms. And suddenly we realize that this old inhabitant of the forest has been doomed to fall victim to the woodsman's ax!

We watch as the ax makes its first gash on the cedar's gnarled trunk. Then we see its noble limbs stripped of their branches as the tree comes crashing to the ground. We cry out against the wanton destruction of this "Tree of God," as it is distinctively known, and express our anger over the demolition of this proud pillar in the forest temple of nature. We are tempted to exclaim with the prophet Zechariah, "*Wail, you juniper, for the cedar has fallen . . . !*" (Zechariah 11:2), as if inviting the sympathy of every less-majestic plant and invoking inanimate things to also resent the offense.

We should not be so quick to complain but should follow the gigantic tree as the workmen of "Hiram king of Tyre" (2 Chronicles 2:3) take it down the mountainside. From there we should watch it being sailed on rafts along the blue water of the Mediterranean. And finally, we should behold it being placed as a glorious and polished beam in the temple of God. As you contemplate its final destination, seeing it in the Holy of Holies as a jewel in the diadem of the almighty King, can you honestly complain that this crown jewel of Lebanon was cut down, removed from the forest, and placed in such a noble setting? The cedar had once stood majestically in nature's sanctuary, but "the glory of this present house will be greater than the glory of the former house" (Haggai 2:9).

So many people are like these cedars of old! God's axes of trials have stripped them bare, and yet we can see no reason for such harsh and difficult circumstances. But God has a noble goal and purpose in mind: to place them as everlasting pillars and rafters in His heavenly Zion. And He says to them, "You will be a crown of splendor in the LORD's hand, a royal diadem in the hand of your God" (Isaiah 62:3). J. R. MACDUFF

> *I do not ask my cross to understand,*
> *My way to see—*
> *Better in darkness just to feel Your hand,*
> *And follow Thee.*

Morning

He breathed on them and said, "Receive the Holy Spirit."
JOHN 20:22

I had an opportunity to preach in a little schoolhouse two miles from my first pastorate—an afternoon meeting. After the morning church service, the rain was pouring in torrents. It seemed useless to go two miles through such a storm, for who would venture out in such weather? But a young woman had come for me in her buggy, and I went with her rather reluctantly.

There were seven men present; the young woman went home to get out of the rain. My first impression was that it was hardly worthwhile to preach a sermon to so small an audience, but I repented of that and gave them the best I had. The dew of heaven was upon us: we were conscious of God's presence, and two of the seven men, who were not Christians, expressed a desire to be saved.

An old farmer arose and said: "My young brother, God is working in our midst. Will you not preach tonight? The clouds are clearing away, and we will go out and tell the people about the meeting." I consented, though it rather upset my plans for the following day. That night about twenty-five persons came, and there were six or seven inquirers and two or three decisions for Christ.

The meetings went on from day to day for two weeks. There were over seventy conversions, and on Sunday morning I baptized forty new members of my church. I could not explain it; no one seemed to be expecting a revival, or praying for it. It seemed like a case of God's sovereignty in giving His *breath-touch* without demanding that anyone should pray for it.

The last day of the meetings solved the mystery. At the close of the service a plainly dressed, gray-haired, motherly woman grasped my hand and said: "This is my home, though I spend most of my time teaching school sixty miles from here. When my niece wrote that you were preaching at three in the afternoon and at seven-thirty in the evening, I dismissed my school a half hour earlier than usual, that I might spend in prayer every minute that you preached. And, sir, *I have come to see what God has been doing. Those you baptized this morning were all my neighbors and friends, and among them my brother, nephew, and niece.*"

Neither my preaching or praying brought that revival. It was the good woman sixty miles away, whose prayers brought the *breath-touch* of God upon dead souls of that community.

Let no day pass without a prayer to God for His *breath-touch* upon the spiritual dry bones of your community.

> *Breathe on me, Breath of God*
> *Till I am wholly Thine,*
> *Till all this earthly part of me*
> *Glows with Thy fire Divine.*

In Wales during the great revival, there was no accounting for the way the Spirit worked. It was all *"a-bend to God."*

~~~~~~ JULY 26 ~~~~~~

Evening

Through the Spirit we eagerly await by faith the righteousness for which we hope.
GALATIANS 5:5

There are times when everything looks very dark to me—so dark that I have to wait before I have hope. Waiting *with* hope is very difficult, but true patience is expressed when we must even wait *for* hope. When we see no hint of success yet refuse to despair, when we see nothing but the darkness of night through our window yet keep the shutters open because stars may appear in the sky, and when we have an empty place in our heart yet will not allow it to be filled with anything less than God's best—that is the greatest kind of patience in the universe. It is the story of Job in the midst of the storm, Abraham on the road to Moriah, Moses in the desert of Midian, and the Son of Man in the Garden of Gethsemane. And there is no patience as strong as that which endures because we see "him who is invisible" (Hebrews 11:27). It is the kind of patience that waits for hope.

Dear Lord, You have made waiting beautiful and patience divine. You have taught us that Your will should be accepted, simply because it *is* Your will. You have revealed to us that a person may see nothing but sorrow in his cup yet still be willing to drink it because of a conviction that Your eyes see further than his own.

Father, give me Your divine power—the power of Gethsemane. Give me the strength to wait for hope—to look through the window when there are no stars. Even when my joy is gone, give me the strength to stand victoriously in the darkest night and say, "To my heavenly Father, the sun still shines."

I will have reached the point of greatest strength once I have learned to wait for hope. GEORGE MATHESON

Strive to be one of the few who walk this earth with the ever present realization—every morning, noon, and night—that the unknown that people call heaven is directly behind those things that are visible.

~~~~~~ JULY 27 ~~~~~~

Morning

Your name will no longer be Jacob, but Israel, because you have
struggled with God and with humans and have overcome.
GENESIS 32:28

Napoleon was once reviewing his troops near Paris. The horse on which he sat was restless, and the Emperor having thoughtlessly dropped the reins from his hand in the eagerness of giving a command, the spirited animal bounded away, and the rider was in danger of being hurled to the ground. A young private standing in the lines leaped forward and, seizing the bridle, saved his beloved Commander from a fall. The Emperor, glancing at him, said in his quick abrupt way, "Thank you, Captain." The private looked up with a smile and asked, "Of what regiment, sir?" "Of my guards," answered Napoleon and instantly galloped to another part of the field.

The young soldier laid down his musket with the remark, "Whoever will may carry that gun; I am done with it," and proceeded at once to join a group of officers who stood conversing at a little distance. One of them, a General, observing his self-possessed approach, angrily said, "What is this insolent fellow doing here?"

"This insolent fellow," answered the young soldier looking the other steadily in the eye, "is a Captain of the Guards." "Why, man," responded the officer, "you are insane;

why do you speak thus?" *"He said it,"* replied the soldier, pointing to the Emperor, who was far down the lines. "I beg your pardon, Captain," politely returned the General, "I was not aware of your promotion."

To those looking on he was still a private, dressed in the coarse rough garb of a common soldier; but in the bold assertion of his dignity, he could meet all the jeers of his comrades and all the scoffs of his superiors with the ready reply, "He said it."

He said it! He said it!

<hr>

JULY 27

Evening

Test me in this . . . and see if I will not throw open the floodgates of heaven and pour out so much blessing that there will not be room enough to store it.

MALACHI 3:10

Here is what God is saying in this verse: "My dear child, I still have floodgates in heaven, and they are still in service. The locks open as easily as before, and the hinges have not grown rusty. In fact, I would rather throw them open to pour out the blessings than hold them back. I opened them for Moses, and the sea parted. I opened them for Joshua, and the Jordan River was stopped. I opened them for Gideon, and the armies of the enemy fled. And I will open them for you—*if you will only let Me.*

"On My side of the floodgates, heaven is still the same rich storehouse as always. The fountains and streams still overflow, and the treasure-rooms are still bursting with gifts. The need is not on *My* side but on *yours.* I am waiting for you to '*test me in this.*' But you must first meet the condition I have set to 'bring the whole tithe into the storehouse' [Malachi 3:10], and thereby *give Me the opportunity to act.*" SELECTED

I will never forget my mother's concise paraphrase of Malachi 3:10. The actual Bible text begins with the words "Bring the whole tithe into the storehouse" and ends with "I will . . . pour out so much blessing that," in effect, "you will be embarrassed over your lack of space to receive it." But my mother's paraphrase was this: "Give all He asks and take all He promises." SAMUEL DICKEY GORDON

God's ability to perform is far beyond our prayers—even our greatest prayers! I have recently been thinking of some of the requests I have made of Him innumerable times in my prayers. And what have I requested? I have asked for a cupful, while He owns the entire ocean! I have asked for one simple ray of light, while He holds the sun! My best asking falls immeasurably short of my Father's ability to give, which is far beyond what we could ever ask. JOHN HENRY JOWETT

All the rivers of Your grace I claim,
Over every promise write my name. [Ephesians 1:8–19.]

~~~~~ JULY 28 ~~~~~

Morning

Why this waste?
MARK 14:4

There is nothing that seems more prodigal than the waste of nature. The showers fall and sink into the ground, and seem to be lost. The rain cometh down from heaven and returneth not thither; the rivers run into the sea, and become absorbed in the ocean's brine. All this seems like a waste of precious material; and yet, science has taught us that no force is ever wasted, but simply converted into another form in which it goes on its way with an altered ministry, but an undiminished force.

Someone has represented in a sort of poetic parable a little raindrop trembling in the air and questioning with the Genius of the sky whether it should fall upon the earth or still linger in the beautiful cloud.

"Why should I be lost and buried in the dirty soil? Why should I disappear in the dark mud, when I may glisten like a diamond or shine like an emerald or ruby in the rainbow's arch?"

"Yes," the Genius agrees; "but, if you fall in the earth you will come forth with a better resurrection in the petal of the flower, in the fragrance of the rose, in the hanging cluster of the vine."

And so, at last, the timid crystal drops one tear of regret, disappears beneath the soil, and is speedily drunk by the parched ground; it has gone out of sight—apparently out of existence. But lo! the root of yonder lily drinks in the moisture; the sap vessels of that damask rose absorb its refreshing draft; the far-reaching rootlet of yonder vine has found that fountain of life—and in a little while that raindrop comes forth in the snowy blossom of the lily, in the rich perfume of the rose, in the purple cluster of the vine, and as it meets once more the Genius of the air it answers back its glad acknowledgment: "Yes, I died, but I have risen, and now I live in a higher ministry, in a larger life, in a better resurrection." A. B. SIMPSON

Pour out thy love like the rush of a river,
Wasting its waters forever and ever,
Through the burnt sands that reward not the giver:
Silent or songful, thou nearest the sea.
Scatter thy life as the summer's shower pouring;
What if no bird through the pearl rain is soaring?
What if no blossom looks upward adoring?
Look to the life that was lavished for thee!

So the wild wind strews its perfumed caresses:
Evil and thankless the desert it blesses;
Bitter the wave that its soft pinion presses;
Never it ceases to whisper and sing.
What if the hard heart give thorns for thy roses?
What if on rocks thy tired bosom reposes?
Sweeter is music with minor-keyed closes,
Fairest the vines that on ruin will cling.

JULY 28

Evening

His way is in the whirlwind and the storm.
NAHUM 1:3

I remember when I was a young person attending school in the vicinity of Mount Pleasant. One day I sat on the side of the mountain and watched a storm as it moved through the valley. The skies were filled with darkness, and thunder began to shake the earth. It seemed as though the lush landscape were completely changed, and its beauty gone forever. But the storm passed quickly and soon moved out of the valley.

If I had sat in the same place the following day and said, "Where is that intense storm and all its terrible darkness?" the grass would have said, "Part of it is in me." The beautiful daisy would have said, "Part of it is in me." And all the other flowers, fruits, and everything that grows in the ground would have said, "Part of the storm has produced the radiance in me."

Have you ever asked the Lord to make you like Him? Have you ever desired the fruit of the Spirit and prayed for sweetness, gentleness, and love? If so, then never fear the fierce storms that even now may be blowing through your life. Storms bring blessings, and rich fruit will be harvested later. HENRY WARD BEECHER

> *The flowers live by the tears that fall*
> *From the sad face of the skies;*
> *And life would have no joys at all,*
> *Were there no watery eyes.*
> *Love the sorrow, for grief will bring*
> *Its own reward in later years;*
> *The rainbow! See how fair a thing*
> *God has built up from tears.*
>
> HENRY S. SUTTON

JULY 29
Morning

Do you not know that your bodies are temples of the Holy Spirit, who is in you, whom you have received from God? You are not your own; you were bought at a price. Therefore honor God with your bodies.
1 CORINTHIANS 6:19–20

The Christian who truly enters into these two verses has solved some of the deepest problems in life. Those who recognize God's absolute proprietorship of their bodies are not long in doubt as to where they should go or what they should do. *Consecration is simply a matter of letting God have what He has paid for, or returning stolen property.*

"You were bought at a price." It was an infinite price that God paid. It was something more than silver and gold—the precious Blood of His only begotten Son (1 Peter 1:18–19). God emphasizes the tremendous cost of redemption as an appeal to the heart of the redeemed. The price He has paid measures His estimate of us. He does not give *a life so dear to Him for a soul that is worth nothing to Him.* He has laid down the gold of His heart—even Jesus Christ. If we would go and stand on Calvary's hill and consider what it has cost heaven to purchase our salvation, we could not long withhold from Him what He rightfully owns—*the full service of spirit, soul, and body.* Yet how many are satisfied to say, "Jesus is mine," who never go on to say, "I am His." *One who takes this higher ground is bound to be careful what he does with property which belongs to another.*

When the thought of His proprietorship becomes uppermost, then we will simultaneously recognize the fact that being His, we are temples of the Holy Spirit. Conscious of God's ownership and thoughtful of our Divine Guest—the Holy Spirit—it is only natural that *we should glorify God in our bodies and in our spirits, which are His.* To glorify Him thus is simply to exhibit the power and character of God in that which is His.

The Christian's greatest joy is found in letting God possess His own property.

JULY 29
Evening

Have you entered the storehouses . . . which I reserve for times of trouble?
JOB 38:22–23

Our trials are great opportunities, but all too often we simply see them as large obstacles. If only we would recognize every difficult situation as something God has chosen to prove His love to us, each obstacle would then become a place of shelter and rest, and a demonstration to others of His inexpressible power. If we would look for the signs of His glorious handiwork, then every cloud would indeed become a rainbow, and every difficult mountain path would become one of ascension, transformation, and glorification.

If we would look at our past, most of us would realize that the times we endured the greatest stress and felt that every path was blocked were the very times our heavenly Father chose to do the kindest things for us and bestow His richest blessings.

God's most beautiful jewels are often delivered in rough packages by very difficult people, but within the package we will find the very treasures of the King's palace and the Bridegroom's love. A. B. SIMPSON

We must trust the Lord through the darkness, and honor Him with unwavering confidence even in the midst of difficult situations. The reward of this kind of faith will be like that of an eagle shedding its feathers is said to receive—a renewed sense of youth and strength. J. R. MACDUFF

> *If we could see beyond today*
> *As God can see;*
> *If all the clouds should roll away,*
> *The shadows flee;*
> *O'er present griefs we would not fret.*
> *Each sorrow we would soon forget,*
> *For many joys are waiting yet*
> *For you and me.*
>
> *If we could know beyond today*
> *As God does know,*
> *Why dearest treasures pass away*
> *And tears must flow;*
> *And why the darkness leads to light,*
> *Why dreary paths will soon grow bright;*
> *Some day life's wrongs will be made right,*
> *Faith tells us so.*
>
> *"If we could see, if we could know,"*
> *We often say,*
> *But God in love a veil does throw*
> *Across our way;*

We cannot see what lies before,
And so we cling to Him the more,
He leads us till this life is o'er;
Trust and obey.

<hr>

JULY 30
Morning

But the LORD will be a refuge for his people,
a stronghold for the people of Israel.
JOEL 3:16

Soldiers may be wounded in battle and sent to the hospital. A hospital isn't a shelf; it is a place of repair.

A soldier on service in the spiritual army is never off his battlefield. He is only removed to another part of the field when a wound interrupts what he meant to do, and sets him doing something else.

Is it not joy, pure joy, that there is no question of *the shelf*? No soldier on service is ever "laid aside"; he is only given another commission to fight among the unseen forces of the field. Never is he shelved as of no further use to his beloved Captain! The soldier must let his Captain say when and for what He needs him most, and he must not cloud his mind with questions. A wise master never wastes his servant's time, nor a commander his soldiers'. So let us settle it once for all and find heart's ease in doing so. *There is no discharge in warfare*—no, not for a single day. We may be called to serve on the visible field, going continually into the invisible both to renew our strength and to fight the kind of battle that can only be fought there. Or we may be called off the visible altogether for a while and drawn deep into the invisible. That dreary word "laid aside" is never for *us*. *We* are soldiers of the King! ROSE FROM BRIER

Place of repair: O blessed place of refuge!
How gladly will I come to meet Him there,
To cease awhile from all the joy of service
To find a deeper joy with Him to share.

Place of repair: for tired brain and body!
How much I need that place just out of sight
Where only He can talk, and be beside me,
Until again made strong by His great might.

Place of repair: when trials press upon me
And God permits the unexpected test,
'Tis there I learn some lesson sweet and precious
As simply on His faithfulness I rest.

Place of repair: the place to take my sorrow,
The thing that hurts and would be hard to bear,
But somehow in the secret place I'm finding
That all the hurt is healed since He is there.

Place of repair: to wait for fresh enduement
I silently with Him alone would stay
Until He speaks again, and says,
"Go forward to help some other sheep to find the way."

Place of repair: O trysting-place most hallowed,
The Lord Himself is just that place to me,
His grace, His strength, His glory and His triumph,
Himself alone my all-sufficiency.

JULY 30
Evening

If anyone gives even a cup of cold water . . . that
person will certainly not lose [his] reward.
MATTHEW 10:42

What shall I do? I expect to pass through this world but once. Therefore any good work, kindness, or service I can render to any person or animal, let me do it now. Let me not neglect or delay to do it, for I will not pass this way again. QUAKER SAYING

It isn't the thing you do, dear,
It's the thing you leave undone,
That gives you the bitter heartache
At the setting of the sun;
The tender word unspoken,
The letter you did not write,
The flower you might have sent, dear,
Are your haunting ghosts at night.

The stone you might have lifted
Out of your brother's way,
The bit of heartfelt counsel
You were hurried too much to say;
The loving touch of the hand, dear,
The gentle and winsome tone,
That you had no time or thought for,
With troubles enough of your own.

These little acts of kindness,
So easily out of mind,
These chances to be angels,
Which even mortals find—
They come in nights of silence,
To take away the grief,
When hope is faint and feeble,
And a drought has stopped belief.

For life is all too short, dear.
And sorrow is all too great,
To allow our slow compassion
That tarries until too late.

And it's not the thing you do,
dear, It's the thing you leave undone,
That gives you the bitter heartache,
At the setting of the sun.

ADELAIDE PROCTOR

Give what you have, for you never know—to someone else it may be better than you can even dare to think. HENRY WADSWORTH LONGFELLOW

~~~~~~~ JULY 31 ~~~~~~~
Morning

Unto him shall the gathering of the people be.
GENESIS 49:10 KJV

What a scene of unimaginable grandeur that will be, when at last *all nations are gathered to His Feet!* That will include representatives from all the European States, from Iceland in the far North to Greece in the South, and from Portugal in the West to hidden saints of God in Soviet Russia in the East. There will be many from Algeria, Morocco, and the Atlas mountains; from Egypt and the Nile Valley; from the sandy deserts and the mountains of the Sahara; from the great lakes in Central Africa, from the banks of the Niger, the Calabar, the Congo, and the Zambesi rivers; and from the uplands of South Africa. There will be *gathered to Christ* many from Palestine, Transjordan, and Arabia; India will contribute her millions; and even from closed lands like Nepal, Sikkim, and Tibet, *Christ will gather His own.*

From the Islands in the Dutch East Indies they will come—Java, Sumatra, Bali, Celebes, Lombok, Soembawa, Borneo, and the rest, and *will be gathered to the feet of the Redeemer.* From the teeming millions of Central Asia, from China, Japan, Korea, Manchukuo, and Mongolia, there will be an immense home-going to the Savior. From the myriad Islands of the Pacific, the peoples of Polynesia and Melanesia will *be gathered to the Lord who redeemed them.*

From Australia and New Zealand there will be multitudes who will *join in the glad song of praise.* From every republic of Central, South, and North America, and from the West Indies Islands—Cuba, Haiti, Jamaica, Puerto Rico, and the Lesser Antilles, *they will come.* From the far-off forests and lakes of Canada *there will be a similar home-going.*

Whether the tongues be those of the white race, or of the red, or of the black, *the gathering to Christ* will be overwhelmingly splendid.

> *From earth's wide bounds, from ocean's farthest coast,*
> *Through gates of pearl streams in the countless host,*
> *Singing to Father, Son, and Holy Ghost, "Hallelujah!"*
>
> BIBLE SOCIETY RECORD

> *I hear ten thousand voices singing*
> *Their praises to the Lord on high;*
> *Far distant shores and hills are ringing*
> *With anthems of their nation's joy:*
>
> *Praise ye the Lord! for He hath given*
> *To lands in darkness hid, His light,*
> *As morning rays light up the heaven,*
> *His word has chased away our night.*
>
> *Hark! Hark! a louder sound is booming*
> *O'er heaven and earth, o'er land and sea;*
> *The angel's trump proclaims His coming—*
> *Our day of endless Jubilee.*
> *Hail to Thee, Lord! Thy people praise Thee;*
> *In every land Thy Name we sing;*
> *On heaven's eternal throne upraise Thee,*
> *Take Thou Thy power, Thou glorious King!*
>
> HYMNS OF CONSECRATION AND FAITH

Evening

With skillful hands he led them.
PSALM 78:72

When you are unsure which course to take, totally submit your own judgment to that of the Spirit of God, asking Him to shut every door except the right one. But meanwhile keep moving ahead and consider the absence of a direct indication from God to be the evidence of His will that you are on His path. And as you continue down the long road, you will find that He has gone before you, locking doors you otherwise would have been inclined to enter. Yet you can be sure that somewhere beyond the locked doors is one He has left unlocked. And when you open it and walk through, you will find yourself face to face with a turn in the river of opportunity—one that is broader and deeper than anything you ever dared to imagine, even in your wildest dreams. So set sail on it, because it flows to the open sea.

God often guides us through our circumstances. One moment, our way may seem totally blocked, but then suddenly some seemingly trivial incident occurs, appearing as nothing to others but speaking volumes to the keen eye of faith. And sometimes these events are repeated in various ways in response to our prayers. They certainly are not haphazard results of chance but are God opening up the way we should walk, by directing our circumstances. *And they begin to multiply as we advance toward our goal,* just as the lights of a city seem to increase as we speed toward it while traveling at night. F. B. MEYER

If you go to God for guidance, He will guide you. But do not expect Him to console you by showing you His list of purposes concerning you, when you have displayed distrust or even half-trust in Him. What He will do, if you will trust Him and go cheerfully ahead when He shows you the way, is to guide you still farther. HORACE BUSHNELL

> *As moves my fragile boat across the storm-swept sea,*
> *Great waves beat o'er her side, as north wind blows;*
> *Deep in the darkness hid lie threat'ning rocks and reefs;*
> *But all of these, and more, my Pilot knows.*

Sometimes when darkness falls, and every light's gone out,
I wonder to what port my frail ship goes;
Although the night be long, and restless all my hours,
My distant goal, I'm sure, my Pilot knows.
THOMAS CURTIS CLARK

AUGUST 1

Morning

Tell me, you whom I love . . . where you rest your sheep at midday.
SONG OF SONGS 1:7

We have lost the art of "resting at midday." Many are slowly succumbing to the strain of life because they have forgotten how to rest. The steady stream, the continuous uniformity of life, is what kills.

Rest is not a sedative for the sick, but a tonic for the strong. It spells emancipation, illumination, transformation. It saves us from becoming slaves even of good works.

One of our Cambridge naturalists told me once of an experiment he had made with a pigeon. The bird had been born in a cage and had never been free; one day his owner took the bird out on the porch of the house and flung it into the air. To the naturalist's surprise the bird's capacity for flight was perfect. Round and round it flew as if born in the air; but soon its flight grew excited, panting, and the circles grew smaller, until at last the bird dashed full against its master's breast and fell to the ground. What did it mean? It meant that, though the bird had inherited the instinct of flight, it had not inherited the capacity to stop, and if it had not risked the shock of a sudden halt the little life would have been panted out in the air.

Isn't that a parable of many a modern life: completely endowed with the instinct of action but without the capacity to stop? Round and round life goes in its weary circle until it is almost dying at full speed. Any shock, even some severe experience, is a mercy if it checks the whirl. Sometimes God stops such a soul abruptly by some sharp blow of trouble, and the soul falls in despair at His Feet, and then He bends over it and says: "Be still, my child; be still, and know that I am God!" until by degrees the despair of trouble is changed into submission and obedience, and the poor, weary, fluttering life is made strong to fly again.

> *When, spurred by tasks unceasing or undone,*
> *You would seek rest afar,*
> *And cannot, though repose be rightly won—*
> *Rest where you are.*

> *Neglect the needless; sanctify the rest;*
> *Move without stress or jar;*
> *With quiet of a spirit self-possessed*
> *Rest where you are.*

> *Not in event, restriction, or release,*
> *Not in scenes near or far,*
> *But in ourselves are restlessness or peace:*
> *Rest where you are.*

> *Where lives the soul lives God; His day, His world,*
> *No phantom mists need mar;*
> *His starry nights are tents of peace unfurled:*
> *Rest where you are.*

Is it so long since we trod the road to our "resting-place," that the path has become a jungle?

~~~~~~ AUGUST 1 ~~~~~~
Evening

Offer yourselves to God as those who have been brought from death to life.
ROMANS 6:13

One night I went to hear a sermon on consecration. Nothing special came to me from the message, but as the preacher knelt to pray, he said, "O Lord, You know we can trust the Man who died for us." That was my message. As I rose from my knees and walked down the street to catch the train, I deeply pondered all that consecration would mean to my life. I was afraid as I considered the personal cost, and suddenly, above the noise of the street traffic, came this message: "You can trust the Man who died for you." I boarded the train, and as I traveled toward home, I thought of the changes, sacrifices, and disappointments that consecration might mean in my life—and I was still afraid.

Upon arriving home, I went straight to my room, fell on my knees, and saw my life pass before my eyes. I was a Christian, an officer in the church, and a Sunday school superintendent, but I had never yielded my life to God with a definite act of my will. Yet as I thought of my own "precious" plans that might be thwarted, my beloved hopes to be surrendered, and my chosen profession that I might have to abandon—*I was afraid*.

I completely failed to see the better things God had for me, so my soul was running from Him. And then for the last time, with a swift force of convicting power to my inmost heart, came that searching message: "*My child, you can trust the Man who died for you. If you cannot trust Him, then whom can you trust?*" Finally that settled it for me, for in a flash of light I realized that the Man who loved me enough to die for me could be absolutely trusted with the total concerns of the life He had saved.

Dear friend, you can trust the Man who died for you. You can trust Him to thwart each plan that should be stopped and to complete each one that results in His greatest glory and your highest good. You can trust Him to lead you down the path that is the very best in this world for you. J. H. M.

> *Just as I am, Thy love unknown,*
> *Has broken every barrier down,*
> *Now to be Thine, yea, Thine alone,*
> *O Lamb of God, I come!*

Life is not wreckage to be saved out of the world but an investment to be used in the world.

Morning

They waited for me as for showers and drank in my words as the spring rain.
JOB 29:23

The LORD *will . . . satisfy your needs in a sun-scorched land. . . . You will*
be like a well-watered garden, like a spring whose waters never fail.
ISAIAH 58:11

Travelers are enthusiastic over a species of palm tree which grows in South America. They call it *the rain tree.* This tree has the remarkable power of attracting, in a wondrous degree, atmospheric moisture, which it condenses and drops on the earth in refreshing dew. It grows straight up in the parched and arid desert and daily distributes its refreshing showers, with the result that around it an oasis of luxuriant vegetation soon springs up. The floodgates of heaven refuse to open, the fountains cease to flow, the rivers evaporate—all true, but the rain tree, getting its moisture from above, renews the garden which it has created about its base, and gives the weary traveler shade and fruit, a new life and a delightful rest!

God would have *us* to be like the rain tree growing alongside the desert highways of the world—sources of new spiritual life. God *Himself* is our atmosphere, and we carry our atmosphere with us wherever we go.

This atmosphere is proof against all infection, and to breathe it is constant health.

Christ's power was in His separateness. He did not withdraw Himself from the world but lived in the very midst of it. No man ever came into such close external contact with the devil. Jesus was not a recluse. He was social—mingling with men, yet He kept intact His separateness from the world. He was *Jesus!* Men felt this! This was His power!

In the secret of Christ's power, we see the secret of *our* power. If we are to have any power in the world we must become partakers of His holiness; we must be *separated* with Him and be *kept separated* and set apart to the same great life.

The angel, grateful for each borrowed sense,
Gazed at the sight:

A girl so white,
With slender fingers tense
Upon the table edge (around his head
The smell of new-baked bread)
The while unhurried tones fell low, and clear,
And near.
Alone, yet not alone, yet not alone,
She fell not prone;
But leaning a little against the wall,
The while the sun grew late,
She knew . . . she knew . . . she knew—why
all Her life she had been separate.
                 "THE ANNUNCIATION" BY FLORENCE G. MAGEE

"To reveal his Son in me" (Galatians 1:16).

~~~~~~ AUGUST 2 ~~~~~~

Evening

I will turn all my mountains into roads.
ISAIAH 49:11

God will make our obstacles serve His purposes. We all have mountains in our lives, and often they are people and things that threaten to block the progress of our spiritual life. The obstacles may be untruths told about us; a difficult occupation; "a thorn in [the] flesh" (2 Corinthians 12:7); or our daily cross. And often we pray for their removal, for we tend to think that if only these were removed, we would live a more tender, pure, and holy life.

"How foolish you are, and how slow to believe . . . !" (Luke 24:25). These are the very conditions we need for achievement, and they have been put in our lives as the means of producing the gifts and qualities for which we have been praying so long. We pray for patience for many years, and when something begins to test us beyond our endurance, we run from it. We try to avoid it, we see it as some insurmountable obstacle to our desired goal, and we believe that if it was removed, we would experience immediate deliverance and victory.

This is not true! We would simply see the temptations to be impatient end. This would not be patience. The only way genuine patience can be acquired is by enduring the very trials that seem so unbearable today.

Turn from your running and submit. Claim by faith to be a partaker in the patience of Jesus and face your trials in Him. There is nothing in your life that distresses or concerns you that cannot become submissive to the highest purpose. Remember, they are *God's* mountains. He puts them there for a reason, and we know He will never fail to keep His promise.

"God understands the way to it and he alone knows where it dwells, for he views the ends of the earth and sees everything under the heavens" (Job 28:23–24). So when we come to the foot of the mountains, we will find our way. F. B. MEYER

The purpose of our trials is not only to test our worthiness but also to increase it, just as the mighty oak is tested by the storms as well as strengthened by them.

AUGUST 3

Morning

Christ in you, the hope of glory.
COLOSSIANS 1:27

The greatest thing that any of us can do is not to live for Christ but to live Christ. What is holy living? It is Christ-life. It is not to be Christians, but Christ-ones. It is not to try to do or be some great thing but simply to have Him and let Him live His own life in us; abiding in Him and He in us, and letting Him reflect His own graces, His own faith, His own consecration, His own love, His own patience, His own gentleness, His own words in us, while we "declare the praises of him who called [us] out of darkness into his wonderful light" (1 Peter 2:9). *This is at once the sublimest and the simplest life that it is possible to live.* It is a higher standard than human perfection, and yet it is possible for a poor, sinful, imperfect man to realize it through the perfect Christ who comes to live within us.

God help us so to live, and thus to make real to those around us, the simplicity, the beauty, the glory, and the power of the Christ life.

"I cannot tell," said the humble shepherd's wife, "what sermon it was that led me into a life of victory. I cannot even explain the creed or the catechism, but I know that something has changed me entirely. Last summer John and I washed the sheep in yonder stream. I cannot tell you where the water went, but I can show you the clean white fleece of the sheep. And so I may forget the doctrine, but I have its blessed fruit in my heart and life."

Two of us were chatting with Sadhu Sundar Singh in my office one morning. The Sadhu had just arrived in London. We knew little concerning him, and my friend was anxious to find out if he knew the doctrine of that "perfect love" of which Saint John speaks.

"Does he understand?" asked my friend, turning to me.

The Sadhu smiled and quietly said: "When I throw a stone at the fruit tree, the fruit tree throws no stone back, but gives me *fruit*. Is it that?" Then he went on to ask: "Should not we, who love the Lord Jesus, be like sandalwood, which imparts its fragrance to the ax which cuts it?" SELECTED

AUGUST 3

Evening

Be courageous; be strong.
1 CORINTHIANS 16:13

Never pray for an easier life—pray to be a stronger person! Never pray for tasks equal to your power—pray for power equal to your tasks. Then doing your work will be no miracle—*you* will be the miracle. PHILLIPS BROOKS

We must remember that Christ will not lead us to greatness through an easy or self-indulgent life. An easy life does not lift us up but only takes us down. Heaven is always above us, and we must continually be looking toward it.

Some people always avoid things that are costly, or things that require self-denial, self-restraint, and self-sacrifice. Yet it is hard work and difficulties that ultimately lead us to greatness, for greatness is not found by walking the moss-covered path laid out for us through the meadow. It is found by being sent to carve out our own path with our own hands.

Are you willing to sacrifice to reach the glorious mountain peaks of God's purpose for you? SELECTED

> *Be strong!*
> *We are not here to play, to dream, to drift;*
> *We have hard work to do, and loads to lift.*
> *Shun not the struggle; face it.*
> > *It's God's gift.*
> > *Be strong!*
> *Say not the days are evil—Who's to blame?*
> *Or fold your hands, as in defeat—O shame!*
> *Stand up, speak out, and bravely,*
> > *In God's name.*
> > *Be strong!*
> *It matters not how deep entrenched the wrong,*
> *How hard the battle goes, the day how long,*
> *Faint not, fight on!*
> > *Tomorrow comes the song.*
> > MALTBIE D. BABCOCK

AUGUST 4

Morning

> The LORD *is good to those whose hope is in him, to the one who seeks*
> *him; it is good to wait quietly for the salvation of the* LORD.
> LAMENTATIONS 3:25–26

It is easier to work than to wait. It is often more important to wait than to work. *We can trust God to do the needed working while we are waiting;* but if we are not willing to wait, and insist upon working while He would have us be still, we may interfere with the effective and triumphant working that He would do in our behalf.

Our waiting may be the most difficult thing we can do; it may be the severest test that God can give us.

Oswald Chambers has said truly: one of the greatest strains in life is the strain of *waiting for God*. God takes the saint like a bow which He stretches; we get to a certain point and say *I cannot stand any more*, but God goes on stretching. He is not aiming at our mark but at His own, and the patience of the saints is that we hold on until He lets the arrow fly straight to His goal. If we are willing to remember God's call and assurance, there need be no strain at all while we are waiting. The stretched bow time may be a time of unbroken rest for us as we are "still before the LORD and wait patiently for him" (Psalm 37:7).

Unless a violin string is stretched until it cries out when the bow is drawn over it, there is no music. A loose violin string with no strain upon it is of no use—it is dead, has no voice. But when stretched till it strains, it is brought to the proper tone, and then only is it useful to the music-maker. A. B. SIMPSON

> In God's eternal plan, a month, a year,
> Is but an hour of some slow April day,
> Holding the germs of what we hope or fear,
> To blossom far away.

The Almighty is tedious, *but He's sure!*

<hr>

AUGUST 4
Evening

Jesus looked up and said, "Father, I thank you that you have heard me."
JOHN 11:41

The sequence of events in this passage seems strange and unusual. Lazarus was still in his tomb, yet Jesus' thanksgiving *preceded* the miracle of raising him from the dead. It seems that thanks would only have been lifted up once the great miracle had been accomplished and Lazarus had been restored to life. But Jesus gave thanks for what He was about to receive. His gratitude sprang forth *before* the blessing had arrived, in an expression of assurance that it was certainly on its way. The song of victory was sung *before* the battle had been fought. It was the Sower singing the song of harvest—it was thanksgiving before the miracle!

Who ever thinks of announcing a victory song as the army is just heading out to the battlefield? And where do we ever hear a song of gratitude and thanksgiving for an answer that has not yet been received?

Yet in this Scripture passage, there is nothing strange, forced, or unreasonable to the Master's sequence of praise before the miracle. *Praise* is actually the most vital preparation to the working of miracles. Miracles are performed through spiritual power, and our spiritual power is always in proportion to our *faith.* JOHN HENRY JOWETT

Praise changes things.

Nothing pleases God more than praise as part of our prayer life, and nothing blesses someone who prays as much as the praise that is offered. I once received a great blessing from this while in China. I had recently received bad news from home, and deep shadows of darkness seemed to cover my soul. I prayed but the darkness remained. I forced myself to endure but the shadows only deepened. Then suddenly one day, as I entered a missionary's home at an inland station, I saw these words on the wall: "Try giving thanks." So I did, and in a moment every shadow was gone, never to return. Yes, the psalmist was right: "It is good to praise the LORD" (Psalm 92:1). HENRY W. FROST

~~~~~ AUGUST 5 ~~~~~

Morning

My God in His lovingkindness will meet me; God will
let me look triumphantly upon my foes.
PSALM 59:10 NASB

It matters not how great the scheme if God draws it out; it matters not how insurmountable the difficulties appear if God undertakes the responsibility. *If we, His children, when we get into tangled corners even by our own folly and sometimes wrongdoing, would only turn to God as a King and as a Father and cast ourselves upon Him,*

He would work for us and lead us out of our troubles safely and in a manner worthy of a King.

> *This morning, Lord, I pray*
> *Safeguard us through the day,*
> *Especially at corners of the way.*
>
> *For when the way is straight,*
> *We fear no sudden fate,*
> *But see ahead the evening's open gate.*
>
> *But few and far between*
> *Are days when all is seen*
> *Of what will come, or yet of what has been.*
> *For unexpected things*
> *Swoop down on sudden wings*
> *And overthrow us with their buffetings.*
>
> *And so, dear Lord, we pray,*
> *Control and guard this day*
> *Thy children at the corners of their way.*
> "CORNERS" BY M. G. L.

Dr. S. D. Gordon says in his writings: "*It is a good thing for us to be put in a tight corner.* To be pushed and hemmed in on every side until you are forced to stand with your back to the wall, facing a foe at every angle, with barely standing room—*that is good.* For one thing, you find out that *no matter how close the fit of that corner may be, it still can hold another in addition to yourself.* Its very tightness brings you and your Lord into the very closest quarters. And *only at closest touch will you find out what a wondrous Friend He is.*

Tight corners are famous places for chamber concerts. The acoustics are wonderful. David's exile Psalms have rung out a strangely sweet melody down all the ages, and out through all the world, and into thousands of hearts.

AUGUST 5

Evening

My grace is sufficient for you.
2 Corinthians 12:9

"God was pleased" (1 Corinthians 1:21) to take my youngest child from this world, under circumstances that caused me severe trials and pain. And as I returned home from the church cemetery, having just laid my little one's body in the grave, I felt a compulsion to preach to my people on the meaning of trials.

I found that the verse "My grace is sufficient for you" was the text of next week's Sunday school lesson, so I chose it as my Master's message to the congregation, as well as His message to me. Yet while trying to write the sermon, I found that in all honesty, I could not say that the words were true in my life. Therefore I knelt down and asked the Lord to make His grace sufficient for me. While I was pleading in this way, I opened my eyes and saw this exact verse framed and hanging on the wall. My mother had given it to me a few days before, when I was still at the vacation resort where our little child had been taken from us. I had asked someone to hang it on the wall at home during my absence but had not yet noticed its words. Now as I looked up and wiped my eyes, the words met my gaze: "My grace *is* sufficient for you."

The word "is" was highlighted in bright green, while the words "my" and "you" were painted in yet another color. In a moment, a message flashed straight to my soul, coming as a rebuke for having prayed such a prayer as, "Lord, make Your grace sufficient for me." His answer was almost an audible voice that said, "How dare you ask for something that *is*? I cannot make My grace any more sufficient than I have already made it. Get up and believe it, and you will find it to be true in your life."

The Lord says it in the simplest way: "My grace *is* [not will be or may be] sufficient for you." The words "my," "is," and "you" were from that moment indelibly written upon my heart. And thankfully, I have been trying to live in the reality of that truth from that day to the present time.

The underlying lesson that came to me through this experience, and that I seek to convey to others, is this: *Never change God's facts into hopes or prayers but simply accept them as realities, and you will find them to be powerful as you believe them.* H. W. Webb Peploe

— 542 —

He giveth more grace when the burdens grow greater,
He sendeth more strength when the labors increase;
To added affliction He addeth His mercies,
To multiplied trials His multiplied peace.

When we have exhausted our store of endurance,
When our strength has failed ere the day is half done,
When we reach the end of our hoarded resources
Our Father's full giving is only begun.

His love has no limit, His grace has no measure,
His power no boundary known unto men;
For out of His infinite riches in Jesus
He giveth and giveth and giveth again.

ANNIE JOHNSON FLINT

AUGUST 6
Morning

No purpose of yours can be thwarted.
JOB 42:2

We believe in the providence of God, but we do not believe half enough in it. Remember that Omnipotence has servants everywhere, set in their places at every point of the road. In the old days of the post horses, there were always swift horses ready to carry onward the king's mails.

It is wonderful how God has His relays of providential agents, how when He has done with one there is always another ready to take his place. Sometimes you have found one friend fail you—he is just dead and buried. "Ah!" you say, "what shall I do?" Well, well, *God knows how to carry on the purposes of His providence;* He will raise up another. How strikingly punctual providence is! You and I make appointments and miss them by half an hour, but *God never missed an appointment yet!* God never is before His time though *we* often wish He were; but He is never behind—no, *not by one tick of the clock.*

When the children of Israel were to go down out of Egypt, all the Pharaohs in the pyramids, if they had risen to life again, could not have kept them in bondage another half minute. "Thus saith the Lord . . . Let my people go!" It was time, and go they must! All the kings of the earth, and all the princes thereof, are in subjection to the kingdom of God's providence, and He can move them just as He pleases. And now, trembler, wherefore are you afraid? "Fear thou not; for I am with thee" (Isaiah 41:10 KJV). *All the mysterious arrangements of providence work for our good.* CHARLES H. SPURGEON

<hr>

AUGUST 6

Evening

*Awake, north wind, and come, south wind! Blow on my
garden, that its fragrance may spread everywhere.*
SONG OF SONGS 4:16

Let us examine the meaning of this prayer for a moment. It is rooted in the fact that in the same way beautiful fragrances may lie *hidden* in a spice plant, certain *gifts* may lie unused or undeveloped in a Christian's heart. Many seeds of a profession of faith may be planted, but from some the air is never filled with the aroma of holy desires or godly deeds. The same winds blow on the thistle and the spice plant, but only *one* of them emits a rich fragrance.

Sometimes God causes severe winds of trial to blow upon His children to develop their gifts. Just as a torch burns more brightly when waved back and forth, and just as a juniper plant smells sweetest when thrown into the flames, so the richest qualities of a Christian often arise under the strong winds of suffering and adversity. Bruised hearts often emit the fragrance that God loves to smell.

> *I had a tiny box, a precious box*
> *Of human love—my perfume of great price;*
> *I kept it close within my heart of hearts*
> *And scarce would lift the lid lest it should waste*
> *Its fragrance on the air. One day a strange*
> *Deep sorrow came with crushing weight, and fell*

Upon my costly treasure, sweet and rare,
And broke the box to pieces. All my heart
Rose in dismay and sorrow at this waste,
But as I mourned, behold a miracle
Of grace Divine. My human love was changed
To Heaven's own, and poured in healing streams
On other broken hearts, while soft and clear
A voice above me whispered, "Child of Mine,
With comfort wherewith you are comforted,
From this time forth, go comfort others,
And you will know blest fellowship with Me,
Whose broken heart of love has healed the world."

AUGUST 7
Morning

I Am Who I Am.
EXODUS 3:14

God is His own equivalent, and God needs nothing but Himself to achieve the great purposes on which He has set His heart.

God gave Moses a blank, and as life went forward for the next forty years, Moses kept filling in the blank with his special need. He *filled in fearlessness* before Pharaoh. He *filled in guidance* across the Red Sea. He *filled in manna* for the whole population. He *filled in water* from the rock. He *filled in guidance* through the wilderness. He *filled in victory* over Amalek. He *filled in clear revelation* at Sinai. And so Moses, for the rest of his life, had little else to do than to go quietly alone, and taking God's blank check-book, signed by God's name, *I Am Who I Am*, write in *I Am guidance; I Am bread*. He presented the check and God honored it.

And whenever you come to live upon God's plan as Moses from that moment did, *you may absolutely trust God*. And when you come down to the hoar-head you will say, *"Not one of all the good promises the* LORD *your God gave you has failed" (Joshua 23:14)*.
A. B. SIMPSON

Joshua had tried God forty years in the brick kilns, forty years in the desert, and thirty years in the Promised Land, and this was his dying testimony. D. L. Moody

> *Whatever life may bring to you,*
> *"God" will ring true to you:*
> *Star in your sky—*
> *Food in your store—*
> *Staff in your hand—*
> *Friend by your side—*
> *Light on your path—*
> *Joy in your heart—*
> *In your ears music—*
> *In your mouth songs.*
> *Yes, rapid as your race may run,*
> *And scorching as may shine your sun,*
> *And bitter as may blow your blast,*
> *And lonely as your lot be cast—*
> *Whatever life may bring to you,*
> *"God" will aye ring true to you.*
>
> Charles Herbert

AUGUST 7
Evening

After they prayed, the place where they were meeting was shaken. And they were all filled with the Holy Spirit and spoke the word of God boldly. . . . With great power the apostles continued to testify to the resurrection of the Lord Jesus.

Acts 4:31, 33

Christmas Evans, a Welsh preacher of the late-eighteenth and early-nineteenth centuries, once wrote the following account in his diary.

"One Sunday afternoon I was traveling by horseback to an appointment. Suddenly as I went along a very lonely road, I was convicted of having a cold heart. I dismounted, tethered my horse to a tree, and found a secluded spot. Then, walking back and forth in agony, I reviewed my life. I waited before God in brokenness and sorrow for three hours. Finally a sweet sense of His forgiving love broke over me, and I received a fresh filling of His Holy Spirit.

"As the sun was setting, I walked back to the road, found my horse, and rode on to my appointment. The following day I preached with so much new power, to a vast gathering of people on a hillside, that revival broke out and ultimately spread through all of Wales."

This explains the great question of the born-again—the password of the early church—"*Did you receive the Holy Spirit when you believed?*" (Acts 19:2).

Oh, the Spirit-filled life; is it thine, is it thine?
Is your soul wholly filled with the Spirit Divine?
As a child of the King, has He fallen on thee?
Does He reign in your soul, so that all men may see
The dear Savior's blest image reflected in thee?

Has He swept through your soul like the waves of the sea?
Does the Spirit of God daily rest upon thee?
Does He sweeten your life, does He keep you from care?
Does He guide you and bless you in answer to prayer?
Is your joy to be led of the Lord ev'rywhere?

Is He near you each hour, does He stand at your side?
Does He clothe you with strength, has He come to abide?
Does He teach you to know that all things may be done
Through the grace and the power of the Crucified One?
Does He witness to you of the glorified Son?

Has He purified you with the fire from above?
Is He first in your thoughts, does He have all your love?
Is His service your choice, and your sacrifice sweet?
Is your doing His will both your drink and your meat?
Do you run at His calling with glad eager feet?

Has He freed you from self and from all of your greed?
Do you hasten to comfort your brother in need?
As a soldier of Christ does your power endure?
Is your hope in the Lord everlasting and sure?
Are you patient and meek, are you tender and pure?

Oh, the Spirit-filled life may be thine, may be thine,
Ever in your soul Shechinah glory may shine;
It is yours to live with the tempests all stilled,
It is yours with God's blest Holy Spirit to be filled;
It is yours, even yours, for your Lord has so willed.

AUGUST 8
Morning

May he be like rain falling on a mown field.
PSALM 72:6

How grateful the soft rain must feel to the mown grass, all cut as it is, and, as we imagine it, so sore! But the rain is healing: and so God says He will come to His people "Like rain falling on a mown field."

There is so much in life that is like the cutting-machine, and the heart becomes sore and needs the healing influences that come from God. No matter what we may call that which is healing to us it is God coming "like rain . . . on a mown field." And may it be with us as with the beautiful lawns we admire: the more cutting and the more rain, the more beautiful we shall be; but *it must not be one, but both.* SELECTED

The absence of joy does not mean the absence of God.

The pruned vine does not suggest an absent vine-dresser, and even if the vine be bleeding it does not mean that he has gone away.

The mower's scythe had passed o'er summer fields,
The grass lay bleeding 'neath the summer sun;

— 548 —

Strong hands swift stored the harvest's wealthy yields,
And left the fields deserted, one by one.

Their glory gone, their beauty swept away,
Still smarting from the swift, keen cut of death,
Their woe the sharp, short work of one brief day
That dawned with sunshine in its balmy breath.
Methought they pleaded to the gentle sky
That smiled above them, bending o'er their grief,
A voiceless pleading in a tearless cry,
A soundless sob soft sighing for relief.

And heaven heard the fervor of their call,
And sent them healing balm at eventide,
Sweet raindrops breathing blessing in their fall,
And weeping gently o'er their wounded pride.

Thus shall He come as rain on new-mown grass,
And withered hopes spring up to grace His path,
New life be born where'er His footsteps pass,
And tender grass spring forth—"God's Aftermath."
FRANCES BROOK

AUGUST 8
Evening

You are my King and my God, who decrees victories for Jacob.
PSALM 44:4

There are no enemies to your growth in grace, or to your Christian work, that were not included in your Savior's victory. Remember, "The LORD said to Joshua, 'Do not be afraid of them, because . . . I will hand all of them . . . over to [you]'" (Joshua 11:6). Also recall the fact that when you resist your enemies, they "will flee from you" (James 4:7). And remember what Joshua said to the people: "Do not be afraid; do not be discouraged. Be strong and courageous" (Joshua 10:25). The Lord is with you, "mighty men of valour" (Joshua 1:14 KJV), and you are mighty because you are one with the Mightiest. So claim victory!

Whenever your enemies are closing in on you, *claim victory!* Whenever your heart and your flesh fail you, look up and claim VICTORY! Be sure you claim your share in the triumph that Jesus won, for He won it not for Himself alone but for us all. Remember that you were in Him when He won it—so *claim victory!*

Count Christ's victory as yours and gather the spoils of the war. Neither the giant "descendants of Anak" (Numbers 13:33) nor fortified cities need intimidate or defeat you. You are a part of the conquering army. *Claim your share in the Savior's victory.* F. B. MEYER

We are children of the King. Therefore which of these most honors our divine Sovereign: failing to claim our rights and even doubting they belong to us, or asserting our privilege as children of the Royal Family and demanding the rights that accompany our inheritance?

<hr />

AUGUST 9

Morning

His praise will always be on my lips.
PSALM 34:1

I heard a joyous strain—
A lark on a leafless bough
Sat singing in the rain.

I heard him singing early in the morning. It was hardly light! I could not understand that song; it was fairly a lilt of joy. It had been a portentous night for me, full of dreams that did disturb me. Old things that I had hoped to forget, and new things that I had prayed could never come, trooped through my dreams like grinning little barefaced imps. Certainly I was in no humor to sing. What could possess that fellow out yonder to be telling the whole township how joyous he was? He was perched on the rail fence by the spring run. *He was drenched.* It had rained in the night and evidently he had been poorly housed. I pitied him. What comfort could he have had through that night bathed in the storm? He never thought of comfort. His song was not bought by any such duplicity. It was in his heart. Then I shook myself: *The shame that a lark has finer poise than a man!* G. A. LEICHLITER

"Nothing can break you as long as you sing."

<hr>

AUGUST 9
Evening

Blessed are those whose strength is in you . . . As they pass through the Valley of Baca, they make it a place of springs.

PSALM 84:5–6

Comfort is not given to us when we are lighthearted and cheerful. We must travel the depths of emotion in order to experience comfort—one of God's most precious gifts. And then we must be prepared to become coworkers with Him.

When the shadows of night—needed night—gather over the garden of our souls, when leaves close up and flowers no longer reflect any sunlight within their folded petals, and when we experience even the thickest darkness, we must remember that we will never be found wanting and that the comforting drops of heavenly dew fall only after the sun has set.

> *I have been through the valley of weeping,*
> *The valley of sorrow and pain;*
> *But the "God of all comfort" was with me,*
> *At hand to uphold and sustain.*
>
> *As the earth needs the clouds and sunshine,*
> *Our souls need both sorrow and joy;*
> *So He places us oft in the furnace,*
> *The dross from the gold to destroy.*

When he leads through some valley of trouble,
    His omnipotent hand we trace;
For the trials and sorrows He sends us,
    Are part of His lessons in grace.

Oft we run from the purging and pruning,
    Forgetting the Gardener knows
That the deeper the cutting and trimming,
    The richer the cluster that grows.

Well He knows that affliction is needed;
    He has a wise purpose in view,
And in the dark valley He whispers,
    "Soon you'll understand what I do."

As we travel through life's shadowed valley,
    Fresh springs of His love ever rise;
And we learn that our sorrows and losses,
    Are blessings just sent in disguise.

So we'll follow wherever He leads us,
    Let the path be dreary or bright;
For we've proved that our God can give comfort;
    Our God can give songs in the night.

AUGUST 10
Morning

But whatever were gains to me I now consider loss for the sake of Christ.
PHILIPPIANS 3:7

If God has called you to be really like Christ, He may draw you into a life of cruci-fixion and humility and put on you such demands of obedience that He will not allow you to follow other Christians, and in many ways He will seem to let other good people do things which He will not let you do.

Other Christians, who seem very religious and useful, may push themselves, pull wires, and work schemes to carry out their plans, but *you cannot do it;* and if you attempt it you will meet with such failure and rebuke from the Lord as to make you sorely penitent.

Others may boast of themselves, of their work, of their success, of their writing, but *the Holy Spirit will not allow you to do any such thing,* and if you begin it He will lead you into some deep mortification that will make you despise yourself and all your good works.

Others will be allowed to succeed in making money . . . but it is likely *God will keep you poor* because He wants you to have something far better than gold, and that is a helpless dependence on Him, that He may have the privilege of supplying your needs day by day out of an unseen treasury.

The Lord will let others be honored and put forward, *and keep you hid away in obscurity* because He wants to produce some choice fragrant fruit for His coming glory.

He will let others be great, *but keep you small.* He will let others do a work for Him and get the credit for it, *but He will make you work and toil without knowing how much you are doing.*

The Holy Spirit will put a strict watch over you . . . rebuking you for little words and feelings or for wasting time.

God is an Infinite Sovereign: *He has a right to do as He pleases with His own.*

Settle it forever, then, that *you are to deal directly with the Lord Jesus—that He is to have the privilege of tying your tongue, chaining your hand, or closing your eyes* in ways that He does not deal with others.

Then, *you will have found the vestibule of heaven.*

Others may. You cannot!

—— AUGUST 10 ——

Evening

[Yet] when he heard that Lazarus was sick, he stayed where he was two more days.
JOHN 11:6

This miraculous story begins with the following declaration: "Jesus loved Martha and her sister and Lazarus" (v. 5). It is as if God were teaching us that at the very heart and foundation of all His dealings with us, no matter how dark and mysterious they may be, we must dare to believe in and affirm His infinite, unmerited, and unchanging love. Yet love permits pain to occur.

Mary and Martha never doubted that Jesus would quickly avert every obstacle to keep their brother from death, "yet when he heard that Lazarus was sick, he stayed where he was two more days."

What a startling word: "*Yet*"! Jesus refrained from going not because He did not love them but because He *did* love them. It was His love alone that kept Him from hurrying at once to their beloved yet grief-stricken home. Anything less than infinite love would have rushed instantly to the relief of those beloved and troubled hearts, in an effort to end their grief, to have the blessing of wiping and stopping the flow of their tears, and to cause their sorrow and pain to flee. Only the power of divine love could have held back the spontaneity of the Savior's tenderheartedness until the angel of pain had finished his work.

Who can estimate the great debt we owe to suffering and pain? If not for them, we would have little capacity for many of the great virtues of the Christian life. Where would our faith be if not for the trials that test it; or patience, without anything to endure or experience and without tribulations to develop it? SELECTED

> Loved! then the way will not be drear;
> For One we know is ever near,
> Proving it to our hearts so clear
>   That we are loved.
>
> Loved when our sky is clouded o'er,
> And days of sorrow press us sore;
> Still we will trust Him evermore,
>   For we are loved.
>
> Time, that affects all things below,
> Can never change the love He'll show;
> The heart of Christ with love will flow,
>   And we are loved.

Morning

And now, do not be distressed and do not be angry with yourselves for selling
me here, because it was to save lives that God sent me ahead of you.

GENESIS 45:5

When you are disappointed or vexed or hedged in or thwarted; when you are seemingly abandoned, *remember, son of God, heir of Heaven, that you are being prepared for the higher life.* You need courage, patience, perseverance, and it is in the hard places that they are developed. You need faith, and you will never have it unless you are brought to circumstances in which you are compelled to act by the invisible rather than the visible. You need those Christian graces of which the Bible speaks and of which the pulpit preaches; and practical life, with its various vicissitudes, is God's school in which you are to acquire these things. Do not be discouraged or cast down.

When you are bestead, remember that God is dealing with you as a good schoolmaster. You will thank Him for His severity by and by.

When God is dealing with you, do not accuse Him. Do not cry out, "Why hast thou forsaken me?" Remember, that to those who are exercised thereby God shows His love and His Fatherhood. Bow yourselves meekly to the chastisements of God, and study not how you can get away from the trouble but how you can rise above it by being made better by it.

> *I knew I had been sold,*
> *For circumstance*
> *Dark as a desert pit*
> *And dismal as the slaver's caravan*
> *Surrounded me,*
> *And seemed to crush me down;*
> *I had been sold.*
>
> *I also had been sent.*
> *The circumstance*
> *Shone with the light Divine,*

And through the wrath of men
God put me in His own appointed place.
He set on high
And none could bow me down.
I Had Been Sent.

"JOSEPH" BY M. MANNINGTON DEXTER

Had *we* no tests, no great hedged-in experiences, *we would never know what a wonderful Deliverer and triumphant Guide we have!*
He never limits us, except to liberate us!

~~~~~ AUGUST 11 ~~~~~

Evening

Though the fig tree does not bud and there are no grapes on the vines, though the olive crop fails and the fields produce no food, though there are no sheep in the pen and no cattle in the stalls, yet I will rejoice in the LORD, *I will be joyful in God my Savior.*
HABAKKUK 3:17–18

I ask you to observe what a disastrous situation is being described in this passage and to notice how courageous is the faith that is expressed. It is as if the writer were actually saying, "Even if I am forced to undergo the extreme condition of not knowing where to find my next meal, and although my house is empty and my fields yield no crops and I see the evidence of divine pestilence where I once saw the fruits of God's plentiful provision, *'yet I will rejoice in the Lord.'*"

I believe that these words are worthy of being *written forever in stone with a diamond tool.* Oh, by God's grace, may they be deeply etched on the tablets of each of our hearts! Although the above verse is very concise, it nevertheless implies or expresses the following thoughts of the writer: that in his time of distress he would flee to God; that he would maintain his spiritual composure under the darkest of circumstances; and that in the midst of everything, he would delight himself with a sacred joy in God and have cheerful expectations of Him.

Heroic confidence! Glorious faith! Unconquerable love! PHILIP DODDRIDGE

> *Last night I heard a robin singing in the rain,*
> *And the raindrop's patter made a sweet refrain,*
> *Making all the sweeter the music of the strain.*
>
> *So, I thought, when trouble comes, as trouble will,*
> *Why should I stop singing? Just beyond the hill*
> *It may be that sunshine floods the green world still.*
>
> *He who faces the trouble with a heart of cheer*
> *Makes the burden lighter. If there falls a tear,*
> *Sweeter is the cadence in the song we hear.*
>
> *I have learned your lesson, bird with spotted wing,*
> *Listening to your music with its tune of spring—*
> *When the storm cloud darkens, it's the time to sing.*
>
> EBEN EUGENE REXFORD

AUGUST 12

Morning

See how he loved him!
JOHN 11:36

He loved, yet lingered. We are so quick to think that delayed answer to prayer means that the prayer is not going to be answered. Dr. Stuart Holden has said truly: "Many a time we pray and are prone to interpret God's silence as a denial of our petitions; whereas, in truth, He only defers their fulfillment until such time as we ourselves are ready to cooperate to the full in His purposes." Prayer registered in heaven is prayer dealt with, although the vision still tarries.

Faith is trained to its supreme mission under the discipline of patience. The man who can wait God's time, knowing that *He* edits his prayer in wisdom and affection, will always discover that He never comes to man's aid one minute too soon or too late.

God's delay in answering the prayer of our longing heart is the most loving thing God can do. He may be waiting for us to come closer to Him, prostrate ourselves at His feet, and abide there in trustful submission *that His granting of the longed-for answer may mean infinitely greater blessing than if we received it anywhere else than in the dust at His feet.*

> *O wait, impatient heart!*
> *As winter waits, her songbirds fed.*
> *And every nestling blossom dead;*
> *Beyond the purple seas they sing!*
> *Beneath soft snows they sleep!*
> *They only sleep. Sweet patience keep*
> *And wait, as winter waits the spring.*

Nothing can hold our ship down when the tide comes in!

The aloe blooms but once in a hundred years; but every hour of all that century is needed to produce the delicate texture and resplendent beauty of the flower.

Faith heard the sound of "the tread of rain," and yet God made Elijah wait!

God never hastens, and He never tarries!

AUGUST 12

Evening

He has given us his very great and precious promises.
2 PETER 1:4

When a shipbuilder erects a boat, does he do so only to keep it on the scaffolding? No, he builds it to sail the seas and to weather the storms. In fact, if he does not think of strong winds and hurricanes as he builds it, he is a poor shipbuilder.

In the same way, when God made you a believer, He meant to test you. And when He gave you promises and asked you to trust them, He made His promises suitable for times of storms and high seas. Do you believe that some of His promises are counterfeit, similar to a life vest that looks good in the store but is of no use in the sea?

We have all seen swords that are beautiful but are useless in war, or shoes made for decoration but not for walking. Yet God's shoes are made of iron and brass, and we can walk all the way to heaven in them, without ever wearing them out. And we could swim the Atlantic a thousand times in His life vest, with no fear of ever sinking. His Word of promise is meant to be tried and tested.

There is nothing Christ dislikes more than for His people to publicly profess Him and then not use Him. He loves for us to make use of Him, for His covenant blessings are not simply meant to be looked at but should be appropriated. Our Lord Jesus has been given to us for our present use. Are you making use of Him as you should?

O beloved, I plead with you not to treat God's promises as something to be displayed in a museum but to use them as everyday sources of comfort. And whenever you have a time of need, trust the Lord. Charles H. Spurgeon

> Go to the depths of God's promise,
> And claim whatsoever you will;
> The blessing of God will not fail you,
> His Word He will surely fulfill.

How can God say no to something He has promised?

AUGUST 13

Morning

He is able to save completely.
Hebrews 7:25

What a magnificent prospect! Does it not take your breath away?
It may well do so; but nevertheless it is true, gloriously and eternally true, for it is written in the Word of God. *Grip that fact; grip it with your whole heart; take*

risks on it; stake your all on it; whisper it to yourself with clenched teeth when you are in the heat of the fight; shout it to the heavens when you see the enemy about to flee; triumph in it; exult in it!

Faith in this one thing can transfigure your whole life and lift you to the heights of victory and glory that once seemed to you as far off and remote as the distant snows of some shining mountain summit seem to the traveler when, through a haze of sunshine, he lifts up his eyes to gaze as at some holy thing up in the blue air.

Remember, *the life of sanctification and spiritual power can never be had cheaply. To bestow it upon us the Lord Jesus paid the price of Calvary.* To receive it we must be at least willing to pay the price of obedience to His simple conditions. Remember, too, *it is the only life worth living.* READER HARRIS

It costs to have a vision, but it costs too much to remember only the price.

~~~~~~ AUGUST 13 ~~~~~~

Evening

If clouds are full of water, they pour rain upon the earth.
ECCLESIASTES 11:3

If we believe the message of this verse, then why do we dread the clouds that darken our sky? It is true that for a while the dark clouds hide the sun, but it is not extinguished and it will soon shine again. Meanwhile those clouds are filled with rain, and the darker they are, the more likely they are to bring plentiful showers.

How can we have rain without clouds? Our troubles have always brought us blessings, and they always will, for they are the dark chariots of God's bright and glorious grace. Before long the clouds will be emptied, and every tender plant will be happier due to the showers. Our God may drench us with grief, but He will refresh us with His mercy. Our Lord's love letters often come to us in dark envelopes. His wagons may rumble noisily across the sky, but they are loaded with benefits. And His rod blossoms with sweet flowers and nourishing fruits. So let us not worry about the clouds. Instead, let us sing because May flowers are brought to us through April clouds and showers.

O Lord, "clouds are the dust of [your] feet"! (Nahum 1:3). Help us remember how near You are during the dark and cloudy days! Love beholds You and is glad. Faith sees the clouds emptying themselves and thereby making the hills on every side rejoice. CHARLES H. SPURGEON

> *What seems so dark to your dim sight*
> *May be a shadow, seen aright*
> *Making some brightness doubly bright.*
>
> *The flash that struck your tree—no more*
> *To shelter thee—lets heaven's blue floor*
> *Shine where it never shone before.*
>
> *The cry wrung from your spirit's pain*
> *May echo on some far-off plain,*
> *And guide a wanderer home again.*

The blue sky of heaven is much larger than the dark clouds.

AUGUST 14

Morning

If it dies, it produces many seeds.
JOHN 12:24

Infinite wisdom takes us in hand and leads us through deep interior crucifixion to our fine parts, lofty reason, brightest hopes, cherished affections, our pious zeal, our spiritual impetuosity, our narrow culture, our creed and churchism, our success, our spiritual experience, our spiritual comforts.

The crucifixion goes on until we are dead and *detached from all creatures, all saints, all thoughts, all hopes, all plans, all tender heart-yearnings, all preferences; dead to all trouble, all sorrow, all disappointments, all praise or blame, success or failure, comforts and annoyances, climates or nationalities;* dead to all desires but Himself.

There is no field without a seed,
Life raised through death is life indeed.
The smallest, lowliest little flower
A secret is, of mighty power.
To die—it lives—buried to rise—
Abundant life through sacrifice.
Wouldst thou know sacrifice?
It is through loss;
Thou can'st not save but by the Cross.
A corn of wheat except it die,
Can never, never multiply.
The glorious fields of waving gold,
Through death are life a hundredfold.
Thou who for souls dost weep and pray,
Let not hell's legions thee dismay.
This is the way of ways for thee,
The way of certain victory.
"THE SOUL WINNER'S SECRET"

Let go of the old grain of wheat if you want a harvest.

AUGUST 14
Evening

You would have no power over me if it were not given to you from above.
JOHN 19:11

Nothing that is not part of God's will is allowed to come into the life of someone who trusts and obeys Him. This truth should be enough to make our life one of ceaseless thanksgiving and joy, because God's will is the most hopeful, pleasant, and glorious thing in the world. It is the continuous working of His omnipotent power for our benefit, with nothing to prevent it, *if* we remain surrendered and believing.

Someone who was passing through the deep water of affliction wrote a friend:

Isn't it glorious to know that no matter how unjust something may be, even when it seems to have come from Satan himself, *by the time it reaches us it is God's will for us* and will ultimately work to our good?

"And we know that in all things God works for the good of those who love him" (Romans 8:28). Think of what Christ said even as He was betrayed: "*Shall I not drink the cup the Father has given me?*" (John 18:11).

We live fascinating lives if we are living in the center of God's will. All the attacks that Satan hurls at us through the sins of others are not only powerless to harm us but are transformed into blessings along the way. HANNAH WHITALL SMITH

> *In the center of the circle*
> *Of the will of God I stand:*
> *There can come no second causes,*
> *All must come from His dear hand.*
> *All is well! for it's my Father*
> *Who my life has planned.*
>
> *Shall I pass through waves of sorrow?*
> *Then I know it will be best;*
> *Though I cannot tell the reason,*
> *I can trust, and so am blest.*
> *God is Love, and God is faithful.*
> *So in perfect Peace I rest.*
>
> *With the shade and with the sunshine,*
> *With the joy and with the pain,*
> *Lord, I trust You! both are needed,*
> *Each Your wayward child to train,*
> *Earthly loss, if we will know it,*
> *Often means our heavenly gain.*
>   I. G. W.

Morning

[Keep] no record of wrongs.
1 CORINTHIANS 13:5

Let it rest!"

Ah! how many hearts on the brink of anxiety and disquietude, by this simple sentence have been made calm and happy!

Some proceeding has wounded us by its want of tact; *let it rest;* no one will think of it again.

A harsh or unjust sentence irritates us; *let it rest;* whoever may have given vent to it will be pleased to see it forgotten.

A painful scandal is about to estrange us from an old friend; *let it rest,* and thus preserve our charity and peace of mind.

A suspicious look is on the point of cooling our affection; *let it rest;* our look of trust will restore confidence.

Fancy! we, who are so careful to remove the briars from our pathway for fear they should wound, yet take pleasure in collecting and piercing our hearts with thorns that meet us in our daily intercourse with one another! How childish and unreasonable we are! GOLD DUST

The rents made by Time will soon mend if you will let God have His way.

Evening

We must go through many hardships to enter the kingdom of God.
ACTS 14:22

The best things in life are the result of being wounded. Wheat must be crushed before becoming bread, and incense must be burned by fire before its fragrance is set free. The earth must be broken with a sharp plow before being ready to receive the seed. And it is a broken heart that pleases God.

Yes, the sweetest joys of life are the fruits of sorrow. Human nature seems to need suffering to make it fit to be a blessing to the world.

Beside my cottage door it grows,
The loveliest, daintiest flower that blows,
    A sweetbrier rose.

At dewy morn or twilight's close,
The rarest perfume from it flows,
    This strange wild rose.

But when the raindrops on it beat,
Ah, then, its odors grow more sweet,
    About my feet.

Often with loving tenderness,
Its soft green leaves I gently press,
    In sweet caress.

A still more wondrous fragrance flows
The more my fingers close
    And crush the rose.

Dear Lord, oh, let my life be so
Its perfume when strong winds blow,
    The sweeter flow.

And should it be Your blessed will,
With crushing grief my soul to fill,
    Press harder still.

And while its dying fragrance flows
I'll whisper low, "He loves and knows
    His crushed brier rose."

If you aspire to be a person of consolation, if you want to share the priestly gift of sympathy, if you desire to go beyond giving commonplace comfort to a heart that is tempted, and if you long to go through the daily exchanges of life with the kind of tact that never inflicts pain, then you must be prepared to pay the price for a costly education—for like Christ, you must suffer. FREDERICK WILLIAM ROBERTSON

AUGUST 16

Morning

Be still, and know that I am God."
PSALM 46:10

Let thy soul walk softly in thee
Like a saint in heaven unshod,
For to be alone with silence
Is to be at home with God.

Quiet hearts are as rare as radium. We need every day to be led by the Divine Shepherd into the green pastures and beside the still waters. We are losing the art of meditation. Inner preparation is necessary to outer service.

"Rest pauses" contribute to the finer music of life. *"Jesus* went out to a mountainside to pray" (Luke 6:12). "As *he* was praying, the appearance of his face changed" (9:29). Therein we have the example of our Lord.

We have yet to learn the power of silence. Not in the college or academy, but in the silence of the soul do we learn the greater lessons of life and become rooted in spiritual inwardness.

The geologist says that certain crystals can only come to their perfect form in stillness. *In the undistracted moment men are in touch with God and everlasting things.*

The strenuousness of life and the increasing distractions of the world demand a zone of silence and the Quiet Hour.

"He said to them, 'Come with me by yourselves to a quiet place and get some rest.' So they went away by themselves in a boat to a solitary place" (Mark 6:31–32). Let *us* find that spot every day, and the fellowship of silence. On such moments infinite issues hinge!

In every life
There's a pause that is better than onward rush,
Better than hewing or mightiest doing;
'Tis the standing still at Sovereign will.

There's a hush that is better than ardent speech,
Better than sighing or wilderness crying;
'Tis the being still at Sovereign will.
The pause and the hush sing a double song
In unison low and for all time long.
O human soul, God's working plan
Goes on, nor needs the aid of man!
Stand still, and see!

Be still, and know!

AUGUST 16

Evening

I waited patiently for the LORD.
PSALM 40:1

Waiting is much more difficult than walking, for waiting requires patience, and patience is a rare virtue. We enjoy knowing that God builds hedges around His people, when we look at the hedge from the aspect of protection. But when we see it growing higher and higher until we can no longer see over it, we wonder if we will ever get out of our little sphere of influence and service, where we feel trapped. Sometimes it is hard for us to understand why we do not have a larger area of service, and it becomes difficult for us to "brighten the corner" where we are. But God has a purpose in all of *His* delays. "The steps of a good man are ordered by the LORD" (Psalm 37:23 KJV).

Next to this verse, in the margin of his Bible, George Mueller made this note: "And the *stops* too." It is a sad mistake for someone to break through God's hedges. It is a vital principle of the Lord's guidance for a Christian never to move from the spot where he is sure God has placed him, until the "pillar of cloud" (Exodus 13:21) moves. SUNDAY SCHOOL TIMES

Once we learn to wait for the Lord's leading in everything, we will know the strength that finds *its highest point in an even and steady walk.* Many of us are lacking the strength we so desire, but God gives complete power for every task He calls us to perform. Waiting—keeping yourself faithful to His leading—this is the secret of strength. And anything that does not align with obedience to Him is a waste of time and energy. Watch and wait for His leading. SAMUEL DICKEY GORDON

Must life be considered a failure for someone compelled to stand still, forced into inaction and required to watch the great, roaring tides of life from shore? No—victory is then to be won by standing still and quietly waiting. Yet this is a thousand times harder to do than in the past, when you rushed headlong into the busyness of life. It requires much more courage to stand and wait and still not lose heart or lose hope, to submit to the will of God, to give up opportunities for work and leave honors to others, and to be quiet, confident, and rejoicing while the busy multitude goes happily along their way.

The greatest life is: "after you have done everything, to stand" (Ephesians 6:13). J. R. MILLER

AUGUST 17

Morning

I have never been eloquent.
EXODUS 4:10

Nothing is more dishonoring to God, or more dangerous for us, than a mock humility. When we refuse to occupy a position which the grace of God assigns us, because of our not possessing certain virtues and qualifications, this is not humility, for if we could but satisfy our own consciences in reference to such virtues and qualifications, we should then deem ourselves entitled to assume the position. If, for instance, Moses had possessed such a measure of eloquence as he deemed needful, we may suppose he would have been ready to go. Now the question is, how much eloquence would he have needed to furnish him for his mission? The answer is, without God no amount of human eloquence would have availed, but with God the merest stammerer would have proved an efficient minister. This is a great practical truth.

Unbelief is not humility, but thorough pride. It refuses to believe God because it does not find in self a reason for believing. This is the very height of presumption. C. H. M.

> *Move to the fore;*
> > *Say not another is fitter than thou.*
> > *Shame to thy shrinking! Up! Face thy task now.*
> > *Own thyself equal to all a soul may,*
> > *Cease thy evading—God needs thee today.*
> *Move to the fore!*
> > *God Himself waits, and must wait till thou come;*
> > *Men are God's prophets though ages lie dumb.*
> > *Halts the Christ Kingdom with conquest so near?*
> > *Thou art the cause, thou soul in the rear.*
> *Move to the fore!*

Find your purpose and fling your life out into it; and the loftier your purpose is, the more sure you will be to make the world richer with every enrichment of yourself. PHILLIPS BROOKS

~~~~~~ AUGUST 17 ~~~~~~

Evening

I have faith in God that it will happen just as he told me.
ACTS 27:25

Anumber of years ago I went to America with a steamship captain who was a very devoted Christian. When we were off the coast of Newfoundland, he said to me, "The last time I sailed here, which was five weeks ago, something happened that revolutionized my entire Christian life. I had been on the bridge for twenty-four straight hours when George Mueller of Bristol, England, who was a passenger on board, came to me and said, 'Captain, I need to tell you that I must be in Quebec on Saturday afternoon.' 'That is impossible,' I replied. 'Very well,' Mueller responded, 'if your ship cannot take me, God will find some other way, for I have never missed an engagement in fifty-seven years. Let's go down to the chartroom to pray.'

"I looked at this man of God and thought to myself, 'What lunatic asylum did he escape from?' I had never encountered someone like this. 'Mr. Mueller,' I said, 'do you realize how dense the fog is?' 'No,' he replied. *My eye is not on the dense fog but on the living God, who controls every circumstance of my life.'*

"He then knelt down and prayed one of the most simple prayers I've ever heard. When he had finished, I started to pray, but he put his hand on my shoulder and told me *not* to pray. He said, 'First, you do not believe God will answer, and second, I BELIEVE HE HAS. Consequently, there is no need whatsoever for you to pray about it.'

"As I looked at him, he said, 'Captain, I have known my Lord for fifty-seven years, and there has never been even a single day that I have failed to get an audience with the King. Get up, Captain, and open the door, and you will see that the fog is gone.' I got up, and indeed the fog was gone. And on Saturday afternoon George Mueller was in Quebec for his meeting." SELECTED

> *If our love were just more simple,*
> *We would take Him at His word;*
> *And our lives would be all sunshine,*
> *In the sweetness of our Lord.*

～～～ AUGUST 18 ～～～
Morning

The angel of the LORD moved on ahead and stood in a narrow place
where was no room to turn, either to the right or to the left.
NUMBERS 22:26

A narrow place!" *You know that place; you have been there—you will very likely be there again before long—some of you may be there at this very moment;* for it is not merely a defile away somewhere among the mountains to the east of Moab. It is a life passage in individual experience—a time when there we are brought face to face with some inevitable question . . . Temptation is such a "narrow place." In the serious crisis of the soul's history, it is alone. *It is a path on which there is room only for itself, and before it there is God. Between these two always the matter has to be settled. Yes, or no, is the hinge on which everything turns. Shall I yield and dishonor God, or shall I resist and triumph in His might? There is no possible compromise; for compromise with sin is itself the most insidious form of sin.* No man can pass through these crises, and be after them what he was before. *He has met God face to face, and he must either be the better or the worse for that experience.* Either, like Jacob at Peniel he can say, "My life is preserved," or like Saul after he had thrown off his allegiance to his God, "Jehovah has departed from me, and is become my enemy." WILLIAM M. TAYLOR

The harder the place, the more He loves to show His power. If you wish to find Him real, come to Him in some great trouble. He has no chance to work until you get in a hard place. He led Israel out of the usual way till He got them to the Red Sea. Then there was room for His power to be manifested. God loves the hard places and the narrow places.

Rejoice if you are in such a place! Even if it is in the very heart of the foe, God is able to deliver you. Let not your faith in Him waver for a moment, and you will find *His omnipotence is all upon your side for every difficulty in which you can be placed.*

"When you get into a tight place," said Harriet Beecher Stowe, "and everything goes against you, till it seems as if you could not hold on a minute longer, never give up then, *for that is just the place and the time that the tide will turn.*"

AUGUST 18

Evening

The LORD *alone led him.*
DEUTERONOMY 32:12

The hill was steep, but cheered along the way
By conversation sweet, climbing with the thought
That it might be so till the height was reached;

But suddenly a narrow winding path
Appeared, and then the Master said, "My child,
Here you will walk safest with Me alone."

I trembled, yet my heart's deep trust replied,
"So be it, Lord." He took my feeble hand
In His, accepting thus my will to yield Him
All, and to find all in Him. One long, dark moment,
And no friend I saw, save Jesus only.

But oh! so tenderly He led me on
And up, and spoke to me such words of cheer,
Such secret whisperings of His wondrous love,
That soon I told Him all my grief and fear,
And leaned on His strong arm confidingly.

And then I found my footsteps quickened,
And light unspeakable, the rugged way
Illumined, such light as only can be seen
In close companionship with God.

A little while, and we will meet again
The loved and lost; but in the rapturous joy
Of greetings, such as here we cannot know,
And happy song, and heavenly embraces,
And tender recollections rushing back
Of life now passed, I think one memory
More dear and sacred than the rest, will rise,
And we who gather in the golden streets,
Will oft be stirred to speak with grateful love
Of that dark day Jesus called us to climb
Some narrow steep, leaning on Him alone.

There is never a majestic mountain without a deep valley, and there is no birth without pain. DANIEL CRAWFORD

Morning

Whatever you want me to do, I'll do for you.

1 SAMUEL 20:4

It is sometimes difficult to realize that the promises of God *are to be taken at their face value.* Too often they are regarded as a part of the general spiritual instruction of the Word, but not to be appropriated for our own need.

We fail to realize because we do not appropriate!

No matter what may be our requirements—guidance, spiritual refreshing, physical or temporal needs—God has given us *some specific word on which to base our faith.*

Then, since the promises are definite, should not our prayers be definite? Prayerfully *search the Word to find the promise that will fit the case. Prove Him!* Back of the word of the Lord is the person and character of God Himself: *God, who cannot lie.*

God honors the person who trusts Him implicitly.

It is not *our* worth, but *Christ's,* which has secured for us *immediate access to the Throne,* "For no matter how many promises God has made, they are 'Yes' in Christ. And so through him the 'Amen' is spoken" (2 Corinthians 1:20).

With such a basis and assurance, *why hesitate to claim the things the Lord has provided?* Can you not trust the *One* who made the promise?

Whatever desire the Father permits to live in the heart of one of His saints, *He will grant the fulfillment thereof.* S. CHADWICK

Prove the immutable promises of God!

─── AUGUST 19 ───

Evening

Sorrowful, yet always rejoicing.

2 CORINTHIANS 6:10

Sorrow was beautiful, but his beauty was the beauty of the moonlight shining through the leafy branches of the trees in the woods. His gentle light made little pools of silver here and there on the soft green moss of the forest floor. And when he sang, his song was like the low, sweet calls of the nightingale, and in his eyes was the unexpectant gaze of someone who has ceased to look for coming gladness. He could weep in tender sympathy with those who weep, but to rejoice with those who rejoice was unknown to him.

Joy was beautiful, too, but hers was the radiant beauty of a summer morning. Her eyes still held the happy laughter of childhood, and her hair glistened with the sunshine's kiss. When she sang, her voice soared upward like a skylark's, and her steps were the march of a conqueror who has never known defeat. She could rejoice with anyone who rejoices, but to weep with those who weep was unknown to her.

Sorrow longingly said, "We can never be united as one." "No, never," responded Joy, with eyes misting as she spoke, "for *my* path lies through the sunlit meadows, the sweetest roses bloom when I arrive, and songbirds await my coming to sing their most joyous melodies."

"Yes, and *my* path," said Sorrow, turning slowly away, "leads through the dark forest, and moonflowers, which open only at night, will fill my hands. Yet the sweetest of all earthly songs—the love song of the night—will be mine. So farewell, dear Joy, farewell."

Yet even as Sorrow spoke, he and Joy became aware of someone standing beside them. In spite of the dim light, they sensed a kingly Presence, and suddenly a great and holy awe overwhelmed them. They then sank to their knees before Him.

"I see Him as the King of Joy," whispered Sorrow, "for on His head are many crowns, and the nailprints in His hands and feet are the scars of a great victory. And before Him all my sorrow is melting away into deathless love and gladness. I now give myself to Him forever."

"No, Sorrow," said Joy softly, "for I see Him as the King of Sorrow, and the crown on His head is a crown of thorns, and the nailprints in His hands and feet are the scars of terrible agony. I also give myself to Him forever, for sorrow with Him must be sweeter than any joy I have ever known."

"Then we are *one* in Him," they cried in gladness, "for no one but He could unite Joy and Sorrow." Therefore they walked hand in hand into the world, to follow Him through storms and sunshine, through winter's severe cold and the warmth of summer's gladness, and to be "sorrowful, yet always rejoicing."

Does Sorrow lay his hand upon your shoulder,
        And walk with you in silence on life's way,
While Joy, your bright companion once, grown colder,
        Becomes to you more distant day by day?
Run not from the companionship of Sorrow,
        He is the messenger of God to thee;
And you will thank Him in His great tomorrow—
        For what you do not know now, you then will see;
He is God's angel, clothed in veils of night,
        With whom "we walk by faith" and "not by
        sight." (2 CORINTHIANS 5:7 KJV)

AUGUST 20
Morning

Whoever wants to save their life will lose it.
MARK 8:35

The laying down of life is not only the foundation of a new life for ourselves but also the foundation of a new life for others, just as the laying down of our Lord's life has brought forth its abundant harvest all through the years.

It is the laying down of life for the sake of the harvest; it is the grain of wheat falling into the ground to die in order that it may not abide alone.

John Coleridge Patterson's life was equipped with every gift to make it rich and happy in his own land, yet he laid it down to go to his hard and toilsome life in the South Seas. Had he been asked, *"Are you regretful for what you have turned your back upon?"* he would have answered, *"The promise has been fulfilled to me."*

An American consul general in China once said to Matthew Culbertson, *"You might have been a major-general if you had stayed at home."* He had been the best man in his class at West Point, but his mother's prayers had borne their fruitage, and he became a missionary. He was the man of military genius in Shanghai's time of need. *"No,"* he said, *"I do not regret it. The privilege of preaching the Gospel to four hundred million of one's fellow creatures is the greatest privilege any man can have on earth."* He had *found* his life!

To be sure, Livingstone lost his life, but he had *found* another—a life which spread through Africa, which abides in Africa, which molded the world's thought of Africa.

Henry Martyn put his hand to the plow with these words, "Now, let me burn out for God!" No "looking back." No relinquishing the handles even for a holiday!

Think of James Gilmore in Mongolia in his uncompanioned life! Mongolia stretches from the Sea of Japan on the east to Turkestan on the west—a distance of three thousand miles; from the southern boundary of Asiatic Russia to the Great Wall of China—nine hundred miles. What a field! But what a plowman! He died in the furrow!

More than two thousand years ago our Lord lost His life and His fame. Or *did He?*

Speak, history! Who are life's victors? Unveil thy long annals and say, Are they those whom the world calls the victors, who won the success of a day? Thy martyrs, or Nero? The Spartans, who fell at Thermopylae's tryst, or the Persians and Xerxes? His judges, or Socrates? Pilate or Christ? William Wetmore Story

~~~~~ AUGUST 20 ~~~~~

Evening

Jacob was left alone, and a man wrestled with him till daybreak.

Genesis 32:24

In this passage, God is wrestling with Jacob more than Jacob is wrestling with God. The "man" referred to here is the Son of Man—the Angel of the Covenant. It was God in human form, pressing down on Jacob to press his old life from him. And by daybreak God had prevailed, for Jacob's "hip was wrenched" (v. 25). As Jacob "fell" from his old life, he fell into the arms of God, clinging to Him but also wrestling until his blessing came. His blessing was that of a new life, so he rose from the earthly to the heavenly, the human to the divine, and the natural to the supernatural. From that morning forward, he was a weak and broken man from a human perspective, but God was there. And the Lord's heavenly voice proclaimed, *"Your name will no longer be Jacob, but Israel, because you have struggled with God and with humans and have overcome"* (v. 28).

Beloved, this should be a typical scene in the life of everyone who has been transformed. If God has called us to His highest and best, each of us will have a time of crisis, when all our resources will fail and when we face either ruin or something better than we have ever dreamed. But before we can receive the blessing, we must rely on God's infinite help. We must be willing to let go, surrendering completely to Him, and cease from our own wisdom, strength, and righteousness. We must be "crucified with Christ" (Galatians 2:20) and yet alive in Him. God knows how to lead us to the point of crisis, and He knows how to lead us through it.

Is God leading you in this way? Is this the meaning of your mysterious trial, your difficult circumstances, your impossible situation, or that trying place you cannot seem to move past without Him? But do you have enough of Him to win the victory?

Then turn to Jacob's God! Throw yourself helplessly at His feet. Die in His loving arms to your own strength and wisdom, and rise like Jacob into His strength and sufficiency. There is no way out of your difficult and narrow situation except at the top. You must win deliverance by rising higher, coming into a new experience with God. And may it bring you into all that is meant by the revelation of "the Mighty One of Jacob" (Isaiah 60:16)! There is no way out *but God.*

> *At Your feet I fall, Yield*
> *You up my all,*
> *To suffer, live, or die*
> *For my Lord crucified.*

AUGUST 21
Morning

Beauty instead of ashes.
ISAIAH 61:3

Oh, not for Thee my fading fires, The ashes of my heart.

May I tell you a tale of the African veld? It concerns the *fire lily.*

A grass fire in a hill country is one of the most wonderful sights in a wonderful land, surpassing in subtle attraction the grandeur of a veld fire on the plain with its roaring flames leaping skyward as they lick up the tall dry grass. Among the mountains where the grass is much shorter, you watch with tireless fascination the long running lines of light on the distant heights—something like the illumination of a town seen from far away. With morning the scene is changed. You lift your eyes to greet the mountains you love, and they answer you with blackened faces. A little longer and these same hills are clothed in springing green, and, from the ashes, one of the first of the flowers, rises the *fire lily* like a little scarlet flame.

"Beauty for ashes!" (KJV). Here are the very words of God incarnate in His works. The matchless message of Isaiah 61:3 comes with a deeper meaning as we consider the *fire lily*. Its story unfolds the Old Testament promise in the radiance of New Testament light, for it shows *by what means* God would make actual in our own experience *the glorious possibility of resurrection life*.

When we surrender our old nature to God that He may carry out the death sentence pronounced upon it, He accepts it in the only way He ever accepted a sacrifice, by turning it to ashes (Psalm 20:3). And where the fire has been, there springs from the ashes of the old life the fire lily of the beauty of Christ. As more ground is daily yielded, on the fire-swept hills of our inner life will be wrought the miracle of life out of death, and the bare slopes will burst with blossom. One unburnt hill will mean a jungle growth of grass and weeds; one valley spared will mean less Christfulness. This is the law of God—both natural and spiritual—*no fire, no fire lily; no ashes, no beauty.* This is the secret of the fire lily. *This is the meaning of surrender.* P. E. SHARP

> But there were only ashes when He came
> Saying, "My daughter, thou hast tried to serve
> In thine own way? but now, stretch forth thy hands
> That I may lead thee out of self's dark cell
> And work My will through thee—
> When thou hast ceased to be."
> I said, "My youth is gone; my strength is gone;
> My life—it lies before Thee bare and sere.
> For very shame I cannot offer Thee
> These ashes that are left me, gray and drear.
> Yet, work Thy will in me
> And teach me not to be."
>
> Then through the ashes of that fading fire
> He breathed His breath; and when the ash had fled,

Laid on some smoldering embers a live coal
That was His life, His love, all flaming red.
"Thy will be done to me, So shall I live in Thee."
AUTHOR UNKNOWN

Before God gives a blessing He writes a sentence of death on the means leading up to it!

AUGUST 21

Evening

He brought me out into a spacious place; he rescued me because he delighted in me.
PSALM 18:19

What is this "spacious place"? What can it be but God Himself—the infinite Being through whom all other beings find their source and their end of life? God is indeed a "spacious place." And it was through humiliation, degradation, and a sense of worthlessness that David was taken to it. MADAME GUYON

"I carried you on eagles' wings and brought you to myself" (Exodus 19:4).

Fearing to launch on "full surrender's" tide,
I asked the Lord where would its waters glide
My little boat, "To troubled seas I dread?"
  "Unto Myself," He said.

Weeping beside an open grave I stood,
In bitterness of soul I cried to God:
"Where leads this path of sorrow that I tread?"
  "Unto Myself," He said.

Striving for souls, I loved the work too well;
Then disappointments came; I could not tell
The reason, till He said, "I am your all;
  Unto Myself I call."

Watching my heroes—those I love the best—
I saw them fail; they could not stand the test,
Even by this the Lord, through tears not few,
Unto Himself me drew.

Unto Himself! No earthly tongue can tell
The bliss I find, since in His heart I dwell;
The things that charmed me once seem all as naught;
Unto Himself I'm brought.

SELECTED

AUGUST 22

Morning

So are you in my hand.

JEREMIAH 18:6

Ole Bull, the world's most noted violinist, was ever wandering about. One day he became lost in the interminable forests. In the dark of the night he stumbled against a log hut, the home of a hermit. The old man took him in, fed and warmed him; after the supper they sat in front of a blazing fireplace, and the old hermit picked some crude tunes on his screechy, battered violin. Ole Bull said to the hermit, "Do you think I could play on that?" "I don't think so; it took me years to learn," the old hermit replied. Ole Bull said, "Let me try it."

He took the old marred violin and drew the bow across the strings, and suddenly the hermit's hut was filled with music Divine; and, according to the story, the hermit sobbed like a child.

We are battered instruments; life's strings have been snapped; life's bow has been bent. *Yet, if we will only let Him take us and touch us,* from this old battered, broken, shattered, marred instrument, He will bring forth music fit for the angels.

I never knew the old, brown violin,
That was so long in some dark corner thrust,

Its strings broken or loose, its pegs run down,
Could ever be of use again. The dust
Of years lay on its shabby case, until
One day a Master took the instrument,
And with caressing fingers touched the wood,
Adjusted pegs and strings; his mind intent
On making music as he drew his bow.
Then from the violin, long silent, sprang
Once more arpeggios, runs, trills. The wood
Quivered, leapt into life, and joyous sang.

I now believe that any broken life,
Jangling with discords, unadjusted, tossed
In some far corner, wasted, thrown aside,
Can yet be of some use; need not be lost
From Heaven's orchestra. A Master's Hand
Scarred with old wounds, can mend the broken
thing if yielded to Him wholly; and can make
The dumb life speak again, and joyous sing
In praise of One who gave His life that none
Need perish. And this message, glad, most
blest, I now believe; for placing in His Hand
My life, I find my world is now at rest.

DOROTHY M. BARTER-SNOW

～～～ AUGUST 22 ～～～

Evening

The rest were to get there on planks or on other pieces of the
ship. In this way everyone reached land safely.

ACTS 27:44

The miraculous story of Paul's voyage to Rome, with its trials and triumphs, is a wonderful example of the light and the darkness through the journey of faith of human life. And the most remarkable part of the journey is the difficult and narrow places that are interspersed with God's extraordinary providence and intervention.

It is a common misconception that the Christian's walk of faith is strewn with flowers and that when God intervenes in the lives of His people, He does so in such a wonderful way as to always lift us out of our difficult surroundings. In actual fact, however, the real experience is quite the opposite. And the message of the Bible is one of alternating trials and triumphs in the lives of "a great cloud of witnesses" (Hebrews 12:1), everyone from Abel to the last martyr.

Paul, more than anyone else, is an example of how much a child of God can suffer without being defeated or broken in spirit. Because of his testimony given in Damascus, he was hunted down by persecutors and forced to flee for his life. Yet we see no heavenly chariot, amid lightning bolts of fire, coming to rescue the holy apostle from the hands of his enemies. God instead worked a simple way of escape for Paul: "His followers took him by night and lowered him in a basket through an opening in the wall" (Acts 9:25). Yes, he was in an old clothes basket, like a bundle of laundry or groceries. The servant of the Lord Jesus Christ was lowered from a window over the wall of Damascus, and in a humble way escaped the hatred of his foes.

Later we find him languishing for months in lonely dungeons, telling of his "sleepless nights and hunger" (2 Corinthians 6:5), of being deserted by friends, and of his brutal, humiliating beatings. And even after God promised to deliver him, we see him left for days to toss upon a stormy sea and compelled to protect a treacherous sailor. And finally, once his deliverance comes, it is not by way of some heavenly ship sailing from the skies to rescue this illustrious prisoner. Nor is there an angel who comes walking on the water to still the raging sea. There is no supernatural sign at all of surpassing greatness being carried out, for one man is required to grab a piece of the mast to survive, another a floating timber, another a small fragment of the shipwreck, and yet another is forced to swim for his life.

In this account, we also find God's pattern for our own lives. It is meant to be good news to those who live in this everyday world in ordinary surroundings and who face thousands of ordinary situations, which must be met in completely ordinary ways.

God's promises and His providence do not lift us from the world of common sense and everyday trials, for it is through these very things that our faith is perfected. And it is in this world that God loves to interweave the golden threads of His love with the twists and turns of our common, everyday experiences. HARD PLACES IN THE WAY OF FAITH

AUGUST 23
Morning

I . . . brought you to myself.
EXODUS 19:4

How we have wondered at those events which stirred us up and set us loose from ties of home and friends; and how we have marveled at the ruthlessness of those providences which sent us headlong from our assured places into the uncertainties of what seemed empty space around and beneath us. *But now we understand that every experience was in God's love and for the fulfillment of His high purposes toward us. No matter what happened, we soon saw His form and heard His heartening cry; and never did we grow weary but we immediately found that strong wings were beneath us. And oh, the wonder of it! when God brought us home to our resting-place beside Himself!* HENRY W. FROST

> *Unto Myself, My dear child, I would bring thee!*
> *Who like Myself thy sure solace can be?*
> *Who can reach down, down so deeply within thee?*
> *Give to thy heart such a full sympathy?*
>
> *Mournest thou sore that thy loved ones have failed thee?*
> *Failed, sadly failed thy true comfort to be?*
> *"Why did they fail" dost thou ask? Let Me whisper—*
> *"That thou should'st find thy heart's comfort in Me."*
>
> *Unto Myself! Ah, no not unto others,*
> *Dearest, or sweetest, or fairest, or best;*
> *Only in Me lieth unchanging solace;*
> *Only in Me is thy promise of rest!*

Child of My love, to Myself I would bring thee!
Not to some place of most heavenly bliss:
Places, like people, may all disappoint thee,
Till thou hast learned to drink higher than this.

Unto Myself, My dear child, I would bring thee!
None like Myself thy full portion can be!
While, in My heart, there is hunger and longing
That I might find choicest treasure in thee.

Unto Myself! To Myself—not My service!
Then to most sweetly and certainly prove
That I can make thee My channel of blessing,
Use thee to shed forth the wealth of My love.

J. DANSON SMITH

AUGUST 23

Evening

By faith Abraham . . . obeyed and went, even though
he did not know where he was going.

HEBREWS 11:8

This is faith without sight. *Seeing* is not faith but reasoning. When crossing the Atlantic by ship, I once observed this very principle of faith. I *saw* no path marked out on the sea, nor could I even see the shore. Yet each day, we marked our progress on a chart as if we had been following a giant chalk line across the water. And when we came within sight of land on the other side of the Atlantic, we knew exactly where we were, as if we had been able to see it from three thousand miles away.

How had our course been so precisely plotted? Every day, our captain had taken his instruments, looked to the sky, and determined his course by the sun. He was sailing using heavenly lights, not earthly ones.

Genuine faith also looks up and sails, by using God's great Son. It never travels by *seeing* the shoreline, earthly lighthouses, or paths along the way. And the steps of faith often lead to total uncertainty or even darkness and disaster, but the Lord will open the way and often makes the darkest of midnight hours as bright as the dawning of the day.

Let us move forth today, not knowing or seeing, but trusting. DAYS OF HEAVEN UPON EARTH

Too many of us want to see our way through a new endeavor before we will even start. Imagine if we could see our way from beginning to end. How would we ever develop our Christian gifts? *Faith, hope, and love cannot be picked from trees, like ripe apples.* Remember, after the words "In the beginning" (Genesis 1:1) comes the word "God." It is our first step of faith that turns the key in the lock of His powerhouse. It is true that God helps those who help themselves, but *He also helps those who are helpless.* So no matter your circumstance, you can depend on Him every time.

Waiting on God brings us to the end of our journey much faster than our feet.

Many an opportunity is lost while we deliberate after He has said, "Move!"

AUGUST 24

Morning

Gideon was threshing wheat. . . . When the angel of the LORD . . . said, "The LORD is with you.
JUDGES 6:11–12

More courage is required when coming to grips with the commonplace problems of the ordinary day than is required to face batteries of destruction on a field of military conflict.

It is much easier to follow on the track of the heroic than to remain true to Jesus in drab mean streets. Human nature unaided by God cannot do it.

The follower of Jesus is a laborer—but a laborer together with God. He is a man with a hoe—but one who has his part in the harvest whose reapers are the angels.

This is the place where Thou didst bid me stand;
And work and wait;
I thought it was a plot of fertile land,

To tend and cultivate:
Flowers and fruit, I said, are surely there,
In rich earth stored,
And I will make of it a garden fair,
For Thee, my Lord!

Lo! it is set where only bleak skies frown,
With rank weeds sown,
And over it the vagrant thistle-down
Like dust is blown;
Long have I labored, but the barren soil
No crop will yield:
This have I won for all my ceaseless toil—
A bare plowed field!

Nay, even here, where thou didst strive and weep,
Some sunny morn
Others shall come with joyous hearts and reap
The full-eared corn;
Yet is their harvest to thy labor due;
On Me 'twas spent—
Are not the furrows driven straight and true?
Be thou content!

"A Tiller of the Soil"

~~~ AUGUST 24 ~~~

Evening

I have received full payment have more than enough.
PHILIPPIANS 4:18

In one of my garden books there is a chapter with a very interesting title: "Flowers That Grow in the Shade." It deals with those areas of a garden that never catch direct sunlight, and it lists the kinds of flowers that not only grow in the dark corners but actually seem to like them and to flourish in them.

There are similarities here to the spiritual world. There are Christians who seem to blossom when their material circumstances become the most harsh and severe. They grow in the darkness and shade. If this were not true, how could we otherwise explain some of the experiences of the apostle Paul?

When he wrote the above verse, he was a prisoner in Rome. The primary mission of his life appeared to have been broken. But it was in this persistent darkness that flowers began to show their faces in bright and fascinating glory. Paul may have seen them before, growing along the open road, but certainly never in the incomparable strength and beauty in which they now appeared. And words of promise opened their treasures to him in ways he had never before experienced.

Among those treasures were such wonderful things as Christ's grace, love, joy, and peace, and it seemed as though they had needed the circumstance of darkness to draw out their secret and inner glory. The dark and dingy prison had become the home of the revealed truth of God, and Paul began to realize as never before the width and the wealth of his spiritual inheritance.

Haven't we all known men and women who begin to wear strength and hopefulness like a regal robe as soon as they must endure a season of darkness and solitude? People like that may be put in prison by the world, but their treasure will be locked away with them, for true treasure cannot be locked out of their lives. Their material condition may look like a desert, but "the desert and the parched land will be glad; the wilderness will rejoice and blossom" (Isaiah 35:1). JOHN HENRY JOWETT

Every flower, even the most beautiful, has its own shadow beneath it as it basks in the sunlight.

Where there is much light, there is also much shade.

~~~~~ AUGUST 25 ~~~~~

Morning

Just believe.
MARK 5:36

An old woman with an halo of silvered hair—the hot tears flowing down her furrowed cheeks—her worn hands busy over a washboard in a room of poverty—praying—for her son John—John who ran away from home in his teens to become a sailor—John, of whom it was now reported that he had become a very wicked man—*praying, praying always,* that her son might be of service to God.

What a marvelous subject for an artist's brush!

The mother believed in two things, the power of prayer and the reformation of her son. So while she scrubbed, she continued to pray. God answered the prayer by working a miracle in the heart *of John Newton.* The black stains of sin were washed white in the blood of the Lamb. *"Though your sins are like scarlet, they shall be as white as snow"* (Isaiah 1:18).

The washtub prayers were heard as are all prayers when asked in His name. John Newton, the drunken sailor, became John Newton, the sailor-preacher. Among the thousands of men and women he brought to Christ was *Thomas Scott,* cultured, selfish, and self-satisfied. Because of the washtub prayers, another miracle was worked, and Thomas Scott used both his pen and voice to lead thousands of unbelieving hearts to Christ—among them, a dyspeptic, melancholic young man, *William Cowper* by name. He, too, was washed by the cleansing Blood and in a moment of inspiration wrote:

> *There is a fountain filled with blood*
> *Drawn from Immanuel's veins,*
> *And sinners, plunged beneath that flood,*
> *Lose all their guilty stains.*

And this song has brought countless thousands to the Man who died on Calvary. Among the thousands was *William Wilberforce,* who became a great Christian statesman and unfastened the shackles from the feet of thousands of British slaves. Among those whom he led to the Lord was *Leigh Richmond,* a clergyman of the Established Church in one of the Channel Islands. He wrote a book, *The Dairyman's Daughter,* which was translated into forty languages and with the intensity of leaping flame burned the love of Christ into the hearts of thousands.

All this resulted because a mother *took God at His Word* and prayed that her son's heart might become as white as the soapsuds in the washtub.

Evening

Before the coming of this faith, we were held in custody . . . locked
up until the faith that was to come would be revealed.

GALATIANS 3:23

G od, in times past, caused people to be kept subject to His law so they would learn the more excellent way of faith. For it was through the law that they would see God's holy standard and thereby realize their own utter helplessness. Then they would gladly learn His way of faith.

God still causes us to be "locked up until faith" is learned. Our own nature, circumstances, trials, and disappointments all serve to keep us submissive and "locked up" until we see that the only way out is His way of faith. Moses attempted the deliverance of his people by using self-effort, his personal influence, and even violence. So God "locked [him] up" for forty years in the wilderness before he was prepared for His work.

Paul and Silas were called of God to preach the gospel in Europe. In Philippi they were "severely flogged, they were thrown into prison, and the jailer . . . fastened their feet in the stocks" (Acts 16:23–24). They were "locked up" to faith. They trusted God and sang praises to Him in their darkest hour, and God brought deliverance and salvation.

The apostle John was also "locked up" to faith, when he was banished to the Isle of Patmos. And if he had never been sent there, he would never have seen such glorious visions of God.

Dear reader, are you in some terrible trouble? Have you experienced some distressing disappointment, sorrow, or inexpressible loss? Are you in a difficult situation? Cheer up! You have been "locked up" to faith. Accept your troubles in the proper way and commit them to God. Praise Him "that in all things God works for the good of those who love him" (Romans 8:28) and that He "acts on behalf of those who wait for him" (Isaiah 64:4). God will send you blessings and help, and will reveal truths to you that otherwise would never have come your way. And many others will also receive great insights and blessings because you were "locked up" to learn the way of faith. C. H. P.

Great things are done when man and mountains meet,
These are not done by walking down the street.

Morning

I will betroth you to me forever.

HOSEA 2:19

"Rise up, my love, my fair one, and come away," He calls (Song of Songs 2:10 KJV)! Away from Egypt's bondage—away . . . *but with Him!* Divinely betrothed!

"My Beloved!" are the words. No other voice would have so aroused her. To *His* voice her heart responds. *Expectation quickens the hearing;* and when we are truly desirous toward Christ, how quickly the accents of His voice are caught!

> *He said: "Wilt thou go with Me*
> *Where shadows eclipse the light?"*
> *And she answered: "My Lord, I will follow Thee*
> *Far, under the stars at night."*
> *But He said: "No starlight pierces the gloom*
> *Of the valley thy feet must tread;*
> *But it leads thee on to a cross and tomb—"*
> *"But I go with Thee," she said.*
>
> *"Count the cost; canst thou pay the price—Be a dumb thing led;*
> *Laid on an altar of sacrifice?" "Bind me there, my Lord,"*
> *   she said. "Bind me that I may not fail—*
> *Or hold with Thy wounded hand;*
> *For I fear the knife and the piercing nail,*
> *And I shrink from the burning brand.*
> *Yet whither Thou goest I will go,*
> *Though the way be lone and dread—"*
> *His voice was tender, and sweet, and low—"Thou shalt go with Me," He said.*
> *And none knew the anguish sore.*
>
> *Or the night of the way she came;*
> *Alone, alone with the cross she bore,*

Alone in her grief and shame.
Brought to the altar of sacrifice,
There as a dumb thing slain:
Was the guerdon more than the bitter price?
Was it worth the loss and pain?

Ask the seed-corn, when the grain
Ripples its ripened gold;
Ask the sower when, after toil and pain,
He garners the hundredfold.
He said (and His voice was glad and sweet):
"Was it worth the cost, My own?"
And she answered, low at His pierced feet,
"I found at the end of the pathway lone
not death, but life on a throne!"

ANNIE CLARKE

"Wilt thou go with this man?" (Genesis 24:58 KJV).

~~~~~ AUGUST 26 ~~~~~

Evening

It is not in me.
JOB 28:14

I remember saying one summer, "What I really need is a trip to the ocean." So I went to the beach, but the ocean seemed to say, *"It is not in me!"* The ocean did not do for me what I thought it would. Then I said, "Perhaps the mountains will provide the rest I need." I went to the mountains, and when I awoke the first morning, I gazed at the magnificent mountain I had so longed to see. But the sight did not satisfy, and the mountain said, *"It is not in me!"*

What I really needed was the deep ocean of God's love, and the high mountains of His truth within me. His wisdom had depths and heights that neither the ocean nor the mountains could contain and that could not be compared with jewels, gold, or precious stones. *Christ is wisdom and He is our deepest need.* Our inner restlessness can only be pacified by the revelation of His eternal friendship and love for us. MARGARET BOTTOME

> *My heart is there!*
> *Where, on eternal hills, my loved one dwells*
> *Among the lilies and asphodels;*
> *Clad in the brightness of the Great White Throne,*
> *Glad in the smile of Him who sits thereon,*
> *The glory gilding all His wealth of hair*
> *And making His immortal face more fair—*
> *there is my treasure and my heart is there.*
> *My heart is there!*
> *With Him who made all earthly life so grand,*
> *So fit to live, and yet to die His plan;*
> *So mild, so great, so gentle and so brave,*
> *So ready to forgive, so strong to save.*
> *His fair, pure Spirit makes the Heavens more fair,*
> *And that is where rises my longing prayer—*
> *there is my treasure and my heart is there.*

FAVORITE POEM OF THE LATE CHARLES E. COWMAN

You can never expect to keep an eagle in the forest. You might be able to gather a group of the most beautiful birds around him, provide a perch for him on the tallest pine, or enlist other birds to bring him the choicest of delicacies, but he will reject them all. He will spread his proud wings and, with his eye on an Alpine cliff, soar away to his own ancestral halls of rock, where storms and waterfalls make their natural music.

Our soul longs to soar as an eagle and will find rest with nothing short of the Rock of Ages. Its ancestral halls are the halls of heaven, made with the rock of the attributes of God. And the span of its majestic flight is eternity! "Lord, YOU have been our dwelling place throughout all generations" (Psalm 90:1). J. R. MACDUFF

"My Home is God Himself"; Christ brought me there.
I placed myself within His mighty arms;
He took me up, and safe from all alarms
He bore me "where no foot but His has trod,"
Within the holiest at Home with God,
And had me dwell in Him, rejoicing there.
O Holy Place! O Home divinely fair!
And we, God's little ones, abiding there.

"My Home is God Himself"; it was not so!
A long, long road I traveled night and day,
And sought to find within myself some way.
Nothing I did or felt could bring me near.
Self-effort failed, and I was filled with fear,
And then I found Christ was the only way,
That I must come to Him and in Him stay,
And God had told me so.

And now "my Home is God," and sheltered there,
God meets the trials of my earthly life,
God compasses me round from storm and strife,
God takes the burden of my daily care.
O Wondrous Place! O Home divinely fair!

And I, God's little one, safe hidden there.
Lord, as I dwell in You and You in me,
So make me dead to everything but Thee;
That as I rest within my Home most fair,
My soul may evermore and only see
My God in everything and everywhere;
My Home is God.

AUTHOR UNKNOWN

Morning

Joseph said to them. . . . "You intended to harm me, but God intended it
for good to accomplish what is now being done, the saving of many lives.
GENESIS 50:19–20

It had been a long road for Joseph; it had been a desperately rough road, too. There was the slimy pit, the brothers' treachery, the slave chains, the terrible palace temptation, and the prison cell. But what a different ending this story has: "So Pharaoh said to Joseph, 'I hereby put you in charge of the whole land of Egypt.' . . . 'Only with respect to the throne will I be greater than you'" (Genesis 41:41–40). And can you not hear Joseph speaking to his brethren: "God intended it for good to accomplish . . . the saving of many lives."

A whole life committed to God in unswerving loyalty is held as a most sacred trust. The processes used in building a great soul are varied and consume much time. Many a long road seems to have no turning. Frequently "the night is dark and we seem to be far from home," but patience cries out, "Lead Thou me on," "Keep Thou my feet; I do not ask to see the distant scene—one step enough for me." *Faith, courage, and patience* are tremendous qualities in a great life, but *the time element* is the factor which is absolutely necessary to work all these out.

Blessed is that life which is so thoroughly rooted down into the life of God that it can feel and know that, though time moves slowly in long drawn-out tests and trials, God's tides move steadily on in accomplishing His glorious purposes. QUESTS AND CONQUESTS

> *O tarry thou His leisure,*
> *Praise when He seems to pause,*
> *Nor think that the Eternal One*
> *Will set His clock by yours;*
> *But wait His time, and trust His date,*
> *It cannot be too soon, or late!*

The turn on the long road comes at last!

Evening

He took him aside, away from the crowd.

MARK 7:33

Paul withstood not only the tests that came while he was active in his service to Christ but also the tests of solitude during captivity. We may be able to withstand the strain of the most intense labor, even if coupled with severe suffering, and yet completely break down if set aside from all Christian activity and work.

This would be especially true if we were forced to endure solitary confinement in a prison cell.

Even the most majestic bird, which soars higher than all others and endures the longest flights, will sink into despair when placed in a cage, where it is forced to helplessly beat its wings against its prison bars. Have you ever seen a magnificent eagle forced to languish in a small cage? With bowed head and drooping wings, it is a sad picture of the sorrow of inactivity.

To see Paul in prison is to see another side of life. Have you noticed how he handled it? He seemed to be looking over the top of his prison wall and over the heads of his enemies. Notice how he even signed his name to his letters—not as the prisoner of Festus, nor of Caesar, and not as a victim of the Sanhedrin, but as *"a prisoner for the Lord"* (Ephesians 4:1). Through it all, he saw only the hand of God at work. To him, the prison became a palace, with its corridors resounding with shouts of triumphant praise and joy.

Forced from the missionary work he loved so well, Paul built a new pulpit—a new witness stand. And from his place of bondage arose some of the most encouraging and helpful ministries of Christian liberty. What precious messages of light came from the dark shadows of his captivity.

Also think of the long list of saints who have followed in the footsteps of Paul and were imprisoned for their faith. For twelve long years, John Bunyan's voice was silenced in an English jail in Bedford. Yet it was there he wrote the greatest work of his life, *Pilgrim's Progress*—read by more people than any other book except the Bible. He once said, "I was at home in prison, and my great joy led me to sit and write and write." And the darkness of his long captivity became a wonderful dream to light the path of millions of weary pilgrims.

Madame Guyon, the sweet-spirited French saint, endured a lengthy time behind prison walls. And like the sounds of some caged birds whose songs are more beautiful as a result of their confinement, the music of her soul has traveled far beyond her dungeon walls to remove the sadness of many discouraged hearts.

Oh, the heavenly consolation that God has caused to flow out of places of solitude!
S. C. REES

Taken aside by Jesus,
    To feel the touch of His hand;
To rest for a while in the shadow
    Of the Rock in a weary land.

Taken aside by Jesus,
    In the loneliness dark and drear,
Where no other comfort may reach me,
    Than His voice to my heart so dear.

Taken aside by Jesus,
    To be quite alone with Him,
To hear His wonderful tones of love
    'Mid the silence and shadows dim.

Taken aside by Jesus,
    Shall I resist the desert place,
When I hear as I never heard before,
    And see Him "face to face"?

AUGUST 28

Morning

Jesus loved Martha and her sister and Lazarus.
JOHN 11:5

Jesus does not want all His loved ones to be of one mold or color. He does not seek uniformity. He will not remove our individuality; He only seeks to glorify it. He loved *"Martha and her sister and Lazarus."*

"Jesus loved Martha." Martha is our biblical example of a practical woman; *"Martha served"* (John 12:2). In that place is enshrined her character.

"And her sister." Mary was contemplative, *spending long hours in deep communion with the unseen.* We need the Marys as well as the Marthas—the deep contemplative souls, whose spirits shed a fragrant restfulness over the hard and busy streets. We need the souls who sit at Jesus' feet and listen to His Word and then interpret the sweet Gospels to a tired and weary world.

"And Lazarus." What do we know about him? Nothing! *Lazarus seems to have been undistinguished and commonplace.* Yet Jesus loved him. What a huge multitude come under the category of "nobodies"! Their names are on the register of births and on the register of deaths, and the space between is a great obscurity. Thank God for the commonplace people! They turn our houses into homes; they make life restful and sweet. Jesus loves the commonplace. Here then is a great, comforting thought: we are all loved—the brilliant and the commonplace, the dreamy and the practical.

"Jesus loved Martha and her sister and Lazarus." Does the wildflower bloom less carefully and are the tints less perfect because it rises beside the fallen tree in the thick woods where mankind never enters? Let us not bemoan the fact that we are not great, and that the eyes of the world are not upon us." J. H. JOWETT

> *Loved! then the way will not be drear,*
> *For One we know is ever near,*
> *Proving it to our hearts so clear*
> *That we are loved.*
>
> *Loved when we sing the glad new song*
> *To Christ, for whom we've waited long,*
> *With all the happy ransomed throng—*
> *Forever loved.*

AUGUST 28
Evening

There He tested them.
EXODUS 15:25 NASB

I once visited the testing room of a large steel mill. I was surrounded by instruments and equipment that tested pieces of steel to their limits and measured their breaking point. Some pieces had been twisted until they broke, and then were labeled with the level of pressure they could withstand. Some had been stretched to their breaking point, with their level of strength also noted. Others had been compressed to their crushing point and measured. Because of the testing, the manager of the mill knew exactly how much stress and strain each piece of steel could endure if it was used to build a ship, building, or bridge.

It is often much the same with God's children. He does not want us to be like fragile vases of glass or porcelain. He wants us to be like these toughened pieces of steel, able to endure twisting and crushing pressure to the utmost without collapse.

God does not want us to be like greenhouse plants, which are sheltered from rough weather, but like storm-beaten oaks; not like sand dunes that are driven back and forth by every gust of wind but like granite mountains that withstand the fiercest storms. Yet to accomplish this, He must take us into His testing room of suffering. And many of us need no other argument than our own experiences to prove that suffering is indeed God's testing room of faith. J. H. M.

It is quite easy for us to talk and to theorize about faith, but God often puts us into His crucible of affliction to test the purity of our gold and to separate the dross from the metal. How happy we are if the hurricanes that blow across life's raging sea have the effect of making Jesus more precious to us! It is better to weather the storm with Christ than to sail smooth waters without Him. J. R. MACDUFF

What if God could not manage to mature your life without suffering?

Morning

Isn't this the carpenter?
MARK 6:3

This is my Son, whom I love; with him I am well pleased.
MATTHEW 3:17

Yes, yes, a carpenter, same trade as mine!
How it warms my heart as I read that line.
I can stand the hard work, I can stand the poor pay,
For I'll see that Carpenter at no distant day.
MALTBIE D. BABCOCK

It suits our best sense that the One who spoke of "putting the hand to the plow" and "taking the yoke upon us" should have made plows and yokes Himself, and people do not think His words less heavenly for not smelling of books and lamps. Let us not make the mistake of those Nazarenes: *that Jesus was a carpenter was* to them poor credentials of divinity, but it has been *Divine credentials to the poor* ever since. Let us not be deceived by social ratings and badges of the schools.

Carey was a cobbler, but he had a map of the world on his shop wall, and outdid Alexander the Great in dreaming and doing.

What thoughts were in the mind of Jesus at His workbench? One of them was that the kingdoms of this world should become the kingdoms of God—*at any cost!*
SELECTED

"*What is that in your hand?*" (Exodus 4:2).

Is it a hoe, a needle, a broom? A pen or a sword? A ledger or a schoolbook? A typewriter or a telegraph instrument? Is it an anvil or a printer's rule? Is it a carpenter's plane or a plasterer's trowel? Is it a throttle or a helm? Is it a scalpel or a yardstick? Is it a musical instrument or the gift of song?

Whatever it is, give it to God in loving service.

Many a tinker and weaver and stonecutter and hard worker has had open windows and a sky, and a mind with wings!

Evening

Carrying his own cross.
JOHN 19:17

"The Changed Cross" is a poem that tells of a weary woman who thought that the cross she must bear surely was heavier than those of other people, so she wished she could choose another person's instead. When she went to sleep, she dreamed she was taken to a place where there were many different crosses from which to choose. There were various shapes and sizes, but the most beautiful one was covered with jewels and gold. "This I could wear with comfort," she said. So she picked it up, but her weak body staggered beneath its weight. The jewels and gold were beautiful, yet they were much too heavy for her to carry.

The next cross she noticed was quite lovely, with beautiful flowers entwined around its sculptured form. Surely this was the one for her. She lifted it, but beneath the flowers were large thorns that pierced and tore her skin.

Finally she came to a plain cross without jewels or any carvings and with only a few words of love inscribed on it. When she picked it up, it proved to be better than all the rest, and the easiest to carry. And as she looked at it, she noticed it was bathed in a radiance that fell from heaven. Then she recognized it as her own old cross. She had found it once again, and it was the best of all, and the lightest for her.

You see, God knows best what cross we need to bear, and we never know how heavy someone else's cross may be. We envy someone who is rich, with a cross of gold adorned with jewels, but we do not know how heavy it is. We look at someone whose life seems so easy and who carries a cross covered with flowers. Yet if we could actually test all the crosses we think are lighter than ours, we would never find one better suited for us than our own. GLIMPSES THROUGH LIFE'S WINDOWS

> *If you, with impatience, give up your cross,*
> *You will not find it in this world again;*
> *Nor in another, but here and here alone*
> *Is given for you to suffer for God's sake.*
> *In the next world we may more perfectly*

Love Him and serve Him, praise Him,
Grow nearer and nearer to Him with delight.
But then we will not anymore
Be called to suffer, which is our assignment here.
Can you not suffer, then, one hour or two?
If He should call you from your cross today,
Saying, "It is finished—that hard cross of yours
From which you pray for deliverance,"
Do you not think that some emotion of regret
Would overcome you? You would say,
"So soon? Let me go back and suffer yet awhile
More patiently. I have not yet praised God."
So whenever it comes, that summons we all look for,
It will seem soon, too soon. Let us take heed in life
That God may now be glorified in us.

"Sermon in a Hospital" by Ugo Bassi's

~~~~~ AUGUST 30 ~~~~~
Morning

I was not disobedient.
Acts 26:19

Whither, O Christ? The *vision did not say; nor did Paul ask, but started on the way.*
If Paul had asked, and if the Lord had said; if Paul had known the long hard
road ahead; if with the heavenly vision Paul had seen stark poverty with cold and hungry mien, black fetid prisons with their chains and stocks, fierce robbers lurking amid
tumbled rocks, the raging of the mob, the crashing stones, the aching eyes, hot fever
in the bones, perils of mountain passes wild and steep, perils of tempest in the angry
deep, the drag of loneliness, the curse of lies, mad bigotry's suspicious peering eyes, the
bitter foe, the weakly, blundering friend, the whirling sword of Caesar at the end—
would Paul have turned his back with shuddering moan and settled down at Tarsus,
had he known? No! and a thousand times the thundering No! *Where Jesus went, there*

Paul rejoiced to go. Prisons were palaces where Jesus stayed; with Jesus near, he asked no other aid; the love of Jesus kept him glad and warm, bold before kings and safe in any storm. *Whither, O Christ? The vision did not say. Paul did not care. He started on the way.* AMOS R. WELLS

"A great *Must* dominated the life of the Son of Man. That *must* will dominate ours if we follow in His footsteps. The Son of Man *must,* and so His followers *must.*"

Lord, I would follow, but—
First I would see what means that wondrous call
That peals so sweetly through life's rainbow hall,
That thrills my heart with quivering golden chords,
And fills my soul with joys seraphical.

Lord, I would follow, but—
First I would leave things straight before I go—
Collect my dues, and pay the debts I owe:
Lest when I'm gone, and none is here to tend,
Time's ruthless hand my garnering o'erthrow.

Lord, I would follow, but—
First I would see the end of this high road
That stretches straight before me fair and broad;
So clear the way I cannot go astray,
It surely leads me equally to God.

Who answers Christ's insistent call
Must give himself, his life, his all,
Without one backward look.
Who sets his hand upon the plow,
And glances back with anxious brow,
His calling hath mistook;
Christ claims him wholly for His own;
He must be Christ's and Christ's alone.

SELECTED

The Spirit of God does not come with a voice like thunder (that may come ultimately) but as a gentle zephyr, yet it can only be described as an imperative compulsion—*This thing must be done!*

∼∼∼ AUGUST 30 ∼∼∼
Evening

Some went out on the sea in ships; they were merchants on the mighty waters.
They saw the works of the LORD, *his wonderful deeds in the deep.*
PSALM 107:23–24

The person who has not learned that every wind that blows can be used to guide us toward heaven has certainly not mastered the art of sailing and is nothing but an apprentice. In fact, the only thing that helps no one is a dead calm. Every wind, whether from the north, south, east, or west, may help us toward that blessed port. So seek only this: *to stay well out to sea*—and then have no fear of stormy winds. May our prayer be that of an old Englishman: "O Lord, send us into the deep water of the sea, for we are so close to shore that even a small breeze from the Devil could break our ship to pieces on the rocks. Again, Lord, send us into the deep water of the sea, where there will be plenty of room to win a glorious victory." MARK GUY PEARSE

Remember, our faith is always at its greatest point when we are in the middle of the trial, and confidence in the flesh will never endure testing. Fair-weather faith is not faith at all. CHARLES H. SPURGEON

∼∼∼ AUGUST 31 ∼∼∼
Morning

You will always be at the top, never at the bottom.
DEUTERONOMY 28:13

Thou shalt be above only, and thou shalt not be beneath.
KJV

This verse came to me first as a very real message from God in a time of great pressure. We had fourteen guests in the Mission house and were almost without domestic help. I had, perforce, to lay aside correspondence and other duties and give my time and attention to cooking and housework, and was feeling the strain.

Then God's Word spoke to me with power: *"Thou shalt be above only, and thou shalt not be beneath,"* and in a moment I saw there was no need to go under—no need to be overwhelmed by my circumstances. No need to trouble because it seemed as if I could not get through and my ordinary work was getting in arrears—somehow, I could be above it all! *"Above only, and not beneath."* How often I used to say as I went about my kitchen, "I refuse to go down," and how the lesson I learned in those difficult days has been an inspiration ever since. Do you wonder that Deuteronomy 28:13 is one of my favorite verses in the Bible?

I see in it the possibility of a life of constant victory—not up today in heights of blessedness, and down in the depths tomorrow. This is a *steady* life. It is the life that has been established and settled by the God of all grace.

"Above only" is a *position* of victory, too. It is that position which is ours in Christ Jesus. "Alive with Christ. . . . in the heavenly realms in Christ Jesus" (Ephesians 2:5–6). "Your life is now hidden with Christ in God" (Colossians 3:3).

When we lived in Alexandria, Egypt, we used to see some fierce squalls of wind and rain, which lashed the sea into fury. The great buoys in the harbor would be covered with spray and foam, but when the wind died down again they were still there in their places, unmoved and steady. "Above only" for they had that within them which kept them on the top. And have we not *power* within us, too, which should insure our *triumph?*

Let us absolutely refuse to come down to live and work on a lower level. A MISSIONARY'S TESTIMONY

"Far above all" (Ephesians 1:21).

~~~~~ AUGUST 31 ~~~~~
Evening

Blessed are those who have not seen and yet have believed.
JOHN 20:29

How important it is for God to keep us focused on things that are unseen, for we are so easily snared by the things we can see! If Peter was ever going to walk on the water, he had to walk, but if he was going to swim to Jesus, he had to swim. He could not do both. If a bird is going to fly, it must stay away from fences and trees, trusting the buoyancy of its wings. And if it tries to stay within easy reach of the ground, it will never fly very well.

God had to bring Abraham to the end of his own strength and let him see that with his own body he could do nothing. He had to consider his own body "as good as dead" (Hebrews 11:12) and then trust God to do all the work. When he looked away from himself and trusted only God, he became "fully persuaded that God had power to do what he had promised" (Romans 4:21).

This is what God is teaching us, and He has to keep results that are encouraging away from us until we learn to trust Him without them. Then He loves to make His Word as real to us in actuality as it is in our faith. A. B. SIMPSON

I do not ask that He must prove
　　His Word is true to me,
And that before I can believe
　　He first must let me see.
It is enough for me to know
　　It's true because He says it's so;
On His unchanging Word I'll stand
　　And trust till I can understand.

E. M. WINTER

～～ SEPTEMBER 1 ～～

Morning

The LORD *makes firm the steps of the one who delights in him.*
PSALM 37:23

The steps of a good man are ordered by the LORD.
KJV

We often make a great mistake thinking that God is not guiding us at all, because we cannot see far ahead. But He only undertakes that *the steps* of a good man should be ordered by the Lord; not next year, but tomorrow; not for the next mile, but the next yard: *as you will acknowledge when you review it from the hilltops of Glory.*

"The *stops* of a good man, as well as his *steps,* are ordered by the Lord," says George Mueller. Naturally an opened door seems more like guidance to us than a closed one. *Yet God may guide by the latter as definitely as by the former.* His guidance of the children of Israel by the pillar of cloud and of fire is a clear case in point. When the cloud was lifted, the Israelites took up their march: it was the guidance of God to move onward. But when the cloud tarried and abode upon the tabernacle, then the people rested in their tents. Both the tarrying and the journeying were guidance from the Lord—the one as much as the other.

I shall never be able to go too fast, if the Lord is in front of me; and I can never go too slowly, if I follow Him always, everywhere.

It is just as dark in advance of God's glorious leading as it is away behind Him.

You may be trying to go faster than He is moving. Wait till He comes up, and then the way will no longer lie in darkness. He has left footprints for us to follow. *Make no footprints of thine own!*

> *Not so in haste, my heart!*
> *Have faith in God and wait:*
> *Although He linger long*
> *He never comes too late.*
>
> *Until He cometh, rest,*
> *Nor grudge the hours that roll,*
> *The feet that wait for God*
> *Are soonest at the goal*
>
> *Are soonest at the goal*
> *That is not gained by speed.*
> *Then hold thee still, my heart,*
> *For I shall wait His lead.*

BAYARD TAYLOR

SEPTEMBER 1
Evening

I will rebuild you with stones of turquoise.
ISAIAH 54:11

The stones in the wall said, "We have come from mountains far away—from the sides of rugged cliffs. Fire and water have worked on us for ages but have only produced crevices. Yet human hands like yours have made us into homes where children of your immortal race are born, suffer, rejoice, find rest and shelter, and learn the lessons that our Maker and yours is teaching. But to come to the point of being used for this purpose, we have endured much. Dynamite has torn at our very heart, and pickaxes have broken and split us into pieces. Often as we lay disfigured and broken in the quarry, everything seemed to be without design or meaning. But gradually we were cut into blocks, and some of us were chiseled with sharper instruments until we had a fine edge. Now we are complete, are in our proper places, and are of service.

"You, however, are still in your quarry. You are not complete, and because of that, as once was the case with us, there is much you do not understand. But you are destined for a higher building, and someday you will be placed in it by angelic hands, becoming a living stone in a heavenly temple."

> *In the still air the music lies unheard;*
> *In the rough marble beauty hides unseen;*
> *To make the music and the beauty needs*
> *The master's touch, the sculptor's chisel keen.*
> *Great Master, touch us with Your skillful hands;*
> *Let not the music that is in us die!*
> *Great Sculptor, hew and polish us; nor let,*
> *Hidden and lost, Your form within us lie!*

Morning

When you walk through the fire, you will not be burned.
ISAIAH 43:2

In giving a lecture on flame a scientist once made a most interesting experiment. He wanted to show that in the center of each flame there is a hollow—a place of entire stillness—around which its fire is a mere wall. To prove this he introduced into the midst of the flame a minute and carefully shielded charge of explosive powder. The protection was then carefully removed, and no explosion followed. A second time the experiment was tried, and by a slight agitation of the hand the central security was lost, and an immediate explosion was the result.

Our safety, then, is only in *stillness of soul.* If we are affrighted and exchange the principle of faith for that of fear, or if we are rebellious and restless, we shall be hurt by the flames, and anguish and disappointment will be the result.

Moreover, God will be disappointed in us if we break down. Testing is the proof of His love and confidence, and who can tell what pleasure our steadfastness and stillness give to Him? If He allowed us to go without testing, it would not be complementary to our spiritual experience. Much trial and suffering mean, therefore, that God has confidence in us, that He believes we are strong enough to endure, that we shall be true to Him even when He has left us without outward evidence of His care and seemingly at the mercy of His adversaries. If He increase the trials instead of diminishing them, it is an expression of confidence in us up to the present, and a further proof that He is looking to us to glorify Him in yet hotter fires through which He is calling us to pass. *Let us not be afraid! We shall be delivered from the transitory and the outward and drawn into closer fellowship with God Himself!*

O God, make us children of quietness! AN ANCIENT LITURGY

Evening

It has been granted to you . . . to suffer for him.
PHILIPPIANS 1:29

God runs a costly school, for many of His lessons are learned through tears. Richard Baxter, the seventeenth-century Puritan preacher, once said, "O God, I thank You for the discipline I have endured in this body for fifty-eight years." And he certainly is not the only person who has turned trouble into triumph.

Soon the school of our heavenly Father will close for us, for the end of the school term is closer every day. May we never run from a difficult lesson or flinch from the rod of discipline. Richer will be our crown, and sweeter will heaven be, if we cheerfully endure to the end. Then we will graduate in glory. THEODORE L. CUYLER

The world's finest china is fired in ovens at least three times, and some many more. Dresden china is always fired three times. *Why* is it forced to endure such intense heat? Shouldn't once or twice be enough? No, it is necessary to fire the china three times so the gold, crimson, and other colors are brighter, more beautiful, and permanently attached.

We are fashioned after the same principle. The human trials of life are burned into us numerous times, and through God's grace, beautiful colors are formed in us and made to shine forever. CORTLAND MYERS

Earth's fairest flowers grow not on sunny plain,
But where some vast upheaval tore in twain
The smiling land.
After the whirlwind's devastating blast,
And molten lava, fire, and ashes fall,
God's still small voice breathes healing over all.
From broken rocks and fern-clad chasms deep,
Flow living waters as from hearts that weep,
There in the afterglow soft dews distill
And angels tend God's plants when night falls still,
And the Beloved passing by the way
Will gather lilies at the break of day.

J. H. D.

They were employed in that work day and night.
1 Chronicles 9:33 KJV

There is a legend of a man who found the barn where Satan kept his seeds ready to be sown in the human heart and on finding the seeds of discouragement more numerous than others, learned that those seeds could be made to grow almost anywhere. When Satan was questioned, he reluctantly admitted that there was one place in which he could never get them to thrive. "And where is that?" asked the man. Satan replied sadly, "In the heart of a grateful man."

The psalmist realized that gratitude plays an essential part in true worship. He sang praises to God at all times; often, in his darkest moments. When in his despair he called on God, his praises soon mingled with his cries of anguish, showing the victory accomplished by his habitual thankfulness.

Sometimes a light surprises the Christian while he sings.

Is it midnight in your experience? Is it an interminable time since the gold and crimson hope died out in the west—and a seemingly longer interval before the hoped-for dawning of day? Midnight! Still, dark, and eerie! It is time to pray! And it is time to sing! Strange how prayer and singing open prison doors—but they do!

Do you need doors to be opened? Try prayer and singing; they go together! They work wonders!

When the heaven is black with wind, the thunder crackling over our heads, then we may join in the paean of the storm-spirits to Him whose pageant of power passes over the earth and harms us not in its march.

The choir of small birds, and night crickets, and all happy things, praise Him all the night long. Not somehow, but triumphantly!

Evening

He saw the disciples straining at the oars.
MARK 6:48

Straining and striving does not accomplish the work God gives us to do. Only God Himself, who always works without stress and strain and who never overworks, can do the work He assigns to His children. When we restfully trust Him to do it, the work will be completed and will be done well. And the way to let Him do His work through us is to so fully abide in Christ by faith that He fills us to overflowing.

A man who learned this secret once said, "I came to Jesus and drank, and I believe I will never be thirsty again. My life's motto has become *'Not overwork but overflow,'* and it has already made all the difference in my life."

There is no straining effort in an overflowing life, and it is quietly irresistible. It is the normal life of omnipotent and ceaseless accomplishment into which Christ invites each of us to enter—today and always. SUNDAY SCHOOL TIMES

Be all at rest, my soul, O blessed secret,
Of the true life that glorifies the Lord:
Not always does the busiest soul best serve Him,
But he that rests upon His faithful Word.
Be all at rest, let not your heart be rippled,
For tiny wavelets mar the image fair,
Which the still pool reflects of heaven's glory—
And thus the image He would have you bear.

Be all at rest, my soul, for rest is service,
To the still heart God does His secrets tell;
Thus will you learn to wait, and watch, and labor,
Strengthened to bear, since Christ in you does dwell.
For what is service but the life of Jesus,
Lived through a vessel of earth's fragile clay,

Loving and giving and poured forth for others,
    A living sacrifice from day to day.

Be all at rest, so then you'll be an answer
    To those who question, "Who is God and where?"
For God is rest, and where He dwells is stillness,
    And they who dwell in Him, His rest will share.
And what will meet the deep unrest around you,
    But the calm peace of God that filled His breast?
For still a living Voice calls to the weary,
    From Him who said, "Come unto Me and rest."
                            FREDA HANBURY ALLEN

In Resurrection stillness there is Resurrection power.

SEPTEMBER 4
Morning

They spring up like flowers.
JOB 14:2

The lotus flower (the spiritual symbol of the East) is rooted in the mud. It is quite as much indebted to the mud and water for its beauty as to the air and sunshine in which it blooms.

We must not scorn the study of root culture, nor neglect it in enthusiasm for the beauties of the orchid; for though that exquisite flower is an air plant, it needs to attach itself to a sturdier growth that is rooted in the ground and draws its nourishment from the soil to feed both itself and its parasite. *The tree will outlive many seasons of orchids!*

"Some time ago in the late autumn," says a writer, "I was in the hothouse of one of our florists. We were in the cellar, and in the dimly lighted place one could see arranged in regular file long rows of flowerpots. The florist explained that in these pots had been planted the bulbs for their winter flowers. It was best for them, he said, that they be rooted in the dark."

Not in the glaring sunlight but in the subdued shadows, their life-giving roots were putting forth. They would be ready for the open day a little later. Then their gay colors would cheer many hearts; then their sweet perfume would laden the winter air.

Rooted in the shadows to bloom in the light! Roots, then roses.

SEPTEMBER 4

Evening

When you hear them sound a long blast on the trumpets, have
the whole army give a loud shout; then the wall of the city will
collapse and the army will go up, everyone straight in.

JOSHUA 6:5

The "loud shout" of steadfast faith is the exact opposite of the groans of wavering faith and the complaints of discouraged hearts. Of all "the secret[s] of the LORD" (Psalm 25:14 KJV), I do not believe there are any more valuable than the secret of this *"loud shout" of faith*. "The LORD said to Joshua, 'See, I have delivered Jericho into your hands, along with its king and its fighting men'" (Joshua 6:2). He did not say, "I *will* deliver" but "I *have* delivered." The victory already belonged to the children of Israel, and now they were called to take possession of it. But the big question still remaining was *how*. It looked impossible, but the Lord had a plan.

No one would normally believe that a shout could cause city walls to fall. Yet the *secret* of their victory lay precisely in just that shout, for it was the shout of faith. And it was a faith that dared to claim a promised victory solely on the basis of the authority of God's Word, even though there were no physical signs of fulfillment. God answered His promise in response to their faith, for when they shouted, He caused the walls to fall.

God had declared, "I *have delivered* Jericho into your hands," and faith believed this to be true. And many centuries later the Holy Spirit recorded this triumph of faith in the book of Hebrews as follows: "By faith the walls of Jericho fell, after the army had marched around them for seven days" (Hebrews 11:30). HANNAH WHITALL SMITH

Faith can never reach its consummation,
Till the victor's thankful song we raise:

In the glorious city of salvation,
  God has told us all the gates are praise.

SEPTEMBER 5

Morning

Then the fire of the LORD *fell and burned up the sacrifice, the wood,*
the stones and the soil, and also licked up the water in the trench.
1 KINGS 18:38

Prayer is one of the most sacred and precious privileges vouchsafed to mortals. The following is a scene from the life of that mighty *Elijah in prayer,* CHARLES G. FINNEY. The summer of 1853 was unusually hot and dry; pastures were scorched. There seemed likely to be a total crop failure. At the church in Oberlin the great congregation had gathered as usual. Though the sky was clear, the burden of Finney's prayer was for rain.

"We do not presume, O Lord, to dictate to Thee what is best for us; yet Thou didst invite us to come to Thee as children to an earthly father and tell Thee all our wants. *We want rain.* Our pastures are dry. The earth is gaping open for rain. The cows are wandering about and lowing in search of water. Even the squirrels are suffering from thirst. Unless Thou givest us rain our cattle will die, and our harvest will come to naught. O Lord, *send us rain, and send it now!* This is an easy thing for Thee to do. *Send it now,* Lord, for Christ's sake."

In a few minutes he had to cease preaching; his voice could not be heard because of the roar and rattle of the rain! LIFE OF FINNEY

Life has outgrown
Faith's childish way,
The proud and scoffing
Folk insist;
And so they laugh
At all who say
God's miracles exist.

Well, let them laugh!
The trusting heart
Has joys which they
Know naught thereof.
And, daily, miracles are wrought
For us who hold
To faith and love!

"MIRACLES" BY JOHN RICHARD MORELAND

The world wants something that has God in it!

~~~~~ SEPTEMBER 5 ~~~~~

Evening

Blessed are all who wait for him!
ISAIAH 30:18

We often hear about waiting *on* God, which actually means that He is waiting until we are ready. There is another side, however. When we wait *for* God, we are waiting until He is ready.

Some people say, and many more believe, that as soon as we meet all His conditions, God will answer our prayer. They teach that He lives in an eternal *now*, that with Him there is no past or future, and that if we can fulfill all He requires to be obedient to His will, *immediately* our needs will be met, our desires satisfied, and our prayers answered.

While there is much truth in this belief, it expresses only one side of the truth. God *does* live in an eternal *now*, yet He works out His purposes over *time*. A petition presented to God is like a seed dropped into the ground. Forces above and beyond our control must work on it until the actual accomplishment of the answer. *The Still Small Voice*

I longed to walk along an easy road,
And leave behind the dull routine of home,
Thinking in other fields to serve my God;
But Jesus said, "My time has not yet come."

—— 615 ——

I longed to sow the seed in other soil,
    To be unshackled in the work, and free,
To join with other laborers in their toil;
    But Jesus said, "It's not My choice for thee."

I longed to leave the desert, and be led
    To work where souls were sunk in sin and shame,
That I might win them; but the Master said,
    "I have not called you, publish here My name."

I longed to fight the battles of my King,
    Lift high His standards in the thickest strife;
But my great Captain had me wait and sing
    Songs of His conquests in my quiet life.

I longed to leave the hard and difficult sphere,
    Where all alone I seemed to stand and wait,
To feel I had some human helper near,
    But Jesus had me guard one lonely gate.

I longed to leave the common daily toil,
    Where no one seemed to understand or care;
But Jesus said, "I choose for you this soil,
    That you might raise for Me some blossoms rare."

And now I have no longing but to do
    At home, or far away, His blessed will,
To work amid the many or the few;
    Thus, "choosing not to choose," my heart is still.
                    SELECTED

And Patience was willing to wait. PILGRIM'S PROGRESS

Morning

Christ in you.
COLOSSIANS 1:27

It is a great secret I tell you today, nay, I can give you—if you will take it from *Him,* not from me—a secret which has been to me, oh, so wonderful! Many years ago I came to Him burdened with guilt and fear; I took that simple secret, and it took away my fear and sin. Years passed on, and I found sin overcame me, and my temptations were too strong for me. I came to Him a second time, and He whispered to me, *"Christ in you."* And I have had victory, rest and sweet blessing ever since . . . I look back with unutterable gratitude to the lonely and sorrowful night, when, mistaken in many things, and imperfect in all, and not knowing but that it would be death in the most literal sense before the morning light, my heart's first full consecration was made, and, with unreserved surrender, I first could say,

Jesus, I my cross have taken,
All to leave and follow Thee:
Destitute, despised, forsaken,
Thou from hence my all shall be.

Never, perhaps, has my heart known such a thrill of joy as when, the following Sunday morning, I gave out these lines, and sang them with all my heart. And, if God has been pleased to use me in any fuller measure, it has been because of that hour. And it will be still, in the measure in which that hour is made the keynote of a consecrated, crucified, and Christ-devoted life. This experience of Christ our Sanctifier marks a definite and distinct crisis in the history of a soul. We do not grow into it, but we cross a definite line of demarcation, as clear as when the hosts of Joshua crossed the Jordan and were over in the Promised Land, and set up a great heap of stones, so that they never could forget that crisis hour. A. B. SIMPSON

Evening

You remain.
HEBREWS 1:11

There are so many people who sit by their fireplace all alone! They sit by another chair, once filled, and cannot restrain the tears that flow. They sit alone so much, but there *is* someone who is unseen and just within their reach. But for some reason, they don't *realize* His presence. Realizing it is blessed yet quite rare. It is dependent upon their mood, their feelings, their physical condition, and the weather. The rain or thick fog outside, the lack of sleep and the intense pain, seem to affect their mood and blur their vision so they do not realize His presence.

There is, however, something even better than *realizing*, and even more blessed. It is completely independent of these other conditions and is something that will abide with you. It is this: *recognizing* that unseen presence, which is so wonderful, quieting, soothing, calming, and warming. So *recognize* the presence of the Master. He is here, close to you, and His presence is real. Recognizing will also help your ability to realize but is never dependent upon it.

Yes, there is immeasurably more—the truth is a presence, not a thing, a fact, or a statement. Some *One* is present, and He is a warmhearted Friend and the all-powerful Lord. This is a joyful truth for weeping hearts everywhere, no matter the reason for the tears, or whatever stream their weeping willow is planted beside. SAMUEL DICKEY GORDON

When from my life the old-time joys have vanished,
  Treasures once mine, I may no longer claim,
This truth may feed my hungry heart, and famished:
  Lord, You remain here! You are still the same!

When streams have dried, those streams of glad refreshing—
  Friendships so blest, so rich, so free;
When sun-kissed skies give place to clouds depressing,
  Lord, You remain here! Still my heart has Thee.

When strength has failed, and feet, now worn and weary,
On happy errands may no longer go,
Why should I sigh, or let the days be dreary?
Lord, You remain here! Could You more bestow?

Thus through life's days—whoe'er or what may fail me,
Friends, friendships, joys, in small or great degree,
Songs may be mine, no sadness need assault me,
Lord, You remain here! Still my heart has Thee.

J. DANSON SMITH

SEPTEMBER 7

Morning

The greatest of these is love.

1 CORINTHIANS 13:13

"I'll master it!" said the ax, and his blows fell heavily on the iron. And every blow made his edge more blunt till he ceased to strike.

"Leave it to me!" said the saw, and with his relentless teeth he worked backward and forward on its surface till his teeth were worn down and broken, and he fell aside.

"Ha, ha!" said the hammer. "I knew you wouldn't succeed! I'll show you the way!" But at the first fierce stroke off flew his head, and the iron remained as before.

"Shall I try?" asked the still, small flame.

They all despised the flame, but he curled gently around the iron and embraced it and never left it till it melted under his irresistible influence.

Hard indeed is the heart that can resist love. "And now these three remain: faith, hope and love. But the greatest of these is love" (1 Corinthians 13:3).

Evening

God is our refuge and strength, an ever-present help in trouble.
PSALM 46:1

Why didn't God help me sooner?" This is a question that is often asked, but it is not His will to act on *your* schedule. He desires to change you through the trouble and cause you to learn a lesson from it. He has promised, "I will be with him *in* trouble, I will deliver him and honor him" (Psalm 91:15). He will be with you *in* trouble all day and through the night. Afterward he will take you out of it, but not until you have stopped being restless and worried over it and have become calm and quiet. Then He will say, "It is enough."

God uses trouble to teach His children precious lessons. Difficulties are intended to educate us, and when their good work is done, a glorious reward will become ours through them. There is a sweet joy and a real value in difficulties, for He regards them not as difficulties but as opportunities. SELECTED

> *Not always out of our troubled times,*
> *And the struggles fierce and grim,*
> *But in—deeper in—to our sure rest,*
> *The place of our peace, in Him.*
>
> ANNIE JOHNSON FLINT

I once heard the following statement from a simple old man, and I have never forgotten it: "When God tests you, it is a good time to test Him by putting His promises to the test and then claiming from Him exactly what your trials have made necessary." There are two ways of getting out of a trial. One is simply to try to get rid of the trial, and then to be thankful when it is over. The other is to recognize the trial as a challenge from God to claim a larger blessing than we have ever before experienced, and to accept it with delight as an opportunity of receiving a greater measure of God's divine grace.

In this way, even the Adversary becomes a help to us, and all the things that seem to be against us turn out to assist us along our way. Surely this is what is meant by the words "In all these things we are more than conquerors through him who loved us" (Romans 8:37). A. B. SIMPSON

SEPTEMBER 8

Morning

I do not want to leave you.
DEUTERONOMY 15:16

Your servant for life.
DEUTERONOMY 15:17

No man ever makes *Him* supreme and suffers loss, for Jehovah will not be left in any man's debt. When a man holds on, God takes away; when a man lets go, He gives, and that liberally.

Make me a captive, Lord,
And then I shall be free.
Force me to render up my sword,
And I shall conqueror be.
I sink in life's alarm
When by myself I stand;
Imprison with Thy mighty arm,
Then strong shall be my hand.

My heart is weak and poor,
Until it Master finds;
It has no spring of action sure,
It varies with the wind.
It cannot freely move
Till Thou hast wrought its chain;
Enslave it with Thy mighty love,
Then deathless I shall reign.

My power is faint and low
Till I have learned to serve:
It wants the needed fire to glow,
It wants the breeze to nerve;
It cannot drive the world
Until itself be driven;
Its flag can only be unfurled
When Thou shalt breathe from heaven.

My will is not my own
Till Thou hast made it Thine;
If it would reach the monarch's throne
It must its crown resign.
It only stands unbent
Amid the clashing strife,
Till on Thy bosom it has leant,
And found in Thee its life.

GEORGE MATHESON

O Master, show me this morning how to yield myself up to Thee completely and then how to ask of Thee things great enough to be *worthy of a King's giving*. Make me equal in my requests to Thy infinite eagerness to give.

Touch with Thy Pierced Hand the hidden springs that will cause every part of my being to fly wide open to Thee, my Lord and my God!

<hr>

SEPTEMBER 8

Evening

Thou hast enlarged me when I was in distress.
PSALM 4:1 KJV

This verse is one of the greatest testimonies ever written regarding the effectiveness of God's work on our behalf during times of crisis. It is a statement of thanksgiving for having been set free not *from* suffering but rather *through* suffering. In stating, "Thou hast enlarged me when I was in distress," the psalmist is declaring that the sorrows of life have themselves been the source of life's enlargement.

Haven't each of us experienced this a thousand times and found it to be true? Someone once said of Joseph that when he was in the dungeon, "iron entered his soul." And the strength of iron is exactly what he needed, for earlier he had only experienced the glitter of gold. He had been rejoicing in youthful dreams, and dreaming actually hardens the heart. Someone who sheds great tears over a simple romance will not be of much help in a real crisis, for true sorrow will be too deep for him. We all need the iron in life to enlarge our character. The gold is simply a passing vision, whereas the iron is the true experience of life. The chain that is the common bond uniting us to others must be one of iron. The common touch of humanity that gives the world true kinship is not joy but sorrow—gold is partial to only a few, but iron is universal.

Dear soul, if you want your sympathy for others to be enlarged, you must be willing to have your life narrowed to certain degrees of suffering. Joseph's dungeon was the very road to his throne, and he would have been unable to lift the iron load of his brothers had he not experienced the iron in his own life. Your life will be enlarged in proportion to the amount of iron you have endured, for it is in the shadows of your life that you will find the actual fulfillment of your dreams of glory. So do not complain about the shadows of darkness—in reality, they are better than your dreams could ever be. Do not say that the darkness of the prison has shackled you, for your shackles are wings—wings of flight into the heart and soul of humanity. And the gate of your prison is the gate into the heart of the universe. God has enlarged you through the suffering of sorrow's chain. GEORGE MATHESON

If Joseph had never been Egypt's prisoner, he would have never been Egypt's governor. The iron chain that bound his feet brought about the golden chain around his neck. SELECTED

～～ SEPTEMBER 9 ～～
Morning

I know whom I have believed.

2 TIMOTHY 1:12

God loves an uttermost confidence in Himself—to be wholly trusted. This is the sublimest of all the characteristics of a true Christian—the basis of all character.

Is there anything that pleases you more than to be trusted—to have even a little child look up into your face and put out his hand to meet yours and come to you confidingly? By so much as God is better than you are, by so much more does He love to be trusted.

There is a Hand stretched out to you; a Hand with a wound in the palm of it. Reach out the hand of your faith to clasp it, and cling to it, for "without faith it is impossible to please God" (Hebrews 11:6). HENRY VAN DYKE

Reach up as far as you can, and God will reach down all the rest of the way. BISHOP VINCENT

> *Not what, but whom I do believe!*
> *That, in my darkest hour of need,*
> *Hath comfort that no mortal creed*
> *To mortal man may give.*
> *Not what, but whom!*
> *For Christ is more than all the creeds,*
> *And His full life of gentle deeds*
> *Shall all the creeds outlive.*
> *Not what I do believe, but whom!*
> *who walks beside me in the gloom?*
> *who shares the burden wearisome?*
> *who all the dim way doth illume,*
> *And bids me look beyond the tomb*
> *The larger life to live?*
> *Not what I do believe, but whom!*
> *Not what,*
> *But whom!*

JOHN OXENHAM

Evening

Some [seed] fell on rocky places, where it did not have much
soil. It sprang up quickly, because the soil was shallow.

MATTHEW 13:5

S hallow! From the context of the teaching of this parable, it seems that we must have something to do with the depth of the soil. The fruitful seed fell on "good soil" (v. 8), or good and honest hearts. I suppose the shallow people are those who "*did not have much soil*"—those who have no real purpose in life and are easily swayed by a tender appeal, a good sermon, or a simple melody. And at first it seems as if they will amount to something for God, but because they "*[do] not have much soil*," they have no depth or genuine purpose, and no earnest desire to know His will in order to do it. Therefore we should be careful to maintain the soil of our hearts.

When a Roman soldier was told by his guide that if he insisted on taking a certain journey, it would probably be fatal, he answered, "It is necessary for me to go—it is not necessary for me to live." That was true depth of conviction, and only when we are likewise convicted will our lives amount to something. But a shallow life lives on its impulses, impressions, intuitions, instincts, and largely on its circumstances. Those with profound character, however, look beyond all these and move steadily ahead, seeing the future, where sorrow, seeming defeat, and failure will be reversed. They sail right through storm clouds into the bright sunshine, which always awaits them on the other side.

Once God has deepened us, He can give us His deepest truths, His most profound secrets, and will trust us with greater power. Lord, lead us into the depths of Your life and save us from a shallow existence!

> *On to broader fields of holy vision;*
> *On to loftier heights of faith and love;*
> *Onward, upward, apprehending wholly,*
> *All for which He calls you from above.*
>
> A. B. SIMPSON

Morning

Spread the sail.
ISAIAH 33:23 KJV

Picture a vessel lying becalmed on a glassy sea—not a breath of air stirs a sail. But, presently, the little pennant far up on the masthead begins to stir and lift! There is not a ripple on the water, not the slightest movement of the air on deck, but there is a current stirring *in the upper air!* At once the sails are spread to catch it!

"So in life," says Dr. Miller, "there are higher and lower currents. Too many of us use only the lower sails and catch only the winds blowing along earthly levels. It would be an unspeakable gain to us all were we to let our lives fall under the influence of these upper currents."

> *Far out to sea, at close of day,*
> *A lonely albatross flew by.*
> *We watched him as he soared away—*
> *A speck against the glowing sky!*
> *Thought I: This lordly feathered one*
> *Is trusting in the faithfulness*
> *Of wind and tide, of star and sun;*
> *And shall I trust the Maker less?*
>
> *O soul of mine, spread wide thy wings:*
> *Mount up; push out with courage strong!*
> *And—like a bird which, soaring, sings—*
> *Let heaven vibrate with thy song!*
> *Spread wide thy wings, o soul of mine,*
> *For God will ever faithful be:*
> *His love shall guide thee; winds Divine*
> *Shall waft thee o'er this troubled sea.*
> *Though dangers threaten in the night,*
> *Though tides of death below thee roll,*

Though storms attend thy homeward flight,
Spread wide thy pinions, o my soul!

Though shadows veil the verdant shore,
And distant seems the hallowed dawn,
Spread wide thy pinions—evermore
Spread wide thy pinions, and press on.

ROBERT CRUMLY

Spread your sails to catch the upper currents!

~~~~ SEPTEMBER 10 ~~~~

Evening

The LORD will vindicate me.
PSALM 138:8

There is a divine mystery in suffering, one that has a strange and supernatural power and has never been completely understood by human reason. No one has ever developed a deep level of spirituality or holiness without experiencing a great deal of suffering. When a person who suffers reaches a point where he can be calm and carefree, inwardly smiling at his own suffering, and no longer asking God to be delivered from it, then the suffering has accomplished its blessed ministry, perseverance has "finish[ed] its work" (James 1:4), and the pain of the Crucifixion has begun to weave itself into a crown.

It is in this experience of complete suffering that the Holy Spirit works many miraculous things deep within our soul. In this condition, our entire being lies perfectly still under the hand of God; every power and ability of the mind, will, and heart are at last submissive; a quietness of eternity settles into the entire soul; and finally, the mouth becomes quiet, having only a few words to say, and stops crying out the words Christ quoted on the cross: "My God, my God, why have you forsaken me?" (Psalm 22:1).

At this point the person stops imagining castles in the sky, and pursuing foolish ideas, and his reasoning becomes calm and relaxed, with all choices removed, because the only choice has now become the purpose of God. Also, his emotions are weaned away from other people and things, becoming deadened so that nothing can hurt, offend, hinder, or get in his way. He can now let the circumstances be what they may, and continue to seek only God and His will, with the calm assurance that He is causing everything in the universe, whether good or bad, past or present, to work "for the good of those who love him" (Romans 8:28).

Oh, the blessings of absolute submission to Christ! What a blessing to lose our own strength, wisdom, plans, and desires and to be where every ounce of our being becomes like a peaceful Sea of Galilee under the omnipotent feet of Jesus! SOUL FOOD

The main thing is to suffer without becoming discouraged. FRANÇOIS FÉNELON

The heart that serves, and loves, and clings,
Hears everywhere the rush of angel wings.

—— SEPTEMBER 11 ——

Morning

The weapons we fight with are not the weapons of the world. On the contrary, they have divine power to demolish strongholds. We demolish arguments and every pretension that sets itself up against the knowledge of God, and we take captive every thought to make it obedient to Christ.

2 CORINTHIANS 10:4–5

He said not,
"Thou shalt not be
Tempested;
Thou shalt not be
Travailed;
Thou shalt not be
Afflicted":
But he said,
"Thou shalt not be
Overcome!"

JULIAN OF NORWICK, A.D. 1373

We are not here to be overcome, but we are to rise unvanquished after every knockout blow *and laugh the laugh of faith—not fear.*

> *Tempested on the sea of life;*
> *Travailed sore, amid earth's strife;*
> *Afflicted often, and sore dismayed;*
> *Look up, faint heart, be not afraid,*
> *Thou shalt not be overcome!*
>
> *God's ways are far beyond our ken;*
> *His thoughts are not the thoughts of men;*
> *And He knoweth what is best for you.*
> *Hope on, my friend, He will bear you through.*
> *Thou shalt not be overcome!*
>
> *Though "The reason why" we cannot see,*
> *Our Father knows—'tis enough that we*
> *But trust His love, when our eyes are dim.*
> *Look up! Holdfast! though the fight is grim.*
> *We shall not be overcome!*

MARY E. THOMPSON

～～～ SEPTEMBER 11 ～～～
Evening

After waiting patiently, Abraham received what was promised.
HEBREWS 6:15

Abraham was tested for a very long time, but he was richly rewarded. The Lord tested him by delaying the fulfillment of His promise. Satan tested him through temptation, and people tested him through their jealousy, distrust, and opposition to him. Sarah tested him through her worrisome temperament. Yet he patiently endured, not questioning God's truthfulness and power or doubting God's faithfulness and love.

Instead, Abraham submitted to God's divine sovereignty and infinite wisdom. And he was silent through many delays, willing to wait for the Lord's timing. Having patiently endured, he then obtained the fulfillment of the promise.

Beloved, God's promises can never fail to be accomplished, and those who patiently wait can never be disappointed, for believing faith leads to realization. Abraham's life condemns a spirit of hastiness, admonishes those who complain, commends those who are patient, and encourages quiet submission to God's will and way.

Remember, Abraham was tested but he patiently waited, ultimately received what was promised, and was satisfied. If you will imitate his example, you will share the same blessing. Selected

~~~~ SEPTEMBER 12 ~~~~
Morning

> *As Jesus started on his way, a man ran up to him and. . . . asked, "What*
> *must I do to inherit eternal life? . . . Jesus looked at him and loved him.*
> *"One thing you lack," he said. "Go, sell everything you have . . . and*
> *you will have treasure in heaven. Then come, follow me." At this the*
> *man's face fell. He went away sad, because he had great wealth.*
> Mark 10:17, 21–22

Such was the preparation necessary before this admirable soul could become a disciple of Jesus Christ. To use the language of Dr. Donald Davidson:

"Strip yourself of every possession, cut away every affection, disengage yourself from all *things,* be as if you were a naked soul, alone in the world; be a mere man merely, and then be God's. *"Sell everything you have and. . . . follow me"!* Reduce yourself down, if I may say so, till nothing remains but your consciousness of yourself, and then cast the self-consciousness at the feet of God in Christ.

"The only way to Jesus is *alone.* Will you strip yourself and separate yourself and take that lonely road, or will you too 'go away sorrowful'?"

We are not told his name—this "rich young ruler"
Who sought the Lord that day;
We only know that he had great possessions
And that—he went away.

He went away; he kept his earthly treasure
But oh, at what a cost!
Afraid to take the cross and lose his riches—
And God and Heaven were lost.

So for the tinsel bonds that held and drew him
What honor he let slip—
Comrade of John and Paul and friend of Jesus—
What glorious fellowship!

For they who left their all to follow Jesus
Have found a deathless fame,
On his immortal scroll of saints and martyrs
God wrote each shining name.

We should have read his there—the rich young ruler—If he had stayed that day;
Nameless—though Jesus loved him—ever nameless because—he went away.

SELECTED

～～～ SEPTEMBER 12 ～～～

Evening

Who is this coming up from the wilderness leaning on her beloved?
SONG OF SONGS 8:5

I once learned a great lesson at a prayer meeting at a southern church. As one man prayed, he asked the Lord for various blessings, just as you or I would, and he thanked the Lord for many blessings already received, just as you or I would. But he closed his prayer with this unusual petition: "And, O Lord, support us! Yes, support us on every leaning side!"

Do you have any "leaning sides"? This humble man's prayer pictured them in a new way and illustrated the Great Supporter in a new light as well. He saw God as always walking alongside the Christian, ready to extend His mighty arm to steady the weak on "every *leaning* side."

> *Child of My love, lean hard,*
> *And let Me feel the pressure of your care;*
> *I know your burden, child. I shaped it;*
> *Balanced it in Mine Own hand; made no proportion*
> *In its weight to your unaided strength,*
> *For even as I laid it on, I said,*
> *"I will be near, and while she leans on Me,*
> *This burden will be Mine, not hers;*
> *So will I keep My child within the circling arms*
> *Of My Own love." Here lay it down, nor fear*
> *To impose it on a shoulder that upholds*
> *The government of worlds. Yet closer come:*
> *You are not near enough. I would embrace your care;*
> *So I might feel My child reclining on My breast.*
> *You love Me, I know. So then do not doubt;*
> *But loving Me, lean hard.*

~~~~~~ SEPTEMBER 13 ~~~~~~

Morning

How precious to me are your thoughts, God! How vast is the sum of them!
PSALM 139:17

Nothing is more beautiful than our Lord's foresight!

There never was anyone so faithful or considerate or farseeing as Jesus. He had great commendation to give a woman because she came "beforehand" with her ministry. It was His own manner to anticipate events. He was always thinking ahead of the disciples.

When He sent His disciples to prepare the Passover, there was found an upper room furnished and prepared. He had thought it all out. His plans were not made only for that day. *He was always in advance of time.* When the disciples came back from fishing, Jesus was on the seashore with a fire of coals and fish laid thereon. He thinks of the morning duties before you are astir; He is there before you. He is waiting long before you are awake. His anticipations are all along the way of life before you.

After the Resurrection, the disciples were bewildered, and the way looked black. But the angel said, "[He] is going ahead of you into Galilee" (Matthew 28:7). He is always ahead, thinking ahead, preparing ahead. Take this text with you into the future, take it into today's experience: "Do not let your hearts be troubled and do not be afraid. . . . I am going there to prepare a place for you" (John 14:27, 2). He is out in the world doing it. *He* will be there *before* you. He will bring you to your appointed place, and you will find *your appointed resources.* You will discover *His insight, His oversight, and His foresight.* You may not always see Him, but you can walk by faith in the dark if you know that He sees you, and you can sing as you journey, even through the night.

JOHN MACBEATH

We mean a lot to Someone;
And 'tis everything to me
That to God His wayward children
Were worth a Calvary.
It's the meaning of my Sunday,
And to Saturday from Monday
It is my hope that one day
My Savior I shall see.
Though the day be dark and dreary,
Here's comfort for the weary—
We mean a lot to Someone
Who died for you and me.

"VALUE"

Evening

In the morning . . . come up. . . . Present yourself to me there on top of the mountain.
EXODUS 34:2

The "morning" is the time I have set to meet with the Lord. *"Morning"*—the very word itself is like a cluster of luscious grapes to crush into sacred wine for me to drink. In the morning! This is when God wants me at my best in strength and hope so that I may begin my daily climb, not in weakness but in strength. Last night I buried yesterday's fatigue, and this morning I took on a new supply of energy. Blessed is the day when the morning is sanctified—set apart to God! Successful is the day when the first victory is won in prayer! Holy is the day when the dawn finds me on the mountaintop with God!

Dear Father, I am coming to meet with You. Nothing on the common, everyday plain of life will keep me away from Your holy heights. At Your calling I come, so I have the assurance that You will meet with me. Each morning begun so well on the mountain will make me strong and glad the rest of the day! JOSEPH PARKER

> *Still, still with You, when the purple morning breaks,*
>   *When the birds awake, and the shadows flee;*
> *Fairer than morning, lovelier than daylight,*
>   *Dawns the sweet consciousness, I am with Thee.*
>
> *Alone with You, amid the misty shadows,*
>   *The solemn hush of nature newly born;*
> *Alone with You in breathless adoration,*
>   *In the calm dew and freshness of the morn.*
>
> *As in a sunrise o'er a waveless ocean,*
>   *The image of the morning star does rest,*
> *So in this stillness, You discerning only*
>   *Your image in the waters of my breast.*

When sinks the soul, subdued by toil, to slumber,
Its closing eyes look up to You in prayer;
Sweet the repose, beneath Your wings o'ershadowing,
But sweeter still to wake and find You there.
HARRIET BEECHER STOWE

My mother made it a habit every day, immediately after breakfast, to spend an hour in her room, reading the Bible, meditating over it, and praying to the Lord. That hour was like a blessed fountain from which she drew the strength and sweetness that prepared her to complete all her tasks. It also enabled her to maintain a genuine peacefulness in spite of the normal trying worries and pettiness that so often accompany life in a crowded neighborhood.

As I think of her life and all that she had to endure, I see the absolute triumph of the grace of God in the ideal Christian lady. She was such a lovely person that I never saw her lose her temper or speak even one word in anger. I never heard her participate in idle gossip or make a disparaging remark about another person. In fact, I never saw in her even the hint of an emotion unbecoming to someone who had drunk from "the river of the water of life" (Revelation 22:1) and who had eaten of "the living bread that came down from heaven" (John 6:51). FREDERICK WILLIAM FARRAR

Give God the fresh blossom of the day. Never make Him wait until the petals have faded.

SEPTEMBER 14

Morning

Surely he will save you from the fowler's snare.
PSALM 91:3

The noblest souls are the most tempted. The devil is a sportsman and likes big game. He makes the deadliest assaults on the richest natures, the finest minds, the noblest spirits. JOHN L. LAWRENCE

Lord!—the fowler lays his net
In Thine evening hour;
When our souls are full of sleep—
Void of full power . . .
Look! The wild fowl sees him not
As he lays it lower!

Creeping round the water's edge
In the dusk of day;
Drops his net, just out of sight,
Weighted lightly!—Stay!
You can see him at his work . . .
Fly to God!—And pray!

Like the wild birds; knowing not
Nets lie underneath!
Gliding near the water's edge—
Fowler's snare" beneath—
Little feet, caught in the net:
Souls lie, near to death.

But the promise still rings clear: "He delivers thee,"
From the snare, however great
He will set thee free.
"Pluck my feet out of the net!" He delivers me.
When Thou dost deliver, Lord,

From the fowler's snare,
Then—the glory is all Thine,
Thou madest us aware,
And though it was stealthy-laid,
We saw it was there!

L. M. WARNER

Those who have the gale of Holy Spirit go forward even in sleep. BROTHER LAWRENCE

SEPTEMBER 14

Evening

*"Whoever wants to be my disciple must deny themselves
and take up their cross and follow me."*
MARK 8:34

The cross that my Lord calls me to carry may assume many different shapes. I may have to be content with mundane tasks in a limited area of service, when I may believe my abilities are suited for much greater work. I may be required to continually cultivate the same field year after year, even though it yields no harvest whatsoever. I may be asked of God to nurture kind and loving thoughts about the very person who has wronged me and to speak gently to him, take his side when others oppose him, and bestow sympathy and comfort to him. I may have to openly testify of my Master before those who do not want to be reminded of Him or His claims. And I may be called to walk through this world with a bright, smiling face while my heart is breaking.

Yes, there are many crosses, and every one of them is heavy and painful. And it is unlikely that I would seek out even one of them on my own. Yet Jesus is never as near to me as when I lift my cross, lay it submissively on my shoulder, and welcome it with a patient and uncomplaining spirit.

He draws close to me in order to mature my wisdom, deepen my peace, increase my courage, and supplement my power. All this He does so that through the very experience that is so painful and distressing to me, I will be of greater use to others.

And then I will echo these words of one of the Scottish Covenantors of the seventeenth century, imprisoned for his faith by John Graham of Claverhouse—*"I grow under the load."* ALEXANDER SMELLIE

> *Use the cross you bear as a crutch to help you on your way,*
> *not as a stumbling block that causes you to fall.*
> *You may others from sadness to gladness beguile,*
> *If you carry your cross with a smile.*

Morning

I consider everything a loss because of the surpassing
worth of knowing Christ Jesus my LORD.
PHILIPPIANS 3:8

The Swedish Nightingale, Jennie Lind, won great success as an operatic singer, and money poured into her purse. Yet she left the stage while she was singing her best, and never returned to it. She must have missed the money, the fame, and the applause of thousands, but she was content to live in privacy.

Once an English friend found her sitting on the steps of a bathing machine on the sea sands with a Bible on her knee, looking out into the glory of a sunset. They talked, and the conversation drew near to the inevitable question: "Oh, Madame Goldschmidt, how is it that you came to abandon the stage at the very height of your success?"

"When every day," was the quiet answer, "it made me think less of this (laying a finger on the Bible) and nothing at all of that (pointing to the sunset), what else could I do?"

May I not covet the world's greatness! It will cost me the crown of life!

Evening

Awake, north wind, and come, south wind! Blow on my
garden, that its fragrance may spread everywhere.
SONG OF SONGS 4:16

Some of the spices and plants mentioned in verse 14 of the above chapter are very descriptive and symbolic. The juice of the aloe plant has a bitter taste but is soothing when applied to the skin, so it tells us of the sweetness of bitter things, the bittersweet, having an important application that only those who have used it will understand. Myrrh is symbolic of death, having been used to embalm the dead. It represents the sweetness that comes to the heart after it has died to self-will, pride, and sin.

What inexpressible charm seems to encircle some Christians, simply because they carry upon their pure countenance and gentle spirit the imprint of the cross! It is the holy evidence of having died to something that was once proud and strong but is now forever surrendered at the feet of Jesus. And it is also the heavenly charm of a broken spirit and a contrite heart, the beautiful music that rises from a minor key, and the sweetness brought about by the touch of frost on ripened fruit.

Finally, frankincense was a fragrance that arose only after being touched with fire. The burning incense became clouds of sweetness arising from the heart of the flames. It symbolizes a person's heart whose sweetness has been brought forth by the flames of affliction until the holy, innermost part of the soul is filled with clouds of praise and prayer.

Beloved, are our lives yielding spices and perfumes—sweet fragrances of the heart?

THE LOVE-LIFE OF OUR LORD

> *A Persian fable says: One day*
> *A wanderer found a lump of clay*
> *So savory of sweet perfume*
> *Its odors scented all the room.*
> *"What are you?" was his quick demand,*
> *"Are you some gem from Samarkand,*
> *Or pure nard in this plain disguise,*
> *Or other costly merchandise?"*
> *"No, I am but a lump of clay."*
>
> *"Then whence this wondrous perfume—say!"*
> *"Friend, if the secret I disclose,*
> *I have been dwelling with the rose."*
> *Sweet parable! and will not those*
> *Who love to dwell with Sharon's rose,*
> *Distill sweet odors all around,*
> *Though low and poor themselves are found?*
> *Dear Lord, abide with us that we*
> *May draw our perfume fresh from Thee.*

Morning

Having loved his own . . . he loved them to the end.
JOHN 13:1

Sadhu Sundar Singh passed a crowd of people putting out a jungle fire at the foot of the Himalayas. Several men, however, were standing gazing at a tree, the branches of which were already alight.

"What are you looking at?" he asked. They pointed to a nest of young birds in the tree. Above it a bird was flying wildly to and fro in great distress. The men said, "We wish we could save that tree, but the fire prevents us from getting near to it."

A few minutes later the nest caught fire. The Sadhu thought the mother bird would fly away. But no! she flew down, spread her wings over the young ones, and in a few minutes was burned to ashes with them.

> *Such love, such wondrous love,*
> *Such love, such wondrous love,*
> *That God should love a sinner such as I,*
> *How wonderful is love like this!*
> *Let us have love heated to the point of sacrifice.*

Evening

Hide in the Kerith Ravine.
1 KINGS 17:3

God's servants must be taught the value of the hidden side of life. The person who is to serve in a lofty place before others must also assume a lowly place before his

God. We should not be surprised if God occasionally says to us, "Dear child, you have had enough of this hurried pace, excitement, and publicity. Now I want you to go and hide yourself—'hide in the Kerith Ravine' of sickness, the 'Kerith Ravine' of sorrow, or some place of total solitude, from which the crowds have turned away." And happy is the person who can reply to the Lord, "Your will is also mine. Therefore I run to hide myself in You. 'I long to dwell in your tent forever and take refuge in the shelter of your wings' [Psalm 61:4]."

Every saintly soul that desires to wield great influence over others must first win the power in some hidden "Kerith Ravine." Acquiring spiritual power is impossible unless we hide from others and ourselves in some deep ravine where we may absorb the power of the eternal God. May our lives be like the vegetation centuries ago that absorbed the power of the sunshine and now gives the energy back after having become coal.

Lancelot Andrews, a bishop of the Church of England and one of the translators of the King James Bible of 1611, experienced his "Kerith Ravine," in which he spent five hours of every day in prayer and devotion to God. John Welsh, a contemporary of Andrews, and a Presbyterian who was imprisoned for his faith by James VI of Scotland, also had his "ravine." He believed his day to be wasted if he did not spend eight to ten hours of isolated communion with God. David Brainerd's "ravine" was the forests of North America while he served as a pioneer missionary to the American Indians during the eighteenth century. And Christmas Evans, a preacher of the late-eighteenth and early-nineteenth centuries, had his long and lonely journeys through the hills of Wales.

Looking back to the blessed age from which we date the centuries, there are many notable "ravines." The Isle of Patmos, the solitude of the Roman prisons, the Arabian Desert, and the hills and valleys of Palestine are all as enduringly memorable as those experienced by the people who have shaped our modern world.

Our Lord Himself lived through His "Kerith Ravine" in Nazareth, in the wilderness of Judea, amid the olive trees of Bethany, and in the solitude of the city of Gadara. So none of us is exempt from a "ravine" experience, where the sounds of human voices are exchanged for the waters of quietness that flow from the throne of God, and where we taste the sweetness and soak up the power of a life "hidden with Christ" (Colossians 3:3).
F. B. MEYER

Morning

Forgive as the LORD *forgave you.*
COLOSSIANS 3:13

A custom way out in the African bush which has no equivalent in this part of the world is "Forgiveness Week." Fixed in the dry season, when the weather itself is smiling, this is a week when every man and woman pledges himself or herself to forgive any neighbor any wrong, real or fancied, that may be a cause for misunderstanding, coldness, or quarrel between the parties.

It is, of course, a part of our religion that a man should forgive his brother. But among recent converts, and even older brethren, this great tenet is, perhaps naturally, apt to be forgotten or overlooked in the heat and burden of work. "Forgiveness Week" brings it forcibly to mind. The week itself terminates with a festival of happiness and rejoicing among the native Christians.

Is it too much to suggest that in this *supposedly more civilized portion of the world* a similar week might be instituted?

Nothing between, Lord—nothing between;
Shine with unclouded ray,
Chasing each mist away,
O'er my whole heart hold sway—
Nothing between.

Let grudges die "like cloudspots in the dawn!"
When God forgives, He forgets!

Evening

He is the Lord*; let him do what is good in his eyes.*
1 Samuel 3:18

If I see God in everything, He will calm and color everything I see! Perhaps the circumstances causing my sorrows will not be removed and my situation will remain the same, but if Christ is brought into my grief and gloom as my Lord and Master, He will "surround me with songs of deliverance" (Psalm 32:7). To see *Him* and to be sure that His wisdom and power never fail and His love never changes, to know that even His most distressing dealings with me are for my deepest spiritual gain, is to be able to say in the midst of bereavement, sorrow, pain, and loss, "The Lord gave and the Lord has taken away; may the name of the Lord be praised" (Job 1:21).

Seeing God in everything is the only thing that will make me loving and patient with people who annoy and trouble me. Then I will see others as the instruments God uses to accomplish His tender and wise purpose for me, and I will even find myself inwardly thanking them for the blessing they have become to me. Nothing but seeing God will completely put an end to all complaining and thoughts of rebellion.
Hannah Whitall Smith

"Give me a new idea," I said,
While thinking on a sleepless bed;
"A new idea that'll bring to earth
A balm for souls of priceless worth;
That'll give men thoughts of things above,
And teach them how to serve and love,
That'll banish every selfish thought,
And rid men of the sins they've fought."

The new thought came, just how, I'll tell:
'Twas when on bended knee I fell,
And sought from Him who knows full well
The way our sorrow to expel.

See God in all things, great and small,
And give Him praise whate'er befall,
In life or death, in pain or woe,
See God, and overcome your foe.

I saw Him in the morning light,
He made the day shine clear and bright;
I saw Him in the noontide hour,
And gained from Him refreshing shower.
At evening, when worn and sad,
He gave me help, and made me glad.
At midnight, when on tossing bed
My weary soul to sleep He led.

I saw Him when great losses came,
And found He loved me just the same.
When heavy loads I had to bear,
I found He lightened every care.
By sickness, sorrow, sore distress,
He calmed my mind and gave me rest.
He's filled my heart with joyous praise
Since I gave Him the upward gaze.

'Twas new to me, yet old to some,
This thought that to me has become
A revelation of the way
We all should live throughout the day;
For as each day unfolds its light,
We'll walk by faith and not by sight.
Life will, indeed, a blessing bring,
If we see God in everything.

A. E. FINN

Morning

Later on, however.

HEBREWS 12:11

It is not a bit of good struggling for the premature unfolding of the Divine mystery. The revelation awaits our arrival at a certain place in the road, and when *Time* brings us to that place and we enter into its experiences, we shall find, to our delighted surprise, that it has become luminous.

And so the only thing we need to be concerned about is to be on the King's high road, stepping out in accordance with His most holy will.

"Light is sown for the righteous" (Psalm 97:11 KJV).

It is the end which justifies all and explains all. It is to the ultimate goal that God's eye is ever turning. At the right moment the shining harvest will appear! What though the seed may seem to perish in the dark cold ground! What will that matter when the blade bursts forth and the ear unfolds and the full corn waves over the golden harvest field?

Luther was once in earnest prayer over some matter of great moment, desiring to know the mind of God in it; and it seemed as though he heard God say to him, "I am not to be traced."

If God is not to be traced, He is to be trusted.

"Afterward Jesus appeared again to his disciples" (John 21:1).

However dark the *nows* may be in your experience, the *afters* of God are worth waiting for!

As we think of God's dealings with His children, we are impressed with *His leisureliness.* God's ways may be hidden, but *wait for God's* afters!

Evening

Where there is no vision, the people perish.
PROVERBS 29:18 KJV

Waiting upon God is vital in order to see Him and receive a vision from Him. And the amount of time spent before Him is also critical, for our hearts are like a photographer's film—the longer exposed, the deeper the impression. For God's vision to be impressed on our hearts, we must sit in *stillness* at His feet for quite a long time. Remember, the *troubled* surface of a lake will not reflect an image.

Yes, our lives must be quiet and peaceful if we expect to see God. And the vision we see from Him has the power to affect our lives in the same way a lovely sunset brings peace to a troubled heart. Seeing God always transforms human life.

Jacob "crossed the ford of the Jabbok" (Genesis 32:22), saw God, and became Israel. Seeing a vision of God transformed Gideon from a coward into a courageous soldier. And Thomas, after seeing Christ, was changed from a doubting follower into a loyal, devoted disciple.

People since Bible times have also had visions of God. William Carey, English pioneer missionary of the eighteenth century who is considered by some to be the Father of Modern Missions, saw God and left his shoemaker's bench to go to India. David Livingstone saw God and left everything in Britain behind to become a missionary and explorer, following the Lord's leading through the thickest jungles of Africa during the nineteenth century. And literally thousands more have since had visions of God and today are serving Him in the uttermost parts of the earth, seeking the timely evangelization of the lost. DR. PARDINGTON

It is very unusual for there to be complete quiet in the soul, for God almost continually whispers to us. And whenever the sounds of the world subside in our soul, we hear the whispering of God. Yes, He continues to whisper to us, but we often do not hear Him because of the noise and distractions caused by the hurried pace of our lives. FREDERICK WILLIAM FABER

Speak, Lord, in the stillness,
While I wait on Thee;

Hushing my heart to listen
   In expectancy.

Speak, O blessed Master,
   In this quiet hour;
Let me see Your face, Lord,
   Feel Your touch of power.

For the words that You speak,
   "They are life," indeed;
Living bread from Heaven,
   Now my spirit feed!

Speak, Your servant hears You!
   Be not silent, Lord;
My soul on You does wait
   For Your life-giving word!

～～～ SEPTEMBER 19 ～～～

Morning

Those who live quietly in the land.
PSALM 35:20

We are to enter into God's chamber, and hide there, and be still. Then God will call us "those who live quietly in the land." Have this stamp upon you. Be quiet outside—you will then be quiet inside. Be quiet in spirit. Beware of soul activities. The dross must be burned out to have the mountain vision. We must get back to God only, and cease to see the human instruments. Hide deeper in God. He must be real—more and more real!

Hide with Christ in God at the Throne; be at the Spring of things!

"In quietness and in confidence shall be your strength" (Isaiah 30:15 KJV). Set yourself to move everything through God, not man. Go direct to Him. Every step with God "in quietness and in confidence" gives you absolute victory over everything!

Keep in step with God.

Get quiet, beloved soul; tell out thy sorrow and complaint to God. Let not the greatest pressure of business divert thee from God. When men rage about thee, go and tell Jesus. Hide thee in His secret place when storms are high.

Get into thy closet, shut thy door, and quiet thyself as a weaned babe. But if thy voice is quiet to man, let it never cease to speak loudly and mightily for man.

We need to be quiet to get the ear of God!

> 'Mid all the traffic of the ways,
> Turmoils without, within,
> Make in my heart a quiet place,
> And come and dwell therein!
>
> A little shrine of quietness,
> All sacred to Thyself,
> Where Thou shalt all my soul possess,
> And I may find myself!
>
> JOHN OXENHAM

Pascal said: "One-half of the ills of life come because men are unwilling to sit down quietly for thirty minutes to think through all the possible consequences of their acts."

~~~~~ SEPTEMBER 19 ~~~~~

Evening

My Father is the gardener.
JOHN 15:1

It is a comforting thought that trouble, in whatever form it comes to us, is a heavenly messenger that brings us something from God. Outwardly it may appear painful or even destructive, but inwardly its spiritual work produces blessings. Many of the richest blessings we have inherited are the fruit of sorrow or pain. We should never forget that redemption, the world's greatest blessing, is the fruit of the world's greatest sorrow. And whenever a time of deep pruning comes and the knife cuts deeply and the pain is severe, what an inexpressible comfort it is to know: "My Father is the gardener."

John Vincent, a Methodist Episcopal bishop of the late-nineteenth and early-twentieth centuries and a leader of the Sunday school movement in America, once told of being in a large greenhouse where clusters of luscious grapes were hanging on each side. The owner of the greenhouse told him, "When the new gardener came here, he said he would not work with the vines unless he could cut them completely down to the stalk. I allowed him to do so, and we had no grapes for two years, but this is now the result."

There is rich symbolism in this account of the pruning process when applied to the Christian life. Pruning *seems* to be destroying the vine, and the gardener *appears* to be cutting everything away. Yet he sees the future and knows that the final result will be the enrichment of the life of the vine, and a greater abundance of fruit.

There are many blessings we will never receive until we are ready to pay the price of pain, for the path of suffering is the only way to reach them. J. R. MILLER

> I walked a mile with Pleasure,
> She chattered all the way;
> But left me none the wiser
> For all she had to say.
>
> I walked a mile with Sorrow,
> And ne'er a word said she;
> But oh, the things I learned from her
> When Sorrow walked with me.

～～ SEPTEMBER 20 ～～

Morning

Shall what is formed say to the one who formed it, "Why did you make me like this?"
ROMANS 9:20

A piece of wood once bitterly complained because it was being cut and filled with rifts and holes, but he who held the wood and whose knife was cutting into it so remorselessly did not listen to the sore complaining. He was making a flute out of the wood he held and was too wise to desist when entreated to do so. He said:

"Oh, thou foolish piece of wood, without these rifts and holes thou wouldst be only a mere stick forever—a bit of hard black ebony with no power to make music or to be of any use. These rifts that I am making, which seem to be destroying thee, will change thee into a flute, and thy sweet music then shall charm the souls of men. My cutting thee is the making of thee, for then thou shalt be precious and valuable, and a blessing in the world."

David could never have sung his sweetest songs had he not been sorely afflicted. His afflictions made his life an instrument on which God could breathe the music of His love to charm and soothe the hearts of men.

> *We are but organs mute till a Master touches the keys—*
> *Verily, vessels of earth into which God poureth the wine;*
> *Harps are we—silent harps that have hung in the willow trees,*
> *Dumb till our heartstrings swell and break with a pulse Divine.*
> *Not till the life is broken is it ready for the Master's use.*

SEPTEMBER 20

Evening

Did I not tell you that if you believe, you will see the glory of God?
JOHN 11:40

Mary and Martha could not understand what their Lord was doing. Each of them had said to Him, "*Lord, if you had been here, my brother would not have died*" (vv. 21, 32). And behind their words we seem to read their true thoughts: "Lord, we do not understand *why* You waited so long to come or *how* You could allow the man You love so much to die. We do not understand *how You could allow such sorrow and suffering to devastate* our lives, when Your presence might have stopped it all. *Why* didn't You come? Now it's too late, because Lazarus has been dead four days!" But Jesus simply had one great truth in answer to all of this. He said, in essence, "You may not understand, but I am telling you that if you *believe*, you will *see*."

Abraham could not understand *why* God would ask him to sacrifice his son, but he trusted Him. Then he *saw* the Lord's glory when the son he loved was restored to him. Moses could not understand *why* God would require him to stay forty years in the wilderness, but he also trusted Him. Then he *saw* when God called him to lead Israel from Egyptian bondage.

Joseph could not understand his brothers' cruelty toward him, the false testimony of a treacherous woman, or the long years of unjust imprisonment, but he trusted God and finally he *saw* His glory in it all. And Joseph's father, Jacob, could not understand *how* God's strange providence could allow Joseph to be taken from him. Yet later he *saw* the Lord's glory when he looked into the face of his son, who had become the governor for a great king and the person used to preserve his own life and the lives of an entire nation.

Perhaps there is also something in your life causing you to question God. Do you find yourself saying, "I do not understand *why* God allowed my loved one to be taken. I do not understand *why* affliction has been permitted to strike me. I do not understand *why* the Lord has led me down these twisting paths. I do not understand *why* my own plans, which seemed so good, have been so disappointing. I do not understand *why* the blessings I so desperately need are so long in coming."

Dear friend, you do not *have* to understand all God's ways of dealing with you. He does not expect you to understand them. You do not expect *your* children to understand everything you do—you simply want them to trust you. And someday you too will *see* the glory of God in the things you do not understand. J. H. M.

> *If we could push ajar the gates of life,*
> *And stand within, and all God's working see,*
> *We might interpret all this doubt and strife,*
> *And for each mystery could find a key.*
>
> *But not today. Then be content, dear heart;*
> *God's plans, like lilies pure and white, unfold.*
> *We must not tear the close-shut leaves apart—*
> *Time will someday reveal the blooms of gold.*

And if, through patient toil, we reach the land
Where tired feet, with sandals loosed, may rest,
When we shall clearly know and understand,
I think that we will say, "God knew best."

SEPTEMBER 21

Morning

Offer your bodies.
ROMANS 12:1

Lend Me *thy body,* our Lord says. For a few brief years, in the body that was prepared for Me I delighted to do My Father's will. By means of that body I came into contact with the children of men—diseased, weary, sin-sick, heavy-laden ones. Those feet carried Me to the homes where sorrow and death had entered; those hands touched leprous bodies, palsied limbs, sightless eyes; those lips told of My Father's remedy for sin, His love for a prodigal world. In that body I bore the world's sin upon the tree, and through its offering once for all My followers are sanctified.

But I need a body still; *wilt thou not lend Me thine? Millions of hearts are longing, with an indescribable hunger, for Me.* On that far-off shore are men, women, and little children sitting in darkness and in the shadow of death—men who have never yet heard of My love. *Wilt thou not lend Me thy body,* that I may cross the ocean and tell them that the light after which they are groping has at last reached them; that the bread for which they have so often hungered is now at their very door?

I want a heart, that I may fill it with Divine compassion; and lips, purged from all uncleanness, wherewith to tell the story that brings hope to the despairing, freedom to the bound, healing to the diseased, and life to the dead. *Wilt thou lend Me thine? Wilt thou not lend Me thy body?* J. GREGORY MANTLE

All that we own is Thine alone, A trust, O Lord, from Thee.

Evening

I consider everything a loss because of the surpassing
worth of knowing Christ Jesus my Lord.
PHILIPPIANS 3:8

The autumn season we are now entering is one of cornfields ripe for harvest, of the cheerful song of those who reap the crops, and of gathered and securely stored grain. So allow me to draw your attention to the sermon of the fields. This is its solemn message: "You must die in order to live. You must refuse to consider your own comfort and well-being. You must be crucified, not only to your desires and habits that are obviously sinful, but also to many others that may appear to be innocent and right. If you desire to save others, you cannot save yourself, and if you desire to bear much fruit, you must be buried in darkness and solitude."

My heart fails me as I listen. But when the words are from Jesus, may I remind myself that it is my great privilege to enter into "the fellowship of his sufferings" (Philippians 3:10 KJV) and I am therefore in great company. May I also remind myself that all the suffering is designed to make me a vessel suitable for His use. And may I remember that His Calvary blossomed into abundant fruitfulness, and so will mine.

Pain leads to plenty, and death to life—it is the law of the kingdom! *In the Hour of Silence*

Do we call it dying when a bud blossoms into a flower? SELECTED

> *Finding, following, keeping, struggling,*
> *Is He sure to bless?*
> *Saints, apostles, prophets, martyrs,*
> *Answer, "Yes."*

Morning

He took up our infirmities.
MATTHEW 8:17

I think perhaps the greatest of all hindrances in our getting hold of God for our bodies is the lack of *knowing Him,* for after all, in its *deepest essence* Divine healing is not a *thing;* it is not an *experience;* it is not an *"it."* It is the *revelation of Jesus Christ* as a living, almighty *Person,* and then the *union* of this living Christ with your *body,* so that there becomes a tie, a bond, *a living link* by which His life keeps flowing into yours, and because He lives you shall *live* also. This is so very real to me that I groan in spirit for those who do not know Him in this blessed union, and I wonder sometimes why He has let me know Him in this gracious manner. There is not an hour of the day or night that I am not conscious of *Someone* who is closer to me than my heart or my brain. I know that *He is living in me,* and it is the continual inflowing of *the life of Another.* If I had not that I could not live. My old constitutional strength gave out long, long ago, but Someone breathed in me gently, with no violence, no strange thrills, but just His wholesome *life.* A. B. SIMPSON

I remember how once I was taken suddenly and seriously ill alone in my study. I dropped upon my knees and cried to God for help. Instantly all pain left me and I was perfectly well. It seems as if God stood right there, and had put out His hand and touched me. The joy of healing was not so great as the joy of meeting God. R. A. TORREY

She only touched the hem of His garment,
As to His side she stole,
Amid the throng that had gathered around Him
And straightway she was whole.

Oh, touch the hem of His garment,
And thou, too, shall be free;
His healing power this very hour,
Will bring new life to thee.

--- SEPTEMBER 22 ---
Evening

Satan has asked to sift you as wheat. But I have prayed
for you, Simon, that your faith may not fail.
LUKE 22:31–32

Our faith is the center of the target God aims at when He tests us, and if any gift escapes untested, it certainly will not be our faith. There is nothing that pierces faith to its very marrow—to find whether or not it is the faith of those who are immortal—like shooting the arrow of the feeling of being deserted into it. And only genuine faith will escape unharmed from the midst of the battle after having been stripped of its armor of earthly enjoyment and after having endured the circumstances coming against it that the powerful hand of God has allowed.

Faith must be tested, and the sense of feeling deserted is "the furnace heated seven times hotter than usual" (Daniel 3:19) into which it may be thrown. Blessed is the person who endures such an ordeal! CHARLES H. SPURGEON

Paul said, "I have kept the faith" (2 Timothy 4:7), but his head was removed! They cut it off, but they could not touch his faith. This great apostle to the Gentiles rejoiced in three things: he had "fought the good fight," he had "finished the race," and he had "kept the faith." So what was the value of everything else? The apostle Paul had won the race and gained the ultimate prize—he had won not only the admiration of those on earth today but also the admiration of heaven. So why do we not live as if it pays to lose "all things . . . that [we] may gain Christ" (Philippians 3:8)? Why are we not as loyal to the truth as Paul was? It is because our math is different—he counted in a different way than we do. What we count as *gain*, he counted as *loss*. If we desire to ultimately wear the same crown, we must have his faith and live it.

Job. . . . blameless and upright; he feared God and shunned evil.
JOB 1:1

Such was Job's character as given by God. He asked Satan, "Have you considered my servant Job? There is no one on earth like him" (v. 8). Satan, in reply, says in effect, "Strip him, and he will curse Thee to Thy face." Satan sought Job's fall; God sought his blessing. Satan gets leave from God to strip Job. With malignant energy he sets to work, and in one day he brings the greatest man in all the East into abject poverty and visits him with sore bereavement. Blow after blow of such a crushing nature and with such rapidity falls upon Job that one marvels at the testimony of the Holy Ghost that: "In all this, Job did not sin by charging God with wrongdoing" (v. 22). *What a triumph for God! What a defeat for Satan!*

"But these strange ashes, Lord? This nothingness,
This baffling sense of loss?"
"Son, was the anguish of My stripping less
Upon the torturing Cross?

"Was I not brought into the dust of death,
A worm, and no man I;
Yea, turned to ashes by the vehement breath
Of fire, on Calvary?

"O Son beloved, this is thy heart's desire:
This and no other thing
Follows the fall of the consuming fire
On the burnt offering.

"Go on and taste the joy set high afar,
No joy like that for thee;

See how it lights thy way like some great star!
Come now, and follow Me!"

A. W. C.

~~~~~ SEPTEMBER 23 ~~~~~

Evening

Whoever believes in me, as the Scripture has said, rivers
of living water will flow from within them.

JOHN 7:38

Some of us are troubled, wondering why the Holy Spirit doesn't fill us. The problem is that we have plenty coming in but we are not giving out to others. If you will give the blessing you have received, planning your life around greater service and being a blessing to those around you, then you will quickly find that the Holy Spirit is with you. He will bestow blessings to you for service, giving you all He can trust you to give away to others.

No music is as heavenly as that made by an aeolian harp. It is a beautiful occurrence of nature, but it has a spiritual parallel. The harp is nothing but a wooden box with strings arranged in harmony, waiting to be touched by the unseen fingers of the wandering wind. As the breath of heaven floats over the strings, notes that are nearly divine float upon the air, as if a choir of angels were wandering about and touching the strings.

In the same way, it is possible to keep our hearts so open to the touch of the Holy Spirit that He may play them as He chooses, while we quietly wait on the pathway of His service. DAYS OF HEAVEN UPON EARTH

When the apostles "were filled with the Holy Spirit" (Acts 2:4), they did not lease the Upper Room and stay there to hold holiness meetings. They went everywhere, preaching the gospel. WILL HUFF

"If I have eaten my morsel alone,"
The patriarch spoke with scorn;
What would he think of the Church were he shown
Heathendom—huge, forlorn, Godless,

Christless, with soul unfed,
While the Church's ailment is fullness of bread,
  Eating her morsel alone?

"Freely you have received, so give,"
  He says, who has given us all.
How will the soul in us longer live
  Deaf to their starving call,
For whom the blood of the Lord was shed,
And His body broken to give them bread,
  If we eat our morsel alone!

ARCHBISHOP WILLIAM ALEXANDER

"Where is your brother Abel?" (Genesis 4:9).

~~~~~~~ SEPTEMBER 24 ~~~~~~~

Morning

He cuts off every branch in me that bears no fruit, while every branch
that does bear fruit he prunes so that it will be even more fruitful.

JOHN 15:2

Only a little more cutting." How strange the words sounded, and then I heard the ring of the gardener's ax as he cut away at the lilac bushes. They were very close to the windows and kept out the sunlight and air; more, they obstructed the view. We watched the process, and as one bush after another fell, one remarked: "Only a little more cutting and we shall get it. These lilac bushes actually shut out the view of the White Mountains!"

I was glad the gardener did the cutting that day, for so much was brought out by the absence of the bushes and suggested by the exclamations that followed: "How lovely that little tree is! I did not see it before!" "What a beautiful evergreen that is! I never noticed it until now!" Have we not heard similar exclamations after severe cuttings and removals in our lives? Have we not said: "I never loved God so much as I have since He took my little one!" "I never saw the beauty of such and such a Scripture until now!"

Ah, He knows! Only trust Him. We shall see it all in the clear light sometime.

God is a zealous Pruner,
For He knows
Who, falsely tender, spares the knife
But spoils the rose.
"The Pruner" by John Oxenham

Give me the courage to submit to the surgery of Thy Spirit. Give me the bravery to part with what I hold most dear if it separates me from Thee. Through Christ, I pray!

～～～ SEPTEMBER 24 ～～～

Evening

When they came to the border of Mysia, they tried to enter Bithynia, but the Spirit of Jesus would not allow them to.

Acts 16:7

What a strange thing for the Lord to prohibit, for they were going into Bithynia to do Christ's work! And the door was shut before them by Christ's own Spirit.

There have been times when I have experienced the same thing. Sometimes I have been interrupted in what seemed to be quite productive work. And at times, opposition came and forced me to go back, or sickness came and forced me to rest in some isolated place.

During such times, it was difficult for me to leave my work unfinished when I believed it was service done in the power of His Spirit. But I finally remembered that *the Spirit requires not only a service of work but also a service of waiting.* I came to see that in the kingdom of Christ, there are not only times for action but times to refrain from action. And I also came to learn that a place of isolation is often the most useful place of all in this diverse world. Its harvest is more rich than the seasons when the corn and wine were the most abundant. So I have learned to thank the blessed Holy Spirit that many a beautiful Bithynia had to be left without a visit from me.

Dear Holy Spirit, my desire is still to be led by You. Nevertheless, my opportunities for usefulness seem to be disappointed, for today the door appears open into a life of service for You but tomorrow it closes before me just as I am about to enter. Teach me to see another door even in the midst of the inaction of this time. Help me to find, even in the area of service where You have closed a door, a new entrance into Your service. Inspire me with the knowledge that a person may sometimes be called to serve by doing nothing, by staying still, or by waiting. And when I remember the power of Your "gentle whisper" (1 Kings 19:12), I will not complain that sometimes the Spirit allows me *not* to go. GEORGE MATHESON

> *When I cannot understand my Father's leading,*
> *And it seems to be but hard and cruel fate,*
> *Still I hear that gentle whisper ever pleading,*
> *God is working, God is faithful, only wait.*

~~~~ SEPTEMBER 25 ~~~~

Morning

My glory was fresh in me, and my bow was renewed in my hand.
JOB 29:20 KJV

It was when Job's glory was fresh in him that his "bow was renewed" in his hand. Freshness and glory! And yet the brilliant music of these words is brought down to *a minor strain* by the little touch "it *was*"—not it *is*.

"All my [fresh] springs are *in thee*" (Psalm 87:7 KJV).

If our glory is to be fresh in us, it all depends upon what the glory in us *is!* There is only one unfailing source—*Christ Himself!* He is "*in you*, the hope of glory" (Colossians 1:27) if you have admitted Him; and He *is* your glory. Then you may sing, "My glory *is* fresh in me."

Jesus Christ is *always fresh!*

And so is the oil with which He anoints us. "I *shall be* anointed with *fresh oil*" (Psalm 92:10 KJV). Fresh oil of joy! Fresh oil of consecration! Fresh oil upon the sacrifice as we offer to God continually *"the fruit of lips that openly profess* his name" (Hebrews 13:15).

> *My heart is parched by unbelief,*
> *My spirit sere from inward strife;*
> *The heavens above are turned to brass,*
> *Arid and fruitless is my life.*
>
> *Then falls Thy rain, O Holy One;*
> *Fresh is the earth, and young once more;*
> *Then falls Thy Spirit on my heart;*
> *My life is green; the drought is o'er!*
> "DROUGHT" BY BETTY BRUECHERT

A desert road? when the Christian has ever at his command *Fresh springs! Fresh oil! Fresh glory!*

SEPTEMBER 25

Evening

> *Why must I go about mourning?*
> PSALM 42:9

Dear believer, can you answer the above question? Can you find any reason why you are so often mourning instead of rejoicing? Why do you allow your mind to dwell on gloomy thoughts? Who told you that night will never end in day? Who told you that the winter of your discontent would continue from frost to frost and from snow, ice, and hail to even deeper snow and stronger storms of despair?

Don't you know that day dawns after night, showers displace drought, and spring and summer follow winter? Then, have hope! Hope forever, for God will not fail you!
CHARLES H. SPURGEON

He was better to me than all my hopes;
    He was better than all my fears;
He made a bridge of my broken works,
    And a rainbow of my tears.

The stormy waves that marked my ocean path,
    Did carry my Lord on their crest;
When I dwell on the days of my wilderness march
    I can lean on His love for the rest.

He emptied my hands of my treasured store,
    And His covenant love revealed,
There was not a wound in my aching heart,
    The balm of His breath has not healed.

Oh, tender and true was His discipline sore,
    In wisdom, that taught and tried,
Till the soul that He sought was trusting in Him,
    And nothing on earth beside.

He guided my paths that I could not see,
    By ways that I have not known;
The crooked was straight, and the rough was plain
    As I followed the Lord alone.

I praise Him still for the pleasant palms,
    And the desert streams by the way,
For the glowing pillar of flame by night,
    And the sheltering cloud by day.

Never a time on the dreariest day,
    But some promise of love endears;
I read from the past, that my future will be
    Far better than all my fears.

Like the golden jar, of the wilderness bread,
Stored up with the blossoming rod,
All safe in the ark, with the law of the Lord,
Is the covenant care of my God.

———— SEPTEMBER 26 ————

Morning

The famine was still severe. . . . They had eaten all the grain. . . . "If
we had not delayed, we could have gone and returned." . . . So the
men took . . . double the amount of silver, and Benjamin also.
GENESIS 43:1–2, 10, 15

Praise God for the famine in our life, that drives us in utter helplessness back to Him!

Praise Him that what we have gets eaten up, and we must turn to Him for more! But how like unto the faltering, fearful family of Israel we act! We could find absolute relief, sufficiency, satisfaction in Jesus Christ; yet we delay, debate, wonder, waste time, and stay hungry. When finally in desperation we are driven to Him we think we must do some great thing to meet His terms, and we try to carry "double the . . . silver" in all sorts of ways, to make sure of what He is yearningly waiting to give us. He does ask us for one thing, and one only: and that is the dearest possession of our lives. With Israel's family the dearest possession was Benjamin. When we lay down our dearest possession, then the treasures of the kingdom are flung open to us and lavished into our life. MESSAGES FOR THE MORNING WATCH

A drying well will often lead the spirit to the river that flows from the throne of God.

———— SEPTEMBER 26 ————

Evening

We live by faith, not by sight.
2 CORINTHIANS 5:7

As believers, "we live by faith, not by sight"—God never wants us to live by our feelings. Our inner self may want to live by feelings, and Satan may want us to, but God wants us to face the facts, not feelings. He wants us to face the facts of Christ and His finished and perfect work for us. And once we face these precious facts, and believe them simply because God says they are facts, He will take care of our feelings.

Yet God never gives us feelings to enable or encourage us to trust Him, and He never gives them to show us that we have already completely trusted Him. God only gives us feelings when He sees that we trust Him apart from our feelings, resting solely on His Word and His faithfulness to His promise. And these feelings that can only come from Him will be given at such a time and to such a degree as His love sees best for each individual circumstance.

Therefore we must choose between facing our feelings or facing the facts of God. Our feelings may be as uncertain and changing as the sea or shifting sand. God's facts, however, are as certain as the Rock of Ages Himself—"Jesus Christ . . . the same yesterday and today and forever" (Hebrews 13:8).

> *When darkness veils His lovely face*
> *I rest on His unchanging grace;*
> *In every strong and stormy gale,*
> *My anchor holds within the veil.*

SEPTEMBER 27

Morning

The LORD *will give you as he promised.*
EXODUS 12:25

God is to be trusted for *what He is,* and not for *what He is not.* We may confidently expect Him to act according to His nature, but never contrary to it. To *dream* that God will do this and that because we wish that He would *is not faith but fanaticism. Faith can only stand upon truth.* We may be sure that God will so act as to honor His own justice, mercy, wisdom, power—in a word, so as to be Himself. Beyond all doubt He will fulfill His promises; and *when faith grasps a promise, she is on sure ground.*

To believe that God will give us *what He has never promised to give is mere dreaming. Faith without a promise revealed or implied is folly.* Yea, though our trust should cry itself hoarse in prayer, it should be nonetheless a vain absurdity if it had no word of God to warrant it. Happily, the promises and unveilings of Scripture are ample for every real emergency; but when unrestrained credence catches at every whim of its own crazy imagination and thinks to see it realized, the disappointment is not to be wondered at.

It is ours to believe the sure things of God's revelation, but we are not to waste a grain of precious reliance upon anything outside of that circle. CHARLES H. SPURGEON

"Faith does not mean that we are trying to believe something that is not so; *it just means that we are taking God at His Word.*"

> *Faith is a thread*
> *Slender and frail,*
> *Easy to tear;*
> *Yet it can lift*
> *The weight of a soul*
> *Up from despair.*
>
> MATTHEW BILLER

～～～ SEPTEMBER 27 ～～～
Evening

I have found a ransom for them.
JOB 33:24

Divine healing is actually divine life. It is the lordship of Christ over the body—or the life of Christ in the framework of the human body. It is the union of the parts of our bodies with His very body, exhibiting His life flowing throughout our bodies.

It is as real as His risen and glorified body. And it is as reasonable as the fact that He was raised from the dead, is a living person with an actual body, and sits today as an understanding soul at God's right hand.

That same Christ, with all His attributes and mighty power, belongs to us. We are members of His body, His flesh, and His bones, and if we will only believe this and receive it, we may actually draw our life from the very life of the Son of God.

Dear God, help me to know and to live this verse: "The body, however, is . . . for the Lord, and the Lord for the body" (1 Corinthians 6:13). A. B. SIMPSON

"*The LORD your God is with you, the Mighty Warrior who saves*" (Zephaniah 3:17). This was the verse that initially brought the truth of divine healing to my mind and my worn-out body more than twenty years ago. It is now a door more wide open than ever and is the gate through which the living Christ enters moment by moment into my redeemed body. He enters to fill, energize, and vitalize me with the presence and power of His own personality, transforming my entire being into "a new heaven and a new earth" (Revelation 21:1).

Another verse reads, "*The Lord your God*" (Luke 10:27). If the Lord is *my* God, then all that is in almighty God is mine. It all resides within me to the extent that I am willing and able to appropriate Him and all that belongs to Him. "God, whose name is the LORD Almighty" (Jeremiah 32:18), is indeed the *all* mighty God and is my *inside* God. Just as the sun is the center of our solar system, He is centered within me, living as the Father, Son, and Holy Spirit. He is the great generator of the power plant at the center of my threefold being, working in the midst of my physical being, including my brain and other parts of my nervous system.

For twenty-one years this truth not only has been a living reality to me but has grown deeper and richer. Now, at the age of seventy, I am in every way a much younger and stronger person than I was at thirty. Today I live using God's strength, accomplishing fully twice as much mentally and physically as I ever did in the past, yet with only half the effort. My physical, mental, and spiritual life is like an artesian well—always full and overflowing. Speaking, teaching, and traveling by day or by night through sudden and violent changes in weather or climate is of no more effort to me than it is for the wheels of an engine to turn when the pressure of the steam is at full force or than it is for a pipe to let water run through it.

> *My body, soul, and spirit thus redeemed,*
> *Sanctified and healed I give, O Lord, to Thee,*
> *A consecrated offering Yours evermore to be.*
> *That all my powers with all their might*
> *In Your sole glory may unite—Hallelujah!*
>
> HENRY WILSON

Morning

Keep yourself pure.
1 TIMOTHY 5:22

Does the judge know the story of the spotless fur that lines his robes of State? Does the society leader realize the sacrifice which makes possible the lovely ermine wrap which lies so gracefully about her shoulders? Do they know that the little animal whose coat they now wear, as he roamed the forest of Asia was as proud as they, aye, inordinately proud of his beautiful snowy coat? And we do not wonder, for it is the most beautiful fur to be found in all the markets of the world!

Such pride does the little carnivore take in his spotless coat, that nothing is permitted to soil it in the slightest degree. Hunters are well acquainted with this fact and take very unsportsmanlike advantage of this knowledge. No traps are set for him. No, indeed! Instead, they seek out his home—a tree stump or rocky cleft and then—be it said to their everlasting shame, they daub filth within and around the entrance. As the dogs are loosed and the chase begins, the little animal naturally turns to his one place of refuge. Reaching it, rather than enter such a place of uncleanness, he turns to face the yelping dogs.

Better to be stained by blood than sully his white coat!

Only a white *coat*, little ermine, but how your act condemns *us! "Made in the image and likeness of God"* with minds and immortal spirits; and yet how often, in order to obtain something we desire, our character is sacrificed on the altars of worldly pleasure, greed, selfishness!

Everything is lost when purity is gone—purity, which has been called *the soul of character.* Keep thyself pure: *every thought, every word, every deed, even the motive behind the deed—all, ermine-pure.*

> *I ask this gift of thee—*
> *A life all lily fair,*

And fragrant as the garden be
Where seraphs are.

SEPTEMBER 28
Evening

In me . . . peace.
JOHN 16:33

There is a vast difference between pleasure and blessedness. Paul experienced imprisonment, pain, sacrifice, and suffering to their very limits, yet through it all he was blessed. All the beatitudes became real in his heart and life, *in the midst* of his difficult circumstances.

Paganini, the great Italian violinist, once stepped onstage only to discover there was something wrong with his violin, just as the audience was ending their applause. He looked at the instrument for a moment and suddenly realized it was not his best and most valuable one. In fact, the violin was not his at all. Momentarily he felt paralyzed, but he quickly turned to his audience, telling them there had been some mistake and he did not have his own violin. He stepped back behind the curtain, thinking he must have left it backstage, but discovered that someone had stolen his and left the inferior one in its place.

After remaining behind the curtain for a moment, Paganini stepped onstage again to speak to the audience. He said, "Ladies and Gentlemen, I will now demonstrate to you that the music is not in the instrument but in the soul." Then he played as never before, and beautiful music flowed from that inferior instrument until the audience was so enraptured that their enthusiastic applause nearly lifted the ceiling of the concert hall. He had indeed revealed to them that the music was not in his instrument but in his own soul!

Dear tested and tried believer, it is your mission to walk onto the stage of this world in order to reveal to all of heaven and earth that the music of life lies not in your circumstances or external things but in your own soul.

If peace be in your heart,
The wildest winter storm is full of solemn beauty,
The midnight flash but shows your path of duty,
Each living creature tells some new and joyous story,
The very trees and stones all catch a ray of glory,
If peace be in your heart.

CHARLES FRANCIS RICHARDSON

～～～ SEPTEMBER 29 ～～～

Morning

On the day when I act . . . they will be my treasured possession.

MALACHI 3:17

And they shall be mine . . . in that day when I make up my jewels.

KJV

Christ died that He might make us a "peculiar people" (1 Peter 2:9 KJV). A great many Christians are afraid that they *will* be peculiar. A few weeks before God took Enoch to heaven, his acquaintances would probably have said that he was a little peculiar; they would have told you that when they had a bridge party and the whole countryside were invited, you would not find Enoch or one of his family present. He was very peculiar.

We are not told that he was a great warrior or a great scientist or a great scholar. In fact, we are not told that he was anything that the world would call great, but he walked with God three hundred and sixty-five years, and he is the brightest star that shone in that dispensation.

If he could walk with God, cannot you and I? He took a long walk one day, and has not come back as yet. The Lord liked his company so well that He said, "Enoch, come up higher."

I suppose that if we asked the men in Elijah's time what kind of a man Elijah was, they would have said, *"He is very peculiar."* The king would have said, "I hate him."

Jezebel did not like him; the whole royal court did not like him and a great number of the nominal Christians did not like him; he was too radical.

I am glad that the Lord had seven thousand that had not bowed the knee to Baal; but I would rather have Elijah's little finger than the whole seven thousand. I would not give much for seven thousand Christians in hiding. They will just barely get into heaven; they will not have crowns.

See that *"no one will take your crown"* (Revelation 3:11). Be willing to be one of Christ's peculiar people, no matter what men may say of you! D. L. MOODY

<hr>

SEPTEMBER 29

Evening

I am a man of prayer.
PSALM 109:4

All too often we are in a "holy" hurry in our devotional time. How much actual time do we spend in quiet devotion on a daily basis? Can it be easily measured in minutes? Can you think of even one person of great spiritual stature who did not spend much of his time in prayer? Has anyone ever exhibited much of the spirit of prayer who did not devote a great deal of time to prayer?

George Whitefield, the English preacher who was one of the leading figures in the eighteenth-century American revival known as the Great Awakening, once said, "I have spent entire days and weeks lying prostrate on the ground, engaged in silent or spoken prayer." And the words of another person, whose life confirmed his own assertion, were these: "Fall to your knees and *grow* there."

It has been said that no great work of literature or science has ever been produced by someone who did not love solitude. It is also a fundamental principle of faith that no tremendous growth in holiness has ever been achieved by anyone who has not taken the time frequently, and for long periods, to be *alone with God.* THE STILL HOUR

"Come, come," He calls you, "O soul oppressed and weary,
  Come to the shadows of My desert rest;

Come walk with Me far from life's noisy discords,
  And peace will breathe like music in your breast."

<center>~~~~~~~~ S E P T E M B E R 3 0 ~~~~~~~~</center>

Morning

Why, my soul, are you downcast?
P SALM 43:5

The other evening I found myself staggering alone under a load that was heavy enough to crush half a dozen strong men. Out of sheer exhaustion I put it down and had a good look at it. I found that it was all borrowed; part of it belonged to the following day; part of it belonged to the following week—and here was I borrowing it that it might crush me *now!* It is a very stupid, but a very ancient blunder. F. W. BOREHAM

You and I are to take our trials, our black Fridays, our lone and long nights, and we are to come to Him and say, "Manage these, Thou Wondrous Friend who canst turn the very night into the morning; *manage these for me!*"

> *Sparrow, He guardeth thee;*
> *Never a flight but thy wings He upholdeth;*
> *Never a night but thy nest He enfoldeth;*
> *Safely He guardeth thee.*
>
> *Lily, He robeth thee;*
> *Though thou must fade, by the Summer bemoaned,*
> *Thou art arrayed fair as monarch enthroned;*
> *Spotless He robeth thee.*
>
> *Hear, thou of little faith;*
> *Sparrow and lily are soulless and dying;*
> *Deathless art thou; will He slight thy faint crying?*
> *Trust, thou of little faith!*

R. G. W.

Evening

He guarded him . . . like an eagle that stirs up its nest and hovers
over its young, that spreads its wings to catch them and carries them
aloft. The LORD *alone led him; no foreign god was with him.*

DEUTERONOMY 32:10–12

Our almighty God is like a parent who delights in leading the tender children in His care to the very edge of a precipice and then shoving them off the cliff into nothing but air. He does this so they may learn that they already possess an as-yet-unrealized power of flight that can forever add to the pleasure and comfort of their lives. Yet if, in their attempt to fly, they are exposed to some extraordinary peril, He is prepared to swoop beneath them and carry them skyward on His mighty wings. When God brings any of His children into a position of unparalleled difficulty, they may always count on Him to deliver them. THE SONG OF VICTORY

When God places a burden upon you, He places His arms underneath you.

There once was a little plant that was small and whose growth was stunted, for it lived under the shade of a giant oak tree. The little plant valued the shade that covered it and highly regarded the quiet rest that its noble friend provided. Yet there was a greater blessing prepared for this little plant.

One day a woodsman entered the forest with a sharp ax and felled the giant oak. The little plant began to weep, crying out, "My shelter has been taken away. Now every fierce wind will blow on me, and every storm will seek to uproot me!"

The guardian angel of the little plant responded, "No! Now the sun will shine and showers will fall on you more abundantly than ever before. Now your stunted form will spring up into loveliness, and your flowers, which could never have grown to full perfection in the shade, will laugh in the sunshine. And people in amazement will say, 'Look how that plant has grown! How gloriously beautiful it has become by removing that which was its shade and its delight!'"

Dear believer, do you understand that God may take away your comforts and privileges in order to make you a stronger Christian? Do you see why the Lord always trains His soldiers not by allowing them to lie on beds of ease but by calling them to difficult marches and service? He makes them wade through streams, swim across rivers, climb steep mountains, and walk many long marches carrying heavy backpacks of sorrow. This is how He develops soldiers—not by dressing them up in fine uniforms to strut at the gates of the barracks or to appear as handsome gentlemen to those who are strolling through the park. No, God knows that soldiers can only be made in battle and are not developed in times of peace. We may be able to grow the raw materials of which soldiers are made, but turning them into true warriors requires the education brought about by the smell of gunpowder and by fighting in the midst of flying bullets and exploding bombs, not by living through pleasant and peaceful times.

So, dear Christian, could this account for your situation? Is the Lord uncovering your gifts and causing them to grow? Is He developing in you the qualities of a soldier by shoving you into the heat of the battle? Should you not then use every gift and weapon He has given you to become a conqueror? CHARLES H. SPURGEON

OCTOBER 1

Morning

In order to keep me from becoming conceited, I was given a thorn in my flesh.
2 CORINTHIANS 12:7

Flowers there are all along life's way; but the thorns are rife also.
"*When the thorns of life have pierced us till we bleed,*" where but to heaven shall we look? To whom shall we go but to Him—the Christ who cures? He was crowned with thorns. He alone can transform our testing, torturing thorns into triumphal experiences of grace and glory. B. McCALL BARBOUR

Your path is thorny and rough? Tramp it! You will find wherever you set your foot upon a thorn, *Another Foot* has been there before and taken off the sharpness. THE MORNING MESSAGE

> *Strange gift indeed!—a thorn to prick,*
> *To pierce into the very quick;*
> *To cause perpetual sense of pain;*
> *Strange gift!—and yet, 'twas given for gain.*
> *Unwelcome, yet it came to stay;*

Nor could it e'en be prayed away.
It came to fill its God-planned place,
A life-enriching means of grace.

God's grace-thorns—ah, what forms they take;
What piercing, smarting pain they make!
And yet, each one in love is sent,
And always just for blessing meant.

And so, whate'er thy thorn may be,
From God accept it willingly;
But reckon Christ—His life—the power
To keep, in thy most trying hour.

And sure—thy life will richer grow;
He grace sufficient will bestow;
And in Heav'n's morn thy joy 'twill be
That, by His thorn, He strengthened thee.

J. Danson Smith

~~~~ OCTOBER 1 ~~~~
Evening

It was good for me to be afflicted.
Psalm 119:71

It is a remarkable occurrence of nature that the most brilliant colors of plants are found on the highest mountains, in places that are the most exposed to the fiercest weather. The brightest lichens and mosses, as well as the most beautiful wildflowers, abound high upon the windswept, storm-ravaged peaks.

One of the finest arrays of living color I have ever seen was just above the great Saint Bernard Hospice near the ten-thousand-foot summit of Mont Cenis in the French Alps. The entire face of one expansive rock was covered with a strikingly vivid yellow lichen, which shone in the sunshine like a golden wall protecting an enchanted castle. Amid the loneliness and barrenness of that high altitude and exposed to the fiercest winds of the sky, this lichen exhibited glorious color it has never displayed in the shelter of the valley.

As I write these words, I have two specimens of the same type of lichen before me. One is from this Saint Bernard area, and the other is from the wall of a Scottish castle, which is surrounded by sycamore trees. The difference in their form and coloring is quite striking. The one grown amid the fierce storms of the mountain peak has a lovely yellow color of a primrose, a smooth texture, and a definite form and shape. But the one cultivated amid the warm air and the soft showers of the lowland valley has a dull, rusty color, a rough texture, and an indistinct and broken shape.

Isn't it the same with a Christian who is afflicted, storm-tossed, and without comfort? Until the storms and difficulties allowed by God's providence beat upon a believer again and again, his character appears flawed and blurred. Yet the trials actually clear away the clouds and shadows, perfect the form of his character, and bestow brightness and blessing to his life.

> *Amidst my list of blessings infinite*
> *Stands this the foremost, that my heart has bled;*
> *For all I bless You, most for the severe.*
>
> HUGH MACMILLAN

~~~ OCTOBER 2 ~~~
Morning

Those who hope in me will not be disappointed.
ISAIAH 49:23

They shall not be ashamed that wait for me.
KJV

"They shall not be ashamed that wait for me." Such is the veritable record of the living God—a record made good in the experience of all those who have been enabled, through grace, to exercise a living faith. We must remember how much is involved in these three words—*"wait for me."* The waiting must be a real thing. It will not do to *say* we are waiting on God, when in reality, our eye is askance upon some human prop. We must absolutely be "shut up" to God. We must be brought to *the end of self* and to *the bottom of circumstance,* in order fully to prove what *God's resources* are. "My soul, wait thou only upon God" (Psalm 62:5 KJV).

Thus it was with Jehoshaphat, in that scene recorded in 2 Chronicles 20. He was wholly wrecked upon God; it was either God or nothing. "We have no power" (v. 12). But what then? "Our eyes are on you" (ibid.). This was enough. Jehoshaphat was in the very best attitude and condition to prove what God was. To have been possessed of creature strength or creature wisdom would only have proved a hindrance to him in leaning exclusively upon the arm and the counsel of the Almighty God. THINGS NEW AND OLD

When you feel at the end of your tether, remember God is at the other end!

<hr>

OCTOBER 2

Evening

He took them with him and they withdrew by themselves.
LUKE 9:10

In order to grow in grace, we must spend a great deal of time in quiet solitude. Contact with others in society is not what causes the soul to grow most vigorously. In fact, one quiet hour of prayer will often yield greater results than many days spent in the company of others. It is in the desert that the dew is freshest and the air is the most pure. ANDREW BONAR

> *Come with Me by yourselves and rest awhile,*
> *I know you're weary of the stress and throng,*
> *Wipe from your brow the sweat and dust of toil,*
> *And in My quiet strength again be strong.*
>
> *Come now aside from all the world holds dear,*
> *For fellowship the world has never known,*

Alone with Me, and with My Father here,
  With Me and with My Father, not alone.

Come, tell Me all that you have said and done,
  Your victories and failures, hopes and fears.
I know how hardened hearts are wooed and won;
  My choicest wreaths are always wet with tears.

Come now and rest; the journey is too great,
  And you will faint beside the way and sink;
The bread of life is here for you to eat,
  And here for you the wine of love to drink.

Then from fellowship with your Lord return,
  And work till daylight softens into even:
Those brief hours are not lost in which you learn
  More of your Master and His rest in Heaven.

OCTOBER 3

Morning

And we know that in all things God works for the good of those who
love him, who have been called according to his purpose.

ROMANS 8:28

The poet Cowper was subject to fits of depression. One day he ordered a cab and told the driver to take him to London Bridge. Soon a dense fog settled down upon the city. The cabby wandered about for two hours and then admitted he was lost. Cowper asked him if he thought he could find the way home. The cabby thought that he could, and in another hour landed him at his door. When Cowper asked what the fare would be, the driver felt that he should not take anything since he had not gotten his fare to his destination. Cowper insisted, saying, *"Never mind that, you have saved my life. I was on my way to throw myself off London Bridge."* He then went into the house and wrote:

God moves in a mysterious way
His wonders to perform;
He plants His footsteps on the sea,
And rides upon the storm.

The plans at the chapel went wrong; the minister was snowed up. The plans of the boy under the gallery went wrong; the snowstorm shut him off from the church of his choice. *Those two wrongs together made a tremendous right, for out of those shattered plans and programs came an event that has incalculably enriched mankind—Spurgeon's conversion.*

A very old Chinese man named Sai had only one son and one horse. Once the horse ran away, and Sai was very worried. Only one horse and lost! Someone said, *"Don't suffer, wait a little."* The horse came back. Not long after this, the only son went out to the field riding the horse. Returning home he fell from the horse and broke his leg. What a sorrow had poor Sai then! He could not eat; he could not sleep; he could not even attend well to the wants of his son. Only one son and crippled! But someone said, *"More patience, Sai!"* Soon after the accident a war broke out. All the young men went to the war; none of them returned. *Only Sai's son, the cripple, stayed at home, and remained to live long to his father's joy.* CHINESE LEGEND

～～～～ OCTOBER 3 ～～～～
Evening

After the earthquake came a fire. . . . And after the fire came a gentle whisper.
1 KINGS 19:12

A woman who had made rapid progress in her understanding of the Lord was once asked the secret of her seemingly easy growth. Her brief response was, *"Mind the checks."*

The reason many of us do not know and understand God better is that we do not heed His gentle "checks"—His delicate restraints and constraints. His voice is "a gentle whisper." A whisper can hardly be heard, so it must be felt as a faint and steady pressure upon the heart and mind, like the touch of a morning breeze calmly moving across the soul. And when it is heeded, it quietly grows clearer in the inner ear of the heart.

God's voice is directed to the ear of love, and true love is intent upon hearing even the faintest whisper. Yet there comes a time when His love ceases to speak, when we do not respond to or believe His message. "God is love" (1 John 4:8), and if you want to know Him and His voice, you must continually listen to His gentle touches.

So when you are about to say something in conversation with others, and you sense a gentle restraint from His quiet whisper, heed the restraint and refrain from speaking. And when you are about to pursue some course of action that seems perfectly clear and right, yet you sense in your spirit another path being suggested with the force of quiet conviction, heed that conviction. Follow the alternate course, even if the change of plans appears to be absolute folly from the perspective of human wisdom.

Also learn to wait on God until He unfolds His will before you. Allow Him to develop all the plans of your heart and mind, and then let Him accomplish them. Do not possess any wisdom of your own, for often His performance will appear to contradict the plan He gave you. God will seem to work against Himself, so simply listen, obey, and trust Him, even when it appears to be the greatest absurdity to do so. Ultimately, "we know that in all things God works for the good of those who love him" (Romans 8:28), but many times, in the initial stages of the performance of His plans:

> In His own world He is content
> To play a losing game.

Therefore if you desire to know God's voice, never consider the final outcome or the possible results. Obey Him even when He asks you to move while you still see only darkness, for He Himself will be a glorious light within you. Then there will quickly spring up within your heart a knowledge of God and a fellowship with Him, which will be overpowering enough in themselves to hold you and Him together, even in the most severe tests and under the strongest pressures of life. WAY OF FAITH

OCTOBER 4

Morning

God chose the weak things of the world. . . . to nullify the
things that are, so that no one may boast before him.

1 CORINTHIANS 1:27–29

Only a blast of rams' horns and a shout—and God made the walls of proud Jericho crumble to their foundations, and the key of all Canaan was in the hand of Israel! (Joshua 6)

Only two women—one, Deborah, inspired courage in the fainting hearts of Israel's men—the other, Jael, with a hammer and nail laid Israel's master low; thus the end came to twenty years of mighty oppression! (Judges 4–5)

Only an ox goad—but with it six hundred Philistines were slain, and Israel delivered by Shamgar's God! (Judges 3:31)

Only a trumpet blast, the smash of a lighted pitcher, a shout—but by these, and Gideon, God delivered Israel from the seven-year yoke of the Midianites! (Judges 6–8)

Only the jawbone of an ass—yet heaps of Philistines fell before it because God strengthened the arm that wielded it! (Judges 15)

Only a sling and a stone sent with unerring precision and directed by Almighty God—and that day Israel's mighty men were put to shame: the giant Philistine was slain, and God's honor was vindicated! (1 Samuel 17)

Only a few ignorant yet wholehearted and consecrated men and women—but by the power of God they were to put men in possession of that Eternal Salvation which would transform its possessors into the likeness of the Son Himself and ultimately land them in Eternal Glory!

If you are one of the base, foolish, weak ciphers of this world, *then the very same power, from the very same Lord, for the very same purpose, will be yours!* W. T.

Under the control of God ordinary instruments become extraordinary.

OCTOBER 4

Evening

The LORD *blessed the latter part of Job's life more than the former part.*
JOB 42:12

Job found his legacy through the grief he experienced. He was tried that his godliness might be confirmed and validated. In the same way, my troubles are intended to deepen my character and to clothe me in gifts I had little of prior to my difficulties, for my ripest fruit grows against the roughest wall. I come to a place of glory only through my own humility, tears, and death, just as Job's afflictions left him with a higher view of God and more humble thoughts of himself. At last he cried, *"Now my eyes have seen you"* (v. 5).

If I experience the presence of God in His majesty through my pain and loss, so that I bow before Him and pray, *"Your will be done"* (Matthew 6:10), then I have gained much indeed. God gave Job glimpses of his future glory, for in those weary and difficult days and nights, he was allowed to penetrate God's veil and could honestly say, *"I know that my redeemer lives"* (Job 19:25). So truly: "The LORD blessed the latter part of Job's life more than the former part." IN THE HOUR OF SILENCE

Trouble never comes to someone unless it brings a nugget of gold in its hand.

Apparent adversity will ultimately become an advantage for those of us doing what is right, if we are willing to keep serving and to wait patiently. Think of the great victorious souls of the past who worked with steadfast faith and who were invincible and courageous! There are many blessings we will never obtain if we are unwilling to accept and endure suffering. There are certain joys that can come to us only through sorrow. There are revelations of God's divine truth that we will receive only when the lights of earth have been extinguished. And there are harvests that will grow only once the plow has done its work. SELECTED

It is from suffering that the strongest souls ever known have emerged; the world's greatest display of character is seen in those who exhibit the scars of sorrow; the martyrs of the ages have worn their coronation robes that have glistened with fire, yet through their tears and sorrow have seen the gates of heaven. CHAPIN

> *I will know by the gleam and glitter*
> *Of the golden chain you wear,*
> *By your heart's calm strength in loving,*
> *Of the fire you have had to bear.*
> *Beat on, true heart, forever;*
> *Shine bright, strong golden chain;*
> *And bless the cleansing fire*
> *And the furnace of living pain!*
>
> ADELAIDE PROCTOR

Morning

Not hidden from the Almighty.
JOB 24:1 KJV

Thy Savior is near thee, suffering, lonely, tempted friend! *Thou art not the plaything of wild chance. There is a purpose in thy life which Jesus is working out.* Let thy spirit flee for rest to Christ and to His pierced hand which opens the book of thy life! Rest thee there! Be patient and trustful! All will work out right. Someday thou wilt understand. In the meantime, trust Him "though sun and moon fail, and the stars drop into the dark."

> *What though the way may be lonely,*
> *And dark the shadows fall;*
> *I know where'er it leadeth,*
> *My Father planned it all.*

> *The sun may shine tomorrow,*
> *The shadows break and flee;*
> *'Twill be the way He chooses,*
> *The Father's plan for me.*

> *He guides my halting footsteps*
> *Along the weary way,*
> *For well He knows the pathway*
> *Will lead to endless day.*

> *A day of light and gladness,*
> *On which no shade will fall,*
> *'Tis this at last awaits me—*
> *My Father planned it all.*

I sing through shade and sunshine,
And trust what'er befall;
His way is best—it leads to rest;
My Father planned it all.

God is working out His purpose.

OCTOBER 5
Evening

Some time later the brook dried up.
1 KINGS 17:7

The education of our faith is incomplete if we have yet to learn that God's providence works through loss, that there is a ministry to us through failure and the fading of things, and that He gives the gift of emptiness. It is, in fact, the material insecurities of life that cause our lives to be spiritually established. The dwindling brook at the Kerith Ravine, where Elijah sat deep in thought, is a true picture of each of our lives. "*Some time later the brook dried up*"—this is the history of our yesterdays, and a prophecy of our tomorrows.

One way or the other, we must all learn the difference between trusting in the gift and trusting in the Giver. The gift may last for a season, but the Giver is the only eternal love.

The Kerith Ravine was a difficult problem for Elijah until he arrived at Zarephath, and suddenly everything became as clear as daylight to him. God's hard instructions are never His last words to us, for the woe, the waste, and the tears of life belong to its interlude, not its finale.

If the Lord had led Elijah directly to Zarephath, he would have missed something that helped to make him a wiser prophet and a better man—living by faith at Kerith. And whenever our earthly stream or any other outer resource has dried up, it has been allowed so we may learn that our hope and help are in God, who made heaven and earth. F. B. MEYER

Perhaps you, too, have camped by such sweet waters,
And quenched with joy your weary, parched soul's thirst;
To find, as time goes on, your streamlet alters
    From what it was at first.

Hearts that have cheered, or soothed, or blest, or strengthened;
Loves that have lavished unreservedly;
Joys, treasured joys—have passed, as time has lengthened,
    Into obscurity.

If then, O soul, the brook your heart has cherished
Does fail you now—no more your thirst assuage—
If its once glad refreshing streams have perished,
    Let Him your heart engage.

He will not fail, nor mock, nor disappoint you;
His comfort and care change not with the years;
With oil of joy He surely will anoint you,
    And wipe away your tears.

J. DANSON SMITH

OCTOBER 6
Morning

Whoever loses their life for my sake will find it.
MATTHEW 10:39

In my early life I entered into a partnership with a friend in the wholesale ice business. For two seasons in succession our ice was swept away by winter freshets. In the winter of which I speak, things had come to a serious pass and it seemed very necessary that we should have ice. The weather became very cold; the ice formed and grew thicker and thicker until it was fit to gather. Then there came an order for thousands of tons of ice which would lift us entirely from our financial stress. Not long before this,

God had showed me that it was His will that I should commit my business to Him and trust Him with it absolutely. I never dreamed what testing was coming. At midnight there came an ominous sound—that of rain. By noon the storm was raging in all its violence; by afternoon I had come into a great spiritual crisis in my life.

I have learned this: *a matter may be seemingly trivial, but the crisis that turns upon a small matter may be a profound and far-reaching one in our lives.*

By midafternoon of that day I had come face to face with the tremendous fact that *down deep in my heart was a spirit of rebellion against God.* And that rebelliousness seemed to develop in a suggestion to my heart like this: "You gave all to God. This is the way He requites you." Then another voice: *"My child, did you mean it when you said you would trust Me? Would I suffer anything to come into your life which will not work out for good for you?"* And then the other voice: "But it is hard! Why should He take your business when it is clean and honest?"

At the end of two hours (during which waged one of the greatest spiritual battles of my life) by the grace of God I was able to cry out, "Take the business; take the ice; take everything; only give me the supreme blessing of a will absolutely submitted to Thee."

And then came peace!

By midnight there came another sound—that of wind. By morning the mercury had fallen to zero, and in a few days we were harvesting the finest ice we ever had. He gave back the ice; He blessed the business; and He led me on and out, until He guided me from it entirely into the place He had for me from the beginning—that of a teacher of His Word. James H. McConkey

Give your life to God, and God will give you back your life!

~~~~~ OCTOBER 6 ~~~~~

Evening

He did not open his mouth.
Isaiah 53:7

What grace it requires when we are misunderstood yet handle it correctly, or when we are judged unkindly yet receive it in holy sweetness! Nothing tests our character as a Christian more than having something evil said about us. This kind of grinding test is what exposes whether we are solid gold or simply gold-plated metal. If we could only see the blessings that lie hidden in our trials, we would say like David, when Shimei cursed him, "Let him curse, for the Lord will return good to me instead of his cursing this day" (2 Samuel 16:11–12 NASB).

Some Christians are easily turned away from the greatness of their life's calling by pursuing instead their own grievances and enemies. They ultimately turn their lives into one petty whirlwind of warfare. It reminds me of trying to deal with a hornet's nest. You may be able to disperse the hornets, but you will probably be terribly stung and receive nothing for your pain, for even their honey has no value.

May God grant us more of the Spirit of Christ, who, "when they hurled their insults at him, . . . did not retaliate. . . . Instead, he entrusted himself to him who judges justly" (1 Peter 2:23). "Consider him who endured such opposition from sinners, so that you will not grow weary and lose heart" (Hebrews 12:3). A. B. SIMPSON

> For you He walked along the path of woe,
> He was sharply struck with His head bent low.
> He knew the deepest sorrow, pain, and grief,
> He knew long endurance with no relief,
> He took all the bitter from death's deep cup,
> He kept no blood drops but gave them all up.
> Yes, for you, and for me, He won the fight
> To take us to glory and realms of light.
>
> L. S. P.

OCTOBER 7
Morning

The Lord is my shepherd.
PSALM 23:1

The great Father above is a Shepherd Chief. I am His and with Him. I want not. He throws out to me a rope, and the name of the rope is love, and He draws me to where the grass is green and the water is not dangerous.

Sometimes my heart is very weak, and falls down, but He lifts it up again and draws me into a good road.

Sometime, it may be very soon, it may be longer, it may be a long, long time, He will draw me into a place between mountains. It is dark there, but I'll draw back not. I'll be afraid not, for it is in there between the mountains that the Shepherd Chief will meet me, and the hunger I have felt in my heart all through this life will be satisfied. Sometimes He makes the love rope into a whip, but afterwards He gives me a staff to lean on.

He spreads a table before me with all kinds of food. He puts His hands upon my head, and all the "tired" is gone.

My cup He fills, till it runs over.

What I tell you is true, I lie not. The roads that are "away ahead" will stay with me through this life, and afterwards I will go to live in the "Big Tepee" and sit down with the Shepherd Chief forever. An American Indian's Version of the Twenty-Third Psalm

Fear not, little flock, He goeth ahead,
Your Shepherd selecteth the path you must tread;
The water of Marah He'll sweeten for thee,
He drank all the bitter in Gethsemane.

Fear not, little flock, whatever your lot,
He enters all rooms, "The doors being shut";
He never forsakes; He never is gone,
So count on His presence in darkness and dawn.
                                        Paul Rader

OCTOBER 7
Evening

Who among you fears the Lord and obeys the word of his
servant? Let the one who walks in the dark, who has no light,
trust in the name of the Lord and rely on [his] God.
                        Isaiah 50:10

What is a believer to do in times of darkness—a darkness of perplexities and confusion—a darkness not of the heart but of the mind? These times of darkness come to a faithful and believing disciple who is walking obediently in the will of God. They come as seasons when he does not know what to do or which way to turn. His sky becomes overcast with clouds, and the clear light of heaven does not shine on his path, so that he feels as if he were groping his way through complete darkness.

Dear believer, does this describe you? What should you do in times of darkness? Listen to God's Word: "Let [him] . . . trust in the name of the LORD and rely on his God." Actually, the first thing to do is nothing. This is a difficult thing for our lowly human nature to do. There is a saying, "When you're rattled, don't rush." In other words, "When you are confused and do not know what to do, do nothing." When you find yourself in a spiritual fog, do not run ahead, but slow the pace of your life. And if necessary, keep your life's ship anchored or tied to the dock.

The right thing is simply to trust God, for while we trust, He can work. Worrying, however, prevents Him from doing anything for us. If the darkness covering us strikes terror in our hearts and we run back and forth, seeking in vain to find a way of escape from the dark trial where God's providence has placed us, then the Lord cannot work on our behalf.

Only the peace of God will quiet our minds and put our hearts at rest. We must place our hand in His as a little child and allow Him to lead us into the bright sunshine of His love. He knows the way out of the dense, dark forest, so may we climb into His arms, trusting Him to rescue us by showing us the shortest and most reliable road. DR. PARDINGTON

Remember, we are never without a pilot—even when we do not know which way to steer.

> Hold on, my heart, in your believing—
>   Only the steadfast wins the crown;
> He who, when stormy winds are heaving,
>   Parts with his anchor, will go down;
> But he who Jesus holds through all,
>   Will stand, though Heaven and earth should fall.
> Hold on! An end will come to sorrow;
>   Hope from the dust will conquering rise;
> The storm foretells a summer's morrow;

The Cross points on to Paradise;
The Father reigns! So cease all doubt;
Hold on, my heart. Hold on, hold out.

Morning

Restore that person gently. But watch yourselves, or you also may be tempted.
GALATIANS 6:1

From the converts in Uganda
Comes to us a story grander,
In the lesson that it teaches,
Than a sermon often preaches.
For they tell what sore temptations
Come to them; what need of patience,
And a need, all else outweighing,
Of a place for private praying.
So each convert chose a corner
Far away from eye of scorner,
In the jungle, where he could
Pray to God in solitude.
And so often went he thither,
That the grass would fade and wither
Where he trod and you could trace
By the paths, each prayer place.

If they hear the evil tiding That a brother is backsliding, And that some are even
saying, "He no longer cares for praying," Then they say to one another, Very
soft and gently, "Brother, You'll forgive us now for showing, On your path
the grass is growing." And the erring one, relenting, Soon is bitterly repenting:
"Ah, how sad I am at knowing
On my path the grass is growing.

But it shall be so no longer; Prayer
I need to make me stronger; On my
path so oft I'm going,
Soon no grass will there be growing."
"Grass on the Prayer Path"

Have a trysting place with God! And keep a little path open!

OCTOBER 8

Evening

Do not be anxious about anything.
Philippians 4:6

Quite a few Christians live in a terrible state of anxiety, constantly fretting over the concerns of life. The secret of living in perfect peace amid the hectic pace of daily life is one well worth knowing. What good has worrying ever accomplished? It has never made anyone stronger, helped anyone do God's will, or provided for anyone a way of escape out of their anxiety or confusion. Worry only destroys the effectiveness of lives that would otherwise be useful and beautiful. Being restless and having worries and cares are absolutely forbidden by our Lord, who said, "So do not worry, saying, 'What shall we eat?' or 'What shall we drink?' or 'What shall we wear?'" (Matthew 6:31). He does not mean that we are not to think ahead or that our life should never have a plan or pattern to it. He simply means that we are not to worry about these things.

People will know that you live in a constant state of anxiety by the lines on your face, the tone of your voice, your negative attitude, and the lack of joy in your spirit. So scale the heights of a life abandoned to God, and your perspective will change to the point that you will look down on the clouds beneath your feet. Darlow Sargeant

It is a sign of weakness to always worry and fret, question everything, and mistrust everyone. Can anything be gained by it? Don't we only make ourselves unfit for action, and separate our minds from the ability to make wise decisions? We simply sink in our struggles when we could float by faith.

Oh, for the grace to be silent! Oh, to "be still, and know that [Jehovah is] God" (Psalm 46:10)! "The Holy One of Israel" (Psalm 89:18) will defend and deliver His own. We can be sure that His every word will stand forever, even though the mountains may fall into the sea. He deserves our total confidence. So come, my soul, return to your place of peace, and rest within the sweet embrace of the Lord Jesus. SELECTED

Peace your inmost soul will fill
When you're still!

OCTOBER 9

Morning

Abraham built an altar there. . . . and took the knife to slay his son. But the
angel of the LORD *called out to him. . . . "Do not lay a hand on the boy."*
GENESIS 22:9–12

Our hardest sacrifices are never so hard as we thought they were going to be, *if* we go on with them to the uttermost that God asks. A sacrifice of self to God's will made halfway, *or even nine-tenths, is a grinding, cruel experience.* When it is made the *whole* way, with the altar built and self laid upon the altar, God always *comes with an unexpected blessing that so overwhelms us with love and joy that the hardship of the sacrifice sinks out of sight.* "Now I know that you fear God, because you have not withheld" (v. 12). Can He say that to *us* today? No one ever knows the full joy of hearing the word from God until the altar has been built and the knife is laid to the sacrifice. MESSAGES FOR THE MORNING WATCH

Is your all on the altar of sacrifice laid?
Your heart, does the Spirit control?
You can only be blest and have peace and sweet rest
As you yield Him your body and soul.

Evening

The LORD longs to be gracious to you; therefore he
will rise up to show you compassion.
ISAIAH 30:18

The greenest grass is found wherever the most rain falls. So I suppose it is the fog and mist of Ireland that makes it "the Emerald Isle." And wherever you find the widespread fog of trouble and the mist of sorrow, you always find emerald green hearts that are full of the beautiful foliage of the comfort and love of God.

Dear Christian, do not say, "Where are all the swallows? They are all gone—they are dead." No, they are not dead. They have simply skimmed across the deep, blue sea, flying to a faraway land; but they will be back again soon.

Child of God, do not say, "All the flowers are dead—the winter has killed them, so they are gone." No! Although the winter has covered them with a white coat of snow, they will push up their heads again and will be alive very soon.

O believer, do not say that the sun has burned out, just because a cloud has hidden it. No, it is still there, planning a summer for you; for when it shines again, it will have caused those clouds to have dropped their April showers, each of them a mother to a sweet May flower.

Above all, remember—when God hides His face from you, do not say that He has forgotten you. He is simply waiting for a little while to make you love Him more. And once He comes, you will rejoice with the inexpressible "joy of the LORD" (Nehemiah 8:10). Waiting on Him exercises your gift of grace and tests your faith. Therefore continue to wait in hope, for although the promise may linger, it will never come too late.
CHARLES H. SPURGEON

> *Oh, every year has its winter,*
> *And every year has its rain—*
> *But a day is always coming*
> *When the birds go north again.*

When new leaves sprout in the forest,
  And grass springs green on the plain,
And tulips boast their blossoms—
  And the birds go north again.

Oh, every heart has its sorrow,
  And every heart has its pain—
But a day is always coming
  When the birds go north again.

It's the sweetest thing to remember,
  If your courage starts to wane,
When the cold, dark days are over—
  That the birds go north again.

~~~ OCTOBER 10 ~~~

Morning

They did not love their lives so much.
REVELATION 12:11

The persecution of the Christians during the reign of Marcus Aurelius was very bitter. The Emperor himself decreed the punishment of forty of the men who had refused to bow down to his image.

"Strip to the skin!" he commanded. They did so. "Now, go and stand on that frozen lake," he commanded, "until you are prepared to abandon your Nazarene-God!"

And forty naked men marched out into that howling storm on a winter's night. As they took their places on the ice, they lifted up their voices and sang:

"Christ, forty wrestlers have come out to wrestle for Thee; to win for Thee the victory; to win from Thee the crown."

After a while, those standing by and watching noticed a disturbance among the men. One man had edged away, broken into a run, entered the temple, and prostrated himself before the image of the Emperor.

The captain of the guard, who had witnessed the bravery of the men and whose heart had been touched by their teaching, tore off his helmet, threw down his spear, and disrobing himself, took up the cry as he took the place of the man who had weakened. The compensation was not slow in coming, for as the dawn broke there were forty corpses on the ice.

Who shall dream of shrinking, by our Captain led?

At least a thousand of God's saints served as living torches to illuminate the darkness of Nero's gardens, wrapped in garments steeped in pitch. *"Every finger was a candle."*

Who follows in their train?

I'm standing, Lord.
There is a mist that blinds my sight.
Steep jagged rocks, front, left, and right,
Lower, dim, gigantic, in the night.
Where is the way?

I'm standing, Lord.
The black rock hems me in behind.
Above my head a moaning wind
Chills and oppresses heart and mind.
I am afraid!

I'm standing, Lord.
The rock is hard beneath my feet.
I nearly slipped, Lord, on the sleet.
So weary, Lord, and where a seat?
Still must I stand?

He answered me, and on His face
A look ineffable of grace,
Of perfect, understanding love,
Which all my murmuring did remove.

I'm standing, Lord.
Since Thou hast spoken, Lord, I see
Thou hast beset; these rocks are Thee;
And since Thy love encloses me,
I stand and sing!

BETTY STAM, MARTYRED IN CHINA

～ OCTOBER 10 ～
Evening

Do not fret.
PSALM 37:1

I believe that this verse is as much a divine command as *"You shall not steal"* (Exodus 20:15). But what does it mean to fret? One person once defined it as that which makes a person rough on the surface, causing him to rub and wear himself and others away. Isn't it true that an irritable, irrational, and critical person not only wears himself out but is also very draining and tiring to others? When we worry and fret, we are a constant annoyance. This psalm not only says, "Do not fret because of those who are evil" but leaves no room for fretting whatsoever. It is very harmful, and God does not want us to hurt ourselves or others.

Any physician can tell you that a fit of anger is more harmful to your system than a fever and that a disposition of continual fretting is not conducive to a healthy body. The next step down from fretting is being quick-tempered, and that amounts to anger. May we set it aside once and for all and simply be obedient to the command *"Do not fret."*
MARGARET BOTTOME

OVERHEARD IN AN ORCHARD

Said the Robin to the Sparrow:
*   "I should really like to know*
Why these anxious human beings
*   Rush about and worry so."*

Said the Sparrow to the Robin:
"Friend, I think that it must be
That they have no Heavenly Father
Such as cares for you and me."
ELIZABETH CHENEY

~~~ OCTOBER 11 ~~~
Morning

Until he to whom it rightfully belongs shall come.
EZEKIEL 21:27

Years ago in Cincinnati Handel's *Messiah* was rendered by perhaps the greatest chorus on earth: Patti, then in her prime, was the leading soprano; Whitney, the bass; Theodore Toedt, the tenor; Carey, the alto; and this quartet was supported by more than four thousand voices.

Just before the "Hallelujah Chorus," a deathlike stillness brooded over that vast assemblage. Suddenly the bass sang, "For He shall reign for ever and ever," the alto lifted it a little higher—"For ever and ever," and the tenor lifted it still higher—"For ever and ever," then Patti broke in as though inspired—"King of Kings, and Lord of Lords." As she broke off, paused, and lifted her eyes, a voice seemed to float down from above as the voice of an Angel flinging out through the great hall the question, "How long shall He reign?"—and the thousand sopranos in unison responded, "For ever and ever." Then the four thousand of the chorus broke forth like the shout of an angelic host, "Hallelujah! Hallelujah! Hallelujah!"

What a day for this poor sin-ruined, storm-torn, heartbroken, groping-in-the-blind world, when He shall take His rightful throne and reign in all hearts and over all lives forever and ever! ELMER ELLSWORTH HELMS

Hail, universal Lord!
Messiah—David's Son!
Take Thou the scepter of the world,
And reign supreme, alone!

Oh, it seems to me like a prophecy of the glad day when every knee shall bow, and all the nations of the earth shall confess that Jesus Christ is Lord, to the glory of God the Father. And from the teeming millions of Asia shall sound the anthem, "King of Kings, and Lord of Lords"; the shout from Europe will give it power; and the deep undertone of Africa's redeemed will lend it volume; and America, and faraway Australia, and the islands of the sea will join the refrain and pour their matchless music into the ear of Christ; and together, from the uttermost parts of the earth, breaking out in triumphant voice, the whole world shall sing, "King of Kings, and Lord of Lords; the Lord God Omnipotent reigneth!"

Come back! Come back! Take the scepter of our lives! Mount the throne of our hearts! All hail the King! My King! *And thine?*

OCTOBER 11

Evening

Dying, and yet we live on.
2 CORINTHIANS 6:9

Last summer I had a flower bed of asters that nearly covered my garden in the country. They were planted late in the season, but how beautiful they were! While the outer portion of the plants were still producing fresh flowers, the tops had gone to seed, and when an early frost came, I found that the radiant beauty of the blossoms had withered. All I could say at this point was, "Oh well, I guess the season has been too much for them, and they have died." So I wished them a fond farewell.

After this I no longer enjoyed looking at the flower bed, for it seemed to be only a graveyard of flowers. Yet several weeks ago one of the gardeners called my attention to the fact that across the entire garden, asters were now sprouting up in great abundance. It appeared that every plant I thought the winter had destroyed had replanted fifty to take its place. What had the frost and the fierce winter wind done?

They had taken my flowers and destroyed them, casting them to the ground. They had walked across them with their snowy feet and, once finished with their work, said, "*This is the end of you.*" And yet in the spring, for every one destroyed, fifty witnesses arose and said, "*It is through 'dying . . . we live on.'*"

As it is in the plant world, so it is in God's kingdom. Through death came everlasting life. Through crucifixion and the tomb came the throne and the palace of the eternal God. Through apparent defeat came victory.

So do not be afraid of suffering or defeat. It is through being "struck down, but not destroyed" (2 Corinthians 4:9) and through being broken to pieces, and those pieces being torn to shreds, that we become people of strength. And it is the endurance of one believer that produces a multitude.

Others may yield to the appearance of things and follow the world. They may blossom quickly and find momentary prosperity, but their end will be one of eternal death.
HENRY WARD BEECHER

> Measure your life by loss and not by gain,
> Not by the wine drunk but by the wine poured forth.
> For love's strength is found in love's sacrifice,
> And he who suffers most has most to give.

～～～～ OCTOBER 12 ～～～～

Morning

May my meditation be pleasing to him.
PSALM 104:34

Isaac went into the fields to meditate. Jacob lingered on the eastern bank of the brook Jabbok after all his company had passed over; there he wrestled with the angel and prevailed. *Moses,* hidden in the clefts of Horeb, beheld the vanishing glory which marked the way by which Jehovah had gone. *Elijah* sent Ahab down to eat and drink while he himself withdrew to the lonely crest of Carmel. *Daniel* spent weeks in ecstasy of intercession on the banks of Hiddekel, which once had watered Paradise. And *Paul,* no doubt in order that he might have an opportunity for undisturbed meditation and prayer, was minded to go afoot from Troas to Assos.

Have you learned to understand the truths of these great paradoxes: the blessing of a curse, the voice of silence, the companionship of solitude?

I walk down the Valley of Silence,
Down the dim voiceless valley alone,
And I hear not the sound of a footstep
Around me, but God's and my own;
And the hush of my heart is as holy
As the bowers whence angels have flown.

In the hush of the Valley of Silence
I hear all the songs that I sing,
And the notes float down the dim Valley
Till each finds a word for a wing,
That to men, like the dove of the deluge
The message of peace they may bring.

But far on the deep there are billows
That never shall break on the beach;
And I have heard songs in the silence
That never shall float into speech;
And I have had dreams in the Valley
Too lofty for language to reach.

Do you ask me the place of the Valley?
To hearts that are harrowed by care
It lieth afar, between mountains,
And God and His angels are there—
One is the dark mountain of sorrow,
And one the bright mountain of prayer.

"THE SONG OF A MYSTIC"

Evening

Joseph's master took him and put him in prison. . . . But . . . the Lord
was with him . . . and gave him success in whatever he did.
Genesis 39:20–21, 23

When God allows us to go to prison because of our service to Him, it is nearly the most blessed place in the world that we could be, because He goes with us. Joseph seems to have known this truth. He did not sulk, become discouraged and rebellious, or engage in self-pity by thinking "everything was against him." If he had done so, the prison warden would never have trusted him.

May we remember that if self-pity is allowed to set in, we will never be used by God again until it is totally removed. Joseph simply placed everything in joyful trust upon the Lord, and as a result, the prison warden placed everything into Joseph's care.

Lord Jesus, when the prison door closes behind me, keep me trusting in You with complete and overflowing joy. Give Your work through me great success, and even in prison make me "free indeed" (John 8:36). Selected

> *A little bird I am,*
> *Shut from the fields of air,*
> *And in my cage I sit and sing*
> *To Him who placed me there;*
> *Well pleased a prisoner to be,*
> *Because, My God, it pleases Thee.*
>
> *My cage confines me round,*
> *Freely I cannot fly,*
> *But though my wings are closely bound,*
> *My soul is at liberty;*
> *For prison walls cannot control*
> *The flight or freedom of the soul.*

I have learned to love the darkness of sorrow, for it is there I see the brightness of God's face. MADAME GUYON

OCTOBER 13
Morning

You may ask . . . and I will do it.
JOHN 14:14

Who is it here who offers to do for us if we will only ask? It is *God Himself!* It is the mightiest doer in the universe who says, "I will do, if you ask."

Think a moment *who* it is that promises: the God who holds the sea in the hollow of His hand; the God who swings this ponderous globe of earth in its orbit; the God who marshals the stars and guides the planets in their blazing paths with undeviating accuracy; the heaven-creating, devil-conquering, dead-raising God. It is this very God who says: *"You may ask . . . and I will do it"!*

Unrivaled wisdom, boundless skill, limitless power, infinite resources are His.

Wouldst thou not rather call forth *Mine omnipotent doing* by thine asking, if to this I have called thee, than even to be busy with thine own doing? JAMES H. MCCONKEY
I will do *marvels!*

OCTOBER 13
Evening

Do not be anxious about anything.
PHILIPPIANS 4:6

Anxiety should never be found in a believer. In spite of the magnitude, quantity, and diversity of our trials, afflictions, and difficulties, anxiety should not exist under any circumstances. This is because we have a Father in heaven who is almighty, who loves His children as He loves His "one and only Son" (John 3:16), and whose complete joy and delight it is to continually assist them under all circumstances. We should heed His Word, which says, "Do not be anxious about anything, but in every situation, by prayer and petition, with thanksgiving, present your requests to God."

"*In every situation*"—not simply when our house is on fire or when our beloved spouse and children are gravely ill, but even in the smallest matters of life. We are to take everything to God—little things, very little things, even what the world calls trivial things. Yes, we are to take *everything*, living all day long in holy fellowship with our heavenly Father and our precious Lord Jesus. We should develop something of a spiritual instinct, causing us to immediately turn to God when a concern keeps us awake at night. During those sleepless nights, we should speak to Him, bringing our various concerns before Him, no matter how small they may be. Also speak to the Lord about any trial you are facing or any difficulties you may have in your family or professional life.

"*By prayer and petition*"—earnestly pleading, persevering and enduring, and waiting, waiting, waiting on God.

"*With thanksgiving*"—always laying a good foundation. Even if we have no possessions, there is one thing for which we can always be thankful—that He has saved us from hell. We can also give thanks that He has given us His Holy Word, His Holy Spirit, and the most precious gift of all—His Son. Therefore when we consider all this, we have abundant reasons for thanksgiving. May this be our goal!

"*And the peace of God, which transcends all understanding, will guard your hearts and your minds in Christ Jesus*" (Philippians 4:7). This is such a wonderful, genuine, and precious blessing that to truly know it, you must experience it, for it "transcends all understanding."

May we take these truths to heart, instinctively walking in them, so the result will be lives that glorify God more abundantly than ever before. George Mueller Life of Trust

Search your heart several times a day, and if you find something that is disturbing your peace, remember to take the proper steps to restore the calm. Francis de Sales

Morning

When he heard that Lazarus was sick, he stayed where he was two more days.
John 11:6

And so the silence of God was itself an answer. It is not merely said that there was no audible response to the cry from Bethany; it is distinctly stated that the absence of an audible response was itself the answer to the cry—it was when the Lord heard that Lazarus was sick that therefore He abode two days still in the same place which He was. I have often heard the outward silence. A hundred times have I sent up aspirations whose only answer has seemed to be the echo of my own voice, and I have cried out in the night of my despair, "Why art Thou so far from helping me?" But I never thought that the seeming farness was itself the nearness of God—that the very silence was an answer.

It was a very grand answer to the household of Bethany. They had asked not too much, but too little. They had asked only the life of Lazarus. They were to get the life of Lazarus and a revelation of eternal life as well.

There are some prayers that are followed by a Divine silence because we are not yet ripe for all we have asked; there are others which are so followed because we are ripe for more. We do not always know the full strength of our own capacity; we have to be prepared for receiving greater blessings than we have ever dreamed of. We come to the door of the sepulcher and beg with tears the dead body of Jesus; we are answered by silence because we are to get something better—a living Lord.

My soul, be not afraid of God's silence; it is another form of His voice. God's silence is more than man's speech. God's negative is better than the world's affirmative. Have thy prayers been followed by a calm stillness? Well! Is not that God's voice—a voice that will suffice thee in the meantime till the full disclosure comes? Has He moved not from His place to help thee? Well, but His stillness makes thee still, and He has something better than help to give thee.

Wait for Him in the silence, and ere long it shall become vocal; death shall be swallowed up in victory! George Matheson

All God's dealings are slow!

Think not that God's silence is coldness or indifference. When birds are on the nest preparing to bring forth life, they never sing. God's stillness is full of brooding. Be not impatient of God!

When the Lord is to lead a soul to great faith, He for a time leaves his prayer unanswered.

OCTOBER 14

Evening

Suddenly an angel of the LORD appeared and a light shone in the cell. He struck Peter on the side and woke him up. "Quick, get up!" he said, and the chains fell off Peter's wrists.

ACTS 12:7

About midnight Paul and Silas were praying and singing hymns to God. . . . Suddenly there was such a violent earthquake that the foundations of the prison were shaken. At once all the prison doors flew open, and everyone's chains came loose.

ACTS 16:25–26

This is the way God works. In our darkest hour, He walks to us across the waves, just as an angel came to Peter's cell when the day of Peter's execution dawned. And when the scaffold was completed for Mordecai's execution, the king's sleeplessness ultimately led to his action favoring God's favored race. (Esther 6.)

Dear soul, you may have to experience the very worst before you are delivered, but you will be delivered! God may keep you waiting, but He will always remember His promise and will appear in time to fulfill His sacred Word that cannot be broken. F. B. MEYER

God has a simplicity about Him in working out His plans, and yet He possesses a resourcefulness equal to any difficulty. His faithfulness to His trusting children is unwavering, and He is steadfast in holding to His purpose. In Joseph's life, we see God work through a fellow prisoner, later through a dream, and finally through lifting Joseph from a prison to the position of governor. And the length of Joseph's prison stay gave him the strength and steadiness he needed as governor.

It is always safe to trust God's methods and to live by His clock. SAMUEL DICKEY GORDON

God in His providence has a thousand keys to open a thousand different doors in order to deliver His own, no matter how desperate the situation may have become. May we be faithful to do our part, which is simply to suffer for Him, and to place Christ's part on Him and then leave it there. GEORGE MACDONALD

Difficulty is actually the atmosphere surrounding a miracle, or a miracle in its initial stage. Yet if it is to be a great miracle, the surrounding condition will be not simply a difficulty but an utter impossibility. And it is the clinging hand of His child that makes a desperate situation a delight to God.

~~~~~ OCTOBER 15 ~~~~~
Morning

This is the confidence we have in approaching God: that if we ask anything according to his will, he hears us. And if we know that he hears us—whatever we ask—we know that we have what we asked of him.

1 JOHN 5:14–15

Prayer can obtain everything: it can open the windows of heaven and shut the gates of hell; it can put a holy constraint upon God and detain an angel until he leave a blessing; it can open the treasures of rain and soften the iron ribs of rocks till they melt into tears and a flowing river; prayer can unclasp the girdles of the north—saying to a mountain of ice, "Be thou removed hence, and cast into the bottom of the sea"; it can arrest the sun in the midst of his course and send the swift-winged winds upon our errands; and to all these strange things and secret decrees, add unrevealed transactions which are above the stars.

When Hudson Taylor was asked if he ever prayed *without any consciousness of joy,* he replied: "Often: sometimes I pray on with my heart feeling like wood; often, too, the most wonderful answers have come when prayer has been a real effort of faith without any joy whatever."

I never prayed sincerely and earnestly for anything but it came; at some time—no matter how distant the day—somehow, in some shape, probably the last I should have devised, *it came.* ADONIRAM JUDSON

For years I've prayed, and yet I see no change.
The mountain stands exactly where it stood;
The shadows that it casts are just as deep;
The pathway to its summit e'en more steep.
Shall I pray on?

Shall I pray on with ne'er a hopeful sign?
Not only does the mountain still remain,
But, while I watch to see it disappear,
Becomes the more appalling year by year.
Shall I pray on?

I shall pray on. Though distant as it seems
The answer may be almost at my door,
Or just around the corner on its way,
But, whether near or far, yes, I shall pray—
I shall pray on.

EDITH MAPES

If thou wilt keep the incense burning there, His glory thou shalt see—sometime, somewhere!

~~~ OCTOBER 15 ~~~

Evening

*The sacrifices of God are a broken spirit; A broken and
a contrite heart, O God, You will not despise.*
PSALM 51:17 NASB

Those people God uses most to bring glory to Himself are those who are completely broken, for the sacrifice He accepts is a "broken and contrite heart." It was not until Jacob's natural strength was broken, when "his hip was wrenched" (Genesis 32:25) at Peniel, that he came to the point where God could clothe him with spiritual power. And it was not until Moses struck the rock at Horeb, breaking its surface, that cool "water [came] out of it for the people to drink" (Exodus 17:6).

It was not until Gideon's three hundred specially chosen soldiers "broke the jars that were in their hands" (Judges 7:19), which symbolized brokenness in their lives, that the hidden light of the torches shone forth, bringing terror to their enemies. It was once the poor widow broke the seal on her only remaining jar of oil and began to pour it that God miraculously multiplied it to pay her debts and thereby supplied her means of support. (2 Kings 4:1–7.)

It was not until Esther risked her life and broke through the strict laws of a heathen king's court that she obtained favor to rescue her people from death. (Esther 4:16.)

It was once Jesus took "the five loaves . . . and broke them" (Luke 9:16) that the bread was multiplied to feed the five thousand. Through the very process of the loaves being broken, the miracle occurred. It was when Mary broke her beautiful "alabaster jar of very expensive perfume" (Matthew 26:7), destroying its future usefulness and value, that the wonderful fragrance filled the house. And it was when Jesus allowed His precious body to be broken by thorns, nails, and a spear that His inner life was poured out like an ocean of crystal-clear water, for thirsty sinners to drink and then live.

It is not until a beautiful kernel of corn is buried and broken in the earth by DEATH that its inner heart sprouts, producing hundreds of other seeds or kernels. And so it has always been, down through the history of plants, people, and all of spiritual life—God uses BROKEN THINGS.

Those who have been gripped by the power of the Holy Spirit and are used for God's glory are those who have been broken in their finances, broken in their self-will, broken in their ambitions, broken in their lofty ideals, broken in their worldly reputation, broken in their desires, and often broken in their health. Yes, He uses those who are despised by the world and who seem totally hopeless and helpless, just as Isaiah said: "The lame will carry off plunder" (Isaiah 33:23).

> Oh, break my heart; but break it as a field
>   Is plowed and broken for the seeds of corn;
> Oh, break it as the buds, by green leaf sealed,
>   Are, to unloose the golden blossom, torn;
> Love would I offer unto Love's great Master,
> Set free the fragrance, break the alabaster.

Oh, break my heart; break it, victorious God,
  That life's eternal well may flow abroad;
Oh, let it break as when the captive trees,
  Breaking cold bonds, regain their liberties;
And as thought's sacred grove to life is springing,
Be joys, like birds, their hope, Your victory singing.

THOMAS TOKE BUNCH

OCTOBER 16

Morning

If . . . God so commands, you will be able.
EXODUS 18:23

Charles G. Finney once said: "When God commands you to do a thing, it is the highest possible evidence, equal to an oath, that we can do it."

The thing that taxes Almightiness is the very thing that you as a disciple of Jesus Christ ought to believe He would do. Sometimes we must be shipwrecked upon the supernatural; we must be thrown upon God; we must lose the temporal—that we may find the Eternal.

"It is God who works" (Philippians 2:13). Men work like men and nothing more is expected of man than what man can do. But God worketh like a God, and with Him nothing is impossible.

There is for us *a source of heightened power.* A most suggestive translation (James Moffatt) of 1 Samuel 2:1 reads: *My heart thrills to the Eternal; my powers are heightened by my God.*

Amos was just a herdsman from Tekoa, but *his powers were heightened* by his God. It happened to Peter. It happened to Paul. Abraham Lincoln faced the impossible when he set out to uproot the slave trade.

We are all in need of more power, more courage, more wisdom than we actually possess. This *"plus extra"* comes to him whose heart thrills over the Eternal, who daily waits for Divine resources.

"Difficulty" is a relative term. It all depends upon the power you have available.

Difficulty diminishes as the power increases, and altogether vanishes when the power rises to Omnipotence. "Our sufficiency is of God." All God's biddings are enablings. *Always provided that we are on the line of God's written Word, in the current of His revealed purpose, there is nothing you may not trust Him for.*

As one of a thousand you may just fail; But as "one, plus God," you are bound to win.

~~~~ OCTOBER 16 ~~~~

Evening

Let us throw off everything that hinders and the sin that so easily entangles.
And let us run with perseverance the race marked out for us.
HEBREWS 12:1

There are certain things that are not sins themselves but that tend to weigh us down or become distractions and stumbling blocks to our Christian growth. One of the worst of these is the feeling of despair or hopelessness. A heavy heart is indeed a weight that will surely drag us down in our holiness and usefulness.

The failure of the children of Israel to enter the Promised Land began with their complaining, or as the Word says it, *"All the Israelites grumbled"* (Numbers 14:2). It may have started with a faint desire to complain and be discontent, but they allowed it to continue until it blossomed and ripened into total rebellion and ruin.

We should never give ourselves the freedom to doubt God or His eternal love and faithfulness toward us in everything. We can be determined to set our own will against doubt just as we do against any other sin. Then as we stand firm, refusing to doubt, the Holy Spirit will come to our aid, giving us the faith of God and crowning us with victory.

It is very easy to fall into the habit of doubting, worrying, wondering if God has forsaken us, and thinking that after all we have been through, our hopes are going to end in failure. But let us refuse to be discouraged and unhappy! Let us "consider it pure joy" (James 1:2), even when we do not feel any happiness. Let us rejoice by faith, by firm determination, and by simply regarding it as true, and we will find that God will make it real to us. SELECTED

The Devil has two very masterful tricks. The first is to tempt us to become *discouraged,* for then we are defeated and of no service to others, at least for a while. The other is to tempt us to *doubt,* thereby breaking the bond of faith that unites us with the Father. So watch out! Do not be tricked either way. G. E. M.

I like to cultivate the spirit of *happiness!* It retunes my soul and keeps it so perfectly in tune that Satan is afraid to touch it. The chords of my soul become so vibrant and full of heavenly electricity that he takes his fiendish fingers from me and goes somewhere else! Satan is always wary of interfering with me when my heart is full of the happiness and joy of the Holy Spirit.

My plan is simply to shun the spirit of *sadness* as I would normally shun Satan, but unfortunately I am not always successful. Like the Devil himself, sadness confronts me while I am on the highway of *usefulness.* And it stays face-to-face with me until my poor soul turns blue and sad! In fact, sadness discolors everything around me and produces a mental paralysis. Nothing has any appeal to me, future prospects seem clouded in darkness, and my soul loses all its aspirations and power!

An elderly believer once said, "*Cheerfulness* in our faith causes any act of service to be performed with *delight,* and we are never moved ahead as swiftly in our spiritual calling as when we are carried on the wings of happiness. *Sadness,* however, clips those wings or, using another analogy, causes the wheels to fall off our chariot of service. Our chariot then becomes like those of the Egyptians at the Red Sea, dragging heavily on its axle and slowing our progress."

~~~~~ OCTOBER 17 ~~~~~

Morning

For he spoke and stirred up a tempest that lifted high the waves.
PSALM 107:25

Stormy wind fulfilling His word. *By the time the wind blows upon us it is His wind for us.* We have nothing to do with what first of all stirred up that wind. It could not ruffle a leaf on the smallest tree in the forest had He not opened the way for it to blow through the fields of air. He commandeth even the winds, and they obey Him. To the winds as to His servants He saith to one, "Go," and it goeth; and to another, "Come," and it cometh; and to another, "Do this," and it doeth it. So, whatever wind blows on us it is His wind for us, *His wind fulfilling His word.*

God's winds do effectual work. *They shake loose from us the things that can be shaken, that those things which cannot be shaken may remain, those eternal things which belong to the Kingdom which cannot be moved.* They have their part to play in stripping us and strengthening us so that we may be the more ready for the uses of Eternal Love. Then can we refuse to welcome them?

Art thou indeed willing for any wind at any time? GOLD BY MOONLIGHT

Be like the pine on the hilltop, alone in the wind for God.

There is a curious comfort in remembering that the Father depends upon His child not to give way. *It is inspiring to be trusted with a hard thing.* You never asked for summer breezes to blow upon your tree. It is enough that you are not alone upon the hill.

And let the storm that does Thy work deal with me as it may.

~~~~~ OCTOBER 17 ~~~~~

Evening

May I never boast except in the cross of our LORD Jesus Christ, through which the world has been crucified to me, and I to the world.

GALATIANS 6:14

They were people who were living to themselves. Their hopes, promises, and dreams still controlled them, but the Lord began to fulfill their prayers. They had asked for a repentant heart and had surrendered themselves with a willingness to pay any price for it, and He sent them sorrow. They had asked for purity, and He sent them sudden anguish. They had asked for meekness, and He had broken their hearts. They had asked to be dead to the world, and He killed all their living hopes. They had asked to be made like Him, so He placed them in the fire "as a refiner and purifier of silver" (Malachi 3:3), until they could reflect His image. They had asked to help carry His cross, yet when He held it out to them, it cut and tore their hands.

They had not fully understood what they asked, but He had taken them at their word and granted them all their requests. They had been unsure whether to follow

Him such a long distance or whether to come so close to Him. An awe and a fear was upon them, as Jacob at Bethel when he dreamed of "a stairway . . . reaching to heaven" (Genesis 28:12), or Eliphaz "amid disquieting dreams in the night" (Job 4:13), or as the disciples when "they were startled and frightened, thinking they saw a ghost" (Luke 24:37), not realizing it was Jesus. The disciples were so filled with awe, they felt like asking Him either to depart from them or to hide His glory.

They found it easier to obey than to suffer, to work than to give up, and to carry the cross than to hang upon it. But now they could not turn back, for they had come too close to the unseen cross of the spiritual life, and its virtues had pierced them too deeply. And the Lord was fulfilling this promise of His to them: "I, when I am lifted up from the earth, will draw all people to myself" (John 12:32).

Now at last their opportunity had come. Earlier they had only heard of the mystery, but now they felt it. He had fastened His eyes of love on them, as He had on Mary and Peter, so they could only choose to follow Him. And little by little, from time to time, with quick glimmers of light, the mystery of His cross shone upon them. They saw Him "lifted up from the earth," and gazed on the glory that radiated from the wounds of His holy suffering. As they looked upon Him, they approached Him and were changed into His likeness. His name then shone out through them, for He lived within them. Their life from that moment on was one of inexpressible fellowship solely with Him above. They were willing to live without possessions that others owned and that they could have had, in order to be unlike others so they would be more like Him.

This is the description of all those throughout the ages who "follow the Lamb wherever he goes" (Revelation 14:4). If they had chosen selfishly for themselves or if their friends had chosen for them, they would have made other choices. Their lives would have shone more brightly here on earth but less gloriously in His kingdom. Their legacy would have been that of Lot instead of Abraham. And if they had stopped along the way or if God had removed His hand from them, allowing them to stray, what would they have lost? What would they have forfeited at their resurrection?

Yet God strengthened them and protected them, even from themselves. Often, in His mercy He held them up when they otherwise would have slipped and fallen. And even in this life, they knew that all He did was done well. They knew it was good to suffer in this life so they would reign in the one to come; to bear the cross below, to wear a crown above; and to know that not their will but His was done in them and through them.

Morning

Some time later the brook dried up.
1 KINGS 17:7

God sent Elijah to the brook, and it dried up. It did not prove equal to the need of the prophet. It failed; God knew it would; He made it to fail. "The brook dried up." This is an aspect of the Divine providence that sorely perplexes our minds and tries our faith. God knows that there are heavenly whispers that men cannot hear till the drought of trouble and perhaps weariness has silenced the babbling brooks of joy. And He is not satisfied until we have learned to depend not upon His gifts, but upon Himself. PERCY AINSWORTH

His camp was pitched where Cherith's stream was flowing—
The man of God! 'Twas God's appointed spot!
When it might fail, he knew not; only knowing
That God cared for his lot.

Full many days on Cherith's bank he camped him,
And from its cool refreshing, drew his share;
And foolish fears of failing streams ne'er damped him;
Was he not God's own care?

Yet, lo, at length, the prospect strangely altered;
The drought e'en Cherith's fountain had assailed;
Slowly but sure, the flowing waters faltered
Until, at last, they failed!

Then came the word from One whose eye beholding
Saw that the stream, the living stream had dried,
Sending him forth, to find by new unfolding,
None of his needs denied.

Perchance thou, too, hath camped by such sweet waters.
And quenched with joy thy weary, parched soul's thirst;
To find, as time goes on, thy streamlet alters
From what it was at first.

Hearts that have cheered, or soothed, or blest, or strengthened,
Loves that have lavished so unstintedly,
Joys, treasured joys—have passed, as time hath
lengthened, into obscurity.

If thus, ah soul, the brook thy heart hath cherished
Doth fail thee now—no more thy thirst assuage—
If its once glad, refreshing streams have perished,
Let Him thy heart engage.

He will not fail, nor mock, nor disappoint thee;
His consolations change not with the years;
With oil of joy He surely will anoint thee,
And wipe away thy tears.

J. DANSON SMITH

～～～ OCTOBER 18 ～～～
Evening

*"Know for certain that for four hundred years your descendants will be
strangers in a country not their own and that they will be . . . mistreated
there. But . . . afterward they will come out with great possessions."*
GENESIS 15:13–14

I can be sure that part of God's promised blessing to me is delay and suffering. The
delay in Abraham's lifetime that seemed to put God's promise well beyond fulfillment

was then followed by the seemingly unending delay experienced by Abraham's descendants. But it was indeed only a delay—the promise was fulfilled, for ultimately they did *"come out with great possessions."*

God is going to test me with delays, and along with the delays will come suffering. Yet through it all God's promise stands. I have His new covenant in Christ, and His sacred promise of every smaller blessing that I need. The delays and the suffering are actually part of the promised blessings, so may I praise Him for them today. May I "be strong and take heart and wait for the LORD" (Psalm 27:14). CHARLES GALLAUDET TRUMBULL

> *Unanswered yet the prayer your lips have pleaded*
> *In agony of heart these many years?*
> *Does faith begin to fail? Is hope departing?*
> *And think you all in vain your falling tears?*
> *Say not the Father has not heard your prayer;*
> *You will have your desire sometime, somewhere.*
>
> *Unanswered yet? No, do not say ungranted;*
> *Perhaps your work is not yet wholly done.*
> *The work began when first your prayer was uttered,*
> *And God will finish what He has begun.*
> *If you will keep the incense burning there,*
> *His glory you will see sometime, somewhere.*
>
> *Unanswered yet? Faith cannot be unanswered,*
> *Its feet are firmly planted on the Rock;*
> *Amid the wildest storms it stands undaunted,*
> *Nor shakes before the loudest thunder shock.*
> *It knows Omnipotence has heard its prayer,*
> *And cries, "It will be done"—sometime, somewhere.*
> OPHELIA G. BROWNING

Morning

Unless a kernel of wheat falls to the ground and dies, it remains only a single seed.
JOHN 12:24

A peasant once came to Tauler to confess; but in place of the peasant confessing to Tauler, Tauler confessed to the peasant. The great preacher said, "I am not satisfied." The peasant replied, "Tauler has to die before he can be satisfied."

That great man, who had thousands listening to him, withdrew to a place of quiet and asked God to work out that death in him.

After he had been there for two years, he came out and assembled his congregation. A great multitude came to hear him, for he had been a wonderful preacher. He began to preach, but he broke down and wept. The audience dispersed saying, "What is the matter with Tauler? He can't preach as he once did. He failed today!"

The next time he preached only a little handful came together—those who had caught a glimpse of something—and he preached to them in a brokenhearted way; *but the power of God came down.* God, by the power of the Spirit, *had put John Tauler to death!* SELECTED

Beloved, are you willing to be crucified with Christ?

> *Higher than the highest heavens,*
> *Deeper than the deepest sea,*
> *Lord, Thy love at last hath conquered:*
> *Grant me now my supplication,*
> *None of self, and all of Thee.*

—— OCTOBER 19 ——

Evening

The ark of the covenant of the LORD went before them.
NUMBERS 10:33

God sometimes does influence us with a simple touch or feeling, but not so we would act on the feeling. If the touch is from Him, He will then provide sufficient evidence to confirm it beyond the slightest doubt.

Consider the beautiful story of Jeremiah, when he felt God leading him to purchase the field at Anathoth. He did not act on his initial feeling but waited for God to completely fulfill His words to him before taking action. Then once his cousin came to him, bringing the external evidence of God's direction by making a proposal for the purchase, he responded and said, *"I knew that this was the word of the LORD"* (Jeremiah 32:8).

Jeremiah waited until God confirmed his feeling through a providential act, and then he worked with a clear view of the facts, which God could also use to bring conviction to others. God wants us to act only once we have His mind on a certain situation. We are not to ignore the Shepherd's personal voice to us, but like "Paul and his companions" (Acts 16:6) at Troas, we are to listen and also examine His providential work in our circumstances, in order to glean the full mind of the Lord. A. B. SIMPSON

Wherever God's finger points, His hand will clear a way.

Never say in your heart what you will or will not do but wait until God reveals His way to you. As long as that way is hidden, it is clear that there is no need of action and that *He holds Himself accountable for all the results of keeping you exactly where you are.* SELECTED

> *For God through ways we have not known,*
> *Will lead His own.*

~~~~~~ OCTOBER 20 ~~~~~~

Morning

They reached the place God had told him about.
GENESIS 22:9

There the LORD bestows his blessing.
PSALM 133:3

Up, up the hill, to the whiter than snow-shine,
Help me to climb, and dwell in pardon's light.
I must be pure as Thou, or ever less
Than Thy design of me—therefore incline
My heart to take men's wrongs as Thou tak'st mine.

Have you come to the *place God told you* of? Have you gone through the sacrifice of death? Are you willing to make the moral decision that the thing die out in you which never was in Jesus?

Up to that whiter than snow-shine; up to that place that is as strong and firm as the Throne of God. Do not say, "That pure, white, holy life is never for me!" Let God lift you; let Him take the shrouds away; let Him lift up; up to the hill, *to the whiter than snow-shine.* And when you get to the top what do you find? A great, strong tableland, where your feet are on a rock; your steps enlarged under you; your goings established. OSWALD CHAMBERS

Jesus offers you "life more abundantly." Grasp the offer! Quit the boggy and dark low ground, and let Him lead you up higher! MOUNTAINTOPS WITH JESUS

`Take the supreme climb!
Jesus lead me up the mountain,
Where the whitest robes are seen,
Where the saints can see the fountain,
Where the pure are keeping clean.

Higher up, where light increases,
Rich above all earthly good,
Where the life of sinning ceases,
Where the Spirit comes in floods.

Lead me higher, nothing dreading,
In the race to never stop;
In Thy footsteps keep me treading,
Give me grace to reach the top.

Courage, my soul, and let us journey on!

—— 718 ——

Evening

*The peace of God, which transcends all understanding, will
guard your hearts and your minds in Christ Jesus.*

PHILIPPIANS 4:7

There is a part of the sea known as "the cushion of the sea." It lies beneath the surface that is agitated by storms and churned by the wind. It is so deep that it is a part of the sea that is never stirred. When the ocean floor in these deep places is dredged of the remains of plant or animal life, it reveals evidence of having remained completely undisturbed for hundreds, if not thousands, of years.

The peace of God is an eternal calm like the cushion of the sea. It lies so deeply within the human heart that no external difficulty or disturbance can reach it. And anyone who enters the presence of God becomes a partaker of that undisturbed and undisturbable calm. ARTHUR TAPPAN PIERSON

> When winds are raging o'er the upper ocean,
> And waves are tossed wild with an angry roar,
> It's said, far down beneath the wild commotion,
> That peaceful stillness reigns forevermore.
>
> Far, far beneath, noise of tempests falls silent,
> And silver waves lie ever peacefully,
> And no storm, however fierce or violent,
> Disturbs the Sabbath of that deeper sea.
>
> So to the heart that knows Your love, O Father,
> There is a temple sacred evermore,
> And all life's angry voices causing bother
> Die in hushed silence at its peaceful door.
>
> Far, far away, the roars of strife fall silent,
> And loving thoughts rise ever peacefully,

And no storm, however fierce or violent,
 Disturbs the soul that dwells, O Lord, in Thee.
HARRIET BEECHER STOWE

Pilgrim was taken to a large upper room that faced the sunrise. And the name of the room was Peace. PILGRIM'S PROGRESS

OCTOBER 21

Morning

Let perseverance finish its work so that you may be
mature and complete, not lacking anything.
JAMES 1:4

Look with Edison at his deafness, with Milton at his blindness, with Bunyan at his imprisonment, and see how patience converted these very misfortunes into good fortunes.

Michelangelo went to Rome to carve statues and found that other artists had taken over all the Carrara marble—all but one crooked and misshapen piece. He sat down before this and studied with infinite patience its very limitations, until he found that by bending the head of a statue here and lifting its arms there, he could create a masterpiece: thus *The Boy David* was produced.

Let us sit down in front of our very limitations and with the aid of patience dare to produce, with God's help, *a masterpiece!*

"I see the stubborn heights,
The bruising rocks, the straining soul."

"I see the goal!"

"I see the tearing plow,
The crushing drag, the beating rain."

"I see the grain!"
"I see compressing walls,
And seething flux, and heats untold."

"I see the gold!"

"I see the cruel blows,
The chisel sharp, the hammer's mace."

"I see My face!"
"OUR VIEW AND HIS" BY PHILIP WENDELL CRANNELL

~~~~~ OCTOBER 21 ~~~~~
Evening

For we know that if the earthly tent we live in is destroyed, we have a building
from God, an eternal house in heaven, not built by human hands.

2 CORINTHIANS 5:1

The owner of the house I have lived in for many years has notified me that he will do little or nothing to keep it in repair. He also advised me to be ready to move.

At first this was not very welcome news. In many respects the surrounding area is quite pleasant, and if not for the evidence of a somewhat declining condition, the house seems rather nice. Yet a closer look reveals that even a light wind causes it to shake and sway, and its foundation is not sufficient to make it secure. Therefore I am getting ready to move.

As I consider the move, it is strange how quickly my interest is transferred to my prospective new home in another country. I have been consulting maps and studying accounts of its inhabitants. And someone who has come from there to visit has told me that it is beautiful beyond description and that language is inadequate to fully describe what he heard while there. He said that in order to make an investment there, he has suffered the loss of everything he owned here, yet rejoices in what others would call a sacrifice. Another person, whose love for me has been proved by the greatest possible

—— 721 ——

test, now lives there. He has sent me several clusters of the most delicious grapes I have ever eaten, and after tasting them everything here tastes very bland.

Several times I have gone to the edge of the river that forms the boundary between here and there and have longed to be with those singing praises to the King on the other side. Many of my friends have moved across that river, but before leaving here they spoke of my following them later. I have seen the smile on their faces as they passed from my sight. So each time I am asked to make some new investment here, I now respond, "I am getting ready to move." SELECTED

The words of Jesus during His last days on earth vividly express His desire to go "back to the Father" (John 16:28). We, as His people, also have a vision of something far beyond the difficulties and disappointments of this life and are traveling toward fulfillment, completion, and an enriched life. We too are going "to the Father." Much of our new home is still unclear to us, but two things are certain. Our "Father's house" (John 14:2) is our home. And it is in the presence of the Lord. As believers, we know and understand that we are all travelers and not permanent residents of this world. R. C. GILLIE

> *The little birds trust God, for they go singing*
> *From northern woods where autumn winds have blown,*
> *With joyous faith their unmarked pathway winging*
> *To summer lands of song, afar, unknown.*

> *Let us go singing, then, and not go crying:*
> *Since we are sure our times are in His hand,*
> *Why should we weep, and fear, and call it dying?*
> *It's merely flying to a Summer Land.*

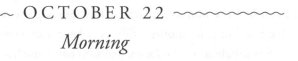

OCTOBER 22

Morning

Understand what the LORD's will is.
EPHESIANS 5:17

It may seem a very terrible thing for the soul to yield itself wholly and unreservedly to the will of Christ. "What is going to happen? What about tomorrow? Will He not put a very heavy burden upon me if I yield, if I take the yoke?" Ah, you have not known my Master; you have not looked into His face; you have not realized His infinite love for you. Why, God's will for you means your fullest happiness! Christ's will and your deepest happiness are synonymous terms. How can you doubt that your Lord has planned for you the very best thing?

The admiral that goes out with his fleet under sealed orders does not know what is in the packet, but he goes out prepared to do the will of the government of his country. And although it seems to you that you take from Christ the sealed packet of His will and know not *what* is in it, yet knowing *who He is* that has *planned your future* you can step out without realizing all that it means, just as you take His promises. *The value of any promise depends upon the promiser, and so it is with His will. Whose* will is it? *Whose* yoke is it?

"My yoke," says the gentle, loving Jesus; "Take *My yoke* upon you." To take His yoke is cheerfully to accept His will for us, not only in the present moment but for the whole future that He has mapped out.

Surrender your will to God. He will never take advantage of you. EVAN H. HOPKINS

"I dare not promise, Lord," I cried,
"For future years close-sealed.
Surrender is a fearful thing—
I long—but dare not yield."
How clear and swift the answer came:
"I only ask of thee
A present of thyself for time
And for eternity."

An easy thing to make a gift!
My fears found swift release.
I gave myself to Him, and found
Past understanding, peace.

BERTHA GERNEAUX WOODS

Evening

Now Moses was tending the flock of Jethro his father-in-law, the
priest of Midian, and he led the flock to the far side of the wilderness
and came to Horeb, the mountain of God. There the angel of the
LORD *appeared to him in flames of fire from within a bush.*

EXODUS 3:1–2

The vision of the Angel of the Lord came to Moses while he was involved in his everyday work. That is exactly where the Lord delights in giving His revelations. He seeks a man traveling an ordinary road, and "suddenly a light from heaven" (Acts 9:3) shines on him. And a "stairway resting on the earth" (Genesis 28:12) can reach from the marketplace to heaven, transforming a life from one of drudgery to one of grace.

Beloved Father, help me to expect you as I travel the ordinary road of life. I am not asking for sensational experiences. Fellowship with me through my everyday work and service, and be my companion when I take an ordinary journey. And let my humble life be transformed by Your presence.

Some Christians think they must always be on the mountaintop of extraordinary joy and revelation, but this is not God's way. Those high spiritual times and wonderful communication with the unseen world are *not* promised to us, but a daily life of communion with Him *is*. And it is enough for us, for He will give us those times of exceptional revelation if it is the right thing for us.

There were only three disciples allowed to see the Transfiguration, and the same three also experienced the darkness of Gethsemane. No one can stay on the mountaintop of favor forever, for there are responsibilities in the valley. Christ fulfilled His life's work not in the glory but in the valley, and it was there He was truly and completely the Messiah.

The value of the vision and the accompanying glory is its gift of equipping us for service and endurance. SELECTED

Morning

They were . . . preparing their nets. Jesus called them.
MATTHEW 4:21

Salome! Had you been with me in the boat,
You would not chide and moan because our boys
Have gone with the Beloved from this our home.
Let me, Salome, tell you how it came.
The night was still—the tide was running strong,
Heavy our nets—the strain reached breaking point,
And while 'twas dark we docked, and as we worked
I felt as though new strength and steady joy
Surged through my being, so I sang a Psalm—
As David sang—a song to greet the morn;
And then my heart was filled with quiet calm.

The boat was soon in order, and we turned
To dry and mend our nets. Then Jesus came—
He called the boys, first John, then James, by name,
And they arose and went to follow Him.
I turned and gazed on Jesus standing there—
He seemed to me all clothed in shining light
As He stood in the pathway with the night
Behind Him and the dawn breaking around,
His form so radiant and glad and free.

And when He climbed the hill our sons went too—
James was behind, and John was by His side;
And when they talked, John scarcely seemed our John—
I felt that he had caught a marvelous light.

And all my being seemed to overflow;
I knew that night had passed—the dawn had come,
And then I knew that we must let them go.
"Zebedee's Sons"

"The share of the man who stayed with the supplies is to be the same as that of him who went down to the battle. All will share alike" (1 Samuel 30:24).

To some Christ calls: "Leave boat and bay,
And white-haired Zebedee";
To some the call is harder: "Stay
And mend the nets for Me."
Selected

OCTOBER 23

Evening

Not one word has failed of all the good promises he gave.
1 Kings 8:56

Someday we will understand that God has a reason behind every no He gives us through the course of our lives. Yet even in this life, He always makes it up to us. When God's people are worried and concerned that their prayers are not being answered, how often we have seen Him working to answer them in a far greater way! Occasionally we catch a glimpse of this, but the complete revelation of it will not be seen until later.

If God says yes to our prayer, dear heart,
And the sunlight is golden, the sky is blue,
While the smooth road beckons to me and you,
And songbirds are singing as on we go,
Pausing to pick the flowers at our feet,
Stopping to drink of the streams that we meet,

Happy, more happy, our journey will grow,
If God says yes to our prayer, dear heart.

If God says no to our prayer, dear heart,
And the clouds hang heavy and dull and gray;
If the rough rocks hinder and block the way,
While the sharp winds pierce us and sting with cold;
Yet, dear, there is home at the journey's end,
And these are the trials the Father does send
To draw us as sheep to His Heavenly fold,
If God says no to our prayer, dear heart.

If only we had the faith not to rush into things but to "be still before the LORD and wait patiently for him" (Psalm 37:7)—waiting for His full explanation that will not be revealed until Jesus Christ comes again! When has God ever taken anything from a person without restoring it many times over? Yet what are we to think if He does not immediately restore what has been taken? Is today His only day to work? Does He have any concerns beyond this little world of ours? Can He still work beyond our death, or does the door of the grave open on nothing but infinite darkness and eternal silence?

Even if we confine our thinking to this life, it is true that God never touches the heart with a trial without intending to bestow a greater gift or compassionate blessing. *The person who knows how to wait has grown to an exceptional degree in God's grace.*
SELECTED

When the frosts are in the valley,
And the mountaintops are gray,
And the choicest blooms are blighted,
And the blossoms die away,
A loving Father whispers,
"This all comes from my hand";
Blessed are you if you trust
When you cannot understand.

If, after years of toiling,
Your wealth should fly away

And leave your hands all empty,
    And your hair is turning gray,
Remember then your Father
    Owns all the sea and land;
Blessed are you if you trust
    When you cannot understand.

Selected

OCTOBER 24

Morning

Return to thy place, and abide with the king.
2 Samuel 15:19 kjv

There is a little fable which says that a primrose growing by itself in a shady corner of the garden became discontented as it saw the other flowers in their gay beds in the sunshine, and begged to be removed to a more conspicuous place. Its prayer was granted. The gardener transplanted it to a more showy and sunny spot. It was greatly pleased, but there came a change over it immediately. Its blossoms lost much of their beauty and became pale and sickly. The hot sun caused them to faint and wither. So it prayed again to be taken back to its old place in the shade. The wise gardener knew best where to plant each flower.

So God, the Divine Husbandman, knows where His children will best grow into what He would have them to be. Some require the fierce storms; some will only thrive spiritually in the shadow of worldly adversity; and some come to ripeness more sweetly under the soft and gentle influences of prosperity, whose beauty rough experiences would mar.

Humbolt, the great naturalist and traveler, said that the most wonderful sight he had ever seen was a primrose flourishing on the bosom of a glacier.

The brightest souls which glory ever knew
Were rocked in storms and nursed when tempests blew.

Evening

I will make you into a threshing sledge, new and sharp.
ISAIAH 41:15

Around the turn of the twentieth century, a bar of steel was worth about $5. Yet when forged into horseshoes, it was worth $10; when made into needles, its value was $350; when used to make small pocketknife blades, its worth was $32,000; when made into springs for watches, its value increased to $250,000. What a pounding the steel bar had to endure to be worth this much! But the more it was shaped, hammered, put through fire, beaten, pounded, and polished, the greater its value.

May we use this analogy as a reminder to be still, silent, and long-suffering, for it is those who suffer the most who yield the most. And it is through pain that God gets the most out of us, for His glory and for the blessing of others. SELECTED

> *Oh, give Your servant patience to be still,*
> *And bear Your will;*
> *Courage to venture wholly on Your arm*
> *That will not harm;*
> *The wisdom that will never let me stray*
> *Out of my way;*
> *The love that, now afflicting, yet knows best*
> *When I should rest.*

Our life is very mysterious. In fact, it would be totally unexplainable unless we believed that God was preparing us for events and ministries that lie unseen beyond the veil of the eternal world—where spirits like tempered steel will be required for special service.

The sharper the Craftsman's knives, the finer and more beautiful His work.

Morning

Whoever dwells in the shelter of the Most High will
rest in the shadow of the Almighty.
PSALM 91:1

It was my practice to rise at midnight for worship. God came to me at that precise time and awoke me from sleep that I might enjoy *Him*. He seemed to pervade my being. My soul became more and more attracted to Him like the waters of a river which pass into the ocean and after a time become one with it. Oh, unutterable happiness! Who could have thought that one should ever find happiness equal to this!

Hours passed like moments, when I could do nothing else but pray. It was a prayer of rejoicing, of possession, when the taste of *God* was so great, so pure, so unblended that it drew and absorbed the soul into a profound state of confiding and affectionate rest in God, without intellectual effort, for I had no sight but of Jesus only. MADAME GUYON

> *A moment in the morning ere the cares of the day begin,*
> *Ere the heart's wide door is open for the world to enter in;*
> *Ah, then, alone with Jesus, in the silence of the morn,*
> *In heavenly sweet communion, let your happy day be born;*
> *In the quietude that blesses with a prelude of repose,*
> *Let your soul be soothed and softened as the dew revives the rose.*

Two men were confessing to each other the causes of their failure in the ministry. "I let my hand slip out of God's hand," said one. The other said, "My soul-life raveled at the point where I ceased to pray, because there were things in my life I could not speak to God about." *Prayer is a handclasp with God.*

Take time for prayer if you have to take it by violence. *Take time to behold Him!*

Evening

Until now you have not asked for anything in my name. Ask
and you will receive, and your joy will be complete.

JOHN 16:24

During the American Civil War, a certain man had a son who enlisted in the Union army. The father was a banker, and although he gave his consent to his son, it seemed as if it would break his heart to let him go.

Once his son had left, he became deeply interested in the plight of soldiers, and whenever he saw one in uniform, his heart went out to him as he thought of his own dear boy. Often to the neglect of his business, he began spending his time and money to care for the soldiers who came home disabled. His friends pleaded with him not to neglect his business in this way, by spending so much time and energy on the soldiers. So he decided to give it all up, taking his friends' advice.

After he had made this decision, however, a young private in a faded, worn uniform stepped into the bank. It was easy to discern from the wounds on his face and hands that he had been in the army field hospital. The poor young man was fumbling in his pocket to find something, when the banker saw him. Perceiving his purpose for coming into the bank, he said to the soldier, "My dear man, I cannot help you today. I am extremely busy. You will have to go to the army headquarters, where the officers will take care of you."

The poor wounded soldier still stood there, not seeming to fully understand what was being said to him. He continued to fumble in his pockets and finally pulled out a scrap of dirty paper. He laid the filthy page before the banker, who read the following words written in pencil:

Dear Father,
    This is one of my friends, who was wounded in the last battle and is coming to you directly from the hospital. Please receive him as you would me.
    Charlie

All the banker's previous resolve to focus solely on his business instead of soldiers quickly flew away. He took the young man to his own magnificent home and gave him Charlie's room and seat at the dinner table. He cared for him until the food, rest, and love had returned him to health, and then sent him back to his place of service to again risk his life for his country's flag. SELECTED

"Now you will see what I will do" (Exodus 6:1).

OCTOBER 26

Morning

Because this widow keeps bothering me, I will see that she gets justice.

LUKE 18:5

We should be careful about what we ask from God; but when once we begin to pray for a thing we should never give up praying for it until we receive it, or until God makes it very clear and definite that it is not His will to grant it. R. A. TORREY

It is said of John Bradford that he had a peculiar art in prayer. When asked his secret, he said: "When I know what I want, I always stop on that prayer until I feel that I have pleaded it with God, and until God and I have had dealings with each other upon it. I never go on to another petition until I have gone through the first."

To the same point Mr. Spurgeon said: "Do not try to put two arrows on the string at once—they will both miss. He that would load his gun with two charges cannot expect to be successful. Plead once with God and prevail, and then plead again. Get the first answer and then go after the second. Do not be satisfied with running the colors of your prayers into one another until there is no picture to look at, but just a huge daub—a smear of colors badly laid on."

Far better would it be to know what our real needs are, and then concentrate our earnest supplications upon those definite objects, taking them thoughtfully one at a time.

"Ask what I shall give thee" (1 Kings 3:5 KJV).

Evening

He went up on a mountainside by himself to pray.
Later that night, he was there alone.
MATTHEW 14:23

Christ Jesus, in His humanity, felt the need of complete solitude—to be entirely by Himself, alone with Himself. Each of us knows how draining constant interchange with others can be and how it exhausts our energy. As part of humankind, Jesus knew this and felt the need to be by Himself in order to regain His strength. Solitude was also important to Him in order to fully realize His high calling, His human weakness, and His total dependence on His Father.

As a child of God, how much more do we need times of complete solitude—times to deal with the spiritual realities of life and to be alone with God the Father. If there was ever anyone who could dispense with special times of solitude and fellowship, it was our Lord. Yet even He could not maintain His full strength and power for His work and His fellowship with the Father without His quiet time. God desires that every servant of His would understand and perform this blessed practice, that His church would know how to train its children to recognize this high and holy privilege, and that every believer would realize the importance of making time for God alone.

Oh, the thought of having God all alone to myself and knowing that God has me all alone to Himself! ANDREW MURRAY

Lamartine, the first of the French Romantic poets and a writer of the nineteenth century, in one of his books wrote of how his mother had a secluded spot in the garden where she spent the same hour of each day. He related that nobody ever dreamed of intruding upon her for even a moment of that hour. It was the holy garden of the Lord to her.

Pity those people who have no such Beulah land! (Isaiah 62:4.) Jesus said, "Go into your room, close the door and pray" (Matthew 6:6), for it is in quiet solitude that we catch the deep and mysterious truths that flow from the soul of the things God allows to enter our lives.

A Meditation

My soul, practice being alone with Christ! The Scripture says, "*When he was alone with his own disciples, he explained everything*" (Mark 4:34). Do not wonder about the truth of this verse, for it can be true of your life as well. If you desire to have understanding, then dismiss the crowd, just as Jesus did. (Matthew 14:22.) Let them "go away one at a time . . . until only Jesus [is] left" (John 8:9) with you. Have you ever pictured yourself as the last remaining person on earth, or the only person left in the entire universe?

If you were the only person remaining in the universe, your every thought would be, "God and I . . . ! God and I . . . !" And yet He is already as close to you as that. He is as near as if no heart but His and yours ever beat throughout the boundlessness of space.

O my soul, practice that solitude! Practice dismissing the crowd! Practice the stillness of your heart! Practice the majestic song "God and I! God and I!" Let no one come between you and your wrestling angel! You will receive conviction yet pardon, when you meet Jesus alone! GEORGE MATHESON

~~~~ OCTOBER 27 ~~~~
Morning

God spoke.
GENESIS 46:2

Any man may hear the voice of God.

When man will listen, God speaks. When God speaks, men are changed. When men are changed, nations are changed.

In the ancient days *God spoke,* and the wonderful things which He told Moses on the mountaintop have inspired mankind for centuries.

Down through the years men of God have heard His voice. *God spoke* to George Mueller, and he became the modern apostle of faith. Hudson Taylor heard Him speak, as he walked by the seashore on a memorable Sabbath morning, and in obedience to that Voice he launched forth into inland China, establishing Mission Stations in every province of that vast country.

God spoke to Dr. A. B. Simpson, and he stepped aside from a well-beaten path, and like Abraham of old "obeyed and went, even though he did not know where he was going" (Hebrews 11:8). Today, The Christian and Missionary Alliance, operating in more than twenty mission fields of the world, is the result of his obedience, and untold numbers have been blessed through his ministry.

Charles Cowman heard the "soft and gentle Voice," when *God spoke* saying, "Get thee out of thy country, and from thy kindred, and from thy father's house, unto a land that I will shew thee" (Genesis 12:1 KJV). The result—The Oriental missionary society, with hundreds of mission stations dotted all over the Orient! And now its activities embrace the wide world.

> *God is not dumb that He should speak no more.*
> *If thou hast wanderings in the wilderness*
> *And find'st not Sinai, 'tis thy soul is poor:*
> *There towers the mountain of the Voice no less,*
> *Which whoso seeks shall find; but he who bends*
> *Intent on manna still, and mortal ends,*
> *Sees it not, neither hears its thundering lore.*
>
> LOWELL

OCTOBER 27

Evening

> *All your waves and breakers have swept over me.*
> PSALM 42:7

> *They are His waves, whether they break over us,*
>   *Hiding His face in smothering spray and foam;*
> *Or smooth and sparkling, spread a path before us,*
>   *And to our haven bear us safely home.*

> *They are His waves, whether for our sure comfort*
>   *He walks across them, stilling all our fear;*

Or to our cry there comes no aid nor answer,
  And in the lonely silence none is near.

They are His waves, whether we are hard-striving
  Through tempest-driven waves that never cease,
While deep to deep with turmoil loud is calling;
  Or at His word they hush themselves in peace.

They are HIS waves, whether He separates them,
  Making us walk dry ground where seas had flowed;
Or lets tumultuous breakers surge about us,
  Rushing unchecked across our only road.

They are His waves, and He directs us through them;
  So He has promised, so His love will do.
Keeping and leading, guiding and upholding,
  To His sure harbor, He will bring us through.
ANNIE JOHNSON FLINT

Stand firmly in the place where your dear Lord has put you, and do your best there. God sends us trials or tests, and places life before us as a face-to-face opponent. It is through the pounding of a serious conflict that He expects us to grow strong. The tree planted where the fierce winds twist its branches and bend its trunk, often nearly to the point of breaking, is commonly more firmly rooted than a tree growing in a secluded valley where storms never bring any stress or strain.

The same is true of human life. The strongest and greatest character is grown through hardship. SELECTED

Morning

You have made your way around this hill country long enough; now turn north.
DEUTERONOMY 2:3

Last summer a party of us lost our way among the lakes of Ontario. A violent storm came up, but we found shelter under a great rock till the storm raged past. Then we resumed our hunt dispiritedly until one said, *"Let us climb this rock; we may spy the trail from the top."* It was a hard climb, but the challenge of the rock restored our courage. As we *conquered the heights* we gained confidence and mastery, and *the hilltop gave us a vision* of our way out.

Get high enough up, you will be above the fog; and while the men down in it are squabbling as to whether there is anything outside the mist, you from your sunny station will see the far-off coasts and haply catch some whiff of perfume from their shores, or see some glinting of glory upon the shining turrets of "a city which hath foundations" (Hebrews 11:10 KJV).

The soul which hath launched itself forth upon God is in a free place, filled with the fresh air of the hills of God.

> *Oh, there are heavenly heights to reach*
> *In many a fearful place,*
> *While the poor, timid heir of God*
> *Lies blindly on his face;*
> *Lies languishing for light Divine*
> *That he shall never see*
> *'Till he goes forward at Thy sign,*
> *And trusts himself to Thee.*
>
> C. A. FOX

We are continually retreating behind our limitations and saying, "Thus far and no farther can I go." God is ever laying His hand upon us and thrusting us into the open, saying, *"You can be more than you are; you must be more than you are."*

OCTOBER 28
Evening

*Because of his great love for us, God, who is rich in mercy, made us alive with
Christ even when we were dead in transgressions. . . . And God raised us up
with Christ and seated us with him in the heavenly realms in Christ Jesus.*

EPHESIANS 2:4–6

This is our rightful place—"seated . . . with him in the heavenly realms in Christ Jesus," yet seated and *still*. But how few of us actually experience this! In fact, most of us believe it is impossible to sit still "in the heavenly realms" while living our everyday life in a world so full of turmoil.

Oh, we believe it may be possible to visit these "heavenly realms" on Sundays or now and then during times of great spiritual emphasis and praise, but to actually be "seated" there *all day, every day*, is a completely different matter. Yet it is clear from the Scriptures that it is meant not only for Sundays but for weekdays as well.

A quiet spirit is of priceless value when performing outward activities. Nothing so greatly hinders the work of God's unseen spiritual forces, upon which our success in everything truly depends, as the spirit of unrest and anxiety.

There is tremendous power in stillness. A great believer once said, "All things come to him who knows how to trust and to be silent." This fact is rich with meaning, and a true understanding of it would greatly change our ways of working. Instead of continuing our restless striving, we would "sit down" inwardly before the Lord, allowing the divine forces of His Spirit to silently work out the means to accomplish our goals and aspirations.

You may not see or feel the inner workings of His silent power, but rest assured it is always mightily at work. And it will work for you, if you will only quiet your spirit enough to be carried along by the current of its power. HANNAH WHITALL SMITH

> There is a point of rest
> At the great center of the cyclone's force,

A silence at its secret source;
A little child might slumber undisturbed,
Without the ruffle of one fair curl,
In that strange, central calm, amid the mighty whirl.

Make it your business to learn to be peaceful and safe in God through every situation.

~~~~~~ OCTOBER 29 ~~~~~~

Morning

We will flee on horses.
ISAIAH 30:16

God is never slow from His standpoint, but He is from ours, because impetuosity and doing things prematurely are universal weaknesses.

God lives and moves in eternity, and every little detail in His working must be like Himself and have in it the majesty and measured movement, as well as the accuracy and promptness, of infinite wisdom. We are to let God do the swiftness and we do the slowness.

The Holy Spirit tells us to "be quick to listen, slow to speak and slow to become angry" (James 1:19), that is, quick to take in from God but slow to give out the opinions, the emotions of the creature.

We miss a great many things from God by not going slow enough with Him. Who would have God change His perfections to accommodate our whims? Have we not had glimpses into God's perfections, insight into wonderful truths, quiet unfoldings of daily opportunities, gentle checks of the Holy Spirit upon our decisions or words, sweet and secret promptings to do certain things?

There is a time for everything in the universe to get ripe—and to go slow with God is the heavenly pace that gathers up all things at the time they are ripe.

What they win, who wait for God, is worth waiting for!
Going slow with God is our greatest safety!

Evening

He will sit as a refiner and purifier of silver.
MALACHI 3:3

Our Father, who seeks to perfect His saints in holiness, knows the value of the refiner's fire. It is with the most precious metals that a metallurgist will take the greatest care. He subjects the metal to a hot fire, for only the refiner's fire will melt the metal, release the dross, and allow the remaining, pure metal to take a new and perfect shape in the mold.

A good refiner never leaves the crucible but, as the above verse indicates, *"will sit" down by it* so the fire will not become even one degree too hot and possibly harm the metal. And as soon as he skims the last bit of dross from the surface and sees his face reflected in the pure metal, he extinguishes the fire. ARTHUR TAPPAN PIERSON

> *He sat by a fire of sevenfold heat,*
> *As He looked at the precious ore,*
> *And closer He bent with a searching gaze*
> *As He heated it more and more.*
> *He knew He had ore that could stand the test,*
> *And He wanted the finest gold*
> *To mold as a crown for the King to wear,*
> *Set with gems with a price untold.*
> *So He laid our gold in the burning fire,*
> *Though we would have asked for delay,*
> *And He watched the dross that we had not seen,*
> *And it melted and passed away.*
> *And the gold grew brighter and yet more bright,*
> *But our eyes were so dim with tears,*
> *We saw but the fire—not the Master's hand,*
> *And questioned with anxious fears.*
> *Yet our gold shone out with a richer glow,*
> *As it mirrored a Form above,*

That bent o'er the fire, though unseen by us,
*   With a look of unspeakable love.*
Should we think that it pleases His loving heart
*   To cause us a moment's pain?*
Not so! for He saw through the present cross
*   The joy of eternal gain.*
So He waited there with a watchful eye,
*   With a love that is strong and sure,*
And His gold did not suffer a bit more heat,
*   Than was needed to make it pure.*

~~~~~ OCTOBER 30 ~~~~~
Morning

Not yours, but God's.
2 CHRONICLES 20:15

There are times when doing nothing is better than doing something. Those are the times when only God can do what is needed. True faith trusts Him then, and Him alone, to do the miracle. Moses and Jehoshaphat knew this secret; they knew the same Lord and the same Divine grace.

As the pursuing Egyptians trapped the helpless Israelites at the Red Sea, Moses said: "Do not be afraid. Stand firm and you will see the deliverance the LORD will bring you. . . . The LORD will fight for you; you need only to be still" (Exodus 14:13–14).

As the Moabites and the Ammonites, a vast multitude, closed in on Judah, King Jehoshaphat said to the helpless people: "Do not be afraid or discouraged because of this vast army. For *the battle is not yours, but God's*. . . . You will not have to fight this battle. Take up your positions; stand firm and see the deliverance the LORD will give you" (2 Chronicles 20:15, 17, emphasis added).

When God alone can win the victory, faith lets God do it all. It is better to trust than to try. SUNDAY SCHOOL TIMES

Faith is the Victory that Overcomes.

The battle is not yours, but God's;
Therefore why fight?
True faith will cease from struggling,
And rest upon His might:
Each conflict into which you come
Was won on Calvary,
'Tis ours to claim what Christ has done,
And "hold" the victory.

H. E. Jessop

Hold thee still.

"And this," says Saint Jerome, "is the hardest precept that is given to man: inasmuch as the most difficult precept of action sinks into nothingness when compared with this command to inaction."

OCTOBER 30

Evening

Let us run with patience.
HEBREWS 12:1 KJV

Running "with patience" is a very difficult thing to do. The word "running" itself suggests the *absence* of patience, or an eagerness to reach the goal. Yet we often associate patience with lying down or standing still. We think of it as an angel who guards the bed of the disabled. Yet I do not believe that the kind of patience a disabled person may have is the hardest to achieve.

There is another kind of patience that I believe is harder to obtain—the patience that runs. Lying down during a time of grief, or being quiet after a financial setback, certainly implies great strength, but I know of something that suggests even greater strength—the power to continue working after a setback, the power to still run with a heavy heart, and the power to perform your daily tasks with deep sorrow in your spirit. This is a Christlike thing!

Many of us could tearlessly deal with our grief if only we were allowed to do so in private. Yet what is so difficult is that most of us are called to exercise our patience not in bed but in the open street, for all to see. We are called upon to bury our sorrows not in restful inactivity but in active service—in our workplace, while shopping, and during social events—contributing to other people's joy. No other way of burying our sorrow is as difficult as this, for it is truly what is meant by running "with patience."

Dear Son of Man, this was *Your* kind of patience. It was both waiting and running at one time—waiting for the ultimate goal while in the meantime doing lesser work. I see You at Cana of Galilee, turning water into wine so the marriage feast would not be ruined. I see You in the desert, feeding the multitude with bread, simply to relieve a temporary need. Yet all the time, You were bearing a mighty grief—not shared or spoken. Others may ask for a "rainbow in the clouds" (Genesis 9:13), but I would ask for even more from You. Make me, in my cloud, a rainbow bringing the ministry of joy to others. My patience will only be perfect when it works in Your vineyard. GEORGE MATHESON

> *When all our hopes are gone,*
> *It is best our hands keep toiling on*
>   *For others' sake:*
> *For strength to bear is found in duty done;*
> *And he is best indeed who learns to make*
> *The joy of others cure his own heartache.*

～～～ OCTOBER 31 ～～～
Morning

Then he lay down under the bush and fell asleep. All at once an angel touched him.
1 KINGS 19:5

God does not chide His tired child when that weariness is a result of toil for Him: "I know . . . your hard work" (Revelation 2:2)—the Greek is "labor to weariness." And what happened? "All at once an angel touched him." There is no wilderness without its angels. Though Elijah knew it not, angels guarded him round about in his blackest depression and were actually placing bread and water at his head while he was asking for death.

A man may have to cry in the midst of an apostate community, "I am the only one left" (1 Kings 19:10); but he is always companied by legions of holy angels. But more than that. Who is this angel? It is the Angel of the Lord, the Jehovah Angel; the One who, centuries later in Gethsemane, had to have an angel to strengthen Him. He touched His exhausted child. Blessed exhaustion that can bring such a touch!

As the psalmist has said (Psalm 127:2), He giveth to His beloved while they sleep. And God does not chide His tired child. THE DAWN

> *Dear child, God does not say today, "Be strong";*
> *He knows your strength is spent; He knows how long*
> *The road has been, how weary you have grown,*
> *For He who walked the earthly roads alone,*
> *Each bogging lowland, and each rugged hill,*
> *Can understand, and so He says, "Be still,*
> *And know that I am God." The hour is late,*
> *And you must rest awhile, and you must wait*
> *Until life's empty reservoirs fill up*
> *As slow rain fills an empty upturned cup.*
> *Hold up your cup, dear child, for God to fill.*
> *He only asks today that you be still.*
> GRACE NOLL CROWELL

OCTOBER 31

Evening

In the same way, the Spirit helps us in our weakness. We do not know what we ought to pray for, but the Spirit himself intercedes for us through wordless groans. And he who searches our hearts knows the mind of the Spirit, because the Spirit intercedes for God's people in accordance with the will of God.
ROMANS 8:26–27

This is a deep mystery of prayer. It is a delicate, divine tool that words cannot express and theology cannot explain, but the humblest believer knows, even when he does not understand.

Oh, the burdens we lovingly bear but cannot understand! Oh, the inexpressible longings of our hearts for things we cannot comprehend! Yet we know they are an echo from the throne of God, and a whisper from His heart. They are often a groan rather than a song, and a burden rather than a floating feather. But they are a blessed burden, and a groan whose undertone is praise and unspeakable joy. They are groans that words cannot express. We cannot always express them ourselves, and often all we understand is that God is praying in us for something that only He understands and that needs His touch.

So we can simply pour from the fullness of our heart the burden of our spirit and the sorrow that seems to crush us. We can know that He hears, loves, understands, receives, and separates from our prayer everything that is in error, imperfect, or wrong. And then He presents the remainder, along with the incense of the great High Priest, before His throne on high. We may be assured that our prayer is heard, accepted, and answered in His name. A. B. SIMPSON

It is not necessary to be continually speaking to God, or always hearing from God, in order to have communion or fellowship with Him, for there is an unspeakable fellowship that is sweeter than words. A little child can sit all day long beside his mother, totally engrossed in his playing, while his mother is consumed by her work, and although both are busy and few words are spoken by either, they are in perfect fellowship. The child knows his mother is there, and she knows that he is all right.

In the same way, a believer and his Savior can continue many hours in the silent fellowship of love. And although the believer may be busy with the ordinary things of life, he can be mindful that every detail of his life is touched by the character of God's presence, and can have the awareness of His approval and blessing.

Then when troubled with burdens and difficulties too complicated to put into words and too puzzling to express or fully understand, how sweet it is to fall into the embrace of His blessed arms and to simply sob out the sorrow that we cannot speak! SELECTED

Morning

Therefore, the promise comes by faith, so that it may be . . . guaranteed.
ROMANS 4:16

The great devotional teacher of the past century, Dr. Andrew Murray, said, *"When you get a promise from God it is worth just as much as fulfillment.* A promise brings you into direct contact with God. Honor Him by trusting the promise and obeying Him." *Worth just as much as fulfillment.* Do we grasp the truth often? Are we not frequently in the state of *trying* to believe, instead of realizing that these promises bring us into contact with God? *"God's promise is as good as His presence."* To believe and accept the promise of God is not to engage in some mental gymnastics where we reach down into our imaginations and begin a process of auto-suggestion, or produce a notional faith in which we argue with ourselves in an endeavor to believe God. It is absolute confidence in and reliance upon God through His Word.

By a naked faith in a naked promise I do not mean *a bare assent* that God is faithful, and that such a promise in the Book of God *may be* fulfilled in me, but *a bold, hearty, steady venturing* of my soul, body, and spirit upon the truth of the promise with an appropriating act. FLETCHER

The faith that will shut the mouths of lions must be more than a pious hope that they will not bite.

Evening

When the cloud remained . . . the Israelites . . . did not set out.
NUMBERS 9:19

This was the ultimate test of obedience. It was relatively easy to fold up their tents when the fleecy cloud slowly gathered over the tabernacle and began to majestically float ahead of the multitude of the Israelites. Change normally seems pleasant, and the people were excited and interested in the route, the scenery, and the habitat of the next stopping place.

Yet having to wait was another story altogether. "When the cloud remained," however uninviting and sweltering the location, however trying to flesh and blood, however boring and wearisome to those who were impatient, however perilously close their exposure to danger—there was no option but to remain encamped.

The psalmist said, "*I waited patiently for the* LORD; *he turned to me and heard my cry*" (Psalm 40:1). And what God did for the Old Testament saints, He will do for believers down through the ages, yet He will often keep us waiting. Must we wait when we are face to face with a threatening enemy, surrounded by danger and fear, or below an unstable rock? Would this not be the time to fold our tents and leave? Have we not already suffered to the point of total collapse? Can we not exchange the sweltering heat for "green pastures . . . [and] quiet waters" (Psalm 23:2)?

When God sends no answer and "the cloud remain[s]," we must wait. Yet we can do so with the full assurance of God's provision of manna, water from the rock, shelter, and protection from our enemies. He never keeps us at our post without assuring us of His presence or sending us daily supplies.

Young person, wait—do not be in such a hurry to make a change! Minister, stay at your post! You must wait where you are until the cloud clearly begins to move. Wait for the Lord to give you His good pleasure! He will not be late! DAILY DEVOTIONAL COMMENTARY

An hour of waiting!
Yet there seems such need
To reach that spot sublime!
I long to reach them—but I long far more
To trust His time!
"Sit still, My children"—
Yet the heathen die,
They perish while I stay!
I long to reach them—but I long far more
To trust His way!
It's good to get,
It's good indeed to give!
Yet it is better still—

O'er breadth, through length, down depth, up height,
To trust His will!

F. M. N.

~~~~~~~~ NOVEMBER 2 ~~~~~~~~

Morning

Your path led through the sea, your way through the mighty waters.
PSALM 77:19

G od's path led through the sea"—just where you would not expect it to be! So when He leads us out by unexpected ways, off the strong solid land, out upon the changing sea, *then* we may expect to see *His ways.* We are with One who finds a path already tracked out, for it makes us perfectly independent of circumstances.

There is an infinite variety in the paths God makes, and He can make them *anywhere!* Think you not that He, who made the spider able to drop anywhere and to spin its own path as it goes, is not able to spin a path for you through every blank or perplexity or depression? God is never lost among our mysteries. He sees the road, "the end from the beginning."

Mystery and uncertainty are only to prepare us for deeper discipline. Had we no stormy sea, we should remain weaklings to the end of our days. God takes us out into the deeps, but He knows the track! He knows the haven! And we shall arrive.

And with Jesus through the trackless deep move on! C. A. FOX

"Oh, the depth of the riches of the wisdom and knowledge of God! How unsearchable his judgments, and his paths beyond tracing out!" (Romans 11:33).

~~~~~~~~ NOVEMBER 2 ~~~~~~~~

Evening

Peter was kept in prison, but the church was earnestly praying to God for him.
ACTS 12:5

Prayer is the link that connects us with God. It is the bridge that spans every gulf and carries us safely over every chasm of danger or need.

Think of the significance of this story of the first-century church: Everything seemed to be coming against it, for Peter was in prison, the Jews appeared triumphant, Herod still reigned supreme, and the arena of martyrdom was eagerly awaiting the next morning so it could drink the apostle's blood. *"But the church was earnestly praying to God for him."* So what was the outcome? The prison was miraculously opened, the apostle freed, the Jews bewildered, and as a display of God's punishment, wicked King Herod "was eaten by worms and died." And rolling on to even greater victory, "the word of God continued to spread and flourish" (vv. 23–24).

Do we truly know the power of our supernatural weapon of prayer? Do we dare to use it with the authority of a faith that not only asks but also commands? God baptizes us with holy boldness and divine confidence, for He is looking not for great people but for people who will dare to prove the greatness of their God! *"But the church was earnestly praying."* A. B. Simpson

In your prayers, above everything else, beware of limiting God, not only through unbelief but also by thinking you know exactly what He can do. Learn to expect the unexpected, *beyond all* that you ask or think.

So each time you intercede through prayer, first be quiet and worship God in His glory. Think of what He can do, how He delights in Christ His Son, and of your place in Him—then expect great things. Andrew Murray

Our prayers are God's opportunities.

Are you experiencing sorrow? Prayer can make your time of affliction one of strength and sweetness. Are you experiencing happiness? Prayer can add a heavenly fragrance to your time of joy. Are you in grave danger from some outward or inward enemy? Prayer can place an angel by your side whose very touch could shatter a millstone into smaller grains of dust than the flour it grinds, and whose glance could destroy an entire army.

What will prayer do for you? My answer is this: Everything that God can do for you. "Ask for whatever you want me to give you" (2 Chronicles 1:7). Frederick William Farrar

Wrestling prayer can wonders do,
Bring relief in dire straits;
Prayer can force a passage through
Iron bars and heavy gates.

[Jesus'] life may also be revealed in our mortal body.

2 CORINTHIANS 4:11

We may have two lives. First, our own life inherited from our parents and given us by our Creator. That life has some value, but how soon it fails and feels the forces of disease, decay, and approaching death!

But we may have another life, or rather the Life of Another—*the life also of Jesus.* How much more valuable and transcendent is this life! It has no weakness nor decay nor limitation. Jesus has a physical life as real as ours, and infinitely greater; He is an actual *man* with a glorified body and a human spirit. And that life belongs to us just as much as the precious blood He shed and the spiritual grace He bestows. He has risen and ascended as our living Head, and He is ever saying to us, *"Because I live, ye shall live also"* (John 14:19 KJV).

Why should we limit Him to what we call the spiritual realm? His resurrection body has in it all the vitality and strength that our mortal frame can ever need. Someday He is to raise us from the dead by virtue of that resurrection life. Why should it be thought *a strange thing* if faith may now *foredate its inheritance* and *claim in advance* part of its physical redemption—a little handful of the soil of that better country—just as a seed is to bring forth more glorious fruit?

This was Paul's experience. Why may it not be *ours*? There was a day at Lystra when, under a shower of stones, Paul's life was ebbing out and he was left for dead outside the city gates. Then it was that *the life also of Jesus* asserted itself, and, calmly rising up in the strength of his Master, he walked back through the streets whose stones were stained by his own blood and quietly went on his way preaching the Gospel as if nothing had happened.

The secret of this life is to live so close to Jesus that we shall breathe His very breath and ever be in touch with His life and love. So let us live by Him. Healing is in His living body. We *receive* it as we abide in Him. We *keep* it only as we abide in Him. A. B. SIMPSON

There are miraculous possibilities for the one who depends on God.

Evening

You who bring good news to Zion, go up on a high mountain.
ISAIAH 40:9

Toys and trinkets are easily earned, but the most valuable things carry a heavy price. The highest places of power are always bought with blood, and you can attain those pinnacles if you have enough blood to pay. That is the condition of conquering holy heights everywhere. The story of true heroics is always the story of sacrificial blood. The greatest values and character in life are not blown randomly across our path by wayward winds, for great souls experience great sorrows.

> *Great truths are dearly bought, the common truths,*
> *Such as we give and take from day to day,*
> *Come in the common walk of easy life,*
> *Blown by the careless wind across our way.*
>
> *Great truths are greatly won, not found by chance,*
> *Nor wafted on the breath of summer dream;*
> *But grasped in the great struggle of our soul,*
> *Hard buffeting with adverse wind and stream.*
>
> *But in the day of conflict, fear, and grief,*
> *When the strong hand of God, put forth in might,*
> *Plows up the subsoil of our stagnant heart,*
> *And brings the imprisoned truth seed to the light.*
>
> *Wrung from the troubled spirit, in hard hours*
> *Of weakness, solitude, and times of pain,*
> *Truth springs like harvest from the well-plowed field,*
> *And our soul feels it has not wept in vain.*

Our capacity for knowing God is enlarged when we are brought by Him into circumstances that cause us to exercise our faith. So when difficulties block our paths, may we thank God that He is taking time to deal with us, and then may we lean heavily on Him.

<hr>

∼∼∼∼ NOVEMBER 4 ∼∼∼∼
Morning

Burst into song.
ISAIAH 49:13

There is a beautiful story which tells of songbirds being brought over the sea. There were thirty-six thousand, mostly canaries. The sea was very calm when the ship first sailed, and the little birds were silent. They kept their little heads under their wings and not a note was heard. But the third day out at sea, the ship struck a furious gale. The passengers were terrified. Children wept. Then a strange thing happened. As the tempest reached its height, the birds began to sing, first one, then another, until the thirty-six thousand were singing as if their little throats would burst.

When the storm rises in its fury, do we then begin to sing? Should not our song break forth in tenfold joy when the tempest begins?

> *I can hear the songbirds singing their refrain*
> *It is morning in my heart;*
> *And I know that life for me begins again,*
> *It is morning in my heart.*
>
> *It is morning, it is morning in my heart,*
> *Jesus made the gloomy shadows all depart;*
> *Songs of gladness now I sing,*
> *For since Jesus is my King,*
> *It is morning, it is morning in my heart.*

O God, wilt Thou teach us to begin the music of heaven! Grant us grace to have many rehearsals of eternal Hallelujahs! "Bless the LORD, O my soul: and all that is within me, bless his holy name" (Psalm 103:1 KJV)!

Try singing! Singing in the storm!

Evening

I was among the exiles by the Kebar River, the heavens were opened and I saw visions of God. . . . There the hand of the LORD was on [me].
EZEKIEL 1:1, 3

There is nothing that makes the Scriptures more precious to us than a time of "captivity." The old psalms of God's Word have sung for us with compassion by our stream at Babel and have resounded with new joy as we have seen the Lord deliver us from captivity and "restore our fortunes, . . . like streams in the Negev" (Psalm 126:4).

A person who has experienced great difficulties will not be easily parted from his Bible. Another book may appear to others to be identical, but to him it is not the same. Over the old and tear-stained pages of his Bible, he has written a journal of his experiences in words that are only visible to his eyes. Through those pages, he has time and again come to the pillars of the house of God and "to Elim, where there were . . . palm trees" (Exodus 15:27). And each of those pillars and trees have become a remembrance for him of some critical time in his life.

In order to receive any benefit from our captivity, we must accept the situation and be determined to make the best of it. Worrying over what we have lost or what has been taken from us will not make things better but will only prevent us from improving what remains. We will only serve to make the rope around us tighter if we rebel against it.

In the same way, an excitable horse that will not calmly submit to its bridle only strangles itself. And a high-spirited animal that is restless in its yoke only bruises its own shoulders. Everyone will also understand the analogy that Laurence Sterne, a minister and author of the eighteenth century, penned regarding a starling and a canary. He told of the difference between a restless starling that broke its wings struggling against the bars of its cage and continually cried, "I can't get out! I can't get out!" and a submissive canary that sat on its perch and sang songs that surpassed even the beauty of those of a lark that soared freely to the very gates of heaven.

No calamity will ever bring only evil to us, if we will immediately take it in fervent prayer to God. Even as we take shelter beneath a tree during a downpour of rain, we may unexpectedly find fruit on its branches. And when we flee to God, taking refuge beneath the shadow of His wing, we will always find more in Him than we have ever before seen or known.

Consequently, it is through our trials and afflictions that God gives us fresh revelations of Himself. Like Jacob, we must cross "the ford of the Jabbok" (Genesis 32:22) if we are ever to arrive at Peniel, where he wrestled with the Lord, was blessed by Him, and could say, "I saw God face to face, and yet my life was spared" (Genesis 32:30).

Make this story your own, dear captive, and God will give you "songs in the night" (Job 35:10) and will turn your "midnight into dawn" (Amos 5:8). NATHANIEL WILLIAM TAYLOR

> *Submission to God's divine will is the softest pillow on which to rest.*
> *It filled the room, and it filled my life,*
> *With a glory of source unseen;*
> *It made me calm in the midst of strife,*
> *And in winter my heart was green.*
> *And the birds of promise sang on the tree*
> *When the storm was breaking on land and sea.*

~~~~~ NOVEMBER 5 ~~~~~
Morning

> *When Joseph saw Benjamin with them, he said to the steward*
> *of his house, "Take these men to my house, slaughter an animal*
> *and prepare a meal; they are to eat with me at noon."*
> GENESIS 43:16

When their brother, who was to be their savior, saw that they had brought with them the dearest treasure of their family, there went forth the instant word for a king's feast to be prepared for them.

That is all that my Savior is waiting for that He may lavish the fullness of His bounty upon me: my bringing to Him the dearest possession of my life—myself—in unconditional surrender to His mastery, confessing my helplessness and awful need. Then He gives the word that *I may come into His own house and eat at His table the best food of which He Himself partakes.*

The surrender of Benjamin, their dearest possession, was the key to all the treasures of the kingdom—yes, even to the recognition of Joseph by the brothers and Jacob. The surrender of the costliest possession of *my life* is the key to the treasures of the Kingdom for me—yes, even to the full recognition and appropriation of *Christ as my whole and only life.*

Oh, Lord Jesus, show me more that I may give up, that I may have more of Thee!
MESSAGES FOR THE MORNING WATCH

> *My friend, beware of me*
> *Lest I should do*
> *The very thing I'd sooner die than do,*
> *In some way crucify the Christ in you.*
>
> *If you are called to some great sacrifice,*
> *And I should come to you with frightened eyes*
> *And cry, "Take care, take care, be wise, be wise!"*
> *See through my softness then a fiend's attack,*
> *And bid me get me straight behind your back;*
> *To your own conscience and your God be true,*
> *Lest I play Satan to the Christ in you.*
>
> *And I would humbly ask of you in turn*
> *That if someday in me Love's fires should burn*
> *To whiteness, and a Voice should call*
> *Bidding me leave my little for God's all,*
> *If need be, you would thrust me from your side—*
> *So keep love loyal to the Crucified.*

Evening

Is anything too hard for the LORD?
GENESIS 18:14

This is God's loving challenge to you and me each day. He wants us to think of the deepest, highest, and worthiest desires and longings of our hearts. He wants us to think of those things that perhaps were desires for ourselves or someone dear to us, yet have gone unfulfilled for so long that we now see them as simply lost desires. And God urges us to think of even the one thing that we once saw as possible but have given up all hope of seeing fulfilled in this life.

That very thing, as long as it aligns with what we know to be His expressed will—as a son was to Abraham and Sarah—God intends to do for us. Yes, if we will let Him, God will do that very thing, even if we know it is such an utter impossibility that we would simply laugh at the absurdity of anyone ever suggesting it could come to pass.

"Is anything too hard for the Lord?" No, nothing is too difficult when we believe in Him enough to go forward, doing His will and letting Him do the impossible for us. Even Abraham and Sarah could have blocked God's plan if they had continued to disbelieve.

The only thing "too hard for the LORD" is our deliberate and continual disbelief in His love and power, and our ultimate rejection of His plans for us. Nothing is impossible for Jehovah to do for those who trust Him. MESSAGES FOR THE MORNING WATCH

———— NOVEMBER 6 ————

Morning

But even if I am being poured out like a drink offering on the sacrifice and service coming from your faith, I am glad and rejoice with all of you. So you too should be glad and rejoice with me.
PHILIPPIANS 2:17–18

The leading symbol of our Christian faith is not an easy chair or a feather-bed: it is a Cross. If we would be His disciples, let us be prepared to live dangerously, to take up the Cross and carry it into the teeth of opposition.

God is at perfect liberty to waste us if He chooses.

When the fight seems fierce and you are tempted to be weary and disconsolate, remember that in the interest of His cause your Leader expects you to turn a glad face to the world—*to rejoice and be exceeding glad!*

I have shamed Thee; craven-hearted
I have been Thy recreant knight;
Own me yet, O Lord, albeit
Weeping whilst I fight!

"Nay," He said, "Wilt thou yet shame Me?
Wilt thou shame thy knightly guise?
I would have my angels wonder
At thy gladsome eyes."

Need'st thou pity, knight of Jesus?
Pity for thy glorious hest?
Oh, let God and men and angels
See that thou are blest!

SUSO

~~~~~~~~~ NOVEMBER 6 ~~~~~~~~~

Evening

Those whom I love I rebuke and discipline.
REVELATION 3:19

God selects the best and most notable of His servants for the best and most notable afflictions, for those who have received the most grace from Him are able to endure the most afflictions. In fact, an affliction hits a believer never by chance but by

God's divine direction. He does not haphazardly aim His arrows, for each one is on a special mission and touches only the heart for whom it is intended. It is not only the grace of God but also His glory that is revealed when a believer can stand and quietly endure an affliction. JOSEPH CARYL

> If all my days were sunny, could I say,
> "In His fair land He wipes all tears away"?
>
> If I were never weary, could I keep
> This blessed truth, "He gives His loved ones sleep"?
>
> If no grave were mine, I might come to deem
> The Life Eternal but a baseless dream.
>
> My winter, and my tears, and weariness,
> Even my grave, may be His way to bless.
>
> I call them ills; yet that can surely be
> Nothing but love that shows my Lord to me!
>   SELECTED

Christians with the most spiritual depth are generally those who have been taken through the most intense and deeply anguishing fires of the soul. If you have been praying to know more of Christ, do not be surprised if He leads you through the desert or through a furnace of pain.

Dear Lord, do not punish me by removing my cross from me. Instead, comfort me by leading me into submission to Your will and by causing me to love the cross. Give me only what will serve You best, and may it be used to reveal the greatest of all Your mercies: bringing glory to Your name through me, according to Your will. A CAPTIVE'S PRAYER

Morning

Every place that the sole of your foot shall tread upon, that have I given unto you.
JOSHUA 1:3 KJV

This blessed inspiring word greeted Israel as they faced the Promised Land. They had the *promise* of it before; *now* they must go forward into it and place their feet upon it. The promise is in the perfect tense and denotes an act just now completed—*"That have I given unto you."*

Our Joshua gives us the same incentive for conquest: *every promise in the New Testament that we put our feet upon is ours!* The upland of spiritual power is yours though Anak may live there! It is yours if you will but go against him and drive him out of his strongholds, in the might of *The Name*.

If we dare to place our foot on anything God has promised, *He makes it real to us.* So take Him as the supply for all your need: believe He is yours, and never doubt it from this moment.

It may be your need is for spiritual cleansing. His promise covers this: *"Now ye are clean through the word which I have spoken unto you"* (John 15:3 KJV). If you can believe this, you shall be sanctified and kept.

Take the promise that suits your need, and step out on it; not touching it timidly on tiptoe, *but placing your foot flat down upon it.* Do not be afraid it will not hold your weight. *Put your whole need on the Word of the eternal* God for your soul, for your body, for your work, for the dear ones for whom you are praying, for any crisis in your life: *then stand upon it forever!*

All the blessed promises of the Old Book are yours, and *why are you so slack to go up and possess your land?* The size of your inheritance depends upon *how much land you have trodden underfoot, really stood on or walked over.* Between you and your possessions that huge mountain looms up. March up to it and make it yours! Go in this thy might and God will get glory; and you, victory. A. B. SIMPSON

Footprints mean possession, but it must be *your own footprints.*

Evening

Whatever was to my profit I now consider loss for the sake of Christ.
PHILIPPIANS 3:7

When George Matheson, the blind Scottish preacher, was buried, they lined his grave with red roses commemorating his life of love and sacrifice. And it was Matheson, this man who was so beautifully and significantly honored, who wrote the following hymn in 1882. It was written in five minutes, during a period he later called "the most severe mental suffering," and it has since become known around the world.

> *O Love that wilt not let me go,*
> *I rest my weary soul in Thee,*
> *I give Thee back the life I owe,*
> *That in thine ocean depths its flow*
> *May richer, fuller be.*
>
> *O Light that followest all my way,*
> *I yield my flickering torch to Thee,*
> *My heart restores its borrowed ray,*
> *That in Thy sunshine's glow its day*
> *May brighter, fairer be.*
>
> *O Joy that seekest me through pain,*
> *I cannot close my heart to Thee,*
> *I trace the rainbow through the rain,*
> *And feel the promise is not vain,*
> *That morn shall tearless be.*
>
> *O Cross that liftest up my head,*
> *I dare not ask to hide from Thee,*
> *I lay in dust life's glory dead,*

And from the ground there blossoms red,
  Life that shall endless be.

There is a legend of an artist who had found the secret of a wonderful red that no other artist could imitate. He never told the secret of the color, but after his death an old wound was discovered over his heart. It revealed the source of the matchless hue in his pictures.

The moral of the legend is that no great achievement can be made, no lofty goal attained, nor anything of great value to the world accomplished, except at the cost of the heart's blood.

NOVEMBER 8

Morning

"In that day," declares the LORD, *"you will call me 'my husband.'"*
HOSEA 2:16

The coming of the Comforter is a holy thing, a solemn act, and must be preceded by an intelligent and solemn covenant between the soul and God. It is the marriage of the soul to the Redeemer, and it is not a "trial marriage." No true marriage is rushed into carelessly. It is carefully considered, and it is based upon complete separation and consecration and the most solemn pledges and vows. So, if the Comforter is come to abide, to be with us and in us evermore, we must come out and be separate for Him, we must consecrate ourselves to Jesus fully and forever, and we must covenant to be the Lord's "for better or for worse," and we must trust Him. The soul that thus truly and solemnly dedicates itself to Him becomes His, and He will come to that soul to abide forever, to be its "shield, and . . . exceeding great reward" (Genesis 15:1 KJV).

Take not back the gift you have voluntarily laid on the altar.

Jesus, Thy life is mine!
Dwell evermore in me;
And let me see

That nothing can untwine
Thy life from mine.

Thy life in me be shown!
Lord, I would henceforth seek
To think and speak
Thy thoughts, Thy words alone,
No more my own.

Thy fullest gift, O Lord,
Now at Thy word I claim,
Through Thy dear Name,
And touch the rapturous chord
Of praise forth-poured.

Jesus, my life is Thine,
And evermore shall be
Hidden in Thee!
For nothing can untwine
Thy life from mine.

FRANCES RIDLEY HAVERGAL

"Thou shalt abide [live] for me many days . . . thou shalt not be for another man: so will I also be for thee" (Hosea 3:3).

～～～～ NOVEMBER 8 ～～～～

Evening

He took Peter, John and James with him and went up onto a mountain to pray.
As he was praying, the appearance of his face changed, and his clothes became as
bright as a flash of lightning. . . . Peter and his companions . . . saw his glory.

LUKE 9:28–29, 32

If you are pleased with me, teach me your ways.

EXODUS 33:13

When Jesus took these three disciples up onto the mountain alone, He brought them into close communion with Himself. They "saw his glory" and said, "It is good for us to be here" (Luke 9:32–33). Heaven is never far from those who linger on a mountain with their Lord.

Who of us in certain moments of meditation and prayer has not caught a glimpse of the heavenly gates? Who has not in the secret place of holy communion felt a surging wave of emotion—a taste of the blessed joy yet to come?

The Master had special times and places for quiet conversation with His disciples. He met with them once on Mount Hermon but more often on the sacred slopes of the Mount of Olives. Every Christian should have his own Mount of Olives. Most of us today, especially those of us in cities, live under great stress. From early morning until bedtime we are exposed to the whirlwind of life. Amid all the turmoil, there is little opportunity for quiet thought, God's Word, prayer, and fellowship of the heart!

Even Daniel needed to have his Mount of Olives in his room amid the roar of idolatrous Babylon. Peter found a rooftop in Joppa, and Martin Luther found an "upper room" in Wittenberg, a place that is still considered sacred.

Joseph Parker, an English Congregationalist preacher of the nineteenth century, once said, "If we, as the church, do not get back to spiritual visions, glimpses of heaven, and an awareness of a greater glory and life, we will lose our faith. Our altar will become nothing but cold, empty stone, never blessed with a visit from heaven." And this is the world's need today—*people who have seen their Lord.* THE LOST ART OF MEDITATION

Come close to Him! Perhaps He will take you today to the mountaintop—the same place He took Peter with his blundering, and James and John, the "Sons of Thunder" (Mark 3:17), who time and again totally misunderstood their Master and His mission. There is no reason why He will not take you, so do not shut yourself out by saying, "Oh, these wonderful visions and revelations of the Lord are only for certain people!" They may be for you! JOHN THOMAS MCNEILL

NOVEMBER 9

Morning

God has made the one as well as the other.

ECCLESIASTES 7:14

Too often we see life's prose, but not its poetry. Too often we miss the inspiration of the songs. How manifold are our sorrows, but how manifold are His gifts!

Sin is here, but so is boundless grace; the devil is here, but so is Christ; the sword of judgment is crossed by Mercy's scepter.

"Judgment and Mercy," according to a lovely Jewish legend, "were sent forth together after the Fall to minister to the sinning but redeemed race," *and together they still act.* One afflicts, the other heals; where one rends, the other plants a flower; one carves a wrinkle, the other kindles a smile; the rainbow succeeds the storm; the succoring wing covers our naked head from the glittering sword.

Gethsemane had its strengthening Angel!

God everlastingly sets Mercies over against Miseries! His interventions are never mistimed. He never comes at the wrong season. *God has the affairs of the world in His hands.* In your blackest crises the angel presences are doubtless in your neighborhood!

God never strikes the wrong note; never sings the wrong song. If God makes music, the music will prove medicinal. JOSEPH PEARCE

> *With mercy and with judgment*
> *My web of time He wove.*
> *And aye the dews of sorrow*
> *Were lustered with His love,*
> *I'll bless the Hand that guided,*
> *I'll bless the Heart that planned,*
> *When throned where glory dwelleth,*
> *In Immanuel's land.*
>
> *Deep waters crossed life's pathway,*
> *The hedge of thorns was sharp;*
> *Now, these lie all behind me—*
>
> *Oh! For a well-tuned harp!*
> *Oh! to join Hallelujahs*
> *With your triumphant band,*
> *Who sing, where glory dwelleth*
> *In Immanuel's land.*

SAMUEL RUTHERFORD

~~~~~ NOVEMBER 9 ~~~~~

Evening

*People will dwell again in his shade; they will flourish
like the grain, they will blossom like the vine.*

HOSEA 14:7

The day ended with heavy showers, and the plants in my garden were beaten down by the pelting storm. I looked at one plant I had previously admired for its beauty and had loved for its delicate fragrance. After being exposed to the merciless storm, its flowers had drooped, all its petals were closed, and it appeared that its glory was gone. I thought to myself, *I suppose I will have to wait till next year to see those beautiful flowers again.*

Yet the night passed, the sun shone again, and the morning brought strength to my favorite plant. The light looked at its flowers and the flowers looked at the light. There was contact and communion, and power passed into the flowers. They lifted their heads, opened their petals, regained their glory, and seemed more beautiful than before. I wondered how this took place—these feeble flowers coming into contact with something much stronger, and gaining strength!

I cannot explain exactly how we are able to receive the power to serve and to endure through communion with God, but I know it is a fact. Are you in danger of being crushed by a heavy and difficult trial? Then seek communion with Christ and you will receive strength and the power to be victorious, for God has promised, "I will strengthen you" (Isaiah 41:10).

YESTERDAY'S GRIEF

*The falling rain of yesterday is ruby on the roses,
    Silver on the poplar leaf, and gold on willow stem;
The grief that fell just yesterday is silence that encloses
    God's great gifts of grace, and time will never trouble them.*

The falling rain of yesterday makes all the hillsides glisten,
    Coral on the laurel and beryl on the grass;
The grief that fell just yesterday has taught the soul to listen
    For whispers of eternity in all the winds that pass.

O faint of heart, storm-beaten, this rain will shine tomorrow,
    Flame within the columbine and jewels on the thorn,
Heaven in the forget-me-not; though sorrow now is sorrow,
    Yet sorrow will be beauty in the magic of the morn.

KATHERINE LEE BATES

~~~ NOVEMBER 10 ~~~
Morning

Righteousness goes before him and prepares the way for his steps.
PSALM 85:13

How I ascertain the will of God: *I seek at the beginning to get my heart into such a state that it has no will of its own* in regard to a given matter.

Nine-tenths of the trouble with people is right here. Nine-tenths of the difficulties are overcome when our hearts are *ready to do the Lord's will,* whatever it may be. When one is truly in this state it is usually but a little way to the knowledge of what His will is.

Having surrendered my own will, I do not leave the result to feeling or simply impressions. If I do so, I make myself liable to great delusions.

I seek the will of the Spirit of God through, or in connection with, *the Word of God.*

The Spirit and the Word must be combined. If the Holy Ghost guides us at all, He will do it according to the Scriptures, and never contrary to them.

Next I take into account *providential circumstances.* These often plainly indicate God's will in connection with His Word and Spirit.

I ask God in prayer to reveal His will to me aright.

Thus, through prayer to God, the study of His Word, and reflection, I come to a deliberate judgment, and if my mind is thus at peace, and continues so after two or three more petitions, I proceed accordingly. In *trivial matters,* and in transactions involving *most important issues,* I have found this method *always effective.* GEORGE MUELLER

~~~~~~ NOVEMBER 10 ~~~~~~
Evening

Against all hope, Abraham in hope believed.
ROMANS 4:18

A braham's faith seemed to be in complete agreement with the power and constant faithfulness of Jehovah. By looking at the outer circumstances in which he was placed, he had no reason to expect the fulfillment of God's promise. Yet he believed the Word of the Lord and looked forward to the time when his descendants would be "as numerous as the stars in the sky" (Genesis 26:4).

Dear soul, you have not been given only one promise, like Abraham, *but a thousand promises.* And you have been given the example of many faithful believers as a pattern for your life. Therefore it is simply to your advantage to rely with confidence upon the Word of God. And although He may delay in sending His help, and the evil you are experiencing may seem to become worse and worse, do not be weak. Instead, be strong and rejoice, for God usually steps forward to save us when we least expect it, fulfilling His most glorious promises in a miraculous way.

He generally waits to send His help until the time of our greatest need, so that His hand will be plainly seen in our deliverance. He chooses this method so we will not trust anything that we may see or feel, as we are so prone to do, but will place our trust solely on His Word—which we may always depend upon, no matter our circumstance. C. H. VON BOGATZKY

Remember, the very time for faith to work is when our sight begins to fail. And the greater the difficulties, the easier it is for faith to work, for as long as we can see certain natural solutions to our problems, we will not have faith. Faith never works as easily as when our natural prospects fail. GEORGE MUELLER

Morning

He was pierced for our transgressions, he was crushed for our iniquities; the punishment that brought us peace was on him, and by his wounds we are healed.

ISAIAH 53:5

He was led like a lamb to the slaughter.

ISAIAH 53:7

Yet it was the LORD's will to crush him.

ISAIAH 53:10

I came alone to my Calvary,
And the load I bore was too great for me;
The stones were sharp and pierced my feet,
And my temples throbbed with the withering heat.

But my heart was faint with the toil that day,
So I sat down to think of an easy way;
Loomed sharply before me that tortuous trail—
No use to try—I would only fail.

I turned back in sorrow, clothed with defeat,
For my load was too heavy; I would retreat
To easier highways, with scenery more fair—

Yet a moment I lingered watching there.

As I held my gaze on that flinty side,
A man came up to be crucified;
He toiled all the way of that painful road,
And the cross that he bore far surpassed my load:

His brow with thorns was pierced and torn;
His face had a look of pain and was worn;
He stopped for a moment and looked on me—
And I followed in rapture to Calvary!
"My Calvary" by Matthew Biller

Haunt the place called Calvary.

—— NOVEMBER 11 ——

Evening

May he be like rain falling on a mown field.
Psalm 72:6

Amos tells of "the king's mowings" (Amos 7:1 kjv). Our King also has many scythes and is constantly using them to mow His lawns. The bell-like sound of the whetstone against the scythe foretells of the cutting down of countless blades of grass, daisies, and other flowers. And as beautiful as they were in the morning, within a few hours they will lie in long, faded rows.

In human life, we try to take a brave stand before the scythe of pain, the shears of disappointment, or the sickle of death. And just as there is no way to cultivate a lawn like velvet without repeated mowings, there is no way to develop a life of balance, tenderness, and sympathy for others without enduring the work of God's scythes.

Think how often the Word of God compares people to grass, and God's glory to its flower. But when the grass is cut, when all the tender blades are bleeding, and when desolation seems to reign where flowers once were blooming, the perfect time has come for God's rain to fall as delicate showers so soft and warm.

Dear soul, God has been mowing you! Time and again the King has come to you with His sharp scythe. But do not dread His scythe—for it is sure to be followed by His shower. F. B. Meyer

When across the heart deep waves of sorrow
Break, as on a dry and barren shore;

—— 769 ——

When hope glistens with no bright tomorrow,
    And the storm seems sweeping evermore;

When the cup of every earthly gladness
    Bears no taste of the life-giving stream;
And high hopes, as though to mock our sadness,
    Fade and die as in some restless dream,

Who will hush the weary spirit's chiding?
    Who the aching void within will fill?
Who will whisper of a peace abiding,
    And each surging wave will calmly still?

Only He whose wounded heart was broken
    With the bitter cross and thorny crown;
Whose dear love glad words of joy had spoken,
    Who His life for us laid meekly down.

Blessed Healer, all our burdens lighten;
    Give us peace. Your own sweet peace, we pray!
Keep us near You till the morn does brighten,
    And all the mists and shadows flee away!

NOVEMBER 12

Morning

Even though refined by fire.
1 PETER 1:7

W hat makes this set of china so much more expensive than that?" asked the customer.

"It has more work on it. It has been put through the fire twice. See, in this one the flowers are in a yellow band; in that one they are on the white background. This had to be put *through the fire a second time* to get the design on it."

"Why is the pattern on this vessel so blurred and marred—the design not brought out clearly?"

"That one was *not burned enough*. Had it remained in the furnace longer *the dark background would have become gold*—dazzling gold, and the pattern would have stood out clear and distinct."

Perhaps some of those who seem to have more than their share of suffering and disappointment are, like the costly china, being *doubly tried* in the fire, that they may be more valuable in the Master's service.

The potter never sees his clay take on rich shades of silver, or red, or cream, or brown, or yellow, until after the darkness and the burning of the furnace. These colors come—*after the burning and darkness*. The clay is beautiful—after the burning and darkness. The vase is made possible—after the burning and darkness.

How universal is this law of life! Where did the bravest man and the purest woman you know get their whitened characters? Did they not get them as the clay gets its beauty—after the darkness and the burning of the furnace? Where did Savonarola get his eloquence? In the darkness and burning of the furnace wherein God discovered deep things to him. Where did Stradivari get his violins? Where did Titian get his color? Where did Angelo get his marble? Where did Mozart get his music, and Chatterton his poetry, and Jeremiah his sermons? They got them where the clay gets its glory and its shimmer—in the darkness and the burning of the furnace. ROBERT G. LEE

> *Thou who didst fashion man on earth, to be*
> *Strong in Thy strength, and with Thy freedom free,*
> *Complete at last Thy great design in me.*
>
> *Cost what it may of sorrow and distress,*
> *Of empty hands, of utter loneliness,*
> *I dare not, Lord, be satisfied with less.*
>
> *So, Lord, reclaim Thy great design in me, Give or reclaim Thy gifts, but let me be*
> *Strong in Thy strength, and with Thy freedom free.*
> *Let us not rebel at the second breath of the flame if He sends it.*

> *These were the potters, and those that dwelt among plants and*
> *hedges: there they dwelt with the king for his work.*
>
> 1 CHRONICLES 4:23 KJV

We may dwell "with the king for his work" anywhere and everywhere. We may be called to serve Him in the most unlikely places and under the most adverse conditions. It may be out in the countryside, far away from the King's many activities in the city. Or it may be "among plants and hedges" of all kinds—hindrances that surround us, blocking our way. Perhaps we will be one of "the potters," with our hands full of all types of pottery, accomplishing our daily tasks.

It makes no difference! The King who placed us *"there"* will come and dwell with us. The hedges, or hindrances, are right for us, or He will quickly remove them. And doesn't it stand to reason that whatever seems to block our way may also provide for our protection? As for the pottery—it is exactly what He has seen fit to place in our hands and is for now *"his work."* FRANCES RIDLEY HAVERGAL

> *Go back to your garden plot, sweetheart!*
> *Go back till the evening falls,*
> *And tie your lilies and train your vines,*
> *Till for you the Master calls.*
>
> *Go make your garden fair as you can,*
> *You will never work alone;*
> *Perhaps he whose plot is next to yours*
> *Will see it and mend his own.*

Brightly colored sunsets and starry heavens, majestic mountains and shining seas, and fragrant fields and fresh-cut flowers are not even half as beautiful as a soul who is serving Jesus out of love, through the wear and tear of an ordinary, unpoetic life. FREDERICK WILLIAM FABER

The most saintly souls are often those who have never distinguished themselves as authors or allowed any major accomplishment of theirs to become the topic of the world's conversation. No, they are usually those who have led a quiet inner life of holiness, having carried their sweet bouquets unseen, like a fresh lily in a secluded valley on the edge of a crystal stream. KENELM DIGBY

NOVEMBER 13

Morning

To him who is able to keep you from stumbling and to present you before his glorious presence without fault and with great joy.

JUDE V. 24

Take that word *keep* and hold it close to your heart tonight and tomorrow. It is one of the great and magnificent messages of the Gospel—He "is able to keep you from stumbling." Put into the word *you* all the weakness, all the unworthiness, all the sinfulness which belongs to man since the Fall; yet He is able to keep you. He does not underrate the disadvantage of its being *you* when He bids His messengers say He is "able to keep you from stumbling." It would be impossible, utterly impossible, were it not undertaken by Infinite love. Look out, and up, then. Look up "from the depth"—the vast depth of your weakness, perhaps of your mysteriously inherited weakness. Look out of your failure under some temptation, inward or outward, inherited so to speak from yourself, from your own unfaithfulness in the past. Look up, out of your ruined purposes—unto Himself.

Being what He is, Keeper of Israel, God of the promises, Lord of the Sacrifice, Prince of life, present Savior, indwelling Power, He is able to keep you, that your feet shall not totter. They shall stand "in a large room" (Psalm 31:8 KJV); they shall hold on straight, until at last they enter, step by step—for it is one step at a time even then—"through the gates into the city" (Revelation 22:14 KJV).

"He shall never give thy feet to tottering." H. C. G. MOULE

We may step firmly down upon the temptation which Another has crushed for us, and we are conquerors in Him.

Behind the dim unknown standeth God within the shadows keeping watch above His own.

Evening

I have chosen him, so that he will direct his children.
GENESIS 18:19

God chooses people He can depend upon. He knew what to expect from Abraham and said of him, "I have chosen him, so that he will direct his children . . . that the LORD will bring about for Abraham what he has promised him." God knew Abraham *would* "direct his children." The Lord can be depended upon, and He desires for us to be just as reliable, determined, and stable. This is simply the meaning of faith.

God is looking for people on whom He can place the weight of His entire love, power, and faithful promises. And His engines are strong enough to pull any weight we may attach to them. Unfortunately, the cable we fasten to the engine is often too weak to handle the weight of our prayers. Therefore God continues to train and discipline us in His school of stability and certainty in the life of faith. May we learn our lessons well and then stand firm. A. B. SIMPSON

God knows that you can withstand your trial, or else He would not have given it to you. His trust in you explains the trials of your life, no matter how severe they may be. God knows your strength, and He measures it to the last inch. Remember, no trial has ever been given to anyone that was greater than that person's strength, through God, to endure it.

NOVEMBER 14

Morning

Enoch walked faithfully with God.
GENESIS 5:22

A day's walk with God will do more to awaken awe, wonder, and amazement in your soul than would a century of travel through the sights of the earth. He chooses for you a way you know not, that you may be compelled into a thousand inter-courses with Him, which will make the journey ever memorable with glory to Him and blessing to you.

> Jesus, these eyes have never seen
> That radiant form of Thine;
> The veil of sense hangs dark between
> Thy blessed face and mine.
>
> I see Thee not, I hear Thee not,
> Yet art Thou oft with me;
> And earth hath ne'er so dear a spot
> As where I meet with Thee.
>
> Like some bright dream that comes unsought
> When slumbers o'er me roll,
> Thine image ever fills my thought
> And charms my ravished soul.
>
> Yet though I have not seen, and still
> Must rest in faith alone,
>
> I love Thee, dearest Lord, and will,
> Unseen but not unknown.
>
> HYMNS OF CONSECRATION AND FAITH

～～～ NOVEMBER 14 ～～～
Evening

Unless a kernel of wheat falls to the ground and dies, it remains
only a single seed. But if it dies, it produces many seeds.

JOHN 12:24

In Northampton, Massachusetts, stands the old cemetery where David Brainerd is buried. Brainerd, a pioneer American missionary, died in 1747 at the age of twenty-nine after suffering from tuberculosis. His grave is beside that of Jerusha Edwards, the daughter of Jonathan Edwards, a Puritan theologian of that day. Brainerd loved Jerusha and they were engaged to be married, but he did not live until the wedding.

Imagine what hopes, dreams, and expectations for the cause of Christ were buried in the grave with the withered body of that young missionary. At that point, nothing remained but memories and several dozen Indian converts! Yet Jonathan Edwards, that majestic old Puritan saint, who had hoped to call Brainerd his son, began to write the story of that short life in a little book. The book took wings, flew across the sea, and landed on the desk of a Cambridge student by the name of Henry Martyn.

Poor Henry Martyn! In spite of his education, brilliance, and great opportunities, he—after reading that little book on the life of Brainerd—threw his own life away! Afterward, what had he accomplished once he set his course toward home from India in 1812? With his health then broken, he dragged himself as far north as the town of Tokat, Turkey, near the Black Sea. There he lay in the shade of a pile of saddles, to cool his burning fever, and died alone at the age of thirty-one.

What was the purpose behind these "wasted lives"? From the grave of a young David Brainerd, and the lonely grave of Henry Martyn near the shores of the Black Sea, have arisen a mighty army of modern missionaries. LEONARD WOOLSEY BACON

Is there some desert, or some boundless sea,
Where You, great God of angels, will send me?
Some oak for me to rend,
Some sod for me to break,
Some handful of Your corn to take
And scatter far afield,
Till it in turn will yield
  Its hundredfold
  Of grains of gold
To feed the happy children of my God?
Show me the desert, Father, or the sea;
Is it Your enterprise? Great God, send me!
And though this body lies where ocean rolls,
Father, count me among all faithful souls.

Morning

Stay here and keep watch with me.
MATTHEW 26:38

When He needed God most in the greatest crisis of His life, Jesus sought a garden. Under the olive trees, with the Passover moon shining down upon Him, He prayed in agony for strength to do God's will. Only those who have been through such agony can realize even in part what that bleak hour of renunciation, for the sake of you and me, meant to Christ.

Are we willing that He should suffer Gethsemane and the Cross for us *in vain?*

"I go to pray," He said to the eight,
"Rest here at the gate."
But He spake to the three entreatingly,
"Will you watch with me as I pray
A stone's throw away?
I suffer tonight exceedingly."
The eight slept well at the garden gate
(As tired men will);
The three tossed fitfully within,
(Twice half-roused by His need of them)
But they slept—
Till the black in the East turned gray,
Till their garments were drenched with the
tears of the day:

Slept
Till He called them—each one by his name—
The three within, and the eight at the gate.

The ground was hard where the eight had slept
(As hard as the road the soldiers stepped);

The grass was bent where the three had dreamt,
But red where the Lord had wept.

MIRIAM LEFEVRE CROUSE

"Couldn't you men keep watch with me for one hour?" (Matthew 26:40).

NOVEMBER 15

Evening

We were under great pressure.

2 CORINTHIANS 1:8

So that Christ's power may rest on me.

2 CORINTHIANS 12:9

God allowed the crisis in Jacob's life at Peniel to totally surround him until he ultimately came to the point of making an earnest and humble appeal to God Himself. That night, he wrestled with God and literally came to the place where he could take hold of Him as never before. And through his narrow brush with danger, Jacob's faith and knowledge of God was expanded, and his power to live a new and victorious life was born.

The Lord had to force David, through the discipline of many long and painful years, to learn of the almighty power and faithfulness of his God. Through those difficult years, he also grew in his knowledge of faith and godliness, which were indispensable principles for his glorious career as the king of Israel.

Nothing but the most dangerous circumstances in which Paul was constantly placed could ever have taught him, and thus the church through him, the full meaning of the great promise of God he learned to claim: "My grace is sufficient for you" (2 Corinthians 12:9). And nothing but the great trials and dangers we have experienced would ever have led some of us to know Him as we do, to trust Him as we have, and to draw from Him the great measure of His grace so indispensable during our times of greatest need.

Difficulties and obstacles are God's challenges to our faith. When we are confronted with hindrances that block our path of service, we are to recognize them as vessels for faith and then to fill them with the fullness and complete sufficiency of Jesus.

As we move forward in faith, simply and fully trusting Him, we may be tested. Sometimes we may have to wait and realize that "perseverance [must] finish its work" (James 1:4). But ultimately we will surely find "the stone rolled away" (Luke 24:2) and the Lord Himself waiting to bestow a double blessing on us for our time of testing.
A. B. SIMPSON

~~~ NOVEMBER 16 ~~~
Morning

This love that surpasses knowledge.
EPHESIANS 3:19

We do not really see the ocean. To do that is beyond our power. Through that vista we glimpse a bit of blue water as though God has painted a picture and framed it with hills and trees. But southward and northward on distance-hidden shores stretches water we have never seen. Bays lie placid by sunlit rocks, and long surges roll in soothing rhythm on smoothly sloping sands. Inlets ripple under tropic moons, and warming currents bear springtime's promise to frozen arctic reefs. Beyond that curved blue line that limits our sight, there rolls an open plain of waters to realms where we have never been, leaving the strands of palmy islands of which we do not know. And this is but the surface! Beneath are miles of depth, fathomless with mysteries beyond the thoughts of men.

God's measureless love is like the ocean. Through the windows of earthly life, we catch a gleam. From the valleys of trouble, we glimpse it near the shore. On the sands of hope we see it, wave on wave. From the headlands of faith we view a broader tide to the line that blends eternity with time. Our happiest days are islands set in its boundless breadth. Yet, as with the ocean, we have never seen it *all!* Even eternity cannot reveal its greatness to the wondering hosts of heaven, nor all the universe exhaust the fountains whence it flows.

We can only see a little of the ocean,
Just a few miles distant from the rocky shore,
But out there—far beyond our eyes' horizon,
There's more—immeasurably more.

We can only see a little of God's loving—
A few rich treasures from His mighty store;
But out there—far beyond our eyes' horizon,
There's more—immeasurably more.

～～～ NOVEMBER 16 ～～～
Evening

They triumphed over him by the blood of the Lamb . . . they did
not love their lives so much as to shrink from death.
REVELATION 12:11

When James and John came to Christ with their mother, asking Him to give them the best place in His kingdom, He did not refuse their request. He told them that the place would be given to them if they could do His work, drink His cup, and be baptized with His baptism (Mark 10:38.)

Are we willing to compete for God's best, with the knowledge that the best things are always achieved by the most difficult paths? We must endure steep mountains, dense forests, and the Enemy's chariots of iron, since hardship is the price of the victor's coronation. Arches of triumph are made not of rose blossoms and strands of silk but of hard blows and bloody scars. The very hardships you are enduring in your life today have been given to you by the Master, for the express purpose of enabling you to win your crown.

Therefore do not always look ahead to your tomorrows for some ideal situation, exotic difficulty, or faraway emergency in which to shine. Rise today to face the circumstances in which the providence of God has placed you. Your crown of glory is hidden in the heart of these things—the hardships and trials pressing in on you this very hour, week, and month of your life. Yet the most difficult things are not those seen and known by the world but those deep within your soul, unseen and unknown by anyone except Jesus. It is in this secret place that you experience a little trial that you would never dare to mention to anyone else and that is more difficult for you to bear than martyrdom.

Beloved, your crown lies there. May God help you to overcome and to wear it. SELECTED

> It matters not how the battle goes,
> The day how long;
> Faint not! Fight on!
> Tomorrow comes the song.

NOVEMBER 17

Morning

> LORD, *come to my aid!*
> ISAIAH 38:14

Are you feeling that life for you has become a tangled skein, tangled with problems that seem to be desperately hard to unravel? If so, examine them and see whether it be not true that somewhere in the tangle there is the golden thread of an obvious present duty. Commence with that thread: *what ought you to do next? Now! Never mind tomorrow!*

> *Father, my life is in tangle,*
> *Thread after thread appears*
> *Twisted and broken and knotted,*
> *Viewed through the lapse of years.*

> *I cannot straighten them, Father;*
> *Oh, it is very hard;*
> *Somehow or other it seemeth,*
> *All I have done is marred.*

I did not see they were getting
Into this tangled state;
How it has happened I know not—
Is it too late, too late?

Is it? "Ah, no!" Thou dost whisper,
"Out of this life of thine
Yet may come wonderful beauty
Wrought by My Power Divine."

Take then, the threads, O my Father,
Let them Thy mind fulfill,
Work out in love a pattern
After Thy holy will!

CHARLOTTE MURRAY

The case looks utterly hopeless. Hope is dead—yea, buried, and the bones are lying scattered at the grave's mouth. *But the eye fixed on the living God can bring a resurrection.* Hope may yet flourish again. The net of terrible entanglement may be broken *by a Father's hand,* and liberty and life abundant may yet be mine!

The Savior can solve every problem,
The tangles of life can undo,
There is nothing too hard for Jesus,
There is nothing that He cannot do.

OSWALD J. SMITH

~~~~~ NOVEMBER 17 ~~~~~

Evening

Listen to what the unjust judge says. And will not God bring about justice
for his chosen ones, who cry out to him day and night? Will he keep putting
them off? I tell you, he will see that they get justice, and quickly.

LUKE 18:6–8

God's timing is not ours to command. If we do not start the fire with the first strike of our match, we must try again. God does hear our prayer, but He may not answer it at the precise time we have appointed in our own minds. Instead, He will reveal Himself to our seeking hearts, though not necessarily when and where we may expect. Therefore we have a need for perseverance and steadfast determination in our life of prayer.

In the old days of flint, steel, and brimstone matches, people had to strike the match again and again, perhaps even dozens of times, before they could get a spark to light their fire, and they were very thankful if they finally succeeded. Should we not exercise the same kind of perseverance and hope regarding heavenly things? When it comes to faith, we have more certainty of success than we could ever have had with flint and steel, for we have God's promises as a foundation.

May we, therefore, never despair. God's time for mercy will come—in fact, it has already come, if our time for believing has arrived. Ask in faith without wavering, but never cease to petition the King simply because He has delayed His reply.

Strike the match again and make the sparks fly. Yet be sure to have your tinder ready, for you will get a fire before long. CHARLES H. SPURGEON

I do not believe there is such a thing in the history of God's eternal kingdom as a right prayer, offered in the right spirit, that remains forever unanswered. THEODORE L. CUYLER

NOVEMBER 18
Morning

But take heart!
JOHN 16:33

Jesus said, "Ye shall have tribulation" (v. 33 KJV)—not difficulties, but tribulation. But "tribulation worketh patience" (Romans 5:3 KJV).

Millstones are used to grind the corn to powder, and they typify the sacredness of the discipline of life.

"No man shall take the nether or the upper millstone to pledge: for he taketh a man's life to pledge" (Deuteronomy 24:6 KJV).

You have been having a snug time in the granary; then God brings you out and puts you under the millstones, and the first thing that happens is the grinding separation of which our Lord spoke: "Blessed are you when people . . . exclude you and . . . reject your name as evil, because of the Son of Man" (Luke 6:22). Crushed forever is any resemblance to the other crowd.

Hands off! when God is putting His saints through the experience of the millstones. We are apt to want to interfere in the discipline of another saint. Do not hinder the production of the bread that is to feed the world!

In the East the women sing as they grind the corn between the millstones. "The sound of the millstones is music in the ears of God." It is not music to the worldling, but the saint understands that His Father has a purpose in it all.

Ill-tempered persons, hard circumstances, poverty, willful misunderstandings, and estrangements are all millstones. Had Jesus any of these things in His life? Had He not! He had a devil in His company for three years! He was continually thwarted and misunderstood by the Pharisees. And is the disciple above his Master?

When these experiences come, remember that God has His eye on every detail.

But beware! lest the tiniest element of self-pity keeps God from putting us anywhere near the millstones. OSWALD CHAMBERS

~~~~~~ NOVEMBER 18 ~~~~~~

Evening

Blessed is he, whosoever shall not be offended in me.
LUKE 7:23 KJV

It is sometimes very difficult not to be offended in Jesus Christ, for the offense may be the result of my circumstances. I may find myself confined to narrow areas of service, or isolated from others through sickness or by taking an unpopular stance, when I had hoped for much wider opportunities. Yet the Lord knows what is best for me, and my surroundings are determined by Him. Wherever He places me, He does so to strengthen my faith and power and to draw me into closer communion with Himself. And even if confined to a dungeon, my soul will prosper.

The offense that causes me to turn from Christ may be emotional. I may be continually confused and troubled over questions I cannot solve. When I gave myself to Him, I had hoped that my skies would always be fair, but often they are overcast with clouds and rain. But I must believe that when difficulties remain, it is that I may learn to trust Him completely—to trust and not be afraid. And it is through my mental and emotional struggles that I am being trained to tutor others who are being tossed by the storm.

The offense causing me to turn away may be spiritual. I had imagined that once within His fold, I would never again suffer from the stinging winds of temptation. Yet it is best for me the way it is, for when I endure temptation His grace is magnified, my own character matures, and heaven seems sweeter at the end of the day.

Once I arrive at my heavenly home, I will look back across the turns and trials along my path and will sing the praises of my Guide. So whatever comes my way, I will welcome His will and refuse to be offended in my loving Lord. ALEXANDER SMELLIE

> *Blessed is he whose faith is not offended,*
> *When all around his way*
> *The power of God is working out deliverance*
> *For others day by day;*
>
> *Though in some prison dark his own soul does fail,*
> *Till life itself be spent,*
> *Yet still can trust his Father's love and purpose,*
> *And rest therein content.*
>
> *Blessed is he, who through long years of suffering,*
> *Not now from active toil,*
> *Still shares by prayer and praise the work of others,*
> *And thus "divides the spoil."*
>
> *Blessed are you, O child of God, who does suffer,*
> *And cannot understand*
> *The reason for your pain, yet will gladly leave*
> *Your life in His blest Hand.*

Yes, blessed are you whose faith is "not offended"
      By trials unexplained,
By mysteries unsolved, past understanding,
      Until the goal is gained.

FREDA HANBURY ALLEN

NOVEMBER 19

Morning

If your son asks.
LUKE 11:11

Henry Gibbud was a mission worker in the city of New York. He was a man of great devotion and wonderful power in prayer. On one occasion he had been working all night in the slums of the great city.

Tired and sleepy at the end of his toil, he made his way in the dark of the morning to the Brooklyn ferry dock. He put his hand in his pocket to pay his fare homeward, but to his dismay he discovered that he did not have the three pennies needed. His heart sank in deep discouragement, but he closed his eyes and began to pray. "Lord, I have been toiling all night in Thy service, trying to bring lost men and women to Thee. I am hungry and sleepy and wish to go home, but I do not have even three pennies for my fare. Will You not help me?"

As he closed his simple prayer, he opened his eyes. They fell upon something shining in the dust at his feet. He reached down and picked up the glittering object and found it was a fifty-cent piece. He paid his fare and went on his way rejoicing.

What was the joy that flooded his heart? It was the fulfillment of the precious promise: *"If a son shall ask"* (KJV).

Have you taken your place in God's presence, not as a stranger, but as a son?

"If a son, then an heir" (Galatians 4:7 KJV).

Heir of a mighty King, heir to a throne,
Why art thou wandering sad and alone?

Heir to the love of God, heir to His grace,
Rise to thy privilege, claiming thy place.

Heir of a Conqueror, why dost thou fear?
Foes cannot trouble thee when He is near.
Child of the promises, be not oppressed,
Claim what belongs to thee, find sweetest rest.

Heir by inheritance! child of thy God!
Right to thy sonship is found in His Word;
Walk with the noble ones, never alone;
Prince of the Royal Blood, come to thy throne.

Heirs! we are joint-heirs with Jesus our Lord!
Heirs of the Covenant, found in His Word!
Rise to thy privilege, heir to His grace!
Heir to the love of God, rise, claim thy place!

SELECTED

~~~~ NOVEMBER 19 ~~~~
Evening

Though you have made me see troubles, many and
bitter, you will restore my life again.

PSALM 71:20

God *makes* you "see troubles." Sometimes, as part of your education being carried out, you must "go down to the depths of the earth" (Psalm 63:9), travel subterranean passages, and lie buried among the dead. But not for even one moment is the bond of fellowship and oneness between God and you strained to the point of breaking. And ultimately, from the depths, He "will restore [your] life again."

Never doubt God! Never say that He has forsaken or forgotten you or think that

He is unsympathetic. He "*will* restore [your] life again." No matter how many twists and turns the road may have, there is always one smooth, straight portion. Even the longest day has a sunset, and the winter snow may stay quite some time, but it will finally melt.

Be steadfast, "because you know that your labor in the Lord is not in vain" (1 Corinthians 15:58). He will turn to you again and comfort you. And when He does, your heart that has forgotten how to sing will break forth in thankful and jubilant song, just like the psalmist who sang, "My tongue will sing of your righteousness" (Psalm 51:14). Selected

> *Though the rain may fall and the wind be blowing,*
> *And chilled and cold is the wintry blast;*
> *Though the cloudy sky is still cloudier growing,*
> *And the dead leaves tell that the summer has passed;*
> *My face is fixed on the stormy heaven,*
> *My heart is as calm as the summer sea,*
> *Glad to receive what my God has given,*
> *Whate'er it be.*
> *When I feel the cold, I can say, "He sends it,"*
> *And His winds blow blessing, I surely know;*
> *For I've never a need but that He will meet it;*
> *And my heart beats warm, though the winds may blow.*

NOVEMBER 20
Morning

Lord, *I know that people's lives are not their own . . . to direct their steps.*
JEREMIAH 10:23

We were at the foot of Mont Blanc in the village of Chamouni. A sad thing had happened the day before. A young physician had determined to reach the heights of Mont Blanc. He accomplished the feat and the little village was illuminated in his honor; on the mountainside a flag was floating that told of his victory.

After they had ascended, and descended as far as the hut, he wanted to be released from his guide; he wanted to be free from the rope, and insisted on going on alone.

The guide remonstrated with him, telling him it was not safe; but he tired of the rope, and declared that he would be free. The guide was compelled to yield. The young man had gone only a short distance when his foot slipped on the ice and he could not stop himself from sliding down the icy steeps. The rope was gone, so the guide could not hold him nor pull him back. Out on the shelving ice lay the body of the young physician.

The bells had been rung, the village had been illumined in honor of his success; but alas, in a fatal moment he refused to be guided; he was tired of the rope.

Do you get tired of the rope? God's providences hold us, restrain us, and we get tired sometimes. We need a guide, and shall until the dangerous paths are over. Never get disengaged from your Guide. Let your prayer be "Lead Thou me on," and sometime the bells of heaven will ring that you are safe at home! CHARLES H. SPURGEON

Oh, tame me, Lord! rebellious nature calm.
Oh, tame me, Lord!
This heart so tossed and filled with wild alarm;
Oh, tame me, Lord!

These human longings, let them end in Thee,
And let me be Thy bond-slave—

Even me.
"THE MARECHAL"

~~~~~ NOVEMBER 20 ~~~~~
Evening

Blessed is the one who waits.
DANIEL 12:12

Waiting may seem like an easy thing to do, but it is a discipline that a Christian soldier does not learn without years of training. Marching and drills are much easier for God's warriors than standing still.

There are times of indecision and confusion, when even the most willing person, who eagerly desires to serve the Lord, does not know what direction to take. So what should you do when you find yourself in this situation? Should you allow yourself to be overcome with despair? Should you turn back in cowardice or in fear or rush ahead in ignorance?

No, you should simply wait—but *wait in prayer*. Call upon God and plead your case before Him, telling Him of your difficulty and reminding Him of His promise to help.

Wait in faith. Express your unwavering confidence in Him. And believe that even if He keeps you waiting until midnight, He will come at the right time to fulfill His vision for you.

Wait in quiet patience. Never complain about what you believe to be the cause of your problems, as the children of Israel did against Moses. Accept your situation exactly as it is and then simply place it with your whole heart into the hand of your covenant God. And while removing any self-will, say to Him, "Lord, 'Not my will, but yours be done' [Luke 22:42]. I do not know what to do, and I am in great need. But I will wait until You divide the flood before me or drive back my enemies. I will wait even if You keep me here many days, for my heart is fixed on You alone, dear Lord. And my spirit will wait for You with full confidence that You will still be my joy and my salvation, 'for you have been my refuge, [and] a strong tower against the foe' [Psalm 61:3]."

MORNING BY MORNING

> *Wait, patiently wait,*
> *God never is late;*
> *Your budding plans are in Your Father's holding,*
> *And only wait His grand divine unfolding.*
> *Then wait, wait,*
> *Patiently wait.*
> *Trust, hopefully trust,*
> *That God will adjust*
> *Your tangled life; and from its dark concealings,*
> *Will bring His will, in all its bright revealings.*

Then trust, trust,
Hopefully trust.
Rest, peacefully rest
On your Savior's breast;
Breathe in His ear your sacred high ambition,
And He will bring it forth in blest fruition.
Then rest, rest,
Peacefully rest!

MERCY A. GLADWIN

～～～ NOVEMBER 21 ～～～

Morning

I was left alone, gazing at this great vision.
DANIEL 10:8

What lonely men were the great prophets of Israel! John the Baptist stood alone from the crowd! Paul had to say, *"Everyone deserted me"* (2 Timothy 4:16). And who was ever more alone than the Lord Jesus?

Victory for God is never won by the multitude. The man who dares to go where others hold back will find himself alone, but he will see the glory of God, and enter into the secrets of eternity. GORDON WATT

I go alone
Upon the narrow way that leads
Through shadowed valleys, over rocky heights,
To glorious plains beyond;
And sometimes when the way is very lone
I cry out for companionship, and long
For fellow-travelers on the toilsome path,
Until a Voice of sweetest music whispers,
"My grace sufficient is, no other guide thou needst but
    Me." And then the path grows brighter as
I go alone.

My Savior knows
The way I take. Himself has trod
The selfsame road. He knows each stone,
Temptations, pitfalls hid by blossoms fair,
The hour of darkness that my life must share,
The wilderness of sorrow, doubt, and fear,
Renunciation's agony, and every pang
Of loneliness and labor's wear; enough for me
That He has known it all, that now He stays
To strengthen, guide and help me. I am glad
My Savior knows.

Thy will be done
Whether on pleasant paths I walk along,
Or crouch amid the lightnings of the storm,
Whether for me the larks of springtime sing,
Or winter's icy blasts my being sting;
Whatever Thou dost send is best for me,
With joyful heart I take it all from Thee,
Rejoicing in Thy sovereignty, and pray
That Thou wilt lead me on my upward way;
The road grows smoother as I travel on.
Thy will be done.

Amy L. Person

The lone wolf travels a lonely path, *but he beats the pack to the kill!*

~~~~~ NOVEMBER 21 ~~~~~

Evening

Commit your way to the Lord.

Psalm 37:5

</div>

Talk to God about whatever may be pressuring you and then commit the entire matter into His hands. Do this so that you will be free from the confusion, conflicts, and cares that fill the world today. In fact, anytime you are preparing to do something, undergoing some trial, or simply pursuing your normal business, tell the Father about it. Acquaint Him with it; yes, even *burden Him with it*, and you will have put the concerns and cares of the matter behind you. From that point forward, exercise quiet, sweet diligence in your work, recognizing your dependence on Him to carry the matter for you. Commit your cares and yourself with them, as one burden, to your God. R. Leighton

> *Build a little fence of trust*
> *Around today;*
> *Fill the space with loving work*
> *And therein stay.*
> *Look not through the protective rails*
> *Upon tomorrow;*
> *God will help you bear what comes*
> *Of joy or sorrow.*
>
> Mary Butts

You will find it impossible to "commit your way to the Lord," unless your way has met with His approval. It can only be done through faith, for if there is even the slightest doubt in your heart that your way is not a good one, faith will refuse to have anything to do with it. Also, this committing of your way to Him must be continuous, not just one isolated action. And no matter how unexpected or extraordinary His guidance may seem and no matter how close to the edge of the cliff He may lead you, never snatch the guiding reins from His hands.

Are you willing to submit all your ways to God, allowing Him to pass judgment on them? There is nothing a Christian needs to more closely examine than his own confirmed views and habits, for we are so prone to taking God's divine approval of them for granted. And that is why some Christians are so anxious and fearful. They have obviously not truly committed their way to the Lord and *left it with Him*. They took it to Him but walked away with it again. Selected

Morning

God does all these things to a person.
JOB 33:29

In a certain old town was a great cathedral. And in that cathedral was a wondrous stained-glass window. Its fame had gone abroad over the land. From miles around people pilgrimaged to gaze upon the splendor of this masterpiece of art. One day there came a great storm. The violence of the tempest forced in the window, and it crashed to the marble floor, shattered into a hundred pieces. Great was the grief of the people at the catastrophe which had suddenly bereft the town of its proudest work of art. They gathered up the fragments, huddled them in a box, and carried them to the cellar of the church. One day there came along a stranger and craved permission to see the beautiful window. They told him of its fate. He asked what they had done with the fragments; and they took him to the vault and showed him the broken morsels of glass. "Would you mind giving these to me?" said the stranger. "Take them along," was the reply, "they are no longer of any use to us." The visitor carefully lifted the box and carried it away in his arms. Weeks passed by; then one day came an invitation to the custodians of the cathedral. It was from a famous artist, noted for his master-skill in glass-craft. It summoned them to his study to inspect a stained-glass window, the work of his genius. Ushering them into his studio he stood them before a great veil of canvas. At the touch of his hand upon a cord the canvas dropped. And there before their astonished gaze shone a stained-glass window surpassing in beauty all their eyes had ever beheld. As they gazed entranced upon its rich tints, wondrous patterns, and cunning workman-ship the artist turned and said: "This window I have wrought from the fragments of your shattered one, and it is now ready to be replaced."

Once more a great window shed its beauteous light into the dim aisles of the old cathedral, but the splendor of the new far surpassed the glory of the old, and the fame of its strange fashioning filled the land.

Do you say that your plans have been crushed? Then know this: Jesus Christ is a matchless life-mender. *Try Him!* JAMES H. McCONKEY

Evening

Do you believe that I am able to do this?
MATTHEW 9:28

God deals with impossibilities. It is never too late for Him to do so, as long as that which is impossible is brought to Him in complete faith by the person whose life and circumstances would be impacted if God is to be glorified. If we have experienced rebellion, unbelief, sin, and ruin in our life, it is never too late for God to deal triumphantly with these tragic things, if they are brought to Him in complete surrender and trust.

It has often been said, and truthfully so, that Christianity is the only religion that can deal with a person's past. God "will repay you for the years the locusts have eaten" (Joel 2:25), and He is trustworthy to do it unreservedly. He does so not because of *what* we are but because of *who* He is. God forgives and heals and restores, for He is "the God of all grace" (1 Peter 5:10). May we praise Him and trust Him. SUNDAY SCHOOL TIMES

Nothing is too hard for Jesus
No man can work like Him.

We have a God who delights in impossibilities and who asks, "Is anything too hard for me?" (Jeremiah 32:27). ANDREW MURRAY

Morning

These are those who. . . . follow the Lamb wherever he goes.
REVELATION 14:4

There are three classes in the Christian life; the men *of the wing*, the men *of the couch*, and the men *of the road*.

The *first* are those who fly before; they are the pioneers of progress; they are in advance of their fellows.

The *second* are those who stand still, or rather lie still; they are the invalids of the human race—they come not to minister but to be ministered unto.

The *third* are those who follow; they are *the ambulance corps of humanity;* they are the sacrificial souls that come on behind. I think with John that these last are the most beautiful souls of all. They are lovely in their unobtrusiveness; they do not wish to lead, choosing rather to be in the rear; they come forward only when others are driven backward. They want no glory from the battle, no wreath for the victory, no honorable mention among the heroes. They seek the wounded, the dying, the dead; they anoint for life's burial; they bring spices for the crucified; they give the cup of cold water; they wash the soiled feet. They break the fall of Adam; of Magdalene. They take in Saul of Tarsus after he becomes blind. They are attracted by defects; they are lured by every form of helplessness.

> *They come out to meet the shadows: they go in the track not of*
> *the lark, but of the nightingale; they follow the Lamb.*

Give me the trouble without the glitter, O Lord! Let others lead! I am content to follow. Help me to serve Thee in the background! Is it not written *they that tarry at home divide the spoil?* I cannot fight Thy battles, but I can nurse Thy wounded. I cannot repel Thy foes, but I can repair Thy fortress. I cannot conduct Thy marches, but I can succor those who have fainted by the way.

Write my name amongst those *who follow Thee!*

O Captain of my Salvation, *put me with the ambulance corps!* GEORGE MATHESON

> *What though the hindmost place is thine,*
> *And thou art in the rear?*
> *This need not cause thy heart a pang,*
> *Nor cost thine eye a tear.*
> *The post of duty is the place*
> *Where oft the Captain shows His face.*
>
> *All cannot charge or lead the van,*
> *All can be brave and true;*

And where the Captain's standards wave
There's work for all to do;
And work from which thou may'st not flee,
Which must be done, and done by thee.

Among the stragglers, faint and few,
Thou dost thy march pursue;
This need not make thy heart to droop,
The weak may yet be true;
Through many a dark and stormy day
The Captain thus holds on His way.

SELECTED

"They will set out last, under their standards" (Numbers 2:31).

~ NOVEMBER 23 ~
Evening

You have shown your people desperate times.
PSALM 60:3

I have always been glad that the psalmist said to God that certain times of life are desperate or difficult. Make no mistake about it, there are difficult things in life.

This summer someone gave me some beautiful pink flowers, and as I took them, I asked, "What kind are they?" My friend answered, "They are rock flowers. They grow and bloom only on rocks where you can see no soil." Then I thought of God's flowers growing in desperate times and hard places, and I somehow feel that He may have a certain tenderness for His "rock flowers" that He may not have for His lilies and roses.
MARGARET BOTTOME

The trials of life are sent to make us, not to break us. Financial troubles may destroy a person's business but build up his character. And a direct blow to the outer person may be the greatest blessing possible to the inner person. So if God places or allows anything difficult in our lives, we can be sure that the real danger or trouble will be what we will lose if we run or rebel against it. MALTBIE D. BABCOCK

> Heroes are forged on anvils hot with pain,
> And splendid courage comes but with the test.
> Some natures ripen and some natures bloom
> Only on blood-wet soil, some souls prove great
> Only in moments dark with death or doom.

God finds His best soldiers on the mountain of affliction.

$$\sim\!\!\sim\!\!\sim \text{ NOVEMBER 24 } \sim\!\!\sim\!\!\sim$$

Morning

> For I know the plans I have for you," declares the LORD, "plans to prosper
> you and not to harm you, plans to give you hope and a future."
>
> JEREMIAH 29:11

> The love of God a perfect plan
> Is planning now for thee,
> It holds "a future and a hope,"
> Which yet thou canst not see.

> Though for a season, in the dark,
> He asks thy perfect trust,
> E'en that thou in surrender "lay
> Thy treasure in the dust,"

> Yet He is planning all the while,
> Unerringly He guides

The life of him, who holds His will
More dear than all besides.

Trust were not trust if thou couldst see
The ending of the way,
Nor couldst thou learn His songs by night,
Were life one radiant day.

Amid the shadows here He works
The plan designed above,
"A future and a hope" for thee
In His exceeding love.

"A future"—abiding fruit,
With loving kindness crowned;
"A hope"—which shall thine own transcend,
As Heaven the earth around.

Though veiled as yet, one day thine eyes
Shall see His plan unfold,
And clouds that darkened once the path
Shall shine with Heaven's gold.

Enriched to all eternity
The steadfast soul shall stand,
That, "unoffended," trusted Him
Who all life's pathway planned.

I have an heritage of bliss,
Which yet I may not see;
The Hand that bled to make it mine,
Is keeping it for me.

FREDA HANBURY ALLEN

Evening

Be still, and know that I am God.
PSALM 46:10

Is there any note in all the music of the world as mighty as the grand pause? Is there any word in the Psalms more eloquent than the word "Selah," meaning pause? Is there anything more thrilling and awe-inspiring than the calm before the crashing of the storm, or the strange quiet that seems to fall upon nature before some supernatural phenomenon or disastrous upheaval? And is there anything that can touch our hearts like the *power of stillness*?

For the hearts that will cease focusing on themselves, there is "the peace of God, which transcends all understanding" (Philippians 4:7); "quietness and trust" (Isaiah 30:15), which is the source of all strength; a "great peace" that will never "make them stumble" (Psalm 119:165); and a deep rest, which the world can never give nor take away. Deep within the center of the soul is a chamber of peace where God lives and where, if we will enter it and quiet all the other sounds, we can hear His "gentle whisper" (1 Kings 19:12).

Even in the fastest wheel that is turning, if you look at the center, where the axle is found, there is no movement at all. And even in the busiest life, there is a place where we may dwell alone with God in eternal stillness.

There is only one way to know God: "Be still, and know." "The LORD is in his holy temple; let all the earth be silent before him" (Habakkuk 2:20). SELECTED

All-loving Father, sometimes we have walked under starless skies that dripped darkness like drenching rain. We despaired from the lack of light from the sun, moon, and stars. The gloomy darkness loomed above us as if it would last forever. And from the dark, there spoke no soothing voice to mend our broken hearts. We would gladly have welcomed even a wild clap of thunder, if only to break the torturing stillness of that mournfully depressing night.

Yet Your soft whisper of eternal love spoke more sweetly to our bruised and bleeding souls than any winds that breathe across a wind harp. It was Your "gentle whisper" that spoke to us. We were listening and we heard You, and then we looked and saw Your face, which was radiant with the light of Your love. And when we heard Your voice and saw Your face, new life returned to us, just as life returns to withered blossoms that drink the summer rain.

NOVEMBER 25
Morning

Take your son . . . whom you love.
GENESIS 22:2

Take now thy son . . . whom thou lovest.
KJV

God's command is "Take *now*," not presently. To go to the height God shows can never be done *presently*. It must be done *now*.

"*Sacrifice him there as a burnt offering on a mountain I will show you*" (v. 2). The mount of the Lord is the very height of the trial into which God brings His servant. There is no indication of the cost to Abraham; his implicit understanding of God so far outreaches his explicit knowledge that he trusts God utterly and climbs the highest height on which God can ever prove him, and remains unutterably true to Him.

There was not conflict; *that was over*. Abraham's confidence was fixed; he did not consult with flesh and blood—his own or anyone else's; he *instantly* obeyed. The point is, that though all other voices should proclaim differently, obedience to the dictates of the Spirit of God at all costs is to be the attitude of the faithful soul.

Always beware when you want to confer with your own flesh and blood—(i.e., your own sympathies, your own insight). When our Lord is bringing us into personal relationship with Himself, it is always the individual relationship He breaks down.

If God has given the command, He will look after everything; your business is to *get up and go!* OSWALD CHAMBERS

"The Holy Spirit says: 'Today'" (Hebrews 3:7).

> *Not of the sunlight,*
> *Not of the moonlight,*
> *Not of the starlight!*

O young Mariner,
Down to the haven
Call your companions,
Launch your vessel
And crowd your canvas,
And, ere it vanishes
Over the margin,
After it, follow it,
Follow the Gleam.

TENNYSON

~~~ NOVEMBER 25 ~~~

Evening

"Take the arrows. . . . Strike the ground." He struck it three times
and stopped. The man of God was angry with him and said,
"You should have struck the ground five or six times."

2 KINGS 13:18–19

How striking and powerful is the message of these words! Jehoash, king of Israel, thought he had done quite well when he struck the ground "three times and stopped." To him, it seemed to be an extraordinary act of his faith, but the Lord and the prophet Elisha were deeply disappointed, *because he had stopped halfway.*

Yes, he did receive something; in fact, he received a great deal—exactly what he had believed God for, in the final analysis. Yet Jehoash did not receive everything that Elisha meant for him to have or that the Lord wanted to bestow on him. He missed much of the meaning of the promise, and the fullness of the blessing. He did receive more than any human could have offered, but he did not receive God's best.

Dear believer, how sobering is the truth of this story! How important it is for us to learn to pray through our circumstances and to fully examine our hearts with God's message to us!

Otherwise, we will never claim all the fullness of His promise or all the possibilities that believing prayer offers. A. B. SIMPSON

"To him who is able to do immeasurably more than all we ask or imagine, according to his power that is at work within us, to him be glory" (Ephesians 3:20–21).

In no other place does the apostle Paul use these seemingly redundant words: "immeasurably more than all." Each word is packed with God's infinite love and power "to do" for His praying believers. Yet there is the following limitation: "according to his power that is at work within us." He will only do as much *for* us as we will allow Him to do *in* us. The same power that saved us, washed us with His blood, filled us with the power of His Holy Spirit, and protected us through numerous temptations will work *for* us to meet every emergency, every crisis, every circumstance, and every adversary. THE ALLIANCE

NOVEMBER 26

Morning

Come with me by yourselves to a quiet place and get some rest.
MARK 6:31

There is one pause in music of which the untrained singer does not know the value—the pause: it is not the cessation of the music; it is a part of it.

Before the tide ebbs or flows, there is always a time of poise when it is neither ebbing nor flowing.

In a Christian life that is to be effective, there will always be the *pause* and the *poise*.

The desert has been God's training school for many of His prophets—Abraham, Moses, Elijah, Paul. But not all who come from Arabia are prophets, and God has other schools. Before the years of witness, there were the years of stillness. Every witness with a great message has these years. Let not the saints shrink from the discipline and training! The sightless days will mean a grander vision; the silent years, the sweeter song. If the Lord puts you in the dark, it is but to strengthen your eyes to bear the glory that He is preparing for you; if He bids you be silent, it is but to tune your tongue to His praise. Remember that the *pause* is part of the music.

The great Composer writes the theme
And gives us each a part to play;

To some a sweet and flowing air,
Smooth and unbroken all the way;

They pour their full heart's gladness out
In notes of joy and service blent;
But some He gives long bars of "rests,"
With idle voice and instrument.

He who directs the singing spheres,
The music of the morning stars,
Needs, for His full creation's hymn,
The quiet of the soundless bars.

Be silent unto God, my soul,
If this the score He writes for thee,
And "hold the rest," play no false note
To mar His perfect harmony.

Yet be thou watchful for thy turn,
Strike on the instant, true and clear,
Lest from the grand, melodious whole
Thy note be missing to His ear.

ANNIE JOHNSON FLINT

～～ NOVEMBER 26 ～～

Evening

> Caleb asked her, "What can I do for you?" She replied, "Do me a
> special favor. Since you have given me land in the Negev, give me also
> springs of water." So Caleb gave her the upper and lower springs.
> JOSHUA 15:18–19

There are both "upper and lower springs" in life, and they are *springs*, not stagnant pools. They are the joys and blessings that flow from heaven above, through the hottest summer and through the most barren desert of sorrow and trials. The land belonging to Acsah was in the Negev under the scorching sun and was often parched from the burning heat. But from the hills came the inexhaustible springs that cooled, refreshed, and fertilized all the land.

These springs flow through the low places, the difficult places, the desert places, the lonely places, and even the ordinary places of life. And no matter what our situation may be, these springs can always be found. Abraham found them amid the hills of Canaan. Moses found them among the rocks of Midian. David found them among the ashes of Ziklag, when his property was gone and his family had been taken captive. And although his "men were talking of stoning him . . . David found strength in the Lord his God" (1 Samuel 30:6).

Isaiah found them in the terrible days when King Sennacherib of Assyria invaded Judah, when the mountains themselves seemed to be thrown into the midst of the sea. Yet his faith could still sing: "There is a river whose streams make glad the city of God, the holy place where the Most High dwells. God is within her, she will not fall" (Psalm 46:4–5).

The Christian martyrs found them amid the flames, the church reformers amid their enemies and struggles, and we can find them each day of the year if we have the Comforter in our hearts and have learned to say with David, *"All my springs of joy are in you"* (Psalm 87:7 NASB).

How plentiful and how precious these springs are, and how much more there is to be possessed of God's own fullness! A. B. SIMPSON

I said, "The desert is so wide!"
I said, "The desert is so bare!
What springs to quench my thirst are there?
Where will I from the tempest hide?"

I said, "The desert is so lone!
No gentle voice, nor loving face
To brighten any smallest space."
I paused before my cry was done!

I heard the flow of hidden springs;
Before me palms rose green and fair;
The birds were singing; all the air
Was filled and stirred with angels' wings!

And One asked softly, "Why, indeed,
Take overanxious thought for what
Tomorrow brings you? See you not
The Father knows just what you need?"

SELECTED

NOVEMBER 27

Morning

Pure nard, an expensive perfume.
JOHN 12:3

Love's reckoning will always be unusual. It was by no means the ordinary thing to do for the homeless Savior; that breaking of the alabaster and that lavish anointing were quite out of the usual way.

Did Mary's heart beat painfully as she glided in with her hoarded treasure? Did she intuitively hide her purpose from all eyes but His, who read its irrepressible meaning? Perhaps she thought only of Him who was her *all*.

Apparently she obtained her spikenard for the very purpose that she might anoint the Lord's body in burial. Possibly it was only an impulse which made her decide to anoint Him beforehand. . . . Let us rejoice that she made the Master's heart glad before it was too late.

One tiny violet of encouragement will mean more to those with whom we live today than will acres of orchids when their pulses are stilled in death.

There were four women who set out later with their spices, only to find the empty tomb.

The opportunity for anointing had passed.

It is passing today! Not in realms of glory will we be able to share in His sufferings, to help in bearing the Cross. Here, and here alone such service may be ours.

O soul of mine, be extravagant in love of Jesus!

There is no fragrance like that of my alabaster box—the box I break for Him!

> I shall not pass this way again,
> But far beyond earth's "where and when,"
> May I look back along the road
> Where on both sides good seed I sowed.
>
> I shall not pass this way again;
> May wisdom guide my tongue and pen,
> And love be mine, that so I may
> Plant roses all along the way.
>
> I shall not pass this way again;
> Grant me to soothe the hearts of men,
> Faithful to friends, true to my
> God; a fragrance on the path I trod.

NOVEMBER 27

Evening

Nothing will be impossible with God.
LUKE 1:37 NASB

High in the snow-covered Alpine valleys, God works one of His miracles year after year. In spite of the extremes of sunny days and frozen nights, a flower blooms unblemished through the crust of ice near the edge of the snow. How does this little flower, known as the soldanelle plant, accomplish such a feat?

During the past summer the little plant spread its leaves wide and flat on the ground in order to soak up the sun's rays, and it kept that energy stored in its roots throughout the winter. When spring came, life stirred even beneath its shroud of snow, and as the plant sprouted, it amazingly produced enough warmth to thaw a small dome-shaped pocket of snow above its head.

It grew higher and higher, and as it did, the small dome of air continued to rise just above its head until its flower bud was safely formed. At last the icy covering of the air compartment gave way, and the blossom burst into the sunshine. The crystalline texture of its mauve-colored petals sparkled like the snow itself, as if it still bore the marks of the journey it had endured.

This fragile flower sounds an echo in our hearts that none of the lovely flowers nestled in the warm grass of the lower slopes could ever awaken. Oh, how we love to see impossible things accomplished! And so does God.

Therefore may we continue to persevere, for even if we took our circumstances and cast all the darkness of human doubt upon them and then hastily piled as many difficulties together as we could find against God's divine work, we could never move beyond the blessedness of His miracle-working power. May we place our faith completely in Him, for He is the God of the impossible. SELECTED

~~~ NOVEMBER 28 ~~~

Morning

He remains faithful forever.
PSALM 146:6

God never forgets His Word. Long ago He promised a Redeemer; and although *He waited four thousand years,* the promise at last was most surely fulfilled.

He promised Abraham a son; and although a quarter of a century of testing intervened, the promise at last came literally true. He promised Abraham the Land of Promise as an inheritance; and although *four hundred years* of trial intervened, at last the land was possessed. *He promised Jeremiah* that after *seventy years* the captives should return from Babylon; and on the very hour, the action answered to the Word. *He promised Daniel* that at a definite time Messiah should appear; and the most extraordinary evidence that we have to offer to the doubting Hebrew today that Jesus is his Messiah, is the literal fulfillment of the prophecy of Daniel.

Just as true are God's promises to the believer. They are all "Yea and Amen" in

Christ Jesus. He has guaranteed them. The promises of God form a great checkbook. Every one is endorsed by the Mediator, and His word and honor are pledged to their fulfillment. To make them "Yea and Amen," *you must sign your name* upon the back of the promise and then *personally appropriate it.*

"Anyone who believes in him will never be put to shame." (Romans 10:11).

NOVEMBER 28

Evening

Where morning dawns, where evening fades, you call forth songs of joy.
PSALM 65:8

Have you ever risen early, climbed a hill, and watched God make a morning? The dull gray gives way as He pushes the sun toward the horizon, and then the tints and hues of every color begin to blend into one perfect light as the full sun suddenly bursts into view. As king of the day, the sun moves majestically across the sky, flooding the earth and every deep valley with glorious light. At this point, you can hear the music of heaven's choir as it sings of the majesty of God Himself and of the glory of the morning.

> *In the holy hush of the early dawn*
> *I hear a Voice—*
> *"I am with you all the day,*
> *Rejoice! Rejoice!"*

The clear, pure light of the morning made me yearn for the truth in my heart, which alone could make me pure and clear as the morning itself and tune my life to the concert pitch of nature around me. And the breeze that blew from the sunrise made me hope in God, who had breathed into my nostrils the breath of life. He had so completely filled me with His breath, mind, and Spirit that I would only think His thoughts and live His life. Within His life I had found my own, but now it was eternally glorified.

What would we poor humans do without our God's nights and mornings! GEORGE MACDONALD

In the early morning hours,
'Twixt the night and day,
While from earth the darkness passes
Silently away;

Then it's sweet to talk with Jesus
In your bedroom still—
For the coming day and duties
Ask to know His will.

Then He'll lead the way before you,
Laying mountains low;
Making desert places blossom,
Sweet'ning sorrow's flow.

Do you want a life of triumph,
Victory all the way?
Then put God in the beginning
Of each coming day.

～～～ NOVEMBER 29 ～～～

Morning

From this day on I will bless you.
HAGGAI 2:19

God has certain dates from which He begins to bless us. On the day of consecration (Genesis 22:16–17), the day when our all is surrendered to Him—on that day untold blessing begins.

Have we come to *that date?*

"It was on the 22nd of July, 1690, that happy day," says Madame Guyon, "that my soul was delivered from all its pains. On that day I was restored, as it were, to perfect liberty. I was *no longer depressed,* no longer borne down under the burden of sorrow. I had thought God lost, and lost forever; but I found Him again. And He returned to me with unspeakable magnificence and purity. In a wonderful manner difficult to explain, *all that which had been taken from me was not only restored, but restored with increase and new advantages. In Thee, O my God, I found it all, and more than all!* The peace which I now possessed was all holy, heavenly, inexpressible. What I had possessed some years before, in the period of my spiritual enjoyment, was consolation, peace—the *gifts* of God, but now that I was fully yielded to the will of God, whether that will was consoling or otherwise, I might now be said to possess not merely consolation, but the God of consolation; not merely peace, but the God of peace.

One day of this happiness, which consisted in simple rest or harmony with God's will, whatever that will might be, was sufficient to counterbalance years of suffering.

Certainly it was not I, myself, who had fastened my soul to the Cross and, under the operations of a providence just but inexorable, had drained, if I may so express it, the blood of the life of nature to the last drop. I did not understand it then; but I understand it *now*. It was the Lord who did it. *It was God that destroyed me, that He might give me true life.*

> *Oh, the Spirit-filled life may be thine, may be thine,*
> *In thy soul evermore the Shechinah may shine;*
> *It is thine to live with the tempests all stilled,*
> *It is thine with the blest Holy Ghost to be filled;*
> *It is thine, even thine, for thy Lord has so willed.*

~~~ NOVEMBER 29 ~~~

Evening

Later on, however . . .
HEBREWS 12:11

There is a legend that tells of a German baron who, at his castle on the Rhine, stretched wires in the air from tower to tower so that the wind might treat them as a wind harp and thereby create music as it blew across them. Yet as the soft breezes swirled around the castle, no music was born.

One night, however, a fierce storm arose, and the hill where the castle sat was struck with the fury of the violent wind. The baron looked out his doorway on the terror of the wind, and the wind harp was filling the air with melodies that rang out even above the noise of the storm. It had taken a fierce storm to produce the music!

Haven't we all known people whose lives have never produced any pleasing music during their days of calm prosperity but who, when fierce winds have blown across their lives, have astonished us by the power and beauty of their music?

> Rain, rain
> Beating against the pane!
> How endlessly it pours
> Out of doors
> From the darkened sky—
> I wonder why!
> Flowers, flowers,
> Springing up after showers,
> Blossoming fresh and fair,
> Everywhere!
> God has now explained
> Why it rained!

You can always count on God to make the "later on" of difficulties a thousand times richer and better than the present, if we overcome them correctly. "No discipline seems pleasant at the time. . . . Later on, however, it produces a harvest of righteousness and peace" (Hebrews 12:11). What a yield!

NOVEMBER 30

Morning

The battle is the LORD's.

1 SAMUEL 17:47

How prone we are to lose sight of this, and to imagine, because we see only our little corner in the conflict, that the battle is ours!

If the battle is the Lord's, then the responsibilities for planning belong to Him.
Everything connected with the line of attack, the method of defense, must belong to Him. We need not be anxious as to the enemy's subtlety, activity, or power.

"As commander of the army of the Lord I have now come" (Joshua 5:14).

He has a full view of the enemy's movements and a perfect knowledge of the enemy's devices. He has anticipated all the enemy's wiles. It is impossible for Him to be deceived or to be taken by surprise. It is His glory that is at stake, the honor of His name that is being assailed. *He is able to withstand the mightiest foe!*

If the battle is the Lord's, the supplies will be all-sufficient. No one knows how much is wanted in the day of battle like that General who has been through many campaigns. *We shall lack nothing to make us victorious warriors.*

The Victory is certain! The Captain on whose side we are has never known defeat. He goes forth conquering and to conquer. The enemy may apparently gain temporary advantage at different points of the battle, but *victory over Christ by Satan is simply impossible!*

But He expects us to *rest* in His wisdom. In the thick of the fight, in the midst of the smoke and din of battle, we may fail to see the wisdom of all God's ways. When we cannot see, it is then that we must *rest in His wisdom.* Let us have confidence in His power, and be obedient to His commands.

I will not fear the battle, if Thou art by my side.

"But thanks be to God, who always leads us . . . in Christ's triumphal procession" (2 Corinthians 2:14).

Queen Victoria said, "We are not interested in the possibilities of defeat. They do not exist!"

～～～NOVEMBER 30～～～
Evening

Should you then seek great things for yourself? Do not seek them.
For I will bring disaster on all people, declares the LORD, *but*
wherever you go I will let you escape with your life.
JEREMIAH 45:5

This is a promise given to you for the difficult places in which you may find yourself—a promise of safety and life even in the midst of tremendous pressure. And it is a promise that adjusts itself to fit the times as they continue to grow more difficult, as we approach the end of this age and the tribulation period.

What does it mean when it says that you will "escape with your life"? It means your life will be snatched from the jaws of the Enemy, as David snatched the lamb from the lion. It does not mean you will be spared the heat of the battle and confrontation with your foes, but it means "a table before [you] in the presence of [your] enemies" (Psalm 23:5), a shelter from the storm, a fortress amid the foe, and a life preserved in the face of continual pressure. It means comfort and hope from God, such as Paul received when he and his friends "were under great pressure, far beyond [their] ability to endure, so that [they] despaired even of life" (2 Corinthians 1:8). And it means the Lord's divine help, such as when Paul's "thorn in the flesh" (2 Corinthians 12:7 KJV) remained, but the power of Christ came to rest upon him, and he learned that God's "grace is sufficient" (2 Corinthians 12:9).

May the Lord "wherever you go . . . let you escape with your life" and help you today to be victorious in your difficulties. DAYS OF HEAVEN UPON EARTH

We often pray to be delivered from afflictions, and even trust God that we will be. But we do not pray for Him to make us what we should be while in the midst of the afflictions. Nor do we pray that we would be able to live within them, for however long they may last, in the complete awareness that we are held and sheltered by the Lord and can therefore continue within them without suffering any harm.

The Savior endured an especially difficult test in the wilderness while in the presence of Satan for forty days and nights, His human nature weakened by the need for food and rest. The three Hebrew young men were kept for a time in the flames of "the furnace heated seven times hotter than usual" (Daniel 3:19). In spite of being forced to endure the tyrant's last method of torture, they remained calm and composed as they waited for their time of deliverance to come. And after surviving an entire night sitting among the lions, "when Daniel was lifted from the den, no wound was found on him, because he had trusted in his God" (Daniel 6:23).

They were able to endure in the presence of their enemies because they dwelt in the presence of their God.

Morning

They saw no one except Jesus.
MATTHEW 17:8

When Samuel Rutherford lay in Aberdeen prison, we are told he used to write at the top of his letters, "God's Palace, Aberdeen."

When Madame Guyon was imprisoned in the castle at Vincennes, she said: "It seems as though I were a little bird whom the Lord has placed in a cage, and that I have nothing now to do but sing."

And prisons shall palaces prove if Jesus abides with me there.

I never had in all my life so great an inlet into the Word of God as now; those Scriptures that I saw nothing in before, are in this place and state [in Bedford Jail] made to shine upon me; Jesus Christ also was never more real and apparent than now; here I have seen and felt Him indeed! JOHN BUNYAN

The New Testament tells of no regret on the part of those who sacrificed themselves for Christ. The apostles never pathetically recite the story of what they gave up for the Christian ministry. The ancient martyrs sometimes kissed the stake at which they suffered so cruelly.

This is the spirit in which we should lose, suffer, and die for Christ's sake.

By thus renouncing all, we gain all. Nothing yields higher interest than loving self-denials for the highest claims.

I have seen the headlight of a giant engine rushing onward through the darkness, heedless of opposition and fearless of danger. I have seen the lightning at midnight leap athwart a storm-swept sky, splintering chaotic darkness with beams of light until the heavens glittered like midday sun. I knew this was grand, but the grandest thing this side of the light that flows from God Almighty's throne is the blessed benediction of a human life that spends itself in forgetful service for a brokenhearted world and finds its home at last in the bosom of the everlasting God.

> *I walk alone, and I am sore afraid;*
> *My way is dark, my path with thorns o'erlaid;*

Draw near me, Lord, and take my trembling hand
And make me brave to join Thy pilgrim band.

Thou hast a band which fears not dark nor death,
Which suffers agony at every breath,
Yet sings with joy e'en in the midst of pain,
With whom the greatest loss is greatest gain.

Who would not walk with such a company?
Who would not sing with such an ecstasy?
Did I say lone and fear? May God forgive
And teach me, e'en through sorrow, how to live.

Life is not life which knows no shrinking fears;
Life is not life which sheds no bitter tears;
This is true life when, through dark suffering,
One learns from Christ and men brave conquering.

Then lead me on thou martyr-host of God!
Then lead me on, O Christ, to Thine abode;
There with Thy holy ones I shall find rest
And learn that death, in life, was God's great best.

HENRY W. FROST

───── ～～～ DECEMBER 1 ～～～ ─────

Evening

There remains, then, a Sabbath-rest for the people of God.

HEBREWS 4:9

[That rest includes victory:] "The LORD gave them rest on every
side. . . . The LORD gave all their enemies into their hands."

JOSHUA 21:44

Thanks be to God! He gives us the victory through our LORD Jesus Christ.
1 CORINTHIANS 15:57

A prominent believer once told of his mother, who was a very anxious and troubled Christian. He would often talk with her for hours, trying to convince her of the sinfulness of worrying, but to no avail. She was like the elderly woman who once said that she had suffered a great deal, especially from the troubles that never came.

Then one morning his mother came to breakfast with a smile adorning her face. He asked her what had happened, and she began describing a dream she had in the night. In her dream, she was walking along a highway with a large crowd of people, all of whom seemed very tired and burdened. The people were all carrying little black bundles, and she noticed that more bundles were being dropped along the way by numerous repulsive-looking creatures that seemed quite demonic in nature. As the bundles were dropped, the people stooped down to pick them up and carry them.

Like everyone else in her dream, she also carried her needless load, being weighted down with the Devil's bundles. After a while, she looked up and saw a Man whose face was loving and bright as He moved through the crowd, comforting the people. Finally He came to her, and she realized it was her Savior. She looked at Him, telling Him how tired she was, and He smiled sadly and said, "My dear child, these bundles you carry are not from me, and you have no need of them. They are the Devil's burdens, and they are wearing out your life. You need to drop them and simply refuse to touch them with even one of your fingers. Then you will find your path easy, and you will feel as if 'I carried you on eagles' wings' [Exodus 19:4]."

The Savior touched her hand, and peace and joy quickly filled her soul. As she saw herself in her dream casting her burdens to the ground and ready to throw herself at His feet in joyful thanksgiving, she suddenly awoke, finding that all her worries were gone.

From that day forward to the end of her life, she was the most cheerful and happy member of her family.

> *And the night will be filled with music,*
> *And the cares that besiege the day,*
> *Will fold their tents like the Arabs,*
> *And will silently steal away.*
> HENRY WADSWORTH LONGFELLOW

Morning

He is altogether lovely.
SONG OF SONGS 5:16

What a glorious fact it is that there is one life that can be held up before the eyes of humanity as *a perfect pattern!* There were lips that never spoke unkindness, that never uttered an untruth; there were eyes that never looked aught but love and purity and bliss; there were arms that never closed against wretchedness or penitence; there was a bosom which never throbbed with sin, nor ever was excited by unholy impulse; there was a man free from all undue selfishness, and whose life was spent in going about doing good.

There was One who loved all mankind, and who loved them more than Himself, and who gave Himself to die that they might live; there was One who went into the gates of death, that the gates of death might never hold us in; there was One who lay in the grave, with its dampness, its coldness, its chill, and its horror, and taught humanity how it might ascend above the grave; there was One who, though He walked on earth, had His conversation in heaven, who took away the curtain that hid immortality from view, and presented to us the Father God in all His glory and in all His love.

Such One is the standard held up in the Church of Christ. The Church rallies round the Cross and gathers around Jesus; and it is because He is so attractive, and lovely, and glorious, that they are coming from the ends of the earth to see the salvation of God. BISHOP MATTHEW SIMPSON

Less than Thyself, Oh do not give. In might Thyself within me live; Come all Thou hast and art.

Oh, there is nothing so admirable, nothing which seems to us in our best moods so worthy of our seeking and so rich in its possession as that holiness which is the summit of true perfection; not a holiness which is distant and frigid, but a holiness which makes the eyes more tender in their softened light, and the lips more affluent of genial speech, and the hand more helpful in its ready service; which makes an end in the human heart of its passions and selfishness, its moroseness and its meanness; which lifts man up to God, and brings God down to man; and which, should it become pervasive and universal, would make every soul a miniature heaven, and change our woeful earth into a Paradise regained. BISHOP NINDE

"And we all, who with unveiled faces contemplate the Lord's glory, are being transformed into his image with ever-increasing glory, which comes from the Lord, who is the Spirit" (2 Corinthians 3:18).

> *The honeysuckle blossoms drenched with rain*
> *That lend enchantment to a summer night;*
> *The purple violet hidden from the sight*
> *Beside the border of a country lane;*
> *The jasmine vine, which hangs its golden chain*
> *Within the forest like a twinkling light,*
> *Have flourished for a time and taken flight—*
> *Their ashes have returned to earth again.*
> *But what of one whose life was like a flower*
> *Which scatters gentle perfume everywhere,*
> *Whose face had caught the radiance of the sky*
> *From looking ever upward till that hour*
> *When the Great Gardener stripped the branches bare?*
> *God smells such fragrance from His throne on high.*
>
> "FRAGRANCE" BY THOMAS KIMBER

~~~ DECEMBER 2 ~~~

Evening

Perfect through sufferings.
HEBREWS 2:10 KJV

Steel is the product of iron *plus* fire. Soil is rock *plus* heat and the crushing of glaciers. Linen is flax *plus* the water that cleans it, the comb that separates it, the flail that pounds it, and the shuttle that weaves it. In the same way, the development of human character requires a *plus* attached to it, for great character is made not through luxurious living but through suffering. And the world does not forget people of great character.

I once heard the story of a mother who brought a crippled boy with a hunched back into her home as a companion for her own son. She warned her son to be very careful not to refer to the other boy's deformity, since this was a sensitive matter to him. And she encouraged him to play with his new friend as if he were a normal child. But after listening to her son play with him for a few minutes, she heard him ask his companion, "Do you know what that is on your back?" The crippled boy was embarrassed, hesitated a moment, but before he could respond, his friend answered the question for him by saying, "It is the box that holds your wings, and someday God is going to break it open, and you will fly away to be an angel."

Someday God is going to reveal this fact to every Christian: the very things they now rebel against are the instruments He has used to perfect their character and to mold them into perfection, so they may later be used as polished stones in His heaven yet to come. CORTLAND MYERS

Suffering is a wonderful fertilizer for the roots of character. The great objective of this life is character, for it is the only thing we can carry with us into eternity. And gaining as much of the highest character possible is the purpose of our trials. AUSTIN PHELPS

The mountain of vision is won by no other road than the one covered with thorns.

～～～ DECEMBER 3 ～～～

Morning

That they may have life . . . to the full.
JOHN 10:10

What a contrast there is between a barren desert and the luxuriant oasis with its waving palms and its glorious verdure! Between gaunt and hungry flocks and the herds that lie down in green pastures and beside the still waters; between the viewless plain and the mountain height with its "land of far distances."

What a difference there is between the aridity of an artificial, irrigated, stinted existence—a desert existence—and a life of abundant rains, crowding vegetation, and harvests that come almost of themselves—*the abundant life!*

The former is like the *shallow stream* where your boat every moment touches bottom or strikes some hidden rock; the latter is where your deep keel never touches ground, and you ride *the ocean's wildest swells!*

There are some Christians who always seem to be kept on scant measure. Their spiritual garments are threadbare, their whole bearing that of people who are poverty-stricken and kept on short allowance—hard up, and on the ragged edge of want and bankruptcy. They come through "by the skin of their teeth" and are "saved so as by fire."

There are other souls who *"have life . . . to the full."* Their love "always protects, always trusts, always hopes, always perseveres" and "never fails" (1 Corinthians 13:7, 8). Their patience has "longsuffering with joyfulness" (Colossians 1:11 KJV). Their peace "transcends all understanding" (Philippians 4:7). Their joy is "inexpressible and glorious" (1 Peter 1:8). Their service is so free and glad that duty is a delight. In a word, this life reaches out into the infinite as well as the eternal, sailing on the shoreless and fathomless seas of God and His infinite grace.

Oh, *where* is such a life to be found? How can the desert place be made to bring forth *life to the full?*

> *"Oh, where is the sea?" the fishes cried,*
> *As they swam the crystal waters through*
> *"We have heard from of old of the ocean tide,*
> *And we long to look on the waters blue.*
> *The wise ones speak of the infinite sea—*
> *Oh, who can tell us if such there be?"*

Are we who live in the sea of the infinite to imitate those silly fishes, and ask, "*Where* is the God who is 'not far from every one of us,' who may be in our inmost hearts by faith, and in whom 'we live, and move, and have our being'?" (Acts 17:27–28 KJV). DEAN FARRAR

"Have you journeyed to the springs of the sea?" (Job 38:16).

The psalmist said: "With you is the fountain of life" (Psalm 36:9). "All my fountains are in you" (Psalm 87:7).

Gushing Fountains!

Evening

"Is your husband all right? Is your child all right?" "Everything is all right," she said.

2 KINGS 4:26

> Be strong, my soul!
> Your loved ones go
> Within the veil. God's yours, e'en so;
>   Be strong.
>
> Be strong, my soul!
> Death looms in view.
> Lo, hear your God! He'll bear you through;
>   Be strong.

For sixty-two years and five months I had my beloved wife, and now, in my ninety-second year, I am left alone. But I turn to the ever present Jesus as I walk around my room, and say, "Lord Jesus, I am alone. Yet I am not alone, for You are with me and are my Friend. Now, Lord, please comfort me, strengthen me, and give to Your poor servant everything that You see I need."

We should never be satisfied until we have come to the place where we know the Lord Jesus in this way—until we have discovered He is our eternal Friend—continually, under all circumstances, and constantly ready to prove Himself as our Friend. GEORGE MUELLER

Afflictions cannot injure when we blend them with submission.

Ice on trees will bend many a branch to the point of breaking. Similarly, I see a great many people bowed down and crushed by their afflictions. Yet every now and then I meet someone who sings in affliction, and then I thank God for my own circumstance as well as his. There is never a song more beautiful than that which is sung in the night. You may remember the story of a woman who, when her only child died, looked toward heaven as with the face of an angel and said, "I give you joy, my sweet child." That solitary, simple sentence has stayed with me for many years, often energizing and comforting me. HENRY WARD BEECHER

E'en for the dead I will not bind my soul to grief;
  Death cannot long divide.
For is it not as though the rose that climbed my garden wall
Has blossomed on the other side?
    Death does hide,
    But not divide;
You are but on Christ's other side!
You are with Christ, and Christ with me;
In Christ united still are we.

～～～ DECEMBER 4 ～～～
Morning

Be ye . . . tenderhearted.
EPHESIANS 4:32 KJV

It is much easier to convince a human soul of its natural impurity than to convince it of its natural hardness and utter destitution of heavenly and Divine tenderness. *The very essence of the Gospel is Divinely imparted tenderness and sweetness of spirit.* Even among intensely religious people, nothing is rarer to find than a continuous and all-pervading spirit of tenderness.

Tenderness of spirit is not the tenderness of mind and manner which results from high culture and a beautiful social training, though these are very valuable in life. No, *it is a supernatural work throughout the whole spiritual being. It is an exquisitely interior fountain of God's own sweetness and tenderness of nature, opened up in the inner spirit to such a degree that it completely inundates the soul, overflowing all the mental faculties and saturating with its sweet waters the manners, expressions, words, and tones of the voice; mellowing the will, softening the judgment, melting the affections, refining the manners, and molding the whole being after the image of Him who was infinitely meek and lowly in heart.*

Tenderness of spirit cannot be borrowed or put on for special occasions; it is emphatically supernatural and must flow out incessantly from the inner fountains of the life.

Deep tenderness of spirit is the very soul and marrow of the Christ life. What specific gravity is to the planet, what beauty is to the rainbow, what perfume is to the rose, what marrow is to the bone, what rhythm is to poetry, what the pulse is to the heart, what harmony is to music, what heat is to the human body—all this, and much more, is tenderness of spirit to religion. It is possible to be very religious, and staunch, and persevering in all Christian duties; possible, even, to be sanctified, to be a brave defender and preacher of holiness, to be mathematically orthodox and blameless in outward life and very zealous in good works, and yet to be greatly lacking in tenderness of spirit—that all-subduing, all-melting love, which is the very cream and quintessence of Heaven and which incessantly streamed out from the voice and eyes of the blessed Jesus.

I would that I could be
A wound-dresser
Of souls—
Reaching the aching heart,
The tortured mind,
Calming them as the night
Calms tired bodies
When she drops the mantle of sleep
Over the world.
As each cold, glittering star
So might I stand in mine,
But with the warmth of a
smile On my face,
And in my eyes
An image of the Soul Divine.

~~~ DECEMBER 4 ~~~
Evening

He went up on a mountainside by himself.
MATTHEW 14:23

One of the blessings of the old-time Sabbath day was the calmness, restfulness, and holy peace that came from having a time of quiet solitude away from the world. There is a special strength that is born in solitude. Crows travel in flocks, and wolves in packs, but the lion and the eagle are usually found alone.

Strength is found not in busyness and noise but in quietness. For a lake to reflect the heavens on its surface, it must be calm. Our Lord loved the people who flocked to Him, but there are numerous accounts in the Scriptures of His going away from them for a brief period of time. On occasion He would withdraw from the crowd and quite often would spend His evenings alone in the hills. Most of His ministry was performed in the towns and cities by the seashore, but He loved the hills more and at nightfall would frequently seclude Himself in their peaceful heights.

The one thing we need today more than anything else is to spend time alone with our Lord, sitting at His feet in the sacred privacy of His blessed presence. Oh, how we need to reclaim the lost art of meditation! Oh, how we need "the secret place" (Psalm 91:1 KJV) as part of our lifestyle! Oh, how we need the power that comes from waiting upon God! SELECTED

> It is good to live in the valley sweet,
>   Where the work of the world is done,
> Where the reapers sing in the fields of wheat,
>   And work till the setting of the sun.
> But beyond the meadows, the hills I see
>   Where the noises of traffic cease,
> And I follow a Voice who calls out to me
>   From the hilltop regions of peace.
>
> Yes, to live is sweet in the valley fair,
>   And work till the setting of the sun;
> But my spirit yearns for the hilltop's air
>   When the day and its work are done.
> For a Presence breathes o'er the silent hills,
>   And its sweetness is living yet;
> The same deep calm all the hillside fills,
>   As breathed over Olivet.

Every life that desires to be strong must have its "Most Holy Place" (Exodus 26:33) into which only God enters.

~~~~~ DECEMBER 5 ~~~~~
Morning

Do not be anxious about anything.
PHILIPPIANS 4:6

I recall an experience in my own Christian life," wrote James H. McConkey. "My father was dying of a disease *brought on by worriment*. A great physician had been summoned from the city. He was closeted with my father for a long time. Then he came out of the sick chamber soberly shaking his head. There was no hope. My father's earthly race was run. My dear mother asked the great doctor to take me aside for a conference; for I myself was breaking in body, and from the same dread enemy which overthrows so many Christian people—*anxious care*.

"The kind physician took me into another room and we sat down for a heart-to-heart talk. Very searchingly, and with all the skill of an expert, did he draw from me the humiliating fact that I was a prey of worriment and suffering from its dread results. In a few keen, incisive sentences, with no attempt at concealment, he told me that I had fallen a victim of the same habit that had been my father's undoing, and that unless I overcame it there was no hope for me even as there was none for him.

"I went upstairs. I threw myself upon my knees in my bedchamber. I cried out in my agony of soul: 'O Christ! He says I must overcome worriment, and Thou alone knowest how I have *tried* to do so. I have fought; I have struggled; I have wept bitter tears. And *I have failed*. Oh, Lord Jesus, unless Thou dost undertake for me now it is all over with me.'

"Then and there I threw myself in utter helplessness upon Christ. Somehow, where before I had been struggling, I now found myself trusting as I had never quite done before. From that time onward Jesus Christ began to give me the beauty of victory for the somber ashes of defeat."

It is God's will that I should cast

On Him my care each day;
He also bids me not to cast
My confidence away.
But, Oh! I am so stupid, that
When taken unawares,
I cast away my confidence,
And carry all my cares.

DECEMBER 5

Evening

LORD, *I know that people's lives are not their own;*
it is not for them to direct their steps.
JEREMIAH 10:23

Lead me in a straight path.
PSALM 27:11

Many people want to direct God instead of surrendering themselves to be directed by Him. They want to show Him the way instead of submissively following where He leads. MADAME GUYON

I said, "Let me walk in the field";
    God said, "No, walk in the town";
I said, "There are no flowers there";
    He said, "No flowers, but a crown."

I said, "But the sky is black,
    There is nothing but noise and din";
But He wept as He sent me back,
    "There is more," He said, "there is sin."

I said, "But the air is thick,
   And smog is veiling the sun";
He answered, "Yet souls are sick,
   And your work is yet undone."

I said, "I will miss the light,
   And friends will miss me, they say";
He answered me, "Choose tonight,
   If I am to miss you, or they."

I pleaded for time to be given;
   He said, "Is it hard to decide?
It will not seem hard in Heaven
   To have followed the steps of your Guide."

I cast one look at the field,
   Then set my face to the town;
He said, "My child, do you yield?
   Will you leave the flowers for the crown?"

Then into His hand went mine,
   And into my heart came He;
And I walk in a light Divine,
   The path I had feared to see.

GEORGE MacDONALD

～～～ DECEMBER 6 ～～～
Morning

He will deliver the needy who cry out.
PSALM 72:12

Bending down to us in infinite love, God says: "My child, *how needy are you?* What heavy burden is upon *you?* What grievous sorrow is darkening your faith? What fear of future ill is shadowing your pathway? What spiritual thirst do you want slaked? What barrenness of soul enriched? What do you need this hour? For I will deliver the needy."

To miss a need may be to miss a miracle!

You are just the one God is looking for—just the one who is ripe for deliverance— just the special individual to whom His promise is made. The human incompleteness meets the Divine completeness, and the want is filled. The deepest yearning in every soul finds in Him the longed-for satisfaction.

Do not be too anxious to be free from needs, unless you want to be free from prayer-power.

We need our needs!

O God, I need Thee!
When morning crowds the night away
And the tasks of waking seize my mind,
I need Thy Poise.

O God, I need Thee!
When clashes come with those
Who walk the way with me,
I need Thy Smile.

O God, I need Thee!
When the path to take before me lies,
I see it—courage flees—
I need Thy Faith.

O God, I need Thee!
When the day's work is done,
Tired, discouraged, wasted;
I need Thy Rest.

I am coming soon. Hold on to what you have, so that no one will take your crown.

REVELATION 3:11

George Mueller, a leader among the Plymouth Brethren, once shared this testimony: "In July 1829 it pleased God to reveal to my heart the truth regarding the return of the Lord Jesus and to show me that I had made a great mistake by sitting back and watching for the complete conversion of the world. It produced the following effect on me: Deep within my soul, I was moved to feel compassion for perishing sinners and for a world lulled to sleep by the wicked Enemy. And I began to think, 'Should I not do whatever I can for the Lord Jesus and try to awake His slumbering church before He returns?'"

There may still be many difficult years of hard work ahead of us before the fulfillment of His prophetic return, but the signs of His coming today are very encouraging. In fact, I would not be at all surprised if I saw the apocalyptic angel spread its wings for its last triumphal flight before today's sunset. Nor would I be surprised if tomorrow morning's news thrilled us with the proclamation that Christ the Lord had arrived atop the Mount of Olives or Mount Calvary to declare His worldwide dominion.

O dead churches, wake up! O Christ, descend! Scarred head, take Your crown! Bruised hands, take Your scepter! Wounded feet, take Your throne! "For thine is the kingdom" (Matthew 6:13 KJV). THOMAS DeWITT TALMAGE

It may be in the evening,
 When the work of the day is done,
And you have time to sit in the twilight,
 And watch the sinking sun,
While the long bright day dies slowly
 Over the sea,
And the hours grow quiet and holy
 With thoughts of Me;
While you hear the village children
 Running along the street—

Among those passing footsteps
　　　May come the sound of My Feet.
Therefore I tell you, Watch!
　　　By the Light of the evening star
When the room is growing darker
　　　As the clouds afar,
Let your door be closed and latched
　　　In your home,
For it may be in the evening
　　　I will come.

DECEMBER 7

Morning

We have given you only what comes from your hand.
1 CHRONICLES 29:14

Who gives himself with his gifts feeds three—
Himself, his hungering neighbor, and Me.
LOWELL

Andrew, I have only five barley loaves left and a couple of fish, but the Master shall have most of it. Here are three loaves, four—but one loaf I should like to keep. You know, Andrew, it is a long way home, but the four loaves and the fishes I will give to Him."

As Andrew explains that the Master would like to have *all*, a struggle goes on in the boy's heart. He looks repeatedly, first at the fifth loaf, then at the Master. "Andrew, take all," he exclaims joyously as the light breaks. "Take all five, and the fishes, too."

What is the fifth loaf that you have not yet surrendered? Let me plead with you to let Him have *all*. PASTOR DOLMAN

Was it the "widow's mite" or "all her living" that caught our Lord's attention (Mark 12)?

It was Martin Luther who wrote: "I have had many things in my hands, and I have lost them all; but whatever I have been able to place in God's hands I still possess."

There is a Divine law in connection with our giving. Christ with a few loaves and fish feeds thousands.

> *Give! as the morning that flows out of heaven;*
> *Give! as the waves when their channel is riven;*
> *Give! as the free air and sunshine are given!*
> *Lavishly, utterly, joyfully give!*
> *Not the waste drops of thy cup overflowing;*
> *Not the faith sparks of thy hearth ever glowing;*
> *Not a pale bud from the June roses blowing:*
> *Give as He gave thee who gave thee to live.*
> *Almost the day of thy giving is over;*
> *Ere from the grass dies the bee-haunted clover*
> *Thou wilt have vanished from friend and from lover:*
> *What shall thy longing avail in the grave?*
> *Give as the heart gives whose fetters are breaking—*
> *Life, love, and hope, all thy dreams and thy waking;*
> *Soon, heaven's river thy soul-fever slaking,*
> *Thou shalt know God and the gift that He gave.*
>
> ROSE TERRY COOKE

～～～ DECEMBER 7 ～～～
Evening

You will see neither wind nor rain, yet this valley will be filled with water, and you, your cattle and your other animals will drink. This is an easy thing in the eyes of the LORD; he will also deliver Moab into your hands.

2 KINGS 3:17–18

To human reason, what God was promising seemed simply impossible, but nothing is too difficult for Him. Without any sound or sign and from sources invisible and seemingly impossible, the water flowed the entire night, and "the next morning . . . there it was . . . ! And the land was filled with water. . . . The sun was shining on the water. . . . [And it] looked red—like blood" (vv. 20, 22).

Our unbelief is always desiring some *outward sign*, and the faith of many people is largely based on sensationalism. They are not convinced of the genuineness of God's promises without some visible manifestation. But the greatest triumph of a person's faith is to "be still, and know that [He is] God" (Psalm 46:10).

The greatest victory of faith is to stand at the shore of the impassable Red Sea and to hear the Master say, "*Stand firm and you will see the deliverance the LORD will bring you today*" (Exodus 14:13), and "*Move on*" (Exodus 14:15). As we step out in faith, without any sign or sound, taking our first steps into the water, we will see the water divide. Continuing to march ahead, we will see a pathway open through the very midst of the sea.

Whenever I have seen God's wondrous work in the case of some miraculous healing or some extraordinary deliverance by His providence, the thing that has always impressed me most was the absolute quietness in which it was done. I have also been impressed by the absence of anything sensational and dramatic, and the utter sense of my own uselessness as I stood in the presence of this mighty God, realizing how easy all this was for Him to do without even the faintest effort on His part, or the slightest help from me.

It is the role of faith not to *question* but to simply *obey*. In the above story from Scripture, the people were asked to "make this valley full of ditches" (2 Kings 3:16 KJV). The people obeyed, and then water came pouring in from some supernatural source to fill them. What a lesson for our faith!

Are you desiring some spiritual blessing? Then dig the ditches and God will fill them. But He will do this in the most unexpected *places* and in the most unexpected *ways*. May the Lord grant us the kind of faith that acts "by faith, not by sight" (2 Corinthians 5:7), and may we expect Him to work although we see no wind or rain. A. B. SIMPSON

~~~ DECEMBER 8 ~~~

Morning

A great door for effective work has opened to me, and there are many who oppose me.

1 CORINTHIANS 16:9

Another expedition of Englishmen was trying to conquer Mt. Everest, the highest peak in the world.

Bitter cold, raging winds, a rarefied atmosphere, blinding blizzards, engulfing avalanches of snow and rock—all these dangers stood between brave men and the top of that towering mountain.

The last expedition came the nearest to success. A little more than two thousand feet below the peak, the main body of the party pitched their highest camp. From that base two men, Mallory and Irvine, equipped with oxygen tanks, attempted a final dash to the top.

They hoped to climb to the peak and return in about sixteen hours. They never came back. Of them the official record of the expedition said in simple words, "When last seen, *they were heading toward the summit.*"

> *Press on! Surmount the rocky steeps,*
> *Climb boldly o'er the torrent's arch;*
> *He fails alone who feeble creeps,*
> *He wins who dares the hero's march.*
> *Be thou a hero! Let thy might*
> *Tramp on eternal snows its way*
> *And through the ebon walls of night*
> *Hew down a passage unto day.*
>
> PARK BENJAMIN

The Kingdom of God will be brought in by Christians who, when last seen, *were heading toward the summit;* Christians who, with Paul, can accept the challenge of the "many adversaries" that guard the open door, even though they go down to defeat in their generation.

$$\sim\!\!\sim\!\!\sim \text{ DECEMBER 8 } \sim\!\!\sim\!\!\sim$$

Evening

As God's chosen people . . . clothe yourselves with . . . kindness.
COLOSSIANS 3:12

There is an old story of an elderly man who always carried a little can of oil with him everywhere he went, and when he would go through a door that squeaked, he would squirt a little oil on the hinges. If he encountered a gate that was hard to open, he would oil the latch. And so he went through life, lubricating all the difficult places, making it easier for all those who came after him. People called the man eccentric, strange, and crazy, but he went steadily on, often refilling his can of oil when it was nearly empty, and oiling all the difficult places he found.

In this world, there are many lives that painfully creak and grate as they go about their daily work. Often it seems that nothing goes right with them and that they need lubricating with "the oil of joy" (Psalm 45:7), gentleness, or thoughtfulness.

Do you carry your own can of oil with you? Are you ready with your oil of helpfulness each morning? If you offer your oil to the person nearest you, it may just lubricate the entire day for him. Your oil of cheerfulness will mean more than you know to someone who is downhearted. Or the oil may be a word of encouragement to a person who is full of despair. Never fail to speak it, for our lives may touch others only once on the road of life, and then our paths may diverge, never to meet again.

The oil of kindness has worn the sharp, hard edges off many a sin-hardened life and left it soft and pliable, ready to receive the redeeming grace of the Savior. A pleasant word is a bright ray of sunshine on a saddened heart. Therefore give others the sunshine and tell Jesus the rest.

We cannot know the grief
That men may borrow;
We cannot see the souls
Storm-swept by sorrow;
But love can shine upon the way
Today, tomorrow;
Let us be kind.
Upon the wheel of pain so many weary lives are broken,
So may our love with tender words be spoken.
Let us be kind.

"Be devoted to one another in love" (Romans 12:10).

Morning

I am carrying on a great project and cannot go down.
NEHEMIAH 6:3

One of Satan's favorite employees is the "switchman." He likes nothing better than to sidetrack one of God's express trains, sent on some blessed mission and filled with the fire of a holy purpose.

Something will come up in the pathway of an earnest soul, to attract its attention, and occupy its strength and thought. Sometimes it is a little irritation and provocation. Sometimes it is some petty grievance we stop to pursue or adjust.

Very often, and *before we are aware of it,* we are absorbed in a lot of distracting cares and interests that quite turn us aside from *the great purpose of our life.*

We may not do much harm, but we have missed our connection. We have gotten off the main line.

Let these things alone. Let distractions come and go, but press forward steadily and irresistibly with your God-given task. The eagle flying in the upper air pays but little or no attention to what is going on in the earth below him. As children of God we are to occupy our rightful place, "in the heavenlies," "far above all" these petty things (Ephesians 1:20–21). God would have us to be "eagle saints." *Let us not stoop from our position!* A. B. SIMPSON

An eagle does not catch flies!

—— DECEMBER 9 ——

Evening

*Our light and momentary troubles are achieving for us
an eternal glory that far outweighs them all.*
2 CORINTHIANS 4:17

The question is often asked, "Why is human life drenched in so much blood and soaked with so many tears?" The answer is found in the word "achieving," for these "momentary troubles are *achieving* for us" something very precious. They are teaching us not only the way to victory but, better still, the law of victory—there is a reward for every sorrow, and the sorrow itself produces the reward. It is the very truth expressed in this dear old hymn, written by Sarah Adams in 1840:

> *Nearer my God to Thee, nearer to Thee,*
> *E'en though it be a cross that raiseth me.*

Joy sometimes needs pain to give it birth. Fanny Crosby was a wonderful American hymn writer who lived from 1820 to 1915 and who wrote more than two thousand hymns. Yet she could never have written the beautiful words "I shall see Him face to face" if not for the fact that she had never gazed upon green fields, evening sunsets, nor even the twinkle in her mother's eye. It was the loss of her own vision that helped her to gain her remarkable spiritual discernment and insight.

It is comforting to know that sorrow stays only for the night and then takes its leave in the morning. And a thunderstorm is very brief when compared to a long summer day. Remember, "Weeping may stay for the night, but rejoicing comes in the morning" (Psalm 30:5). Songs in the Night

> *There is a peace that springs soon after sorrow,*
> *Of hope surrendered, not of hope fulfilled;*
> *A peace that does not look upon tomorrow,*
> *But calmly on the storm that it has stilled.*
>
> *A peace that lives not now in joy's excesses,*
> *Nor in the happy life of love secure;*
> *But in the unerring strength the heart possesses,*
> *Of conflicts won while learning to endure.*
>
> *A peace there is, in sacrifice secluded,*
> *A life subdued, from will and passion free;*
> *It's not the peace that over Eden brooded,*
> *But that which triumphed in Gethsemane.*

Morning

We live by faith, not by sight.
2 CORINTHIANS 5:7

F aith is taking God at His word. Faith is not belief without evidence. It is belief on the very best of evidence—the Word of Him "who does not lie" (Titus 1:2). Faith is so rational that it asks no other evidence than this all-sufficient evidence. To ask other than the Word of Him who cannot lie is not *rationalism,* but consummate *irrationalism.* R. A. TORREY

When we can *see,* it is *not faith but reasoning.*

Look at the faith of the master mariner! He looses his cable, he steams away from the land. For days, weeks, or even months, he sees neither sail nor shore; yet on he goes day and night without fear, till one morning he finds himself exactly opposite the desired haven toward which he had been steering.

How had he found his way over the trackless deep? He has trusted in his compass, his nautical almanac, his glass, and the heavenly bodies; and obeying their guidance, without sighting land, he has steered so accurately that he has not changed a point to enter port.

It is a wonderful thing—that sailing or steaming without sight. Spiritually it is a blessed thing to leave altogether the shores of sight and feeling; to say "Good-bye" to inward feelings, cheering providences, signs, tokens, and so forth. It is glorious to be far out on the ocean of Divine love, believing in God, and steering for Heaven straightaway, by the direction of the Word of God. CHARLES H. SPURGEON

DECEMBER 10

Evening

If we are distressed, it is for your comfort and salvation; if we are comforted,
it is for your comfort, which produces in you patient endurance of the same

sufferings we suffer. And our hope for you is firm, because we know that
just as you share in our sufferings, so also you share in our comfort.

2 Corinthians 1:6–7

Are there some people in your circle of friends to whom you naturally go in times of trials and sorrow—people who always seem to say just the right words and who give you the very counsel you so desire? If so, you may not realize the high cost they have paid to become so skilled at binding up your gaping wounds and drying your tears. Yet if you were to investigate their past, you would find they have suffered more than most other people.

They have watched the silver cord on which the lamp of life hung slowly unravel. They have seen the golden bowl of joy smashed at their feet, and its contents spilled. They have experienced raging tides, withering crops, and darkness at high noon, but all this has been necessary to make them into the nurses, physicians, and ministers of others.

Cartons containing spices from the Orient may be cumbersome to ship and slow in coming, but once they arrive the beautiful fragrances fill the air. In the same way, suffering is trying and difficult to bear, but hiding just below its surface is discipline, knowledge, and limitless possibilities. Each of these not only strengthens and matures us but also equips us to help others. So do not worry or clench your teeth, simply waiting with stubborn determination for the suffering to pass. Instead, be determined to get everything you can from it, both for yourself and for the sake of those around you, according to the will of God. Selected

> *Once I heard a song of sweetness,*
> *As it filled the morning air,*
> *Sounding in its blest completeness,*
> *Like a tender, pleading prayer;*
> *And I sought to find the singer,*
> *Where the wondrous song was borne;*
> *And I found a bird, quite wounded,*
> *Pinned down by a cruel thorn.*
>
> *I have seen a soul in sadness,*
> *While its wings with pain were furled,*

Giving hope, and cheer and gladness
    That should bless a weeping world
And I knew that life of sweetness,
    Was of pain and sorrow borne,
And a stricken soul was singing,
    With its heart against a thorn.

You are told of One who loved you,
    Of a Savior crucified,
You are told of nails that held Him,
    And a spear that pierced His side;
You are told of cruel scourging,
    Of a Savior bearing scorn,
And He died for your salvation,
    With His brow against a thorn.

You "are not above the Master."
    Will you breathe a sweet refrain?
And His grace will be sufficient,
    When your heart is pierced with pain.
Will you live to bless His loved ones,
    Though your life be bruised and torn,
Like the bird that sang so sweetly,
    With its heart against a thorn?

                                    SELECTED

DECEMBER 11

Morning

The LORD binds up the bruises of his people and heals the wounds he inflicted.

ISAIAH 30:26

When some friend has proved untrue—betrayed your simple trust; used you for his selfish end, and trampled in the dust the Past, with all its memories, and all its sacred ties, the light is blotted from the sky—for something in you dies.

Bless your false and faithless friend, just smile and pass along—God must be the judge of it: He knows the right and wrong . . . Life is short—don't waste the hours by brooding on the past; His great laws are good and just; Truth conquers at the last.

Red and deep our wounds may be—but after all the pain—God's own finger touches us, and we are healed again . . . With faith restored, and trust renewed—we look toward the stars—the world will see the smiles we have—but God will see the scars. "SCARS" BY PATIENCE STRONG

Love grows stronger when assailed;
Love conquers where all else has failed.
Love ever blesses those who curse;
Love gives the better for the worse.
Love unbinds others by its bonds;
Love pours forgiveness from its wounds.

Lord, let me love like Thee!

DECEMBER 11

Evening

Praise the LORD, all you servants of the LORD who minister by
night in the house of the LORD. . . . May the LORD bless you
from Zion, he who is the maker of heaven and earth.
PSALM 134:1, 3

You may see this as a strange time to worship—"minister[ing] by night in the house of the LORD." Indeed, worshiping at night, during the depth of our sorrows, is a difficult thing. Yet therein lies the blessing, for it is the test of perfect faith. If I desire to know the true depth of my friend's love, I must see how he responds during the winter seasons of my life. And it is the same with divine love.

It is easy for me to worship in the summer sunshine, when the beautiful melodies of life seem to fill the air, and the lush fruit of life is still on the trees. But when the songbirds cease and the fruit falls from the trees, will my heart continue to sing? Will I remain in God's house at night? Will I love Him simply for who He is? Am I willing to "keep watch for one hour" (Mark 14:37) with Him in His Gethsemane? Will I help Him carry His cross up the road of suffering to Calvary? Will I stand beside Him in His dying moments, with Mary, His mother, and John, the beloved disciple? Would I be able, with Joseph of Arimathea and Nicodemus, to take the dead Christ from His cross?

If I can do these things, then my worship is complete and my blessing glorious. Then I have indeed shown Him love during the time of His humiliation. My faith has seen Him in His lowest state, and yet my heart has recognized His majesty through His humble disguise. And at last I truly know that I desire not the gift but the Giver. Yes, when I can remain in His house through the darkness of night and worship Him, I have accepted Him for Himself alone. GEORGE MATHESON

> *My goal is God Himself, not joy, nor peace,*
> *Nor even blessing, but Himself, my God;*
> *It's His to lead me there, not mine, but His—*
> *"At any cost, dear Lord, by any road!"*
>
> *So faith bounds forward to its goal in God,*
> *And love can trust her Lord to lead her there;*
> *Upheld by Him, my soul is following hard*
> *Till the Lord has fulfilled my deepest prayer.*
>
> *No matter if the way is sometimes dark,*
> *No matter though the cost is often great,*
> *He knows the way for me to reach the mark,*
> *The road that leads to Him is sure and straight.*
>
> *One thing is sure, I cannot tell Him no;*
> *One thing I do, I press towards my Lord;*
> *Giving God my glory here, as I go,*
> *Knowing in heaven waits my Great Reward.*

He who promised is faithful.

HEBREWS 10:23

God's power will keep God's promises! Promises for the soul, promises for the body, promises for others, promises for our work, promises for our business, promises for time and for eternity: *these are all ours!* It is not your weakness that can defeat God's promise, nor your strength that can fulfill the promise: He that spoke the Word will Himself make it good. *It is neither your business nor mine to keep God's promises:* that is His grace.

The signed check is given us. How foolish if we fear to present it! *Never yet has one single check been dishonored!* "He who promised is faithful."

I take; He undertakes!

We may pray much over a promise and yet never obtain it. *Asking* is not *taking*. *Beseeching* is not *claiming*.

> *I clasp the hand of Love Divine,*
> *I claim the gracious promise mine,*
> *And add to His my countersign.*
> *I take, He undertakes.*
>
> *I simply take Him at His Word;*
> *I praise Him that my prayer is heard*
> *And claim my answer from the Lord.*
> *I take, He undertakes.*
>
> A. B. SIMPSON

Remember what you take *is all you will* ever get.

Evening

I am already being poured out like a drink offering, and the time for my departure is near. I have fought the good fight, I have finished the race, I have kept the faith.

2 TIMOTHY 4:6–7

Just as old soldiers compare their battle scars and stories of war when they get together, when we arrive at our heavenly home, we will tell of the goodness and faithfulness of God, who brought us through every trial along the way. I would not like to stand with the multitude clothed in robes made "white in the blood of the Lamb" (Revelation 7:14) and hear these words: "'These are they who have come out of the great tribulation'—*all except you.*"

How would *you* like to stand there and be pointed out as the only saint who never experienced sorrow? Never! You would feel like a stranger in the midst of a sacred fellowship. Therefore may we be content to share in the battle, for we will soon wear a crown of reward and wave a palm branch of praise. CHARLES H. SPURGEON

During the American Civil War, at the battle of Lookout Mountain, Tennessee, a surgeon asked a soldier where he was hurt. The wounded soldier answered, "*Right near the top of the mountain.*" He was not thinking of his gaping wound but was only remembering that he had won the ground near the top of the mountain.

May we also go forth to higher endeavors for Christ, never resting until we can shout from the mountaintop, "I have fought the good fight, I have finished the race, I have kept the faith."

> *Finish your work, then rest,*
>   *Till then rest never;*
> *Since rest for you with God*
> *Is rest forever.*

God will examine your life not for medals, diplomas, or degrees but for battle scars. A medieval singer once sang of his hero:

> *With his trusty sword for aid;*

Ornament it carried none,
But the notches on the blade.

What nobler medal of honor could any godly person seek than the scars of service, personal loss for the crown of reward, disgrace for the sake of Christ, and being worn out in the Master's service!

~~~~~~ DECEMBER 13 ~~~~~~

Morning

The peace of God, which transcends all understanding, will
guard your hearts and your minds in Christ Jesus.
PHILIPPIANS 4:7

There are depths in the ocean, I am told, which no tempest ever stirs—beyond the reach of all storms that sweep and agitate the surface of the sea. And there are heights in the blue sky above, to which no cloud ever ascends, where no tempest ever rages, where all is perpetual sunshine, where naught exists to disturb the deep serenity. *Even at the center of the cyclone there is rest.*

Each of these is an emblem of the soul which Jesus visits, to whom He speaks peace, whose fear He dispels, whose lamps of hope He trims.

During the test of a submarine it remained submerged for many hours. When it had returned to the harbor, the commander was asked: "Well, how did the storm affect you last night?" The Commander looked at him in surprise and said: "Storm? We knew nothing of any storm!"

Dwell deep. When doubts assail and stealthy shadows creep
Across your sky, and fill you with a sense of doom,
And thunders roar, and lightnings frighten with their glare,
And old foundations seem to crumble 'neath your feet,
Dwell deep and rest your soul amid eternal things.
Upon the surface storms may rage, and billows break
On every beach of life, and fling disaster

Far and wide; but if your soul is dwelling quiet
In the depths, naught can harm you evermore. Therefore
Dwell deep, and rest your head upon the heart of God.

"When he giveth quietness, who then can make trouble?" (Job 34:29 KJV).

DECEMBER 13
Evening

I will give you the treasures of darkness.
ISAIAH 45:3 NASB

In the famous lace shops of Brussels, there are special rooms devoted to the spinning of the world's finest lace, all with the most delicate patterns. The rooms are kept completely dark, except for the light that falls directly on the developing pattern, from one very small window. Only one person sits in each small room, where the narrow rays of light fall upon the threads he is weaving, for lace is always more beautifully and delicately woven when the weaver himself is in the dark, with only his work in the light.

Sometimes the darkness in our lives is worse, because we cannot even see the web we are weaving or understand what we are doing. Therefore we are unable to see any beauty or any possible good arising from our experience. Yet if we are faithful to forge ahead and "*if we do not give up*" (Galatians 6:9), someday we will know that the most exquisite work of our lives was done during those days when it was the darkest.

If you seem to be living in deep darkness because God is working in strange and mysterious ways, do not be afraid. Simply go forward in faith and in love, never doubting Him. He is watching and will bring goodness and beauty from all of your pain and tears. J. R. MILLER

The shuttles of His purpose move
  To carry out His own design;
Seek not too soon to disapprove
  His work, nor yet assign
Dark motives, when, with silent tread,

You view some somber fold;
For lo, within each darker thread
There twines a thread of gold.

Spin cheerfully,
Not tearfully,
He knows the way you plod;
Spin carefully,
Spin prayerfully,
But leave the thread with God.

CANADIAN HOME JOURNAL

～～ DECEMBER 14 ～～
Morning

They feast on the abundance of your house.
PSALM 36:8

Ask the eagle that splashes in the glory of the sun if it ever longs for its cage away down among the dim, distant earth scenes. If it ever stops to look at the old cage of former days, it is to sing its doxology of deliverance and soar away to its home near the sun.

The life of the Spirit-filled heart is *the winged life.* The unsurrendered life is the life of the cage. The best that the cage can give is a momentary thrill that soon gives place to a pitiful beating against the bars.

Our precious Savior, by His death on the Cross, proclaims "liberty to the captives" (Isaiah 61:1 KJV), and you may be *set free;* free, not to take refuge on the branches of a nearby tree but to rise and walk in heaven's own light, above the world and sin, with heart made pure, and garments white, and Christ enthroned within!

"They feast on the abundance of your house." The song in your heart will daily be: *"Thou, O Christ, art all I want; More than all in Thee I find."*

Forget the past, throw off your last fear, and leap boldly forward to *complete emancipation!*

O Christ, in Thee my soul hath found,
And found in Thee alone,
The peace, the joy I sought so long;
The bliss till now unknown.

I sighed for rest and happiness,
I yearned for them, not Thee;
But while I passed my Savior by,
His love laid hold on me.

I tried the broken cisterns, Lord,
But ah! the waters failed.
E'en as I stooped to drink they'd fled,
And mocked me as I wailed.

Now none but Christ can satisfy,
None other name for me;
There's love, and life, and lasting joy,
Lord Jesus, found in Thee!

DECEMBER 14

Evening

One of his disciples said to him, "LORD, teach us to pray. . . ." He
said to them, "When you pray, say: 'Your kingdom come.'"
LUKE 11:1–2

When one of the disciples said, "Teach us to pray," the Lord raised His eyes to the far horizon of His Father's world. He brought the ultimate goal of eternal life together with everything God desires to do in the life of humankind and packed it all into a powerful prayer that followed these words: "This, then, is how you should pray" (Matthew 6:9). And what a contrast between His prayer and what we often hear today!

How do we pray when we follow the desires of our own hearts? We say, "Lord, bless *me*, then my family, my church, my city, and my country." We start with those closest to us and gradually move outward, ultimately praying for the expansion of God's kingdom throughout the world.

Our Master's prayer, however, begins where we end. He taught us to pray for the world *first* and our personal needs second. Only after our prayer has covered every continent, every remote island of the sea, every person in the last hidden tribe, and every desire and purpose of God for the world are we taught to ask for a piece of bread for ourselves.

Jesus gave Himself for us and to us, paying a holy and precious price on the cross. After giving His all, is it too much for Him to ask us to do the same thing? No man or woman will ever amount to anything in God's kingdom or ever experience any of His power, until this lesson of prayer is learned—that Christ's business is the supreme concern of life and that all of our personal considerations, no matter how important or precious to us, are secondary. DR. FRANCIS

When Robert Moffat, the nineteenth-century Scottish explorer and missionary to South Africa, was once asked to write in a young lady's personal album, he wrote these words:

> *My album is a savage chest,*
> *Where fierce storms brood and shadows rest,*
> *Without one ray of light;*
> *To write the name of Jesus there,*
> *And see the savage bow in prayer,*
> *And point to worlds more bright and fair,*
> *This is my soul's delight.*

"His kingdom will never end" (Luke 1:33), or as an old Moravian version says, "His Kingdom shall have no frontier."

Missionary work should never be an afterthought of the church, because it is Christ's forethought. HENRY JACKSON VAN DYKE

Morning

*Whoever wants to be my disciple must deny themselves
and take up their cross and follow me.*

MATTHEW 16:24

In the light of eternity, who are those who shall stand before the throne arrayed in white robes? Are they those who have come out of ease and pleasure, out of untroubled calm and unbroken human relationships? Nay, rather they are those who have come out of great tribulation. Had Milton not been blind, neither he nor we could have seen so clearly, and he could never have written,

My vision Thou hast dimmed, that I may see Thyself, Thyself alone.

Out of blindness he learned the lesson so needed today by those cut off from an active life, that "They also serve who only stand and wait."

If Tennyson had not lost his friend Hallam, we should never have had his "In Memoriam."

One cannot have a victory without a battle! Character without conflict! Perfect love without suffering!

As we visit the pearl fisheries, we find that life without pain leaves no pearl; that the life lived in sluggish ease, unwounded, without suffering or long-continued friction, forms no jewel.

As we pass the dwellings of men we find that, without suffering, *the pearl of great price,* the highest human character, is not formed.

Suffering is linked with joy for those who take it aright. *If you suffer without succeeding, it is that someone else may succeed. If you succeed without suffering, it is because someone else has suffered.*

"*Is there no other way, O God,
Except through sorrow, pain and loss,*

To stamp Christ's image on my soul?
No other way except the Cross?"

And then a voice stills all my soul,
As stilled the waves on Galilee:
"Canst thou not bear the furnace heat,
If 'mid the flames I walk with thee?

"I bore the Cross, I know its weight, I drank the cup I hold
for thee; Canst thou not follow where I lead?
I'll give the strength—lean thou on me."
SELECTED

DECEMBER 15

Evening

Trust in him.
PSALM 37:5

The word *trust* is the heart of faith and is the Old Testament word given to the infant, or early, stages of faith. The word *faith* conveys more an act of the will, while the word *belief* conveys an act of the mind or intellect, but trust is the language of the heart. The words *faith* and *belief* refer more to a truth believed or to something expected to happen.

Trust implies more than this, for it sees and feels and it leans on those who have a great, living, and genuine heart of love. Therefore let us "trust also in him" (Psalm 37:5 KJV), through all the delays, in spite of all the difficulties, and in the face of all the rejection we encounter in life. And in spite of our feelings and evidence to the contrary, and even when we cannot understand our way or our situation, may we still "trust also in him; [for] he shall bring it to pass." The way will open, our situation will be changed, and the end result will be peace. The cloud will finally be lifted, and the light of eternal noonday will shine at last.

Trust and rest when all around you
    Puts your faith to stringent test;
Let no fear or foe confound you,
    Wait for God and trust and rest.

Trust and rest with heart abiding,
    Like a birdling in its nest,
Underneath His feathers hiding,
    Fold your wings and trust and rest.

～～～ DECEMBER 16 ～～～
Morning

"I have come that they may have life, and have it to the full."
JOHN 10:10

What a breathtaking truth! "I have come." Just another way of saying, *"Before Abraham was born, I am!"* (John 8:58). All others began to be; our Lord is *pretemporal,* definitely coming out of the eternities for a definite purpose: "That they may have life." This quality of life which the Biologist from Eternity gives, increases in *quantity* forever—*"To the full!"*

The abundant life which Christ offers is the possession alone of those whom He designates "my sheep." It is not an entering into material blessedness. It is a spiritual fullness conditional altogether upon likeness to the Lord and walking in that obedience toward God wherein He walked. Its first condition is the acceptance of the Cross whereby the world is crucified unto the believer and the believer unto the world. But, as this separation is recognized and accepted and the life is wholly yielded and kept subject to the will of the Father, the Master's incoming and indwelling meets every longing and every need. Then alone will be understood the meaning of the promise of our text: "I have come that they may have life, and have it to the full."

Have *we* come to the fountain of life? Are *we* drinking of its fullness? Are *we* living in His love? This is *the life of our spirit; the health of our body; the secret of our joy!*

May we seek this overflowing life, and become *"channels only,"* with *"all His*

wondrous power flowing through us" so that He can use us every day and every hour!
EVAN H. HOPKINS

Come to the everlasting spring and drink freely. It never runs dry!

> *Though millions their thirst are now slaking,*
> *It never runs dry,*
> *And millions may still come partaking,*
> *It never runs dry!*

DECEMBER 16

Evening

> *There was also a prophet, Anna. . . . She never left the temple*
> *but worshiped night and day, fasting and praying.*
> LUKE 2:36–37

There is no doubt that it is by praying that we learn to pray, and that the more we pray, the better our prayers will be. People who pray in spurts are never likely to attain to the kind of prayer described in the Scriptures as "powerful and effective" (James 5:16).

Great power in prayer is within our reach, but we must work to obtain it. We should never even imagine that Abraham could have interceded so successfully for Sodom if he had not communed with God throughout the previous years of his life. Jacob's entire night of wrestling at Peniel was certainly not the first encounter he had with his God. And we can even look at our Lord's most beautiful and wonderful prayer in John 17, before His suffering and death, as the fruit of His many nights of devotion, and of His rising often before daybreak to pray.

If a person believes he can become powerful in prayer without making a commitment to it, he is living under a great delusion. The prayer of Elijah, which stopped the rain from heaven and later opened heaven's floodgates, was only one example of a long series of his mighty pleadings with God. Oh, if only we Christians would remember that perseverance in prayer is necessary for it to be effective and victorious!

The great intercessors, who are seldom mentioned in connection with the heroes and martyrs of the faith, were nevertheless the greatest benefactors of the church. Yet their becoming the channels of the blessings of mercy to others was only made possible by their abiding at the mercy seat of God.

Remember, we must pray to pray, and continue in prayer so our prayers may continue. CHARLES H. SPURGEON

DECEMBER 17

Morning

I will repay you for the years the locusts have eaten.
JOEL 2:25

I will restore to you the years that the locust hath eaten.
KJV

How many years we are not told; only this: *"I will restore the years."*

Human lives are often laid bare—barren patches produced by our own failures; a wilderness stretching across our life. But what comfort in these words: *"I will restore to you the years that the locust hath eaten."*

Have you been brooding over some sorrow? Has it darkened your life as a swarm of locusts might darken the sun at midday? And have you cried out in your anguish, "The sun will never shine again"? But read the word He has promised: *"I will restore to you the years that the locust hath eaten."*

Turn to Him, dear reader—turn to the One whom you may have been inclined to forget when you lived in the larger house. He is waiting; and if He does not see fit to give you back the earthly possession once so highly prized by you, remember this: *in a higher and better way He will restore those years.*

The years that the locust hath eaten sometimes take another form: years spent away from God in pursuit of worldly pleasure and self-gratification! How many have tried this! No wonder the fields are bare! *Can* God restore these years? Did He not restore the years for Naomi?

God can!

The blue water lily abounds in several of the canals in Alexandria, Egypt, which at certain seasons become dry; and the beds of these canals, which quickly become burnt as hard as bricks by the action of the sun, are then used as carriage roads. When, however, the water is admitted again, the lily resumes its growth with redoubled vigor and splendor.

DECEMBER 17

Evening

May God himself, the God of peace, sanctify you through and through.
May your whole spirit, soul and body be kept blameless at the coming of our
Lord Jesus Christ. The one who calls you is faithful, and he will do it.
1 Thessalonians 5:23–24

Many years after I first read that "without holiness no one will see the Lord" (Hebrews 12:14), I began following this truth and encouraging everyone with whom I spoke to do the same. Ten years later God gave me a clearer view than I had ever seen before of the way to obtain holiness—namely, by faith in the Son of God. Immediately I began sharing with everyone, "We are saved from sin *and* made holy by faith." I testified to this in private, in public, and in print, and God confirmed it through a thousand other witnesses. I have now declared this truth continuously for more than thirty years, and God has continued to confirm my work. John Wesley in 1771

I knew Jesus, and He was very precious to me, but I found something deep within me that would not stay pleasant, patient, and kind. I did what I could to keep those traits suppressed, but they were still there. Finally I sought Jesus for help, and when I gave Him my will, He came to my heart and removed everything that would not stay pleasant, patient, and kind. And then *He* shut the door. George Fox

At this very moment, my entire heart does not have even a hint of thirst after my acceptance by God. I am alone with Him and He fills every void. I do not have one wish, one will, or one desire, except in Him. He has set my feet in His large room. And I am in awe, standing amazed that He has conquered everything within me, through His love. Lady Huntington

Suddenly I felt as if a hand—not weak but omnipotent, and not of wrath but of love—were laid on my forehead. Yet I did not feel it as much outwardly as inwardly. It seemed to be pressing in on my entire being and sending a holy, sin-consuming energy throughout me as it moved downward, my heart as well as my head was aware of the presence of this soul-cleansing energy. Under its power I fell to the floor, and in the joyful wonder of the moment, I cried out in a loud voice. This hand of power continued to work without and within me, and wherever it moved, it seemed to leave the glorious influence of the Savior's image. And for several minutes, the deep ocean of God's love swallowed me, as all its waves and billows rolled over me. BISHOP HAMLINE

Some of my views on holiness, as I once wrote them, are as follows: Holiness appears to me to have a sweet, calm, pleasant, charming, and serene nature, all of which brings an inexpressible purity, radiance, peacefulness, and overwhelming joy to the soul. In other words, holiness makes the soul like a field or garden of God, with every kind of pleasant fruit and flower, and each one delightful and undisturbed, enjoying a sweet calm and the gentle and refreshing rays of the sun. JONATHAN EDWARDS

> Love's resistless current sweeping
> All the regions deep within;
> Thought and wish and senses keeping
> Now, and every instant clean:
> Full salvation! Full salvation!
> From the guilt and power of sin.

～～～ DECEMBER 18 ～～～
Morning

You are . . . a light for those who are in the dark.
ROMANS 2:19

We are kindled that we might kindle others. I would like, if I might have my choice, to burn steadily down, with no guttering waste, and as I do so to communicate God's fire to as many unlit candles as possible and to burn on steadily until the socket comes in view; then to light in the last flicker, twenty, thirty, or a hundred candles at once, so that as one expires they may begin burning and spreading light which shall shine until Jesus comes.

> Let me burn out for Thee, dear Lord,
> Burn and wear out for Thee;
> Don't let me rust, or my life be
> A failure, my God, to Thee.
> Use me, and all I have, dear Lord,
> And get me so close to Thee
> That I feel the throb of the great heart of God,
> Until I burn out for Thee.
>
> BESSIE F. HATCHER

~~~~ DECEMBER 18 ~~~~
Evening

In all these things we are more than conquerors through him who loved us.
ROMANS 8:37

The gospel and the gift of God are structured so wonderfully that the very enemies and forces that are marshaled to fight against us actually help pave our way to the very gates of heaven and into the presence of God. Those forces can be used in the same way an eagle uses the fierce winds of a storm to soar to the sky. At first he sits perfectly still, high on a cliff, watching the sky as it fills with darkness and as the lightning strikes all around him. Yet he never moves until he feels the burst of the storm, and then with a screech he dives toward the winds, using them to carry him ever higher.

This is also what God desires of each of His children. He wants us to be "more than conquerors," turning storm clouds into chariots of victory. It is obvious when an army becomes "more than conquerors," for it drives its enemies from the battlefield and confiscates their food and supplies. This is exactly what this Scripture passage means. There are spoils to be taken!

Dear believer, after experiencing the terrible valley of suffering, did you depart with the spoils? When you were struck with an injury and you thought you had lost everything, did you trust in God to the point that you came out richer than you were before? Being "more than [a] conqueror" means taking the spoils from the enemy and appropriating them for yourself. What your enemy had planned to use for your defeat, you can confiscate for your own use.

When Dr. Moon, of Brighton, England, was suddenly struck with blindness, he said, "Lord, I accept this 'talent' of blindness from You. Help me to use it for Your glory so that when You return, you may receive it 'back with interest' [Matthew 25:27]." Then God enabled him to invent the Moon Alphabet for the blind, through which thousands of blind people were enabled to read the Word of God and thereby come to the glorious saving knowledge of Christ. SELECTED

God did not remove Paul's "thorn in the flesh" (2 Corinthians 12:7 KJV). The Lord did something much better—He conquered it and made it Paul's servant. The ministry of *thorns* has often been a greater ministry to humankind than the ministry of *thrones*. SELECTED

~~~ DECEMBER 19 ~~~
Morning

Though he was rich, yet for your sake he became poor.
2 CORINTHIANS 8:9

The poorest man that ever walked the dirt roads of earth! Born in poverty, reared in obscurity, *yet He enriched all mankind!*

For twenty years He worked as a carpenter in that village which bore the scorn of men: "Can there any good thing come out of Nazareth?" (John 1:46 KJV).

As far as we know He never possessed the value of one penny. In the wilderness without food, by Jacob's well without water, in the crowded city without a home—thus *He lived, and loved, and died!*

> *The foxes find rest,*
> *And the birds have their nests*
> *In the shade of the forest tree,*
> *But Thy couch was the sod,*

O Thou Son of God,
In the desert of Galilee.

He preached without price and wrought miracles without money. His parish was the world. He sought breakfast from a leafing fig tree. He ate grain as He walked through the field of corn. *Without money,* did I say? He sent Peter to the sea for the fish that they might have money for the tax! He had no cornfields or fisheries, yet He could spread a table for five thousand and have bread and fish to spare! No beautiful carpets to walk on, yet the waters supported Him!

So poor was He that He must needs bear His own cross through the city, till fainting He fell. His value was thirty pieces of silver—the price of a slave, the lowest estimate of human life. But, on God's side, *no lower price than His infinite agony* could have made possible our Redemption! When He died, few men mourned; but a black crepe was hung over the sun. *His crucifixion was the crime of crimes!*

It was not merely human blood that was spilled on Calvary's hill!

He did not have a house where He could go
When it was night—when other men went down
Small streets where children watched with eager eyes,
Each one assured of shelter in the town,
The Christ sought refuge anywhere at all:
A house, an inn, the roadside, or a stall!

He borrowed the boat in which He rode that day,
He talked to throngs along the Eastern lake;
It was a rented room to which He called
The chosen twelve the night He bade them break
The loaf with Him, and He rode, unafraid,
Another's colt in that triumph-parade.

A man from Arimathea had a tomb
Where Christ was placed when nails had done their deed.
Not ever in the crowded days He knew,
Did He have coins to satisfy a need.

They should not matter, these small things I crave.
Make me forget them, Father, and be brave!
"THE TRANSIENT" BY HELEN WELSHIMER

DECEMBER 19

Evening

And so you will bear testimony to me.
LUKE 21:13

Life is a steep climb, and it is always encouraging to have those ahead of us "call back" and cheerfully summon us to higher ground. We all climb together, so we should help one another. The mountain climbing of life is serious, but glorious, business; it takes strength and steadiness to reach the summit. And as our view becomes better as we gain altitude, and as we discover things of importance, we should "call back" our encouragement to others.

If you have gone a little way ahead of me, call back—
It will cheer my heart and help my feet along the stony track;
And if, perhaps, Faith's light is dim, because the oil is low,
Your call will guide my lagging course as wearily I go.

Call back, and tell me that He went with you into the storm;
Call back, and say He kept you when the forest's roots were torn;
That, when the heavens thunder and the earthquake shook
*   the hill,*
He bore you up and held you where the lofty air was still.

O friend, call back, and tell me for I cannot see your face;
They say it glows with triumph, and your feet sprint in the race;
But there are mists between us and my spirit eyes are dim,
And I cannot see the glory, though I long for word of Him.

But if you'll say He heard you when your prayer was but a cry,
And if you'll say He saw you through the night's
    sin-darkened sky—
If you have gone a little way ahead, O friend, call back—
It will cheer my heart and help my feet along the stony track.

SELECTED

~~~ DECEMBER 20 ~~~

Morning

Here is your God!

ISAIAH 40:9

</div>

He became the Son of Man that *we* might become the sons of God. Here is a man who was born in an obscure village, child of a peasant woman. He had neither wealth nor influence, neither training nor education; yet in infancy He startled a king; in boyhood He puzzled the doctors. In manhood He walked upon the billows and hushed the sea to sleep. He healed the multitudes without medicine and made no charge for His services. He never wrote a book, *yet all the libraries of the world could not hold the books that could be written about Him.* He never wrote a song, *yet He has furnished the theme of more songs than all songwriters combined.* He never founded a college, *yet all the colleges together cannot boast of as many students as He.*

"*Though he was rich, yet for your sake he became poor*" (2 Corinthians 8:9).

How poor? Ask Mary! Ask the Wise Men! He slept in another's manger. He cruised the lake in another's boat. He rode on another man's ass. He was buried in another man's tomb.

While still a young man, the tide of popular opinion turned against Him. His friends ran away from Him. One of them denied Him; another betrayed Him and turned Him over to His enemies. He went through the mockery of a trial. He was nailed upon the Cross between two thieves. His executioners gambled for His coat.

Yet, *all the armies that ever marched, all the navies that were ever built, all the parliaments that ever sat, all the kings that ever reigned, put together,* have not affected the life of man as powerfully as has *this one solitary life!*

<div align="center">

—— 861 ——

</div>

Great men have come and gone, *yet He lives on!* Death could not destroy Him! The grave could not hold Him!

"Look how the whole world has gone after him!" (John 12:19).

"Let us also go" (John 11:16).

"If you seek him, he will be found by you" (1 Chronicles 28:9).

Find Him!

~~~ DECEMBER 20 ~~~

Evening

"I am not alone, for my Father is with me."

JOHN 16:32

It is certainly unnecessary to say that turning conviction into action requires great sacrifice. It may mean renouncing or separating ourselves from specific people or things, leaving us with a strange sense of deprivation and loneliness. Therefore the person who will ultimately soar like an eagle to the heights of the cloudless day and live in the sunshine of God must be content to live a relatively lonely life.

There are no birds that live in as much solitude as eagles, for they never fly in flocks. Rarely can even two eagles be seen together. And a life that is dedicated to God *knows divine fellowship*, no matter how many human friendships have had to be forfeited along the way.

God seeks "eagle people," for no one ever comes into the full realization of the best things of God in his spiritual life without learning to walk alone with Him. We see Abraham alone "in the land of Canaan, while Lot lived among the cities . . . near Sodom" (Genesis 13:12). Moses, although educated in all the wisdom of Egypt, had to spend forty years alone with God in the desert. And Paul, who was filled with all the knowledge of the Greeks and who sat "at the feet of Gamaliel" (Acts 22:3 KJV), was required, after meeting Jesus, to go immediately "into Arabia" (Galatians 1:17) to learn of the desert life with God.

May we allow God to isolate us, but I do not mean the isolation of a monastery. It is in the experience of isolation that the Lord develops an independence of life and of faith so that the soul no longer depends on the continual help, prayers, faith, and care of others. The assistance and inspiration from others are necessary, and they have a place in a Christian's development, but at times they can actually become a hindrance to a person's faith and welfare.

God knows how to change our circumstances in order to isolate us. And once we yield to Him and He takes us through an experience of isolation, we are no longer dependent upon those around us, although we still love them as much as before. Then we realize that He has done a new work within us and that the wings of our soul have learned to soar in loftier air.

We must dare to be alone, in the way that Jacob had to be alone for the Angel of God to whisper in his ear, "Your name will no longer be Jacob, but Israel" (Genesis 32:28); in the way that Daniel had to be left alone to see heavenly visions; and in the way that John had to be banished to the Isle of Patmos to receive and record "the revelation of Jesus Christ, which God gave him" (Revelation 1:1).

He has "trodden the winepress alone" (Isaiah 63:3) for us. Therefore, are we prepared for a time of "glorious isolation" rather than to fail Him?

~~~~~ DECEMBER 21 ~~~~~

Morning

Save yourself.
MATTHEW 27:40

Save Yourself! These words have a familiar ring in the Master's ears. He had heard them in all their variations throughout the whole period of His public ministry. When a messenger came to Peraea carrying tidings of the passing of Lazarus, His disciples tried to dissuade Him from going to Bethany, *to save Himself.*

An anxious family waited on Him in Capernaum and begged Him to return to Nazareth *to save Himself.*

Certain Greeks approached Him during the Last Passover and evidently afforded Him an opportunity to slip out of the picture gracefully, *to save Himself.*

In Gethsemane His final decision was made, quite in accord with all of His previous decisions. He would *not* save Himself. Now, agonizing on the cross, He heard the malefactors suggesting that He save Himself—and them. His critics and crucifiers joined the chorus and cried, "Come down from the cross and *save yourself!*" (Mark 15:30).

But He who taught His disciples to deny themselves and to save their lives by losing them had definitely determined to give Himself. THE UPPER ROOM

When a Roman soldier was told by his guide that if he insisted on taking a certain journey it would probably be fatal, he answered, "It is necessary for me to go; it is not necessary for me to live."

That was depth. When we have convictions like that, we shall come to something worthy of our name Christian.

> *More than half beaten, but fearless,*
> *Facing the storm and the night,*
> *Reeling and breathless, but fearless,*
> *Here in the lull of the fight.*
> *I who bow not but before Thee,*
> *God of the fighting clan,*
> *Lifting my fists I implore Thee,*
> *Give me the heart of a man!*
>
> *What though I stand with the winners,*
> *Or perish with those that fall?*
> *Only the cowards are sinners;*
> *Fighting the fight, that is all.*
> *Strong is my foe, who advances,*
> *Snapped is my blade, O Lord;*
> *See their proud banners and lances,*
> *But spare me the stub of a sword!*

Evening

I will give him . . . the land he set his feet on, because
he followed the LORD wholeheartedly.
DEUTERONOMY 1:36

Every difficult task that comes across your path—every one that you would rather not do, that will take the most effort, cause the most pain, and be the greatest struggle—brings a blessing with it. And refusing to do it regardless of the personal cost is to miss the blessing.

Every difficult stretch of road on which you see the Master's footprints and along which He calls you to follow Him leads unquestionably to blessings. And they are blessings you will never receive unless you travel the steep and thorny path.

Every battlefield you encounter, where you are required to draw your sword and fight the enemy, has the possibility of victory that will prove to be a rich blessing to your life. And every heavy burden you are called upon to lift hides within itself a miraculous secret of strength. J. R. MILLER

> *I cannot do it alone;*
> *The waves surge fast and high,*
> *And the fogs close all around,*
> *The light goes out in the sky;*
> *But I know that we two*
> *Will win in the end,*
> *Jesus and I.*
>
> *Cowardly, wayward, and weak,*
> *I change with the changing sky;*
> *Today so eager and bright,*
> *Tomorrow too weak to try;*
> *But He never gives in,*
> *So we two will win,*
> *Jesus and I.*

I could not guide it myself,
    My boat on life's wild sea;
There's One who sits by my side,
    Who pulls and steers with me.
And I know that we two
    Will safe enter port,
Jesus and I.

DECEMBER 22

Morning

He persevered because he saw him who is invisible.
HEBREWS 11:27

The life of Moses was a much-enduring one. He endured the banishment from palatial surroundings and the most brilliant court then in existence; he endured the forfeiture of privilege and the renunciation of splendid prospects; he endured the flight from Egypt and the wrath of the king; he endured the lonely exile in Midian, where for years he was buried alive; he endured the long trudge through the wilderness at the head of a slave people, whom he sought to consolidate into a nation; he endured the ill manners and the countless provocations of a forward and perverse generation; he endured the lonely death on Nebo and the nameless grave that angels dug for him there! And here we have the secret of his wondrous fortitude disclosed to us:

"He persevered because he saw him who is invisible."

He realized the presence of God. He lived in the consciousness, "Thou God seest me." He looked up and had an habitual regard to the heavenly and eternal. In the upper chambers of his soul, there was a window that opened skyward and commanded a view of things unseen. As an old author puts it, "He had a greater view than Pharaoh in his eye, and this kept him right." Yes, and this will keep any of us right: to live under the sense that God is overlooking us—to walk by faith and not by sight. "There is nothing," says a great modern preacher, "that enables a man so well to carry on things that are terraqueous and material, as to have in ascendancy every day that part of his nature which dwells with the invisible." S. LAW WILSON

Evening

A thick and dreadful darkness came over him.

GENESIS 15:12

In this Scripture passage, the sun had finally gone down, and the eastern night had swiftly cast its heavy veil over the entire scene. Worn out by the mental conflict, and the exertion and the cares of the day, Abraham "fell into a deep sleep" (v. 12). During his sleep, his soul was oppressed with "a thick and dreadful darkness," which seemed to smother him and felt like a nightmare in his heart.

Do you have an understanding of the horror of that kind of darkness? Have you ever experienced a terrible sorrow that seems difficult to reconcile with God's perfect love—a sorrow that comes crashing down upon you, wrings from your soul its peaceful rest in the grace of God, and casts it into a sea of darkness that is unlit by even one ray of hope? Have you experienced a sorrow caused by unkindness, when others cruelly mistreat your trusting heart, and you even begin to wonder if there is really a God above who sees what is happening yet continues to allow it? If you know this kind of sorrow, then you know something of this "thick and dreadful darkness."

Human life is made of brightness and gloom, shadows and sunshine, and dark clouds followed by brilliant rays of light. Yet through it all, God's divine justice is accomplishing His plan, affecting and disciplining each individual soul.

Dear friend, if you are filled with fear of the "thick and dreadful darkness" because of God's dealings with humankind, learn to trust His infallible wisdom, for it is equal to His unchanging justice. And know that He who endured the "dreadful darkness" of Calvary and the feeling of having been forsaken on the cross is ready to accompany you "through the valley of the shadow of death" (Psalm 23:4 KJV) until you can see the sun shining on the other side.

May we realize that "we have this hope as an anchor for the soul, firm and secure" and that "it enters the inner sanctuary behind the curtain" (Hebrews 6:19). And may we know that although it is unseen within His sanctuary, our anchor will be grounded and will never yield. It will hold firm until the day He returns, and then we too will follow it into the safe haven guaranteed to us in God's unchangeable Word. F. B. MEYER

The disciples thought that the angry sea separated them from Jesus. In fact, some of them thought something even worse—they thought that the trouble they were facing was a sign that He had forgotten them and did not care about them.

O dear friend, that is when your troubles can cause the most harm. The Devil comes and whispers to you, "God has forgotten you" or "God has forsaken you," and your unbelieving heart cries out, as Gideon once did, "If the LORD is with us, why has all this happened to us?" (Judges 6:13). God has allowed the difficulty to come upon you, in order to bring you closer to Himself. It has come not to separate you from Jesus but to cause you to cling to Him more faithfully, more firmly, and more simply. F. S. WEBSTER

We should abandon ourselves to God more fully at those times when He seems to have abandoned us. Let us enjoy His light and comfort when it is His pleasure to give it to us, but may we not attach ourselves to His gifts. May we instead attach ourselves to Him, and when He plunges us into the night, where *pure faith* is required, may we still press on through the agonizing darkness.

> *Oh, for faith that brings the triumph*
> *When defeat seems very near!*
> *Oh, for faith that brings the triumph*
> *Into victory's ringing cheer—*
> *Faith triumphant; knowing not defeat or fear.*
> HERBERT BOOTH

DECEMBER 23

Morning

"What do I still lack?"
MATTHEW 19:20

When Jesus answered the rich young ruler's question, the young man said: "All these I have kept. . . . What do I still lack?" Then Jesus told him what his lack was and "he went away sad" (v. 22). The interview was over; Jesus asked for the Master Key, and the young man refused to give it.

Has Jesus the keys to your life? Has He the key to the Library of your life, or do you just read what you please? Has He the key to the Dining room of your life—do you feed your soul on His Word? Has He the key to the Recreation compartment, or do you just go where you please? Have you given Christ the Master Key to your life?

We may have all of the Holy Ghost, but has He all of us? Are there spaces yet to be filled with the Holy Ghost—spaces, places, rooms, and closets in our spiritual house into which He has not "fully come" because we have not yet given up all the keys from cellar to attic of our spiritual homestead?

The House of the Lord has many chambers,
Large and lofty, or low and small;
And some who turn from the world's broad highways
And find the door to the entrance hall,
Are satisfied with its shade and coolness,
To know they have come to the House of a Friend,
And, resting there in the peace and quiet,
They think they have fared to their journey's end.

And some are content with the antechamber,
That opens out of the entrance hall,
With the winds that blow from the spicy gardens,
The musical splash of the fountain's fall;
They feast on the fruits of the Spirit's giving
And muse on the thought of the joys to come,
And resting there in the peace and quiet,
Are glad that the Lord has brought them home.

But those who have heeded His invitation
To come up higher and enter in
To the upper room of the Master's dwelling,
To stores of treasures their way shall win.
What eye hath seen them? What mind conceived them?
What heart hath dreamed of the things concealed,
The joys prepared for the Lord's beloved,
To those who seek them alone revealed?

Clothed with His glory they leave His presence,
Girt with His power they walk abroad
Who find the door to the inner chamber,
The secret place of the Most High God.
"The Inner Chamber" by Annie Johnson Flint

~~~ DECEMBER 23 ~~~

Evening

The journey is too much for you.
1 Kings 19:7

What did God do with Elijah, His tired servant? He allowed him to sleep and then gave him something good to eat. Elijah had done tremendous work and in his excitement had run "ahead of Ahab['s chariot] all the way to Jezreel" (1 Kings 18:46). But the run had been too much for him and had sapped his physical strength, ultimately causing him to become *depressed*. Just as others in this condition need sleep and want their ailments treated, Elijah's physical requirements needed to be met.

There are many wonderful people who end up where Elijah did—"under a juniper tree" (1 Kings 19:4 KJV)! When this happens, the words of the Master are very soothing: "Get up and eat, for the journey is too much for you." In other words, "I am going to refresh you."

Therefore may we never confuse physical weariness with spiritual weakness.

I'm too tired to trust and too tired to pray,
Said I, as my overtaxed strength gave way.
The one conscious thought that my mind possessed,
Is, oh, could I just drop it all and rest.

Will God forgive me, do you suppose,
If I go right to sleep as a baby goes,
Without questioning if I may,
Without even trying to trust and pray?

Will God forgive you? Think back, dear heart,
When language to you was an unknown art,
Did your mother deny you needed rest,
Or refuse to pillow your head on her breast?

Did she let you want when you could not ask?
Did she give her child an unequal task?
Or did she cradle you in her arms,
And then guard your slumber against alarms?

Oh, how quickly a mother's love can see,
The unconscious yearnings of infancy.
When you've grown too tired to trust and pray,
When overworked nature has quite given way:

Then just drop it all, and give up to rest,
As you used to do on mother's breast,
He knows all about it—the dear Lord knows,
So just go to sleep as a baby goes;

Without even asking if you may,
God knows when His child is too tired to pray.
He judges not solely by uttered prayer,
He knows when the yearnings of love are there.

He knows you do pray, He knows you do trust,
And He knows, too, the limits of poor, weak dust.
Oh, the wonderful sympathy of Christ,
For His chosen ones in that midnight tryst,

When He told them, "Sleep and take your rest,"
While on Him the guilt of the whole world pressed—
You have trusted your life to Him to keep,
Then don't be afraid to go right to sleep.

ELLA CONRAD COWHERD

Morning

Buried with him . . . in order that . . . we too may live a new life.

ROMANS 6:4

No one enters into the experience of entire sanctification without going through a "white funeral," (i.e., the burial of the old life. If there has never been this crisis of death, sanctification is nothing more than a vision). There must be a "white funeral," the death that has only one resurrection—a resurrection into the life of Jesus. Nothing can upset this life; it is one with God, for one purpose, to be a witness to Him.

Have I come to my last days really? I have come to them in sentiment, but have I come to them *really*? You cannot go to your funeral in excitement nor die in excitement. Death means stopping being. Do I agree with God that I stop being the striving earnest kind of Christian I have been? We skirt the cemetery and all the time refuse to go to death. It is not striving to go to death, it is dying—"baptized into his death" (v. 3).

Have I had a "white funeral," or am I sacredly playing with my soul? Is there a place marked in my life as the last day, a place that the memory goes back to with a chastened and extraordinary grateful remembrance—Yes, it was then, that I made an agreement with God. "This is the will of God, even your sanctification." When you realize what the will of God is, you will enter into sanctification as naturally as can be. Are you willing to go through the "white funeral" now?

Do you agree with Him that this is your last day on earth? That moment depends on you. MY UTMOST FOR HIS HIGHEST BY OSWALD CHAMBERS

Evening

He went out to the field one evening to meditate.

GENESIS 24:63

We would be better Christians if we spent more time alone, and we would actually accomplish more if we attempted less and spent more time in isolation and quiet waiting upon God. The world has become too much a part of us, and we are afflicted with the idea that we are not accomplishing anything unless we are always busily running back and forth. We no longer believe in the importance of a calm retreat where we sit silently in the shade. As the people of God, we have become entirely too practical. We believe in having "all our irons in the fire" and that all the time we spend away from the anvil or fire is wasted time. Yet our time is never more profitably spent than when we set aside time for quiet meditation, talking with God, and looking up to heaven. We can never have too many of these open spaces in life—hours set aside when our soul is completely open and accessible to any heavenly thought or influence that God may be pleased to send our way.

Someone once said, "Meditation is the Sunday of the mind." In these hectic days, we should often give our mind a "Sunday," a time in which it will do no work but instead will simply be still, look heavenward, and spread itself before the Lord like Gideon's fleece, allowing itself to be soaked with the moisture of the dew of heaven. We should have intervals of time when we do nothing, think nothing, and plan nothing but simply lie on the green lap of nature and "rest a while" (Mark 6:31 KJV).

Time spent in this way is not lost time. A fisherman does not say he is losing time when he is mending his nets, nor does a gardener feel he has wasted his time by taking a few minutes to sharpen the blades on his mower. And people living in cities today would do well to follow the example of Isaac and as often as possible visit the fields of the countryside, away from the hustle and bustle of the city. After having grown weary from the heat and noise of the city, communion with nature is very refreshing and will bring a calming, healing influence. A walk through a field, a stroll by a seashore, or a hike across a meadow sprinkled with daisies will purge you of the impurities of life and will cause your heart to beat with new joy and hope.

> *The little cares that worried me,*
> *I lost them yesterday,*
> *Out in the fields with God.*

A poem for Christmas Eve:

Bells across the Snow

O Christmas, merry Christmas,
    Has it really come again,
With its memories and greetings,
    With its joy and with its pain!
Minor chords are in the carol
    And a shadow in the light,
And a spray of cypress twining
    With the holly wreath tonight.
And the hush is never broken
    By laughter light and low,
As we listen in the starlight
    To the "bells across the snow."

O Christmas, merry Christmas,
    It's not so very long
Since other voices blended
    With the carol and the song!
If we could but hear them singing,
    As they are singing now,
If we could but see the radiance
    Of the crown on each dear brow,
There would be no cry to cover,
    No hidden tear to flow,
As we listen in the starlight
    To the "bells across the snow."

O Christmas, merry Christmas,
    This nevermore can be;
We cannot bring again the days
    Of our unshadowed glee,
But Christmas, happy Christmas,
    Sweet herald of goodwill,

With holy songs of glory
 Brings holy gladness still.
For peace and hope may brighten,
 And patient love may glow,
As we listen in the starlight
 To the "bells across the snow."

FRANCES RIDLEY HAVERGAL

DECEMBER 25

Morning

Good tidings of great joy.
LUKE 2:10 KJV

Tidings of glory! all the sky aflame, all Heaven hymning one imperial Name! Radiant glimpses of a Throne, a Crown, all splendor focused on one little town! Tidings of joy, good tidings of great joy! Supernal ecstasy without alloy! The death of sorrow and the end of pain, the bliss, bliss, bliss eternally to reign! News of Salvation! Jesus, Savior, Christ, bearer of mercy ample, and unpriced herald of freedom from the chains of sin, come to our hearts, Lord Jesus, enter in! Tidings to all the people, yea, to all! To kings and shepherds, to the great and small, to rich and poor, to ignorant and wise, to each his blessing from the liberal skies! Oh, for the ready eye and quickened ear, the Advent light to see, and song to hear! To every man and woman, girl and boy, in all the world, *good tidings of great joy!* AMOS R. WELLS
 He gave us the best that He had!

To Bethlehem they went to be enrolled;
And there, in Caesar's census book of old,
His name was written 'mong the sons of men
As Caesar's subject: "Jesus"—followed then
By "Son of Mary, born in David's Town,
Of David's line"—the record thus set down.

In a world's book of life, a place they gave
To "Jesus" who was born a world to save.
They numbered Him with sinful men and poor,
Though He was Son of God, Divine and pure.

A heavenly census book His name alone
Bears, on the title page; for 'tis His own,
That Book of Life; and there, writ clear and plain
Are names of those born in that King's domain;
All who alive forevermore shall be
Are there enrolled for all eternity.
Since He was numbered once with sinful men,
We may be numbered as God's own again.
Though Caesar's book has long since passed away,
The Lamb's blest Book of Life shall stand for aye.
"THE CENSUS BOOKS" BY KAY MCCULLOUGH

Was it merely the son of Joseph and Mary who crossed the world's horizon nineteen hundred years ago? Your own heart must answer—*"My Lord and my God!"*

DECEMBER 25
Evening

"They will call him Immanuel" (which means "God with us").
MATTHEW 1:23

Prince of Peace.
ISAIAH 9:6

There's a song in the air!
   There's a star in the sky!
There's a mother's deep prayer,
   And a baby's low cry!

And the star rains its fire
     While the beautiful sing,
For the manger of Bethlehem cradles a King.

Anumber of years ago a remarkable Christmas card was published by the title "If Christ Had Not Come." It was based on our Savior's own words, "If I had not come," in John 15:22. The card pictured a minister falling asleep in his study on Christmas morning and then dreaming of a world into which Jesus had never come.

In his dream, he saw himself walking through his house, but as he looked, he saw no stockings hung on the chimney, no Christmas tree, no wreaths of holly, and no Christ to comfort and gladden hearts or to save us. He then walked onto the street outside, but there was no church with its spire pointing toward heaven. And when he came back and sat down in his library, he realized that every book about our Savior had disappeared.

The minister dreamed that the doorbell rang and that a messenger asked him to visit a friend's poor dying mother. He reached her home, and as his friend sat and wept, he said, "I have something here that will comfort you." He opened his Bible to look for a familiar promise, but it ended with Malachi. There was no gospel and no promise of hope and salvation, and all he could do was bow his head and weep with his friend and his mother in bitter despair.

Two days later he stood beside her coffin and conducted her funeral service, but there was no message of comfort, no words of a glorious resurrection, and no thought of a mansion awaiting her in heaven. There was only "dust to dust, and ashes to ashes," and one long, eternal farewell. Finally he realized that *Christ had not come*, and burst into tears, weeping bitterly in his sorrowful dream.

Then suddenly he awoke with a start, and a great shout of joy and praise burst from his lips as he heard his choir singing these words in his church nearby:

O come, all ye faithful, joyful and triumphant,
     O come ye, O come ye to Bethlehem!
Come and behold Him, born the King of angels,
     O come let us adore Him, Christ the Lord!

Let us be glad and rejoice today, because He *has* come. And let us remember the proclamation of the angel: "I bring you good news that will cause great joy *for all the people.* Today in the town of David a Savior has been born to you; he is the Messiah, the Lord" (Luke 2:10–11).

> *He comes to make His blessing flow,*
> *Far as the curse does go.*

May our hearts go out to the unconverted people of foreign lands who have no blessed Christmas day. "Go and enjoy choice food and sweet drinks, and SEND SOME TO THOSE WHO HAVE NOTHING PREPARED. This day is holy to our Lord" (Nehemiah 8:10).

DECEMBER 26
Morning

Then my head will be exalted above the enemies who surround me.
PSALM 27:6

There is an old Scottish mansion quite close to where I have a little summer home in the north of Scotland, which has in it a room noted for the sketches and pictures that from time to time have been drawn upon the walls by visiting artists. It is a room to which people came from the ends of the world, and it all began in this way.

That room had been redecorated. Its plaster walls had been repainted. There was an accident in that room with a syphon of soda water which burst and covered the newly decorated plaster wall with stain. The woman of the house was, of course, not unnaturally irritated at such an accident to her newly decorated room, and she was not slow to express her irritation.

There was a great artist staying in the house, no less than Sir Edwin Landseer. He did not say anything to her, but when even the next day her irritation had not altogether abated—for the stain had dried, and it looked even worse then, and was seen to be permanent—he stayed at home when the rest of the party in the house went out on the moors. He took a piece of charcoal, and with a few deft touches and strokes he transformed that disfigurement into a thing of priceless beauty. He made it the background of a waterfall, and he put in the surrounding crags and one or two fir trees, a noble stag.

It is regarded, indeed, that sketch upon the wall, as one of Landseer's most successful sketches of Highland life. The point is this. That which was a disfigurement has become a thing of permanent beauty and pricelessness.

I do not care where you have failed. I do not care if it is in the deepest motive of your being. I do not care how far you have fallen. I do not care how deeply you have disfigured and defaced the image of God—the great Craftsman, the great Master and Lord of us all, can turn your soul from that very failure into a positive endowment for future service. J. STUART HOLDEN

Let God do it for you!

───ᔕᔕᔕᔕ─── DECEMBER 26 ───ᔕᔕᔕᔕ───

Evening

"Sit here while I go over there and pray."
MATTHEW 26:36

It is a very difficult thing to be kept in the background during a time of crisis. In the Garden of Gethsemane, eight of the eleven remaining disciples were left behind to do nothing. When Jesus went ahead to pray, Peter, James, and John went with Him to watch, but the rest sat down to wait. I believe that the ones left behind must have complained. They were *in* the garden, but that was all, for they had no part in the cultivation of its flowers. It was a stormy time of crisis and great stress, yet they were not allowed to participate.

You and I have certainly had that experience and felt the same disappointment. Perhaps you have seen a great opportunity for Christian service arise, and some people are sent immediately to the work, while still others are being trained to go. Yet *you* are forced to do nothing but sit and wait. Or perhaps sickness and poverty has come your way, or you have had to endure some terrible disgrace. Whatever your situation, you have been kept from service, and now you feel angry and do not understand why you should be excluded from this part of the Christian life. It seems unjust that you have been allowed to enter the garden but have found no path assigned to you once inside.

Be still, dear soul—things are not what they seem! You are *not* excluded from any part of the Christian life. Do you believe that the garden of the Lord only has places for those who walk or those who stand? No! It also has a place set apart for those who are compelled to *sit*. Just as there are three voices in a verb—active, passive, and neuter—there are three voices in Christ's verb "live." There are active people, who go straight to the battle, and struggle till the setting of the sun. There are passive people, who stand in the middle and simply report the progress of the fight. Yet there are also neuter people—those who can neither fight nor be spectators of the fight but must simply lie down and wait.

When this experience comes, do not think that you have been turned aside. Remember, it is *Christ himself* who says to you, "Sit here." *Your* place in the garden has *also* been set apart. God has selected it especially for you, and it is not simply a place of waiting. There are some lives He brings into this world neither to do great work nor to bear great burdens. Their job is simply to be—they are the neuter verbs, or the flowers in the garden that have no active mission. They have won no major victories and have never been honored with the best seats at a banquet—they have simply escaped the sight of people like Peter, James, and John.

However, *Jesus* is delighted by the sight of them, for through their mere fragrance and beauty, they have brought Him joy. And just their existence and the preservation of their loveliness in the valley has lifted the Master's heart. So you need not complain if you are one of these flowers! Selected

DECEMBER 27
Morning

In repentance and rest is your salvation, in quietness and trust is your strength.
Isaiah 30:15

Desert sweetened." It was only a sign in a wayside fruit stand. But the golden grapefruit that it advertised took on new value! So will any life that follows the formula given by the Master: "Come with me by yourselves to a quiet place and get some rest" (Mark 6:31). It was in the loneliness of desert reaches that some of the mightiest of the Old Testament prophets received their message: "Thus saith the Lord." In the desert Jesus met and mastered temptation. Out of a three-year desert retreat came Paul to be the greatest missionary of all time!

"Desert sweetened!" A quiet place at the beginning and the close of day. A "little chapel of silence"—"where, though the feet may join the throng, the soul may enter in and pray." Sunshine and silence—synonyms for the desert. May they bring special gifts of calm and courage and confidence—because we have kept our appointment with Christ in these moments of devotion! SELECTED

The road to the Promised Land of spiritual power always leads through desert places where "the still small voice" has a chance to be heard. GLENN RANDALL PHILLIPS

In the secret of His presence how my soul delights to hide!
Oh, how precious are the lessons which I learn at Jesus' side!
Earthly cares can never vex me, neither trials lay me low;
For when Satan comes to tempt me, to the secret place I go.
When my soul is faint and thirsty, 'neath the shadow of His wing
There is cool and pleasant shelter and a fresh and crystal spring;
And my Savior rests beside me, as we hold communion sweet:
If I tried I could not utter what He says when thus we meet.
Only this I know: I tell Him all my doubts, my griefs, and fears.
Oh, how patiently He listens! and my drooping soul He cheers.
Do you think He ne'er reproves me? What a false friend He would be
If He never, never told me of the sins which He must see!
Would you like to know the sweetness of the secret of the Lord?
Go and hide beneath His shadow; this shall then be your reward.
And whene'er you leave the silence of that happy meeting-place,
You must mind and bear the image of the Master in your face.

ELLEN LAKSHMI GOREH

His neck was put in irons.
PSALM 105:18

The irons of sorrow and loss, the burdens carried as a youth, and the soul's struggle against sin all contribute to developing an iron tenacity and strength of purpose, as well as endurance and fortitude. And these traits make up the indispensable foundation and framework of noble character.

Never run from suffering, but bear it silently, patiently, and submissively, with the assurance that it is God's way of instilling iron into your spiritual life. The world is looking for iron leaders, iron armies, iron tendons, and muscles of steel. *But God is looking for iron saints*, and since there is no way to impart iron into His people's moral nature except by letting them suffer, He allows them to suffer.

Are the best years of your life slipping away while you suffer enforced monotony? Are you afflicted with opposition, misunderstandings, and the scorn of others? Do your afflictions seem as thick as the undergrowth confronting someone hiking through a jungle? Then take heart! Your time is not wasted, for God is simply putting you through His iron regimen. Your iron crown of suffering precedes your golden crown of glory, and iron is entering your soul to make it strong and brave. F. B. MEYER

> But you will not mind the roughness, nor the steepness
>   of the way,
> Nor the cold, unrested morning, nor the heat of the noonday;
> And you will not take a turning to the left or the right,
> But go straight ahead, nor tremble at the coming of the night,
>   For the road leads home.

Morning

Your love for me was wonderful.
2 SAMUEL 1:26

I s it too much to hope that when we see our blessed Lord in the glory, when the trials and the toils and the sacrifices are all at an end—Is it too much to desire that He should say something like this to us: *"Your love for me was wonderful"?* I tell you it will make the toils of the road and all the renunciations and willing sacrifices of life seem as nothing to have some such words of commendation from the lips of our Savior and to hear Him say to the one who has sought to be faithful at all cost: "Well done. You were never popular on earth, and nobody knew much about you. The life you lived to My glory in the uninspiriting sphere of duty seemed to be wasted and its sacrifice to be worthless by those who knew it, *but your love for Me was wonderful!* Men said you made mistakes and were narrow-minded and did not catch the spirit of the age. Men thought you were a fanatic and a fool and called you so; men crucified you as they crucified Me, but *your love for Me was wonderful!"*

> *Savior, Thy dying love Thou gavest me,*
> *Nor should I ought withhold,*
> *Dear Lord, from Thee:*
> *In love my soul would bow,*
> *My heart fulfill its vow,*
> *Some offering bring Thee now,*
> *Something for Thee.*

He is altogether lovely.

Evening

Rejoice in the Lord always. I will say it again: Rejoice!
PHILIPPIANS 4:4

Sing a little song of trust,
    O my heart!
Sing it just because you must,
    As leaves start;
As flowers push their way through dust;
Sing, my heart, because you must.

Wait not for an eager throng—
    Bird on bird;
It's the solitary song
    That is heard.
Every voice at dawn will start,
Be a nightingale, my heart!

Sing across the winter snow,
    Pierce the cloud;
Sing when mists are drooping low—
    Clear and loud;
But sing sweetest in the dark;
He who slumbers not will hark.

And when He hears you sing, He will bend down with a smile on His kind face. As He cheerfully listens, He will say, "Sing on, dear child. I hear you and I am coming to deliver you. I will carry that load for you. So just lean hard on Me, and the road will get smoother by and by."

Morning

A cloud as small as a man's hand is rising from the sea.
1 KINGS 18:44

The fields were parched for lack of rain. The foliage of the green bay tree wilted in the sun. The earth was dry like powder, and gray dust covered leaf and blade. There was no freshness anywhere. As far as eye could see, nature seemed to have dressed herself in sackcloth and ashes. We have never seen such drought as that which had fallen upon Israel in the days of Elijah the Tishbite. There had been no rain for three and a half years. The fields had not yielded their increase, and little children cried for food.

Elijah was on Mount Carmel praying for rain. "Go," he said to his servant, "and look out toward the sea and tell me if any sign of rain appears." Seven times he went and surveyed the western horizon, where the sky seemed to drop into the glittering Mediterranean. The seventh time he returned and said, "A cloud as small as a man's hand is rising from the sea."

A very little cloud it was, but sufficient to assure Elijah that God was answering prayer and that the day of refreshment had come for all the land of Israel.

It is not always so with men. When we cry to God we are impatient to see God's finished answer all at once. We rise from our knees, and because the heavens do not hang heavily with clouds, we are too quick to think that God is withholding His showers of blessing. *But God usually gives us by slow degrees the things we need.*

We grow impatient because we have not the sensibility of soul to detect *the faint beginnings* of God's mercies. The first gray tints that touch the eastern skies are a promise of the coming day. The first flickering ray of light that steals across our soul when we cry to God is the beginning of His answer. The first indefinable feeling of comfort that slips into the distressed soul is *a little cloud* bearing promise of refreshing showers.

"I knelt and prayed," said a young woman, "and it seemed that I saw a light across my way, and *then I was sure* that the thing perplexing me would come out all right." The light that shone for a moment in the heart's secret places was the harbinger of great happiness and blessing.

Broken heart, crying to God for comfort, take courage from moments which come like respites when the weight of sorrow is for a little while lightened! How delicately God deals with us! These are intimations of the peace which in the process of God's providence shall at last come.

Perplexed heart, crying to God for guidance, be assured by the events that seem to turn your life in a particular direction and by the light that every now and then falls on your problems—be assured that *God is beginning* to answer your prayer!

O Guilty heart, crying to God for forgiveness, let your desires for purity, your bitterness of soul, the faint whisperings of Divine love heard only by the spirit's ear—let all of these tell you that God is already hearing and answering. Our skies are dotted with *little clouds, faint beginnings* of God's mercies. *They assure the waiting heart of greater clouds just beyond* the horizon, laden with His blessings. COSTEN J. HARRELL
Watch for God's faint beginnings!

DECEMBER 29

Evening

*Come on . . . ! We have seen the land, and it is very good. Aren't you
going to do something? Don't hesitate to go there and take it over. . . .
God has put into your hands, a land that lacks nothing whatever.*
JUDGES 18:9–10

Come on!" This command indicates that there is something definite for us to do and that nothing is ours unless we take it. "The children of Joseph, Manasseh and Ephraim, *took their inheritance*" (Joshua 16:4 KJV). The house of "Jacob will *possess inheritance*" (Obadiah 17). "The upright shall have good things *in possession*" (Proverbs 28:10 KJV).

We need to have appropriating faith when it comes to God's promises and should make His Word our own personal possession. A child was once asked what appropriating faith was, and he answered, "It is taking a pencil and underlining every 'me,' 'my,' and 'mine' in the Bible."

Pick any word you want that He has spoken and say, "That word is my word." Put your finger on a promise and say, "It is mine." How much of God's Word have you received and endorsed, and how much have you been able to say, "This has been done in my life"? By how many of His promises have you signed your name and said, "This has been fulfilled to me"?

"My son, . . . you are always with me, and *everything* I have *is yours*" (Luke 15:31). Do not miss your inheritance through your own neglect.

When faith goes to the market, it always takes a basket.

Morning

He came to a broom bush, sat down under it and prayed that he might die.

1 KINGS 19:4

This is Elijah! One is startled, perplexed, disappointed. A while ago we saw him on Mount Carmel surrounded by the thronging thousands of Israel, undismayed by the bold audacity of the worshipers of Baal, and confidently appealing to God to vindicate His own honor, and confound Baalim. Here he is, the prey of deep depression, forgetful of the past, giving all up, wanting God to take away his life. God has not once failed him. Not to any extent at all has one single foe prevailed against him. He should not have lost heart, should not have fled, should not have asked God to take away his life; all this was wrong. He should have remembered how God had wonderfully stood by him in the past, and have firmly trusted Him still. Is not his privilege ours also? May not God's people trust Him fully, firmly, and under all circumstances, and at all times? God is not "afar off," neither has He forgotten to be gracious; and that which He has promised He will unfailingly remember, and do. Are we not always in His hands and under His care? Should we ever have a single fear? Why should we be cast down, or disquieted? J. T. W.

Have faith in God, the sun will shine, though dark the cloud may be today!
Have faith in God!

Evening

So Peter was kept in prison, but the church was earnestly praying to God for him.
ACTS 12:5

Peter was in prison awaiting his execution, and the church had no human power or influence that could save him. There was no earthly help available, but help could be obtained by way of heaven. So the church gave themselves to fervent and persistent prayer. And God sent an angel, who "struck Peter on the side and woke him up" (v. 7). Then the angel led him past "the first and second guards and [they] came to the iron gate leading to the city. It opened for them by itself" (v. 10), and Peter was free.

Perhaps there is some "iron gate" in your life, blocking your way. Like a caged bird, you have often beaten against the bars, but instead of helping your situation, you have become even more tired and exhausted and caused yourself more heartache. There is a secret for you to learn—the secret of *believing* prayer.

Then when you come to the iron gate, it will open as it did for Peter: "by itself."

How much wasted energy and painful disappointment will be saved once you learn to pray as the early church did in the "upper room" (Acts 1:13 KJV)! Insurmountable difficulties will disappear and adverse circumstances will turn favorable once you learn to pray—not with your own faith but with the faith of God. Many of your loved ones have been bound by Satan and imprisoned by him for years, and they are simply waiting for the gates to be opened. They will be set free in Christ when you pray fervently and persistently in faith to God. C. H. P.

Emergencies call for intense prayer. *When the person himself becomes the prayer* nothing can resist its touch. Elijah bowed to the ground on Mount Carmel with his face between his knees, and *he* became the prayer.

Spoken prayer is not always needed, for prayer can often be too intense for words. In the case of Elijah, his entire being was in touch with God and was aligned with Him against the powers of evil. And Elijah's evil enemies could not withstand this kind of prayer in human form—something that is greatly needed today. THE BENT-KNEE TIME

"Wordless groans" (Romans 8:26) are often prayers that God cannot refuse. CHARLES H. SPURGEON

For here we do not have an enduring city, but we
are looking for the city that is to come.
HEBREWS 13:14

A great world conqueror was leading his victorious army back to Italy—and home. Onward they marched over rivers and plains, and through wooded forests until they reached the foothills of the towering Alps. Here the thinning ranks of the worn and tired soldiers began to falter as they trudged on over the rocky defiles of the mighty mountain passes. As they climbed higher and still higher, the blinding snow and storms well-nigh discouraged the stoutest hearts. Stopping on an eminence where he could overlook all his men and be heard by them, and pointing upward across the mighty barrier, the great general shouted, "Men, beyond those Alps lies Italy!"

Italy! Waving fields, beautiful orchards, sparkling fountains! Mothers and fathers, wives and children, sweethearts! Home! Ah, sweet home!

Fainting hearts revived. Tired muscles found new strength. Onward and upward that brave army pressed against every obstacle—and won! They reached home.

Another scene. All over the world are members of Prince Emmanuel's army. Many have won decisive battles with the enemy, great victories over sin. They have struggled along life's rugged highway, and many have become worn and weary in the conflict. Long have they marched, homeward bound. But now they have reached great mountains of difficulties, strifes, wars, threatened dissolution of all social and moral standards—the mighty Alps on the stream of time. To this vast army their Captain shouts, "Christian soldiers, beyond these mountains of difficulty lies Home!"

Heaven! Waving fields of living, green, kingly forests with never-fading foliage, sparkling fountains! The Tree of Life and the River of Life! Long lost friends, mothers and fathers, brothers and sisters, husbands, wives, children, loved ones! Thank God, we are nearing our heavenly home!

I've been to the rim of the world, and beyond,
but I'm headin' home tonight.

E. W. PATTEN

Homing!

<div align="center">~~~~~ DECEMBER 31 ~~~~~</div>

Evening

Thus far the LORD has helped us.

1 SAMUEL 7:12

The words "thus far" are like a hand pointing in the direction of the *past*. It had been "a long time—twenty years in all" (v. 2), but even if it had been seventy years, "Thus far the LORD has helped"! Whether through poverty, wealth, sickness, or health; whether at home or abroad, or on land, sea, or air; and whether in honor, dishonor, difficulties, joy, trials, triumph, prayer, or temptation—"Thus far the LORD has helped"!

We always enjoy looking down a long road lined with beautiful trees. The trees are a delightful sight and seem to be forming a temple of plants, with strong wooden pillars and arches of leaves. In the same way you look down a beautiful road like this, why not look back on the road of the years of your life? Look at the large green limbs of God's mercy overhead and the strong pillars of His loving-kindness and faithfulness that have brought you much joy. Do you see any birds singing in the branches? If you look closely, surely you will see many, for they are singing of God's mercy received "thus far."

These words also point *forward*. Someone who comes to a certain point and writes the words "thus far" realizes he has not yet come to the end of the road and that he still has some distance to travel. There are still more trials, joys, temptations, battles, defeats, victories, prayers, answers, toils, and strength yet to come. These are then followed by sickness, old age, disease, and death.

Then is life over after death? No! These are still yet to come: arising in the likeness of Jesus; thrones, harps, and the singing of psalms; being "clothed in white garments" (Revelation 3:5 NASB), seeing the face of Jesus, and sharing fellowship with the saints;

and experiencing the glory of God, the fullness of eternity, and infinite joy. So dear believer, "be strong and take heart" (Psalm 27:14), and with thanksgiving and confidence lift your voice in praise, for:

> *The Lord who "thus far" has helped you*
> *Will help you all your journey through.*

When the words "thus far" are read in heaven's light, what glorious and miraculous prospects they reveal to our grateful eyes! CHARLES H. SPURGEON

The shepherds of the Alps have a beautiful custom of ending the day by singing an evening farewell to one another. The air is so pure that the songs can be heard for very long distances. As the sun begins to set, they gather their flocks and begin to lead them down the mountain paths while they sing, "'Thus far has the LORD helped us.' Let us praise His name!"

Finally, as is their beautiful custom, they sing to one another the courteous and friendly farewell "Good night! Good night!" The words then begin to echo from mountainside to mountainside, reverberating sweetly and softly until the music fades into the distance.

Let us also call out to one another through the darkness until the night becomes alive with the sound of many voices, encouraging God's weary travelers. And may the echoes grow into a storm of hallelujahs that will break in thundering waves around His sapphire throne. Then as the morning dawns, we will find ourselves on the shore of the "sea of glass" (Revelation 4:6), crying out with the redeemed hosts of heaven, "To him who sits on the throne and to the Lamb be praise and honor and glory and power, for ever and ever!" (Revelation 5:13).

> *This my song through endless ages,*
> *Jesus led me all the way.*

"AND AGAIN THEY SHOUTED: 'HALLELUJAH!'" (Revelation 19:3).

Note: Some contributors are not listed, due to partial name information given in original edition.

of the popular allegorical novel *Pilgrim's Progress*. 1/21, 3/5, 3/23, 4/12, 6/23, 6/27, 8/27, 9/5, 10/20

Bushnell, Horace (1802–76). Graduate of Yale and pastor of North Congregational Church of Hartford, Connecticut. 7/31

Butterfield, Mary 3/9

Butts, Mary 11/21

C

Caryl, Joseph 11/6

Chadwick, S. 3/25

Champness, Thomas 3/28

Cheney, Elizabeth 10/10

Christian, London 3/10

Clark, Thomas Curtis 7/31

Clarke, Adam (1762–1832). Irish Wesleyan minister. Wrote *Commentary on the Holy Scriptures*. 3/24

Collyer, Robert (1823–1912). Anglo-American Unitarian clergyman. 5/25

Cowherd, Ella Conrad 12/23

Crawford, Daniel (1870–1926). Scottish author and missionary to central Africa. 6/3, 6/14, 8/18

Cuyler, Theodore L. (19th century). American Presbyterian minister and devotional writer. 9/2, 11/17

D

David. Sixth-century Welsh patron saint. 6/20

Deck, Northcote 6/21

de Sales, Francis (1567–1622). French Roman Catholic missionary, bishop, and author. 2/8, 10/13

Digby, Kenelm (1603–65). English diplomat, scientist, and author. 11/12

Doddridge, Philip (1702–51). English-born Nonconformist preacher whose theology fell somewhere between Calvinism and Arminianism. 8/11

Drummond, Henry (1851–97). Scottish preacher and writer, known especially for his book entitled *The Greatest Thing in the World*. 6/13

E

Edwards, Jonathan (1703–58). American theologian, author, and preacher, known for his famous sermon "Sinners in the Hands of an Angry God." 12/17

Emerson, Ralph Waldo (1803–82). Popular essayist and poet, born in Boston. 1/21

Evans, Christmas (1766–1838). Welsh-born Baptist preacher. 1/4, 8/7

F

Faber, Frederick William (1814–63). Anglican preacher and composer of hymns, including "Faith of Our Fathers." 7/8, 9/18, 11/12

Farrar, Frederick William (1831–1903). Anglican preacher and dean of Canterbury. 9/13, 11/2

I

Ignatius (died c. 107). Early church bishop, author, and martyr. 6/19

J

Jackson, Helen Hunt (1830–85). American author of *Ramona* and other stories, books, and poems about Native-Americans. 3/11

James, J. Angell 7/20

Jarvis, Mary Rowles 4/7

Johnson, Annie Porter 4/16

Jowett, John Henry (1863–1923). English preacher who pastored Fifth Avenue Presbyterian Church, New York, and Westminster Chapel, London. 1/11, 2/14, 3/3, 3/15, 3/22, 4/3, 7/27, 8/4, 8/24

K

Keen, S. A. 3/26

Kilbourne, E. A. 7/12

L

Larcom, Lucy (1826–93). Massachusetts-born poet and teacher. 6/12

Leighton, R. (Robert) (1611–84). Scottish preacher and prelate. 1/29, 4/12, 11/21

Linn, Edith Willis 2/15

Longfellow, Henry Wadsworth (1807–82). Well-known American poet, author of such famous poems as "The Song of Hiawatha" and "The Village Blacksmith." 7/30, 12/1

M

Machen, J. Gresham (1881–1937). Baltimore-born Presbyterian theologian. 2/29

MacDonald, George (1824–1905). Scottish author of novels, sermons, poems, and children's stories, such as the Curdie books and *At the Back of the North Wind*. 7/15, 10/14, 11/28, 12/5

Macduff, J. R. (19th century). Scottish minster and devotional writer. Author of *Comfort Ye, Comfort Ye*. 2/6, 3/10, 4/22, 6/10, 7/25, 7/29, 8/26, 8/28

Maclaren, Alexander (1826–1910). English pastor of the Union Chapel, Manchester. 1/17, 1/25, 2/20, 7/10

Macmillan, Hugh 10/1

Matheson, George (1842–1906). Scottish preacher, author, and composer of hymns, including "O Love That Wilt Not Let Me Go." 1/8, 1/15, 2/3, 2/24, 4/8, 5/8, 5/30, 7/26, 9/8, 9/24, 10/26, 10/30, 12/11

McAdam, A. E. 6/26

McLeod, Malcolm J. 5/21

McNeill, John Thomas (1885–1975). Canadian preacher, lecturer, and author. 11/8

Merritt, Stephen 3/30

Meyer, F. B. (Frederick Brotherton) (1847–1929). English Baptist preacher and author of more than seventy books. 1/5, 1/10, 1/14, 2/2, 3/8, 4/11, 4/16, 6/24, 6/25, 7/11, 7/16, 7/31, 8/2, 8/8, 9/16, 10/5, 10/14, 11/11, 12/22, 12/27

Miller, J. R. (James Russell) (1840–1912). American Presbyterian minister and writer of devotional books, the most popular being *Devotional Hours with the Bible.* 1/26, 3/11, 3/15, 5/28, 6/19, 7/8, 9/19, 12/13, 12/21

Miller, Joaquin (1841–1913). American poet, best known for his poems on the American West. 2/11

Moffat, Robert (1795–1883). Scottish missionary to South Africa and father-in-law of David Livingstone, who shared his mission. 12/14

Moule, H. C. G. (Hendley Carr Glyn) (1841–1920). Leader of evangelicals and bishop in the Church of England. 2/20

Mueller, George (1805–98). Plymouth Brethren preacher, author, and founder of Christian orphanages. 1/4, 1/17, 2/7, 4/15, 6/10, 7/18, 8/16, 10/13, 11/10, 12/3

Murray, Andrew (1828–1917). South African missionary, pastor, and author of popular devotional books, such as *With Christ in the School of Prayer.* 7/22, 10/26, 11/2, 11/22

Myers, Cortland 9/2, 12/2

P

Parker, Joseph (1830–1902). English author and Congregational preacher. 1/5, 9/13

Parker, Theodore (1810–60). Massachusetts preacher and social reformer. 6/12

Parkhurst, Charles (Henry) (1842–1933). Massachusetts-born Presbyterian clergyman. 7/19

Pearse, Mark Guy 3/12, 5/2, 8/30

Peploe, H. W. Webb 8/5

Phelps, Austin 12/2

Pierson, Arthur Tappan (1837–1911). New York born preacher, missionary, and writer. Worked as editor for *The Scofield Reference Bible.* 2/25, 4/29, 10/20, 10/29

Porter, Bessie 7/1

Proctor, Adelaide (1825–64). London-born poet and hymn writer, published in Charles Dickens's periodicals. 7/30, 10/4

R

Rees, S. C. 8/27

Rexford, Eben Eugene (1848–1916). American poet and author, known for gardening books. 8/11

Richardson, Charles Francis 9/28

Richter, Julius (1862–1940). German professor and author of *History of Protestant Missionary Activities.* 7/9

Roach, J. 2/14

Robertson, Frederick William (1816–53). London-born preacher and author. 6/6, 8/15

Rossetti, Christina (1830–94). London-born poet and author. 5/14

Ruskin, John (1819–1900). Well-known English writer and art critic. 1/22, 5/4

Rutherford, Samuel (1600–61). Scottish preacher whose writings supporting Covenant theology were hailed by Charles Spurgeon. 3/10, 7/2, 7/3

S

Sargeant, Darlow 10/8

Shairp, John Campbell (1819–85). Scottish teacher and author. 7/10

Shipton, Anna 3/19

Simpson, A. B. (Albert Benjamin) (1844–1919). Canadian minister, author, and founder of the Christian and Missionary Alliance. 1/27, 2/17, 3/18, 4/8, 4/9, 4/21, 4/28, 5/6, 5/18, 5/27, 6/2, 6/18, 6/30, 7/6, 7/20, 7/29, 8/31, 9/7, 9/9, 9/27, 10/6, 10/19, 10/31, 11/2, 11/13, 11/15, 11/25, 11/26, 12/7

Smellie, Alexander (1857–1923). English writer and scholar. 9/14, 11/18

Smetham, James 6/26

Smith, Hannah Whitall (1832 –1911). Author well known for *The Christian's Secret of a Happy Life*. 1/29, 4/4, 4/7, 6/9, 8/14, 9/4, 9/17, 10/28

Smith, J. Danson 1/14, 2/5, 5/17, 9/6, 10/5

Smith, May Riley (1842–1927). American poet. 4/27

Snow, Laura A. Barter (early 20th century). English devotional writer and editor. Author of *Just for Me*. 2/1

Spurgeon, Charles Haddon (1834–92). Popular English-born Baptist preacher, evangelist, and founder of a pastor's college and an orphanage. Known for his Calvinist theology and his authorship, which included *The Treasury of David*. 1/2, 1/8, 2/16, 2/26, 3/8, 4/6, 4/10, 4/12, 4/19, 5/3, 5/22, 6/1, 6/14, 6/16, 7/9, 7/23, 8/12, 8/13, 8/30, 9/22, 9/25, 9/30, 10/9, 11/17, 12/12, 12/16, 12/30, 12/31

Stowe, Harriet Beecher (1811–96). Connecticut-born author of *Uncle Tom's Cabin* and sister of author Henry Ward Beecher. 9/13, 10/20

Sturm, Julius (1816–96). German clergyman and poet. 7/9

Sutton, Henry S. 7/28

T

Talmage, Thomas DeWitt (1832–1902). New Jersey–born Dutch Reformed and Presbyterian preacher and author. 12/6

Taylor, James Hudson (1832–1905).

English missionary to China
and founder of the China Inland
Mission. 2/8

Taylor, Nathaniel William (1786–1858).
Connecticut-born preacher,
theologian, and Yale University's
first professor of theology. 6/7, 11/4

Trumbull, Charles Gallaudet (1872–
1941). Connecticut-born author
and an editor of the *Sunday School
Times.* 1/17, 1/24, 7/16, 10/18

Trumbull, Henry Clay (1830 –1903).
American Congregational
clergyman, Civil War chaplain, and
edtior of the *Sunday School Times.*
1/20, 7/2

U

Upham, Thomas C. (1799–1872). New
Hampshire–born philosopher and
educator. 7/13

V

Van Dyke, Henry Jackson (1852–1933).
Pennsylvania-born pastor and
author of *The Story of the Other Wise
Man.* 2/2, 12/14

Vaughan, Abbott Benjamin (1830–90).
American lawyer and author. 1/25,
4/27

Von Bogatzky, C. H. (1690–1775).
German hymn writer and author
of popular devotional *The Golden
Treasury for the Children of God.* 11/10

W

Watkinson, William L. (19th century)
English Wesleyan preacher and
writer. 5/16

Webster, F. S. 12/22

Wesley, John (1703–91). English-born
preacher, missionary, theologian,
author, and one of the founders of
the Methodist movement with his
brother Charles Wesley and George
Whitefield. 12/17

White, Aphra 2/3, 4/23

Whitefield, George (1714–70). English
revivalist, evangelist, and friend of
John and Charles Wesley. 7/18, 9/29

Wilson, Antoinette 5/23

Wilson, Henry 9/27

Winter, E. M. 8/31

Z

Zinzendorf, Nicholaus Ludwig (1700–
60). Moravian bishop and author
born into Austrian nobility. 1/1

NOTES

NOTES

NOTES

NOTES